Perspectives
on
Contemporary Issues

Readings Across the Disciplines
Third Edition

KATHERINE ANNE ACKLEY

University of Wisconsin at Stevens Point

THOMSON

HEINLE

Australia   Canada   Mexico   Singapore   Spain   United Kingdom   United States

For my newest grandchildren
Che-Aaron James White
Celia Fatima Yahi

THOMSON

HEINLE

Perspectives on Contemporary Issues, Third Edition
Readings Across the Disciplines
Katherine Anne Ackley

Publisher: *Michael Rosenberg*
Acquisitions Editor: *Dickson Musslewhite*
Developmental Editor: *Michell Phifer*
Production Editor: *Eunice Yeates-Fogle*
Marketing Manager: *Katrina Byrd*
Executive Marketing Manager: *Ken Kasee*
Director of Higher Education
  Marketing: *Lisa Kimball*

Senior Print Buyer: *Mary Beth Hennebury*
Cover Design: *Gina Petti*
Composition: *ATLIS Graphics & Design*
Project Management: *Hearthside
  Publishing Services*
Printer: *Malloy Lithographing*

CONTENTS

should be able to determine its general purpose or aim. A clearly implied or stated purpose helps the writer to shape the writing, and it helps the reader to understand and evaluate the work.

Try to Determine the Intended Audience. Writers make assumptions about the people they are writing for, and these assumptions influence the tone they use, the evidence they select, the way in which they organize and develop their writing, and even their sentence structure, word choices, and diction level. Knowing whom the writer is addressing helps you to understand the writer's point of view and to explain the choices the writer has made in writing the piece. In writing for college courses, students usually assume a general audience of people like themselves who are reasonably intelligent and interested in what they have to say. However, professional writers or scholars often write for specific audiences, depending on the publications in which their writing appears. Writers want to know if their audiences will be sympathetic or opposed to their positions. Knowing the likely positions of readers helps a writer to make decisions about what tone to use and what details to include. Knowing if an audience is familiar with a subject or if the audience is specialized or general also governs what kind of evidence and how much to include.

Where the writing is published gives you a good idea of who the audience is. Take, for instance, the essays by Susan R. Lamson and William F. Buckley Jr., in chapter 10, "Television." You know from the headnote that accompanies "TV Violence: Does It Cause Real-Life Mayhem?" that the piece was first published in *American Hunter.* Readers of *American Hunter* very likely would support those who blame the high rate of violent crimes in America on television violence, rather than on the ready availability of guns in America. When you combine the knowledge of who author Susan R. Lamson is writing for with the information that she is director of federal affairs for the National Rifle Association, you can guess that she will answer "yes" to the question she poses in her title. Likewise, Buckley's essay, "Don't Blame Violence on the Tube," was first published in *TV Guide,* a weekly magazine listing television programs for television viewers. Writing as a longtime host of his own television show for an audience of television viewers, Buckley likely assumes an audience that is more sympathetic than not to his position that television violence does not cause real-life violence.

Locate the Thesis Statement or Main Idea. The thesis states the main idea of the entire essay. Sometimes it is embodied in a single sentence, the thesis statement, and sometimes it is stated in several sentences. If the main idea is not explicitly stated, it should be clearly implied. The thesis statement answers the question, What is the main point of this essay? Whether the thesis is explicit or implicit, it is a necessary component of a clearly written work. A thesis helps the writer to focus the writing and guides the organization and development of key ideas. It also helps to provide direction to the reader and assists in the reader's understanding of the piece.

Locate Key Ideas and Supporting Evidence or Details. For this step in your critical reading, you should underline or highlight the major points of the essay. One important tool for an active, critical reader is a pen or pencil. As you read, underline, star, or in some way highlight major points of development. Look for topic sentences of paragraphs. The thesis statement answers the question, What is this essay about? In the same way, the topic sentence answers the question, What is this paragraph about? If a topic sentence is not clearly stated, it should be clearly implied.

Make Marginal Notes as You Read. In the margins, write your response to a passage or make note of words, phrases, or entire passages you think are important to the piece. Make notes about the evidence or details that support major points. If you have a question about something the author says, write it in the margin for later consideration. If you are not sure of the meaning of the word, circle it and look it up in a dictionary after you have finished reading. Finally, if you are struck by the beauty, logic, or peculiarity of a passage, note marginal comments on that as well.

Summarize What You Have Read. This is the point at which you test your understanding of what you have read. Go back now and look at your underlinings and notations. Then try to state in your own words what the writing is about and the main points the writer made. If you can accurately summarize a piece of writing, then you probably have a good idea of its meaning. Summarizing also helps you to recall the piece later, perhaps in class or in small-group discussions. Incidentally, summarizing is also a good strategy for your own study habits. After reading an assignment for any of your courses, try to write or tell someone a summary of your reading. If you cannot express in your own words the major ideas of what you have just read, it should be reread.

Evaluate What You Have Read. When you are sure that you understand what you have read and can summarize it objectively, you are ready to respond. You can evaluate something in a number of ways, depending on its purpose. First, consider whether the author achieves the stated or implied purpose and whether the thesis or main idea is thoroughly explained, developed, or argued. Has the writer supplied enough details, examples, or other evidence? If you are evaluating an argument or persuasion essay, is the evidence convincing to you? Does the piece make a logical and reasonable argument? Are you persuaded to the writer's position?

What questions do you have about any of the writer's assertions? Do you wish to challenge her or him on any points? If the purpose of the essay is to describe, has the writer conveyed the essence of the subject to you with appropriately vivid language? For any piece of writing, you can assess how well written it is. Is it organized? Is the writing clear to you? Does the introduction give you enough information to get you easily into the essay, and does the conclusion leave you satisfied that the writer has accomplished the purpose for the essay? In the section on writing a critique in chapter 3, you will find a more detailed discussion of how to evaluate a passage or entire essay.

GUIDELINES FOR READING CRITICALLY

- Consider what the title tells you about the essay.
- Try to learn something about the author.
- Determine the purpose of the writing.
- Determine the audience for which the piece was written.
- Locate the thesis statement or main idea.
- Locate key ideas and supporting evidence or details.
- Make marginal notes as you read, including not only a summary of key ideas but also your questions about the content.
- Summarize what you have read.
- Evaluate what you have read.

It is helpful in both your own writing and in evaluating the writing of others to be familiar with common kinds of writing and the strategies writers use for organizing and developing their ideas. If you understand what strategies are available to a writer and what elements make those strategies work, you can better evaluate how well a selection is written. The next section explains some of those common strategies.

ORGANIZING AND DEVELOPING IDEAS

Writers use many different strategies for organizing and developing their ideas, depending on their purposes. Whether they pursue persuasive, expository, or expressive purposes, writers must be focused and clear if they want to engage their readers. They can achieve clarity or coherence with good organization and logical development of ideas. Writers seldom use any one method or even consciously think about any particular pattern or mode of development. Instead, they first decide what their purpose for writing is, and then they use whatever patterns best achieve their purpose.

In your college courses, you will often be asked to write. Your history or communications instructor may require a paper on a subject relevant to the course. You may need to answer essay questions on exams in a philosophy or music course. In biology or English, you may be asked to argue a position on a controversial issue. Your art professor may ask you to write a description of a painting, or your math professor may test your understanding by asking you to explain in writing how to solve a problem. Whatever your purpose, some fairly standard models can help you to organize your writing.

Argument/Persuasion.   Argument is a mode of persuasion in which the goal is either to convince readers of the validity of the writer's position (argument) or move readers to accept the author's view and even act on it (persuasion). In argument, writers set forth an assertion (often called a *proposition*) and offer proof intended to convince readers that the assertion is a valid or true one. In persuasion, a writer goes a step further and offers a course of action, with the ultimate goal of making readers take action. The supporting evidence or proof must be so convincing that readers cannot help but agree with the validity of the author's position. The reasoning process must be so logical that readers inevitably draw the same conclusions that the author does from the evidence.

A writer's primary concern in argument is to maintain an assertion in which she strongly believes. This position or assertion should be stated clearly at the beginning of the essay. It is helpful to have an explanation about why the writer believes as she does, for example, that the position is worth upholding or endorsing because it has some bearing on the lives of readers or the common good of a community or society. The argument will be most effective if it is organized with the least-convincing or least-important point first, building to its strongest point. This pattern lends emphasis to the most-important points and engages readers in the unfolding process of the argument as the writer moves through increasingly compelling proofs.

A successful argument also gives evidence of some sort for every important point. Evidence may include statistics, observations or testimony of experts, personal narratives, or other supporting proof. A writer needs to convince readers by taking them from some initial position on an issue to the writer's position, which readers will share if the argument succeeds. The only way to do this is to provide evidence that convinces readers that the position is a right or true one.

Many of the essays in this textbook are arguments. Some of the arguments are paired so that you can read varying perspectives on an issue and decide which, if either, you side with. For instance, the following pairs of essays provide opposing views on the same topic:

- Susan R. Lamson's "TV Violence: Does It Cause Real-Life Mayhem?" and William Buckley Jr.'s "Don't Blame Violence on the Tube" (chapter 10)
- William Lutz's "With These Words I Can Sell You Anything" and John O'Toole's "What Advertising Isn't" (chapter 11)
- William S. Pollack's "The Columbine Syndrome: Boys and the Fear of Violence" and Gary Kleck's "There Are No Lessons to Be Learned from Littleton" (chapter 14)
- Ruth Macklin's "Human Cloning? Don't Just Say No" and Charles Krauthammer "Of Headless Mice . . . and Men" (chapter 20)
- The *Economist* opinion piece "Science and Profit" and Tom Fiedler's "AIDS Fight Boils Down to Dollars vs. Lives" (chapter 21).

In addition, the *Time* magazine forum "Tough Talk on Entertainment" (chapter 9) provides an excellent example of a wide variety of positions on a single issue. Indeed, most of the chapters contain clusters of essays that argue different positions on the same topic. Thus chapter 10 focuses on the role television viewing plays in influencing behavior, and chapter 11 looks at the manipulative powers of advertising. Several essays in chapter 14 discuss school shootings, all of the essays in chapter 20 focus on the human genome project and the possibility of cloning, and chapter 26 features readings on the benefits and drawbacks of globalization.

Cause–Effect Analysis.   A writer who wants to explain why something happened or show what happened as a result of something—or perhaps both—is doing cause and effect analysis. This type of analysis is used frequently in news broadcasts and magazine and newspaper articles to explain phenomena, such as the chain of events that led to a particular action, the effects of a particular event or crisis, or both causes and effects of a specific situation. Cause and effect analysis is also used frequently to argue. A writer might use the strategy of causal analysis in arguing that offering sex education in schools or making contraceptives readily available to high school students would be more effective in reducing the number of teenage pregnancies than prohibiting explicit sex scenes on prime time television. The writer would have to sort out possible causes to explain the high rate of teenage pregnancies, determine which likely are most responsible and which are contributing factors, and then conjecture likely results if the recommendation were followed. Wayne M. Barrett and Bernard Rowe use cause–effect analysis in "What's Wrong with America and Can Anything Be Done about It?" (chapter 14) as they seek to explain America's social problems. Both Susan R. Lamson in "TV Violence: Does It Cause Real-Life Mayhem?" and William F. Buckley Jr. in "Don't Blame Violence on the Tube" (chapter 10) use cause–effect analysis as a strategy in their arguments.

Comparison/Contrast.   Another strategy for developing ideas is to show similarities and differences between two elements. Comparison and contrast can be useful in an argument piece in which the writer supports one of two possible choices and needs to explain reasons for that choice. In an expository essay, that is, one with the purpose of explaining something, comparison and contrast can be useful to demonstrate a thorough understanding of the subject. Comparing or contrasting usually promotes one of two purposes: to show each of two subjects distinctly by considering both side by side or to evaluate or judge two things. An analogy is a useful kind of comparison when seeking to explain a complicated or unfamiliar subject by showing its similarities to a less-complicated or more familiar subject. In "Crack and the Box" (chapter 10), Pete Hamill makes an unusual comparison when he argues that television viewing is as addictive and deadening as drug addiction.

Classification/Division.   Classification is sorting information and ideas into categories or groups; division is breaking information, ideas, or concepts into parts in order to better understand them. A writer may use classification to explain how a particular class of people, things, or ideas can be separated into groups and labeled according to common characteristics that distinguish them from other groups. A writer may use division to make a large, complex subject easier to understand by dividing it into smaller, more manageable parts. Thus, William Lutz, in "With These Words I Can Sell You Anything," classifies advertisement strategies according to the type of "weasel words" they employ.

Definition.   Writers often need to define as they inform or argue. Definition is the process of making clear a precise meaning or significance. In definition, a writer conveys the essential characteristics of something by distinguishing it from all other things in its class. You are familiar with dictionary definitions of words. Writers employ a similar technique to clarify or to explain, but usually in more detail than dictionaries give. In addition to providing brief definitions of terms, a writer may provide an extended definition, that is, take the meaning of a word beyond its dictionary definition or beyond the limits of a simple definition. An extended definition may go for a paragraph or two or even for the length of an entire essay. A writer using abstract terms or concepts unfamiliar to an audience will find the extended definition a useful tool. In his examination of a particular phenomenon that has arisen from a series of school shootings in the United States, William S. Pollack defines the term "Columbine Syndrome" in his article of the same name.

Exemplification.   Examples and illustrations are crucial to writing, no matter what the primary purpose. Without examples, writing stays at the general or abstract level and leaves readers only vaguely understanding what a writer means. Examples make meaning clear and help make writing more interesting, livelier, and more engaging than in an essay without details. Examples may be brief and numerous or extended and limited in number, and they may take the form of narratives. Much of Joe Saltzman's essay, "Dick Tracy Never Had It This Good!" consists of examples that both illustrate and argue his thesis. It would be difficult to find an effective piece of writing that does not use examples of some sort.

Narration.   Narration is the re-creation of an experience for a specific purpose. It may be a brief anecdote, a story, or a case history. Writers use narration for a variety of purposes: to explain, to illustrate a particular point, to report information, to entertain, or to persuade. Often a narrative is only one part of a written work, but occasionally it may be the entire means of development. Journalists are accustomed to asking themselves a series of questions when they write their stories to ensure they give complete narratives: What happened? To whom did it happen? When did it happen? Where did it happen? Why did it happen? How did it happen; that is, under what circumstances or in what way did it happen? Narration is often combined with description.

Description.   Description depicts in words a person, place, or thing by appealing to the senses, that is, by evoking through words certain sights, smells, sounds, or tactile sensations. Description is an almost indispensable part of writing; it is certainly inextricably linked with narration. As with narration and all other kinds of writing, description has a purpose. The purpose of description may be objective—to convey information without bias—or it may be subjective—to express feelings, impressions, or attitudes about a person, place, or thing.

ILLUSTRATION: READING CRITICALLY

An example can show how a reader might apply the guidelines for critical reading. Such a discussion follows the essay "The Hollow Curriculum" by Robert N. Sollod. Read the essay first, noticing words and passages that are underlined and addressed in the comments. These marginal notes reflect Kari Kolb's observations as she prepared to write her critique of the eassay (see chapter 3). After you have read the essay, write a response to the personal response question before you read the discussion. Then read the discussion and prepare for class or small-group discussion of the questions. For class, take into consideration the ways in which your own critical reading might differ from the comments following "The Hollow Curriculum." Would you add anything? What other words or passages would you underline or highlight? What other marginal comments would you make?

You will find another essay after the discussion of "The Hollow Curriculum," which you can use to practice critical reading. As you prepare for class discussion of Ronald Dahl's "Burned Out and Bored," apply the guidelines for critical reading. As with all essays in this textbook, a personal response question and questions for class or small-group discussion follow the essay.

THE HOLLOW CURRICULUM

Robert N. Sollod

University teacher: clinical psychology

Robert N. Sollod is a professor of clinical psychology at Cleveland State University. He was a member of the Task Force on Religious Issues in Graduate Education and Training for the American Psychological Association when he wrote this essay for the March 18, 1992, issue of The Chronicle of Higher Education, *a professional publication for faculty, staff, and administrators in colleges and universities.*

The past decade in academe has seen widespread <u>controversy over curricular reform.</u> We have explored many of the deeply rooted, core assumptions that have guided past decisions about which subjects should be emphasized in the curriculum and how they should be approached. Yet I have found myself

His subject

repeatedly <u>disappointed by the lack of significant discussion concerning the place of religion and spirituality in colleges' curricula and in the lives of educated persons.</u>

His main idea—an intriguing observation

I do not mean to suggest that universities should indoctrinate students with specific viewpoints or approaches to life; that is not their proper function. <u>But American universities now largely ignore religion and spirituality, rather than considering what aspects of religious and spiritual teachings should enter the curriculum and how those subjects should be taught.</u> The curricula that most undergraduates study do little to rectify the fact that many Americans are ignorant of religious and spiritual teachings, of their significance in the history of this and other civilizations, and of their significance in contemporary society.

Thesis— Assumes something about university life that he will have to prove. Example: Advocates of multiculturalism exclude religion and spirituality

<u>Omitting this major facet of human experience and thought contributes to a continuing shallowness and imbalance in much of university life today.</u>

Let us take <u>the current discussions of multiculturalism</u> as one example. It is hardly arguable that an educated person should approach life with knowledge of several cultures or patterns of experience. Appreciation and understanding of human diversity are worthy educational ideals. <u>Should such an appreciation exclude the religious and spiritually based concepts of reality that are the backbone upon which entire cultures have been based?</u>

Analogy   4

<u>Multiculturalism that does not include appreciation of the deepest visions of reality reminds me of the travelogues that I saw in the cinema as a child</u>—full of details of quaint and somewhat mysterious behavior that evoked some superficial empathy but no real, in-depth understanding. Implicit in a multicultural approach that ignores spiritual factors is a kind of <u>critical and patronizing attitude.</u> It assumes that we can understand and evaluate the experiences of other cultures without comprehension of their deepest beliefs.

Traditionalists also ignore religion

<u>Incomprehensibly, traditionalists who oppose adding multicultural content to the curriculum also ignore the religious and theological bases of the Western civilization that they seek to defend.</u> Today's advocates of Western traditionalism focus, for the most part, on conveying a type of rationalism that is only a single strain in Western thought. Their approach does not demonstrate sufficient awareness of the contributions of Western religions and spirituality to philosophy and literature, to moral and legal codes, to the development of governmental and political institutions, and to the mores of our society.

Uses personal experience: His undergraduate classes in 1960s omitted religious concerns

Nor is the lack of attention to religion and spirituality new. I recall taking undergraduate philosophy classes in the 1960s in which Plato and Socrates were taught without reference to the fact that they were contemplative mystics who believed in immortality and reincarnation. Everything that I learned in my formal undergraduate education about Christianity came through studying a little Thomas Aquinas in a philosophy course, and even there we focused more on the logical sequence of his arguments than on the fundamentals of the Christian doctrine that he espoused.

I recall that Dostoyevsky was presented as an existentialist with hardly a nod given to the fervent Christian beliefs so clearly apparent in his writings. I even recall my professors referring to their Christian colleagues, somewhat disparagingly, as "Christers." I learned about mystical and spiritual interpretations of Shakespeare's sonnets and plays many years after taking college English courses.

Uses clinical psychology as an example of how religion is omitted from college courses

8   We can see the significance of omitting teaching about religion and spirituality in the discipline of psychology and, in particular, in my own field of clinical psychology. I am a member of the Task Force on Religious Issues in Graduate Education and Training in Division 36 of the American Psychological Association, a panel chaired by Edward Shafranske of Pepperdine University. In this work, I have discovered that graduate programs generally do not require students to learn anything about the role of religion in people's lives.

Almost no courses are available to teach psychologists how to deal with the religious values or concerns expressed by their clients. Nor are such courses required or generally available at the undergraduate level for psychology majors. Allusions to religion and spirituality often are completely missing in textbooks on introductory psychology, personality theory, concepts of psychotherapy, and developmental psychology.

Clinical training ignores religion

Recent attempts to add a multicultural perspective to clinical training almost completely ignore the role of religion and spirituality as core elements of many racial, ethnic, and national identities. Prayer is widely practiced, yet poorly understood and rarely studied by psychologists. When presented, religious ideas are usually found in case histories of patients manifesting severe psychopathology.

Yet religion important in lives of many people

Yet spiritual and mystical experiences are not unusual in our culture. And research has shown that religion is an important factor in the lives of many Americans; some studies have suggested that a client's religious identification may affect the psychotherapeutic relationship, as well as the course and outcome of therapy. Some patterns of religious commitment have been found to be associated with high levels of mental health and ego strength. A small number of psychologists are beginning to actively challenge the field's inertia and indifference by researching and writing on topics related to religion and spirituality. Their efforts have not as yet, however, markedly affected the climate or curricula in most psychology departments.

Effects of 12   Is it any wonder that religion for the typical psychotherapist is a mysterious and taboo topic? It should not be surprising that therapists are not equipped even to ask the appropriate questions regarding a person's religious or spiritual life—much less deal with psychological aspects of spiritual crises.

Effects of
omitting
religion:
Psychotherapists
not equipped
to deal with
patients'
spiritual crises

Another
example

Or consider the field of political science. Our scholars and policy makers have been unable to predict or understand the major social and political movements that produced upheavals around the world during the last decade. That is at least partly because many significant events—the remarkable rise of Islamic fundamentalism, the victory of Afghanistan over the Soviet Union, the unanticipated velvet revolutions in Eastern Europe and in the Soviet Union, and the continuing conflicts in Cyprus, Israel, Lebanon, Northern Ireland, Pakistan, Sri Lanka, Tibet, and Yugoslavia—can hardly be appreciated without a deep understanding of the religious views of those involved. The tender wisdom of our contemporary political scientists cannot seem to comprehend the deep spirituality inherent in many of today's important social movements.

Far from being an anachronism, religious conviction has proved to be a more potent contemporary force than most, if not all, secular ideologies. Too often, however, people with strong religious sentiments are simply dismissed as "zealots" or "fanatics"—whether they be Jewish settlers on the West Bank, Iranian demonstrators, Russian Baptists, Shiite leaders, antiabortion activists, or evangelical Christians.

Students learn
to separate
their spiritual
lives from their
intellectual lives

Most sadly, the continuing neglect of spirituality and religion by colleges and universities also results in a kind of segregation of the life of the spirit from the life of the mind in American culture. This situation is far from the ideals of Thoreau, Emerson, or William James. Spirituality in our society too often represents a retreat from the world of intellectual discourse, and spiritual pursuits are often cloaked in a reflexive anti-intellectualism, which mirrors the view in academe of spirituality as an irrational cultural residue. <u>Students with spiritual interests and concerns learn that the university will not validate or feed their interests. They learn either to suppress their spiritual life or to split their spiritual life apart from their formal education.</u>

Sollod contends that ignorance of religions and spiritual worldviews leads to loss of ethics and moral standards. Is this an exaggeration? What is his proof? What he wants colleges/universities to do Recommended action:
- *Curricula need to be evaluated*
- *Leaders at all levels need to be involved*
- *Campus organizations should hold forums*
How practical is his proposal?

16   Much has been written about the <u>loss of ethics, a sense of decency, moderation, and fair play in American society. I would submit that much of this loss is a result of the increasing ignorance, in circles of presumably educated people, of religious and spiritual world views.</u> It is difficult to imagine, for example, how ethical issues can be intelligently approached and discussed or how wise ethical decisions can be reached without either knowledge or reference to those religious and spiritual principles that underlie our legal system and moral codes.

Our colleges and universities should <u>reclaim one of their earliest purposes</u>—to <u>educate and inform students concerning the spiritual and religious underpinnings of thought and society. To the extent that such education is lacking, our colleges and universities are presenting a narrow and fragmented view of human experience.</u>

Both core curricula and more advanced courses in the humanities and social sciences should be evaluated for their coverage of religious topics. Active leadership at the university, college, and departmental levels is needed to encourage and carry out needed additions and changes in course content. Campus organizations should develop forums and committees to examine the issue, exchange information, and develop specific proposals.

National debate and discussion about the best way to educate students concerning religion and spirituality are long overdue.

Personal Response

Describe the degree to which you are spiritual or religious. How important is religion in your life?

Questions for Class or Small-Group Discussion

1. Sollod gives examples of how an understanding of religion and spirituality would help someone trained in his field, psychology, and how it would help political scientists. In what other disciplines or fields do you think such training would be important? Explain how it would enhance the understanding of people trained in those fields.

2. Discuss whether you agree with Sollod that religion and spirituality have a place in the college curriculum.

3. Sollod calls for campus organizations to develop forums and committees to examine the place of religion and spirituality on the college campus and to develop specific proposals on the issue (paragraph 18). Conduct your own class forum or create a class committee to consider the issues that Sollod raises. Where do people learn about spirituality? How do you think a person could benefit from learning about religion and spirituality in college courses?

DISCUSSION OF "THE HOLLOW CURRICULUM"

The Title.   The word *curriculum* in the title indicates that Sollod's subject is education. The title does not reveal what educational level this curriculum refers to, but the word *hollow* indicates a critical stance toward the curriculum. On the basis of the title, we can expect to read what the author finds wrong with curriculum and why he considers it hollow.

The Author.   The headnote points out that the author teaches at a state university, that his area of expertise is clinical psychology, and that his special interests include religious issues in education. It suggests that Sollod is active in his profession: He served at the national level on a task force for his discipline's professional organization, the American Psychological Association, at the time he wrote this essay for a publication that is read by higher-education professionals. We can gather from this information that Sollod has experience teaching at the college level and is particularly well versed in the subjects of religion and education.

The Audience.   The headnote also says that "The Hollow Curriculum" was first published in *The Chronicle of Higher Education,* a professional publication for faculty, staff, and administrators in colleges and universities. Sollod writes for a specialized audience of his professional peers, people like himself who work in higher education. His audience is made up of people who are familiar with issues in higher education and who are therefore likely to have informed opinions on his subject. Because they are in higher education, his readers are also likely to be well-educated people. Because of this audience and the nature of the publication, Sollod writes in a formal style, avoiding informal language such as slang or colloquialisms. He uses words and terms that are familiar to his audience and specific to his field, and his sentence structure is appropriate for college-educated adults.

Purpose and Main Idea.   Sollod states his subject at the end of the first paragraph: "the lack of significant discussion concerning the place of religion and spirituality in colleges' curricula and in the lives of educated persons." His purpose and thesis, or main idea, appear in paragraph 2. Sollod believes that "American universities now largely ignore religion and spirituality." He thinks they should consider "what aspects of religious and spiritual teachings should enter the curriculum and how those subjects should be taught." Furthermore, he asserts that not teaching religion and spirituality contributes to "a continuing shallowness and imbalance in much of university life today." Sollod's purpose, then, is to argue this position.

Key Ideas and Supporting Evidence.   Sollod primarily uses **exemplification** and **cause–effect analysis** to develop his **argument.** Beginning in paragraph 3 ("Let us take the current discussions of multiculturalism as one example."), he gives examples of ways in which omitting religion and spirituality weakens college curricula. In addition to multiculturalism (paragraphs 3–4), Sollod discusses advocates of Western traditionalism, using personal experience to illustrate the long tradition of omitting religious and spiritual teachings from the curriculum (paragraphs 5–7).

Next, Sollod cites the effects of omitting religion and spirituality in his own field, clinical psychology (paragraphs 8–9). Once again, he brings in the matter of multiculturalism, this time in reference to the training of clinical psychologists (paragraph 10). Sollod goes on to note that "religion is an important factor in the lives of many Americans," and he refers to studies of the effects of religion on therapy and on mental health (paragraph 11). He concludes his discussion of clinical psychologists by noting that religion for many of them "is a mysterious and taboo topic," making them ill prepared to be therapists (paragraph 12).

Sollod moves next to the example of political science (paragraph 13). He blames the inability of scholars and policy makers "to predict or understand the major social and political movements . . . during the last decade" on their lack of understanding of "the religious views of those involved." As he builds to his conclusion, Sollod laments "the segregation of the life of the spirit from the life of the mind in American culture" (paragraph 15). He blames "the loss of ethics, a sense of decency, moderation, and fair play in American society" on "ignorance . . . of religious and spiritual world views" (paragraph 16).

Sollod's argument turns to **persuasion** as he states a course of action he believes colleges and universities must take: Reclaim one of the earliest goals of higher education, to educate students about "the spiritual and religious underpinnings of thought and society" (paragraph 17). In his concluding paragraphs (18–19), Sollod makes recommendations for ways to get religion and spirituality back into the college curriculum.

Summary.   In "The Hollow Curriculum," Robert N. Sollod argues that omitting courses on religion and spirituality in colleges and universities weakens the curriculum and leaves students ill prepared for their professions. He cites the example of the controversy over including multiculturalism in the curriculum, pointing out that both those who would change the curriculum and those who would adhere to the traditional curriculum ignore the importance of religious and spiritual issues in the matter of cultural or ethnic identity. Sollod says this omission is not a new development, recalling that his own undergraduate career over thirty years earlier lacked any real information on religion and spirituality. In his own field, clinical psychology, graduate students receive no training in how to deal with patients' spiritual lives—either the importance to patients or related crises patients may experience. As for the field of political science, Sollod argues that knowledge of religious and spiritual issues would help experts to make sense of social and political movements, motivations for which are often closely tied to religious views. Most of all, Sollod laments the way in which many students are forced to separate their spiritual lives from their intellectual lives. He concludes by calling for colleges and universities to reclaim one of their earliest goals, educating students about religion and spirituality. Sollod suggests that educators, administrators, and students alike can help to correct what he views as a grievous omission in the academic lives of America's college and university students.

Evaluation of Content and Structure.   Sollod's essay as a whole is organized sensibly and developed well in clear, straightforward prose. He makes a convincing case for the inclusion of courses on religion and spirituality in college and university curricula. His introduction both explains and introduces the context for his subject, curriculum reform in higher education. This element also establishes his own position on the subject. He anticipates opposition by quickly pointing out that he does not want to impose religious beliefs on students, just educate them. He states his main idea clearly and provides relevant examples throughout the essay, all focused on that main idea. He selects wisely his examples of areas in which instruction about religion and spirituality are missing and the effects of that void on students. The topic of multiculturalism ties in directly to his opening sentence, and his use of personal experiences as both a student and a teacher lets him speak with authority from positions that are directly relevant to his main idea. He makes a sensible point with his final example, political science. Sollod's plan for actions that students, teachers, and administrators can take to correct what he sees as a major lack in the higher education curriculum brings the essay to its conclusion.

Despite the admirable construction of the essay, Sollod is guilty of exaggeration and hasty generalization at times. For instance, what evidence does he supply to support his statement in paragraph 16 that educated people are ignorant "of religious and spiritual world views"? Further, his call for the inclusion of more courses on religion and spirituality, a move that would require a widespread review of core curricula, is impractical. Sollod has a good idea but needs more evidence to support his assertions. He also overlooks the realities of college curricula that are already overburdened by general degree requirements that allow very little room for additional courses.

BURNED OUT AND BORED

Ronald Dahl

Ronald Dahl is a professor of psychiatry and pediatrics at the University of Pittsburgh Medical Center. This essay appeared in the "My Turn" section of the December 15, 1997, issue of Newsweek. Each week, "My Turn" features an opinion piece by a guest writer.

Each summer, no matter how pressing my work schedule, I take off one day exclusively for my son. We call it dad–son day. This year our third stop was the amusement park, where he discovered (at the age of nine) that he was tall enough to ride one of the fastest roller coasters in the world. We blasted through face-stretching turns and loops for ninety seconds. Then, as we stepped off the ride, he shrugged and, in a distressingly calm voice, remarked that it was not as exciting as other rides he'd been on. As I listened, I began to sense something seriously out of balance.

Throughout the season, I noticed similar events all around me. Parents seemed hard pressed to find new thrills for nonchalant kids. I saw this pattern in my family, in the sons and daughters of friends and neighbors and in many of my patients with behavioral and emotional problems. Surrounded by ever-greater stimulation, their young faces were looking disappointed and bored.

By August, neighborhood parents were comparing their children's complaints of "nothing to do" to the sound of fingernails on a chalkboard. They were also shelling out large numbers of dollars for movies, amusement parks, video arcades, camps, and visits to the mall. In many cases the money seemed to do little more than buy transient relief from the terrible moans of their bored children. This set me pondering the obvious question: "How can it be so hard for kids to find something to do when there's never been such a range of stimulating entertainment available to them?"

4   What really worries me is the intensity of the stimulation. I watch my eleven-year-old daughter's face as she absorbs the powerful onslaught of arousing visuals and gory special effects in movies. Although my son is prohibited from playing violent video games, I have seen some of his third-grade friends at an arcade inflicting blood-splattering, dismembering blows upon on-screen opponents in distressingly realistic games. My four-year-old boy's high-tech toys have consumed enough batteries to power a small village for a year.

Why do children immersed in this much excitement seem starved for more? That was, I realized, the point. I discovered during my own reckless adolescence that what creates exhilaration is not going fast, but going faster. Accelerating from 0 to 60 mph in a few seconds slams the body backward with powerful sensations, but going 60 for hours on the interstate causes so little feeling of speed that we fight to stay awake. At a steady velocity of 600 mph we can calmly sip coffee on an airplane. Thrills have less to do with speed than changes in speed.

Since returning to school, the kids have been navigating ever more densely packed schedules. The morning rush to make the school bus is matched by a rapid shuttle through after-school sports, piano, foreign-language programs and social activities. Dinner is, too often, a series of snacks eaten on the run. Then, if they manage to get their homework done, the kids want to "relax" in front of highly arousing images on the television or computer screen.

I'm concerned about the cumulative effect of years at these levels of feverish activity. It is no mystery to me why many teenagers appear apathetic and burned out, with a "been there, done that" air of indifference toward much of life. As increasing numbers of friends' children are prescribed medications—stimulants to deal with inattentiveness at school or antidepressants to help with the loss of interest and joy in their lives—I question the role of kids' boredom in some of the diagnoses.

8   My own work—behavioral pediatrics and child psychiatry—is focused on the chemical imbalances and biological underpinnings to behavioral and emotional disorders. These are complex problems. Some of the most important research concentrates on genetic vulnerabilities and the effects of stress on the developing brain. Yet I've been reflecting more and more on how the pace of life and the intensity of stimulation may be contributing to the rising rates of psychiatric problems among children and adolescents in our society.

The problem of overstimulation arises frequently in my work on children's sleep. Although I diagnose and treat many unusual neurologically based sleep disorders, the most common is deceptively simple—many kids and adolescents don't get enough sleep. There are myriad factors in delaying bedtime despite the need to get up early for school. Even when tired, children often find stimulation through exciting activities. Fighting off tiredness by going faster can turn into a habit—and habits can be very hard to change. Most important, as thrills displace needed rest, sleep-deprived kids have trouble with irritability, inattention, and moodiness. Ironically, stimulants can seem to help children with these symptoms.

Our research also suggests that difficulties in turning down one's emotions after a stressful event may be a major factor leading to adolescent mood disorders. Constant access to high stimulation may also create patterns of emotional imbalance. An adolescent moving too fast emotionally for too long can experience the same sense of stillness as the airline passenger traveling at break-neck speed.

My wait at the airport for a flight home from a scientific meeting gave me time to think more about this fast-track phenomenon. I fleetingly considered my own need to slow down and the disturbing truth in the cliché that each year goes by more quickly. I realized with sadness how soon my children will be grown, and I sensed the fear that I may miss chapters of their childhood amid my hectic, overfilled life. In these images, I saw clearly the need to help our children find alternatives to the thrill-seeking fast lane by leading a slower version of life ourselves. I became convinced that nothing could be so important as finding a more balanced path, rediscovering slower, simpler pleasures before we all become burned out and bored to death.

Personal Response

Do you feel "apathetic and burned out" (paragraph 7), as Dahl suggests so many people do, especially teenagers? If you do, explain what you think accounts for that feeling. If you do not, explain how you avoid the kind of frenzied life Dahl says too many people lead.

Questions for Class or Small-Group Discussion

1. To what extent do you agree with Dahl that children today experience too much stimulation? Can you give examples of children like his, who seem to want more and more exciting stimulation (paragraph 4)?

2. Comment on Dahl's remark that "thrills have less to do with speed than changes in speed" (paragraph 5).

3. Based on your own experience and observations, what is your opinion of Dahl's comments about the effects of overstimulation and fatigue on children (paragraphs 7–10)?

4. Dahl concludes by noting that adults need to change their own lives in order to help "children find alternatives to the thrill-seeking fast lane." Discuss ways you think people can find "a more balanced path" and slow down their lives (paragraph 11).

Writing Topics

1. Write your own "My Turn" column on the subject of Ronald Dahl's essay. Does the title "Burned Out and Bored" describe your own position on the subject, or is another title more appropriate for your piece?

2. Explain what adults might do if they feel their lives are too hectic so they could move toward "a slower version of life." If you personally feel that your life is too fast paced, explain what you could do to slow its pace (paragraph 11).

3. Using examples of children or teenagers you know or have observed, either support or refute Dahl's assertion that young people's lives are overstimulated, which leads to demands for ever-greater stimulation and results in boredom and apathy.

CHAPTER 2
WRITING A SUMMARY

Students often must write both informal exercises and formal papers based on readings in their textbooks. In writing assignments for the course using this textbook, for instance, you will find frequent use for information or ideas discussed in the readings. For formal writing assignments, you may be instructed to choose among the writing topics that end each chapter, or you may be asked to suggest your own topic for a paper on a reading or readings. You may choose to argue in favor of or against a position another author takes; you may use information from one or more of the readings to write an essay suggested by a particular chapter; you may decide to compare and contrast two or more essays in a chapter or explain various perspectives on an issue. At some point, you may want to use some of the readings from this or another textbook in combination with other print and Internet resources in a research paper.

This and the next three chapters introduce several specific types of assignments and provide guidelines for writing them. This chapter focuses on the summary, chapter 3 on writing a critique, and chapter 4 on writing a synthesis. In all of these assignments, you may be called on to paraphrase, quote, and document material on which you are writing. The guidelines for paraphrasing, quoting, and documenting sources are explained in chapter 5. All illustrations of handling source material follow MLA (Modern Language Association) documentation style. (Note: If your instructor prefers that you use APA style or gives you a choice of styles, guidelines for APA documentation style appear in chapter 7.)

WRITING A SUMMARY

Summarizing produces an objective restatement of a written passage in your own words in a much shorter version than the original. The purpose of a summary is to highlight the central idea or ideas and major points of a work. A summary does not attempt to restate the entire reading. You might summarize an entire book in the space of a paragraph or perhaps even a sentence, although you will not do full justice to a lengthy work that way. Many reasons call for summarizing. Your instructor may ask you to write a summary of an essay, or a passage from one, to gauge your understanding. Such an assignment may be informal, something that you write in class as a quiz or an ungraded journal entry, or you may be assigned a formal summary, a longer piece that you write out of class in detail and with care. Many kinds of writing include summaries as part of the development of their main ideas. For instance, if you are asked to report on an individual or group research project for a science class, you will probably summarize your purpose, methodology, data, and conclusions. If you write an argumentative paper, you may need to summarize either opposing viewpoints or your own supporting evidence. A research paper often includes summaries of information from source materials, and the research process itself necessitates summarizing portions of what you read. Reviews of books or articles almost always include summaries of the works under discussion, and essay questions on an examination often require summaries of information or data. Across the curriculum, no matter what course you are taking, you will probably be asked to summarize.

Summaries serve useful purposes. Professors summarize as they lecture in order to convey information in a condensed way when a detailed review would take far too much time. Textbook chapters often present summaries of chapter contents as part of chapter introductions (as in parts 2 through 5 of this textbook). In this textbook, some of the questions for small-group and class discussion following the readings ask you to summarize major points or portions of readings, in order to facilitate your understanding of the text. That process, in turn, enhances the quality of your classroom experience and develops your abilities to follow the discussion intelligently and to make useful contributions to the discussion yourself. Your instructor may ask you to write a summary of a piece you have read as a formal assignment. Summarizing is also an excellent strategy to enhance your own study habits. After reading an assignment for any of your courses, try to write a summary of the reading. If you cannot put into your own words the major ideas of what you have just read, you may need to go back and reread the material.

Outside the classroom and the academic environment, summaries routinely give brief introductions, overviews, and conclusions of subjects at hand. In business, industry, law, medicine, scientific research, government, or any other field, both managers and workers often need quick summaries to familiarize themselves with the high points or essence of information. Knowing how to summarize accurately is a skill that you will find useful in both your academic writing and in your profession or job.

A Summary Is Not a Substitute for Analysis.   A summary, instead, is a brief, concise, objective restatement of the important elements of a piece of writing of any length, from a paragraph to an entire book. A summary may be brief, as in a one-paragraph abstract that precedes a report or long paper and gives a very short overview of it, or it may be several paragraphs in length, depending on the length of the writing or writings being summarized. You may summarize as an informal exercise for your own purposes or as a formal assignment that you hand in to your instructor for evaluation.

Abstract.   An abstract is a short, concise summary of the essential points of a text. Here is an example of an **abstract** of Joan DeGuire North's essay "Strangers in a Strange Land: Women in Higher Education Administration" (chapter 15):

Strangers in a Strange Land:

Women in Higher Education Administration

Joan DeGuire North

Abstract

Four differences between women and men seem to make male administrators and managers look more successful and accomplished than women administrators and managers. Men appear to claim three-fourths of talk time in meetings, while women listen intently, following their lead. In language patterns, women appear more tentative, while men speak with greater authority, even when they are unsure of themselves. Many women approach their work with both feeling and thought, and feeling is often unwelcome in the workplace. Finally, women tend to approach problems inductively, while men seem more deductive. These four differences affect both the perception and performance of women in positions of authority in the workplace.

This abstract provides a broad outline of North's thesis, major points, and conclusion. In her essay, she discusses or develops each of these components at length, providing examples and supporting evidence where necessary. You can see how an abstract, like summaries of other lengths, is useful for getting a quick overview of a report or essay.

Informal and Formal Summaries.   For an example of an informal summary that would help a student prepare for a class discussion or recall key elements of an article, see the summary of Robert N. Sollod's "The Hollow Curriculum," located in the discussion that follows that reading in chapter 1. For an example of a formal summary, see the summary following Arthur Levine's "The Making of a Generation," later in this chapter. The summaries of both Sollod's and Levine's articles underscore the need for a close, critical reading of the text in order to fairly represent what a writer says.

The trick in summarizing accurately is knowing what is important, and therefore must be included, and what is secondary, and therefore should be omitted. Here you see the usefulness of the guidelines for critical reading. When you read critically, you identify the main idea or thesis of the selection, and you highlight or in some way mark major points. A summary must include the main idea of what you are summarizing, and it should include major points, and only major points. Thus, if you learn to read critically, you can write a summary.

When you are asked to summarize, begin by carefully reading the work. Make note of its thesis or main idea. Then as you read, make marginal notes and underline, circle, or in some way mark the key supporting points or major ideas in the development of that thesis. After you have finished reading, look at your notes and state in one sentence, in your own words, the thesis and each major point. Do not include details or minor supporting evidence unless leaving them out would misrepresent or unfairly represent what you are summarizing. If the writing you are summarizing comes to any important conclusions, note them as well in one sentence in your own words. If you are writing a formal summary or an abstract, edit what you have written before turning it in to your instructor. Make sure that sentences are complete and that you have written in smooth and coherent language.

GUIDELINES FOR WRITING A SUMMARY

- On your first reading, locate the thesis or central idea of the work or passage you are summarizing.
- Make notes about key points as you read, either in the margin, by highlighting, or on a separate piece of paper.
- When you have finished reading, look over your notes, and write in your own words a one-sentence summary of the thesis or central idea.
- Write in your own words a one-sentence summary of each major point the author has used to develop, illustrate, or support the thesis or central idea. State only essential details related to each major point.
- Do not include minor points unless you believe their omission would give an unfair representation of what you are summarizing.
- Where appropriate, write in your own words a one-sentence summary of any conclusion from the piece.
- Keep your summary short, succinct, and focused on the central idea and major points of the piece you are summarizing.

ILLUSTRATION: MAKING MARGINAL NOTES AND SUMMARIZING

Arthur Levine's "The Making of a Generation" is reprinted here, along with examples of the kinds of marginal notes a student might make when reading and preparing to write a formal summary of an essay. The notes highlight the central idea and major points of the selection, so that when the student is ready to write a summary, he or she will already have marked the important points to include. Following the essay, the chapter presents questions for discussion, writing topics suggested by Levine's piece, and a sample summary of the essay.

THE MAKING OF A GENERATION

Arthur Levine

Arthur Levine is chair of the Institute for Educational Management and a member of the senior faculty of the Harvard Graduate School of Education. This essay appeared in the September/October 1993 issue of Change *magazine.*

Levine states his thesis in his first sentence.

Introduction provides background. Levine explains a previous survey he took and what he told students then that generations of college students before them were likely to have named as the most influential social or political events in their lives.

Every college generation is defined by the social events of its age. The momentous occurrences of an era—from war and economics to politics and inventions—give meaning to lives of the individuals who live through them. They also serve to knit those individuals together by creating a collective memory and a common historic or generational identity. In 1979, I went to twenty-six college and university campuses, selected to represent the diversity of American higher education, and asked students what social or political events most influenced their generation. I told them that the children who came of age in the decade after World War I might have answered the Great Depression. The bombing of Pearl Harbor, World War II, or perhaps the death of Franklin Roosevelt might have stood out for those born a few years later. For my generation, born after World War II, the key event was the assassination of John F. Kennedy. We remember where we were when we heard the news. The whole world seemingly changed in its aftermath.

The Me Generation

For students in the 1979 survey, Vietnam and Watergate were the most influential events.

I asked what stood out for that generation of undergraduates on the eve of the 1980s. They said Vietnam and Watergate. These events had defined their world. Few could remember a time in their lives when there had been no war, and Watergate seemed a confirmation about the way the world worked in business, government, and all sectors of society. On Watergate, students' comments echoed one another:

"Government doesn't give a damn."

"All politicians are crooks."

"Nixon was like all of us, only he got caught."

"It happens all the time."

"I don't trust government as far as I can throw the Capitol building."

"Nixon was a victim, that's all."

"The whole thing was out of proportion."

For three out of four students, the effects of Watergate and Vietnam had been distinctly negative, causing undergraduates to turn away from politics, politicians, and government. Most said they had no heroes.

Effects of those events included distrust of government, politics, and all social institutions.

4   Trust in all social institutions had declined among college students. A plurality of undergraduates described the major social institutions of society—Congress, corporations, labor unions, and the rest—as dishonest and immoral. They expressed a belief that there was nothing left to hold onto: "Everything is bad."

This distrust led to an emphasis on the self, hence the label "the me generation."

In response, the students had turned inward, and the refuge they had chosen was "me." They described the mood on campus this way:

"People only care about me, me, me."

"We're just interested in staying alive."

"We're part of the me generation."

"Concerns today are not about social issues, but about me."

"People are looking out for number one."

"The me generation is not concerned with the good of society, but with what's good for themselves."

Students in the earlier survey felt optimistic about their personal futures but much less optimistic about their collective future.

Ninety-one percent of the undergraduates interviewed were optimistic about their personal futures, but only 41 percent expressed hope about their collective future together. Student interests focused increasingly on being well-off financially. At the same time they had become more and more vocationally oriented, seeking careers in the platinum professions: law, medicine, and business. They had adopted what might be called a Titanic ethic: a sense that they were riding on a doomed ship called the United States or the world, and as long as it remained afloat, they would go first class.

The Current Generation

The findings of the 1979 study were so telling that I decided to repeat it this academic year. Once again I, along with several colleagues, visited a diverse selection of colleges and universities across the country. We followed the same approach as the

Levine explains
the selection
criteria and
numbers
involved in his
recent survey of
college
undergraduates.

original study, meeting with intentionally heterogeneous groups consisting of eight to ten students on each campus. The number of institutions was raised to twenty-eight to reflect the changing character of higher education since 1979. (This was part of a larger study including a survey of 10,000 undergraduates, a survey of 300 chief student affairs officers, and interviews with undergraduate student body presidents, newspaper editors, vice presidents and deans of students, and others.) Again we asked the undergraduate groups what social and political events had most influenced their generation. They gave five common answers.

Levine highlights
each of the five
commonly cited
answers and
discusses each
in turn.

Students cited
the Challenger
explosion most
often.

8   **Challenger.**   The most frequent answer was the *Challenger* explosion. Once a student mentioned it, members of the group commonly nodded in affirmation or said "yes." It was the equivalent of the Kennedy assassination for this generation. The students all knew where they had been when they heard the news. Many had watched it on television in school. Those who had not, saw it "on the news over and over and over again." Some had been scheduled to have teacher–astronaut Christa McAuliffe teach them from space. For a number it was the first time they had ever seen an adult, their own teacher, break down and cry. It was a first brush with death for quite a few.

That students answered the *Challenger* explosion surprised me. When I thought about the responses students might give to my question, the Shuttle disaster was not on the list. My generation had witnessed other fatalities in the space program, and while the *Challenger* explosion was a very sad occurrence, it did not seem to me to be a defining moment for the nation.

Students
explained that
the explosion
destroyed both
their idealism
and their sense
of safety.

I asked them why they had selected the *Challenger.* Beyond the fact that it was the first shared generational tragedy, students talked of a shattering of both their idealism and their sense of safety:

"I always thought NASA was perfect."

"There were smashed dreams because of it."

"My hopes were in it. There was an Asian, a black, and a woman."

"Thought America invincible."

"Burst my bubble."

"It was something good and then it blew up."

"NASA fell off its pedestal."

Students also said the *Challenger* explosion had marked a "wake-up call" or "reality check" for them and the nation. For some it was "a sign of a lot of things wrong" with the United States, such as in manufacturing, and for others it highlighted the decline of America due to its inability to compete economically and technologically. As one student put it, until then "I thought we were the best; we're really only second class."

The second-most-common answer was the fall of communism.

End of the Cold War.   The fall of communism was a second event students cited. They spoke in terms of "pride," "hope," "drama," "energy," and "a closer world." The symbol that stood out for them was the razing of the Berlin Wall.

12 Today's undergraduates are the last Cold War generation. They had studied Russia in school as an evil power to be feared. Although none of the eighteen-to-twenty-four-year-old undergraduates had seen Khrushchev bang his shoe at the U.N. or lived through the Cuban Missile Crisis, and only a small minority had engaged in duck-and-cover exercises in school, most had seen films like *The Day After,* which warned of the danger of a nuclear war. As a group, the students interviewed had been scared of the Soviet Union and afraid of the prospect of nuclear holocaust. In this sense the fall of communism was an extremely positive event.

The fall of communism has left many students worried about the instability of Central and Eastern Europe and about the Soviet nuclear arsenal.

However, the students were quite somber about the results. They regularly talked of the instability of Central and Eastern Europe, but in recent months, their focus shifted to U.S. involvement in a potential Vietnam-like ground war in Bosnia. They noted almost as frequently the danger of a now uncontrolled Soviet nuclear arsenal. They often worried whether the world was, in retrospect, a better place because of the demise of communism. One student put it this way: "For my generation, every silver lining brings a cloud."

Mentioned third most often by students was the Gulf War.

Persian Gulf War.   The third event students mentioned was the 1991 Gulf War, which they described as "our first war"— "Every generation has a war: this was ours." Like the *Challenger* explosion, they had watched it on television. TVs in student lounges, which were usually tuned to soap operas, had stayed fixed on the war. With the rise of CNN, students joked that friends would drop by and say, "You want to watch the war for a while?" and off they would go.

Despite fear of a draft and another potential Vietnam, students said the Gulf War had pulled them together. Many knew people who had been called up to serve in the Gulf. On their campuses, demonstrations against the war had tended to be tiny or absent in comparison to those in favor. The initial student reaction was pride: "We're still number one"; and "We can get things done." This seemed to be generally true among both liberal and conservative undergraduates. Students talked of flags and yellow ribbons appearing in profusion on many campuses.

16   By the 1992–1993 academic year, undergraduate reactions had changed, with students becoming much more critical:

"It's still a mess."

"We didn't finish the job."

"We botched another one."

"No reason to be there."

"Only a political show."

"Bush just wanted to be a hero."

"People were risking their lives and then had to return and not get jobs."

"We were in there to keep our oil prices down."

"Did it for economic interest only."

Many students were critical of the U.S. involvement in the GulfWar.

Few students were willing to speak out in favor of the Gulf War in spring of 1993 or to offer noneconomic rationales for it. In conversation after conversation, students disavowed the U.S. role as world peace officer. They rejected the notion that when "anything goes wrong, we have to straighten it out."

The AIDS epidemic has angered many young people, yet they act as if they could never get the disease. Some report that they are simply tired of hearing about it.

AIDS.   A fourth event the students cited was the AIDS epidemic. AIDS has been a fact of life for this generation as long as sexuality has been a possibility for them. Many reported lectures, pamphlets, films, and condom demonstrations in school. They commonly lamented, "I hear about it all the time"; "I'm tired of it."

But more than being tired, the students were often angry. They frequently compared their situation with that of the baby boomers, complaining, "When the boomers had sex, they got laid. When we have sex, we get AIDS." One student said it this way: "Free love is more expensive [now]."

Nonetheless, even though undergraduates resented a sword dangling over their heads, they acted as if it were not there. Though most said they knew what constituted safe sex, only a minority said they practiced it consistently. Students interviewed felt AIDS could not happen to them. They felt immortal. Very few knew anyone who had been diagnosed as HIV positive. Women undergraduates regularly expressed a greater fear of rape and pregnancy than AIDS.

20   **Rodney King.**   The final event students mentioned was the verdict in the Rodney King beating trial and the riots that followed. Minorities—African Americans, Hispanics, and Asian Americans—cited it most frequently, but by no means exclusively. Students expressed polar opinions; some had been appalled by the verdict, and others repulsed by the subsequent violence. The only commonality was the strong negative reaction:

The fifth most commonly cited event was the Rodney King beating trials and the riots that followed the verdict. Those events left students bitter and hostile about the judicial system and the police.

"I lost faith in the judicial system."

"I lost faith in the police."

"I lost confidence in people."

"It was a lesson in how to buy off a jury."

"Everything is politics."

"I used to believe the civil rights movement made a difference."

"Racism lives."

"Laws were created, but minds were not changed."

"Another shock to the system."

"Rioting inexcusable."

"Lawless."

"Verdict really disturbed me."

"I was glad. It's the only way to get people to see."

"It reminded me that society treats me differently."

"Police jobs are stressful."

What Do These Events Mean?

Levine concludes that the five events that are significant to this generation of college undergraduates are all quite recent, and most are viewed negatively. That the events are so recent suggests to Levine that the events their parents found significant have little or no meaning to today's students.

What stands out about the five events the students cited is first how recent they were. Most of today's freshmen were born in 1975—after John F. Kennedy's death, the end of the Great Society, the assassinations of Martin Luther King Jr., and Robert Kennedy, the moon landing, the Watergate break-in and Richard Nixon's resignation, and the end of the war in Vietnam. They were a year old when Jimmy Carter was elected president, four when the hostages were taken in Iran, five when Ronald Reagan entered the White House, ten when Gorbachev came to power, and thirteen when George Bush became president. More than 40 percent have never heard of Hubert Humphrey, Ralph Nader, or Barry Goldwater.

As a consequence, the events that stand out to their parents and faculty have little meaning to current undergraduates. Those events do not stir the same anger, elation, frustration, or vivid emotions in students that they do in older adults. They are at best history to contemporary undergraduates.

Today's students really know only two presidents of the United States, Ronald Reagan and George Bush. They have lived through three wars, Granada, Panama, and Iraq. The longest war in their lives lasted six weeks. They are living through a period of profound demographic, economic, global, and technological change.

24   In addition to being recent, the five events the students cited were at least in part negative. They described three—the *Challenger* explosion, AIDS, and the Rodney King affair—in wholly negative terms, and their initial optimism about the fall of communism and the Gulf War has faded significantly. In general, students thought they were living in a deeply troubled nation in which intractable problems were multiplying and solutions were growing more distant:

Today's students are bothered by the nation's problems and believe, somewhat resentfully, that they will have to fix them.

"Our experience is of flaws, problems, decline. We're not number one in anything. Our generation grew up with that."

"The world seems to be falling apart."

"We don't have anything that stable to hold onto."

The students interviewed shared a sense that their "generation would be called on to fix everything." As a group, they rejected the likelihood of broadscale solutions. For them the five events they cited showed that such solutions are unlikely to occur and unlikely to work. They also dismissed the possibility that answers would come from government. They saw Congress as bankrupt, but held out hope for the Clinton presidency in its earliest days.

An Increased, if Guarded, Optimism

Despite their negativity, today's students feel optimistic about their personal futures and have replaced superheroes with local heroes.

Yet the students I interviewed expressed some optimism about the future. Again, more than nine out of ten were optimistic about their personal fates, but the level of optimism about our collective future shot up to 55 percent. This is in large measure because students have shifted their focus. While they were rather negative about the future of the country, they were remarkably optimistic about the future of their communities. Today's students emphasize the local in their thinking and their action.

Heroes are back too. More than three out of four students had heroes, but those heroes were local—Mom and Dad, my teacher, my neighbor, the person leading the community cleanup campaign.

28   Participation in service activities increased dramatically as well. Prior to coming to college about half of all current

Although they have some optimism, students also are afraid and angry about the job market, the economy, and possible environmental disasters, among other things.

undergraduates had been engaged in some form of community service. Such programs are booming on college campuses today as well, particularly in the area of environmentalism, a common interest among today's undergraduates. Even on some campuses in which political action was low or absent, recycling bins have appeared at the behest of students.

Nonetheless, fear and anger were a part of the conversation with every student group I interviewed. Current undergraduates were afraid of being unable to find jobs, of living in an economy in which they will do less well than their parents, of facing a mounting national debt, of having to contend with environmental disasters, and much, much more. They felt put upon, cheated, and robbed of the opportunity that had been given to previous generations. They especially resented the baby boomers for their advantages. They criticized the students of the 1980s for their "me-ism."

In conclusion, this generation seems torn between looking out for themselves and working for the common good.

For most of the students interviewed, the real struggle was choosing between making money and performing good deeds. Six out of eight undergraduates said it was essential or very important to be very well-off financially, but five out of eight said it was essential or very important to have a career that would make a meaningful social contribution. The big issue facing students I interviewed was how to choose. Most didn't want to be Donald Trump, but the prospect of Mother Teresa was not all that appealing either. Above all, this is a generation torn between doing good and doing well.

Personal Response

What motivates you when thinking about choosing a career? Do you think you will be driven by financial desires or by other reasons?

Questions for Class or Small-Group Discussion

1. Discuss the five events that Levine discovered have had the most impact on today's generation of undergraduate students. Are they events you would have named? If not, what other events would you name? How have these events affected you personally? Share your answer with your classmates.

2. Respond to the remark that students feel that "their 'generation would be called on to fix everything' " (paragraph 25). Do you believe that your generation can fix the problems created by previous generations? Do you think you should have to? If your generation does not do it, then who will?

3. Discuss to what degree you and your classmates feel optimistic about the future. Are you more or less hopeful about the future of the global community than you are about your own personal future and that of your community?

4. Describe to what extent you fear the future. What problems do you foresee? What makes you fearful?

5. Three-fourths of the students Levine interviewed said they had heroes. If you have heroes, who are they? Do you and your classmates have the same heroes?

Writing Topics

1. Using Levine's essay as a starting point, explain what social or political event has had the most influence on your life. Argue for its importance as a key influence by explaining the event's impact on you personally and how you believe it has affected society in general.

2. Explain the degree to which you feel optimistic about either your personal future or the future of your country and why.

3. Argue for or against taking an optimistic viewpoint about the future of your community by identifying aspects or characteristics of it that support your position.

4. If you have heroes, state who they are and defend your reasons for regarding them as heroes. Include a definition of *hero* in your argument.

SUMMARY OF ARTHUR LEVINE'S "THE MAKING OF A GENERATION"

> In "The Making of a Generation," Arthur Levine reports the results of his 1993 survey of undergraduates at twenty-eight American colleges and universities to support his thesis that college students are defined by the key social and political events of their age. To provide background for the report and comparative analysis that follows, Levine first explains the results of his 1979 survey of college students, who cited the Vietnam War and the Watergate scandal as most significantly affecting them. Those events produced a generation of people preoccupied with themselves rather than with the larger society.
>
> The event cited most frequently by students in Levine's 1993 survey was the *Challenger* explosion.

When asked why that event had had such a profound effect on them, most reported that the tragedy had both disillusioned them and shaken their sense of safety. The second event cited was the fall of communism, which students viewed positively, though their enthusiasm had been dampened somewhat by the instabilities in many Central and Eastern European countries that erupted as a result of that fall. In third, fourth, and fifth places, respectively, were the Persian Gulf War, which many viewed critically; the AIDS epidemic, which both terrifies and angers many young people; and the verdict in the Rodney King beating trial and the riots that followed, which left many students feeling disillusioned about the police, the judicial system, and humanity in general.

According to Levine, his survey reveals that while many of today's generation of college undergraduates feel as if their personal success is manageable, they are uncertain about the future of their society and find themselves torn between choosing a career that provides personal financial security and one that makes some meaningful contribution to society.

Exercise

Read Martha Barnett's "Lessons in Democracy" and then summarize it, following the guidelines for writing a summary outlined previously. Your instructor will tell you whether you are to hand in your summary. Prepare for class discussion by considering your responses to the questions that follow the essay.

LESSONS IN DEMOCRACY

Martha W. Barnett

Martha W. Barnett received her Juris Doctor from the University of Florida, where she was an editor of the University of Florida Law Review. Her primary areas of practice have been administrative and governmental law. As president of the American Bar Association (ABA), she wrote this essay for the January 2001 issue of the ABA Journal, *a magazine for lawyers published by the ABA. Barnett wrote the piece before the 2000 presidential election was decided, but she knew that it would be published after the outcome was known.*

As I write this article, the eyes of the world are on my hometown of Tallahassee, Florida. For the first time in more than a century, the outcome of the election of the next president of the United States hinges upon a few hundred Florida votes. By the time you read this the results will be final, and in the spirit of majority rule, the American people will unite behind our president. Meanwhile, we have learned about the resilience and strength of our democratic system and have identified some areas that deserve rethinking and perhaps changing.

Our democracy has been called an experiment, and if that is true, it is fortunately an evolving one. The concept of separate but equal branches of government embodied in our courts, our legislatures and our executive offices provides the flexibility we need to deal with new and unforeseen developments. We have the tools to keep our disputes from becoming the kinds of crises that have plagued other forms of government.

There were moments that appeared to threaten crisis. Some scenes broadcast made it seem as if we stood at the brink of turmoil. But it did not materialize. The key difference between our election process and those that have plummeted into violence is the fundamental trust our citizens place in the rule of law and in the legitimacy of our trusted court system. Rather than taking our fights to the streets, Americans take them to our courts.

4   There are other lessons as well. On Election Day plus one, my son and I discussed why he and I voted for different candidates. I said, "It doesn't matter how you voted. The important thing is that you voted—every vote counts." It almost seems prophetic now. If the lukewarm interest of some of the American people in elections has been ignited, this event was worth every heated moment. For too long, too many have taken this fundamental right for granted and left it up to others.

The ABA historically has supported the National Voting Rights Act, the National Voter Registration Act, and other efforts to increase voter registration and participation. We believe that each citizen has a responsibility to actively participate in our nation's electoral process. Participation is more than just casting a vote. It includes such things as engaging in the debate on campaign finance reform, the method of selecting the president, ballot procedures and a myriad of other issues that contribute to the underlying issue—the public trust and confidence in the electoral process and our elected officials.

The ABA has considered many of these issues. For example, we've long been on record calling for campaign finance reform. As recently as the 2000 annual meeting, the House of Delegates passed a resolution supporting partial public financing of presidential campaigns and urging Congress to limit or eliminate various kinds of campaign contributions. Last year's federal elections cost about $3 billion. The impact of such large sums of money can be insidious.

It has been more than 25 years since there have been significant revisions in the laws governing campaign financing. Yet how campaigns are conducted has changed dramatically, especially with the advent of technology, the electronic media, issue advertising and soft money contributions. Our laws must be updated to address the realities of the modern campaign era to ensure the continued integrity of the campaign finance system.

8   Another issue that has long been on the ABA's agenda—and that now has found some currency with the general public—is the electoral college, an institution that is now more than 200 years old. It was a compromise between those who believed in the direct election of the president and those who wanted to ensure that knowledgeable people in each state elected the president. The ABA first addressed the issue in 1967, calling "for the election of president and vice president by direct, nationwide popular vote."

In 1989, the association adopted ballot integrity standards. While technological advances have pervaded all aspects of society, there has not been the same surge in the electoral process. Issues of funding, tradition and the tangible ballot have led to continuing the status quo in many jurisdictions. I have called upon our Standing Committee on Election Law to revisit these issues and give particular attention to the need for reform as a result of the inevitable intersection of technology and the election process.

We live in interesting times. We were participants, or at the very least witnesses, to history in the making. Regardless of who has won this particular election, the real winners are the American people. The overriding lesson we have learned is that democracy does work. I, for one, am proud to be part of it!

Personal Response

Whether you voted in the 2000 presidential election or not, what were your views of the controversy over the decision of that election?

Questions for Class or Small-Group Discussion

1. Share your recollection of what went on during the period following the 2000 presidential election in an effort to come to a collective understanding of the surrounding controversies.

2. What "lessons in democracy" does Barnett believe Americans learned as a result of the 2000 presidential election? Do you agree with her?

3. In her discussion of campaign finance reform, Barnett notes that the 2000 election cost several billion dollars, and she writes: "The impact of such large sums of money can be insidious" (paragraph 6). What examples does she give of the insidious impact of large sums of money? What other examples can you give?

4. Barnett states that the ABA is in favor of "the election of the president and vice president by direct, nationwide popular vote" (paragraph 8). What reasons does she cite to explain why the ABA favors direct popular vote over the Electoral College? To what extent do you agree with the ABA on this issue?

Writing Topics

1. Argue your position on the issue of the Electoral College. Do you favor continuing it, reforming it, or abolishing it in favor of election by direct popular vote?

2. Argue your position on the issue of campaign finance reform.

3. With Barnett's "Lessons in Democracy" in mind, explain an event other than the 2000 presidential election that you believe demonstrates "that democracy does work" (paragraph 10).

CHAPTER 3

WRITING A CRITIQUE

THE CONNECTION BETWEEN READING CRITICALLY AND WRITING A CRITIQUE

Recall the guidelines for reading critically outlined in chapter 1: The final step is to evaluate what you have read. A critique is the written form of an evaluation of a passage or an entire work. Reading critically is the biggest aid to writing a critique; applying the guidelines for reading critically is a crucial part of preparing to write a critique. You will need to understand not only the purpose of the piece and its central idea but also the main points the writer makes. Reading critically enriches your understanding of a work and its components, enabling you to focus your critique.

WRITING A CRITIQUE

When you write a critique, your goal is to make a formal analysis of and response to a piece of writing, whether a selected passage or an entire essay. Your purpose encompasses both explaining and evaluating a piece of writing. In general, a critique includes these components: (1) an introduction; (2) an objective, a concise summary of the work or passage; (3) an objective analysis of the author's presentation; (4) a subjective response detailing your opinion of the author's views; and (5) a conclusion. A critique differs from a summary, which is an objective restatement in your own words of the original material. When you summarize, you leave out your personal or subjective viewpoint. In a critique, you begin objectively but then add your own subjective response to the work.

A Note on Verb Tense.   Whenever you write about or refer to another person's work, use the present tense: "Ronald Dahl **argues** . . ." or "Dahl **asserts** that. . . ." Use the past tense only to refer to something that happened before the time span of the essay: "Dahl's essay **is** a response to a comment his son **made** after a roller coaster ride they **took** together one summer day."

Introduction.   The first paragraph of your critique should name the author and title of the work that you are critiquing. Do not neglect this information, as it immediately tells readers the subject of your critique. Then give a very brief overview of the piece in two to four sentences. Your intent in the introduction is not to summarize the piece but to tell readers its purpose. Generally, stating the thesis or central idea of the piece along with a highlight or two and/or its major conclusion(s) will be enough to convey its essence and provide background for the rest of your paper. Finally, your introduction should state your own thesis. In one sentence, indicate your assessment of the passage or work that you examined. Your thesis statement should be worded to reveal your position to readers before they begin reading the body of your paper.

Summary.   The first section in the body of your critique should offer an objective summary of the piece. This summary states the original author's purpose and includes key ideas and major points. Where appropriate, include direct quotations that are particularly important to the development of the piece. Do not write anything evaluative or subjective at this point. Your purpose here is to give a fair and accurate summary of the intent and main points of the work you are analyzing.

Analysis.   Once you have summarized the work by stating its purpose and key points, begin to analyze the work. Your goal is to examine how well the author has achieved the purpose and consider the validity or significance of the author's information. Do not try to look at every point the author makes; rather, limit your focus to several important aspects of the piece. Remain as objective as possible in this section, saving your personal opinion of the author's position for the response section of your critique. Different purposes for writing—persuasive, expository, and expressive—require application of different criteria to judge a writer's success in achieving the intended purpose. In general, however, certain considerations help in the assessment of any piece of writing. Questions about validity, accuracy, significance, and fairness help you to evaluate any author's success or failure.

Assessing Persuasive Writing.   Look again at the discussion of argumentative writing in chapter 1, which provides not only a statement of the purpose of argument or persuasion but also a number of strategies for writing an argumentative paper. In assessing the success of another writer's argument, you should gauge how well that writer has used the standard strategies for argumentation. Furthermore, pay attention to the writer's use of language. Finally, assess the validity of the argument by examining the evidence the writer presents to support his position and the logic of his conclusions.

Examining a Writer's Language.   In particular, make sure that the writer defines any words or terms that may be unclear, abstract, or ambiguous. Ask yourself if the writer's language seems intended to intimidate or confuse readers or if the writer attempts to manipulate readers by relying on emotionally loaded words. Does the writer make sarcastic remarks or personal attacks? Ultimately, examine a writer's evidence to evaluate credibility and fairness. Good writers do not rely on manipulative language, unclear terms, or loaded or sarcastic words to achieve their purposes.

Examining a Writer's Evidence.   A writer should support any generalizations or claims with ample, relevant evidence. As a critical reader, consider the value or significance of that evidence. Evidence may be supplied in the form of statistics, facts, examples, or appeals to authorities. Keep in mind that statistics can be manipulated to conform to the needs of the person using them, so make sure that they are based on a large and representative sample, that the method of gathering the statistics yields accurate results, and that the statistics come from reliable sources. Look closely at statements of facts, as well; they should give accurate, complete, and trustworthy information. Examples are specific instances or illustrations that reveal a whole type, and they should give believable, relevant, reliable, and representative support for an author's thesis. Finally, authorities are people who have the training or experience needed to make trustworthy and reliable observations on matters relating to their areas of expertise. In completing a critique, make sure, as far as possible, that the piece under study appeals to believable and credible authorities.

Judging a Writer's Logic.   Argumentative or persuasive writing must portray a logical, reasonable, and accurate reasoning process supplemented by relevant, sensible supporting proofs. You will be in a good position to evaluate a writer's reasoning process if you are mindful of any pitfalls that undermine the success of the argument. Look for these **common flaws** or **fallacies** in any writing you analyze:

- **Hasty generalization.** A writer makes a hasty generalization if she draws a broad conclusion on the basis of very little evidence. Such a writer probably has not explored enough evidence and has jumped too quickly to conclusions. Assuming that all politicians are corrupt because of the bad behavior of one is an example of making a hasty generalization. Condemning all films with violent content because of one film that has received widespread criticism for its graphic violence is another example.
- **Oversimplification.** In oversimplification, the arguer offers a solution that is too simple for the problem or issue being argued. For instance, arguing that the problem of homelessness could be solved by giving jobs to homeless people overlooks the complexity of the issue. Such a suggestion does not take into account such matters as drug or alcohol dependency that sometimes accompanies life on the streets or a range of other problems faced by people who have lost their homes and learned to live outdoors.
- **False analogy.** A writer may falsely claim that, because something resembles something else in one way, it resembles it in all ways. This warning does not deny that analogy has a place in argument. It can be an extremely useful technique by emphasizing a comparison that furthers an argument, especially for a difficult point. Explaining a difficult concept in terms of a simpler, more familiar one can give helpful support to readers. However, make sure that the analogy is true and holds up under close scrutiny. A controversial analogy that is sometimes used is the comparison of America's internment of American citizens of Japanese descent during WW II to Hitler's concentration camps. On some levels the comparison is justified: people in the U.S.

internment camps were held against their will in confined areas guarded by armed soldiers, they often lost all of their property, and some were even killed in the camps. On the other hand, they were not starved to death, extermi- nated, or used as subjects of medical experiments. The analogy is useful for making a point about the unfair treatment of American citizens during wartime, but many would argue that the analogy breaks down on some very important points.

- *Non sequitur.* This Latin term, meaning "does not follow," refers to infer- ences or conclusions that do not follow logically from available evidence. Non sequiters also occur when a person making an argument suddenly shifts course and brings up an entirely new point.

- *Ad hominem* **arguments.** This Latin term means "against the man" or "to- ward the person" and applies to arguments that attack the character of the arguer rather than the argument itself. *Ad hominem* arguments often occur in politics, for instance, when opponents of a candidate refer to personal characteristics or aspects of the candidate's private life as evidence of her or his unsuitability to hold office. Arguing that a candidate would not make a good senator because she is a single parent or that a candidate would not be effective as mayor because he is homosexual ignores the more important questions of qualifications for the office, the candidate's stand on issues rel- evant to the position, the candidate's experience in political office, and sim- ilar substantive considerations.

- **Circular reasoning or begging the question.** This error makes a claim that simply rephrases another claim in other words. It assumes as proof the very claim it is meant to support.

- **Emotionally charged language.** Writers may rely on language guaranteed to appeal to their audiences on an emotional level rather than an intellectual level. Writers do not have to avoid appeals to the emotions entirely, but they should limit their use of such appeals. Arguments on ethical or moral issues such as abortion or capital punishment lend themselves to emotional appeals.

- **Either/or reasoning.** If a writer admits only two sides to an issue and asserts that his is the only possible correct one, the writer has probably not given full thought to the subject or is unaware of the complexity of the issue. Most ar- guable topics are probably complex, and few are limited to either one or an- other right viewpoint.

- **Red herring.** A red herring diverts the audience's attention from the main is- sue at hand to an irrelevant issue. Writers of mystery fiction often use red her- rings to distract readers from identifying the stories' criminals. That is part of the fun of reading a mystery. But an argumentative writer who tries to use red herrings probably does not have enough relevant supporting evidence or does not recognize the irrelevance of the evidence. These are legitimate rea- sons for faulting an argument.

- *Post hoc, ergo propter hoc* **reasoning.** This Latin term means "after this, therefore because of this." It applies to reasoning that assumes that Y happened due to X simply because it came after X. Accusing a rock group of causing the suicide of a fan because the fan listened to the group's music just before committing suicide is an example of such reasoning. Although the music might be a small factor, other factors are more likely to account for the suicide, such as a failed love relationship, feelings of low self-worth, or personal despair for a variety of reasons.

Response. In this part of your critique, express your own position relative to that of the writer of the piece and give reasons why you believe as you do. You may find yourself in total agreement or absolutely opposed to the author's position, or you may place yourself somewhere in between. You may agree with some points the author makes but disagree with others. No matter what position you take, you must state your viewpoint clearly and provide reasons for your position.

Conclusion. The final paragraph of your critique should reiterate in several sentences your overall assessment of the piece, the conclusions you have drawn from your analysis, and your personal response to the work. This section is not the place to introduce new material; rather, it is an opportunity to provide an overall summary of your paper. You want your readers to feel that you have given them a thorough and thoughtful analysis of the work under consideration and that you have brought a satisfying closure to your comments.

GUIDELINES FOR WRITING A CRITIQUE

- Begin with an introduction. The introduction familiarizes readers with the work under discussion, provides a context for the piece, and states your thesis.
- Summarize main points. The summary tells readers what major points the writer makes to support her position.
- Analyze how well the writer has achieved her purpose. The analysis tells readers what aspects of the work you have examined, depending on the kind of writing you are considering. In general, assess the overall presentation of evidence, judging its validity, accuracy, significance, and fairness.
- Explain your response to the piece. The response section tells readers your personal viewpoint by explaining the extent to which you agree or disagree with the author.
- Conclude with your observations of the overall effectiveness of the piece and your personal views on the subject. The conclusion summarizes for readers the results of your analysis and your overall judgment of the piece.

ILLUSTRATION: CRITIQUE

Kari Kolb

English 150

September 20, 2001

A Critique of "The Hollow Curriculum"

In his essay "The Hollow Curriculum," Robert Sollod addresses the controversial subject of religion in the public school system, particularly at the college level. Sollod believes that by failing to acknowledge religious histories and teachings, universities contribute to the declining morality of society. He recommends an evaluation of course offerings in terms of ways in which courses on religion or spirituality can be integrated into higher education curriculum. Such a project would involve not only university faculty and administrators but also American citizens nationwide. While it may be true that recent years have seen a moral or ethical decline in the general public, Sollod's assertion that this decline is due to religious ignorance is not only unfounded but also untrue.

Sollod begins his piece by exploring the lack of religious and spiritual emphasis in the national curriculum and in the lives of college alumni. After explaining the religious background of America's history, he goes on to look at other cultures as well. Noting that much of multicultural appreciation depends on understanding others' cultures, Sollod points out that many other civilizations have built the foundation of their culture upon religious and

Kolb 2

spiritual beliefs. He does not endorse one particular faith; rather, he suggests that all-inclusive religious studies would enrich the careers and lives of college students. Sollod continues by warning that a lack of religious studies has resulted in "the loss of ethics, a sense of decency, moderation, and fair play in American society" (15). His proposed solution includes a curriculum assessment of current course offerings in religion and spirituality, active leadership of faculty and administrators across the university to initiate curriculum change, and the involvement of students in the form of debates and committees (15).

Sollod has a solid sense of his audience, made up primarily of faculty and staff in higher education. By implication, what he proposes is of interest to students as well. Sollod draws readers into his argument with a series of questions and then offers information in a simple yet authoritative manner. He provides detailed examples, explaining how religious understanding would enhance all areas of study, ranging from the broad fields of political science and psychology to the ideas of Shakespeare and Socrates. This wide-ranging analysis enables Sollod to reach his large and somewhat diverse audience. He bases much of his reasoning upon the idea that "religious and spiritually based concepts . . . are the backbone upon which entire cultures have been based" (12). Sollod's valid argument is made even more credible when he extends it to include familiar examples, such as conflicts in the former Soviet Union, Ireland, and the Middle East. At times, Sollod relies on emotional

Kolb 3

appeals, seen most often in his occasional use of loaded words and phrases such as "continuing shallowness and imbalance" (12) and "mysterious and taboo" (14). In general, though, he makes a fair and logical argument, and he concludes with a rational solution to what he sees as a serious problem.

I agree with Sollod when he states that the college curriculum would be greatly enhanced by the addition of courses in religion and spirituality or the incorporation of such material in traditional courses. Such courses would provide a solid grounding for most professions and promote a greater cultural understanding in general. I do believe, however, that Sollod exaggerates in his statement that the loss of ethics in American society is "a result of the increasing ignorance, in circles of presumably educated people, of religious and spiritual world views" (15). Here, Sollod makes an inaccurate generalization, with no evidence or clear reasoning to back up his stance. On the contrary, statistics show that in the past thirty years, religion has not only sustained itself, but it has also diversified. According to a recent survey, "Some 375 ethnic or multiethnic religious groups have already formed in the United States in the last three decades. Sociologists of religion believe the numbers will only increase in the coming years" (Beckman). These religious groups are not only the creations of immigrants, but they also reflect America's growing diversity. In fact, as Joanne Beckman of Duke University explains, almost half of the baby boomer

Kolb 4

generation has dropped out of their traditional
churches and are "just as willing to sample Eastern
religions, New Age spiritualism, or quasi-religious
self-help groups. . . . [F]or [these] seekers,
spirituality is a means of individual expression,
self-discovery, inner healing, and personal growth."
Although the deterioration of moral values is a
frustrating problem in our society, it cannot, as
Sollod suggests, be attributed entirely to a lack of
religious appreciation and diversity.

    "The Hollow Curriculum" endorses a controversial
proposal that has prompted much deliberation: the
addition of, or increase in, religious and spiritual
studies in our national curriculum. Although Sollod
does well in arguing his position on the subject, he
assumes, without proof, that much of university life is
shallow and that university curricula is unbalanced.
Further, he makes a hasty generalization when he places
the blame of America's ethical undoing on the lack of
"knowledge or reference to those religious and
spiritual principles that underline our legal system
and moral codes" (15). In this generalization, he
neglects to recognize the growing religious and
spiritual diversity of the American people. This
omission weakens the foundation of his argument—that an
increase in religious studies will benefit all areas of
life—by overlooking evidence showing that, despite an
increase in spiritual awareness, the loss of ethics
remains a problem in our society. Sollod thus
undermines his own position and leaves his readers,
though inspired by his zeal, understandably skeptical.

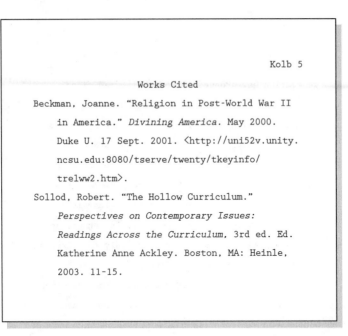

```
                                              Kolb 5
                        Works Cited
    Beckman, Joanne. "Religion in Post-World War II
         in America." Divining America. May 2000.
         Duke U. 17 Sept. 2001. <http://uni52v.unity.
         ncsu.edu:8080/tserve/twenty/tkeyinfo/
         trelww2.htm>.
    Sollod, Robert. "The Hollow Curriculum."
         Perspectives on Contemporary Issues:
         Readings Across the Curriculum, 3rd ed. Ed.
         Katherine Anne Ackley. Boston, MA: Heinle,
         2003. 11-15.
```

Exercise

Read Linda Lee's "Who Needs College?" and prepare for class discussion by writing a critique of the essay. The questions for response and discussion after the essay may help you in your critique. Your instructor may want you to hand in your critique or use it for class discussion.

WHO NEEDS COLLEGE?

Linda Lee

Linda Lee is an editor and writer for the New York Times. *An article she wrote for the Education Life supplement of that publication in 1998, called "What's the Rush? Why College Can Wait," was the basis for her book* Success Without College: Why Your Child May Not Have to Go to College Right Now—And May Not Ever Have to Go *(2000). In addition to contributing to the* Times, *Lee is the author of several books. This brief essay, which touches on some of the ideas explained in her book, appeared in the "Full Circle" column of the June 12, 2001, issue of* Family Circle.

Do you, like me, have a child who is smart but never paid attention in class? Now it's high-school graduation time. Other parents are talking Stanford this and State U. that. Your own child has gotten into a pretty good college. The question is: Is he ready? Should he go at all?

In this country two-thirds of high school graduates go on to college. In some middle-class suburbs, that number reaches 90 percent. So why do so many feel the need to go?

America is obsessed with college. It has the second-highest number of graduates worldwide, after (not Great Britain, not Japan, not Germany) Australia. Even so, only 27 percent of Americans have a bachelor's degree or higher. That leaves an awful lot who succeed without college, or at least without a degree. Many read books, think seriously about life and have well-paying jobs. Some want to start businesses. Others want to be electricians or wilderness guides or makeup artists. Not everyone needs a higher education.

4   What about the statistics showing that college graduates make more money? First, until the computer industry came along, all the highest-paying jobs *required* a college degree: doctor, lawyer, engineer. Second, on average, the brightest and hardest-working kids in school go to college. So is it a surprise that they go on to make more money? And those studies almost always pit kids with degrees against those with just high school. An awful lot have additional training, but they are not included. Ponder for a moment: Who makes more, a plumber or a philosophy major?

These are tough words. I certainly wouldn't have listened to them five years ago when my son was graduating from high school. He had been smart enough to get into the Bronx High School of Science in New York and did well on his SATs. But I know now that he did not belong in college, at least not straight out of high school.

But he went, because all his friends were going, because it sounded like fun, because he could drink beer and hang out. He did not go to study philosophy. Nor did he feel it incumbent to go to class or complete courses. Meanwhile I was paying $1,000 a week for this pleasure cruise.

Eventually I asked myself, "Is he getting $1,000 a week's worth of education?" Heck no. That's when I began wondering why everyone needs to go to college. (My hair colorist makes $300,000 a year without a degree.) What about the famous people who don't have one, like Bill Gates (dropped out of Harvard) and Walter Cronkite (who left the University of Texas to begin a career in journalism)?

8   So I told my son (in a kind way) that his college career was over for now, but he could reapply to the Bank of Mom in two years if he wanted to go back. Meanwhile, I said, get a job.

If college is so wonderful, how come so many kids "stop out"? (That's the new terminology.) One study showed only 26 percent of those who began four-year colleges had earned a degree in six years. And what about the kids who finish, then can't find work? Of course, education is worth a great deal more than just employment. But most kids today view college as a way to get a good job.

I know, I know. What else is there to do? Won't he miss the "college experience?" First off, there are thousands of things for kids to do. And yes, he will miss the college experience, which may include binge drinking, reckless driving and sleeping in on class days. He can have the same experience in the Marine Corps, minus the sleeping in, and be paid good money for it and learn a trade and discipline.

If my son had gone straight through college, he would be a graduate by now. A number of his friends are, and those who were savvy enough to go into computers at an Ivy League school walked into $50,000-a-year jobs. But that's not everyone. An awful lot became teachers making half that. And some still don't know what they want to do.

12   They may, like my son, end up taking whatever jobs they can get. Over the last two years, he's done roofing, delivered UPS packages and fixed broken toilets. His phone was turned off a few times, and he began to pay attention to details, like the price of a gallon of gasoline.

But a year ago he began working at a telecommunications company. He loves his work, and over the last year, he's gotten a raise and a year-end bonus. He tells me now he plans to stay there and become a manager.

So, just about on schedule, my son has had his own graduation day. And although I won't be able to take a picture of him in cap and gown, I couldn't be any more proud. He grew up, as most kids do. And he did it, for the most part, in spite of college.

Personal Response

Respond to the questions posed by Lee in her first paragraph. Are you ready for college? Should you go at all? What would you do if you were not in college?

Questions for Class or Small-Group Discussion

1. Lee states in paragraph 3 that "not everyone needs a higher education." Do you agree with her? Discuss your response to her statement.

2. In paragraph 5, Lee says that her son "did not belong in college, at least not straight out of high school." Explore the implications of that statement by considering the advantages and disadvantages of postponing entry into college after high school graduation.

3. Summarize Lee's "case against college." What is her strongest argument? How do you respond to that point?

4. What is your reaction to Lee's characterization of "the college experience" in paragraph 10? Is it true of your own experience in college? Would you describe the college experience differently? If so, how would you describe it?

CHAPTER 4
WRITING A SYNTHESIS

A synthesis draws conclusions from, makes observations on, or shows connections between two or more sources. In writing a synthesis, you attempt to make sense of the ideas of two or more sources by extracting information that is relevant to your purpose. The ability to synthesize is an important skill, for people are continuously bombarded with a dizzying variety of information and opinions that need sorting out and assessment. To understand your own thinking on a subject, it is always useful to know what others have to say about it. You can see the importance of reading and thinking critically when synthesizing the ideas of others. The sources for a synthesis may be essays, books, editorials, lectures, movies, group discussions, or any of the myriad forms of communication that inform academic and personal lives. At minimum, you will be required in a synthesis to reflect on the ideas of two writers or other sources, assess them, make connections between them, and arrive at your own conclusions on the basis of your analysis. Often you will work with more than two sources; certainly you will do so in a research paper.

Your purpose for writing a synthesis will be determined by the nature of your assignment, although syntheses are most commonly used to either explain or argue. Perhaps you want to explain how something works or show the causes or effects of a particular event. You may argue a particular point, using the arguments of others as supporting evidence or as subjects for disagreement in your own argument. You may want to compare or contrast the positions of other writers for the purpose of stating your own opinion on the subject. When you write a research paper, you most certainly must synthesize the ideas and words of others. Whether your research paper is a report or an argument, you must sort through and make sense of what your sources say. Sometimes you will want to read many sources to find out what a number of people have to say about a particular subject in order to discover your own position on it.

Synthesis, then, involves not only understanding what others have to say on a given subject but also making connections between them, analyzing their arguments or examples, and/or drawing conclusions from them. These are processes you routinely employ in both your everyday life and in your courses whenever you consider the words, ideas, or opinions of two or more people or writers on a topic. Beginning with chapter 8, each chapter in parts 2 through 5 ends with a list of suggestions for synthesis on the basis of the readings in that chapter. These topics ask you to argue, to compare and contrast, to explore reasons, to explain something, to describe, or to report on something, using at least two of the essays in the chapter.

In all cases, no matter what your purpose is for writing the synthesis, you will need to state your own central idea or thesis early in your paper. In preparation for writing your essay, you will complete a very helpful step if you locate the central idea or thesis of each of the works under analysis and summarize their main points. The summary is itself a kind of synthesis, in that you locate the key ideas in an essay, state them in your own words, and then put the ideas back together again in a shortened form. This process helps you understand what the authors believe and why they believe it. Furthermore, your own readers benefit from a summary of the central idea or chief points of the articles you are assessing. As you write your essay, you will not only be explaining your own view, opinion, or position, but you also will be using the ideas or words of the authors whose works you are synthesizing. These will have to be documented, using the appropriate formatting for documenting sources illustrated in this chapter and in chapter 5.

GUIDELINES FOR WRITING A SYNTHESIS

- **Determine your purpose for writing by asking yourself what you want to do in your essay.** Without a clear purpose, your synthesis will be a loosely organized, incoherent jumble of words. Although your purpose is often governed by the way in which the assignment is worded, make sure you understand exactly what you intend to do.
- **Consider how best to accomplish your purpose.** Will you argue, explain, compare and contrast, illustrate, show causes and effects, describe, or narrate? How will you use your sources to accomplish your purpose?
- **Read each source carefully and understand its central purpose and major points.** If you are unclear about the meaning of an essay, reread it carefully, noting passages that give you trouble. Discuss these passages with a classmate or with your instructor if you still lack a clear understanding.
- **Write a one-sentence statement of the central idea or thesis and a brief summary of each source you will use in your paper.** This process will help clarify your understanding of your sources and assist you in formulating your own central idea. These statements or summaries can then be incorporated appropriately into your synthesis.
- **Write a one-sentence statement of your own thesis or central purpose for writing the synthesis.** This statement should be a complete sentence, usually in the first paragraph of your essay. The thesis statement helps you focus your thoughts as you plan your essay by limiting the nature and scope of what you intend to accomplish. It also is a crucial aid to your readers, because it is essentially a succinct summary of what you intend to do.
- **Develop or illustrate your thesis by incorporating the ideas of your sources into the body of your paper, either by paraphrasing or directly quoting.** Part of your purpose in writing a synthesis is to demonstrate familiarity with your sources and to draw on them in your own essay. This goal requires that you make reference to key ideas of the sources.
- **Document your sources.** Keep in mind the guidelines for documenting all borrowed material.

ILLUSTRATION: SYNTHESIS

Following are two examples of a synthesis paper, each written by a student. The first is annotated with marginal comments, whereas the second has no marginal commentary. Note that in both papers, a "Works Cited" list appears at the end. The works cited page gives full bibliographic information for each source. Notice that works are listed alphabetically and that each citation conforms in punctuation and spacing to the MLA style of documentation (chapter 6). For a discussion of paraphrasing and quoting, see chapter 5. For more on formatting of the works cited list, see chapter 6.

ILLUSTRATION: SYNTHESIS

Konrad 1

Elizabeth Konrad

Professor Lee

English 102

November 28, 2002

The Place of Spirituality in the College Curriculum

The opening paragraph provides background information and indicates that the issue raises controversy.

Education today is more complicated than ever before. The rapid rate at which knowledge increases and the almost constantly changing nature of our society and the jobs required to sustain it put great pressure on both institutions of higher education and students alike. Colleges consider how best to adapt and change their curricula to meet the needs of students preparing to enter the workforce, while students are conflicted not only about what they should study but also about the relevance of their studies to their futures. One controversy centers on what subjects are appropriate in the college curriculum, including how much, if any, emphasis should be given to students' spiritual lives as they prepare for their professional lives. Given the increasingly complicated and troubled

The thesis statement in the last sentence of the first paragraph is a straightforward declarative sentence that makes clear the position of the author.

Konrad 2

nature of contemporary society, colleges and
universities should give as much consideration to
students' spiritual development as they do to their
intellectual development.

Research indicates that many college students
are worried about America's future. One such study
is that of Arthur Levine, a professor in the Harvard
Graduate School of Education, who profiles today's
college undergraduates and their views of the future
in a report of his 1993 survey of undergraduates at
twenty-eight campuses. In his survey, Levine asked
what social and political events had most
influenced their lives. Levine's survey reveals
that many of today's generation of college
undergraduates have negative feelings about the
significant events that have affected their lives.
They also feel somewhat overwhelmed by the
knowledge that they are inheriting a "deeply
troubled nation" whose problems they will be
expected to find solutions for (27). This sense of
fear about their futures and students' resentment at
the state of the country whose problems they will
inherit suggest a real need for the kind of
emotional support that a strong spirituality or deep
religious belief can provide. The support that comes
from a solid understanding of the role of religion
in people's lives would very likely be a comfort to
students as they complete their education. It would
also help them prepare for a future in which they

Levine's survey is summarized briefly, and its relevance to the subject of the paper is explained clearly.

Only a page number is given in the citation because Levine's name is mentioned in the text.

Elizabeth expresses her own conclusion about the implications of Levine's survey for her own thesis.

Konrad 3

may have to make decisions that will affect others
as well as themselves.

Proponents of including courses that teach
students about religious values in college curricula
point out that "some patterns of religious
commitment have been found to be associated with
high levels of mental health and ego strength"
(Sollod 16). Given that today's young people are
tomorrow's problem solvers, it makes sense to
nurture good mental health and the kind of self-
confidence that comes from spirituality or religious
beliefs. As Levine notes in the conclusion to his
report, "The big issue facing students [he]
interviewed was how to choose" between "making money
and performing good deeds" (28). College-level
courses on religion and spirituality may help
students make the choices that best benefit the
larger society.

Courses in religion and spirituality might also
help address some of the criticisms leveled at
colleges, such as the complaint that too many
college classrooms are isolated from one another,
making most of them, according to Gerald Graff, like
"a set of ships passing in the night" (40). Graff
cites the critic Kenneth Burke as having once
"compared the intellectual life of a culture to a
parlor in which different guests are forever
dropping in and out," adding: "As the standard
curriculum represents the intellectual life,
however, there is no parlor; the hosts congregate in

Robert Sollod's name is not mentioned in the text, so in the citation, his last name is given along with the page number where the quotation appears in the source.

The quotation from Levine uses brackets to indicate that a word has been changed for consistent grammar in the sentence.

The first time an author's name is used, his or her full name is given. For second and subsequent references, use the last name only.

Konrad 4

separate rooms with their acolytes and keep their
differences and agreements to themselves" (37).
Educators have responded to such criticism by
offering cross-curricular or interdisciplinary
courses and by team-teaching classes. As a result,
students gain a sense of community beyond the
individual classroom and see connections among the
courses they take. This is the kind of community
that courses in spirituality and religion encourage.

Robert N. Sollod would likely agree that
schools should do more to meet students' personal
needs, as he makes clear in "The Hollow Curriculum"
when he argues that college "curricula [. . .] do
little" to correct the lack of "religious and
spiritual teachings" (14). Sollod believes that an
understanding of religion and spirituality would
help professionals in many fields. Most colleges and
universities ignore these important aspects of
students' lives, resulting in "a kind of segregation
of the life of the spirit from the life of the mind
in American culture" (Sollod 16). A happy joining of
the life of the spirit and the life of the mind
would surely be of benefit in an age often criticized
for its lack of a strong moral center and
intellectual activity.

Despite the many courses colleges currently
offer, they would do well to add a component to the
curriculum that meets the spiritual needs of
students. Students themselves express anger about
the state of the world they are being educated to

Notice that Elizabeth balances her own observations or general remarks with both paraphrases and quotations from her source materials.

Naming the source as well as author provides additional helpful information for readers.

The three spaced dots are ellipsis points and indicate that words have been omitted from the original. Rather than quote the entire sentence, Elizabeth touches on the essence of Sollod's article and stresses the point relevant to her own central idea.

Konrad 5

take major roles in, and they are confused about
whether to serve society at large or to look after
only themselves. Some educators are calling for
colleges and universities to help students make
connections between the courses they take and to
realize the place of these courses in their larger
contexts. Others call for colleges to pay attention to
the spiritual lives of their students. Offering
courses on spirituality and religion would thus benefit
students, satisfy educators, and ultimately serve the
greater need of a troubled and complex nation.

The conclusion makes reference to the ideas of each of the three authors mentioned in the text of the paper and restates Elizabeth's own position on the subject.

Konrad 6

Works Cited

Ackley, Katherine, ed. <u>Perspectives on
    Contemporary Issues: Readings Across the
    Disciplines</u>, 2nd ed. Fort Worth: Harcourt,
    2000.

Graff, Gerald. "Ships in the Night." Ackley
    285-292.

Levine, Arthur. "The Making of a Generation."
    Ackley 20-28.

Sollod, Robert N. "The Hollow Curriculum." Ackley
    14-17.

Novak 1

Barbara Novak

English 150

September 24, 2003

The Shock-Proof Generation

Arthur Levine, an education faculty member at
Harvard, firmly believes that "every college generation
is defined by the social events of its age" (26). To
confirm his belief Levine questioned university
students about "what social or political events most
influenced their generation" (26). The Great Depression
influenced those who grew up after World War I. Those
born after World War II were affected by the
assassination of John F. Kennedy. Students surveyed in
1979 rallied around Vietnam and Watergate. Those
questioned in 1993 remembered the explosion of the
Challenger. What modern political or social events
will the youth of today be influenced by?

Psychiatric professor Ronald Dahl might suggest
that the events that have the greatest impact on
today's youth will be more stunning and dramatic than
ever. While observing his own young children and
their friends, Professor Dahl could not help but
notice that despite "ever-greater stimulation, their
young faces were looking disappointed and bored"
(19). Dahl believes that the over-stimulation of
today's youth has resulted in a generation with a
previously unprecedented threshold for excitement.
Consequently, it takes increasingly shocking,
violent, or thrilling events to stimulate young
people. Consistent with their insatiable appetite for

Novak 2

excitement, the upcoming generation, described by
Dahl as "burned out and bored," will be influenced by
political and social events that are more violent,
thrilling, or fast-paced than those remembered by
previous generations.

The widely publicized tragedy at Columbine High
School is one example of a political and social event
shocking enough to influence the current generation of
young Americans. Two high school students, Eric
Harris and Dylan Klebold, entered their own school on
April 20, 1999, and executed a carefully planned
rampage of terror. Fifteen members of the school
community were killed before the young men took their
own lives (Pellegrini). The violence carried out that
day by Harris and Klebold reached a climactic point
high enough to actually have a shocking effect on
modern over-stimulated youth. Therefore, the calamity
that occurred at Columbine High School will be an
occurrence indicated by most of today's youth as an
event that defines their generation.

Dahl writes: "What really worries me is the
intensity of the stimulation. I watch my eleven-year-
old daughter's face as she absorbs the powerful
onslaught of arousing visuals and gory special
effects in movies" (19). Over-exposure to such
violence, whether in video games, television, movies,
or music lyrics, leads to de-sensitization of the
viewer. Prior to, as well as after, the events in
Littleton there were numerous school shootings;
however, the impact of these paled in

comparison to that of Columbine. If an increase in exposure to violence creates youth who are increasingly tolerant of violence, it can be inferred that the power of the events at Columbine was greater than that of other school shootings because it was phenomenally more violent. If Dahl's beliefs regarding today's youth are correct, the social and political events that define this generation will become increasingly violent simply because it will take more violence to obtain a reaction.

Dahl also poses the following question: "Why do [small] children immersed in this much excitement seem starved for more? That was, I realized, the point. I discovered during my own reckless adolescence that what creates exhilaration is not going fast, but going faster [. . .]. Thrills have less to do with speed than changes in speed" (19). The unthinkable actions carried out by Eric Harris and Dylan Klebold were attempts to create exhilaration by changing the speed of a normal day at Columbine High School. Unfortunately, Harris and Klebold were raised in a world of "ever-greater stimulation" (Dahl 19). Therefore, the efforts necessary to create exhilaration were nearly as enormous as the impact of the shooting.

Recognizing the tragedy at Columbine High School as an event that will define a generation allows it to be examined as an indicator of the problems that exist within that age group. The future of our nation lies upon the shoulders of the young. It is crucial

Novak 4

to be aware of the immense effects of the violent and
negative images that bombard this group on a daily
basis. Realizing the over-stimulation that is
occurring among young Americans will help not only to
prevent another tragedy like Columbine, but it will
also ensure that the next generation will have the
ability to successfully handle the problems of the
future.

Novak 5

Works Cited

Ackley, Katherine, ed. Perspectives on
    Contemporary Issues: Readings Across the
    Disciplines, 3rd ed. Boston: Heinle,
    2003.

Dahl, Ronald. "Burned Out and Bored." Ackley
    18-20.

Levine, Arthur. "The Making of a Generation."
    Ackley 26-33.

Pellegrini, Frank. "Colorado Shootings: Now, the
    Aftermath." Time 21 Apr. 99. 20 Sept. 01.
    <http://www.time.com/time/daily/0,2960,
    23427,00.html>

CHAPTER 5

IN-TEXT CITATIONS, PARAPHRASING, AND QUOTING

No matter what your purpose or pattern of development, if you draw on the writing of someone else, you must be fair to the author of the material you borrow. If you paraphrase an author's words or, occasionally, quote them exactly as they appear in the original text, you must cite your source. In any case, when you are using the ideas or words of another, you must give credit to your source. In academic writing, credit is given by naming the author of the borrowed material, its title, the place and date of publication, and the page number or numbers where the information is located.

This chapter introduces some basic skills needed to incorporate the words and ideas of others into your own written work. It begins with a discussion of documenting sources, goes on to provide guidelines and examples for paraphrasing and quoting, illustrates some useful tools for handling source material and integrating source materials, and ends with directions for documenting sources from collections of essays, such as this textbook. The guidelines in this chapter follow MLA (Modern Language Association) documentation style. (Note: If your instructor prefers that you use APA style or gives you a choice of styles, guidelines for APA documentation style appear in chapter 7.) MLA style is used primarily in the humanities disciplines, such as English and philosophy, whereas other disciplines have their own guidelines. If you learn the skills necessary for paraphrasing, quoting, and documenting the material located in this textbook, you will be prepared to incorporate library and Internet resources, as well as other materials, into long, complex research papers. For more discussion of MLA style, with sample works cited entries for a broad range of both print and nonprint sources, including the Internet, see chapter 6.

IN-TEXT CITATIONS USING MLA STYLE

The MLA style of documentation requires that you give a brief reference to the source of any borrowed material in a parenthetical note that follows the material. This parenthetical note contains only the last name of the authority and the page number or numbers on which the material appears or only the page number or numbers if you mention the author's name in the text.

The parenthetical citation is placed within the sentence, after the quotation or paraphrase, and before the period. If punctuation appears at the end of the words you are quoting, ignore a comma, period, or semicolon but include a question mark or exclamation mark. In all cases, the period for your sentence follows the parenthetical citation.

The name or title that appears in the parenthetical citation in your text corresponds to an entry in the Works Cited page at the end of your paper. This entry contains complete bibliographic information about the work you reference, including the full name of the author, the complete title, the place of publication, and the date of publication.

Treat World Wide Web sources as you do printed works. Because many Web sources do not have page numbers, omit page numbers. Some authorities recommend naming the title of Internet source material in the text and placing the author's name in the parentheses, or repeating the author's name in the parentheses, even if it is used in the text.

GUIDELINES FOR DOCUMENTING SOURCES

- Provide a citation every time you paraphrase or quote directly from a source.
- Give the citation in parentheses following the quotation or paraphrase.
- In the parentheses, give the author's last name and the page number or numbers from which you took the words or ideas. Do not put any punctuation between the author's last name and the page number.
- If you name the author as you introduce the words or ideas, the parentheses will include only the page number or numbers.
- At the end of your paper, provide an alphabetical list of the authors you quoted or paraphrased and give complete bibliographic information, including not only author and title but also where you found the material. This element is the Works Cited page.

Illustration: In-text Citations.   The following examples show formats for citing sources in the text of your paper. The works cited format for many of the references illustrated here can be found in the section on creating a Works Cited page in chapter 6.

- **Book or article with one author.** Name the author followed by the page number:

    (Sollod 15)

- **Book or article with two authors.** Name both authors followed by the page number:

    (Barrett and Rowe 78)

- **Book or article with three or more authors.** If three, name all three or just the first and "et al." (Latin for "and others"). If more than three, name just the first and "et al." In either case, add the page number:

    (Fletcher, Miller, and Caplan 78) or (Fletcher et al. 78)

Note: Reproduce the names in the order in which they appear on the title page. If they are not listed alphabetically, do not change their order.

- **Article or other publication with no author named.** Give a short title followed by the page number:

  ("Teaching" 10)

Note: If you cite two anonymous articles beginning with the same word, use the full title of each to distinguish one from the other.

- **Two works by the same author.** Give the author's name followed by a comma, a short title and the page number:

  (Heilbrun, "Hamlet's Mother" 123)

- **Works by people with the same last name.** If your list of works cited has works by authors with the same last name, include the first name of the author in the parenthetical citation and then the page number or numbers.

  (Gregory Smith 16)

PARAPHRASING

Paraphrasing is similar to summarizing in that you restate in your own words something someone else has written, but a paraphrase restates everything in the passage rather than highlighting just the key points. Summaries give useful presentations of the major points or ideas of long passages or entire works, whereas paraphrases are most useful in clarifying or emphasizing the main points of short passages.

To paraphrase, express the ideas of the author in your own words, being careful not to use phrases or key words of the original. Paraphrases are sometimes as long as the original passages, though often they are slightly shorter. The purpose of paraphrasing is to convey the essence of a sentence or passage in an accurate, fair manner and without the distraction of quotation marks. If your paraphrase repeats the exact words of the original, then you are quoting, and you must put quotation marks around those words. A paper will be more interesting and more readable if you paraphrase more often than you quote. Think of your own response when you read something that contains quotations. Perhaps, like many readers, you will read with interest a paraphrase or short quotation, but you may skip over or skim quickly long passages set off by quotation marks. Readers generally are more interested in the ideas of the author than in his skill at quoting other authors.

GUIDELINES FOR PARAPHRASING

- Restate in your own words the important ideas or essence of a passage.
- Do not repeat more than two or three exact words of any part of the original, unless you enclose them in quotation marks.

- If you must repeat a phrase, clause, or sentence exactly as it appears in the original, put quotation marks around those words.
- Keep the paraphrase about the same length as the original.
- Give the source of the paraphrased information either in your text or in parentheses immediately after the paraphrase.
- Try to paraphrase rather than quote as often as possible, saving direct quotations for truly remarkable language, startling or unusual information, or otherwise original or crucial wording.

Illustration: Paraphrasing.   This section provides examples of paraphrases using selected passages from the sources indicated.

1. **Source:** Graff, Gerald. *Beyond the Culture Wars: How Teaching the Conflicts Can Revitalize American Education.* New York: W. W. Norton, 1992.

   Original (page 118): But the most familiar representation of the sentimental image of the course as a scene of conflict-free community is the one presented on untold numbers of college catalog covers: A small, intimate class is sprawled informally on the gently sloping campus greensward, shady trees overhead and ivy-covered buildings in the background. Ringed in a casual semicircle, the students gaze with rapt attention at a teacher who is reading aloud from a small book—a volume of poetry, we inevitably assume, probably Keats or Dickinson or Whitman. The classroom, in these images, is a garden occupying a redemptive space inside the bureaucratic and professional machine.

   Paraphrase: Gerald Graff notes that many colleges project a common sentimental image of campus life as an idyllic community set among ivy-covered buildings and characterized by small classes, attentive students, and poetry-reading instructors. The classroom becomes a haven from conflict and stress (118).

Comment: Even when you put material into your own words, you must cite the source and give a page number where the paraphrased material is located.

2. **Source:** Dahl, Ronald. "Burned Out and Bored." *Newsweek* 15 Dec. 1997: 8.

   Original (page 8): What really worries me is the intensity of the stimulation. I watch my eleven-year-old daughter's face as she absorbs the powerful onslaught of arousing visuals and gory special effects. Although my son is prohibited from playing violent video games, I have seen some of his third-grade friends at an arcade inflicting blood-splattering, dismembering blows upon on-screen opponents in distressingly realistic games. . . . Why do children immersed in this much excitement seem starved for more? That was, I realized, the point.

Paraphrase: Dahl believes that the overstimulation of today's youth has resulted in a generation with a previously unprecedented threshold for excitement. It takes increasingly more violent, more shocking, and more thrilling events to stimulate young people (8).

Comment: When it is clear that you are paraphrasing from the same source in two or more consecutive sentences *and* you have named the author or source in the first sentence, you need give only one parenthetical citation at the end of the series of sentences.

---

3. **Source:** Watkins, Wes. "English Should Be America's Official Language." *Washington Window* 20 Feb. 1998. 5 Dec. 2002 <www.house.gov/watkins/wwenglsh.htm>.

   Original: This assimilation has always included the adoption of English as the common means of communication. Unfortunately, our government now sends mixed signals which contribute to linguistic division in our country. This division of the United States into separate language groups contributes to racial and ethnic conflicts. Designating English as the official language will halt this harmful process.

   Paraphrase: According to Congressman Wes Watkins, who favors making English America's official language, when the government supports the choice of people to speak their native language, it helps create racial tension. Watkins believes that making English America's official language would ease that tension (Watkins).

Comment: For Internet or other electronic sources without pagination, many instructors recommend that you repeat the author's name in parentheses after all paraphrases and direct quotations, even if the name is already included in the text.

QUOTING

When you want to include the words of another writer, but it is not appropriate to either paraphrase or summarize, you will want to quote. Quoting requires that you repeat the exact words of another, placing quotation marks before and after the material being quoted. A crucial guideline requires that you copy the words exactly as they appear in the original text. To omit words or approximate the original within quotation marks is sloppy or careless handling of your source material.

Be selective in the material you choose to quote directly, however. You should usually paraphrase the words of another, restating them in your own language, rather than relying on exactly copying the words. How do you know when to quote rather than paraphrase? You should quote only words, phrases, or sentences that are particularly striking or that must be reproduced exactly because you cannot convey them in your own words without weakening their effect or changing their intent. Quote passages or parts of passages that are original, dramatically worded, or in some way essential to your paper. Otherwise, rely on paraphrasing to refer to the ideas of others. In either case, document your source by identifying the original source and the location of your information within that source.

GUIDELINES FOR QUOTING

- Be selective: Quote directly only words, phrases, or sentences that are particularly striking and whose beauty, originality, or drama would be lost in a paraphrase.
- Quote directly passages that are so succinct that paraphrasing them would be more complicated or take more words than a direct quotation would require.
- Enclose the exact words you are quoting between quotation marks.
- Do not change one word of the original unless you indicate with brackets, ellipses, or other conventions that you have done so.
- Provide the source of your quoted material either in your text or in parentheses following the material.

Illustration: Quoting. This section provides examples of quotations using selected passages from Gerald Graff's "Ships in the Night." The source for all examples in this section is the following:

> Graff, Gerald. *Beyond the Culture Wars: How Teaching the Conflicts Can Revitalize American Education.* New York: W. W. Norton, 1992.

1. **Original** (page 106): To some of us these days, the moral of these stories would be that students have become cynical relativists who care less about convictions than about grades and careers.

   Quotation: Gerald Graff suggests that "students have become cynical relativists who care less about convictions than about grades and careers" (106).

COMMENTS

- Place double quotation marks before and after words taken directly from the original.
- When the quoted material is an integral part of your sentence, do not capitalize the first letter of the first word.

- Where possible, name the author whose ideas or words you are quoting or paraphrasing.
- In parentheses after the quotation, give the page number in the source where the quotation is located (hence the phrase "parenthetical citation"). This example contains only the page number because the author's name is mentioned in the text. If the text had not given the author's name, it would be included in the parenthetical citation.

2. **Original** (page 118): The more fundamental question we should be asking in most cases is not how *much time* teachers are spending in the classroom but *under what conditions.*

   Quotation: Gerald Graff believes that "[t]he more fundamental question [. . .] is not *how much* time teachers are spending in the classroom but *under what conditions*" (118).

COMMENTS

- When a quotation preceded by *that* forms an integral part of your sentence, do not capitalize the first word in the quotation, even when it is capitalized in the original. In this example, because the *t* in *the* is capitalized in the original, the bracket around the lowercased *t* in the quotation indicates that the letter has been changed.
- If some text is italicized in the original, you must italicize it in your quotation.
- Use brackets around ellipsis points.

3. **Original** (page 109): Among the factors that make academic culture more confusing today than in the past is not only that there is more controversy but that there is even controversy about what can legitimately be considered controversial. Traditionalists are often angry that there should even be a debate over the canon, while revisionists are often angry that there should even be a debate over "political correctness," or the relevance of ideology and politics to their subjects.

   Quotation: In discussing the factors that confuse people about college curricula today, Gerald Graff notes: "Traditionalists are often angry that there should even be a debate over the canon, while revisionists are often angry that there should even be a debate over 'political correctness' [. . .]" (109).

COMMENTS

- If your direct quotation is preceded by introductory text and a colon or comma, capitalize the first letter of the first word of the quotation.
- If you quote something that appears in quotation marks in the original source, use single marks within the double quotes.
- If an ellipsis comes at the end of a quotation, the closing quotation mark follows the third period, with no space between the period and quotation mark. The parenthetical citation follows as usual.

Combination of paraphrase and direct quotation. The following example illustrates how one can combine paraphrasing and quoting for a balanced handling of source material.

4. **Original** (page 118): But the most familiar representation of the sentimental image of the course as a scene of conflict-free community is the one presented on untold numbers of college catalog covers: A small, intimate class is sprawled informally on the gently sloping campus greensward, shady trees overhead and ivy-covered buildings in the background. Ringed in a casual semicircle, the students gaze with rapt attention at a teacher who is reading aloud from a small book—a volume of poetry, we inevitably assume, probably Keats or Dickinson or Whitman. The classroom, in these images, is a garden occupying a redemptive space inside the bureaucratic and professional machine.

   Paraphrase and Quotation: Gerald Graff thinks that colleges project an image different from the realities of academic life. College catalog covers, he says, foster "the sentimental image of the course as a scene of conflict-free community" when they portray students sitting outside on a sunny day, mesmerized by the instructor who stands before them, reading someone's words of insight or wisdom. According to him, the classroom becomes "a garden occupying a redemptive space inside the bureaucratic and professional machine" (118).

Here are two more examples of correctly handled direct quotations:

5. Jack Santino in "Rock and Roll as Music; Rock and Roll as Culture" maintains that "[s]uch things as suicide, drugs, sex, and violence *are* teenage concerns" and that, "while artists have a responsibility not to glamorize them, that does not mean these themes should not be explored" (196).

6. In "Rock and Roll as Music; Rock and Roll as Culture," Jack Santino observes: "Furthermore, such things as suicide, drugs, sex, and violence *are* teenage concerns. While artists have a responsibility not to glamorize them, that does not mean these themes should not be explored" (196).

COMMENTS

- Notice the difference between examples 5 and 6. The first integrates the quoted material into the sentence with the word *that,* so the first words in each of the quoted passages do not require a capital first letter. In the second example, the quotation is introduced and set off as a separate sentence, so the first word after the quotation mark begins with a capital letter.

INTEGRATING SOURCE MATERIALS INTO YOUR PAPER

When quoting or paraphrasing material, pay special attention to your treatment of source materials. Authors have developed many ways of skillfully integrating the words and ideas of other people with their own words. Your paper should not read as if you simply cut out the words of someone else and pasted them in your paper.

> **Caution: Never incorporate a quotation without in some way introducing or commenting on it.** A quotation that is not introduced or followed by some concluding comment, referred to as a "bald" or "dropped" quotation, detracts from the smooth flow of your paper.

You can achieve smooth integration of source materials into your text if you keep the following suggestions in mind:

- **Mention the cited author's name in the text of your paper to signal the beginning of a paraphrase or quotation.** The first time you mention the name, give both first and last names. After the first mention, give only the last name:

  > **Robert Sollod** points out in "The Hollow Curriculum" that colleges would not think of excluding courses on multiculturalism from today's curriculum, given the importance of "appreciation and understanding of human diversity." **Sollod** asks: "Should such an appreciation exclude the religious and spiritually based concepts of reality that are the backbone upon which entire cultures have been based?" (A60).

- **Mention the source if no author is named.** This practice gives credit to the source while providing an introduction to the borrowed material:

  > A *U.S. News & World Report* article notes that, although no genes determine what occupation one will go into, groups of genes produce certain tendencies—risk-taking, for instance—that might predispose one to select a particular kind of work ("How Genes Shape Personality" 64).

- **Give citations for all borrowed material.** State the authority's name, use quotation marks as appropriate, give the source and page number in a parenthetical citation, give some sort of general information, and/or use a pronoun to refer to the authority mentioned in the previous sentence. **Do not rely on one parenthetical citation at the end of several sentences or an entire paragraph:**

Regna Lee Wood has also researched the use of phonics in teaching children to read. **She** believes that the horrible failure of our schools began years ago. Wood notes that "it all began in 1929 and 1930 when hundreds of primary teachers, guided by college reading professors, stopped teaching beginners to read by "matching sounds with letters that spell sounds" (52). **She** adds that since 1950, when most reading teachers switched to teaching children to sight words rather than sound them by syllable, "fifty million children with poor sight memories have reached the fourth grade still unable to read" (52).

- **Vary introductory phrases and clauses.** Avoid excessive reliance on such standard introductory clauses as "Smith says," or "Jones writes." For instance, vary your verbs and/or provide explanatory information about sources, as in the following examples:

  Jerry Baker notes the following:
  Professor Xavier argues this point convincingly:
  According to Dr. Carroll, chief of staff at a major health center:
  As Marcia Smith points out,

- **The first mention of an authority in your text (as opposed to the parenthetical citation) should include the author's first name as well as last name.** The second and subsequent references should give the last name only (never the first name alone).

  First use of author's name in your paper: Susan Jaspers correctly observes that . . .
  Second and subsequent mentions of that author: Jaspers contends elsewhere that . . .

- **Combine quotations and paraphrases.** A combination provides a smoother style than quoting directly all of the time:

  Arthur Levine's 1993 survey of college students reveals that today's generation of young people differs from those he surveyed in 1979. Levine discovered that today's college students "are living through a period of profound demographic, economic, global, and technological change." Since these students of the 90s see themselves living in a "deeply troubled nation," they have only guarded optimism about the future (32–33).

- **For long quotations (more than four lines) set the quoted material off from the text (referred to as a block quotation).** Write your introduction to the quotation, generally followed by a colon. Then begin a new line indented ten spaces from the left margin, and type the quotation, double-spaced as usual.

- **Do not add quotation marks for block quotations indented and set off from the text.** If quotation marks appear in the original, use double quotation marks, not single. If you quote a single paragraph or part of one, do not indent the first line any more than the rest of the quotation.

- **For block quotations, place the parenthetical citation after the final punctuation of the quotation.** See the following example of a block quotation:

  > In her article exploring the kind of workforce required by a high-tech economy, Joanne Jacobs suggests that many of today's high school graduates lack crucial skills necessary for jobs in the rapidly growing technical and computer industries. For instance, a number of corporations agreed on the following prerequisites for telecommunications jobs:
  >
  > - Technical reading skills (familiarity with circuit diagrams, online documentation, and specialized reference materials).
  > - Advanced mathematical skills (understanding of binary, octal, and hexadecimal number systems as well as mathematical logic systems).
  > - Design knowledge (ability to use computer-aided design to produce drawings) (39–40).

USING ELLIPSIS POINTS, BRACKETS, SINGLE QUOTATION MARKS, AND "QTD. IN"

This section offers some additional guidelines on the mechanics of handling source materials and incorporating them into your paper.

Ellipsis Points

- **If you want to omit original words, phrases, or sentences from your quotation of source material, use ellipsis points to indicate the omission.** Ellipsis points consist of three spaced periods, with spaces before, between, and after the periods. In quotations, ellipses are most frequently used within sentences, almost never at the beginning, but sometimes at the end. In every case, the quoted material must form a grammatically complete sentence, either by itself or in combination with your own words.

  MLA style calls for the use of brackets around ellipsis points to distinguish between your ellipses and the spaced periods that sometimes occur in works. In that case, leave a space before the second and third periods but no space before the first or after the third. Use an ellipsis mark to indicate that you have left words out of an otherwise direct quotation:

  > **Original:** The momentous occurrences of an era—from war and economics to politics and inventions—give meaning to lives of the individuals who live through them.
  >
  > **Quotation with ellipses in the middle:** Arthur Levine argues, "The momentous occurrences of an era [. . .] give meaning to lives of the individuals who live through them" (26).
  >
  > **Quotation with ellipses at the end:** Use ellipsis marks at the end of a quotation only if you have dropped some words from the end of the final sentence quoted. In that case, include four periods. When the

ellipsis coincides with the end of your own sentence, leave a space before the first bracket, and immediately follow the last bracket with the sentence period and the closing quotation mark.

> You know the old saying, "Eat, drink, and be merry [...] ."

If a parenthetical reference follows the ellipsis at the end of your sentence, leave a space before the first bracket, and immediately follow the last bracket with the closing quotation mark, a space, the parenthetical reference, and the sentence period.

> According to recent studies, "Statistics show that Chinese women's status has improved [...]" (*Chinese Women* 46).

- **Ellipsis points are not necessary** if you are quoting a fragment of a sentence, that is, a few words or a subordinate clause, because context will clearly indicate the omission of some of the original sentence.

  > Sociobiologists add that social and nurturing experiences can "intensify, diminish, or modify" personality traits (Wood and Wood 272).

Brackets

- The *MLA Handbook* says that "[u]nless indicated in brackets or parentheses . . . , changes must not be made in spelling, capitalization, or interior punctuation of the source" (3.9.1). Although you should look for ways to integrate source material into your text that avoid overuse of brackets, the following guidelines apply when changing source material is unavoidable.
- **If you want to change a word or phrase to conform to your own sentence or add words to make your sentence grammatically correct, use brackets to indicate the change.** The brackets enclose only the changed portion of the original.

  > **Original:** They were additional casualties of our time of plague, demoralized reminders that although this country holds only two percent of the world's population, it consumes 65 percent of the world's supply of hard drugs.
  > **Quotation:** According to Pete Hamill in his essay "Crack and the Box," America "holds only two percent of the world's population, [yet] it consumes 65 percent of the world's supply of hard drugs" (267).
  > **Original:** In a miasma of Walt Disney images, Bambi burning, and Snow White asleep, the most memorable is "Cinderella."
  > **Quotation:** Louise Bernikow recalls spending Saturday afternoons at the theatre when she was growing up "[i]n a miasma of Walt Disney images, [...] the most memorable [of which] is 'Cinderella'" (17).
  > **Note:** This example illustrates the use not only of brackets but also of ellipsis points and single and double quotation marks.

- **Use brackets if you add some explanatory information or editorial comment, or use them to indicate that you have changed the capitalization in the quoted material.**

Original: Marriage is another dying institution[...]. "If we live to-gether," the attitude goes, "why should I commit myself? Why should I assume responsibility?"

Quotation: Even the perspective toward marriage carries the atti-tude, " '[W]hy should I commit myself? Why should I assume respon-sibility?' " (Barrett and Rowe 346).

Original: Then, magically, the fairy godmother appears. She comes from nowhere, summoned, we suppose, by Cinderella's wishes.

Quotation: Louise Bernikow points out that "[s]he [the fairy god-mother] comes from nowhere, summoned [...] by Cinderella's wishes" (19).

- **The Latin word *sic* (meaning "thus") in brackets indicates that an error occurs in the original source of a passage you are quoting.** Because you are not at liberty to change words when quoting word for word, reproduce the error but use [*sic*] to indicate that the error is not yours.

  Original: Thrills have less to do with speed then changes in speed.

  Quotation: Dahl makes this observation: "Thrills have less to do with speed then [*sic*] changes in speed" (18).

Single quotation marks

- **If you quote text that itself appears in quotation marks in the original, use single marks within the double that enclose your own quotation.**

  Original: This set me pondering the obvious question: "How can it be so hard for kids to find something to do when there's never been such a range of stimulating entertainment available to them?"

  Quotation: Dahl is led to ask this question: " 'How can it be so hard for kids to find something to do when there's never been such a range of stimulating entertainment available to them?' " (18–19).

- **Occasionally you will have to quote something that is already a quotation within a quotation,** where the original contains single quotation marks within double quotes. In that case, use double quotation marks within single within double:

  Original: In my interviews with the chief witness, he swears he heard Smith say: " 'It wasn't me! I didn't do it!' "

  Quotation: Johnson records an interview with a chief witness in the case. Smith is said to have proclaimed, " ' "It wasn't me! I didn't do it!" ' " (23).

Qtd. in

If you quote or paraphrase material that is already quoted, use the abbreviation "qtd." with the word "in." Use "qtd. in" whenever you quote or paraphrase the published account of someone else's words or ideas. The Works Cited page will include not the original source of the material you quoted or paraphrased but rather the in-direct source, the one where you found the material. You will likely be using the single quotation marks within the double because you are quoting what someone else has quoted.

1. **Original:** Printed in bold letters at the entrance of the show is a startling claim by Degas' fellow painter Auguste Renoir: "If Degas had died at 50, he would have been remembered as an excellent painter, no more; it is after his 50th year that his work broadened out and that he really becomes Degas."

   Quotation: Impressionist painter Auguste Renoir observed of Degas: " 'If Degas had died at 50, he would have been remembered as an excellent painter, no more; it is after his 50th year that his work broadened out and that he really becomes Degas' " (qtd. in Benfey).

2. **Original:** Teen suicide is nearly four times more common today than it was a few decades ago, says Dr. Janice Grossman, a suicide expert.

   Quotation: According to Dr. Janice Grossman, an expert on suicide, "Teen suicide is nearly four times more common today than it was a few decades ago" (qtd. in Arenofsky).

GUIDELINES FOR INTEGRATING SOURCE MATERIALS INTO YOUR PAPER

- Avoid "bald" or "dropped" quotations by introducing all direct quotations.
- Use the author's name, where appropriate, to signal the beginning of a paraphrase or quotation.
- Cite sources for all borrowed material.
- Name a source, if the article does not list an author's name.
- Vary the way you introduce source material.
- Try combining direct quotations and paraphrases in the same sentence.
- Become familiar with appropriate uses of ellipsis points, brackets, single quotation marks, and "qtd. in."

DOCUMENTING SOURCES IN A COLLECTION OF ESSAYS

You have been reading about and looking at examples of one important component of source documentation: in-text citations. The other component is the alphabetical list, appearing at the end of your paper, of all the works you quoted from or paraphrased. This is the list of works cited. Each entry in the list begins with the author's name, last name first, followed by the title of the article, book, or other source and information about its place and date of publication. The author's name (or title of the work, if it is published anonymously) in the text's parenthetical citation refers to one item in this list at the end of the paper.

You will find more discussion of documenting sources in chapter 6, but the brief treatment here gives useful guidelines for short papers using materials reprinted in a collection of essays, such as this textbook. Although the examples in this section illustrate how to document materials reprinted in the second edition of this textbook, the guidelines apply to any collection of essays. Because *Perspectives on Contemporary Issues* is a collection of other people's works, not the editor's, you will probably not have occasion to use the words or ideas of Ackley herself. However, because you are not reading the essays in their original source, you must indicate that you have read them in her book.

You may prefer an acceptable alternative to constructing a Works Cited page: Cite bibliographic information about the source parenthetically in your text, just as you do for author and page numbers. If you are writing about one of the readings from this book, or even two or three of them, your instructor may prefer that you provide information that would otherwise appear on a Works Cited page in parenthetical citations. A fairly simple difference distinguishes a formal Works Cited page from parenthetical citations of full publishing details: The former is more appropriate when the sources are not the focus or subject of the paper but rather provide supporting or illustrative material, as in a synthesis or research paper. The latter is more appropriate when the source is the focus of the paper, its main subject, as in a summary or critique.

Citing One Source.   Suppose your paper quotes or paraphrases a statement from Robert Hughes's essay "Behold the Stone Age." After you write either the exact words of Hughes or your paraphrase of his words, put a parenthesis, then give his last name and the page number where you read the words *with no punctuation between them,* and then close the parenthesis: (Hughes 161). Do not write the word *page* or *pages* nor insert a comma between the author's name and the number of the page. If Hughes's piece is the only one you use in your paper, write "Work Cited" at the end of your paper and enter complete bibliographic information for the Hughes article:

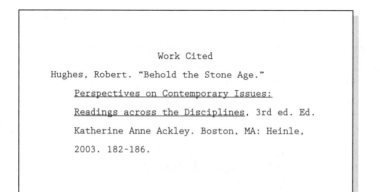

```
                    Work Cited
      Hughes, Robert. "Behold the Stone Age."
          Perspectives on Contemporary Issues:
          Readings across the Disciplines, 3rd ed. Ed.
          Katherine Anne Ackley. Boston, MA: Heinle,
          2003. 182-186.
```

Citing Two or More Sources.   If you draw material from two or more essays from Ackley (or from any collection of essays), you do not need to repeat the full information for the collection with the citation for each essay. Instead, list the collection by the editor's name, giving full bibliographic information. Then list separately each article you use by author and title, but after each essay title, give only the collection editor's name and the inclusive page numbers of the essay. You may, if you wish, follow the model for citing one source.

For example, suppose in a paper on the "Arts" chapter of this textbook, you use information or words from the Hughes article, Harold M. Williams's "Don't Ignore the Arts," and Norman Cousins's "The Poet and the Computer." Here is how your works cited page might look:

Works Cited

Ackley, Katherine Anne, ed. <u>Perspectives on
    Contemporary Issues: Reading across the
    Disciplines</u>. 3rd ed. Boston, MA: Heinle,
    2003.

Cousins, Norman. "The Poet and the Computer."
    Ackley 187-189.

Hughes, Robert. "Behold the Stone Age." Ackley
    182-186.

Williams, Harold M. "Don't Ignore the Arts."
    Ackley 190-195.

You may also do your Works Cited page this way:

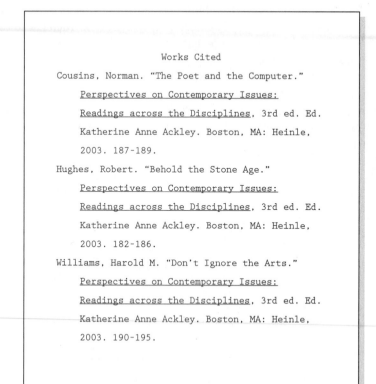

```
                        Works Cited
Cousins, Norman. "The Poet and the Computer."
     Perspectives on Contemporary Issues:
     Readings across the Disciplines, 3rd ed. Ed.
     Katherine Anne Ackley. Boston, MA: Heinle,
     2003. 187-189.
Hughes, Robert. "Behold the Stone Age."
     Perspectives on Contemporary Issues:
     Readings across the Disciplines, 3rd ed. Ed.
     Katherine Anne Ackley. Boston, MA: Heinle,
     2003. 182-186.
Williams, Harold M. "Don't Ignore the Arts."
     Perspectives on Contemporary Issues:
     Readings across the Disciplines, 3rd ed. Ed.
     Katherine Anne Ackley. Boston, MA: Heinle,
     2003. 190-195.
```

Parenthetical Documentation of Source Material.   When a single reading is the primary focus of your paper (or it concentrates on two or three readings), that is, the paper deals with limited primary sources, as opposed to secondary source materials that provide illustration or supporting evidence, you can provide full bibliographic information parenthetically the first time you mention each source. Then you do not have to construct a separate Works Cited page. This technique may be convenient when your paper focuses on just one work, for instance, if you were to write a formal summary or critique of one reading or a paper on one or two works of literature. At the first mention of the source, provide full publication information in a parenthetical citation:

> According to Robert Hughes in "Behold the Stone Age" (in Katherine Anne Ackley, ed., <u>Perspectives on Contemporary Issues: Reading across the Disciplines</u>, 3rd ed. [Boston, MA: Heinle, 2003] 182-186), early cave paintings suggest something significant about the importance of art for humans.

Notice that the author's name and the title of the work are mentioned in the text of the paper and not in the parenthetical citation. Brackets indicate parentheses within parentheses. After this first documentation of full publishing information, parenthetical citations will give only author and page number or just page number.

CHAPTER 6
WRITING A RESEARCH PAPER USING MLA STYLE

No matter what course you write a research paper for, your goal is the same: to skillfully support a carefully formulated thesis with documented evidence. Writing such a paper can seem both overwhelming and exciting, especially if you have never written one before. This chapter presents a brief overview of the key steps in discovering a topic, researching it, and writing a paper incorporating the sources you have used. Keep in mind the discussion in chapter 5 on paraphrasing, quoting, and documenting sources. A research paper is likely to be much longer than a writing assignment generated from readings in this book, but otherwise little difference separates the processes of using materials from this textbook and using materials from other sources in terms of accuracy and fairness to your sources.

DEFINING YOUR PURPOSE

Your instructor will tell you whether your purpose in the research paper is to argue, explain, analyze, or come to some conclusion about something. In an argumentative paper, you will make a judgment about your topic on the basis of what you find in your research. You will begin your research with an idea of what your position is, then research your subject extensively, arrive at an informed opinion, and finally defend that position by presenting evidence that seems valid (that is, logical and convincing) to you. If you want to go a step further and convince your audience to adopt your position or to act on suggestions you propose, then your purpose is persuasion.

Caution: In addition to proving the validity of your own position, you must also present some opposing arguments. Obviously you cannot present every aspect and every position of an issue, but you must demonstrate that you are aware of the major viewpoints on your subject and that the position you have taken is a reasonable one. Ignoring an opposing opinion is a major fault in argumentation, because it suggests that you have not explored enough aspects of the topic to warrant the position you are taking.

The subjects for argumentative papers are virtually unlimited, but they often include controversial issues, such as those addressed in this textbook, topics with widely varying opinions. On the other hand, an informative paper does not necessarily address a controversial subject. If you are to write an explanatory paper, you will gather information about your topic and present it in such a way that your reader fully understands it. You will explain, describe, illustrate, or narrate something in full detail, such as what a black hole is, how photosynthesis works, the circumstances surrounding a historical event, significant events in the life of a famous person, and the like.

No matter what your purpose, though, you will have one central idea, most often articulated early in the paper in the form of a single thesis statement. You will take a position on your topic and defend or illustrate it convincingly with evidence from your source materials. Because the argumentative paper is a common research assignment, much of the discussion in this chapter will be about selecting an appropriate topic on which to base an argument.

DISCOVERING A TOPIC

Once you know your purpose, the next, and perhaps most important, step in writing a research paper is to find a subject you will be comfortable working with for many weeks and then narrow it to a specific topic. Some instructors assign topics, but most leave the choice to students. The freedom to choose your own research paper topic can be intimidating because so much depends on selecting the right topic. You want a topic that not only holds your interest but that also offers you an opportunity to investigate it in depth.

The process of discovering what you will write about involves first determining the broad subject you are particularly interested in pursuing. Once you have settled on the subject, you will need to narrow it to one specific aspect of that subject. For many research paper assignments, that topic will have to be arguable, one that requires you to investigate both sides and arrive at and defend your own position. This position will be worded in the form of a hypothesis or thesis, stated most often as a declarative statement but sometimes as a question. Discovering your final topic takes time, so do some serious thinking about this important step as soon as the paper is assigned. You will be reshaping, narrowing, and refining your topic for much of the research process, so you do not want to switch subjects halfway through.

Asking Questions.   One of the best ways to approach the research project is to ask questions about a subject that interests you and that seems worth investigating. As you read through the suggestions for discovering a topic that follow, from brainstorming to generating topics from controversy, think in terms of questions that you might ask about the initial subjects you come up with. Try to think in terms of questions that can be answered in a research paper as opposed to a short essay. As you narrow your field of potential topics, look for those about which you can ask questions whose answers are neither too broad nor too narrow. You want the topic that you ultimately select to be challenging enough that your paper will be interesting to you as well as to your audience. Avoid topics about which questions are unanswerable or highly speculative. Your goal in the research process will be to arrive at an answer, insofar as that is possible, to your question.

Here are examples of questions that would be appropriate to ask about topics that students have selected for research papers:

- Should the Electoral College be abolished?
- Does America need an official language?

- Should research into human cloning continue?
- Do advertising images of women set up impossible standards of femininity?
- Is hormone replacement therapy a safe choice for women?
- Which plays a more prominent role in determining behavior, genes or environment?
- What role does phonics education play in the teaching of reading?
- How dangerous is secondhand smoke?
- Was King Arthur a real person?
- What tactics have succeeded in the effort to combat terrorism?

Brainstorming.   As you consider various suggestions for generating a research paper topic, you can apply a useful technique for discovery that you have probably used before in your writing classes. Most students are familiar with **brainstorming** or **freewriting,** which involves simply writing without stopping, putting on paper everything that occurs to you as you think about your subject. To brainstorm or freewrite, spend five or ten minutes listing on a blank sheet of paper all of the subjects you are interested in without stopping to think too hard about what you are doing. Then select one or more of the subjects on your list and brainstorm for another five to ten minutes in order to find out what you already know about your subject.

Generating a Topic from Personal Interest.   One way to find a topic for your research paper is to begin with subjects you already know well, are interested in, or think you would like to improve your knowledge. Begin by writing down such things as hobbies, sports, issues in your major, contemporary social issues, or topics in classes you are taking. Consider topics that attracted your interest in high school or in previous college classes, any reading you have already done on subjects that appeal to you, or the kinds of things that capture your attention when you watch television news, read news magazines or newspapers, or select nonfiction books for leisure-time reading.

Narrowing Your Subject to a Specific Topic.   Most research paper assignments are short enough that you simply must narrow your focus to avoid a too shallow or too hopelessly general treatment of your topic. Keep in mind the distinction between **subject** and **topic:** Subject is the general area under investigation, whereas topic is the narrow aspect of that subject that you are investigating. For example, Jack the Ripper is a subject, but entire books have been written on the notorious 1888 murders in the Whitechapel area of London. A suitable topic on the subject would be to explore the controversy surrounding the alleged links of the Duke of Clarence with the murders, taking a position in favor of the theory most plausible to you.

One way to get a sense of how a general topic can be narrowed is to look at the table of contents of a book on a subject that interests you. Notice the chapter headings, which are themselves subtopics of the broad subject. Chapters themselves are often further subdivided. You want to find a topic that is narrow enough that you can fully explore it without leaving unanswered questions, yet broad enough that you can say enough about it in a reasonably long paper.

To narrow your subject to a topic, take a general subject and go through the brainstorming process again, this time listing everything that comes to mind about that particular subject. What subtopics does your subject have? What questions can you ask about your general subject? How might you narrow your focus on that subject? Ultimately, you want to generate an idea that gives focus to your preliminary library search.

Generating Topics from Personal Opinions.   Virtually any topic can be turned into an argument, but opinions are always subject to debate. So one way to generate a research paper topic is to begin with your own strongly held opinions.

Caution: Avoid a topic that is based entirely on opinion. Evaluative statements are especially good for argumentative papers, because they are likely to have differing opinions. Once you say that something is the best, the most significant, the most important, or the greatest, for instance, you have put yourself in the position of defending that statement. You will have to establish your criteria for making your judgment and defend your choice against what others might think. Here are some ideas for this particular approach:

- The most influential person in the twentieth century (or in America, in the world, in a particular field such as education, government, politics, arts, entertainment, or the like)
- The most significant battle in the Civil War (or World War I, World War II, the Korean War, the Vietnam War, the Gulf War)
- The greatest basketball (or football, tennis, soccer, baseball) player (either now playing or of all time)
- The greatest or worst president
- The best movie, book, or album of all time
- The business or industry with the greatest impact on American life in the last decade (or last twenty years, last fifty years, or century)

Because your conclusion on any of these or similar topics is your opinion, you need to establish criteria for your conclusion, clearly describe the process you used to make it, and explain the logical basis for that process.

Generating Topics from Commonly Held Opinions.   Another possibility for a research paper topic is to take a commonly held opinion (though not necessarily one that you share), especially one based on stereotyped assumptions about a group or class of people, and explore the validity of that belief. Your goal is to determine whether the commonly held opinion is a valid, partially valid, or invalid position. Even if you cannot arrive at a definitive evaluation of the validity of the statement, you can still present the evidence you find and explain why your research does not reach a conclusion. Here are examples of commonly held beliefs:

- Watching violence on television produces violent behavior.
- People who were abused as children often grow up to be abusers themselves.
- Men naturally perform mechanical tasks better than women do.

- Women naturally perform better at nurturing children than men do.
- Young people do not have much hope for a bright future.
- Women are more emotional than men.
- People stay on welfare because they are too lazy to work.
- Homosexuals could become "straight" if they wanted to.
- Homeless people could get off the streets if they really tried.

When determining the validity of a commonly held opinion or belief, your research focuses on gathering evidence without bias. Although you may want to interview people about their opinions on a particular belief, the basis of your conclusion must rest on clearly reliable evidence.

Generating Topics from Controversy.   Yet another way to discover a topic you find intriguing enough to commit many hours of time is to think of controversial issues that always generate heated debate. These topics may be frequently discussed in newspapers, news magazines, and on television news programs and talk shows. They may be issues on which candidates for public office, from local county board members to state and federal officials, are pressed to take stands. Here are some examples of controversial statements:

- Affirmative action laws are unfair to white males and should be repealed.
- Media coverage of celebrity trials should be banned.
- Birth parents should always have a legal right to take back children they have given up for adoption.
- Children whose parents are on welfare should be placed in state-run orphanages.
- Women should be barred from participating in combat duty.
- Graphic violence in the movies (or in video games or MTV videos) poses a serious threat to the nation's moral values.
- The federal government should stop funding projects in the arts and the humanities.
- The federal government should provide unlimited funds to support research to find a cure for AIDS.
- Children who commit murder should be tried as adults no matter what their age.

DEVELOPING A WORKING BIBLIOGRAPHY

Now that you have narrowed your topic, you are ready to start the actual research process. First, you need to locate potential sources. A working bibliography is a list of the sources you **might** use in your research paper, those that look particularly promising during a preliminary search. At this point, you will not have had time to read or even carefully skim all potential sources, let alone imagine how they fit together to support your hypothesis. Your goal is to find the sources that bear most directly on your topic and select from them the most useful ones to read carefully, taking notes as you read. One obvious place to start looking for sources is the library; another source is the Internet.

For the working bibliography, some instructors require that you prepare a separate bibliography card for each source with promise. Others suggest that you simply make a list of titles and locations of potential sources and wait until you have looked at them more closely before filling out bibliography cards. If you use your computer to locate sources, you can make a list of potentially useful sources in a special file. Your instructor may have a preference, but most allow students to use the methods that best suit them.

USING THE LIBRARY

Card Catalog.   Begin your library search for sources on your general subject or topic (if you have sufficiently narrowed your focus) by reviewing the **online catalog** or **main card catalog** for titles of potential sources. The catalog cross-references sources by name of author, by title, and by subject matter. In this searching stage, you probably will not know titles of works or authors, so you will begin by looking under subject headings for titles that sound relevant to your research subject. The card catalog gives titles of books, audio-visual materials, and government documents housed in the library. Jot down the titles and call numbers of materials that look promising and then locate them. One advantage of using your library is that you can physically examine a book, flip through its table of contents, check its index, read the author's credentials, and skim some of the text. If it seems to suit your purpose, you can check it out and take it home with you.

Computer Databases.   Many libraries provide access to computer databases or CD-ROMs that list books and periodical articles related to particular subject areas. You can search these resources by subject, author, title, or keywords. Generally, such a listing provides the full name of the author, the title, and complete bibliographic information (publisher and year for books; title of magazine or journal, month and year of issue, and page numbers for articles). Often, computer services provide abstracts of articles and sometimes entire texts that you can download and print out or send for via mail or fax for a fee.

Indexes.   In addition to books and other materials listed in the card or online catalog of the library, you should look into both general and specialized indexes for additional titles of sources. These resources are usually located in the reference room. Here are titles of some **general indexes:**

- *Bibliographic Index* lists by subject bibliographies that appear in books, pamphlets, and periodical articles.
- *Biography Index* lists articles and books on important people; it also lists the people included in the index by profession or occupation.
- *Essay and General Literature Index* focuses on material in the social sciences and humanities, organized according to author, subject, and title. It lists periodical articles, individual essays, and book chapters on particular subjects.

- *Monthly Catalog of United States Government Publications* indexes all government-generated materials.
- *General Science Index* is arranged by subject and lists articles in general science periodicals.
- *Periodical Abstracts* provides abstracts of articles from over 1,600 periodicals, covering the humanities, social sciences, general science, and general interest. It is updated monthly and is available in electronic format.
- *Reader's Guide to Periodical Literature* is a standard reference tool for locating articles in popular magazines. Organized by both subject and author, it provides titles of articles, authors, names of publications, and dates of publication. It publishes supplements every two weeks, so you can find very recent articles. It is also available in electronic format.

Specialized indexes list articles on particular subjects or areas that appear in professional journals, written by and published for specialists in those areas. Indexes cover specific areas of interest in the humanities, fine arts, social sciences, and natural and applied sciences. A look at just a few of the titles of specialized indexes gives you an idea of the resources available in your library's reference room:

- *Art Index* collects titles of articles on archaeology, art history, architecture, and the fine arts.
- *Biological Abstracts* gives brief summaries of articles on biology and biomedicine.
- *Business Index* is a good source for current material on business topics.
- *The Directory of On-Line Databases* provides a current listing of databases in all fields.
- *Historical Abstracts* contains abstracts of articles on world history.
- *Humanities Index* lists titles of periodical articles on a broad range of topics in the social sciences and humanities.
- *MLA International Bibliography of Books and Articles on the Modern Languages and Literatures* provides titles of articles on languages and literature, arranged by nationality and literary period.
- *Philosopher's Guide to Sources, Research Tools, Professional Life, and Related Fields* is useful for all sorts of information on philosophical topics.
- *Psychological Abstracts* presents abstracts of articles and books in all areas of the social sciences.
- *Political Science: A Guide to Reference and Information Sources* cites current sources on a range of topics in political science.

USING ELECTRONIC SOURCES

Although you do not want to miss the pleasure of going to the library for sources for your research paper, the Internet can be another valuable tool in your search for potential sources. Most colleges and universities make computers readily available to their students, so even if you do not own a computer, you will likely have access to one in your campus library or computing services center.

Locating Material on the Internet.   To find Internet materials, you can use any of a number of equally good search engines available on the Web. Search engines collect many sites in their data banks; they return sites that match the keywords you type to begin your search. You can usually focus an Internet search much more specifically than one pursued through a card catalog or an index located in the reference room of your library. Among the most popular search engines are **Alta Vista,** which gives access to probably the largest Web index, with approximately four million articles from fourteen thousand Usenet newsgroups, and **Yahoo** and **WebCrawler,** both of which are easy to search and suitable for both experienced and novice Internet users. **Magellan** is an online guide to the Internet that includes original editorial content, a directory of rated and reviewed Internet sites, a vast database of yet-to-be-reviewed sites, and a powerful search engine that helps you find sites that interest you. **Excite** rates each site it lists. **SEARCH.COM** is a collection of tools designed to find all kinds of information, from World Wide Web sites to phone numbers to movies to stock quotes. **Four11** is the Internet's largest white pages directory with over eight million listings, including e-mail addresses and Web sites.

Although it cannot replace the library, the Internet does offer resources that a library does not. The same could be said of the library, of course. A fair conclusion notes that each offers excellent but different kinds of materials for the researcher. In the following essay, Mark Horowitz describes his experiences on the Internet. He quickly revised a skeptical opinion of chances for locating "good history" when he first searched the Web. The essay is an interesting glimpse of what one can find on the Internet and nowhere else.

FINDING HISTORY ON THE NET

Mark Horowitz

Mark Horowitz has written for the Atlantic, The New York Times magazine, American Heritage, and other publications. This essay was first published in the October 1995 issue of American Heritage.

The Internet doesn't sound like a promising place to find good history. Cyberspace is too young and ephemeral to compete with a good research library or a well-stocked bookstore, but on my first visit to the World Wide Web, I stumbled onto a site called "On the Lower East Side: Observations of Life in Lower Manhattan at the Turn of the Century" (http://140.190.128.190:80/SMC/Dept/history/Contents.html) and unexpectedly found myself transported back a hundred years.

Designed as an on-line "hypertextbook" by professors at St. Mary's University of Minnesota, "On the Lower East Side" combines contemporary descriptions of New York immigrant life with wonderful photographs and drawings from the period. It wasn't the photos or even the unfamiliar texts that moved me but a ghostly period map that materialized slowly on my screen after I clicked an icon. At home in Los Angeles I gently touched my finger to the street corner where my grandfather was born a century ago.

In fact there is a great deal of history on the Net, but, as with everything else online, finding it can be difficult. The Internet is mostly a collection of private obsessions on public display, and nowhere is this more true than in the public newsgroups and mailing lists where users exchange views on every possible subject. Of the thousands of newsgroups, soc.history is by far the most active history discussion. Recently George Washington's religious beliefs were the hot topic.

4   Military affairs, however, tend to dominate the history newsgroups with special emphasis on Germany and World War II. Over at soc.history.war.world-war-ii people were arguing the relative capabilities of the German V-1 and V-2 missiles. For the more imaginative, alt.history.what-if deals with questions like "What if Hitler had invested in jet technology?" and "What if Hilter gets into art school?" though my favorite recent thread was the less well-contested "What if Christie Brinkley made out with Boris Yeltsin?"

When you least expect it, moments of true feeling burst through. On soc.history.war.vietnam, for example, after some fairly predictable discussions about land reform, air combat tactics, and Jane Fonda, there was this response to an argument about the origins of the pejorative term *REMF*, which refers to rear-echelon troops. "I can remember watching from a hill to the south of Bong Son," someone had typed in, "as the mortars came in on the REMFs at LZ English. And the unknown and unhonored REMFs that pulled a bunch of boonie-rats out of a C-130 that crashed while taking off at English. And what was left of the REMFs when LZ Tom was overrun. . . . I'll always be proud of being Airborne, of having pounded the bush, but if you were in country, you're OK."

Historical discussions are also flourishing on countless listservs, or mailing lists, which you can join only by sending a precisely worded e-mail request and which tend to be more academic and less freewheeling than newsgroups. There are lists devoted to Western American history (AMWEST-H), Southern history (H-SOUTH), colonial history (EARAM-L), legal and constitutional history (H-LAW), and the history of Kansas (KANSAS-L). There are a maritime history list (MARHST-L), a list for students of the 1960s (SIXTIES-L), and separate ones for most American wars, including the Civil War (H-CIVWAR), World War II (WWII-L), and Vietnam (VWAR-L). To search for a list by subject, or for instructions on joining one, check out "Your Personal Network" (http://www.ypn.com./search/search.html). And if you subscribe to the Prodigy online service, check out *American Heritage*'s own "American Heritage Picture Gallery," a weekly feature there.

The Internet remains so ad hoc and eccentric that trying to find specific information usually leads to disappointment. Random window-shopping, on the other hand, always produces delightful surprises, and the rich graphic capabilities and endless hypertextual links of the World Wide Web are a rambler's paradise.

JOURNAL ARTICLE WITH ONE AUTHOR

Weaver, Constance. "Weighing the Claims about
Phonics First." The Education Digest 56
(April 1991): 19-22.

NEWSPAPER ARTICLE WITH AUTHOR NAMED

Warrick, Pamela. "Questions of Life and Death."
The Los Angeles Times 4 Aug. 1991: E1+.

MAGAZINE ARTICLE WITH NO AUTHOR NAMED

"Another Challenge to Coffee's Safety." Science
News 20 October 1990: 253.

JOURNAL ARTICLE WITH TWO AUTHORS

Fabes, Richard A., and Jeremiah Strouse. "Formal
versus Informal Sources on Sex Education:
Competing Forces in the Sexual Socialization
of Adolescents." Adolescence 20 (1985):
250-61.

GOVERNMENT DOCUMENT

United States. Cong. House. Committee on Armed

    Services. <u>Women in the Military: Hearing before</u>

    <u>the Military Personnel and Compensation</u>

    <u>Subcommittee</u>. 101st Cong., 2nd sess. 20 Mar.

    1990: 14-56.

Using a Computer for a Working Bibliography.   If you store bibliographic information about your sources in a computer file and follow the formatting guidelines for the Works Cited page, you will save time later in the process when you put your paper in its final form. Record information in the proper format and alphabetize your list, placing new items in the appropriate alphabetical positions. Then, when you need to assemble the Works Cited page, just move the list to the file where you store your paper (or keep the list in the same file). Here is how a list of the works on the previous sample bibliography cards would look in a computer file:

"Another Challenge to Coffee's Safety." <u>Science</u>

    <u>News</u> 20 Oct. 1990: 253.

Fabes, Richard A., and Jeremiah Strouse. "Formal

    versus Informal Sources on Sex Education:

    Competing Forces in the Sexual Socialization

    of Adolescents." <u>Adolescence</u> 20 (1985):

    250-61.

Heilbrun, Carolyn G. <u>Hamlet's Mother and Other</u>

    <u>Women</u>. New York: Ballantine, 1990.

United States. Cong. House. Committee on Armed

    Services. <u>Women in the Military: Hearing</u>

    <u>before the Military Personnel and</u>

    <u>Compensation Subcommittee</u>. 101st Cong., 2nd

    sess. 20 Mar. 1990: 14-56.

```
Warrick, Pamela. "Questions of Life and Death."
    Los Angeles Times 4 Aug. 1991: E1+.
Weaver, Constance. "Weighing the Claims about
    Phonics First." Education Digest 56 (April
    1991): 19-22.
```

EVALUATING SOURCES

Before you begin taking notes from any source, carefully assess its reliability. Ideally, your research should rely on unbiased, current, well-documented sources written by people with the authority to discuss the subject. However, you are likely to find a great number of sources that are written from particular perspectives that are out of date or incomplete, that are written by people with no authority whatsoever, or that do not document their own sources. Part of your job as a researcher is to try to discover these aspects of your sources, to reject those that are completely unreliable, and to use with caution sources about which you lack complete confidence. While you may never know for sure how much to trust a particular source, you can check certain things to help in your assessment.

Check for Bias. Try to find out if the author, publication, organization, or person being interviewed is known to give fair coverages. People, organizations, and publications often promote particular perspectives, which you should recognize and take into account. You need not reject sources outright if you know they take particular positions on subjects, especially controversial issues. However, your own paper should be as unbiased as possible, which requires acknowledgment of the known biases of your sources.

Check the Date of Publication. In general, an increasingly recent publication or update of a Web site provides an increasingly reliable source. For many subjects, current information is crucial to accurate analysis. If you are researching issues such as global warming, morality at high governmental levels, or controversial treatments for AIDS victims, for instance, you need the most recent available information. However, if you are examining a historical matter, such as the question of Richard III's guilt in his two young cousins' deaths or whether King Arthur of Britain is an entirely mythical figure, you can rely in part on older materials. You still want to look for the latest theories, information, or opinions on any subject you research, though.

Check the Author's Credentials. Find out if the author has sufficient education, experience, or expertise to write or speak about your subject. You can do this in a number of ways. Any book usually gives information about an author, from a sentence or two to several paragraphs, either on the dust jacket or at the beginning or end of the book. This information reveals the author's professional status, other books the author has published, and similar information that helps to establish her authority. You can also look up the author in sources like *Contemporary Authors, Current Biography,* and *Who's Who.* Other checks on an author's reliability might review what professionals in other sources say about her or to note how often her name shows up on reference lists or bibliographies on your subject.

Check the Reliability of Your Source.   In evaluating a book, determine if the publishing house is a respectable one. For a magazine, find out if it is published by a particular interest group. Evaluation of a book could include reading some representative reviews to see how it was received when first published. Both the *Book Review Digest* and *Book Review Index* will help you locate reviews.

Check the Thoroughness of Research and Documentation of Sources. If your source purports to be scholarly, well-informed, or otherwise reliable, check to see how the evidence was gathered. Determine whether the source reports original research or other people's work and what facts or data support its conclusions. Look for references either at the ends of chapters or in a separate section at the end of a book. Almost all journal articles and scholarly books document sources, whereas few magazine articles and personal accounts do. Also, consider how statistics and other data are used. Statistics are notoriously easy to manipulate, so check how the author uses them and confirm his fair interpretation.

Reliability of Internet Sources.   As with print sources, you must take care to evaluate any material you locate on the Internet before you use it in your paper. The Internet may pose more difficulty, because its resources may offer fewer clues than a book or journal article might give. However, searching the Internet will turn up many useful sources, such as scholarly projects, reference databases, text files of books, articles in periodicals, and professional sites. You must use your judgment when selecting sources for your research paper. Remember that anyone with some knowledge of the Internet can create a Web site, so be very cautious about accepting the authority of anything you find on the Internet. In general, personal sites are probably not as reliable as professional sites and those of scholarly projects. Reference databases can be extremely useful tools for locating source materials. For an excellent guide to evaluating Web sources available on the Internet, go to **http://www. science.widener.edu/~withers/evalout.html.** This site was prepared by Jan Alexander and Marsha Tate, reference librarians at the Wolgram Memorial Library, Widener University.

Suppose, for example, that Shawn Ryan is interested in finding information on the Internet for his paper on King Arthur (located later in this chapter). When he first enters the keywords "Arthurian legend," a search engine returns almost two million matches. Obviously, he cannot look at every match, but he can begin his search by scrolling through the first page of matches, picking a site that sounds promising, and going to that site. The list shows several entries that appear to be newsgroups or personal sites, whereas two will take him to the sites of a scholarly society and a scholarly project associated with a university. Because he is looking for sources for a research paper, as opposed to satisfying general curiosity, Shawn prefers the scholarly sites.

Both of the scholarly sites provide enormously useful information. The entry labeled "Arthurian Web Sites" takes him to the home page of the North American branch of the International Arthurian Society, whose journal, *Arthuriana,* Shawn can read on the Web. Furthermore, the site offers manuscripts, reviews, and scholarly essays, including the titles of over two hundred sources listed under the heading "Nonfiction and Research." In addition, the site offers links to other Arthurian sites.

As with print sources, Shawn has to judge the trustworthiness and reliability of an Internet source on the basis of who created the site, the credentials of the authorities, and the kind of information it gives. For instance, he particularly likes the information available at the Web site for the Camelot Project at the University of Rochester. Shawn determines that this site is a reliable source for several reasons. According to its home page, the Camelot Project aims to create a database of Arthurian texts, bibliographies, and other information. This goal tells Shawn that the site is not devoted to one person's opinions or to an informal collection of materials. Rather, it has a legitimate, scholarly aim, making it a valuable source of relevant materials for his paper. The Camelot Project itself is sponsored by the University of Rochester and the Robbins Library, associations that assure a certain level of reliability and scholarly appropriateness. Finally, the material at the site is continually updated, the most recent change occurring just one month before Shawn visited the site. Thus, Shawn has found a source that he is confident he can trust and that is sure to lead him to other reliable sources.

QUESTIONS TO ASK WHEN EVALUATING SOURCES

- Is the publication known to be fair, or does it have a bias or slant?
- Does the source seem one sided, or does it try to cover all perspectives on an issue?
- Does the site include current or outdated material?
- Does the authority have respectable credentials?
- If your source is a book, is the publishing house a respectable one? What kind of reviews did the book get?
- Depending on the nature of the source, does it offer adequate documentation for its information?
- If the source relies on research data, how was evidence gathered? Are statistics used fairly, or are they misrepresented?

TAKING NOTES

When you find an article, book, pamphlet, Web site, or other source you believe will be important or informative in your research, take notes from that source. Note cards are useful for recording several kinds of information: direct quotations, paraphrases, summaries of several pages or entire articles, and personal thoughts on your subject. Note taking is crucial to the success of your paper. You must take accurate and careful notes, reproducing an author's words exactly as they appear if you quote, or completely restating the author's words if you paraphrase. In either case, you will give a citation in your paper, so **you must record the source and page number for any notes.**

When taking notes, some students are tempted to write every detail as it appears in the original, thinking that they will paraphrase the material at some later time. They must then spend valuable time later rephrasing material when they should be concentrating on writing their papers, or else they take the easier route and use the direct quotations. The result may be a paper that is too full of direct quotations and lacking in effective paraphrases. Remember that you should quote directly only language that is particularly well expressed or material that you do not feel you can adequately restate in your own words. Your final paper should have far more paraphrases than direct quotations.

Note Cards.   Where you record your notes does not matter, as long as you develop an efficient system. The important consideration is the accuracy and fairness of your notes. Traditionally, researchers have been told to use 4 × 6 cards, because they are large enough to record ideas, summaries, quotations, or major points. When the note-taking part of the research ends, the researcher can shuffle the cards about, arranging them in the order that makes sense for the research paper. Many people like the note card system and work well with this system.

Word Processor.   If you work better with a word processor, then by all means use one. A word processor can be very helpful for organizing and sorting notes. Most programs allow you to arrange your notes in numerical order. However, make sure to develop a filing system for your notes. If your program lets you create folders, you can keep your notes from different sources under specific headings, each with its own subheadings. Place the subject heading at the beginning of your notes, and put the page number at the end. Make sure that your notes clearly identify sources for all information.

GUIDELINES FOR TAKING NOTES

- **Write both the author's last name and the page number from which the information is taken.** That is all the information you need, as long as you have a bibliography card or file for the source that lists complete bibliographic information.

- **Place a subject heading at the top of each card or note in a computer file.** This labeling system will help you sort and arrange your cards when you write your paper.
- **Record only one idea or several small, related ones in each note.** This practice will help you to organize your notes when you begin writing.
- **Place quotation marks before and after the material taken directly from a source.** Don't rely on memory to determine whether words are identical to the original or paraphrased.
- **Use notes to summarize.** A note may refer to an entire passage, an article, or a book without giving specific details. Make a note to remind you that the information is a summary.
- **Use notes to record original ideas that occur to you while you are reading.** Make sure you identify your own ideas.

Paraphrasing and Quoting.   See chapter 5 for directions and summary guidelines for both paraphrasing source material and quoting directly. Chapter 5 also discusses some common tools for handling source material: ellipsis points, brackets, single quotation marks, and "Qtd. In." Sample research papers located later in this chapter also give examples of correct handling of source material.

AVOIDING PLAGIARISM

Giving proper credit to your sources is a crucial component of the research process. It is also one of the trickiest aspects of the process, because it requires absolute accuracy in note taking. Many students have been disheartened by low grades on papers that took weeks to prepare, because they were careless or inaccurate in handling and documenting source materials.

Simply defined, **plagiarism** is borrowing another person's words without giving proper credit. The worst form of plagiarism is deliberately using the words or important ideas of someone else without giving any credit to that source. Handing in a paper someone else has written or copying someone else's paper and pretending it is yours are the most blatant and inexcusable forms of plagiarism, crimes that on some campuses carry penalties like automatic failure in the course or even immediate expulsion from school. Most student plagiarism is not deliberate, but rather results from carelessness either in the research process, when notes are taken, or in the writing process, when notes are incorporated into the student's own text. Even this unintentional plagiarism can result in a failing grade, however, especially if it appears repeatedly in a paper.

Keep the following standards in mind when you take notes on your source materials and when you write your research paper:

- **You commit plagiarism if you use the exact words or ideas of another writer without putting quotation marks around the words or citing a**

source. The reader of your paper assumes that words without quotation marks or a source citation are your own words. To use the words of another without proper documentation suggests that you are trying to pass the words off as your own without giving credit to the writer.

- **You commit plagiarism if you use the exact words of another writer without putting quotation marks around those words, even if the paper cites the source of the material.** Readers assume that words followed by a parenthetical citation are paraphrased from the original, that is, that they are your own words and that the general idea was expressed by the author of the source material.

- **You commit plagiarism if you paraphrase by changing only a few words of the original or by using the identical sentence structure of the original, with or without a source.** Again, readers assume that words without quotation marks followed by a parenthetical citation are your own words, not those of someone else. In a paraphrase, the *idea* is that of another; the *words* are your own.

- **You inaccurately handle source material when you use quotation marks around words that are not exactly as they appear in the original.** Readers assume that all words within quotation marks are identical to the original.

Obviously, accuracy and fairness in note taking are essential standards. Great care must be taken when you read your source materials and again when you transfer your notes to your final paper.

GUIDELINES FOR AVOIDING PLAGIARISM

- **For direct quotations, write the words exactly as they appear in the original.** Put quotation marks before and after the words. Do not change anything.

- **For paraphrased material, restate the original thought in your own words, using your own writing style.** Do not use the exact sentence pattern of the original, and do not simply rearrange words. You have to retain the central idea of the paraphrased material, but do so in your own words.

- **When using borrowed material in your paper, whether direct quotations or paraphrases, acknowledge the source by naming the author or work as you introduce the material.** Doing so not only tells your reader that you are using borrowed material but also often provides a clear transition from your own words and ideas to the borrowed material that illustrates or expands on your ideas.

- **Provide an in-text citation for any borrowed material.** Give the author's last name if it is not mentioned in the text of the paper, followed by page number(s). If the source material is anonymous, use a shortened version of the title in place of a name.

- **Assemble all sources cited in your paper in an alphabetical list at the end of the paper.** This is your list of works cited, containing only those works actually used in the paper.

ILLUSTRATION: PLAGIARISM, INACCURATE DOCUMENTATION, AND CORRECT HANDLING OF SOURCE MATERIAL

The passage that follows is from page 8 of Jean Kilbourne's "Beauty and the Beast of Advertising." Complete bibliographic information follows, as it would appear on a bibliography card and on the Works Cited page of a research paper:

```
Kilbourne, Jean. "Beauty and the Beast of
     Advertising." Media&Values Winter 1989:
     8-10.
```

Note that the title of the magazine is correct as written, with the ampersand (&) instead of "and" and with no spaces between the words.

> "You're a Halston woman from the very beginning," the advertisement proclaims. The model stares provocatively at the viewer, her long blonde hair waving around her face, her bare chest partially covered by two curved bottles that give the illusion of breasts and cleavage.
>
> The average American is accustomed to blue-eyed blondes seductively touting a variety of products. In this case, however, the blonde is about five years old.
>
> Advertising is an over $130 billion a year industry and affects all of us throughout our lives. We are each exposed to over 1,500 ads a day, constituting perhaps the most powerful educational force in society. The average adult will spend 1½ years of his/her life watching television commercials. But the ads sell a great deal more than products. They sell values, images, and concepts of success and worth, love and sexuality, popularity and normalcy. They tell us who we are and who we should be. Sometimes they sell addictions.

Now look at each of these sentences from a hypothetical research paper using information from the Kilbourne article. The commentary that follows identifies plagiarism, inaccurate handling of the original, or correct handling of source material:

1. Advertising is an over $130 billion a year industry and affects us throughout our lives.

   [This is **plagiarism:** Quotation marks are needed around words identical to the original and a source must be cited.]

2. We are each exposed to over 1,500 ads a day (Kilbourne 8).

   [This is **plagiarism:** Quotation marks are needed around words taken directly from the original.]

3. The average American is used to blue-eyed blondes seductively selling a variety of things (Kilbourne 8).

   [This is **plagiarism:** Original words are changed only slightly and the original sentence structure is retained.]

4. Kilbourne's analysis of advertising begins with the following quotation from a popular advertisement: "You're a Halston woman from the very beginning" (8).

   [This is **inaccurate documentation:** Single quotation marks are needed within the double marks to indicate that quotation marks are in the original.]

5. In her analysis of the ways in which advertising uses women's bodies to sell products, Jean Kilbourne argues that ads sell much more than just products. Ads "sell values, images, and concepts of success and worth" (8).

   [This is **correct:** The text acknowledges the author and the general idea of the article is adequately summarized. Quotation marks enclose material taken directly from the original.]

Students are sometimes frustrated by these guidelines governing note taking and plagiarism, arguing that virtually everything in the final paper will be in quotation marks or followed by citations. But keep in mind that your final paper is a synthesis of information you have discovered in your research with your own thoughts on your topic, thoughts that naturally undergo modification, expansion, and/or revision as you read and think about your topic. Probably half of the paper will be your own words. These words will usually include all of the introductory and concluding paragraphs, all topic sentences and transitional sentences within and between paragraphs, and all introductions to direct quotations. Furthermore, you need give no citation for statements of general or common knowledge, such as facts about well-known historical or current events. If you keep running across the same information in all of your sources, you can assume it is general knowledge.

GUIDELINES FOR HANDLING SOURCE MATERIAL

- **Introduce or provide a context for quoted material.** "Bald" or "dropped" quotations occur when you fail to integrate quotations smoothly into your text. The abrupt dropping of a quotation disrupts the flow of your text.
- **Name your authority or, when no author is named, use title of the source.** Provide this information either in the text itself or in the parenthetical citation. Rely on standard phrases such as "one writer claims," "according to one expert," and the like to introduce quotations or paraphrases.
- **Use both first and last names of author at the first mention in your text.** After that, use just last name. Always use last name only in parenthetical citations (unless you have sources by two authors with the same last name).

- **Acknowledge source material when you first begin paraphrasing.** Make sure you give some kind of signal to your reader when you begin paraphrasing borrowed material. This is particularly important if you paraphrase more than one sentence from a source. Otherwise, your reader will not know how far back the citation applies.
- **Quote sparingly.** Quote directly only those passages that are vividly or memorably phrased, so that you could not do justice to them by rewording them; that require exact wording for accuracy; or that need the authority of your source to lend credibility to what you are saying.
- **Intermingle source material with our own words.** Avoid a "cut-and-paste" approach to the research process. Remember that source materials serve primarily to support your generalizations. Never run two quotations together without some comment or transitional remark from you.
- **Make sure that direct quotations are exact.** Do not change words unless you use brackets or ellipses to indicate changes. Otherwise, be exact. For instance, if your source says "$2 million," do not write "two million dollars."
- **Make sure that paraphrases are truly your own words.** Do not inadvertently commit plagiarism by failing to paraphrase fairly.

DOCUMENTING SOURCES

Following the Appropriate Style. The examples of documentation and sample research papers that appear in this chapter all follow MLA (Modern Language Association) documentation style. That style governs because this textbook is often used in English courses, and English is located within the discipline of the humanities. However, your instructor may permit you to choose the style appropriate to the major field you intend to study. Chapter 7 gives guidelines for writing a research paper using APA (American Psychological Association) style. That style is probably as commonly used as MLA in undergraduate course papers. In addition to MLA and APA, other frequently used documentation styles are CBE (Council of Biology Editors) and Chicago. Following this summary of the chief differences among those four styles, the chapter lists stylebooks that give additional guidelines.

SUMMARY OF DIFFERENCES AMONG DOCUMENTATION STYLES

- **MLA:** Used by writers in the many areas of the humanities (English, foreign languages, history, and philosophy); requires parenthetical in-text citations of author and page number that refer to an alphabetical list of works cited at the end of the paper.
- **APA:** Used by writers in the behavioral and social sciences (education, psychology, and sociology); requires parenthetical in-text citations of author and date of publication that refer to an alphabetical list of references at the end of the paper.

- **CBE:** Used by writers in technical fields and the sciences (engineering, biology, physics, geography, chemistry, computer science, and mathematics); requires either a name–year format or a citation-sequence format. The name–year format places the author's last name and the year of publication in parentheses, referring to an alphabetical list of references at the end of the paper.
- **Chicago:** Used by some areas of the humanities, notably history, art, music, and theatre; requires a superscript number [1] for each citation, all of which are numbered sequentially throughout the paper; no number is repeated. Numbers correspond either to footnotes at the bottoms of pages or a list of notes at the end of the paper. The first note gives complete information about the source, with shortened information for each subsequent reference to that source. A bibliography follows the notes, giving the same information, except for the page number, as in the first citation of each source. The information is also punctuated and arranged differently from the note copy.

Style Guides.   To find full details on a particular documentation style, consult the following style guides:

MLA

Gibaldi, Joseph. *MLA Handbook for Writers of Research Papers.* 5th ed. New York: Modern Language Association of America, 1999.

APA

American Psychological Association. *Publication Manual of the American Psychological Association.* 5th ed. Washington: American Psychological Association, 2001.

CBE

CBE Style Manual Committee. *Scientific Style and Format: The CBE Manual for Authors, Editors, and Publishers.* 6th ed. Chicago: Council of Biology Editors, 1994.

CHICAGO

The Chicago Manual of Style. 14th ed. Chicago: U of Chicago P, 1993.
Turabian Kate L. *A Manual for Writers of Term Papers, Theses, and Dissertations.* 6th ed. Rev. John Grossman and Alice Bennet. Chicago: U of Chicago P, 1996.

Internet Citation Guides.   Many research resources are available on the Internet, including guides for citing such sources. Your university librarian may have created a Web site where you will find the names and URLs (Uniform Resource Locators) of sites that give directions for citing electronic sources. Keep in mind that Internet sites constantly change. URLs that were correct when this book was published may no longer be correct, or the sites may have ceased functioning. However, the ease of changing and updating Internet sites means that they may have more current information than print guides offer. If you doubt the reliability and currency of a Web site, consult with your instructor about the advisability of using the site. Here is an excerpt of a list, in alphabetical order, prepared by Susan Barribeau of the University of Wisconsin-Madison Memorial Library:

APA Style Electronic Formats (by Dr. Mary Ellen Guffey; formats and examples provided)
http://www.westwords.com/GUFFEY/apa.html

Bibliographic Formats for Citing Electronic Information (APA and MLA styles; based on Li and Crane's book, *Electronic Styles: A Handbook for Citing Electronic Sources*
http://www.uvm.edu/~ncrane/estyles

A Brief Citation Guide for Internet Sources in History and the Humanities (by Melvin E. Page; this guide is based on the Turabian style and provides sample citations)
http://h-2net.msu.edu/~africa.citation.html

Brief Guide to Citing Government Publications (gives examples of print and electronic resources based on the Chicago/Turabian style)
http://www.lib.memphis.edu/gpo/citeweb.htm

Citation Formats for Internet Resources: Examples and Links (a list of references and links to citation resources)
http://www.cc.emory.edu/WHSCL/citation.formats.html

Citing Electronic Resources (from Purdue University's On-Line Writing Lab)
http://owl.english.purdue.edu/Files/110.html

Cómo citar recursos electrónic (by Assumpció Estivill and Cristobal Urbana, Spanish-language guide to citing electronic sources)
http://www.ub.es/div5/biblio/citae-e.htm

MLA Style (guidelines authorized by the Modern Language Association of America)
http://www.mla.org/main_stl.htm

MLA Style Citations of Electronic Sources (by Dr. Janice R. Walker; includes a style sheet of citation examples)
http://www.cas.usf.edu/english/walker/mla.html

CITING SOURCES IN THE TEXT
Recall from the discussion in chapter 5 on documenting sources with in-text citations and the discussion in this chapter on taking notes that a crucial task of the

researcher is to accurately identify sources for all borrowed material. This section expands the discussion from chapter 5 with illustrations of treatments for several types of sources. It also includes guidelines for creating a list of works cited that incorporates a variety of sources, including electronic sources. These examples follow MLA guidelines as they appear in Joseph Gibaldi's *MLA Style Manual and Guide to Scholarly Publishing,* 2nd edition (New York: Modern Language Association of America, 1998). Chapter 5 gives basic examples for in-text citations of books, periodical articles, and Internet sources.

In-Text Citations.   Remember that you must name your source for any borrowed material. The parenthetical citation must give enough information to identify the source by directing your reader to the alphabetized list of works cited at the end of your paper. The citation should also give the page number or numbers, if available, on which the material appears.

Author-Page Format.   Recall from chapter 5 that MLA guidelines call for the author-page format when acknowledging borrowed material in the text of your paper. You must name the author (or source, if no author is named) and give a page number or numbers where the borrowed material appears in the source. The author's name or title you give in your text directs readers to the correct entry in the Works Cited list, so the reference must correspond to its entry on that list.

As a reminder of the information covered in chapter 5, consider this example of in-text citations from one of the sample research papers at the end of this chapter. In her research paper, Erin Anderson uses the following source:

> Longley, Lawrence D., and Neal R. Peirce. The Electoral College Primer 2000. New Haven, CT: Yale UP, 1999.

When Erin quotes from that source in her paper, this is how she documents it:

> In The Electoral College Primer 2000, Lawrence D. Longley and Neal R. Peirce explain their opposition to the electoral college system. They assert that in an "advanced democratic nation, where . . . popular choice is the most deeply ingrained of government principles," a voting system where popular votes don't necessarily mean electoral votes is "irrational" (132).

For her second and subsequent references to this source, she does the following:

> Longley and Peirce also explain the "faithless elector" issue. The Constitution nowhere requires the chosen electors to vote for the winner of the popular vote. However, in the history of the Electoral College, only nine votes of the over 20,000 cast have been known to go "'against instructions'" (113).

Many papers must accommodate some exceptions to the basic author-page parenthetical citation. For instance, nonprint sources such as a lecture, a telephone conversation, a television documentary, or a recording call for text discussion to name the source or identification in parentheses after the material.

Citing an Entire Work.   You may want to refer to an entire work rather than to part of it. In that case, name the work and the author in the text of your paper, without a parenthetical citation:

> Sir Arthur Conan Doyle's <u>Hound of the Baskervilles</u> features Watson to a much greater degree than do the earlier Holmes stories.

Citing Volume and Page Number of a Multivolume Work.   If you refer to material from more than one volume of a multivolume work, state the volume number, followed by a colon, and then the page number. Do not use the words or abbreviations for *volume* or *page*. The two numbers separated by a colon explicitly indicate volume and page. Your works cited entry will state the number of volumes in the work.

> Edgar Johnson's critical biography of Charles Dickens concludes with a rousing tribute to the author's creative imagination: "[T]he world he [Dickens] created shines with undying life, and the hearts of men still vibrate to his indignant anger, his love, his tears, his glorious laughter, and his triumphant faith in the dignity of man" (2: 1158).

> **Works Cited Entry:**
> Johnson, Edgar. <u>Charles Dickens: His Tragedy and Triumph</u>. 2 vols. New York: Simon, 1952.

If you draw material from just one volume of a multivolume work, your works cited entry states which volume, and your in-text citation gives only the page number:

> The works of Charles Dickens fervently proclaim "his triumphant faith in the dignity of man" (1158).

> **Works Cited Entry:**
> Johnson, Edgar. <u>Charles Dickens: His Tragedy and Triumph</u>. Vol. 2. New York: Simon, 1952.

Citing a Work by a Corporate Author or Government Agency.   Cite the author's or agency's name followed by a page reference, just as you would for a book or periodical article. However, if the title of the corporate author is long, put it in the body of the text to avoid an extensive parenthetical reference:

> Testifying before a subcommittee of the U.S. House Committee on Public Works and Transportation, a representative of the Environmental Protection Agency argued that pollution from second-hand smoke within buildings is a widespread and dangerous threat (173–174).

Documenting Internet Sources.   According to the MLA online guidelines, works on the World Wide Web are cited just like printed works when citing sources in your text. A special consideration with Web documents is that they generally do not have fixed page numbers or any kind of section numbering. If your source lacks numbering, MLA says that you have to omit numbers from your parenthetical references.

In that case, in your parenthetical citation, give the author's last name, if known (Plonsky), or the title if the original gives no author's name ("Psychology with Style"). If an author incorporates page numbers, section numbers, or paragraph numbers, you may cite the relevant numbers. Give the appropriate abbreviation before the numbers: (Plonsky, pars. 5–6). (*Pars.* is the abbreviation for *paragraphs.*) For a document on the World Wide Web, the page numbers of a printout should normally not be cited, because the pagination may vary in different printouts.

Remember that the purpose of the parenthetical citation is to indicate the location of the quotation or paraphrase in the referenced work and to point to the referenced work in the list of works cited. Whatever entry begins the reference in the works cited list (i.e., author's last name or title of work), that same entry should also appear in the parenthetical reference. A citation for an Internet source should reference the site in the body of the text, if possible, rather than including parenthetical information. For example, here is Erin's Internet source:

> Geraghty, Jim. "Do Elections Need New Rules?" Policy.com News and Events: Daily Briefing. 22 Nov. 2000. 29 Nov. 2000 <http://www.policy.com/news/dbrief/dbriefarc834.asp>.

In her paper, she documents the source this way:

> Former First Lady Hillary Clinton has given her support for the abolition of the Electoral college; in fact, she is reported to have said that she would "be willing to co-sponsor a measure to abolish the Electoral College" (Geraghty).

When mentioning the name of an author for a World Wide Web source in the text rather than in the parenthetical citation, it is sometimes difficult to tell when material borrowed ends, especially when paraphrasing. Some instructors recommend that students repeat the author's name in the parenthetical citation, even when it is mentioned in the text. The same holds true when citing a source that has no author, just a title.

CREATING A WORKS CITED PAGE

The Works Cited page of a research report lists in alphabetical order all of the sources you cite in your paper. It comes at the end of your paper, beginning on a separate page. Include an entry for every work quoted from, paraphrased, summarized, or otherwise alluded to in your paper. **Do not include on your list of works cited any sources you read but did not use in the paper.** You may want to include a list of useful works that informed your understanding of the topic but that you did not quote or paraphrase from in your final paper; to do so, create a separate page entitled "Works Consulted" using the same format as for the Works Cited page. Place the Works Consulted page last in your paper. Shawn Ryan's paper on the King Arthur legend includes a list of works consulted.

GENERAL GUIDELINES FOR CREATING A WORKS CITED LIST

- Begin your list of works cited on a new page.
- Center the title "Works Cited" one inch from the top of the page.
- Continue the page numbers of the text, with a separate number for each of the Works Cited pages.
- Begin the first line of each entry flush with the left margin. Indent the second and subsequent lines within each entry five spaces.
- Begin with the author's last name, followed by a comma and then the first name. For a source with two or more authors, invert only the first name. List the other name or names in normal order.
- Underline the titles of books, journals, magazines, and newspapers. Do not use italics or quotation marks. [**Note:** MLA guidelines recommend underlining instead of italics because printers are not uniform in the way they reproduce italics. Underlining has therefore become a convention that is understood to represent italics. However, if your instructor approves, and if your printer clearly distinguishes italics from regular print, you may use italics for the titles of books and journals.]
- Double-space within and between all entries.
- Place a period at the end of each entire entry.

The remainder of this section gives guidelines for creating works cited entries for books, periodicals, and electronic sources, supplemented by models for miscellaneous types of entries. The numbers on the list in each section (books, periodicals, electronic sources, miscellaneous) correspond to the numbered illustrations that follow each list on subsequent pages.

GUIDELINES FOR CREATING A WORKS CITED LIST FOR BOOKS

- Begin with author's last name, followed by a comma, and then the first name, followed by a period. For a source with two or more authors, invert the first author's name with a comma before and after the first name, then write the word *and* and put the other author's name in normal order.
- Underline the title of the book.
- State the place of publication, the publisher, and the date the book was published: Place: Publisher, date.
- Separate each item in an entry by a period: Author. Title. Publication information and date. Note that each period is followed by two spaces.
- For essays in collections, begin by listing the author of the essay, then the title within quotation marks, the book it appears in, the editor's name, and publication information for the book. Put the inclusive page numbers of the essay at the end of the entry.

> • **Shorten publishers' names and drop such words as *Inc., Co.,* and *Press*.** Abbreviate *University* and *Press* for university presses, as "U of Wisconsin P" for University of Wisconsin Press or "Oxford UP" for Oxford University Press.

This list will help you locate the illustrated works cited entries that follow:

1. Book with a single author

2. Article in a collection

3. Collection or anthology

4. Book with two or more authors

5. Two works by the same author

6. Reprint of a book

7. Preface, foreword, introduction, or afterword to a book

8. Edition of a book

9. Multivolume work

1. BOOK WITH A SINGLE AUTHOR

Author's name. <u>Title of Book</u>. Place of publication. City: Publisher, date of publication.

Leonardi, Susan J. <u>Dangerous by Degrees: Women at Oxford and the Somerville College Novelists</u>. New Brunswick: Rutgers UP, 1989.

2. ARTICLE IN A COLLECTION

Name the author, the title of the article, the title of the collection, the editor or coeditors of the collection, publication information, and the **inclusive page numbers** of the entire article. Follow this format:

Author's name. "Title of Article." <u>Title of Collection</u>. The abbreviation *Ed.* Editor's name in normal order. Place of publication: Name of publisher, date of publication. Inclusive page numbers on which the article appears.

Rose-Bond, Sherry, and Scott Bond. "Sherlockiana." <u>Encyclopedia Mysteriosa: A Comprehensive Guide to the Art of Detection in Print, Film, Radio, and Television</u>. Ed. William L. DeAndrea. New York: Prentice, 1994. 327–330.

If the edition has two or more editors, use the abbreviation *Eds.* followed by both editors' names:

Spacks, Patricia Meyer. "Sisters." Fetter'd or Free?: British Women Novelists, 1670–1815. Eds. Mary Anne Schofield and Cecilia Macheski.
Athens, OH: Ohio UP, 1986. 136–151.

3. COLLECTION OR ANTHOLOGY

Use this format when you cite the ideas of the editor(s) or when you refer to the entire collection. Name the editor, followed by the abbreviation *ed.* Treat the rest of the
entry as you would for a book.

Editor's name, ed. Title of Collection. Place of publication: Publisher, date
of publication.
Salwak, Dale, ed. The Life and Work of Barbara Pym. Iowa City: U of Iowa P,
1987.

For two or more editors, list the first editor's name in inverted order, followed by a
comma, the word *and,* and the second editor's name in normal order.

Schofield, Mary Anne, and Cecilia Macheski, eds. Fetter'd or Free?: British
Women Novelists, 1670–1815. Athens, OH: Ohio UP, 1986.

4. BOOK WITH TWO OR MORE AUTHORS

List the names of the authors in the same order as they are listed on the title page,
even if they are not in alphabetical order.

First author's name in inverted order, and second author's name in nor-
mal order. Name of Book. Place of publication: Publisher, date of
publication.
Gilbert, Sandra M., and Susan Gubar. The Madwoman in the Attic: The
Woman Writer and the Nineteenth-Century Literary Imagination. New
Haven: Yale UP, 1979.

5. TWO WORKS BY THE SAME AUTHOR

List the books in alphabetical order by title. For the second and subsequent books by
the same author, type three hyphens followed by a period in place of the name.

Heilbrun, Carolyn. Hamlet's Mother and Other Women. New York: Ballantine, 1990.
---. Writing a Woman's Life. New York: Ballantine, 1988.

6. REPRINT OF A BOOK

Follow the same format as for books, but add the date of the first publication after
the title.

Author's name. Title of Book. First date of publication. Place of publication
of this edition: Publisher, date of publication.

> Symons, Julian. <u>Bloody Murder: From the Detective Story to the Crime Novel: A History</u>. 1972. 1985. London: Pan Macmillan, 1992.

If a different publisher produced earlier editions, you have the option of naming the place of publication and publisher for the other editions as well as for the current one.

> Symons, Julian. <u>Bloody Murder: From the Detective Story to the Crime Novel: A History</u>. London: Faber, 1972. London: Viking, 1985. London: Pan Macmillan, 1992.

7. Preface, Foreword, Introduction, or Afterword to a Book

If you use material from the preface, foreword, introduction, or afterword of a book, your works cited entry begins with the name of the person who wrote the selection you use, not necessarily with the author of the book (though sometimes they are the same person). You will need to indicate what part of the book you cite (preface, foreword, introduction, or afterword), then name the book and author and give complete bibliographic information. Finally, give the inclusive page numbers of the preface, foreword, introduction, or afterword. Follow this model:

> Author of introduction. Introduction. <u>Title of Book</u>. By author's name in normal order. Place of publication: Publisher, date of publication. Inclusive page numbers on which the introduction appears.
> Green, Richard Lancelyn. Introduction. <u>The Adventures of Sherlock Holmes</u>. By Arthur Conan Doyle. 1892. Oxford: Oxford UP, 1993. xi–xxxv.

8. Edition of a Book

Use this format for a book prepared for publication by someone other than the author.

> Doyle, Arthur Conan. <u>The Adventures of Sherlock Holmes</u>. The Oxford Sherlock Holmes. Ed. Richard Lancelyn Green. Oxford: Oxford UP, 1994.

9. Multivolume Work

If you draw material from two or more volumes of a work, cite the total number of volumes in the entire work. When you refer to the work in the text of your paper, your parenthetical reference gives the volume number and page number.

> Johnson, Edgar. <u>Charles Dickens: His Tragedy and Triumph</u>. 2 vols. New York: Simon, 1952.

If you refer to only one volume of a multivolume work, state the number of that volume in the works cited entry. Your parenthetical in-text citation supplies page number only, not volume and page.

> Johnson, Edgar. <u>Charles Dickens: His Tragedy and Triumph</u>. Vol. 2. New York: Simon, 1952.

Periodicals in a Works Cited List.   Periodicals are magazines or journals that are published frequently and at fixed intervals. Distinguish between journals and magazines by considering audience, subject matter, and frequency of publication. Journals are fairly specialized, are usually written for people in a specific profession, are more technical and research oriented than magazines, and generally appear much less frequently than magazines, perhaps bimonthly or four times a year. Magazines, on the other hand, are intended for general audiences, are not heavily research oriented, and usually appear in monthly or even weekly editions.

GUIDELINES FOR CREATING WORKS CITED
ENTRIES FOR PERIODICALS

- Place the author's name first, in inverted order.
- If the article is published anonymously, begin the entry with the title. For placing the entries in alphabetical order on the list, ignore *The, A,* and *And* at the beginnings of titles.
- State both the title of the article and the name of the periodical in which it appears.
- Enclose the article title in quotation marks and underline the name of the periodical.
- Entries for articles in periodicals have three main divisions: the author's name, the title of the article, and publication information, that is, title of the periodical, the date the article was published, and inclusive page numbers.
- Periods separate the main parts of the entry followed by two spaces: Author. Article title. Publication information.
- Follow the date with a colon and the inclusive page numbers of the article.
- Do not use the abbreviations *p.* or *pp.* for pages.

The following illustrated works cited entries are represented in this section:

10. Article in a journal with continuous pagination

11. Article in a journal with separate pagination

12. Article in a weekly or biweekly magazine

13. Article in a monthly or bimonthly magazine

14. Article in a quarterly magazine

15. Magazine article with no author

16. Newspaper article

10. ARTICLE IN A JOURNAL WITH CONTINUOUS PAGINATION

Use this format for journals that continue pagination throughout the year.

Author's name. "Title of Article." <u>Name of Periodical</u> volume number (date): inclusive page numbers of article.

Groff, Patrick. "The Maturing of Phonics Instruction." <u>Education Digest</u> 52 (March 1991): 402–408.

11. ARTICLE IN A JOURNAL WITH SEPARATE PAGINATION

Use this format for journals that begin each issue with page 1. Give the issue number as well as the volume number.

Author's name. "Title of Article." <u>Name of Periodical</u> volume number.issue number (date): inclusive page numbers of article.

Hamby, Alonozo L. "An American Democrat: A Reevaluation of the Personality of Harry S. Truman." <u>Political Science Quarterly</u> 106.1 (Spring 1991): 33–35.

12. ARTICLE IN A WEEKLY OR BIWEEKLY MAGAZINE

Author's name. "Title of Article." <u>Name of Magazine</u> complete date, beginning with the day and abbreviating the month, page number(s).

Bazell, Robert. "Sins and Twins." <u>New Republic</u> 21 Dec. 1987: 17–18.

13. ARTICLE IN A MONTHLY OR BIMONTHLY MAGAZINE

Author's name. "Title of Article." <u>Name of Magazine</u> date, including month and year: page number(s).

Barrett, Wayne M., and Bernard Rowe. "What's Wrong with America and Can Anything Be Done about It?" <u>USA Today Magazine</u> Nov. 1994: 18–21.

14. ARTICLE IN A QUARTERLY MAGAZINE

Fletcher, John C., Franklin G. Miller, and Arthur L. Caplan. "Facing Up to Bioethical Decisions." <u>Issues in Science and Technology</u> Fall 1994: 75–80.

15. MAGAZINE ARTICLE WITH NO AUTHOR

"Teaching for Millions." <u>Success</u> Oct. 1992: 10.

16. NEWSPAPER ARTICLE

Following the author's name and article title, give the name of the newspaper, underlined. If the city where the newspaper is published is not included in its name, add that information in brackets after the name. Then give the date, beginning with the day, and abbreviating the month. Follow the date with a colon and the page number(s) where the article appears. If the newspaper has more than one section and each section is paginated separately, give both section and page number. If you gather material from a special edition of the newspaper, indicate that fact, as well.

> Schemo, Diana Jean. "Between the Art and the Artist Lies the Shadow." <u>The New York Times</u> 1 Jan. 1995: sec. 4: 1.

For an article in any periodical that does not appear on consecutive pages, give only the first page number followed by a plus sign.

> Dew, Diane. "Moral Responsibility: The Best Contraceptive." <u>Milwaukee Journal</u> 28 Sept. 1986: J6+.

Creating a Works Cited List for Electronic Sources.   As with other types of sources you cite in your research paper, your works cited entries for electronic sources should provide enough information that your reader can locate them. These sources pose a particular problem that books, periodicals, and other print media do not: They change frequently, with updates, moves to new sites, or even removal from the Internet. References to electronic works require slightly more and certainly different information than print sources require. You still need to supply the author's name, if known, and the title of the site, but you also must provide the date the site was created or updated or the date of the posting. If the source is a posting, state the name of the listserv, newsgroup, or forum where it appeared. Give the date that you accessed the material. Finally, provide the URL (Uniform Resource Locator) of the site. See the guidelines that follow for additional details.

Keep in mind that electronic sources are not uniform in the amount of information they provide. A site may not incorporate page numbers, an author's name, reference markers such as paragraph or page breaks, or other conventional print references. You can supply only the information that is available at any particular site. Use common sense: Include as much information as you have available to you.

GUIDELINES FOR CREATING A WORKS CITED LIST FOR ELECTRONIC SOURCES

- **Name the author, editor, or compiler, if known, in reversed order.** Use the abbreviation *ed.* following the name of an editor.
- **State the title of the work, following conventional punctuation rules.** For instance, use quotation marks for titles of poems, articles, or other short works within a scholarly project. Do the same for the title of a posting, that is, the information in the subject line. (Indicate that the source is an online posting.) If you cite a book, underline the title.
- **State the title of the scholarly project, database, periodical, or professional or personal site, underlined.** If the site gives no title, give a description of the site (e.g., Home page) but do not underline it or enclose it in quotation marks.

- Name the editor of the scholarly project or database, if the site gives the information.
- Supply any identifying information, such as version, volume, or issue number.
- Give the date the electronic publication was created or the date of its latest update. If you are citing a posting to a newsgroup, discussion group, or forum, give the date of the posting.
- For a posting to a discussion list or forum, give the name of the list or forum.
- If pages are numbered, give the number range or total number of pages.
- Supply the name of any institution or organization sponsoring or associated with the site.
- State the date when you accessed the source.
- Give the electronic address, or URL, of the source, in angle brackets.
- Place a period at the end of the entry.

This section provides illustrations of the following works cited entries:

17. Scholarly project
18. Professional site
19. Article in a reference database
20. Online article
21. Article with author named, scholarly journal (specialized readership)
22. Article in magazine (general readership)
23. Article in magazine with more than one page, starting page number given
24. Article with no author named
25. Personal site
26. Posting to a discussion group
27. E-mail message

17. SCHOLARLY PROJECT

Virtual London: Monuments and Dust. Ed. Michael Levenson. 28 Nov. 1998. U of Virginia. 2 Feb. 1999 <http://jefferson.village.virginia.edu/mhc/london/london.html>.

18. PROFESSIONAL SITE

The Camelot Project. 3 Mar. 1999. U of Rochester. 4 Apr. 1999 <http://www.lib.rochester.edu/camelot/cphome.stm>.

19. ARTICLE IN A REFERENCE DATABASE

"Fresco." Britannica Online. Vers. 97.l.l. Mar. 1997. Encyclopaedia Britannica, 29 Mar. 1997 <http://www.eb.com:180>.

20. ONLINE ARTICLE

Benfey, Christopher. "Better Late than Ever." Slate. 18 Dec. 1996. n. pag. 28 Nov. 2000. <http://slate.msn.com/Art/96-12-18/Art.asp>.

The following four examples are from an Online Source of Full-Text Articles

21. ARTICLE WITH AUTHOR NAMED, SCHOLARLY JOURNAL (SPECIALIZED READERSHIP)

Barnett, Martha W. "Lessons in Democracy." *ABA Journal* 87 (Jan. 2001): 8. 10 Mar. 2001. Online. EBSCO.

22. ARTICLE IN MAGAZINE (GENERAL READERSHIP)

Arenofsky, Janice. "Teen Suicide." *Current Health* Dec. 1997: 16+. Online. EBSCO. 23 April 2001.

23. ARTICLE IN MAGAZINE WITH MORE THAN ONE PAGE, STARTING PAGE NUMBER GIVEN

Philonoe. "Procrustes and the Culture Wars." American Scholar Summer 99: 5+. 14 Nov 2000. Online. EBSCO.

24. ARTICLE WITH NO AUTHOR NAMED

"Yelling 'Fire.' " *New Republic* 3 April 2000: 9. 6 April 2000. Online. EBSCO.

25. PERSONAL SITE

Taylor, Andrew. Home page. 21 Sept. 2001 <http://www.thenet.co.uk/~hickafric/ataylor1.html>.

26. POSTING TO A DISCUSSION GROUP

Walton, Hilary. "New Pym Biography." Online posting. 2 Feb. 2001. Pym-1. 3 Feb. 1999 <pym-1@onelist.com>.

27. E-MAIL MESSAGE

Konrad, Lucas. "Antique Fire Trucks." E-mail to author. 3 Mar. 2001.

Works Cited Formats for Sources Other than Books, Periodicals, and Electronic Sources. The following illustrated works cited entries are represented in this section:

28. Congressional record

29. Government document

30. Lecture

31. Letter

32. Personal interview

33. Reprint of an article provided by an information service

34. Telephone interview

35. Pamphlet

36. Television or radio program

37. Sound recording

38. Article in a reference book

28. CONGRESSIONAL RECORD

United States. Senate. <u>Transportation Systems for Alaskan Natural Gas</u>. 95th Cong., 1st sess. S-2411. Washington: GPO, 1977.

United States. House. Committee on Public Works and Transportation. Subcommittee on Public Buildings and Grounds. <u>To Prohibit Smoking in Federal Buildings</u>. 103rd Cong., 1st sess. H. R. 881. Washington: GPO, 1993.

29. GOVERNMENT DOCUMENT

U.S. Department of Health and Human Services. <u>Caffeine and Pregnancy</u>. Rockville, MD: HHS Publications, 1981.

30. LECTURE

Schilling, Brian. "The Role of First Responders in Medical Emergencies." Lecture at Whitko High School, 22 Dec. 2001.

31. LETTER

White, Jeremy. Letter to author. 1 Oct. 2001.

32. PERSONAL INTERVIEW

Yahi, Mourad. Personal interview. 10 Nov. 2001.

33. REPRINT OF AN ARTICLE PROVIDED BY AN INFORMATION SERVICE

Koop, C. Everett. "Life and Death and the Handicapped Newborn." <u>Law &
Medicine</u> (Summer 1989): 101–113. <u>Medical Science of Social Issues
Resources Series</u>. Boca Raton: SIRS, 1989. Art. 50.

34. TELEPHONE INTERVIEW

Yahi, Laurel. Telephone interview. 12 Jan. 2001.

35. PAMPHLET

Tweddle, Dominic. <u>The Coppergate Helmet</u>. York, UK: Cultural Resource
Management, 1984.

36. TELEVISION OR RADIO PROGRAM

News program:

<u>60 Minutes</u>. CBS. WSAW, Wausau. 17 Dec. 2001.

Series with episode titles:

"Lights Out." <u>ER</u>. NBC. WNBC, Atlanta. 23 Sept. 1999.

Radio program:

<u>On the Air</u>, WOWO, Fort Wayne. 12 Apr. 2001.

37. SOUND RECORDING

To cite a compact disc, list first the aspect of the recording you want to emphasize:
composer, conductor, or performer. Give that name first, then the title of the recording or selection, the manufacturer, and the year of issue (write *n.d.* if no date appears
on the package or disc). If you are not using a compact disc, state the medium, such
as audiotape or audiocassette. Do not enclose the name of the medium in italics or
quotation marks.

Uchida, Mitsuko, pianist. Piano Sonatas D, KV 284, Sonata in B flat, KV 570,
and Rondo in D, KV 485. By Wolfgang Amadeus Mozart. Philips, 1986.

38. ARTICLE IN A REFERENCE BOOK

Treat an entry in an encyclopedia or dictionary as you would an article in a collection,
but do not cite the book's editor. If the article is signed, begin with the author's name,
followed by the title of the entry; otherwise, begin with the title. For familiar reference books such as standard encyclopedias and dictionaries that are frequently updated and reissued, you need not give publication information. Just list the edition
(if stated) and year of publication.

Watkins, Calvert. "Indo-European and the Indo-Europeans." <u>American Heritage Dictionary of the English Language</u>. 3rd ed. 1991.

When citing less-familiar books, give full publication information.

Rose-Bond, Sherry, and Scott Bond. "Sherlockiana." <u>Encyclopedia Mysteriosa: A Comprehensive Guide to the Art of Detection in Print, Film, Radio, and Television</u>. Ed. William L. DeAndrea. New York: Prentice, 1994.
327–330.

SAMPLE PAGES FROM STUDENT RESEARCH PAPERS

Title Page.   Although MLA style does not require a separate title page, some instructors ask for it. If your instructor requires a title page, follow these guidelines:

- Center your title about one-third to halfway down the page.
- Do not underline your title, enclose it in quotation marks, capitalize every let-
ter, or place a period after it.
- Capitalize the first letter of every important word in the title.
- Beneath the title, double-space, type the word *by*, double-space again, and
center your own name.
- Drop farther down the page and center your instructor's name, the course
name, and the date. (See the example on page 119.)

Pagination and Spacing.   The entire paper should be double-spaced, with each
page numbered in the upper right-hand corner, one-half inch from the top and flush
with the right margin. MLA style requires that pagination begin with page 1 and recommends that you include your last name before the page number.

FIRST PAGE OF A RESEARCH PAPER WITH A SEPARATE TITLE PAGE

If your instructor requires a separate title page, follow these guidelines for the first
text page of your paper:

- Type your last name and the number 1 in the upper right-hand corner, one-
half inch from the top of the page, flush with the right margin.
- Drop down two inches from the top of the page and center your title, exactly
as it appears on your title page.
- Do not underline your title, enclose it in quotation marks, capitalize every letter, or place a period after it.
- Capitalize the first letter of every important word in the title.
- Double-space and begin the body of your paper. (See the example on page
123.)

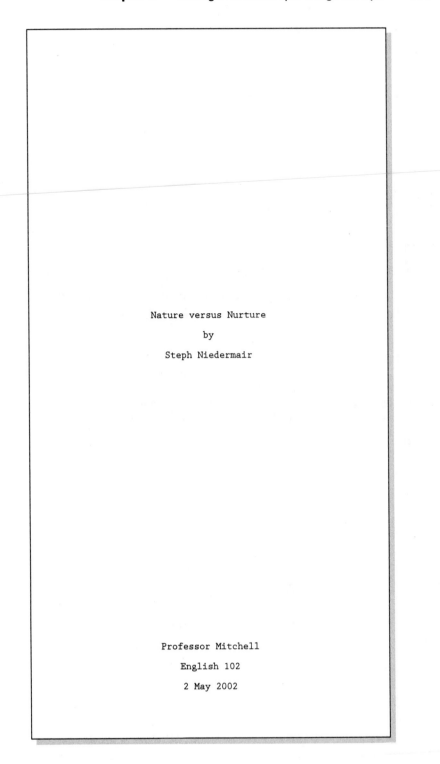

Nature versus Nurture

by

Steph Niedermair

Professor Mitchell

English 102

2 May 2002

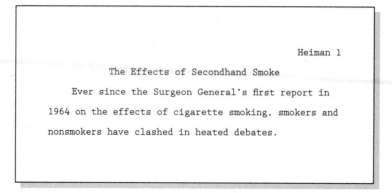

```
                                              Heiman 1
              The Effects of Secondhand Smoke
         Ever since the Surgeon General's first report in
     1964 on the effects of cigarette smoking, smokers and
     nonsmokers have clashed in heated debates.
```

FIRST PAGE OF A RESEARCH PAPER WITHOUT A SEPARATE TITLE PAGE

If your instructor does not require a separate title page, follow these guidelines:

- Place your name, your instructor's name, the course title, and the date in the upper left-hand corner, one inch from the top of the paper and flush with the left margin.
- Double-space between each line.
- Double-space below the date and center your title.
- Do not underline your title, enclose it in quotation marks, capitalize every letter, or place a period after it.
- Capitalize the first letter of every important word in the title.
- Double-space again and begin the body of your paper.

```
                                              Phonics 1

         Cory L. Vandertie
         Professor Kathy Mitchell
         English 102
         19 April 2002
                      The Phonics Controversy
             In recent years, school officials, teachers, and
         parents have been wrestling with the issue of how
         best to teach reading, with the controversy often
         centering on the conflict
```

Outline Page.   If your instructor requires a formal outline, place it immediately after the title page. Your instructor will tell you how detailed your outline should be, but follow these basic directions in most cases:

- Begin your outline with the thesis statement of your paper.
- Double-space between all lines of the outline.
- Use uppercase roman numerals (I, II, III) for each major division of your outline and capital letters (A, B, C) for each subdivision under each major division. If you find it necessary to further subdivide, use arabic numerals (1, 2, 3) under capital letters and lowercase letters (a, b, c) under arabic numerals.
- Do not number the outline page unless it runs to two or more pages. If your outline is two or more pages long, number all pages after the first in lowercase roman numerals (ii, iii, iv), placed in the upper right-hand corner, one-half inch from the top of the page and flush with the right margin.
- End with a statement summarizing your conclusion.

Here are outline pages from two student papers, the first with a fairly brief outline, the second with more detail.

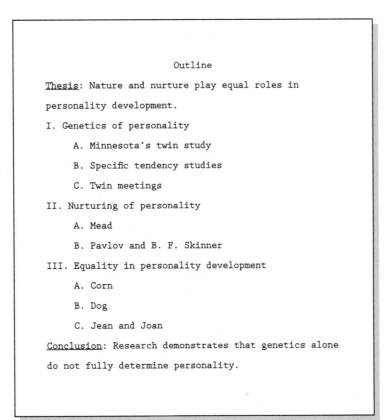

```
                        Outline
    Thesis: Nature and nurture play equal roles in
    personality development.
    I. Genetics of personality
            A. Minnesota's twin study
            B. Specific tendency studies
            C. Twin meetings
    II. Nurturing of personality
            A. Mead
            B. Pavlov and B. F. Skinner
    III. Equality in personality development
            A. Corn
            B. Dog
            C. Jean and Joan
    Conclusion: Research demonstrates that genetics alone
    do not fully determine personality.
```

Outline

Thesis: Parents, educators, and reading experts disagree on the issue of whether phonics instruction is beneficial to beginning readers.

I. Introduction

    A. Rudolph Flesch's observations

    B. National Assessment of Education Progress reports

II. Background

    A. Introduction to phonics

    B. Failure of schools to teach reading

    C. Regna Lee Wood

III. Phonics instruction

    A. How phonics works

    B. Problems associated with the teaching of phonics

    C. Factors associated with teaching phonics

        1. Direct

        2. Systemic

        3. Intensive

IV. Negative effects of phonics instruction

    A. Lack of information and knowledge

    B. Hooked on Phonics

V. Positive effects of phonics instruction

    A. Present-day improvements over early techniques

    B. Myths about phonics dispelled

    C. Andrew Schuster's story

VI. Jeanne Sternlicht Chall's research

    A. History of research

    B. The Great Debate

Conclusion: The debate over the benefits of phonics remains unresolved.

Introductory Paragraphs and Body of the Paper.   As for any other kind of writing assignment, begin with an introduction that provides background information that clearly portrays the topic of your paper or the direction your argument will take, or that in some way sets the stage for what follows. State your thesis or central idea early in the paper. If your topic is controversial, explain the nature of the controversy. Once you have introduced your topic sufficiently, begin developing your argument. Here are the opening pages of Steph Niedermair's paper, "Nature versus Nurture."

Steph's introduction explains something of the nature of the controversy between those who believe environment plays a dominant role in personality development and those who believe heredity plays a dominant role.

Steph's thesis indicates that she sides with those who believe both play equal roles. Readers can expect to see a development in the rest of the paper of each of these positions, as well as persuasive evidence from a variety of authorities in support of Steph's thesis.

Neidermair 1

Nature versus Nurture

"Nature versus nurture" is one of the most heatedly debated topics in the area of human biology today. Most scientists and nurturists agree that temperament and environment interact in some way to form personality. Their opinions differ, however, when it comes to how much and in what ways each factor influences personality and behavior. Geneticists are convinced that most of one's personality is formed at the moment of conception. On the other hand, nurturists claim that people who believe that genes are in control of personality do not take into consideration the fact that society and environment have a major effect on personality development. A review of both sides of the issue leads me to the conclusion that the human personality is so complex that it can be explained by neither heredity nor environment but rather by a combination of both.

Sociobiologists, for example, are convinced that nature and nurture are of equal importance. They agree with the geneticists' view that babies

Here, Steph has combined a direct quotation and a paraphrase. The parenthetical citation tells the source and the page number on which the quoted and paraphrased material is found.

Neidermair 2

are born with a predisposed personality. But they
add that social and nurturing experiences can
"intensify, diminish, or modify" personality traits
(Wood and Wood 272). Gerald McClearn, a psychologist

The information about Gerald McClearn establishes his credentials.

and twin researcher at Pennsylvania State
University, explained personality development
realistically when he said, " 'A gene can produce a
nudge in one direction or another, but it does not
directly control behavior. It doesn't take away a
person's free will' " (qtd. in "How Genes Shape

McClearn's words are in both single and double quotation marks because he was quoted in the anonymous article "How Genes Shape Personality."

Personality" 62). This component of an individual's
free will is crucial to understanding the relative
roles of nature and nurture in personality
development.

      The debate began over a century ago when Sir
Francis Galton conducted the first twin studies, and
it continues today with the work on human biology
that is being done in many university research
laboratories. The "nature versus nurture"
controversy is being heavily studied at the
University of Minnesota's Twin Research Center, for
instance, where scientists are trying to quantify
genetic and environmental factors that influence
human behavior. Most research involves studying both
identical and fraternal twins, some of whom were

Paragraph 3 is phrased entirely in Steph's own words. She has done enough reading in her sources to know that twins are crucial to research in the area of personality formation and human behavior and that the University of Minnesota twin studies are common knowledge. Thus, paragraph 3 does not require any documentation.

The words qtd. in in the citation for McClearn's words mean "quoted in." Steph did not read his words in the original but as they were quoted in the article "How Genes Shape Personality."

Steph does not need to give a citation at the end of the first sentence in paragraph 4, because she has named her authority, and her second sentence clearly indicates that she is still paraphrasing from that same authority. The parenthetical citation gives the source.

Note that the title of the Gallagher article "Manner Born," is included because Steph's Works Cited page mentions two articles by Winifred Gallagher.

Neidermair 3

reared together and some of whom were reared apart. Identical twins who were reared apart are ideal for these studies because they share the same genetic codes but not the same environments. At the University of Minnesota, the twins go through six days of physical, psychological, and intellectual testing.

Winifred Gallagher reports that these twins answer 15,000 questions about their interests, values, principles, and eating habits. She explains that the Multidimensional Personality Questionnaire (MPQ), developed by Auke Tellegen of the University of Minnesota, evaluates eleven traits that can be broken down into three categories: "positive emotionality," "negative emotionality," and "constraint" ("Manner Born" 61). For their tests, Tellegen and a team of scientists gathered 407 pairs of twins. Of these, 261 pairs were identical, 44 of whom had been reared apart. The other 146 pairs were fraternal, of whom 27 sets had been reared apart (Konner 64). From the MPQ, scientists obtained approximate percentages relating to how much of each of the eleven traits was caused by genetics. The results looked like this: extroversion—61%; conformity—60%; worry—55%; creativity—55%; paranoia—55%; optimism—54%; cautiousness—51%; aggressiveness—48%; ambitiousness—46%; orderliness—43%; and intimacy—33% ("How Genes Shape Personality" 62). These percentages vary from person to person, but most times when twins are subjected

Neidermair 4

to testing, the results are remarkably alike for

each person. Minnesota scientists have concluded

that this data shows that genes are more influential

than nurture on most personality traits (Bazell 17)

Complete bibliographic information for the Bazell article is given on Steph's Works Cited page.

Theodore Reich, a psychiatric geneticist at

Washington University in St. Louis, is not surprised

by new evidence showing that genes influence

personality. He says that, after all, people have

been breeding animals to obtain certain traits or

behaviors for many years (Holden 601). The genetics

of personality gets even more complicated when one

takes into consideration the fact that each trait

tested by MPQ is not controlled by one gene alone.

In the following excerpt from Missy Heiman's paper, "The Effects of Secondhand Smoke," notice the parenthetical references to testimony recorded in the *Congressional Record* and to a government document:

Heiman 3

According to an investigation into whether to

prohibit smoking in federal buildings conducted by

the United States House Subcommittee of the

Committee on Public Works and Transportation, almost

To cite a government document, state the committee or agency name followed by a page reference. For agencies or committees with long names, a better option is to place the name in the text of your paper, rather than interrupt the flow of your text with a long parenthetical reference.

Heiman 4

50 million nonsmokers over the age of 35 are
regularly passive smokers, that is, they are exposed
to environmental tobacco smoke (ETS) (412).
According to biochemical markers, ETS is the
equivalent of smoking two cigarettes a day (Hayward
7), so a person who chooses not to smoke is
subjected to the same harmful effects of smoking as
a smoker is. Since much of people's time is spent
indoors, it is difficult for nonsmokers to escape ETS
if they live or work with smokers. The Environmental
Protection Agency (EPA), in testimony before a
subcommittee of the U.S. House Committee on Public
Works and Transportation, has shown that pollutant
levels are higher indoors than out, causing real
concern for the health of nonsmokers: "[We have]
concluded that the widespread exposure to
environmental tobacco smoke in the U.S. presents a
serious and substantial public health risk"
(173-174).

The risk includes adults and children alike. An
estimated 50,000 adult Americans die from secondhand
smoke each year: 35,000 from heart disease, 3,000
from lung cancer, and 12,000 from other types of
cancers ("Pros/Cons" 142). Those 50,000 nonsmoking
people are paying a price that people used to think
was reserved only for smokers. In Wisconsin alone,
more than 10 percent of lung cancer deaths are
attributed to passive smoke (Hayward 7). Nationally,
according to Dr. Randolph D. Smoak, Jr.,

To refer to something by its initials, write out the full term the first time you mention it and place the initials in parentheses immediately after, as "environmental tobacco smoke (ETS)" and "Environmental Protection Agency (EPA)."

Missy uses brackets to insert the words "We have" in the quotation from the EPA.

Heiman 5

The words of Dr. Randolph D. Smoak Jr. are quoted in the source Missy read. His words also include a phrase in quotation marks. As a result, Missy's quotation of Smoak's words begins with a triple set of quotation marks: single within double to indicate the passage is quoted in her source and double within the single to indicate the phrase is quoted within the quotation.

" ' "Passive smoking" is the third leading cause of premature death in the United States, exceeded only by direct smoking and alcohol' " (qtd. in "Pros/Cons" 142). Those lives could have been saved had smoking been permitted only outdoors.

Children are also victims of passive smoke. The EPA concluded in 1993 that secondhand smoke can cause respiratory problems in children ("Second Hand" 130). Besides respiratory ailments, children are subject to many other risks from secondhand smoke, such as increased chances of chronic middle-ear infections, worsened conditions in asthmatics, or even increased chances of developing asthma ("Second Hand" 133). The question is, do smokers have the right to endanger the lives and well-being of children and adults by smoking in public places? Representative Henry Waxman, a Democrat from California who is the main sponsor of the Smoke-Free Environment Act, declares, " 'Smokers do not have the right to jeopardize the health of nonsmokers, particularly children' " ("Pros/Cons"

"Second Hand" and "Pros/Cons" are short titles for articles with no authors' names.

142). Representative Waxman's Act was approved by the House committee in May 1994. It prohibits smoking in buildings visited by ten or more people per week, except in designated areas that must have separate ventilation systems.

Works Cited Page.   The Works Cited pages for Steph Niedermair's and Missy Heiman's papers illustrate how to cite some of the most common sources used in undergraduate research papers, including books, weekly news magazine articles, newspaper articles, journal articles, essays in a collection, and government documents.

Niedermair 10

Works Cited

Bazell, Robert. "Sins and Twins." <u>New Republic</u> 21
    Dec. 1987: 17-18.

Gallahger, Winifred. "How We Become What We Are."
    <u>Atlantic Monthly</u> Sept. 1994: 38-40+.

---. "To the Manner Born." <u>Rolling Stone</u> 19 Nov.
    1987: 56+.

Holden, Constance. "The Genetics of Personality."
    <u>Science</u> 237 (1987): 598-601.

"How Genes Shape Personality." <u>U.S. News & World
    Report</u> 13 Apr. 1987: 58-62.

Konnert, Melvin. "Under the Influence." <u>Omni</u> Jan.
    1990: 62-64+.

Macionis, John J. "Socialization." <u>Sociology</u>.
    Englewood Cliffs, NJ: Prentice, 1993. 131.

Wood, Samuel E., and Ellen R. Green Wood. "Child
    Development." <u>The World of Psychology</u>.
    Needham Heights, NJ: Allyn, 1993. 272.

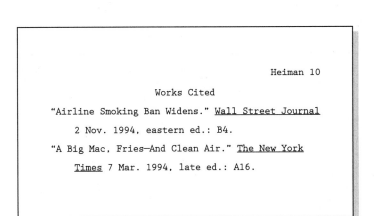

Heiman 10

Works Cited

"Airline Smoking Ban Widens." <u>Wall Street Journal</u>
    2 Nov. 1994, eastern ed.: B4.

"A Big Mac, Fries—And Clean Air." <u>The New York
    Times</u> 7 Mar. 1994, late ed.: A16.

Heiman 11

Hayward, Julie. <u>Exposure to Tobacco Smoke:</u>
    <u>Effects on Children and Nonsmoking Adults</u>.
    Madison: Wisconsin Dept. of Health and
    Social Services, August 1989.

Hilts, Philip J. "McDonald's Bans Smoking at All
    the Sites It Owns." <u>The New York Times</u> 24
    Feb. 1994, late ed.: A16.

Nieves, Evelyn. "Going Smoke-Free: More Malls
    Joining in the Bans on Tobacco." <u>The New</u>
    <u>York Times</u> 2 Aug. 1993, late ed.: A1+.

"Pros & Cons: Should H.R. 3434, the Smoke-Free
    Environment Act, Be Approved?" <u>Congressional</u>
    <u>Digest</u> May 1994: 142-160.

"Second-Hand Smoke." <u>Congressional Digest</u> May
    1994: 130-141.

Schmitt, Eric. "Military Tightens Its Rules
    against Smoking." <u>The New York Times</u> 9 Mar.
    1994, late ed.: A13.

"Travel Adviser." <u>Travel Holiday</u> Apr. 1994: 18.

U.S. House. Committee on Public Works and
    Transportation. Subcommittee on Public
    Buildings and Grounds. <u>To Prohibit Smoking</u>
    <u>in Federal Buildings</u>. 103rd Cong., 1st
    sess. H.R. 881. Washington: GPO, 1993.

Here are two examples of complete student papers that implement the MLA style guidelines introduced in this chapter.

Arthur of Camelot: The Once and Future King

by

Shawn Ryan

Professor Zackary

English 102

1 May 2001

Outline

Thesis: An examination of some of the research on Arthurian legend suggests that the evidence supports the theory that a man like Arthur did exist.

I. The birth of Arthur

    A. The legend

    B. Evidence of Tintagel

II. The places and people most important to Arthur

    A. Camelot

    B. Glastonbury Abbey

    C. Lancelot and Perceval

III. Arthur's impact on society

    A. His image

    B. The difference between the man and the legend

Conclusion: Arthur's existence as a man is indeterminable, but Arthur's presence in the minds and hearts of people everywhere gives credence to his existence as a leader of nations.

Ryan 1

Arthur of Camelot: The Once and Future King

North and west the wind blew beneath the morning sun, over endless miles of rolling grass and far scattered thickets . . . [and] Dragonmount, where the dragon had died, and with him, some said, the Age of Legend--where prophecy said he would be born again.

(Jordan 13)

Ryan 2

Tales of Britain's legendary sixth-century King
Arthur have long been an inspiration to writers and
poets. In the works of the fifteenth-century writer
Sir Thomas Malory, the nineteenth-century poet
Alfred, Lord Tennyson, and authors of today, we find
references to the glorious tales of chivalry and
heroism found in the earliest legends of the hero of
the Round Table, King Arthur. Robert Jordan's <u>The
Wheel of Time</u>, published in 1992, uses many of the
names and legends associated with Arthur. Though most
people have likely at some point heard various
aspects of Arthurian legend, they may not be aware
that they are hearing a new spin on an old tale.
<u>Camelot</u> the musical, Disney's <u>The Sword in the Stone</u>,
and Steven Spielberg's <u>Star Wars</u> all have their roots
in the tales of King Arthur. So many stories revolve
around this great king that some may not realize the
controversy surrounding him. However, much is
mysterious about King Arthur, even whether he
existed. Scholars and amateurs alike have done
extensive research to determine the historical basis
of King Arthur and to establish whether he was
mythical or real. An examination of some of the
research on Arthurian legend suggests that the
evidence supports the theory that a man like Arthur
did exist.

The search for evidence begins with what may be
the murkiest part of the legend, the birth of King
Arthur and his ascension to the throne of Britain.
According to Sir Thomas Malory's <u>The Arthurian Tales:</u>

Ryan 3

The Greatest of Romances, King Utherpendragon had
fallen in love with the wife of the Duke of Cornwall
and waged war so that he could kill her husband and
thus marry her legally. The Duke hid his wife in the
castle Tintagel, and that night Merlin, the King's
wizard, transformed Uther so that he appeared to be
the Duke of Cornwall. After the transformation, Uther
made love to the Duke's wife and she became pregnant.
Soon after the adultery had been committed, the Duke
was slain on the battlefield, and Uther took the
Duke's wife to be his bride. Their child, Arthur, was
still young when his father died. Malory explains
that, at Merlin's prompting, the child Arthur pulled
the sword Caliburn (Excalibur in more recent
versions) from an anvil and was proclaimed King.
Finally he commanded the armies of Britain to defeat
those who opposed his rule, and they won a great
victory for their king (1-14). Other versions of the
story vary from this one, but most of the places and
major characters are the same. Despite all the
anecdotal evidence, this story, with its magical
transformations and a holy sword embedded in an
anvil, are difficult to believe.

Tintagel itself may be the easiest point of
reference to begin a quest for the truth of Arthur's
birth, since archeological records are generally
accurate and reliable. Interestingly, there are ruins
of a building from around the alleged time of Arthur
(approximately AD 500-600), but they are only the
ruins of a Celtic monastery, not those of a castle or

Ryan 4

even a fort (Alcock 249). This is to be expected,
because during the hundreds of years since the time
when Arthur was believed to live, many stories have
been invented to complete the life history of a great
man. Authors who write stories about heroes and
leaders bestow upon them great powers or deeds,
coupled with an equally great or fantastic birth, and
we can expect no less from monks and poets who copied
the histories of Arthur from their very beginnings.
It will be assumed that, if Tintagel is a
fabrication, searching for evidence of the other
persons or items from the same story would not be
within the scope of this paper.

If the stories surrounding Arthur's birth are
fabricated, then we are left with two very prominent
places associated with his life and death, Camelot
and Glastonbury Abbey. Camelot has been a tremendous
source of controversy when it is linked to the
Arthurian legends. For many centuries, Camelot was
believed to be a fictional location, similar to
Tintagel. Only recently, in the past few decades,
have archeologists found proof of a massive fortified
city that would fit the time period of Camelot. South
Cadbury in Somerset has many remnants of various hill
forts. Michael Wood notes that "a late local
tradition connected Arthur with one of these hill
forts. . . . On top of the fort they found the
18-acre area had been refortified with a drystone
wall, inside which had been timber buildings
including the feasting hall of a Dark Age warlord."

Ryan 5

This fort, according to Wood, also had similarities to Roman military architecture and contained Mediterranean pottery, which would have been in use at the time of Arthur (49).

Despite this promising evidence, some skeptics doubt that Camelot is a legitimate historical Arthurian landmark. Richard Barber, for instance, claims that the source of the name Camelot is derived from a tenth-century village named Camel, "so the name Camelot in connection with Cadbury is wholly wide of the mark, even in the general sense of Arthur's court" (135). However, this does not necessarily mean that the South Cadbury site could not have been from Arthur's time. Even Michael Wood, who claims that the site is strongly connected to Arthur, admits that the name "Camelot" may have been invented by a twelfth-century French poet (49). Whether the *name* "Camelot" came before or after the period in which Arthur lived, evidence associated with the *place* Camelot does show that a very powerful leader ruled from that site during the relevant time period of Arthurian legend. This proof is our first piece of evidence in support of the existence of a real King Arthur.

Glastonbury Abbey is the last place that our search for the historical Arthur takes us to, and it is the second most discussed site, after Camelot, that is associated with Arthur. In the legend, Arthur was said to be buried at Avalon. This name itself

brings up controversy, specifically because there is
no record of such a place ever existing. One theory
is that it may be a man's name, Aballach, father of
Modron, who appears as the ruler of Avalon in
Geoffrey [Monmouth's] Life of Merlin (Barber 125). A
second opinion is that it comes from the Welsh word,
afallenau, or "apple trees," since the island of
Avalon was said to be a rich and plentiful land
(Barber 125). This difference of opinion only begins
to scratch the surface of the controversy surrounding
this supposed burial site of Arthur.

One of the most puzzling questions surrounding
the Glastonbury site is that there is no proof of
anything relating to the story told by the monks who
claimed to find Arthur's remains. Barber describes
this situation and the interesting flaws in the
stories told by the different parties involved.
According to him, in 1191 monks from Glastonbury
Abbey made a claim to the world that they had found
the burial site of King Arthur, thanks to a tip from
the late King Henry II. Gerald of Wales was there
right after the announcement and took careful notes
of the findings (Barber 127). The monks said that
there were two sets of bones, one male and one
female, both found inside a hollowed out tree trunk,
separated with a wooden divider. Secondly, Barber
notes, there was a lead cross with these words
inscribed on it: " 'Here lies buried the famous king
Arthurus with Wennevereia his second wife in the

island of Avallonia' " (127). However, the monks'
claim was likely political in origin and has several
flaws. First, Barber points out, the dates for the
discovery are not clear; taking into account the poor
methods of recording events in the Middle Ages, there
is still a significant discrepancy in the dating of
the supposed finds. Secondly, King Richard took the
throne after Henry II, who had funded the Abbey.
Richard ceased funding the Abbey 1 year before the
monks' claim that Arthur's tomb was discovered, and
the discovery is suspected to have been falsified to
increase pilgrimage and donations to the Abbey.
Finally, two firsthand accounts of the event record
different sayings on the lead cross found on the
coffin. The monks, it seems, changed their story
later, claiming that the lead cross had the words
"the Once and Future King" inscribed upon it instead
of the statement that the king and queen lay buried
there, presumably because they wanted to embellish
the story (Barber 132). Clearly there is a lack of
evidence at Glastonbury for any final judgment to be
made, so we will assume that the burial site of King
Arthur has yet to be discovered.

　　Because of the very inconclusive evidence
regarding the sites of the supposed legendary
occurrences, we are forced to turn to the characters
themselves for proof of Arthur's existence. The
easiest place to begin is with his knights, since
they were documented in military records throughout
history. These records show us that

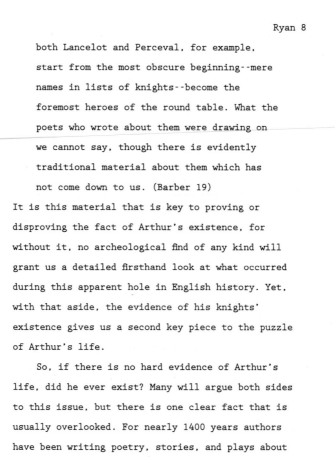

Ryan 8

both Lancelot and Perceval, for example,

start from the most obscure beginning--mere

names in lists of knights--become the

foremost heroes of the round table. What the

poets who wrote about them were drawing on

we cannot say, though there is evidently

traditional material about them which has

not come down to us. (Barber 19)

It is this material that is key to proving or

disproving the fact of Arthur's existence, for

without it, no archeological find of any kind will

grant us a detailed firsthand look at what occurred

during this apparent hole in English history. Yet,

with that aside, the evidence of his knights'

existence gives us a second key piece to the puzzle

of Arthur's life.

So, if there is no hard evidence of Arthur's

life, did he ever exist? Many will argue both sides

to this issue, but there is one clear fact that is

usually overlooked. For nearly 1400 years authors

have been writing poetry, stories, and plays about

this man whom they have named Arthur. These literary

works, in turn, have inspired people to strive for

the values of the Round Table, the beauty of Camelot,

and the glories of Britain during the time of Arthur.

In people's minds Arthur is real, and he may be one

of the last great heroes that any society can look to

as the ideal person. Only because Arthur is so

intertwined in legend and tale can he fit this

Ryan 9

persona. His story and the legends surrounding him have had a tremendous impact on countless people's imaginations throughout history, perhaps more than any other person living or dead. Here is where the importance of Arthur lies, in the hearts and minds of people all around the globe. Even if the actual man King Arthur did not exist and did not save Britain from the barbarian hordes, the image of what he represents--courage, strength, valor, honor, love, devotion--cannot help but have inspired many real kings and world leaders to accomplish feats of equal or greater importance.

Our conclusion, then, rests on a philosophical dilemma centering on the nature of existence and the influence of legend: "Historically speaking, Arthurian fact is far clearer than Arthur himself" (Ashe et al. 65). An archaeologist might argue that because there is no physical proof of King Arthur of Camelot, he never existed. However, a sociologist or a philosopher could argue that because of the influence of the *idea* of Arthur on those who came after the time in which he flourished, he has become the equal of any person living or dead. Besides, no person can at this time definitively prove that Arthur did not exist, and this may well be enough evidence to prove his existence. No record books show names tied to places during his apparent reign, and although wars with barbarians clearly did take place, no leader or ruler is named alongside an English victory. There is historical evidence that a great and powerful

Ryan 10

general, if not a king, did rule England at the time of Arthur, but it is impossible to determine from the records available if this ruler was Arthur. Because such physical proof is missing from various historical and archeological records, we are left to evaluate Arthur's impact on society.

Countless movies, books, and stories have had their roots in the legend of this mysterious man, and people of all ages are attracted to the tales of heroism and romance that surround him. To these people Arthur exists, at least in spirit, and the values that he stood for guide some of their lives. To say that Arthur doesn't exist is to take a shallow look at all of the data surrounding him. The majority of evidence for Arthur's existence is not buried in Camelot or Tintagel but in the minds and hearts of people around the world. Although he may not be born again in the flesh, as a prophecy at Glastonbury Abbey states, he is reborn every time a new child hears the legend of the great King Arthur of Camelot. This is Arthur's kingdom, and until more proof can be discovered, this is where he always has been.

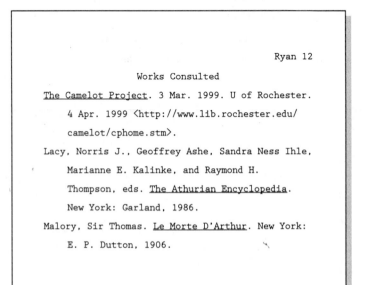

Ryan 11

Works Cited

Alcock, Leslie. <u>Arthur's Britain: History and</u>
  <u>Archeology AD 367-634</u>. New York: Viking
  Penguin, 1971.

Ashe, Geoffrey, Leslie Alcock, C. A. Ralegh
  Radford, Philip Rahtz, and Jill Racy. <u>The</u>
  <u>Quest for Arthur's Britain</u>. New York:
  Praeger, 1968.

Barber, Richard. <u>The Figure of Arthur</u>. Totowa,
  NJ: Rowman and Littlefield, 1972.

Jordan, Robert. <u>The Shadow Rising</u>. New York: Tom
  Doherty, 1992.

Malory, Sir Thomas. <u>The Arthurian Tales: The</u>
  <u>Greatest of Romances</u>. London: Norrcena
  Society, 1906.

Wood, Michael. <u>In Search of the Dark Ages</u>. New
  York: Facts on File, 1987.

Ryan 12

Works Consulted

<u>The Camelot Project</u>. 3 Mar. 1999. U of Rochester.
  4 Apr. 1999 <http://www.lib.rochester.edu/
  camelot/cphome.stm>.

Lacy, Norris J., Geoffrey Ashe, Sandra Ness Ihle,
  Marianne E. Kalinke, and Raymond H.
  Thompson, eds. <u>The Athurian Encyclopedia</u>.
  New York: Garland, 1986.

Malory, Sir Thomas. <u>Le Morte D'Arthur</u>. New York:
  E. P. Dutton, 1906.

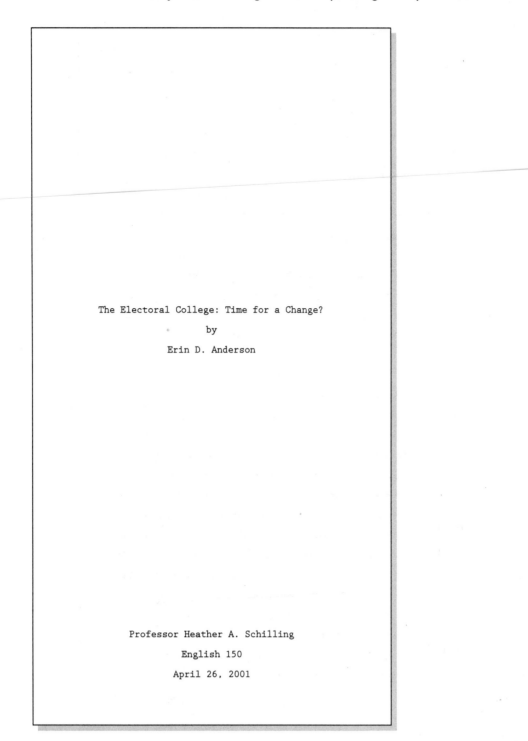

The Electoral College: Time for a Change?

by

Erin D. Anderson

Professor Heather A. Schilling

English 150

April 26, 2001

Anderson 1

The Electoral College: Time for a Change?

The electoral college system, which has been in
place for over 200 years, is one of the most widely
debated of all governmental policies; in fact, over
850 proposals for its change or abolishment have been
offered in Congress (Vile 109). However, only two of
these reforms have ever been enacted. Questions are
once again being raised concerning whether another
alternative would better suit modern America or if
reform would do more harm than good. People have many
contrasting opinions about the popular direct voting
proposal, which would abolish the Electoral College
altogether. In light of the year 2000 election, which
placed in the White House a candidate who had half a
million fewer popular votes than his opponent, should
the electoral college be abolished?

The electoral college system has its origins in
the Constitutional Convention that took place in
Philadelphia in 1787. The Framers themselves were
ambivalent when it came to how the President should
be elected, which made the process of determining how
to choose the President a complicated one. In fact,
Pennsylvania delegate James Wilson declared that the
presidential selection issue was " 'the most difficult
of all [. . .]' " of those discussed, one that " 'has
greatly divided the house, and will also divide
people out of doors' " (qtd. in Sayre and Parris 23).
Proposals were made for election by Congress,
election by the people, and election by state
governments (Sayre and Parris 23). However, as the

issue remained unsolved and the end of the Convention
was nearing, the Brearly Committee on Unfinished Parts
suggested the electoral college system.

The following very brief summary of this system
was adapted from Shlomo Slonim's "Electoral College":
Instead of a direct popular election, this system
provided for indirect election of the President
through a college of electors, in which each state
receives a number of electoral votes based on its
total number of Senators and Representatives. On the
first Tuesday in November of election years, the
general population technically casts ballots for the
electors that represent their choice for President
and Vice President. The electors themselves are
individuals "pledged to support a particular
candidate's election in the electoral college" (543).
Popular vote totals are used to determine which party
slate will become that state's electors. On the
Monday following the second Wednesday in December,
the electors meet in their respective state capitals
and cast their ballots for President and Vice
President. A majority of the 538 electoral votes is
needed in order to be selected or the matter is put
up to vote in the House of Representatives. Under
this system, "Popular will is expressed state by
state, rather than by a national referendum" (Slonin
543-544). An added feature of the electoral college
system is the winner-takes-all unit rule system.
Although the Constitution leaves the choice of how
the states' electoral votes are cast up to the states

themselves, every state except Maine and Nebraska has chosen over time to award all of a state's electoral votes to the winner of the popular vote (Cronin xii).

Michael Glennon proposes in his comprehensive guide to the electoral college that the debate by the Framers of the Constitution about presidential selection was rooted in a disagreement on two essential issues: first, the extent and view of democracy to be used in determining the winner, and second, the degree of federalism to be considered (6). These two issues continue to lie at the center of the debate. On one hand are those who desire the abolishment of the electoral college; in their view, direct democracy, where the will of the people is directly translated into policy, is the key principal. On the other hand, those who support the Electoral College as it is believe that federalism is of ultimate importance and that democracy is still supported through the electoral college, but in a different way.

Many people vehemently argue in support of the electoral college system. As explained in William C. Kimberling's The Electoral College, the main arguments center on two requirements that are placed on candidates in order to be chosen President. First, winning a majority in the electoral college means that the candidate has *"sufficient* popular vote to [. . .] govern," even if his/her support is not the majority of the voting population. Secondly, the votes the winner has secured must be "sufficiently

Anderson 4

distributed across the country" (7). According to
Kimberling, these two requirements together ensure
that whoever is chosen will be able to handle
governing the nation (7).

A second strong argument used in support of the
Electoral College is that it promotes the important
Constitutional concept of federalism. Judith A. Best,
distinguished professor of political science at State
University of New York at Cortland, refers to
federalism as one of the two essential principles of
the "constitutional solar system [. . .] around which
everything else [. . .] rotates" (65). She believes
that this federal principal, based on state-by-state
victories and therefore, electoral votes, provides
for a better overall assessment of the strengths and
weaknesses of the competing candidates than a direct
popular vote would because it ensures that the
winning candidate has "broad, cross-national support"
(67). This requirement of broad support promotes the
pulling together of "coalitions of states and
regions," rather than the candidate's having support
just from specific regions of the country
(Kimberling 12).

In response to those who claim that the electoral
college is undemocratic, Best points out that
"politics and mathematics are two very different
disciplines" (18). Those who support abolishing the
Electoral College in favor of direct election claim
that numbers themselves determine who the President
should be. However, Best believes that in a political

decision as important as electing a President, the
"will of the people" is not necessarily the same as
the "will of the majority" (19). She points out that
one of the basic principals of the Constitution is
majority rule with minority consent; in her view, the
Electoral College better provides for the minority.

However, over time many have expressed opposition
to the indirect and complex electoral college system.
Their main criticism is the possibility of a
"minority President," that is, one elected without
the majority of the popular vote but with a majority
of the electoral votes. Other criticisms leveled
against the electoral college system include the "so-
called faithless electors," the winner-takes-all unit
rule, and the possibility of decreased voter turnout
(Kimberling 9). In addition, critics say that the
electoral college does not accurately reflect the
national popular will and that rural states are over
represented in the current system because each state
receives two electoral votes regardless of size plus
those attributed to population (Kimberling 9).

In The Electoral College Primer 2000, Lawrence D.
Longley and Neal R. Peirce explain their opposition
to the electoral college system. They assert that in
an "advanced democratic nation, where [. . .] popular
choice is the most deeply ingrained of government
principles," a voting system where popular votes
don't necessarily mean electoral votes is
"irrational" (132). In addition, they point out that
even if a direct popular vote were to choose a

Anderson 6

candidate who proved less than ideal in the long run,

the candidate would still be the choice of the people

(132). Longley and Peirce also explain the "faithless

elector" issue. The Constitution nowhere requires the

chosen electors to vote for the winner of the popular

vote. However, in the history of the Electoral

College, only nine votes of the over 20,000 cast have

been known to go " 'against instructions' " (113).

    Critics of the electoral college system see the

2000 election as a prime example of the minority

President criticism. The election of governor George

Bush by the electoral college despite Vice President

Al Gore's winning the popular vote (50,996,582 to

Bush's 50,456,062) is seen by many as a problem.

Because of the complicated nature of the electoral

college system and what many see as its drawbacks,

several reform proposals have been brought to

Congress. These proposals generally fall into four

categories: the district system, the proportional

system, the automatic plan, and the direct popular

election. Wisconsin's Role in Electing the President

describes the four main Electoral College

alternatives. The district system would eliminate the

unit rule and provide that two of each state's

electoral votes would be determined by popular vote,

while the rest would be allocated on a district-by-

district basis. The proportional system would divide

the state's electoral votes in "direct proportion to

the popular vote" of the state. The automatic plan

would simply eliminate the role of the actual elector

Anderson 7

and provide that the electoral votes would automatically be signed to the winner of the popular election. Finally, direct popular election would abolish the Electoral College altogether, instead requiring a "nationwide popular vote," with the winner receiving at least 40% of the votes (Watchke 12).

The direct voting alternative is by far the most popular proposal alternative. However, this alternative has its own set of pros and cons which must be evaluated before making a judgment about which presidential election system should be in place.

Proponents of a direct voting system have several arguments as to why a direct popular vote would be preferable to the electoral college system. They argue that it provide an increased and more direct democracy for the people, an increased authority for the President, and a simpler, one-person-one-vote system that would eliminate the intermediate electoral college in the Presidential selection procedure. In addition, they feel that the electoral college system is out of date because America is faced with a different set of circumstances and challenges than when it was created.

Those in favor of direct election believe this system is the only way to achieve a true democracy. Former First Lady Hillary Clinton has expressed her belief that abolition of the Electoral college is

Anderson 8

important in a democracy; in fact, she said that she
would "be willing to co-sponsor a measure to abolish
the electoral college" (Geraghty). Another argument
is that a popular vote would give more authority to
the President because the vote totals would be a
direct communication of the will of the people,
rather than an indirect translation that takes
electoral votes into account (Sayre and Parris 69).
Thirdly, in the words of Yale Law School professor
Akhil Amar, the Electoral College is a "brilliant
18th-century device that cleverly solved [. . .]
18th-century problems." However, he sees that " '[a]s
we approach the 21st century, we confront a different
cluster of problems, and our constitutional machinery
[. . .] does not look so brilliant' " (qtd. in Sung).
Finally, those in defense of direct election often
cite public opinion surveys that reflect popular
support for abolishment of the Electoral College. One
such survey, conducted by the trusted Gallup
Organization and released on November 16, 2000,
revealed that 61% of Americans would like to see
direct popular vote in place of the electoral college
system ("Americans Have Long Questioned").

Direct voting also seems to have its drawbacks,
however. Its opponents claim that direct election
would lead to manipulation in campaigns, jeopardize
the two-party system with a multitude of candidates,
cause even more runoffs and recounts, and sacrifice
the federalist system currently in place.

Anderson 9

Curtis Gans, director of the Committee for the Study of the American Electorate, suggests that a direct popular vote system would greatly change the way campaigns are run. With such a system, where the goal is to win over the masses rather than focus on groups of states all around the nation, he believes even more of the election funds would go toward mass television advertising, leading to the " 'handing [of the] American presidential campaign to whatever media adviser could outslick the other' " (qtd. in Sung). This, in turn, would lead to increased " 'opponent bashing,' " a factor that already has been leading citizens to " 'tune out politics' " (qtd. in Sung).

According to Wallace Sayre and Judith Parris, direct elections, especially those including a popular vote runoff provision, would tend to "encourage a multitude of minor party candidacies" because, depending on the proposal, these minor party candidates would not need to win entire states in order to receive part of the vote (73). They believe, therefore, that many candidates would tend to run as "spoilers," with the goal of forcing a runoff. In order to protect the two-party system, which is an important basis of American government, they insist that the electoral college system must stay in place.

Judith Best reflects on the increase in recounts and runoffs that she feels would follow from a direct voting system: "If the advocates of direct nonfederal election stuck with a majority requirement for victory, nearly every general election would be

Anderson 10

turned into a national primary followed by a runoff election" (57). She believes that with the lifting of the state division, focusing only on the national vote, "a recount of every ballot box in the country" could be necessary, because recounts and challenges in one state would no longer be limited in scope, but could demand a national result questioning (57).

Thomas Cronin brings up an important point that makes one question whether the current system should be abolished. He argues that while there are some imperfections in the electoral college system, no one can be sure of the effects of abandoning it in place of a direct vote (viii). President John F. Kennedy himself opposed abolishment, explaining that " '[i]f it is proposed to change the balance of power of one of the elements of the [governmental] solar system, it is necessary to consider the others' " (qtd. in Glennon 76). Therefore, because changes would undoubtedly have a holistic effect on the intricate political system, it is necessary to carefully weigh this decision.

After weighing arguments for both the current electoral college system and the direct voting alternative, I tend to agree with Cronin. Although the Electoral College may be complex and does have its imperfections, there is no way of knowing just what other effects and problems may result from its abolishment. Even in light of the 2000 presidential election, in which President George W. Bush did not win the majority of the popular vote, I see the

Anderson 11

electoral college system as a way to moderate the
will of the people in general with the good of the
government. I also very much support the argument
that the electoral college ensures that the candidate
who is victorious has proven that he or she has
secured enough voter support to warrant the
presidential office. It is very important that the
winner has both a sufficient popular vote and a
sufficient distribution of votes across the country, a
fact that he or she demonstrates by securing enough
states' electoral votes to win the election.

However, the current electoral college system
could better represent the population in general.
Adopting the relatively small change that Maine and
Nebraska have made to their system, which selects two
electoral votes a popular vote and determines the
remainder of the electoral votes by Congressional
district, would help to improve the system. This
would not be such an extreme change as abolishing the
Electoral College altogether, yet it would represent
the popular vote more closely because of the district
divisions. Thus, the benefits of the current Electoral
College would almost entirely remain in place, while
those who want the election to more closely reflect
the popular will would also be appeased.

The 2000 presidential election was an anomalous
one, and the extremely close margins of support, both
in the popular vote and the Electoral College count,
have caused an increase in discussion about the
electoral college system. One even sees divisions

Anderson 12

among party lines regarding support for or opposition against this system. However, one must note that the conflict in the 2000 election was not completely rooted in the Electoral College itself. Many believe that the recounts and challenges would still have taken place even with a system of direct election.

In conclusion, Michael Glennon, author of <u>When No Majority Rules</u>, reflects on the essential dilemma in electing America's President: "Just as Winston Churchill concluded about democracy, the electoral college is probably the worst possible method of choosing the President—except for all the others" (3). Indeed, there is no perfect solution that will satisfy both those desiring voting and those who support the Electoral College. However, weighing both the pros and cons in the arguments over the current system, I believe that the Electoral College should be kept in place, yet modified slightly to better represent the people. Such a compromise would reflect what was at the very heart of the Constitution when it was established over two centuries ago and what will carry this country and its citizens through the coming centuries.

Anderson 13

Works Cited

"Americans Have Long Questioned Electoral
College." <u>Gallup Poll Releases</u>. 16 Nov 2000.
29 Nov. 2000 <http://www.gallup.com/poll/
releases/pr001116.asp>.

Best, Judith A. <u>The Choice of the People?:
Debating the Electoral College</u>. Lanham, MD:
Rowman & Littlefield, 1996.

Cronin, Thomas E. "The Electoral College
Controversy." Foreword. Best vii-xxv.

Geraghty, Jim. "Do Elections Need New Rules?"
<u>Policy.com News and Events: Daily Briefing</u>.
22 Nov. 2000. 29 Nov. 2000
<http://www.policy.
com/news/dbrief/dbriefarc834.asp>.

Glennon, Michael J. <u>When No Majority Rules: The
Electoral College and Presidential
Succession</u>. Washington, D.C.: Congressional
Quarterly, 1992.

Kimberling, William C. <u>The Electoral College</u>.
Washington, D.C.: National Clearinghouse on
Election Administration, Federal Election
Commission, May 1992.

Longley, Lawrence D., and Neal R. Peirce. <u>The
Electoral College Primer 2000</u>. New Haven,
CT: Yale UP, 1999.

Power, Max S. "Logic and Legitimacy: On
Understanding the Electoral College
Controversy." Ed. Donald R. Matthews.
<u>Perspectives on Presidential Selection</u>.
Washington, D.C.: Brookings, 1973. 204-237.

Anderson 14

Sayre, Wallace S., and Judith H. Parris. <u>Voting</u>
<u>for President: The Electoral College and the</u>
<u>American Political System</u>. Washington, D.C.:
Brookings, 1972.

Slonim, Shlomo. "Electoral College." <u>Encyclopedia</u>
<u>of the American Presidency</u>. Eds. Leonard W.
Levy and Louis Fisher. New York: Simon &
Schuster, 1994. 542-547.

Sung, Ellen. "Time to Reform the Electoral
College?" <u>Policy.com News and Events: Daily</u>
<u>Briefing</u>. 31 July 2000. 21 Nov. 2000
<http://www.policy.com/news/dbrief/
dbriefarc770.asp>.

Vile, John R. "Electoral College Reform."
<u>Encyclopedia of Constitutional Amendments,</u>
<u>Proposed Amendments, and Amending Issues,</u>
<u>1789-1995</u>. Santa Barbara, CA: ABC-CLIO,
1996. 109-112.

Watchke, Gary. <u>Wisconsin's Role in Electing the</u>
<u>President</u>. Madison, WI: Wisconsin
Legislative Reference Bureau, Mar. 2000.

CHAPTER 7

WRITING A RESEARCH PAPER USING APA STYLE

The documentation style of the American Psychological Association (APA), also referred to as the *author–date system,* is used widely in the behavioral and social sciences. It differs from that of the Modern Language Association (MLA), used primarily in the humanities, in some significant ways. APA style cites sources in parenthetical notes in the sentences to which they refer, as does MLA style, but the contents of the notes differ. In the APA system, the year of publication is given in the parenthetical note, and page numbers are given only for quotations, not for paraphrases. Finally, sources are listed at the end of the paper on a page called *References* rather than *Works Cited,* and formatting for that page is quite different from formatting in MLA style.

This chapter gives general guidelines for both parenthetical citations and composing a references page using APA style. The guidelines are accompanied by sample pages from a student research paper using APA documentation style. See also Joan North's essay "Strangers in a Strange Land: Women in Higher Education Administration," chapter 15, for an example of a lengthy paper using APA formatting. For a detailed guide to preparing a research report in the social sciences using APA format, see Mark Plonsky's *Psychology with Style: A Guide to Writing Research Reports Using APA Style* at the end of this chapter. Professor Plonsky's directions for handling citations in the text and assembling the references page restate the general guidelines outlined here but provide additional examples. The rest of his guidelines address such matters as preparing an abstract, writing an introduction, describing methods, reporting research results, and discussing those results.

PARENTHETICAL CITATIONS USING APA STYLE

- For a quotation, include the author's last name, a comma, the year the work was published, another comma, and the page number, preceded by the abbreviation *p.* or *pp.:*

    Many experts agree that "it is much easier and more comfortable to teach as one learned" (Chall, 1989, p. 21).

- If the source has two authors, name them both, and separate their names with an ampersand (&):

  President Truman and his advisors were aware that the use of the bomb was no longer required to prevent an invasion of Japan by the Soviets (Alperovitz & Messer, 1991, 1992).

- Omit from the parenthetical citation any information given in the text:

  Samuel E. Wood and Ellen R. Green Wood (1993a) note that sociobiologists believe that social and nurturing experiences can "intensify, diminish, or modify" personality traits (p. 272).

- If the author's name is given in the text, follow it with the year of publication in parentheses:

  Nancy Paulu (1988) believes that children who are taught phonics get off to a better start than those who are not taught phonics.

- For works with three to five authors, name all of the authors the first time you refer to the work, but give only the last name of the first author followed by "et al." in subsequent citations. For a work with six or more authors, give only the first author's last name, followed by "et al." for all citations, including the first.

- If the author's name is repeated in the same paragraph, it is not necessary to repeat the year. However, if the author is cited in another paragraph, give the year of the work again.

- For summaries and paraphrases, give author and year but not the page number where the information appears:

  Minnesota scientists have concluded that this data shows that genes are more influential than nurture on most personality traits (Bazell, 1987).

- If the source names no author, cite a short form of the title:

  The twins were both born with musical abilities, but their unique experiences determined whether they acted on this ability ("How Genes Shape Personality," 1987).

  Note: The first letter of each word in the short title is capitalized, but in the references list, only the first letter of the first word is capitalized.

- If you use two or more sources by the same author and they were published in the same year, add lowercase letters to refer to their order on the references page:

  Wood and Wood (1993a) observe that . . .
  Other authorities (Wood & Wood, 1993b) agree, pointing out that . . .

- If one of your sources quotes or refers to another, and you want to use the second source in your paper, use the words *cited in*, followed by the source you read and the year the source was published. If you quote directly, give the page number of the source you read on which the quotation appeared:

  Gerald McClearn, a psychologist and twin researcher at Pennsylvania State University, explained personality development realistically when he said: " 'A gene can produce a nudge in one direction or another, but it does not directly control behavior. It doesn't take away a person's free will' " (cited in "How Genes Shape Personality," 1987, p. 62).

SAMPLE PAGES FROM A STUDENT RESEARCH PAPER USING APA STYLE

Here is a shortened version of Cory L. Vandertie's research paper entitled "The Phonics Controversy," illustrating in-text citations using APA style. Cory's outline appeared in chapter 4's discussion of outlines.

In papers written in APA style, provide a shortened version of the title, known as a running head, in the upper right-hand corner of the page along with the page number. If your instructor requires a separate title page, the title page is numbered 1.

Phonics 1

Cory L. Vandertie

Professor Kathy Mitchell

English 102

19 April 2000

The Phonics Controversy

The introductory paragraphs provide background for the research topic.

        In recent years, school officials, teachers, and parents have been wrestling with the issue of how best to teach reading, with the controversy often centering on the conflict over the effectiveness of phonics in such instruction. Rudolph Flesch, in his best-selling 1955 book *Why Johnny Can't Read*, was one of the first educators to advocate the use of phonics in reading classes. His book not only brought national attention to the reading problems of America's children but also endorsed the use of phonics to overcome those problems (cited in Groff,

Cory read about the Flesch book in Groff's book.

Phonics 2

1989). Neither the problem of children's inability to read effectively nor the effectiveness of phonics instruction has been satisfactorily addressed in the 40 years since Flesch's book, however. According to

Write the author's full name the first time it is mentioned.

Regna Lee Wood (1992), literacy rates continue to decline. In "That's Right—They're Wrong: Decline in Reading Ability Due to Abandonment of Phonics," Wood

Although only the first letter of the first word in the title of a work is capitalized in the references list, in your paper you must capitalize as you would other titles.

includes these startling results of studies by the National Assessment of Educational Progress (NAEP): "Twenty years of NAEP reading tests show that most 7th-graders today can't read 6th-grade lessons; most 8th-graders can't read 7th-grade lessons; and most 11th-graders can't read 9th-grade lessons written with 6th-grade vocabularies" (p. 52). Statistics such as these have created tension among educators as they debate how to improve reading skills.

Give the page number on which a direct quotation appears in the source.

The declining literacy rate is an alarming indicator that something must be done differently in our schools. Wood (1992) points out that in 1930, only 3 million Americans could not read, but in 1990,

This is a new paragraph, so the date of Wood's publication needs to be mentioned again.

30 to 35 million U.S. citizens could not read and were considered to be truly illiterate. She also reports that two out of every three 17-year-olds

This is a paraphrase, so no page number need be given.

The pronoun she clearly indicates that Cory is referring to Wood, mentioned in the previous sentence.

Phonics 3

could not read well enough to do high school work in any subject. Educators and parents who are concerned about this dramatic increase in the illiteracy rate and the inability of the majority of students to read at their own grade levels cannot refuse to explore all possible explanations for the failure of our schools to teach reading adequately. One avenue for exploration that may prove fruitful is the phonics controversy. Parents, teachers, and reading experts familiar with phonics all differ sharply in their views, compounding the dilemma of whether phonics instruction should be included in American schools. What role *does* phonics education play in the teaching of reading?

More than 450 years ago, phonics instruction was introduced to help young readers learn more about the relationship between letters and sound (Groff, 1989). Some researchers think that phonics has been used to teach reading since the time of ancient Greeks. Chall (1989) describes the method "as a tool for helping beginners identify words accurately so that they can read texts with comprehension earlier and more efficiently" (p. 4). Groff agrees that phonics instruction can be very useful for the development of children's word recognition skills. The problem is how to convince parents and teachers of the benefits of phonics. Wood (1992) believes that the horrible failure of our schools to teach children to read skillfully began

Cory asks a question as his thesis, reflecting the controversy over teaching phonics. He will answer the question in the course of the paper.

The year of Groff's publication has already been mentioned in this paragraph, so it is not repeated here.

Phonics 4

years ago. She writes that "[the failure of schools

to teach reading] began in 1929 and 1930 when

hundreds of primary teachers, guided by college

reading professors, stopped teaching beginners to

read by matching sounds with letters that spell

sounds" (p. 52).

The brackets indicate that Cory has added his own words to the direct quotation.

Phonics is not the entire answer to the

question of how best to teach children to read,

however. Most reading experts agree that "the most

the application of phonics can do is help children

produce the approximate pronunciation of words"

(Groff, 1989, p. 6). Roberts (1989), writing for

Parents magazine, reports that phonics may not help

all children learn to pronounce words. He explains

that anyone who has a visual or auditory handicap

will find it harder to read using phonics. For

instance, Roberts points out that a child who has

suffered from an ear infection that caused temporary

hearing loss at an early age may find it difficult to

learn to read by using phonics because of missing

out on experiencing sound discrimination.

For a smooth transition and to avoid too many parenthetical interruptions, mention author and source in text whenever you can.

* * * * *

In conclusion, many experts believe that we

have the ability and the knowledge to educate our

schoolchildren more effectively by using phonics.

But while both traditional and experimental evidence

supports the use of phonics, the debate continues.

Educators who are not familiar with phonics

instruction must be enlightened, perhaps with

in-service workshops from experts on phonics

Phonics 5

instruction. Parents, too, may need to be convinced.
Reading experts must be willing to work together to
resolve some of the issues in the phonics debate,
perhaps by putting together a combination of approaches
to the teaching of reading that includes phonics. The
bottom line is that we all must work to find a solution
to the appalling rate of adult illiteracy in this
country and the unsettling inability of students to
read at their own grade levels. We must find solutions
to these problems, or we risk jeopardizing not only our
children's futures but our own.

APA STYLE REFERENCES LIST

- Bibliographic entries for all works cited in a paper are listed in alphabetical order on a page entitled *References.*
- The first line of each entry in the references list is indented five spaces, and the second and subsequent lines are flush with the left margin.
- Give the last names and only the initials of the first and middle names of authors.
- The year of publication, in parentheses, follows the author's name.
- For a book, capitalize only proper nouns and the first word of the title and subtitle; underline the title.
- If a book is edited, place the abbreviation *Ed.* or *Eds.* in parentheses after the name(s) of the editor(s).
- If a citation names two or more authors, each name is reversed and an ampersand (&), not the word *and,* is placed before the last name.
- For an article, book chapter title, or title of an essay in a collection, capitalize as for a book title and do not use quotation marks or underlining.
- Capitalize the first letters of all important words in the name of the periodical and underline it.
- Use the abbreviations *p.* and *pp.* for inclusive page numbers of articles in magazines and journals, except when volume and issue number is given. If volume number is given, place it after name of the periodical and underline it. If an issue number is also given, place it in parentheses after the volume number:

  Hamby, A. L. (1991, Spring). An American Democrat: A reevaluation of the personality of Harry S. Truman. Political Science Quarterly, 106, 33–55.

- If two or more works by the same author appear on the references list, put them in chronological order. Repeat the author's name each time, followed by the date in parentheses.
- If you cite two works of one author published in the same year, alphabetize them by title, and give each entry a lowercase letter: (1996a), (1996b).

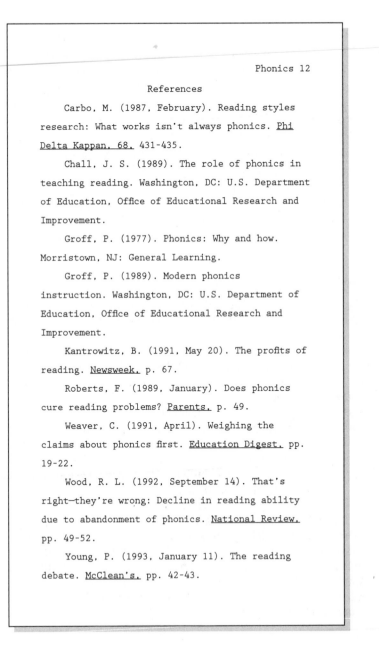

Phonics 12

References

Carbo, M. (1987, February). Reading styles research: What works isn't always phonics. <u>Phi Delta Kappan, 68,</u> 431-435.

Chall, J. S. (1989). The role of phonics in teaching reading. Washington, DC: U.S. Department of Education, Office of Educational Research and Improvement.

Groff, P. (1977). Phonics: Why and how. Morristown, NJ: General Learning.

Groff, P. (1989). Modern phonics instruction. Washington, DC: U.S. Department of Education, Office of Educational Research and Improvement.

Kantrowitz, B. (1991, May 20). The profits of reading. <u>Newsweek,</u> p. 67.

Roberts, F. (1989, January). Does phonics cure reading problems? <u>Parents,</u> p. 49.

Weaver, C. (1991, April). Weighing the claims about phonics first. <u>Education Digest,</u> pp. 19-22.

Wood, R. L. (1992, September 14). That's right—they're wrong: Decline in reading ability due to abandonment of phonics. <u>National Review,</u> pp. 49-52.

Young, P. (1993, January 11). The reading debate. <u>McClean's,</u> pp. 42-43.

PSYCHOLOGY WITH STYLE
A GUIDE TO WRITING RESEARCH REPORTS
USING APA STYLE

Mark Plonsky

Mark Plonsky is a professor of psychology at the University of Wisconsin at Stevens Point. He has been teaching Experimental Psychology, where APA formatting is typically required, for fifteen years, and he has published a dozen articles in peer-reviewed scientific journals. Plonsky developed these guidelines for preparing research reports for his courses and has made them available on the Internet for both students and instructors. His guide follows closely the formatting recommendations of the Publication Manual of the American Psychological Association, *5th ed., and is written specifically for undergraduate students. After the instructions for citations and quotations, he presents his material in outline form to make it easier for students to locate the information they need. Plonsky welcomes comments or suggestions at <mplonsky@uwsp.edu>.*

Citations in the Text

1. If you use someone's words or ideas, you must give him or her credit with a citation. This is particularly important, because the penalties for plagiarism are severe.
2. There are numerous ways to formally cite a reference in the text. Examples include **Some fact (last name, year); Last name (year) noted that . . . ; or In (year), last name reported that . . . .** For more ideas, pay close attention to the articles you read.
3. The first time the reference is cited in the text, spell out all of the authors' last names. For example, **Miller, Rosellini, and Seligman (1975) suggested that. . . .** With articles that have three or more authors use the Latin abbreviation for "and others" (et al.) when the reference is cited a second (or third) time. For example, **Miller et al. (1975) suggested that . . .** or **. . . some fact (Miller et al., 1975).**
4. If the citation is in parenthesis and you need to use the word *and,* use the ampersand (&) instead of writing out the word. For example, **Some (e.g., Estes & Skinner, 1940) have suggested that . . . ,** as compared to Estes and Skinner (1940) have suggested. . . Note also that the opposite applies as well, that is, if the citation is not in parentheses, you must use the word *and.*
5. Multiple citations in parentheses are placed alphabetically and are separated by a semicolon and a space. For example, **Some fact (Carlson, 1972; Moon, 1968; Partin, 1980).**

6. If you cite something secondhand, you must make it clear, for example, **Some fact (Smith, as cited in Jones, Year).** Note that in this example, only the Jones reference would be placed in the reference section.

Quotations

1. You must give page numbers for direct quotations. For example, **Smith (1978) noted that "the world is round" (p. 1).**
2. Use direct quotations sparingly. Three or four quotations in a ten-page paper is about the upper limit.
3. Display a quotation of more than forty words as a freestanding block of text indented five spaces from the left margin. Omit the quotation marks and include the page number in parenthesis after the last period. Also, if the long quotation is more than one paragraph, indent the first line of the second and any subsequent paragraphs five spaces.

Research Reports
The order of the sections of the manuscript are as follows:

A. Title Page

1. See Appendix 1 of this chapter for an example of a title page.
2. The manuscript page header is the first thing that appears on the title page. It consists of the first two or three words of the title and is followed by the page number. It is used by the editors and reviewers to identify the pages of the manuscript. Place it in the upper right-hand corner of all pages of the manuscript (except for any figures). Thus, the manuscript page header should appear as the first line of the title page, right justified with the number "1" double-spaced below it or five spaces to the right of it. If you are using a word processor, you can have it put this manuscript page header on all pages automatically.
3. The running head comes next and is no more than fifty characters (including punctuation and spaces). It typically consists of a couple of keywords from the title. Type this running head flush left and in all capital letters. For example, Running head: ABORTION ATTITUDES IN COLLEGE STUDENTS (note that the *R* in *running* is capitalized, but the *h* in *head* is not).
4. The title should summarize the main idea of the study in ten to twelve words. A good recipe to work with when reporting the results of an experiment is **(Dependent Variable) as a Function of (Independent Variable) or The Effects of (Independent Variable) on (Dependent Variable).** With other types of research you should try to include the variables of interest in the title (and be careful not to imply causality). Also, it is a good idea to include the species if you are working with animals or some details about the type of population if you are working with humans.
5. When typing the title, center it on the page and capitalize only the first letter of important words. On the next double-spaced line is the author's name followed by the institutional affiliation.

6. Below that, type whatever additional information your instructor requires. For the purposes of my course, I ask students to include something like **In partial fulfillment of the requirements for PSY389, Instructor's Name, and Date.**

B. Abstract

1. The abstract page is page 2.
2. Center the word *Abstract* on this page, then begin typing on the very next line (i.e., do not insert any blank lines here).
3. Type this section as a single (double-spaced) paragraph in block format (i.e., do not use indentation).
4. The purpose of this section is to provide a brief (100 to 120 words), comprehensive summary of the study. The abstract is very important because it is all that many people will read.
5. The abstract should include a brief description of the problem being investigated, the methods used, the results, and their implications.
6. It is a good idea to write this section last (after all of the other sections are written). Another hint is to take the lead sentence or two from the introduction, method, results, and discussion sections and integrate them to form the abstract.
7. Avoid citing references in the abstract.

C. Introduction

1. The introduction begins on page 3.
2. Start this page by retyping the title (centered), then begin typing the section using normal (five-space indented) paragraphs. **Do not type the word *Introduction.***
3. The main purpose of this section is to tell the reader why you performed the study. You have to inform the reader of the research question, indicate why it is important, and explain how it is unique when compared to previous studies.
4. Start your introduction with broad statements and then get more and more specific. For example, you might begin by defining any relevant terms. Then go on to review the relevant literature. Avoid an exhaustive and historical review. Then go on to make clear the connection between previous research and the present work.
5. You might include any hypotheses and the rationale for them.
6. The final paragraph usually contains a statement that clearly and explicitly states why the study was performed, such as **The purpose of this study was to . . .** or **The present study was designed to investigate the . . . .** Be especially careful not to use a sentence of this type earlier in your introduction.
7. Thus, this section should contain an absolute minimum of four paragraphs: the general introduction, the literature review, the statement of connection of the present study to the literature, and the explicit statement of purpose.

D. Methods

1. Do not purposely start a new page for this section. Simply center the word *Method* and continue typing (without inserting any blank lines).
2. The purpose of this section is to describe in detail how you performed the study. Someone should be able to replicate your study based on the information you provide in this section.
3. Make it sound professional; that is, do not make it sound like a class project. Assume you are writing for submission to a scientific journal.
4. Avoid unnecessary details like "the data were displayed on the computer screen and recorded on the data sheet(s)." These are empty words that add nothing to your report.
5. For an experiment, this section is typically divided into four subsections: **subjects, apparatus, design,** and **procedure.** The order of design followed by procedure is arbitrary. In other words, you could have the procedure come before the design. Sometimes researchers combine the design and procedure sections. Ask your instructor what he or she prefers.
6. For a survey study (i.e., one in which the participants are simply asked a set of questions), the design section is not necessary (and the survey itself may be included as an appendix).

Subjects/Participants

7. This section is labeled as subjects or participants depending on whether animals or humans are used in the study. If animals are used, use the term *subjects.* If humans are used, use the term *participants.*
8. Do not purposely start a new page for this section. Type the appropriate title for this subsection flush with the left margin and underline it. On the next line, begin typing normal paragraphs.
9. Indicate who participated in the study, how many, and how were they selected.
10. Include any details that are relevant to the study (e.g., gender, age, ethnicity, strain, weight).
11. If the subjects were human, what type of reward or motivation was used to encourage them to participate?

Apparatus

12. Do not purposely start a new page for this section. Type the word *Apparatus* flush with the left margin and underline it. On the next line, begin typing normal paragraphs.
13. Describe what materials were used and how they functioned in the study.
14. If you used a piece of equipment, you must give the model number, company, and state where the company resides (as a two-letter abbreviation).
15. You must give the dimensions (and perhaps other descriptive details) of any important items used in the study.
16. Standard equipment such as furniture, stopwatches, and pencils and paper can usually be mentioned without providing a lot of details. In fact, you may often simply mention these items in passing as part of the procedure.

17. Be careful **not** to describe procedures in this section. You should make clear what purpose the apparatus served, but do not give a lot of details on the use of the apparatus at this point. One hint in this regard is to avoid using action verbs in this section.

Design

18. Do not purposely start a new page for this section. Type the word *Design* flush with the left margin and underline it. On the next line, begin typing normal paragraphs.
19. Describe the design and clearly spell out the independent and dependent variables. Indicate what the levels of the independent variables were, and whether the factor(s) were repeated, matched, or independent.
20. Describe how the subjects were assigned to groups.
21. Describe any control procedures used.

Procedure

22. Do not purposely start a new page for this section. Type the word *Procedure* flush with the left margin and underline it. On the next line, begin typing normal paragraphs.
23. Carefully summarize each step in the execution of the study.
24. Indicate what a typical test, trial, or session involved.
25. Describe any phases that the study had or any instructions that the subjects received.
26. When referring to groups, try to use descriptive labels. For example, instead of saying **Group 1** or **the experimental group,** you might say **the drugged group.** Another technique in this regard is to use abbreviations that emphasize meaning. For example, "There were three groups, including, the control group, which received 0 mg/kg of morphine (M0), a low-dose group receiving 1 mg/kg of morphine (M1), and a high-dose group receiving 4 mg/kg of morphine (M4)."

E. Results

1. Do not purposely start a new page for this section. Simply center the word *Results* and continue typing on the very next double-spaced line (i.e., do not insert any extra blank lines here).
2. Look carefully at the results. That is, take a good hard look at all those numbers you collect. Think of different ways to summarize them, as well as to make sense of them. This section will be easier to write if you make any tables and/or figures you intend to use first.
3. Briefly state the main findings in words. That is, first give a general description, then go into details.
4. When presenting the results of statistical tests, give descriptive statistics before the corresponding inferential statistics. In other words, give means and/or percentages (perhaps referring to a table or figure) before talking about the results of any statistical tests you performed.

5. When presenting means, it is reasonable to use one additional digit of accuracy than what is contained in the raw data. In other words, if the raw data consisted of whole numbers, then the means should contain one decimal place.
6. When presenting nominal or ordinal data, give the percentages rather than frequencies (because percentages are independent of the sample size).
7. The general format for presenting an inferential statistic is: *Statistic* (df) = value, *probability* = value. Note that if the statistics are generated with a computer, you can give the exact p values. Also, if the computer output says the probability is .0000, then report it as .001.
8. When actually presenting the results, try to emphasize the meaning of the statistics. That is, clearly describe what it is you are testing and what significance means for the variables involved. Here are examples of the correct way to present the results of several common statistical tests:

> An examination of the number of hours of television viewing and the frequency of aggressive acts for each of the 20 children revealed a direct correlation between television viewing and instances of aggressive behavior. An analysis using Pearson's correlation coefficient supported this observation, r (59) = .63, $p < 0.05$.

> The control group remembered a mean of 14 words on the memory test, whereas the drugged group had a mean of 12. This difference was tested using an independent group's t test, and was shown to be nonsignificant, t (18) = 1.23, $p > 0.10$. Thus, the data fail to support the notion of a drug effect on memory.

> The mean scores for the short, medium, and long retention intervals were 5.9, 10.3, and 14.2, respectively. A one-way analysis of variance revealed a significant effect of retention interval, F (2, 34) = 123.07, $p < .001$.

> Where 60% of the males agreed that their map-reading skills were strong, only 35% of the females did. A 2 × 2 chi-square analysis revealed that this was a significant difference, x^2 (1, N = 119) = 10.51, $p < .025$, suggesting that there was a relationship of gender to confidence in map-reading skills.

9. Do not discuss the implications of the results in this section.
10. Do not talk about the meaning of the alpha level or the null hypothesis, and what chance factors have to do with it. Because you are writing for the scientific community, you can assume the reader will have a working knowledge of statistics.
11. If you are presenting a lot of material here, you may wish to employ subheadings (as is done in the methods section). These subheadings should have meaning and relevance to the data and should help to organize your presentation of it. In other words, they should **not** be organized by the type of analysis employed. Because this is not expected by the reader, it is a good

idea to precede the subheadings with a paragraph informing the reader of the logical organization of this section.

12. In cases where the reader would expect something to be significant, and it is not, you should address the issue.

13. Do not provide raw data unless, for some reason, you require a single-subject approach.

14. Be careful with the word *prove*. Because statistical tests are based on probability and can be in error, they do not really prove anything.

15. You can only use wording that implies causality if you actually manipulated the independent variable (i.e., performed an experiment). For example, suppose you manipulated whether subjects received a drug (while employing appropriate control procedures, etc.) and found a significant difference in memory performance (with the drug users performing more poorly than nonusers). In this case, you would be able to conclude that the drug **caused** the difference in memory ability; it impaired it. As another example, suppose that you compared drug use (as determined from the results of a survey) with memory ability and found a correlation (greater use went along with poorer memory performance). Because correlation doesn't say much about causality, we could only conclude that there is a **relationship** between drug use and memory ability.

F. Discussion

1. Do not purposely start a new page for this section. Simply center the word *Discussion* and continue typing.

2. The purpose of this section is to evaluate and interpret the results, especially with respect to the original research question.

3. Start off with a brief, nontechnical summary of the results. In other words, tell the reader about the main findings without using statistical terminology.

4. Then go on to discuss the implications of the results. In other words, whatever was found needs to be discussed.

5. It is also important to discuss how the results relate to the literature you cited in the introduction. In other words, emphasize any theoretical consequences of the results.

6. You might (or might not) also mention any limitations of the study and any suggestions for future research in this section.

7. Finally, you need a concluding paragraph in which you make a final summary statement of the conclusions you have drawn.

8. Thus, this section should contain an absolute minimum of three paragraphs: the nontechnical summary, the discussion of the results and their implications, and the concluding paragraph.

G. References

1. Start on a new page. Center the word *References* at the top. As usual, double-space.

2. Any citations made in the manuscript must be presented in this section and vice versa. That is, if something is not cited in the text, then it should not

appear in this section. This is a list of only the works you referred to in your paper, not a bibliography.

3. In any of the previous sections, whenever you say something like **studies have shown** you must provide a citation. This section tells the reader where they can find these citations.

4. This section is alphabetized by last name of the first author involved in the study.

5. A normal paragraph indentation (i.e., five-space indented) is employed for each reference.

6. For each author, give the last name followed by a comma and the first (and middle) initials followed by periods.

7. Separate the names of multiple authors with commas and the last author with an ampersand (&) rather than the word *and*.

8. After the author(s) comes the year (in parentheses and followed by a period).

9. For a journal reference, underline the title of the journal, volume number, and adjacent punctuation marks with a single unbroken line. Note that issue numbers are typically **not** included. Also, capitalize the first letters of the important words of the journal title.

10. For a book reference, underline just the title. Only capitalize the first letter or the first word of the title. Include the city, state (as a two-letter abbreviation without periods), and the publisher's name.

H. Other Sections

1. After the preceding sections come any tables, the page(s) with the figure captions, and finally any figures, respectively. Each belongs on a separate page (multiple figure captions can appear on one page, however).

2. Tables and the figure captions page have a short title (or manuscript page header) and page number just like all the other typed pages. Note that figures are not typed, and so do not have a short title and page number.

3. Tables and figures should be able to stand alone (i.e., you should not have to read the manuscript to be able to understand a table or figure). A big help in this regard is the table title or the figure caption. Use these wisely to explain what is going on in the table or figure. Do not be afraid to be a little bit verbose in your table titles and figure captions.

4. Tables and figures should not duplicate the same information. Likewise, you should not repeat the data point values in a table or figure in the text of the manuscript.

5. Tables and figures are more expensive to include in the manuscript than text. Therefore, if you include one, it should include a reasonable number of data points (unless it illustrates a particularly complex result). If you only have a few data points to present, do it in the text of the manuscript rather than in a table or figure.

6. Tables and figures are most often used to present results, but may also be used to present other information, such as the design or a theoretical schema.

7. If you include a table or figure, you must introduce it in the text in the results section (e.g., **Table 1 displays the . . .**) **and** describe to the reader what should be seen in it.

Tables

8. See Appendix 3 of this chapter for an example table.
9. Note that APA-style tables do not contain any vertical lines, so do not draw them in or use your word processor to generate them.
10. Type the table number and then (on the next double-spaced line) type the table title flush left and underlined. Note that there are no periods after the table number or title.
11. When using columns with decimal numbers, make the decimal points line up.

Figure Captions

12. See Appendix 4 of this chapter for an example.
13. Start on a new page. Center the phrase **Figure Captions** at the top.
14. Type each figure caption flush left in block format.
15. Underline the word *figure,* the number, and the adjacent period, for example, *Figure 1.* **The effects of . . . .**

Figures

16. *Figures* is the technical term for graphs, charts, drawings, and pictures.
17. Figures (other than pictures) may be drawn in black and white only (using a ruler and preferably on graph paper) or they may be generated with a computer graphics program (keeping it in two dimensions).
18. Center each figure on the page vertically as well as horizontally, and arrange for the figure to use the bulk of the page.
19. If the figure is a chart or graph, verbally label the axes (do not use X and Y) and provide a key if necessary (e.g., explaining what open vs. filled circles are).
20. On the back of each figure (with a pencil), write the short title, the figure number, and the word *TOP* to indicate how the figure should appear on the page.
21. Do not put the figure caption on the figure, as that is what the figure captions page is for.

APPENDIX I: EXAMPLE TITLE PAGE

```
                                        Attitudes Towards Abortion
                                                              1
            Running head: ABORTION ATTITUDES IN COLLEGE STUDENTS




                            Attitudes Towards Abortion
                            in Midwestern College Students
                                  Mark Plonsky
                      University of Wisconsin--Stevens Point




            In partial fulfillment of the requirements for PSY 389
                              Instructor's Name
                                    Date
```

APPENDIX 2: EXAMPLE REFERENCES SECTION

Attitudes Towards Abortion 12

References

Anisman, H., Remington, G., & Sklar, L. S. (1979). Effects of inescapable shock on subsequent escape performance: Catecholaminergic and cholinergic mediation of response initiation and maintenance. Psychopharmacology, 61(1), 107-124.

Beck, A. T. (1967). Depression: Clinical, experimental, and theoretical aspects. New York: Hoeber.

Cicero, T. J. (1979). A critique of animal analogues of alcoholism. In E. Majchrowicz & E. P. Noble (Eds.), Biochemistry and pharmacology of ethanol (Volume 2, pp. 31-59). New York: Plenum Press.

Dorworth, T. R., & Overmier, J. B. (1977). On "learned helplessness": The therapeutic effects of electroconvulsive shocks. Physiological Psychology, 5, 355-358.

U.S. Department of Health, Education, and Welfare. (1971). Alcohol and health. Washington, D.C.: U.S. Government Printing Office.

APPENDIX 3: EXAMPLE TABLE

Table 1

Average Ages Sexual Information Was Acquired Compared
With the Youngest and Oldest Ages Subjects Believed
the Information Should Be Acquired

Information	Age acquired Mean	SD	Youngest age Mean	SD	Oldest age Mean	SD
How babies are made	10.1	2.9	8.5	2.8	11.9	2.7
How babies are born	10.0	3.1	8.4	3.1	11.6	2.8
Sexual intercourse	11.6	2.6	10.4	2.6	13.1	2.6
Menstruation	11.6	2.2	9.9	2.1	12.6	2.1
Nocturnal emissions	12.5	2.6	10.8	2.6	13.4	2.7
Masturbation	13.0	2.6	11.4	2.8	14.0	2.6
Birth control	13.9	2.4	12.0	2.2	14.3	2.4
Homosexuality	13.4	2.8	11.3	2.8	14.1	2.5
Genital terminology	12.4	2.9	10.4	3.3	13.1	3.3
Orgasm	14.0	2.3	12.5	2.7	15.0	2.6
STD's	14.1	2.3	12.0	2.4	14.7	2.4

STD's = Sexually transmitted diseases

APPENDIX 4: EXAMPLE FIGURE CAPTIONS PAGE

Attitudes Towards Abortions 15

Figure Captions

<u>Figure 1.</u> Mean activity counts as a function of maternal diet and age of the rat at the time of testing.

<u>Figure 2.</u> Number of people arrested for drunken driving as related to the day of the week.

PART 2

THE ARTS, MEDIA STUDIES, AND POPULAR CULTURE

CHAPTER 8

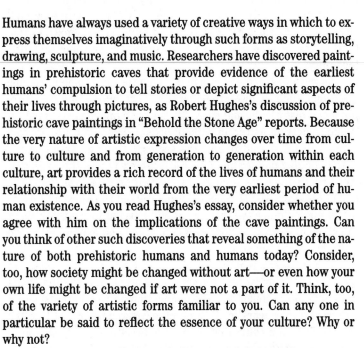

THE ARTS

Humans have always used a variety of creative ways in which to express themselves imaginatively through such forms as storytelling, drawing, sculpture, and music. Researchers have discovered paintings in prehistoric caves that provide evidence of the earliest humans' compulsion to tell stories or depict significant aspects of their lives through pictures, as Robert Hughes's discussion of prehistoric cave paintings in "Behold the Stone Age" reports. Because the very nature of artistic expression changes over time from culture to culture and from generation to generation within each culture, art provides a rich record of the lives of humans and their relationship with their world from the very earliest period of human existence. As you read Hughes's essay, consider whether you agree with him on the implications of the cave paintings. Can you think of other such discoveries that reveal something of the nature of both prehistoric humans and humans today? Consider, too, how society might be changed without art—or even how your own life might be changed if art were not a part of it. Think, too, of the variety of artistic forms familiar to you. Can any one in particular be said to reflect the essence of your culture? Why or why not?

Despite the persistence of art throughout time, the role of the artist in society and the relative value of art often are hotly debated topics. Tastes change and differ from generation to generation and individual to individual, as do values and beliefs about what is important to sustain and nurture a society and the standards by which people judge the merits of works of art. Determining what makes an artwork "good" or "bad" is often a subjective response to the art rather than a conscious application of objective standards. For instance, do you have trouble determining whether a new movie, painting, or song is a good or bad one? How do you judge such works?

Although this chapter focuses on the visual arts, literature is also a significant art form. Indeed, some would claim that imaginative writing, whether it be a short story, a novel, a poem, or some other form of creative expression, is just as crucial to the nurturing of the human soul as are visual arts and music. Certainly this is Norman Cousins's position in "The Poet and the Computer."

Elsewhere in this textbook, in the section on the natural sciences, several people, whose chief interests are science and scientific writing, explore the nature of human intelligence as measured by an ability to create metaphor and to think in imaginative ways. Whatever its form, imagination and creativity are clearly important components of human identity. As you read Cousins's essay, think about the degree to which you would describe yourself as creative. Do you agree with him that humans' imaginative capabilities are as essential to their identities as is their scientific ingenuity?

As you will see, the essays in this chapter raise some intriguing questions, such as, given the quantity of art, music, and literature produced historically and currently, how can one measure quality? Would society be better off without artists, or would it lose its soul without them? Harold M. Williams seems to think so, for he asserts in the opening paragraph of his essay "Don't Ignore the Arts" that "the arts define what is meant by civilization." He explains in the rest of his essay why he feels so strongly about the place of the arts in the curriculum. As you read what Williams has to say, think about the place of the arts in your own education, and explore your own attitude toward the arts.

This chapter's readings touch on some broad issues related to the role of the artist and the nature of art, too, including Diana Jean Schemo's thoughts on the connection between artists' moral nature and their work in "Between the Art and the Artist Lies the Shadow." Do you think that an artist's private morality should in any way influence the way you perceive his or her work?

The subject of art and artists is so vast that these few readings serve only to indicate the breadth and depth of possible related topics and issues. As you consider the points made by the writers in this section on art and the one that follows on music, also think about the kinds of imaginative writing you like to read and perhaps write yourself. Think about the role all these forms of expression play in humans' lives: How might their absence affect people? Do you think your life would be impoverished without art, music, and literature? Why or why not?

BEHOLD THE STONE AGE

Robert Hughes

Robert Hughes has been art critic for Time *magazine for over thirty years and author of at least sixteen books, including* The Art of

Australia (1966), Heaven and Hell in Western Art (1969), The Shock of the New (1981), and The Fatal Shore (1987). He has made dozens of TV documentaries, mainly for the BBC and other English production companies, since the mid-1960s. He became widely known in 1981 as the creator and host of the much-acclaimed television history series on modern art, The Shock of the New. His 1997 television series on American art and architecture, Americana Visions, received equal attention and acclaim, earning him the prestigious Richard Dimbley Award from the British Academy of Film and Television Arts for "the most important personal contribution to factual television" of 1996–97. In 2000, Hughes was honored by the London Sunday Times as Writer of the Year. Hughes wrote this cover story for the February 13, 1995, issue of Time.

Not since the Dead Sea Scrolls has anything found in a cave caused so much excitement. The paintings and engravings, more than 300 of them, amount to a sort of Ice Age Noah's ark—images of bison, mammoths, and woolly rhinoceroses, of a panther, an owl, even a hyena. Done on the rock walls with plain earth pigments—red, black, ocher—they are of singular vitality and power, and despite their inscrutability to modern eyes, they will greatly enrich our picture of Cro-Magnon life and culture.

When the French government last month announced that a local official, Jean-Marie Chauvet, had discovered the stunning Paleolithic cave near Avignon, experts swiftly hailed the 20,000-year-old paintings as a trove rivaling—and perhaps surpassing—those of Lascaux and Altamira. "This is a virgin site—it's completely intact. It's great art," exulted Jean Clottes, an adviser to the French Culture Ministry and a leading authority on prehistoric art. It has also reopened some of the oldest and least settled of questions: When, how, and above all why did Homo sapiens start making art?

In the span of human prehistory, the Cro-Magnon people who drew the profusion of animals on the bulging limestone walls of the Chauvet cave were fairly late arrivals. Human technology—the making of tools from stone—had already been in existence for nearly two million years. There are traces of symbolism and ritual in burial sites of Neanderthals, an earlier species, dating back to 100,000 B.P. (before the present). Not only did the placement of the bodies seem meaningful, but so did the surrounding pebbles and bones with fragmentary patterns scratched on them. These, says Clottes, "do indicate that the Neanderthals had some creative capacity."

4   Though the dates are vastly generalized, most prehistorians seem to agree that art—communication by visual images—came into existence somewhere around 40,000 B.P. That was about the time when Cro-Magnons, Homo sapiens, reached Ice Age Europe, having migrated from the Middle East. Some experts think the Cro-Magnons brought a weapon that made Neanderthals an evolutionary has-been: a more advanced brain, equipped with a large frontal lobe "wired" for associative thinking. For art, at its root, is association—the power to make one thing stand for and symbolize another, to create the agreements by which some marks on a surface denote, say, an animal, not just to the markmaker but to others.

Among the oldest types of art is personal decoration—ornaments such as beads, bracelets, pendants, and necklaces. The body was certainly one of the first surfaces for symbolic expression. What did such symbols communicate? Presumably the wearer's difference from others, as a member of a distinct group, tribe, or totemic family: that he was a bison-man, say, and not a reindeer-man.

The Cro-Magnons were not the inarticulate Alley Oops of popular myth. They were nomadic hunter–gatherers with a fairly developed technology. They wore animal-skin clothing and moccasins tailored with bone needles, and made beautiful (and highly efficient) laurel-leaf-shaped flint blades. Living in small groups, they constructed tents from skins, and huts from branches and (in what is now Eastern Europe) mammoth bones.

Most striking was their yearning to make art in permanent places—the walls of caves. This expansion from the body to the inert surface was in itself a startling act of lateral thinking, an outward projection of huge cultural consequence, and Homo sapiens did not produce it quickly. As much time elapsed between the first recognizable art and the cave paintings of Lascaux and Altamira, about fifteen to twenty millenniums, as separates Lascaux (or Chauvet) from the first TV broadcasts. But now it was possible to see an objective image in shared space, one that was not the property of particular bodies and had a life of its own; and from this point the whole history of human visual communication unfolds.

8   We are apt to suppose that Cro-Magnon cave art was rare and exceptional. But wrongly; as New York University anthropologist Randall White points out, more than 200 late–Stone Age caves bearing wall paintings, engravings, bas-relief decorations, and sculptures have been found in southwestern Europe alone. Since the discovery of Lascaux in 1940, French archaeologists have been finding an average of a cave a year—and, says professor Denis Vialou of Paris's Institute of Human Paleontology, "there are certainly many, many more to be discovered, and while many might not prove as spectacular as Lascaux or Chauvet, I'd bet that some will be just as exciting."

No doubt many will never be found. The recently discovered painted cave at Cosquer in the south of France, for instance, can be reached only by scuba divers. Its entrance now lies below the surface of the Mediterranean; in the Upper Paleolithic period, from 70,000 B.P. to 10,000 B.P., so much of Europe's water was locked up in glaciers that the sea level was some 300 feet lower than it is today.

Why the profuseness of Cro-Magnon art? Why did these people, of whom so little is known, need images so intensely? Why the preponderance of animals over human images? Archaeologists are not much closer to answering such questions than they were a half-century ago, when Lascaux was discovered.

Part of the difficulty lies in the very definition of art. As anthropologist Margaret Conkey of the University of California, Berkeley puts it, "Many cultures don't really produce art, or even have any concept of it. They have spirits, kinship, group identity. If people from highland New Guinea looked at some of the Cro-Magnon cave art, they wouldn't see anything recognizable"—and not just because there are no woolly rhinos in New Guinea either. Today we can see almost anything as an aesthetic configuration and pull it into the eclectic orbit of late-Western "art experience"; museums have trained us to do that. The paintings of Chauvet strike us as aesthetically impressive in their power and economy of line, their combination of the sculptural and the graphic—for the artists used the natural bulges and bosses of the rock wall to flesh out the forms of the animals' rumps and bellies. But it may be that aesthetic pleasure, in our sense, was the last thing the Ice Age painters were after.

12   These were functional images; they were meant to produce results. But what results? To represent something, to capture its image on a wall in colored earths and animal fat, is in some sense to capture and master it; to have power over it. Lascaux is full of nonthreatening animals, including wild cattle, bison, and horses, but Chauvet pullulates with dangerous ones—cave bears, a panther, and no fewer than fifty woolly rhinos. Such creatures, to paraphrase Claude Lévi-Strauss, were good to think with, not good to eat. We can assume they had a symbolic value, maybe even a religious value, to those who drew them, that they supplied a framework of images in which needs, values, and fears—in short, a network of social consciousness—could be expressed. But we have no idea what this framework was, and merely to call it *animistic* does not say much.

Some animals have more than four legs, or grotesquely exaggerated horns; is that just style, or does it argue a state of ritual trance or hallucination in the artists? No answer, though some naturally occurring manganese oxides, the base of some of the blacks used in cave paintings, are known to be toxic and to act on the central nervous system. And the main technique of Cro-Magnon art, according to prehistorian Michel Lorblanchet, director of France's National Center of Scientific Research, involved not brushes but a kind of oral spray-painting—blowing pigment dissolved in saliva on the wall. Lorblanchet, who has re-created cave paintings with uncanny accuracy, suggests that the technique may have had a spiritual dimension: "Spitting is a way of projecting yourself onto the wall, becoming one with the horse you are painting. Thus the action melds with the myth. Perhaps the shamans did this as a way of passing into the world beyond."

Different hands (and mouths) were involved in the production, but whose hands? Did the whole Cro-Magnon group at Chauvet paint, or did it have an élite of artists, to be viewed by nonartists as something like priests or professionals? Or does the joining of many hands in a collaborative work express a kind of treaty between rival groups? Or were the paintings added to over generations, producing the crowded, palimpsest-like effect suggested by some of the photos? And so on.

A mere picture of a bison or a woolly rhino tells us nothing much. Suppose, France's Clottes suggests, that 20,000 years from now, after a global cataclysm in which all books perished and the word vanished from the face of the earth, some excavators dig up the shell of a building. It has pointy ogival arches and a long axial hall at the end of which is a painting of a man nailed to a cross. In the absence of written evidence, what could this effigy mean? No more than the bison or rhino on the rock at Chauvet. Representation and symbolism have parted company.

16   Chauvet cave could be viewed as a religious site—a Paleolithic cathedral. Some have even suggested that a bear's skull found perched on a rock was an "altar." Says

Henry de Lumley, director of France's National Museum of Natural History: "The fact that the iconography is relatively consistent, that it seems to obey certain rules about placement and even the way animals are drawn . . . is evidence of something sacred." Yet nobody lived in the cave, and no one in his right mind could imagine doing so; the first analyses of the contents have yielded no signs of human habitation, beyond the traces of animal-fat lamps and torches used by temporary visitors, and some mounds of pigmented earth left behind by the artists.

Modern artists make art to be seen by a public, the larger (usually) the better. The history of public art as we know it, across the past 1,000 years and more, is one of increasing access—beginning with the church open to the worshippers and ending with the pack-'em-in ethos of the modern museum, with its support-system of orientation courses, lectures, films, outreach programs, and souvenir shops. Cro-Magnon cave art was probably meant to be seen by very few people, under conditions of extreme difficulty and dread. The caves may have been places of initiation and trial, in which consciousness was tested to an extent that we can only dimly imagine, so utterly different is our grasp of the world from that of the Cro-Magnons.

Try to imagine an art gallery that could be entered only by crawling on your belly through a hole in the earth; that ramified into dark tunnels, a fearful maze in the earth's bowels in which the gallerygoer could, at any moment, disturb one of the bears whose claw marks can still be seen on the walls; where the only light came from flickering torches, and the bones of animals littered the uneven floor. These are the archaic conditions that, one may surmise, produced the array of cave fears implanted in the human brain—fears that became absorbed into a later, more developed culture in such narratives as that of the mythical Cretan labyrinth in whose core the terrible Minotaur waited. Further metabolized, and more basically misunderstood, these sacred terrors of the deep earth undergird the Christian myth of hell. Which may, in fact, be the strongest Cro-Magnon element left in modern life.

Personal Response

Describe your own interests in the visual arts by explaining whether you like art in general and who, if any, are your favorite artists and works of art.

Questions for Class or Small-Group Discussion

1. This essay raises a number of questions about the purpose and nature of Cro-Magnon art. What implications do you think those questions have for art today? Explain your answer.

2. What impact, if any, do you think the discovery of the paintings in a Paleolithic cave in France will have on people today? What do you think modern humans can learn from them?

3. In what ways has art remained essentially the same since the period that Hughes describes in this essay? What significant changes do you see? Be as specific as possible in your answer.

4. Hughes describes the paintings in the French cave and theorizes why they were painted. Can you offer any other plausible reasons for the cave paintings? Explain your answer in detail.

THE POET AND THE COMPUTER

Norman Cousins

Norman Cousins (1915–1990) was editor of the Saturday Review for thirty-five years. He wrote twenty-five books and numerous essays on a wide range of subjects, including Talks with Nehru *(1951),* Who Speaks for Man? *(1953), and* Present Tense *(1967). More recently,* The Celebration of Life *(1974) and* The Anatomy of Illness *(1979) describe his experiences with and recovery from an illness described as fatal by doctors. A holistic health pioneer, Cousins served on the medical faculty at UCLA from 1978 until his death. In 1990, he received the Albert Schweitzer Prize for Humanitarianism for his efforts on behalf of international peace. In this essay, which first appeared in* Beyond Literacy: The Second Gutenberg Revolution *(1989), Cousins argues for the crucial importance of not only the poet but of all imaginative creativity in the electronic age.*

"A poet," said Aristotle, "has the advantage of expressing the universal; the specialist expresses only the particular." The poet, moreover, can remind us that man's greatest energy comes not from his dynamos but from his dreams. The notion of where a man ought to be instead of where he is; the liberation from cramped prospects; the intimations of immortality through art, all these proceed naturally out of dreams. But the quality of man's dreams can only be a reflection of his subconscious. What he puts into his subconscious, therefore, is quite literally the most important nourishment in the world.

Nothing really happens to a man except as it is registered in the subconscious. This is where event and feeling become memory and where the proof of life is stored. The poet, and I use the term to include all those who have respect for and speak to the human spirit, can help to supply the subconscious with material to enhance its sensitivity, thus safeguarding it. The poet, too, can help to keep man from making himself over to the image of his electronic marvels. The danger is not so much that man will be controlled by the computer as that he may imitate it.

There once was a time, in the history of this society, when the ability of people to convey meaning was enriched by their knowledge of and access to the work of creative minds from across the centuries. No more. Conversation and letters today, like education, have become enfeebled by emphasis on the functional and the purely contemporary. The result is a mechanization not just of the way we live but of the way we think and of the human spirit itself.

4   The delegates to the United States Constitutional Convention were able to undergird their arguments with allusions to historical situations and to the ideas of philosophers, essayists, and dramatists. Names such as Thucydides, Aristotle, Herodotus, Plutarch, or Seneca were commonly cited to support their positions. They alluded to fictional characters from Aristophanes, Marlowe, or Shakespeare to lend color to the exploration of ideas. The analytical essays by Hamilton, Madison, and Jay that appeared in *The Federalist Papers* were an excursion into the remote corners of history.

Men such as Jefferson, Adams, Franklin, and Rush could summon pertinent quotations from Suetonius or Machiavelli or Montaigne to illustrate a principle. If they referred to Bacon's opinion of Aristotle, they didn't have to cite particulars; they assumed such details were common knowledge. Their allusions were not the product of intellectual ostentation or ornamentation but the natural condiments of discourse, bringing out the full flavor of the cultivated intelligence.

The same was true of correspondence. People regarded letters as an art form and a highly satisfying way of engaging in civilized exchange. The correspondence of Jefferson and Adams and Priestley was not so much a display of personal matters as a review of the human condition. It was not unusual for the writers to range across the entire arena of human thought as a way of sharing perceptions. Allusion was common currency. Today, we rarely turn to letters as a way of embarking on voyages of intellectual discovery.

The essential problem of man in a computerized age remains the same as it has always been. That problem is not solely how to be more productive, more comfortable, more content, but how to be more sensitive, more sensible, more proportionate, more alive. The computer makes possible a phenomenal leap in human proficiency; it demolishes the fences around the practical and even the theoretical intelligence. But the question persists, and indeed grows, whether the computer makes it easier or harder for human beings to know who they really are, to identify their real problems, to respond more fully to beauty, to place adequate value on life, and to make their world safer than it now is.

8   Electronic brains can reduce the profusion of dead ends involved in vital research. But they can't eliminate the foolishness and decay that come from the unexamined life. Nor do they connect a man to the things he has to be connected to, the reality of pain in others; the possibilities of creative growth in himself; the memory of the race; and the rights of the next generation.

The reason these matters are important in a computerized age is that there may be a tendency to mistake data for wisdom, just as there has always been a tendency to confuse logic with values and intelligence with insight. Unobstructed access to facts can produce unlimited good only if it is matched by the desire and ability to find out what they mean and where they would lead.

Facts are terrible things if left sprawling and unattended. They are too easily regarded as evaluated certainties rather than as the rawest of raw materials crying to be processed into the texture of logic. It requires a very unusual mind, Whitehead said, to undertake the analysis of a fact. The computer can provide a correct number, but it may be an irrelevant number until judgment is pronounced.

To the extent, then, that man fails to make the distinction between the intermediate operations of electronic intelligence and the ultimate responsibilities of human decision and conscience, the computer could obscure man's awareness of the need to come to terms with himself. It may foster the illusion that he is asking fundamental questions when actually he is asking only functional ones. It may be regarded as a substitute for intelligence instead of an extension of it. It may promote undue confidence in concrete answers. "If we begin with certainties," Bacon said, "we shall end in doubts; but if we begin with doubts, and we are patient with them, we shall end in certainties."

12   The computer knows how to vanquish error, but before we lose ourselves in celebration of victory, we might reflect on the great advances in the human situation that have come about because men were challenged by error and would not stop thinking and probing until they found better approaches for dealing with it. "Give me a good fruitful error, full of seeds, bursting with its own corrections," Ferris Greenslet wrote. "You can keep your sterile truth for yourself."

Without taking anything away from the technicians, it might be fruitful to effect some sort of junction between the computer technologist and the poet. A genuine purpose may be served by turning loose the wonders of the creative imagination on the kinds of problems being put to electronic tubes and transistors. The company of poets may enable the men who tend the machines to see a larger panorama of possibilities than technology alone may inspire.

Poets remind men of their uniqueness. It is not necessary to possess the ultimate definition of this uniqueness. Even to speculate on it is a gain.

Personal Response

What are some examples of your creativity? Do you consider yourself a *poet* as Cousins defines the term?

Questions for Class or Small-Group Discussion

1. Do you agree or disagree with the central argument of this essay? Explain your answer. Do you think Cousins is an alarmist, or does he have good cause for concern?

2. Discuss Cousins's lament that too few people today recognize "allusions to historical situations and to the ideas of philosophers, essayists, and dramatists" (paragraph 4). Do you agree with Cousins that this lack of knowledge is a cause for concern? What does he think was gained when history, philosophy, and literature were common knowledge?

3. How many names in paragraphs 4 and 5 do you recognize? In class, go through the list and try to identify them. For those whose names no one recognizes, volunteer to find out who they are and report back to your classmates.

4. Cousins defines "the poet" to include "all those who have respect for and speak to the human spirit" (paragraph 2). Who do you think are today's poets? What do they contribute to culture?

DON'T IGNORE THE ARTS
Harold M. Williams

Harold M. Williams, former chairman of the United States Securities and Exchange Commission, served as president and chief executive officer of the J. Paul Getty Trust, Santa Monica, California, for fifteen years until his retirement in 1998. He is author of The Getty Center: Design Process, Making Architecture *(1997), a two-volume chronicle of the building of the Getty Center from site and architect selection through design and construction. This essay first appeared in* USA Today *in 1995.*

It is difficult to imagine a society without the arts. What dark and empty souls would populate an environment without paintings, statues, architecture, drama, music, dances, or poems? The arts define what is meant by *civilization.* They are part of the foundation and the framework of culture. As a universal language through which individuals can express common aspirations, the arts are a channel to understanding and appreciating other cultures. To be conversant with the arts is to be a civilized person.

The arts are a basic and central medium of human communication and understanding. They are how people talk to each other. The arts are the languages of civilization—past and present—through which they express their anxieties, hungers, hopes, and discoveries. They are the means of listening to dreams—of expressing imagination and feelings.

The arts reaffirm humanity. They are the glue that holds society together. While improvement in the three *Rs* may enable Americans to compete more effectively in the world economically and technologically, they do not feed the human spirit. The most vital stages in the history of any society are marked by a flourishing of the arts. When most material goods have turned to dust, it is the arts that remain as testimony to the dreams and passions of the past.

4   Nobel Prize-winning physicist Richard Feynman decided to learn how to draw at the age of forty-four. He eventually got quite good at it, even though he confessed to having been terrible at art in high school. Later, Feynman, who was a brilliant teacher and thinker in mathematics and physics at California Institute of Technology, explained why he had taken up art so late in life. He wanted to express the awe he felt about the glories of the universe, he said. Art, he felt, might be the only way he could reveal this emotion to someone who might share it.

Feynman, of course, wasn't the first or last scientist to seek a perspective on his life through the arts. He discovered late what many others are lucky enough to know intuitively—that the arts are key to building the metaphorical bridges that link individuals to their own creative powers and to each other.

Americans live in a society that is communicating more and more through visual images. Daily, they are bombarded by a constantly changing torrent of messages from billboards, architecture, magazines, four-color newspapers, television, and films. New technology controlled by computers combines words, pictures, and sound to convey information at a breathtaking pace. Computers, with their power to manufacture and animate images, are creating entirely new art forms.

Consider, also, that American civilization is increasingly diverse, mixing cultures from Europe, Africa, the Far East, and Latin America. Each group sends its own messages and images, jostling to preserve and advance its own identity. Meanwhile, many of the surviving messages from past civilizations exist in visual form.

8   In short, to be educated is to be visually literate—to understand the historical and cultural context of the message, make aesthetic judgments about what one sees, and sort out these images in order to tell the good from the bad, the fake from the genuine, and interpret accurately the signals of other cultural groups in search of common humanity. Armed with an ability to make judgments, an educated person will learn to construct sound value systems for any event or object, whether it is art or not.

It seems fair to ask then, if the arts occupy such a central role in human life, shouldn't they have a central place in education? If children are not taught to look and understand what they see, isn't this a failure to prepare them for life in contemporary society? Aren't they being sent into the modern world without a complete education?

If a purpose of education is to ensure the continuity of the democratic system and its values from one generation to the next, then why aren't schools teaching the things that bring Americans closest to the core of their cultural experience? If the United States is spending its resources on a back-to-basics education, why the tendency to ignore something as basic to human development and culture as the study of the arts?

Access to the wealth of American culture and the cultivation of the sensibilities, human imagination, and judgment are not peripheral educational aims. The arts represent a form of thinking and a way of knowing and, as such, their presence in the schools is as basic as anything can be.

12   Ernest Boyer of the Carnegie Foundation for the Advancement of Teaching put it well in his study, *High School.* "The arts are essential parts of the human experience, they are not a frill. We recommend that *all* students study the arts to discover how human beings communicate not only with words, but through music, dance, and the visual arts. During our visits we found the arts to be shamefully neglected. Courses in the arts were the last to come and first to go."

In 1988, the National Endowment for the Arts released the results of a two-year study, *Toward Civilization: A Report on Arts Education.* Its assessment was that "basic arts education does not exist in the United States today."

With the emphasis on improving the three *Rs*, many schools have cut back on what they consider to be "frills," including the arts. The result is that "the artistic heritage that is ours and the opportunities to contribute significantly to its evolution are being lost to our young people." Not only does the absence or meagerness of the arts in the schools deny children access to the vast treasury of American and world culture, but without it there is no replenishing of the infrastructure to assure the cultural future of the country.

If the arts are so basic to becoming an educated person, why are they ignored in American schools? Elliot W. Eisner of Stanford University examined this question in his book, *The Enlightened Eye.* Among the reasons why the arts are ignored were, first, because there is a tendency to regard them as dealing with emotion, rather than the mind, and useful primarily as a release from the serious work of getting educated. This view fails to recognize that creation of images is a matter of mind that calls for inventive problem-solving capacities, analytic and synthetic forms of reasoning, and the exercise of judgment. Psychologists and educators recognize that intelligence extends beyond verbal and mathematical reasoning.

16   A second cause is that they are not assessed formally and, as a consequence, do not promote students' academic upward mobility. The arts carry little, if any, weight in college admissions decisions. If arts courses are viewed by college admissions offices as not having much value, it is to be expected that they will be of little importance to schools, upwardly mobile students, or their parents. The attitude on the part of universities carries through into teacher training, which pays little, if any, attention to preparing general education teachers to present the arts competently in the classroom.

A third reason follows from the view held by many art educators that, to the extent that art is taught, it should focus on developing the students' creative abilities. As such, many have resisted including any structure or content for fear it would stifle creativity. The result is programs lacking substance and perceived as not worthy of inclusion in the curriculum.

There are values to be realized in addition to the direct benefits of arts education. Skillfully taught and integrated into the curriculum, the arts can help to achieve many of the aims of educational reform. Studying them can empower children to see and make valid judgments about their environment. The arts also can provide an effective bridge to understanding and appreciating other cultures.

Further, a growing body of evidence from the classroom indicates that strengths gained in the study of art carry over into other subject areas. One of the most convincing testimonials to this comes from New Jersey Assemblywoman Maureen Ogden: "Compare two similar schools; one with strong arts curricula and one without. You'll soon discover that there are nonartistic benefits that make the school with arts curricula a higher performance environment. Most importantly, in such settings the kids are excited about learning. Teachers attribute higher test scores in other traditional subjects to the integration of the arts for learning science, math, reading, and the like. And if that isn't enough, go into a multicultural setting and you will witness a common language that enhances cultural understanding and appreciation. You can see a path to heightened self-esteem that permeates those tough social programs areas we would prefer to ignore."

20   There are reports that students' vocabulary and writing skills improve after having been in a substantive art program. Teachers involved in these initiatives have come to recognize their worth, and faculty in some schools have begun to correlate arts education more closely with other studies such as history or biology.

In 1993, the UCLA Center for the Study of Evaluation conducted an evaluation of the educational impact of the Los Angeles Music Center's Artist in Residence and Teacher (ART) Partnerships. The report found improvement and growth in all areas of the study, including students' cognitive, thinking, and social skills, self-expression, and attitude development.

In cognitive skills, students learned from the factual knowledge and abilities presented by the artists and showed overall improvement in academic knowledge and skills. Their thinking skills also improved, as they made progress in problem-solving. Moreover, they were able to use the information and skills learned in other subjects, as well as outside of school. In the area of self-expression, students improved in both written and oral communication. They learned how to express themselves better in writing, speaking in front of others, and acting out their feelings. Finally, attitude development showed improvement, with gains in motivation and self-confidence, as well as work habit/cooperation report card grades.

What does all this signify for America's schools and children? It means that it is possible to make a difference, that the arts do change lives, and that youngsters will grow through the arts, transforming their own lives and that of their community.

24   During the early 1980s, the J. Paul Getty Trust surveyed the state of art education in America's public schools. The picture generally was bleak. The results were consistent with the later findings reported by Elliot Eisner and the National Endowment for the Arts study. Nevertheless, through discussions with art experts and educators, it was found that there were some exciting trends afoot. New ideas and lines of research were developing that, fortified by subsequent research, were beginning to jell into a comprehensive strategy called discipline-based art education, a humanities-based approach that embraced content from art production, history, criticism, and aesthetics. There even were a few schools struggling in isolation to nurture a version of such an integrated, sequential art program into maturity.

In 1982, the trust, through the Getty Center for Education in the Arts, committed itself to helping make such an approach to art education a reality. We are engaged in a long-term effort to serve as a catalyst in furthering the theory and practice of art education in the United States.

Our experience has confirmed the potential of discipline-based art education programs to develop intellectual skills and create opportunities to explore creative self-expression. It now is known, for instance, that involving students in analyzing works of art, whether their own or others, requires functioning at the highest cognitive levels of mental activity.

Children confronted by a work of art in the context of a comprehensive learning program tend to be fascinated and excited by the challenge and mystery of it. Many classroom teachers who have had to learn art content through in-service training in order to participate in a discipline-based program have reported a renewed enthusiasm for their profession.

28   Students asked to consider art from the standpoints of the artist, historian, critic, and aesthetician soon become more perceptive about visual images and more open to different ways of thinking about the same image. The quality of art produced by students improves measurably as they learn about other artists, are required to solve problems, and assess other works of art.

Opening Children's Imaginations

Art history opens the child's imagination to other eras and cultures. If students of the next century are to work and live productively side by side with others from different cultures, they must respect and appreciate cultural differences and, at the same time, discern what they share in common with other peoples. The arts are one of the best ways of achieving this practical goal.

Learning how to critique and judge art sharpens critical faculties by obliging the student to think independently, creatively, and to make reasoned judgments based on his or her knowledge and trained observations. Finally, consideration of aesthetic issues teaches them to be able to deal with the nature and meaning of art in their own lives.

The ability to think critically and creatively and to make informed judgments is vital for young people preparing for the twenty-first century. The world is changing rapidly and so is the workplace. The likelihood of multiple careers during one's lifetime will demand flexibility and imagination. In an increasingly multicultural society, young people need language skills and a tolerance of other peoples and customs based on informed understanding.

32   Computer-based technology requires that workers be able to deal with ever more complex and fast-paced systems of symbols and images—the world of Nintendo and MTV grown up. To cope and compete in these surroundings, young people must become visually literate, versed in the language of the arts. Even today, exciting interactive multimedia programs are beginning to enhance the ways children learn. Before long, they permanently may alter the basic nature of the traditional classroom.

There are reasons to be optimistic about the future. Especially encouraging is the number of people who have joined forces to ensure that arts education is a significant part of national education reform. In the spring of 1994, Congress passed Goals 2000: Educate America Act. This law makes the arts one of the core subjects to be included in the curriculum. It marked the first time in three decades that the arts have been included in federal education legislation.

Also in 1994, the first set of national voluntary curriculum standards for what children should know and be able to do in dance, music, theater, and the visual arts were completed and presented to the Secretary of Education. These are significant for two reasons. First, they expect youngsters not only to be able to create and perform in the arts, but also to understand the entire body of work that makes up human intellectual and cultural heritage. They recognize that, when the arts are studied, students involve themselves in a particular set of processes, influences, and meanings. The standards also recognize that art is expressed in various styles, reflects different historical circumstances, and draws on a multitude of social and cultural resources.

In another significant development for arts education, and one that supports the national arts standards, the National Assessment of Educational Progress is developing a new arts assessment to be administered in 1996 to 4th-, 8th-, and 12th-grade students nationwide. The national arts assessment will enable parents, educators, and the general public to evaluate the condition and progress of student achievement in the arts just as is done for all of the other academic subjects named in the National Education Goals.

36   The national voluntary standards in the arts, the new national arts assessment, and state curriculum frameworks of more than thirty states that recommend a comprehensive approach to arts education instruction reflect a recognition among educational policy makers and the public that the cognitive and affective contributions of the arts are significant enough to be part of every child's schooling from kindergarten through 12th grade.

Americans can have any kind of schools they want, if they make up their minds to do it. They have the freedom to be outspoken advocates for including the arts and humanities in the curriculum. They can form alliances with like-minded individuals and groups. They can seek out successful programs and hold them up as examples. When they finally succeed in raising the arts and humanities to their rightful, and necessary, place in education, they have done a great service not only to countless generations of students to come, but to the cause of democracy.

Personal Response

Describe the art education you have experienced. Are you satisfied with the quality and quantity of that instruction? In what ways have you benefited—or not—from the art instruction you have received? Do you anticipate taking any more courses in the arts?

Questions for Class or Small-Group Discussion

1. What do you think Williams means when he says: "The arts define what is meant by *civilization*. [. . .] To be conversant with the arts is to be a civilized person" (paragraph 1)? Do you agree or disagree with him?

2. Explain what this statement means to you: "[T]he arts are key to building the metaphorical bridges that link individuals to their own creative powers and to each other" (paragraph 5). Do you agree with Williams on this point, or do you think he is overstating the importance of the arts?

3. Find the reasons Williams gives to explain why the arts have been ignored in American schools (paragraph 15), and then comment on those reasons.

4. What, according to Williams, "are [the] values to be realized in addition to the direct benefits of art education" (paragraph 18)? Are you persuaded by his evidence?

BETWEEN THE ART AND THE ARTIST LIES THE SHADOW

Diana Jean Schemo

Diana Jean Schemo writes for the New York Times *on a wide variety of topics, both national and international. Among her hundreds of articles are pieces on such subjects as art, education, refugees from Kosovo, Chilean politics, and repression in South America. Her articles are often reprinted by major newspapers across the nation. "Between the Art and the Artist Lies the Shadow" first appeared in the January 1, 1995, issue of the* Times.

Reports of the death of the playwright John Osborne last week, which chronicled a life of unrelenting venom, probably did not stir a great amount of soul-searching among those who loved his work. The author of the 1956 play *Look Back in Anger* seemed to have looked forward, sideways, up, and down in anger through his life, and gave rise to a school of British playwrights of such familiar bitterness they had their own acronym, the A.Y.M.—Angry Young Men.

But why do suggestions that other artists whose work we admire—writers, composers, painters, actors, and singers—had politics or personal habits we find despicable stir uneasiness within? Why can the knowledge of the anti-Semitism of Edgar Degas or T. S. Eliot, or allegations of the near-criminal opportunism of Bertolt Brecht or of Picasso's misogyny cause such profound turmoil in many people?

For some, the disparity between the beauty of art and the human foibles of an artist undoubtedly causes no alarm. The poet Kenneth Koch, among many others, argues that art exists on its own plane, and should be considered independent of the person who created it. Art may well be like nature, wrapped in its own splendor and mystery, no more beholden to moral tribulations than the crocuses that herald spring. Perhaps, unlike Dorothy in *The Wizard of Oz*, one should never trouble over the befuddled shaman behind the curtains who fashions our illusions, but thank genius for its gifts and ignore the rest.

4   After all, discarding art on a political basis lands us in dubious company of both left and right, from Josef Stalin to Joseph McCarthy. And while mores shift through age and place, true art defies time; centuries after the scandal wore off Michelangelo's homosexuality, the Sistine Chapel still takes the breath away.

Logically, we can recount the intellectual arguments with ease: that the composer's gifts have more to do with an intuitive ability to imagine complex patterns of sound than to form sound political judgments; that an ear for language and rhythm, which can make a fine writer, has nothing to do with an eye for morality, let alone humanity.

But while good art requires skills such as these, art at its best connects words, sounds, movement, or color to emotions crystalized within us. It allows us to glimpse something sublime within human reach, to fulfill the unuttered promise of experience, to find the poetry in our loneliness. We come to believe the person capable of elevating the mundane acts of our lives, fitting them into the grander record of human experience, must also possess a greater measure of wisdom.

We discover a writer and feel as if we've made a new friend, welcoming his witticisms, stacking them on our night tables. We follow the progression of his thinking, wonder about his observations on the way to work, and feel a twinge of pride for having recognized talent. We want to know more. We want to know everything about the person behind the curtains, as if putting together the pieces of their lives will unravel the mystery of their creations.

8   And the art we love becomes intensely intimate.

Like the gloriously extravagant writer of radio scripts in Mario Vargas Llosa's *Aunt Julia and the Script Writer,* when we are about to be swallowed by the muck of life, we turn to art. We fall in love and hear Puccini in our heads. We grow old and find "The Love Song of J. Alfred Prufrock" ineffably moving:

> *There will be time, there will be time*
> *To prepare a face to meet the faces that you meet;*
> *There will be time to murder and create,*
> *And time for all the works and days of hands*
> *That lift and drop a question on your plate.*

William Styron's severe depression, recounted in his slender volume, *Darkness Visible* (Random House, 1990), culminated in his contemplating suicide through a wrenching, sleepless night. He found the strength to prevail upon hearing Brahms's "Alto Rhapsody," which seemed to draw him back into the human family. (Styron left it at that, never addressing the question of politics. But what if his savior had been Richard Strauss, who had headed the Reich Music Chamber under Hitler, in charge of making sure that no "subversive" music or Jewish musicians were heard in the concert halls and opera houses of Nazi Germany?)

And so to learn that Eliot was an anti-Semite becomes a kind of betrayal, as if we were taken in by fine phrases alone. The exhilaration of personal discovery one might have felt gives way to shame at having not picked up on some fundamental flaw that, on some level, we reason, must have been transmitted in the work.

12   "If you're dealing with a writer, more so than an artist or a musician, you can find symptoms of the despicable private trait, which is often a blemish on the work," said George Stade, a professor of English and comparative literature at Columbia University and author of *Confessions of a Lady-Killer* (Norton, 1979). He noted that Eliot's

"Gerontion," for example, contains an anti-Semitic caricature of the rootless Jew as landlord of Europe; his "Sweeney Among the Nightingales" speaks of "Rachel, née Rabinovitch," who "tears at the grapes with murderous paws."

Professor Stade said the relation between talent and integrity bothered him more when he was fifteen than it does now, though he confessed that recent allegations that Brecht signed his name to other people's work has lowered his esteem for the playwright. "It's like a person you fall in love with for his or her physical beauty, who you're then disappointed to find isn't a good person," Professor Stade said.

More disturbing than the prospect that one fell for a pretty face are the doubts about one's own character that may arise. Does finding that literature that resonates to our very core was written by a philanderer suggest there is a liar or a cheat crouching silently within us?

Philip Larkin, the English poet laureate, maintained that most people, faced with contradictory judgments about an artist and his work, will adjust their views until the two elements fall in line rather than accept the ambiguity. Thus a fine poet who was a misanthrope and racist—as the posthumous publication of Larkin's own correspondence suggests he was—will come to be seen as either a bitter poet or a good person, Larkin contends.

16   It is usually not that simple. We almost don't want to know, we long for the state of unknowing appreciation. We want to say, "Come back. All is forgiven," but we can't.

And so at times we flatter ourselves with the notion that we are rising above petty strictures to value art in all its breadth and mystery, and we listen to Strauss with pleasure. Or it's possible to admit this is a shameful indulgence, and listen guiltily, as if we are holed up in the pantry with chocolate ice cream. The only other choice is to avoid the work as sham altogether.

Still, the private questions persist—testimony to the power of art, and its limits.

Personal Response

Is your regard for a work of art (of any kind) in any way influenced by what you know about the artist? Give an example to illustrate your answer.

Questions for Class or Small-Group Discussion

1. Schemo's concluding statement suggests that questions about artists' political beliefs or private morality are "testimony to the power of art, and its limits." Discuss your perception of the limits of art in this context.

2. Discuss the ways in which artists' private behavior or personal beliefs affect your own responses to their art. Give examples from as many different kinds of art as you can.

3. If you discovered that an artist whom you have always admired holds views you strongly disagree with or has done something you think is horrible, do you think you would continue to appreciate his or her art? Why or why not? What sorts of things would make you change your attitude toward that art?

4. Conduct a classroom debate on Kenneth Koch's argument "that art exists on its own plane, and should be considered independent of the person who created it" (paragraph 3).

PERSPECTIVES ON THE ARTS

Suggestions for Synthesis

1. Drawing on at least two of the selections in this chapter, explain your viewpoint on the importance of art. Be sure to defend your position by supplying evidence not only from the essays but also from your own observations.

2. Taking Norman Cousins's definition of *poet* in "The Poet and the Computer" and Diana Jean Schemo's "Between the Art and the Artist Lies the Shadow" as starting points, argue who you think today's most creative people are. Your argument might highlight a particular group of people (artists, scientists, musicians, television talk show hosts) or a particular person. In either case, give supporting evidence to substantiate your viewpoint.

3. Invite two artists from the community or campus to speak to your class on what art means to them and how they see the place of art in America today. Then write an essay in which you not only synthesize their remarks but provide a reasoned critique of them, as well.

4. Using Diana Jean Schemo's observations in "Between the Art and the Artist Lies the Shadow" as background, survey a group of your friends and acquaintances for their opinions of the place of an artist's private beliefs and behavior in judging the artist's work. Then report the results of your survey in an essay that synthesizes Schemo's comments and those of the people you interview.

5. In "Don't Ignore the Arts," Harold M. Williams asks, "Shouldn't [the arts] have a central place in education?" (paragraph 9). Drawing on the comments of two or more writers in this chapter, answer that question.

Additional Writing Topics

1. In "Behold the Stone Age," Robert Hughes points out that the oldest form of art is personal decoration. The body is still being used as a surface for symbolic expression by some young people, who use such techniques as branding, piercing, and tattooing. Defend or attack these practices by considering their relative artistic or creative merits.

2. Define *excellence* in relation to a specific art form (for instance, a painting, a novel, a poem, a song, or a film) by stating the criteria you use for judging that abstract quality and by giving examples you believe best illustrate it.

3. Explore the question of what makes some art live for all time and other art disappear. That is, what makes a "timeless" work of art? Select a particular painting as an example and explain, in as much detail as possible, why you believe as you do.

4. Define *art* (an admittedly abstract term but one that people never tire of wrestling with), and explain what you think is gained by a culture's interest in and support of art and what you think would be lost without it. As an alternative, argue that nothing is gained by a culture's art and that little or nothing would be lost without it. Make sure you explain why you feel as you do on this subject.

5. Write a response to Norman Cousins's statement that "the danger is not so much that man will be controlled by the computer as that he may imitate it" (paragraph 2 of "The Poet and the Computer"). Agree or disagree with Cousins, stating why and giving examples to support your position.

6. In paragraph 13 of "The Poet and the Computer," Norman Cousins writes: "It might be fruitful to effect some sort of junction between the computer technologist and the poet." Support or argue against that statement by explaining whether you think such a junction is possible or even desirable and, if so, how it might be effected.

7. Expand on either or both of these statements from Harold M. Williams's "Don't Ignore the Arts": "The arts define what is meant by *civilization*" (paragraph 1) and "The arts reaffirm humanity" (paragraph 3).

Research Topics

1. Taking into consideration Diana Jean Schemo's "Between the Art and the Artist Lies the Shadow" and the revelations about the private lives of people she mentions or an artist you know of, do your own research, and then argue your position on the connection between the artist's public life and private behavior. As an alternative, do the same thing for any public figure such as a sports star or a performer, who has committed or been accused of an immoral act. Consider whether evidence of immorality affects or alters in any way the quality of a person's work.

2. In recent years, some people have been highly critical of what they see as obscenity or immorality in contemporary art. The works of Robert Mapplethorpe, for instance, were the object of such widespread, heated public debate that the National Endowment for the Arts was threatened with funding cuts because of similar projects it had supported with grants. Research the issue of censorship in the arts, and write an opinion paper on the subject. Consider: Does society have a moral obligation to limit what people can say, do, or use in their art, or do First Amendment rights extend to any subject or medium an artist wants to use?

3. Robert Hughes in "Behold the Stone Age" offers his theory about the nature and purpose of prehistoric art based on an interpretation of cave drawings recently discovered in France. Such discoveries of prehistoric cave drawings that are fairly sophisticated in technique and meaning have led some art historians to suggest that art did not necessarily develop progressively, as has been commonly believed. Research this topic by reading about some of the prehistoric cave drawings that have been discovered and the theories of art historians about their importance. Then weigh the evidence and arrive at your own opinion about the nature and purpose of prehistoric art or its place in the historical development of art.

4. Harold M. Williams states in "Don't Ignore the Arts" that "a growing body of evidence from the classroom indicates that strengths gained in the study of art carry over into other subject areas" (paragraph 19). Research the role of the arts in strengthening students' abilities in other subject areas. You may want to begin by locating the studies Williams cites in his essay and then continuing your search to find more recent studies.

CHAPTER 9

MUSIC, FILM, AND MEDIA STUDIES

The essays in this chapter cover a fairly wide spectrum of topics that are nonetheless closely related. All are concerned with controversial aspects of popular culture that are in some ways essentially timeless but also absolutely contemporary. The readings do not and cannot cover every aspect of music, film, and media studies, but they raise some of the issues frequently addressed in the discussions of popular music, Hollywood films, and other media. They provide plenty of subjects for you to consider in classroom discussion and in your own writing. Note that, although the writers represented in this chapter touch on the subjects of television and advertising, those facets of popular culture are so pervasive in our society that each also has a separate chapter devoted to it following this one.

Music has been an integral part of humans' lives from their earliest existence. Song and instrumental music have spoken to, soothed, excited, and otherwise influenced humans of virtually all cultures and time periods in a seemingly endless variety of styles, subject matter, and methods of delivery. Each new musician, composer, or singer hopes to create a style uniquely his or her own, often acknowledging the influence of a previous form or artist. Sometimes a wholly new form of musical expression is created, from which generations of musicians and music lovers in turn take their inspiration.

The subject of contemporary music, though, gives rise to sometimes-heated debate, especially when rock and roll or alternative music is discussed. Isabelle Leymarie, who wrote "Rock 'n' Revolt" about a decade ago, addresses an issue that is still hotly discussed: the connection between rock and roll music and actual violence. Some people are firmly convinced that certain lyrics of both mainstream and alternative music actually cause violence by promoting and glorifying it. Others argue just as vehemently that such music simply reflects popular culture, rather than influencing it. Following Leymarie's essay, Leonard Pitts Jr. expresses his views on what he sees as a decline in standards in contemporary music since the days when Elvis Presley shocked parents across the nation with his gyrating hips. Indeed, in "The Lessons of Presley's Hips," Pitts asserts that "pop culture fell into the toilet sometime in the last generation." In his short commentary, written for his regular newspaper column, Pitts minces no words in stating his opinion of the current pop music scene. As you read about the kinds of music that Leymarie cites as having been banned or stigmatized and the examples that Pitts gives, think about the music you like. Have you ever been criticized for the kinds of music you like (or perhaps perform)? Are you critical of certain kinds of music yourself? Where do you stand on the issue of the connection between rock lyrics and violent behavior? Do you believe that pop musicians have no standards of decency?

By its very nature, popular culture reflects the interests and tastes of large segments of the population. Makers of Hollywood films, contemporary music, and other products of the entertainment industry hope to tap into or even to create trends that will have widespread appeal and thus result in huge profits. Because of its high visibility, ready availability, and ease of access to all age groups, the entertainment industry has always been closely scrutinized and subject to attack by its critics. Popular Hollywood films are particularly prime targets for both criticism and praise. Hollywood watchdogs and film critics pay attention not only to the craft of film production but also to the content of films. The current ratings system evolved in response to alarm at the exposure of young viewers to graphic sex and violence, sometimes unwittingly, before such guidelines were in place. In recent years, many people have been sharply critical of the entire entertainment industry, especially Hollywood films, for what they see as irresponsible depiction of shocking images, excessive violence, and unnecessarily graphic sex. Defenders have been just as heated in their responses.

Strongly critical of one aspect of Hollywood, Michael Medved, in "Hollywood Poison Factory," argues that many of the movies produced when he wrote the article in the early 1990s posed a threat to mainstream American values. His fairly conservative viewpoint may differ sharply from your own, or you may find yourself agreeing with him. As you read Medved's observations, think about the movies you have seen recently. Do they contain scenes of graphic sex and violence? Do they contain foul and abusive language? If so, do such things bother you as they do Medved? Louise Bernikow is also critical of a certain type of Hollywood film as well as the fairy tales the films are based on. Her essay, "Cinderella: Saturday Afternoon at the Movies," is a feminist analysis of a specific fairy tale and the Disney movie version that she remembers from her childhood. The essay is a classic example of the kind of critique of popular culture that many writers were making during the 1970s and 1980s. Although the film she refers to was produced years ago, it is still in circulation, and the fairy tale she recalls is very likely familiar to you as well.

Peter H. Gibbon's "The End of Admiration: The Media and the Loss of Heroes" switches focus slightly to the subject of the role that journalists play in building or destroying the reputations of public figures. He suggests that journalists, by encouraging cynicism and celebrity worship, discourage hero worship and idealism. He believes that, with the media's central bias toward bad news, journalists have made it difficult if not impossible for Americans to have heroes. Consider his words carefully as you read his essay. Is he on target with his critique, or does he overgeneralize or ignore positive examples to prove his point? Can you supply examples to either support or refute his argument?

The final readings in this chapter focus on one particular aspect of popular culture, media violence and its influence on people, especially young people. First is an excerpt from a book by one of the most well-known contributors in the debate over the role media violence plays in forming children's characters and values. Sissela Bok's "Aggression: The Impact of Media Violence" discusses a topic that is often quite volatile. Finally, "Tough Talk on Entertainment," a *Time* magazine forum on the subject of the entertainment industry, presents divergent voices on the issue of what to do about vulgarity and violence in movies and other forms of popular culture. Consider your own position on this controversial issue as you read the differing perspectives of these representative voices.

ROCK 'N' REVOLT

Isabelle Leymarie

Isabelle Leymarie is a Franco-American jazz pianist, dancer, and musicologist. She holds a Ph.D. from Columbia University in ethnomusicology. Formerly an assistant professor of African-American Studies at Yale University, she currently resides in Paris. Her study, "Salsa and Migration," appeared in an anthology of writing on Puerto Rico entitled The Commuter Nation *(1992). She has written several books, including* La Salsa et le Latin Jazz *(1993) and* Musiques Caraïbes *(Caribbean Music) (1996). This essay first appeared in the February 1993 issue of* UNESCO Courier.

Rock, a musical and social phenomenon of unprecedented scope and intensity, raises in acute form the question of the relationship between music and violence. Its history has been fraught with violence. Jim Morrison, leader of The Doors, apostle of sex, alcohol, and LSD, died young, of a heart attack in his bathtub in Paris. Stars Jimi Hendrix and Janis Joplin both died of drug overdoses. Acid rock has become synonymous with punks and English football riots. The fans of Metallica and Guns n' Roses have burned cars, and during a recent concert in Montreal they wrecked a stadium and injured twelve people. The Sex Pistols proclaimed in their song "Anarchy in the UK:" "I wanna destroy passers-by, for I wanna be anarchy." John Phillips, a member of The Mamas and The Papas, was reported by musicologist David Tame as claiming that any rock group can whip a crowd into a hysterical frenzy by carefully controlling a sequence of rhythms. In 1967 he went ahead and did just that in Phoenix. When Hell's Angels roughed up spectators during a Rolling Stones concert in California, rocker Mick Jagger remarked that "Something like this happens every time I play that song."

Although physically less conspicuous, violence is also expressed in the lyrics of urban music such as rap (a recent hit by star rapper Ice-T is entitled "Cop Killer") and free jazz ("We are not angry young men, we are enraged!" proclaimed saxophonist Archie Shepp in the late 1960s). Here, violence is palpable in lyrics, song titles, public statements by musicians, and in the music itself: the mega-volumes, "fuzz" effects, and distortions of rock, the hammer beats of rap, the shrieking saxophones and cascading notes of jazz, and the amplified bass of reggae. Violence is also associated with other types of music. In Stanley Kubrick's film *A Clockwork Orange,* the hero, Alex, driven crazy by the sounds of Beethoven, jumps out of a window. In Cuba during the 1920s and 1930s, concerts by rival bands playing the popular music known as *son* degenerated into brawls which had to be broken up by the police.

Violence, in more controlled forms, is present in many musical traditions, old and new: in the wailing of women in the funeral lamentations of Macedonia; in certain Senegalese songs whose lyrics pour out a stream of bitter invective against new wives brought into a household; in the drumbeats of African *griot* storytellers which once stimulated the ardor of warriors and today perform a similar role for the participants in traditional wrestling matches. It is found in martial music, in hunting calls, and in filmed thrillers where it plays a crucial role in setting the mood.

4   Violence is also present in classical music such as Handel's "Saul," Beethoven's *Eroica Symphony,* in operas generally, such as those of Verdi, who once said that he sought to express "passions above all else" and almost all of whose heroines die tragic deaths, in Mahler's *Fourth Symphony,* in Berlioz's *Symphonie Fantastique,* with its dramatic *Dies irae,* and in Stravinsky's *The Rite of Spring,* in which a virgin, sacrificed to the gods, dances herself to death (a riot broke out during the first performance). One could continue the list indefinitely.

An Extraordinary Power

Is it possible, asks musicologist Gilbert Rouget in his book on music and trance, that music may be endowed with a magical power capable of whipping people into the state of madness which the ancient Greeks called *mania?* Or does it have no objective reality? Rouget cites Timotheus of Miletus, who lived in the fourth century B.C. and once said that music "was capable of tempting Alexander away from a banquet to take up arms, and then of luring him back again to his guests with a lilting harmony." Rouget also quotes Boethius, who claimed that the Dorian mode inspired virtue, whereas the Phrygian mode aroused passion and violence, and refers to Aristotle's theory of the ethos of modes, which was similar to that of Boethius. He concludes that music can induce a trance in some cases and calm in others, and that it "derives its power from its integration into a given set of representations."

It is true that in order to grasp the symbolism in a particular type of music it is essential to be familiar with the set of representations into which it is integrated and the context in which it is performed. In the West, for example, the major modes evoke elation and rejoicing and the minor modes inspire melancholy, while in the East other modes such as Arab *maqam* and Indian *ragas* evoke totally different emotional moods. Similarly, drums and trumpets are regarded as martial instruments and flutes are associated with pastoral. All this is bound up with mental associations that are to a large extent culturally determined.

Leibniz spoke of the "anxiety-causing effect" of dissonance, and yet today dissonances, which have become commonplace in contemporary music, have lost much of their disquieting character (even Chopin's mazurkas, when first performed, were criticized for their "dissonance"). Verdi's use of double basses to introduce the final scene of *Othello,* Berlioz's use of percussion instruments in the *Symphonie Fantastique,* and Alfred Hitchcock's use of violins to heighten dramatic tension, are all illustrations of the way in which musical choices are both personal and culturally determined.

8   And yet music, when considered as a group of organized sounds and hence as a purely acoustic phenomenon, is also known to produce certain physiological and psychological effects which have been scientifically documented. Certain rhythms and sound frequencies, for example, can accelerate or slow down the human metabolic rate and even induce hypnosis. John Diamond, a specialist in behavioral physiology, has shown how the relative strength of certain muscles, a function which is easily measurable, varies according to the type of music to which people are listening. Animals and plants are also known to react physically to music. According to studies carried out in India, Russia, and the United States, plants seem to hate "heavy metal" rock music and twist themselves as far away as possible from the offending loudspeaker, while they adore classical violin and will grow even more lushly to the sounds of disco.

Noise engenders violence; it can even drive people to suicide. Some artificial noises, especially those which emanate from continuous-frequency engines, have been found to have a pathological effect on the body's cellular structure, and can sometimes cause cancer, while natural sounds, like those of waves, the warbling of birds, and certain types of classical or African music, can create a sense of well-being and even a healing effect by harmonizing with our biorhythms.

In recent years, the practice of music therapy has enjoyed considerable popularity. Members of the Research Group in Pediatric Anaesthesiology at the Hospital

for Sick Children in Paris and doctors in many American hospitals have used carefully selected types of music to reduce their patients' dependency on tranquillizers.
In *The Burmese Harp* (1956), a fine film by the Japanese director Kon Ichikawa, a
soldier-musician saps his comrades' will to fight whenever he plays and sings.

Study of the relationship between music and violence also raises the question of
the political aspect of music. In many parts of the world, musicians such as the bards
of Nepal, the *griots* or the musicians of Ethiopia are perceived as pariahs or as socially inferior, and are believed to lead dissolute lives and be addicted to drugs and
alcohol. Music has often been used as an instrument of domination. In some African
societies, *mirliton* reed pipes and other instruments provide a musical accompani-
ment during the ritual parading of masks, which women and children must not see
and which perpetuate male dominance.

12   The French writer Jacques Attali has observed that in Western societies the upper classes have always encouraged artistic creation, but only in order to maintain
the established order and legitimize their own authority. In the 1950s, the Dominican
dictator Rafael Trujillo y Molina encouraged the practice of the *merengue,* a dance
closely related to the samba, but gave orders that the musicians should sing his
praises and exiled those who opposed him. In many countries, music has become a
form of propaganda or been appropriated by the Church, and judgments about music
have been an endorsement of manipulation and intolerance.

Authoritarian colonial regimes arbitrarily associated drums with violence and
debauchery, and long banned black music. The "New Age" writer Corinne Hélène
claims that jazz and juvenile delinquency go hand in hand. But this baseless claim is
fraught with prejudice, for how can the beautiful and expressive phrasing of a Sarah
Vaughan or an Ella Fitzgerald be associated with juvenile delinquency? Why should
jazz as a whole be connected with this social problem when most young jazz musicians are now graduates of music conservatories and universities and the overwhelming majority of jazz fans are intellectuals? How indeed, when music, for many
deprived black and Hispanic adolescents of America's urban ghettos, far from leading to delinquency, is often a lifeline?

In the United States, moral-majority pressure groups have stigmatized some rock
records as "obscene," in the hope of getting them withdrawn from the market, but
they also tried to ban the Robert Mapplethorpe photo exhibition and other artistic
events which did not correspond with their ideals. On the other hand, some kinds of
music such as "Muzak," which supposedly increase consumer sales and induce
people in restaurants to eat more but are actually a form of audio-brainwashing and
noise pollution, are broadcast all day long in shopping centres and other public
areas.

Jacques Attali has also remarked that "show business, the star system, and the
hit parade are signs of deep-rooted institutional and cultural colonization." In this
context music, through a sometimes violent protest against official art and the mechanization of society, becomes a means of fighting authority. "Music exists,"
adds Jacques Attali, "to help us hear the sound of change. It forces us to invent new

categories, to come up with a new momentum capable of rejuvenating a view of society that has become ossified, trapped, moribund." This is partly true of rock and its rebellious anti-establishment stance, and of jazz, rap, and reggae—all musical forms which proclaim their black identity and have rejected old models along with the hypocrisy and inhumanity of materialism. In certain ritualized settings, notably during festivals, subversive songs are often used to express grievances against the establishment.

A Yearning for Harmony

16 Does music engender violence or does it express violence? And if it does express violence, does it, by sublimating violent impulses and dissipating tensions, play a cathartic role and "soothe the savage breast"? Music, for Attali, is the "audible tape of society's vibrations and signs." It is undeniably deeply rooted in the collective psychology: rock, rap, free jazz, and reggae all express the violence of the cultures which have bred them. But people and their environment are inseparable: the pent-up violence in the individual affects society and vice versa. While music reflects the collective *gestalt* of a society, its particular form of expression also reflects the emotions of the musician.

In China, Egypt, India, and ancient Greece, music was believed to possess a certain ethical value and the power to uplift or debase the soul. In ancient China, the imperial government existed in harmony with the twelve celestial tones, and during the Confucian Chin dynasty, certain "virtuous" songs and musical instruments were reputed to temper the harshness of the regime. Classical music is also imbued with spirituality: Mozart's Don Giovanni brings down divine vengeance upon himself by assassinating a nobleman and burns in hell for it. Liszt aspired to compose inspirational works, and although Wagner's *Tetralogy* (the four-opera *Ring* cycle) expresses both the fall of humanity cut adrift from the gods and the distress of the artist faced with the world's misfortunes, Wagner had a deeply moral view of art.

The French sociologist Jean Duvignaud has written that art expresses "nostalgia for a lost form of communication in the shape of a forbidden dream that is continually revived by the irrepressible desire of the human emotional impulse." He goes on to say that a successful work of art "rebuilds behind the self a unity which pieces together the shards of a divided humanity." Now that idealism has been demolished and the philosophy of music has become a thing of the past, while the media (which tend to put the visual image before the musical message) bombard us with vulgar and iconoclastic music, it is more than ever incumbent on musicians and artists in general to adopt an ethical position. The most influential creators of the twentieth century, notably the film-makers whose art is one of our era's most powerful forms of expression—artists such as Kurosawa, Ozu, and Satyajit Ray—have been passionate humanists.

Musical eurhythmics presupposes both inner and outer harmony, peace with oneself and with the universe. Violence, in its latent form, is an intrinsic part of human nature and of the universe generally. But when violence is unleashed and expressed, often in a paroxysm, in music or other art forms, it is a symptom either of social unrest or of inner imbalance or torment, emotional deprivation, and arrested development.

20   And just as the wind can rise from a gentle breeze to a raging hurricane, so music can enchant or destroy us. It is for musicians to create works which enrich life, which contribute to the harmony of humanity, without compromising the quality of their art (some forms of therapeutic music, such as "New Age" music, do not really have any aesthetic value).

However, when music achieves perfection, it allows us to catch a glimpse of the divine; it becomes, according to a Buddhist belief, the most refined art, the path to enlightenment. According to the Taoist sage, Zhuangzi, "Music allows man to remain pure, simple, sincere, and in this way to rediscover his primitive emotions." (A few centuries later, Wagner would also use music to explore primitive forms of expression.) The great violinist Yehudi Menuhin once observed that "music creates order out of chaos." Nietzsche's humorous conclusion was that "Without music, life would be a mistake."

Personal Response

Describe your favorite kind of music and why it appeals to you. Are you ever criticized for listening to it? What characteristic of this music do you think produces negative or even hostile reactions in some people?

Questions for Class or Small-Group Discussion

1. How would you answer Leymarie's question, "Does music engender violence or does it express violence" (paragraph 16)? Discuss whether you think music creates violent behavior or simply reflects the culture that produces it.

2. Leymarie gives examples of the ways in which certain mental associations with music "are to a large extent culturally determined" (paragraphs 6 and 7). Can you give other examples of the point she makes in this section of her essay?

3. Give examples of musicians or musical groups who have made political statements through their music (paragraphs 11–15), especially those who use music as "a means of fighting authority" (paragraph 15). Discuss the effect you see from their political statements.

4. Leymarie discusses her subject objectively for the most part, but she offers her own opinions from time to time, as for instance, when she says that "New Age" music does "not really have any aesthetic value." Find passages in which she makes her own subjective comments, and discuss whether you agree with her opinions or not.

THE LESSONS OF PRESLEY'S HIPS

Leonard Pitts Jr.

Leonard Pitts Jr. has written a twice-weekly column on pop culture, social issues, and family life for the Miami Herald *since 1994 and KRT News Service since 1995 and is now syndicated by Tribune*

Media Services. He has also freelanced for national magazines and written and produced numerous radio programs. A 1992 Pulitzer Prize finalist, he has won a number of awards, including the 2001 American Society of Newspaper Editors Awards for distinguished writing. He is author of the book Becoming Dad: Black Men and the Journey to Fatherhood *(1999). This article appeared in syndication in August 2000.*

Last week, my 15-year-old son asked me to explain Elvis Presley's hips.

What was the big deal, he asked. Why was there such an outcry, such public anger, over this guy's gyrating pelvis?

I didn't have to reach too far for an answer. I explained how each rhythmic thrust of this white country boy's hips came like a dagger to the heart of American hypocrisy on the dangerous subjects of sex and race. Told how he liberated a nation in spite of itself, got it all shook up so that nearly half a century later, he's a pop culture demigod while the people who decried his music seem short-sighted, censorious—quaint.

4   Easy question. Except, as I thought about it later, it occurred to me that while the answer I'd given was correct, it was also incomplete. Because if it's true that Elvis' hips represent a victory by the forces of progress, amity and good rockin' tonight, it's also perversely true that we've been hobbled by that victory ever since.

More to the point, that victory is part of the reason pop culture fell into the toilet sometime in the last generation. And that instead of climbing out, it's doing the backstroke. Indeed, that it swims proudly in matters excretory, masturbatory, penile, puerile, bigoted and foul. From the potty-mouthed tykes of "South Park" to the hateful gay-bashing of rapper Eminem to the lewd butt-worshipping of the music video channel, it's become nearly impossible to absorb popular culture without also absorbing slop that would embarrass a reasonably respectable pig.

Worse, you can't even complain about it without worrying that people will think you some priggish, humorless prude. Which is why, over the years, the complaining has nearly stopped. Granted, when a given piece of work offends a particular constituency—if an Eminem insults gays, let's say—you can expect representatives of that group to register a complaint. But a general sense of outrage? No. That's a capacity we seem to have lost.

It's a loss that traces directly to the fight over the hips of Elvis. Not that they were the only battleground. The same war was waged, after all, over Little Richard's mascara, the Beatles' hair, Lenny Bruce's language, the Smothers Brothers' politics. Now, like Elvis, all those people stand vindicated, acclaimed as performers who changed the architecture of art and hurried the Zeitgeist along. And history's judgment of the people who fought them has been harsh. They seem, in hindsight, stuffy, silly, self-righteous and out of touch.

8   It's a verdict that unavoidably colors any attempt to offer honest criticism of the state of pop culture today. We've learned to fear history's hindsight—this present raunch, might one day be judged genius—so instead of complaining, we nod and smile at stuff we hate. Like Bill Clinton, we obsess over legacy.

Take, for example, the recent Entertainment Weekly cover story about the sewer pop culture has become. Writer Lisa Schwarzbaum seemed ill at ease with her own premise, worried that, in pronouncing certain aspects of the culture offensive, she might damage her reputation as an arbiter of edgy entertainment. Writing the piece "makes me sound like Bill Bennett with a wedgie," she fretted.

As a former full-time critic of pop music, I understand the apprehension. I also understand that something's wrong when people are too fearful of history's judgment to voice honest misgivings.

Understand: The issue is not freedom of speech. Pop culture has an absolute constitutional right to swim in the toilet and I'm opposed to ham-handed government attempts to take that right away. We ought to understand by now that taste is, by definition, subjective; I may draw the line in a different place than you.

TACTLESS

12   But here's the question: What happens when no one has the guts to draw the line anywhere?

We're finding the answer now and it's not pretty. We've become a people too cool to take offense, too jaded for questions of decency and so filled with attitude that we disconnect from our own feelings, our own barometers of right and wrong. We took the wrong lessons from Elvis' hips.

And we're getting the pop culture we deserve.

Personal Response

What do you think of Pitts's use of the term *sewer* to describe popular culture today?

Questions for Class or Small-Group Discussion

1. In what way did "Elvis's hips represent a victory," according to Pitts (paragraph 2)? What do you understand Pitts to mean when he says, "[T]hat victory is part of the reason pop culture fell into the toilet some time in the last generation" (paragraph 3)? Discuss your response to that remark. Can you think of other examples that would illustrate his point?

2. To what extent to you agree with Pitts's opinion that "we seem to have lost" the capacity to be outraged by anything in popular music today (paragraph 4)? Do you agree that we as a culture are "too cool to take offense, too jaded for questions of decency, ... [too] disconnect[ed] from our own feelings ... of right and wrong" (paragraph 10)?

3. Pitts says in paragraphs 8 and 9: "Understand: The issue is not freedom of speech. ... But here's the question: What happens when no one has the guts to draw the line anywhere?" Discuss your understanding of his point here and the extent to which you agree with him.

HOLLYWOOD POISON FACTORY

Michael Medved

Michael Medved is a film critic, best-selling author and nationally syndicated radio talk show host, who served for twelve years as cohost of Sneak Previews, *a weekly PBS program. He is author of eight nonfiction books, including* The Shadow Presidents: The Secret Histories of the Chief Executives and their Top Aides *(1979),* Hospital: The Hidden Lives of a Medical Center Staff *(1983), and* Saving Childhood: Protecting Our Children from the National Assault on Innocence *(with Diane Medved, 1998). This article, which appeared first in the November 1992 issue of* Imprimis, *was based on a series of lectures Medved gave at Hillsdale College in Michigan. The lectures led to a contract for his book* Hollywood vs. America: Popular Culture and the War on Traditional Values *(1992). Medved's Web site is located at <http://www. michaelmedved.com>.*

America's long-running romance with Hollywood is over. For millions of people, the entertainment industry no longer represents a source of enchantment, of magical fantasy, of uplift, or even of harmless diversion. Popular culture is viewed now as an implacable enemy, a threat to their basic values and a menace to the raising of their children. The Hollywood dream factory has become the poison factory.

This disenchantment is reflected in poll after poll. An Associated Press Media General poll released in 1990 showed that 80 percent of Americans objected to the amount of foul language in motion pictures; 82 percent objected to the amount of violence, 72 percent objected to the amount of explicit sexuality, and by a ratio of three to one they felt that movies today are worse than ever.

Hollywood no longer reflects—or even respects—the values that most Americans cherish.

4   Take a look, for example, at the most recent Oscars. Five very fine actors were nominated for best actor of the year. Three of them portrayed murderous psychos: Robert DeNiro in *Cape Fear,* Warren Beatty in *Bugsy,* and Anthony Hopkins in *The Silence of the Lambs* (this last a delightful family film about two serial killers–one eats and the other skins his victims). A fourth actor, Robin Williams, was nominated for playing a delusional homeless psycho in *The Fisher King.* The most wholesome character was Nick Nolte's, a good old-fashioned manic-depressive-suicidal neurotic in *The Prince of Tides.*

These are all good actors, delivering splendid performances, compelling and technically accomplished. But isn't it sad when all this artistry is lavished on films that are so empty, so barren, so unfulfilling? Isn't it sad when at the Academy Awards—the annual event that celebrates the highest achievement of which the film industry is capable—the best we can come up with is movies that are so floridly, strangely whacked out?

I repeat: The fundamental problem with Hollywood has nothing at all to do with the brilliance of the performers, or the camera work, or the editing. In many ways, these things are better than ever before. Modern films are technically brilliant, but they are morally and spiritually empty.

The Messages

What are the messages in today's films? For a number of years I have been writing about Hollywood's antireligious bias, but I must point out that this hostility has never been quite as intense as in the last few years. The 1991 season boasted one religion-bashing movie after another in which Hollywood was able to demonstrate that it was an equal-opportunity offender.

8   For Protestants there was *At Play in the Fields of the Lord*, a lavish $35 million rain forest spectacle about natives and their wholesome primitive ways and the sick, disgusting missionaries who try to ruin their lives. And then for Catholics there was *The Pope Must Die*, which was re-released as *The Pope Must Diet*. It didn't work either way. It features scenes of the Holy Father flirting with harlot nuns and hiding in a closet pigging out on communion wafers. For Jews there was *Naked Tango*, written and directed by the brother of the screenwriter for *The Last Temptation of Christ*. This particular epic featured religious Jews operating a brutal bordello right next door to a synagogue and forcing women into white slavery.

And then most amazingly there was *Cape Fear*, which was nominated for a number of the most prestigious Academy Awards. It wasn't an original concept. *Cape Fear* was a remake of a 1962 movie in which Robert Mitchum plays a released convict intent on revenge who tracks down his old defense attorney. Gregory Peck portrays the defense attorney, a strong, stalwart, and upright man who defends his family against this crazed killer. In the remake, by *Last Temptation* director Martin Scorsese, there is a new twist: The released convict is not just an ordinary maniac, but a "Killer Christian from Hell." To prevent anyone from missing the point, his muscular back has a gigantic cross tattooed on it, and he has biblical verses tattooed on both arms.

When he is about to rape the attorney's wife, played by Jessica Lange, he says, "Are you ready to be born again? After just one hour with me, you'll be talking in tongues." He carries a Bible with him in scenes in which he is persecuting his family, and he tells people that he is a member of a Pentecostal church.

The most surprising aspect of this utterly insulting characterization is that it drew so little protest. Imagine that DeNiro's character had been portrayed as a gay rights activist. Homosexual groups would have howled in protest, condemning this caricature as an example of bigotry. But we are so accustomed to Hollywood's insulting stereotypes of religious believers that no one even seems to notice the hatred behind them.

12   The entertainment industry further demonstrates its hostility to organized religion by eliminating faith and ritual as a factor in the lives of nearly all the characters it creates. Forty to 50 percent of all Americans go to church or synagogue every week. When was the last time you saw anybody in a motion picture going to church, unless that person was some kind of crook, or a mental case, or a flagrant hypocrite?

Hollywood even removes religious elements from situations in which they clearly belong. The summer of 1991 offered a spate of medical melodramas like *Regarding Henry, Dying Young*, and *The Doctor*. Did you notice that all these characters go into the operating room without once invoking the name of God, or whispering one little prayer, or asking for clergy? I wrote a nonfiction book about hospital life once, and I guarantee that just as there are no atheists in foxholes, there are no atheists in operating rooms—only in Hollywood.

Religion isn't Hollywood's only target; the traditional family has also received surprisingly harsh treatment from today's movie moguls. Look again at *Cape Fear*. The remake didn't only change the killer; it also changed the hero, and this brings me to the second message that Hollywood regularly broadcasts. As I mentioned, the original character Gregory Peck plays is a decent and honorable man. In the remake, Nick Nolte's character is, not to put too fine a point on it, a sleazeball. He is repeatedly unfaithful to his wife; when his wife dares to question that practice, he hits her. He tries to beat up his daughter on one occasion because she is smoking marijuana. He is not a likable person. That a happily married, family defending hero—the kind of person that people can identify with—is transformed into a sadistic, cheating, bitter man, says volumes about the direction of American movies.

Did you ever notice how few movies there are about happily married people? There are very few movies about married people at all, but those that are made tend to portray marriage as a disaster, as a dangerous situation, as a battleground—with a long series of murderous marriage movies.

16   There was *Sleeping with the Enemy*, in which Patrick Bergin beats up Julia Roberts so mercilessly that she has to run away. When he comes after her, she eventually kills him. There was also *Mortal Thoughts*, in which Bruce Willis beats up *his* wife and he is killed by his wife's best friend. In *Thelma and Louise*, there is another horrible, brutal, and insensitive husband to run away from. In *A Kiss Before Dying*, Matt Dillon persuades twin sisters to marry him. He kills the first one and then tries to kill the second, but she gets to him first.

In *She-Devil*, Roseanne Barr torments her cheating husband Ed Begley Jr., and in *Total Recall*, Sharon Stone pretends to be married to Arnold Schwarzenegger and tries to kill him. When he gets the upper hand, she objects, "But you can't hurt me! I'm your wife." Arnold shoots her through the forehead and says, "Consider that a divorce." And then there was a more recent film, *Deceived*, starring Goldie Hawn. The advertisement for the movie says, "She thought her life was perfect," and, of course, her model husband turns out to be a murderous monster. *Deceived* is an appropriate title, because we all have been deceived by Hollywood's portrayal of marriage. It even applies to television. The *New York Times* reports that in the past TV season there were seven different pregnancies. What did six of the seven pregnancies have in common? They were out of wedlock. The message is that marriage is outmoded, it is dangerous, oppressive, unhealthy.

But is it true? Recently, I made an interesting discovery. The conventional wisdom is that the divorce rate in America stands at 50 percent. This figure is used repeatedly in the media. But the 1990 U.S. Census Bureau has a category listing the number of people who have ever been married and who have ever been divorced. Less than 20 percent have been divorced! The evidence is overwhelming that the idea of a 50 percent divorce rate is more than a slight overstatement; it is a destructive and misleading myth.

Yet for years Hollywood has been selling divorce. Remember *The Last Married Couple in America,* starring the late Natalie Wood? That may be a Hollywood prophecy, but it is not the reality of the American heartland. In this matter, as in so many others, by overstating the negative, the film industry leads viewers to feel terrified and/or insecure, and their behavior is adversely affected. I know many people who say, "I'm reluctant to get married because I know there's a 50 percent chance I'm going to get divorced." Wouldn't it make a difference if they knew there was an 80 percent chance of staying together?

Rekindling Our Love Affair with Hollywood

20 There are many indications that the entertainment industry may be eager to reconnect with the grass roots—and to entertain an expanded notion of its own obligations to the public. The industry has, in some areas, behaved responsibly. In the past five years it changed its message about drugs. No longer is it making movies in which marijuana, cocaine, and other drugs are glamorized. Hollywood made a decision. Was it self-censorship? You bet. Was it responsible? Yes.

We can challenge the industry to adopt a more wholesome outlook, to send more constructive messages. We can clamor for movies that don't portray marriage as a living hell, that recognize the spiritual side of man's nature, that glorify the blessings in life we enjoy as Americans and the people who make sacrifices to ensure that others will be able to enjoy them.

The box-office crisis put Hollywood in a receptive mood. Already two film corporations have committed to a schedule of family movies for a very simple reason: They are wildly successful. Only 2 percent of movies released in 1991 were G-rated—just fourteen titles—but at least eight of these fourteen proved to be unequivocally profitable. (By comparison, of more than 600 other titles, *at most* 20 percent earned back their investment.) Look at *Beauty and the Beast,* my choice for Best Movie of 1991. It was a stunning financial success. We need many more pictures like this, and not just animated features geared for younger audiences. Shouldn't it be possible to create movies with adult themes but without foul language, graphic sex, or cinematic brutality? During Hollywood's golden age, industry leaders understood that there was nothing inherently *mature* about these unsettling elements.

People tell me sometimes, "Boy, the way you talk, it sounds as though you really hate movies." The fact is that I don't. I'm a film critic because I *love* movies. And I want to tell you something: All of the people who are trying to make a difference in this business love movies and they love the industry, despite all its faults. They love what it has done in the past, and they love its potential for the future. They believe that Hollywood can be the dream factory again.

24 When I go to a screening, sit in a theater seat, and the lights go down, there's a little something inside me that hopes against all rational expectation that what I'm going to see on the screen is going to delight me, enchant me, and entice me, like the best movies do. I began by declaring that America's long-running romance with Hollywood is over. It is a romance, however, that can be rekindled, if this appalling,

amazing industry can once again create movies that are worthy of love and that merit the ardent affection of its audience.

Personal Response

Respond to Medved's question, "Shouldn't it be possible to create movies with adult themes but without foul language, graphic sex, or cinematic brutality" (paragraph 22)? Is this statement a possible goal? Would you prefer movies to be less brutal, foul, and sexually graphic, or do those things not bother you?

Questions for Class or Small-Group Discussion

1. Discuss the extent to which you think that Medved is unfair or generalizing too much on the basis of just a few films. Can you give examples of movies from the early 1990s that either support or refute his allegation? What about films today? Does Medved's critique apply to them as well?

2. Medved refers several times to the film *Cape Fear.* If you have seen that film, discuss whether you agree with Medved's analysis of it. If you have not seen it, rent the videotape and watch it, perhaps with some of your classmates. Then prepare your own response to the film, keeping in mind Medved's comments. As an alternative, do the same for any of the other films that Medved refers to or for the most recent film that you have seen.

3. What is your response to Medved's allegation that Hollywood films reveal antireligion and antifamily biases? Can you supply examples of recent films that disprove his claim? Can you give examples of films that support his assertion? Has any film accurately portrayed your own family? Were you surprised at Medved's comments about the divorce rate (paragraph 18)?

4. What other values would you say Hollywood projects in the films it produces? Do you see a continuation or an increase of the trend toward more family entertainment, as Medved indicates in the section subtitled "Rekindling Our Love Affair with Hollywood"?

5. What do you think Medved has in mind when he longs for a return to Hollywood as "a dream factory"? Do you agree with Medved on this point, that films should be a source of "enchantment, of magical fantasy, of uplift" (paragraph 1)? Can you think of any films that might fit that ideal?

CINDERELLA: SATURDAY AFTERNOON AT THE MOVIES

Louise Bernikow

Louise Bernikow's work has centered on women's culture. Her personal essays reflecting on women's psychology, women's friendships,

and the ties between women are collected in Among Women
*(1980), from which this piece is taken. Her other books include the
following:* Let's Have Lunch: Games of Sex and Power *(1981),*
Alone in America: The Search for Happiness *(1986),* The
Women in Our Lives: Cinderella, Scarlett, Virginia, and Me
(1989), The American Women's Almanac: An Inspiring and Irreverent Women's History *(1997), and* Bark if you Love Me: A
Woman-Meets-Dog Story *(2001).*

No, Cinderella, said the stepmother,
you have no clothes and cannot dance.
That's the way with stepmothers.
        (Anne Sexton, "Cinderella")

Turn and peep, turn and peep,
No blood is in the shoe,
The shoe is not too small for her,
The true bride rides with you.
        (Grimms' Cinderella*)*

I begin with a memory of movies and mother, a dark theatre and a Saturday afternoon. In a miasma of Walt Disney images, Bambi burning and Snow White asleep, the
most memorable is "Cinderella." I carry her story with me for the rest of my life. It is
a story about women alone together and they are each other's enemies. This is more
powerful as a lesson than the ball, the Prince, or the glass slipper. The echoes of "Cinderella" in other fairy tales, in myth and literature, are about how awful women are
to each other. The girl onscreen, as I squirm in my seat, needs to be saved. A man will
come and save her. Some day my Prince will come. Women will not save her; they will
thwart her. There is a magical fairy godmother who does help her, but this, for me,
has no relation to life, for the fairy is not real, and the bad women are. The magical
good fairy is a saccharine fluff.

There are two worlds in the Cinderella cartoon, one of women, one of men. The
women are close by and hostile, the men distant and glittering. Stepsisters and stepmother are three in one, a female battalion allied against Cinderella. The daughters
are just like their mother. All women are alike. Lines of connection, energy fields,
attach sisters to mother, leaving Cinderella in exile from the female community
at home.

Father is far off. On film, neither he nor the Prince has much character. Father
is her only tie, her actual blood tie, but the connection does her no good. Daddy is
King in this world; I cannot keep Daddy and King apart in my memory. My own father
was as far off, as full of authority, as surrounded by heraldry, the trumpets of fantasy,
to me, to my mother. King Daddy.

4   The Prince is rich and handsome. Rich matters more than handsome. The girl
among the cinders, dressed in rags, will escape—I am on her side, I want her to escape, get away from the cinders and the awful women—because the Prince will lift

her out. The world of the Prince is the world of the ball, music, fine clothes, and good feeling. Were everything to be right at home, were the women to be good to one another and have fun together, it would not be sufficient. The object is the ball, the Prince, the big house, the servants. Class mobility is at stake. Aspiration is being titillated.

To win the Prince, to be saved, requires being pretty. All the women care about this. Being pretty is the ticket, and because Cinderella is pretty, the stepmother and stepsisters want to keep her out of the running. There is no other enterprise. Cinderella does not turn up her nose and hide in a corner reading a book. Being pretty, getting to the ball, winning the Prince is the common ground among the women. What we have in common is what keeps us apart.

Cinderella must be lonely. Why, I wonder, doesn't she have a friend? Why doesn't she go to school? Why doesn't her father tell the awful women to stop? A hurt and lonely girl, with only a prince to provide another kind of feeling. Why doesn't she run away? Why can't the situation be changed? It is as though the house they live in is the only world, there is no other landscape. Women are always in the house, being awful to each other.

Magic. Cinderella has a fairy godmother who likes her and wants her to be happy. She gives the girl beautiful clothes. She doesn't have to instruct Cinderella or give her advice about how to waltz or how to lift her skirt or even give her directions to the palace. Only the clothes and the accoutrements—and a prohibition about coming home at midnight. A powerful woman who wants Cinderella to be pretty and successful in the social world. I know, at whatever age it is that I watch this story unfold, that the mother beside me is not the woman on the screen. Her feelings on such matters are, at best, mixed up. She is not so powerful.

8   I am stirred and confused by the contrast between bad and good women and the way it all seems to revolve around the issue of being pretty. Some women are hostile and thwarting, others enabling and powerful. The stepmother hates Cinderella's prettiness; the fairy godmother adorns it. I look sideways at my mother, trying to decide which kind of woman she is, where she stands on the business of pretty. Often, she braids my hair and settles me into polka dot, parades me before my beaming father. It is good to be pretty. Yet, onscreen, it is bad to be pretty—Cinderella is punished for it. In the enterprise of pretty, other women are your allies and your enemies. They are not disinterested. The heat around the issue of pretty, the urgency and intensity of it, is located among the women, not the men, at whom it is supposedly aimed. Luckily, we move on to the ball and the lost slipper.

This is one of the oldest and most often-told stories, varying significantly from one version to another, one country to another, one period to another. What appears on movie theatre screens or television on Saturday afternoons comes from as far away as China, as long ago as four hundred years. Each teller, each culture along the way, retained some archetypal patterns and transformed others, emphasized some parts of the story, eradicated others. Disney took his version of Cinderella from one written down by a Frenchman named Perrault in the seventeenth century. Perrault's is a "civilized" version, cleaned up, dressed up, and given several pointed "lessons" on top of the original material.

Many of the details about fashionability that we now associate with the story come from Perrault. His has the atmosphere of Coco Chanel's dressing rooms, is modern and glamorous. He concocted a froufrou, aimed at an aristocratic audience and airily decorated with things French. He named one of the sisters Charlotte and set the action in a world of full-length looking glasses and inlaid floors. He invented a couturière called Mademoiselle de Poche to create costumes for the ball, linens and ruffles, velvet suits and headdresses. Disney dropped the French touches.

Perrault's story is set in a world of women with their eyes on men. Even before the King's ball is announced, the stepmother and stepsisters are preoccupied with how they look. They are obsessed with their mirrors, straining to see what men would see. Once the ball is on the horizon, they starve themselves for days so that their shapes shall be, when laced into Mademoiselle de Poche's creations, as extremely slender as those in our own fashion magazines. The ball—and the prospects it implies—intensifies the hostility toward Cinderella. They have been envious. Now, they must keep the pretty girl out of competition. Most of the action of Perrault's story is taken up with the business of the ball.

12   Cinderella is a sniveling, self-pitying girl. Forbidden to go to the ball, she does not object but, instead, dutifully helps her stepsisters adorn themselves. She has no will, initiates no action. Then, magically, the fairy godmother appears. She comes from nowhere, summoned, we suppose, by Cinderella's wishes. Unlike the fairy godmother in other versions of the story, Perrault's and Disney's character has no connection to anything real, has no meaning, except to enable Cinderella to overcome the opposition of the women in her home, wear beautiful clothes, and get to the ball. Cinderella stammers, unable to say what she wants—for she is passive, suffering, and good, which comes across as relatively unconscious. The fairy divines Cinderella's desire and equips her with pumpkin/coach, mice/horses, rats/coachmen, lizards/footmen, clothes, and dancing shoes. She adds the famous prohibition that Cinderella return by midnight or everything will be undone.

These details of the fairy godmother's magic—the pumpkin, image of All Hallows' Eve; midnight, the witching hour; mice, rats, and lizards originated with Perrault. They are specific reminders of an actual and ancient female magic, witchcraft. Since Perrault wrote his story in the seventeenth century, it is not surprising to find echoes of this magic, which was enormously real to Perrault's audience.

Thousands had been burned at the stake for practicing witchcraft, most of them women. A witch was a woman with enormous power, a woman who might change the natural world. She was "uncivilized" and in opposition to the world of the King, the court, polite society. She had to be controlled. Perrault's story attempts to control the elements of witchcraft just as various kings' governments had, in the not too recent past, controlled what they believed to be an epidemic of witchcraft. Perrault controls female power by trivializing it. The witchcraft in this story is innocent, ridiculous, silly, and playful. It is meant to entertain children.

The prohibition that Cinderella return by midnight is also related to witchcraft. She must avoid the witching hour, with its overtones of sexual abandon. The fairy godmother acts in this capacity in a way that is familiar to mothers and daughters—she controls the girl, warns her against darkness, uses her authority to enforce restraint, prevent excess, particularly excess associated with the ball, the world of men, sexuality.

16   Cinderella's dancing shoes are glass slippers. Perrault mistranslated the fur slipper in the version that came to him, substituting *verre* for *vire* and coming up glass. No pedant came along to correct the mistake, for the glass slipper is immensely appropriate to the story in its modern form and the values it embodies. Call it dainty or fragile, the slipper is quintessentially the stereotype of femininity. I wonder how Cinderella danced in it.

The rags-to-riches moment holds people's imagination long after the details of the story have disappeared. It appeals to everyone's desire for magic, for change that comes without effort, for speedy escape from a bad place—bad feelings. We all want to go to the ball, want life to be full of good feeling and feeling good. But Cinderella's transformation points to a particular and limited kind of good feeling—from ugly to beautiful, raggedy to glamorous. The object of her transformation is not actually pleasure (she does not then walk around her house feeling better) but transportation to the ball with all the right equipment for captivating the Prince.

Transformed, Cinderella goes to the ball, which is the larger world, the kingdom ruled by kings and fathers. The stepmother has no power in that world and does not even appear. This part of the story focuses on men, who are good to Cinderella as forcefully as women have been bad to her. Perrault embellishes Cinderella's appearance in a way that would have been congenial to the French court. In fact, she seems to have gone to the French court. The story is suffused with perfume and "fashionability." The Prince is taken with Cinderella and gives her some candy—"citrons and oranges," according to the text. How French. She, forever good, shares the candy with her stepsisters, who do not, of course, know who she is.

Cinderella has a wonderful time. As readers, hearers, watchers, we have a wonderful time along with her. More than the music and the dancing, the aura of sensual pleasure, everyone's good time comes from the idea that Cinderella is a "knockout." This is exciting. Perrault's word for what happens is that the people are *étonnés*, which means stunned. Cinderella is a showstopper, so "dazzling" that "the King himself, old as he was, could not help watching her." He remarks on this to his Queen, whose reactions we are not told. Being "stunning" is being powerful. This is the way women have impact, the story tells us. This is female power in the world outside the home, in contrast to her former powerlessness, which was within the home, which was another country. This tells me why women spend so much time trying to turn themselves into knockouts—because, in Cinderella and in other stories, it *works*.

20   Presumably, Cinderella's giddiness over her own triumph at the ball makes her forget her godmother's command and almost miss her midnight deadline. Lest we lose the idea that all men adore Cinderella, Perrault adds a courtier at the end of the

story, as the search for the missing Cinderella is carried out, and has him, too, say how attractive Cinderella is. She fulfills, then, the masculine idea of what is beautiful in a woman. She is the woman men want women to be.

Cinderella flees at midnight and loses her shoe. Perrault plays this part down, but Disney has a visual festival with the glinting glass slipper on the staircase and the trumpet-accompanied quest to find its owner. Perrault's Prince sends a messenger to find the shoe's owner, which puts the action at some distance, but Disney gives us a prince in all his splendor.

Cinderella is a heroine and in the world of fairy tales what the heroine wins is marriage to the Prince. Like any classic romance, wafted by perfume and fancy clothes, the young girl is lifted from a lowly powerless situation (from loneliness and depression, too) by a powerful man. He has no character, not even a handsome face, but simply represents the things that princes represent, the power of the kingdom.

Opposition to achieving this triumph comes from the women in the house; help comes from daydream and fantasy. The only proper activity for women to engage in is primping. What is expected of them is that they wait "in the right way" to be discovered. Cinderella obeys the rules. Her reward is to be claimed by the Prince. The lesson of Cinderella in these versions is that a girl who knows and keeps her place will be rewarded with male favor.

24   Like a saint, she shows neither anger nor resentment toward the women who treated her so badly. In fact, she takes her stepsisters along to the castle, where she marries each off to a nobleman. Now everyone will be happy. Now there will be no conflict, no envy, no degradation. If each woman has a prince or nobleman, she will be content and the soft humming of satisfaction will fill the air. Women otherwise cannot be alone together.

This is the sort of story that poisoned Madame Bovary's imagination. In Flaubert's novel, a woman married to a country doctor, with aspirations for a larger life, goes to a ball where a princely character pays her some attention. The ball and the Prince, seen by Emma Bovary as possibilities for changing everyday life, haunted her uneasy sleep. The ball was over. Wait as she might for its return, for a second invitation, all she got was a false prince—a lover who did not lift her from the ordinariness of her life—and then despair.

The romance depends on aspiration. The Prince must be able to give the heroine something she cannot get for herself or from other women. He must represent a valuable and scarce commodity, for the women must believe there is only one, not enough to go around, and must set themselves to keeping other women from getting it. In "Cinderella," like other fairy tales and other romances, the world of the Prince represents both actual and psychological riches.

Perrault's Cinderella is the daughter of a gentleman, turned into a peasant within the household. She has been declassed by female interlopers, reduced to the status of servant, for she belongs to her father's class only precariously. One of the ways women exercise their power, the story tells us, is by degrading other women. Cinderella will be saved from her female-inflicted degradation first by another female, the fairy godmother, who puts her on the road to her ultimate salvation. At the end of the story, she is restored to her class position, or, better, raised to an even higher position by the Prince.

28   Her fall from class is represented not only by her tattered clothes, but by the work she is forced to do. She is the household "drudge" and housework is the image of her degradation. Her work has no value in the story; it is the invisible, repetitious labor that keeps things going and makes it possible for the sisters and stepmother to devote themselves to *their* work, which is indolence on the one hand and trying to be beautiful for men on the other. Historically, indolence has been revered as the mark of a lady. What is "feminine" and "ladylike" is far removed from the world of work. Or the world of self-satisfying work. A man prides himself on having a wife who does not work; it increases his value in the eyes of other men; it means he provides well; it enforces conventional bourgeois "masculinity." A lady has long fingernails, neither the typewriter nor the kitchen floor has cracked them. She has porcelain skin; neither the rough outdoors nor perspiration has cracked that. Out of the same set of values comes the famous glass slipper.

The stepmother's class position is as precarious as Cinderella's is. The story does not tell, but we can imagine that whether she was married before to a poorer man or one equally a gentleman, her status and security are now tied to the man she has married and the ones she can arrange for her daughters. History, experience, and literature are full of landless, propertyless women trying to secure marriage to stand as a bulwark against poverty, displacement, and exile, both actual and psychological. The actual situation bears emphasis. The economic reality behind the fairy tale and the competition among the women for the favor of the Prince is a world in which women have no financial lives of their own. They cannot own businesses or inherit property. The kingdom is not theirs. In order to survive, a woman must have a husband. It is in the interest of her daughters' future—and her own—that the stepmother works to prevent competition from Cinderella. She is not evil. Within the confines of her world and the value systems of that world, she is quite nice to her own daughters, only cruel to Cinderella.

Still, the stepmother is an archetypal figure in fairy tales, always a thwarter, often a destroyer of children. Psychologists, and Bruno Bettelheim in particular, have a psychological explanation for this. The "bad" stepmother, Bettelheim points out, usually coexists with the "good" mother, representing two aspects of a real mother as experienced by a child. The stepmother is shaped by the child's unacceptable anger against her own mother. But there are real facts of life at work in these stepmother stories, too, especially as they describe what can happen among women at home. To a man's second wife, the daughter of the first marriage is a constant reminder of the first wife. The second wife is continually confronted with that memory and with the understanding that wives are replaceable, as they frequently and actually *were* in a world where women died young in childbirth, and men remarried, moved on.

A woman marries a man who has a daughter and comes to his household, where the daughter's strongest connection is to her father; the stepmother's strongest connection is to the husband. The Eternal Triangle appears, husband/father at the center, mediating the relationship, stepmother and daughter as antagonists, competing for the husband/father's attention and whatever he may represent. Anxious, each in her own way and equally displaced, they face each other with enmity. The masculine imagination takes prideful pleasure in the story, placing, as it does, husband/father at center stage, making him King, arbiter of a world of women. . . .

32   I am writing an essay about Cinderella, spending mornings at the typewriter, afternoons in libraries, interpreting information on index cards of various colors and sheets of yellow paper. I discover something bizarre woven in the story as we now know it: that the story took root in ancient China. The remnants of that culture, especially of the ancient practice of foot-binding, are in the story, in the value of the small foot, in the use of the shoe to represent the potential bride. I see, then, the historical truth behind the terrible moment at the end of "Cinderella."

The Prince brings the slipper to the house of Cinderella's father. First one stepsister, then the other attempts to slip her foot into it, but each foot is too large. The first stepsister's toe is too large. The stepmother hands her daughter a knife and says, "Cut off the toe. When you are Queen you won't have to walk anymore." The second stepsister's heel is too large and her mother repeats the gesture and the advice.

Mutilation. Blood in the shoe, blood on the knife, blood on the floor and unbearable pain, borne, covered, masked by the smile. It is too familiar, frightening in its familiarity. The mother tells the daughter to mutilate herself in the interests of winning the Prince. She will not have to walk. Again, indolence enshrined. As mothers, in fact, did in China until the twentieth century—among the upper classes as unquestioned custom and among peasants as great sacrifice and gamble.

It began when the girl was between five and seven years old. The bandages were so tight, the girl might scream. Her mother pulled them tighter and might have tried to soothe her. Tighter. At night, in agony, the girl loosens them. She is punished, her hands tied to a post to prevent unlacing. The bones crack. The pain is constant. Tighter. She cannot walk. Tighter. By her adolescence, the girl has learned to bind her feet herself and the pain has lessened. She has, as a reward, special shoes, embroidered and decorated, for her tiny feet.

36   I translate the actual foot-binding, the ritual interaction of mother and daughter, to metaphor. A black mother straightens her daughter's hair with a hot iron, singeing the scalp, pulling and tugging. The daughter screams. My mother buys me a girdle when I am fifteen years old because she doesn't like the jiggle. She slaps my face when I begin to menstruate, telling me later that it is an ancient Russian custom and she does not know its origin. I sleep with buttons taped to my cheeks to make dimples and with hard metallic curlers in my hair. Tighter. I hold myself tighter, as my mother has taught me to do.

Is the impulse to cripple a girl peculiar to China between the eleventh and twentieth centuries? The lotus foot was the size of a doll's and the woman could not walk without support. Her foot was four inches long and two inches wide. A doll. A girl-child. Crippled, indolent, and bound. This is what it meant to be beautiful. And desired. This women did and do to each other.

Pain in the foot is pain in every part of the body. A mother is about to bind her daughter's feet. She knows the pain in her own memory. She says: "A daughter's pretty legs are achieved through the shedding of tears."

This women did to each other.
This women do.
Or refuse to do.
. . . .

Personal Response

Select a film for children that you recall from your childhood and discuss what you remember most about it. Do you think it has the same kinds of messages Bernikow finds in "Cinderella"?

Questions for Class or Small-Group Discussion

1. Discuss whether you agree with Bernikow's interpretation that "Cinderella" is chiefly "about how awful women are to each other" (paragraph 1).

2. Discuss whether you think it is true that "rich matters more than handsome" (paragraph 4) for men in today's society, whereas being pretty is most important for women (paragraph 5).

3. Do you agree that females' power resides in their being "stunning" (paragraph 19), whereas other kinds of power in women are feared? Discuss your own perceptions of powerful women: Do you view power in women differently from or the same as the way you see it in men?

4. Bernikow sees a parallel between the stepsisters in "Cinderella" cutting off parts of their feet to win the Prince and the practice of foot-binding in China, and she interprets foot-binding as a metaphor for other interactions between mothers and daughters (paragraphs 36–38). To what extent do you agree with her in this interpretation? Do women today go through painful rituals to make themselves appealing to men? Do men go through painful rituals in order to appeal to women?

5. Can you name any current books or recent Hollywood films that have the same sorts of messages that Bernikow sees in "Cinderella"? What other fairy tales or children's stories reinforce Bernikow's point about female rivalry and male power? What would happen if you reversed the sex roles in "Cinderella"?

THE END OF ADMIRATION:
THE MEDIA AND THE LOSS OF HEROES

Peter H. Gibbon

Peter H. Gibbon is a research associate at Harvard University's Graduate School of Education. He has done extensive research on the educational systems of Japan, China, and Germany and is currently at

work on a book about the disappearance of public heroes in Ameri-
can society. This piece, based on a talk he delivered at a seminar on
the history of journalism hosted by Hillsdale College, appeared in the
May 1999 issue of Imprimis.

I travel around the country talking to Americans about the loss of public heroes. I point out that New York City's Hall of Fame for Great Americans attracts only a few thousand visitors each year, while Cleveland's Rock and Roll Hall of Fame draws over one million.

I describe a 25-foot stained glass window in the Cathedral of St. John the Divine—dedicated in the 1920s to four athletes who exemplified good character and sportsmanship—and I offer a quick list of titles of contemporary books on sports: *Shark Attack,* on the short and bitter career of college coaches; *Meat on the Hoof,* about the mercenary world of professional football; *Personal Fouls,* on the mistreatment of college athletes; *The Courts of Babylon,* on the venality of the women's professional tennis circuit; and *Public Heroes, Private Felons,* on college athletes who break the law.

I contrast two westerns: *High Noon,* which won four Academy Awards in 1959, and *Unforgiven,* which was voted "Best Picture" in 1992. The hero of *High Noon,* Will Kane, is a U.S. marshal. The hero of *Unforgiven,* Will Munny, is a reformed killer and alcoholic reduced to pig farming.

4   I mention that our best-selling postage stamps feature Elvis Presley and Marilyn Monroe and that our most popular TV show was, until it left the air recently, *Seinfeld.*

I remind my audiences that Thomas Jefferson is now thought of as the president with the slave mistress and Mozart as the careless genius who liked to talk dirty.

I add that a recent biography of Mother Teresa is titled *The Missionary Position.*

I offer some reasons for the disappearance of public heroes. Athletes have given up on being team players and role models. Popular culture is often irreverent, sometimes deviant. Revisionist historians present an unforgiving, skewed picture of the past. Biographers are increasingly hostile toward their subjects. Social scientists stridently assert that human beings are not autonomous but are conditioned by genes and environment.

8   Hovering in the background are secularism, which suggests that human beings are self-sufficient and do not need God, and modernism—a complex artistic and literary movement that repudiates structure, form, and conventional values.

Finally, in an age of instant communication, in which there is little time for reflection, accuracy, balance or integrity—the media creates the impression that sleaze is everywhere, that nothing is sacred, that no one is noble, and that there are no heroes.

Nothing to Admire

Radio, television, and computers offer news with such speed that newspaper and magazine circulation has plummeted, and readers have smaller vocabularies. I recently wrote an op-ed piece syndicated in several newspapers. My title, *"Nil Admirari,"* which means "nothing to admire," came from the Roman lyric poet Horace.

None of the newspapers used the title, and one editor reminded me that newspaper stories are now aimed at a sixth-grade reading level.

In the Age of Information, the image reigns. There are 81 television sets for every 100 Americans. In the typical household, the television is on six hours a day. Television has become our chief source of local and national news, and broadcast journalists have become more prominent and more powerful than columnists. There used to be three channels. Now, there are over one hundred. When we weary of television channels, we can turn to countless radio stations, videotapes, and web pages.

12   This explosion of information means we now have a vast menu of choices that allows us to be transported to many different worlds and provides us with educational opportunities undreamed of thirty years ago. It also means that we spend more time in front of television and computer screens and less time reading to our children. It is no wonder that our children have shorter attention spans and smaller vocabularies.

A Wired World

Along with this vast menu of choices is the absence of gatekeepers. As parents, we need to realize that there are dangers that come with too many choices and too few guides. We need to remind ourselves that their well-being depends not only on nutrition, sunlight, and exercise; on friendship, work, and love; but also on *how they see the world.* Subtly and powerfully, the media helps shape their world view.

The media has a liberal bias, but its *central* bias is toward bad news. Accidents, crimes, conflict, and scandal are interesting. Normality is boring. The prevalence of bad news and the power of the image encourage children—and us—to overestimate the chance of an accident, the risk of disease, the rate of violence, the frequency of marital infidelity. The average policeman, for example, never fires a gun in action, and most Americans are monogamous.

In a wired world with no restraint, the media can misinform us. It can also make us suspicious, fearful, and cynical. It can lead us to lose faith in our nation, repudiate our past, question our leaders, and cease to believe in progress.

16   We know the worst about everyone instantly. Over and over again, we see clips of George Bush vomiting, Dan Quayle misspelling "potato," Gerald Ford tripping. No longer do we want our child to grow up and become president. We harbor dark suspicions about the personal conduct of scoutmasters, priests, and coaches. We think army sergeants harass their subordinates. We have trouble calling any public figure a hero. A wired world becomes a world without heroes, a world of *nil admirari,* with no one to admire.

Americans tell pollsters the country is in moral and spiritual decline. In the midst of peace and prosperity, with equality increasing and health improving, we are sour. With our military powerful and our culture ascendant, pessimism prevails.

Crusaders or Rogues?

Should we blame journalists? It is certainly tempting. Just as we blame teachers for the poor performance of students, so we can blame reporters for the nation's malaise.

But just as teachers are not responsible for poverty and disintegrating families, journalists are not responsible for satellites, fiber optic cables, transistors, and microprocessors—the inventions that make possible instant information. Journalists did not cause the sexual revolution. They did not invent celebrity worship or gossip. Nor did they create leaders who misbehave and let us down.

At the same time, in the world of *nil admirari,* journalists are not innocent, and they know it. Roger Rosenblatt, a veteran of the *Washington Post, Time, Life,* and the *New York Times Magazine,* says, "My trade of journalism is sodden these days with practitioners who seem incapable of admiring others or anything." In his memoir, former presidential press secretary and ABC News senior editor Pierre Salinger writes, "No reporter can be famous unless they have brought someone down." And *New Yorker* writer Adam Gopnik comments, "The reporter used to gain status by dining with his subjects; now he gains status by dining on them."

20   Journalists can also be greedy. Eager for money, some reporters accept handsome speaking fees from organizations they are supposed to be covering. Some are dishonest, making up quotations, even inventing stories. No longer content with anonymity, many reporters seek celebrity, roaming the talk shows and becoming masters of the sound bite. They write autobiographies and give interviews to other journalists.

Just as our president is enamored of Hollywood, so are our journalists. Larry King recently spent a full hour interviewing singer Madonna. *Sixty Minutes* devoted much of a show to "bad boy" actor Sean Penn. Actors, supermodels, and musicians are no longer just entertainers. They are treated like philosopher–kings, telling us how to live. In a recent interview, actress Sharon Stone, star of *Basic Instinct,* advises parents to make condoms available to their teenagers.

Aggressive and anxious for ratings, television news shows feature hosts and guests who come armed with hardened opinions. Many are quick to judge and prone to offer easy solutions for complex problems. "Talking heads" argue, yell, interrupt, and rarely make concessions.

But in the world of *nil admirari,* journalists are now reviled more often than revered. In the 1980s, muckraker Steven Brill skewered lawyers. In his new magazine, *Brill's Content,* he lambastes journalists. In *Right in the Old Gazoo,* former Wyoming Senator Alan Simpson accuses journalists of becoming "lazy, complacent, sloppy, self-serving, self-aggrandizing, cynical and arrogant beyond belief." In *Breaking the News,* writer James Fallows comments that while movies once portrayed journalists as crusaders, they are now portrayed as rogues "more loathsome than . . . lawyers, politicians, and business moguls."

24   How much of this is new?

Since the founding of America, reporters have been harsh critics of public figures. George Washington did not like reading in pamphlets that the essence of his education had been "gambling, reveling, horse racing and horse whipping." Thomas Jefferson did not relish the label "effeminate." Abraham Lincoln did not appreciate being portrayed by cartoonists as a baboon.

Throughout our history, reporters have also received harsh criticism. Just after the Civil War, abolitionist Harriet Beecher Stowe claimed the press had become so vicious that no respectable American man would ever again run for president. In 1870, the British critic and poet Matthew Arnold toured America and concluded, "If one were searching for the best means . . . to kill in a whole nation . . . the feeling for what is elevated, one could not do better than take the American newspaper." At the turn of the century, novelist Henry James condemned what he called the "impudence [and] the shamelessness of the newspaper and the interviewer." In the early decades of the 20th century, "yellow journalism," "muckraking," and "debunking" became household words to describe newspaper stories that exaggerated and distorted events to make them more sensational.

Nor is the media's fascination with celebrities new. When silent screen idol Rudolph Valentino and educational reformer Charles William Eliot died within a day of each other in 1926, high-minded Americans complained that the press devoted too many columns to a celebrity and too few to a hero of education. Between 1925 and 1947, millions of Americans listed to Walter Winchell's radio program, *The Lucky Strike Hour* and read his column in the *New York Mirror.* Winchell hung out at the Stork Club, collecting gossip about celebrities and politicians from tipsters. He urged all newspaper offices to post these words on their walls: "Talk of virtue and your readers will become bored. Hint of gossip and you will secure perfect attention."

In short, media critics have always called reporters cynical. Reporters have always collected gossip and featured celebrities. And high-minded Americans have always warned that journalists could lower the nation's moral tone.

An Empire of Information

28   From the outset, thoughtful critics conceded that journalists had an obligation to inform and expose. But those same critics were afraid that reporters would eliminate privacy and slander leaders; that by repeating gossip and emphasizing crime and corruption, newspapers would coarsen citizens; and that journalists would become more influential than ministers, novelists, professors, and politicians. They were right.

Journalists *have* become more powerful than ministers, novelists, professors, and politicians. They preside over an empire of information unimaginable to our ancestors—an empire that reaches small villages in India and can change governments in China; an empire characterized by staggering choice, variety, and technological sophistication.

An empire of information ruled by the modern media *has* eliminated privacy. With recorders and cameras, reporters freely enter dugouts, locker rooms, board rooms, hotel rooms. There are neither secrets nor taboos. Some listen in on private telephone conversations and sift through garbage for incriminating documents.

Early critics were also right to worry that journalists could contribute to a decline in taste and judgment, could destroy the feeling for the elevated, could eliminate appetite for the admirable. The empire they have created is slick, quick, hardhitting, entertaining, and inescapable. It makes us more knowledgeable, but it also leaves us overwhelmed, convinced that the world is a sleazy place, and mistrustful of authority and institutions. It all but extinguishes our belief in heroism.

Hope for the Future

32   Are there reasons to be hopeful about the future of America and the future of the media? I believe there are. Intent on exposing our faults, we forget what we do well.

America is much better and healthier than the country portrayed in the media and in pessimistic opinion polls. The American people are basically hardworking, idealistic, compassionate, and religious.

American journalism is still biased, but it is slowly becoming more balanced. We have the *Washington Times* as well as the *Washington Post, U.S. News & World Report* as well as *Newsweek, National Review* as well as the *Nation,* the *Wall Street Journal* as well as the *New York Times.* We have prominent conservative and liberal commentators.

In the late 1990s, newspaper and television journalists have become more self-critical. Some recognize the need to become less cynical, less greedy, less celebrity oriented, less combative; and a few recognize the need to report the normal and the good rather than only the sensational and the deviant.

Reporters, editors, and publishers are influential, but they are not all-powerful. In America, the consumer is king. We choose our sources of information just as we purchase cars and potato chips. When CNN interrupted its coverage of the Lorena Bobbitt trial to report on the Chernobyl nuclear disaster, the number of angry callers caused the network's switchboard to crash. Reporters could be more courageous and less concerned with profits, but American citizens could be more high-minded.

36   In the Age of Information, journalists and citizens face the same challenges. We need to study the past so as not to become arrogant, to remember the good so as not to become cynical, and to recognize America's strengths so as not to dwell on her weaknesses. We need to be honest and realistic without losing our capacity for admiration—and to be able to embrace complexity without losing our faith in the heroic.

Personal Response

Gibbon states that "we have trouble calling any public figure a hero" (paragraph 16). Are there public figures whom you admire as heroes, and if so, what makes them heroic? If you cannot think of any public hero whom you would regard as a hero, explore reasons why this is so.

Questions for Class or Small-Group Discussion

1. Comment on the effectiveness of the series of contrasts Gibbon makes in the first six paragraphs. Then discuss the explanations he gives to account for them in the next several paragraphs. Do you accept his explanations? Are there any that you would challenge?

2. Gibbon alleges that journalists can be greedy and dishonest, seeking celebrity status for themselves (paragraphs 19–20). To what extent do you agree with Gibbon? Can you name journalists who either support or refute his claims?

3. In paragraph 28, Gibbon briefly summarizes both positive and negative views of journalists over time, with emphasis on the negative. He concludes that those who feared the worst "were right." To what extent do you agree with Gibbon that the worst fears of critics of journalists have been realized?

4. Discuss the following from paragraph 31: "The empire they created is slick, quick, hard-hitting, entertaining, and inescapable. It makes us more knowledgeable, but it also leaves us overwhelmed, convinced that the world is a sleazy place, and mistrustful of authority and institutions. It all but extinguishes our belief in heroism." To what extent do you agree with Gibbon? Do you think he is wrong or unfair in any part of this passage?

AGGRESSION: THE IMPACT OF MEDIA VIOLENCE

Sissela Bok

Born in Sweden and educated in Switzerland, France, and the United States, Sissela Bok earned a Ph.D. in philosophy from Harvard University. She has been a professor of philosophy at Brandeis University and is currently a Distinguished Fellow at the Harvard Center for Population and Development Studies. Widely known for her writings on topics in bioethics, applied ethics, biography and autobiography, and public affairs, her books include Lying: Moral Choice in Public and Private Life *(1978),* Secrets: On the Ethics of Concealment and Revelation *(1983),* A strategy for Peace: Human Values and the Threat of War *(1989),* Alva Myrdal: A Daughter's Memoir *(1991),* Common Values *(1995), and* Mayhem: Violence as Public Entertainment *(1998), from which the following is taken.*

Even if media violence were linked to no other debilitating effects, it would remain at the center of public debate so long as the widespread belief persists that it glamorizes aggressive conduct, removes inhibitions toward such conduct, arouses viewers, and invites imitation. It is only natural that the links of media violence to aggression should be of special concern to families and communities. Whereas increased fear, desensitization, and appetite primarily affect the viewers themselves, aggression directly injures others and represents a more clear-cut violation of standards of behavior. From the point of view of public policy, therefore, curbing aggression has priority over alleviating subtler psychological and moral damage.

Public concern about a possible link between media violence and societal violence has further intensified in the past decade, as violent crime reached a peak in the early 1990s, yet has shown no sign of downturn, even after crime rates began dropping in 1992. Media coverage of violence, far from declining, has escalated since then, devoting ever more attention to celebrity homicides and copycat crimes. The latter, explicitly modeled on videos or films and sometimes carried out with meticulous fidelity to detail, are never more relentlessly covered in the media than when they are committed by children and adolescents. Undocumented claims that violent copycat crimes are mounting in number contribute further to the ominous sense of threat that these crimes generate. Their dramatic nature drains away the public's attention from other, more mundane forms of aggression that are much more commonplace, and from . . . other . . . harmful effects of media violence.

Media analyst Ken Auletta reports that, in 1992, a mother in France sued the head of a state TV channel that carried the American series *MacGyver,* claiming that her son was accidentally injured as a result of having copied MacGyver's recipe for making a bomb. At the time, Auletta predicted that similar lawsuits were bound to become a weapon against media violence in America's litigious culture. By 1996, novelist John Grisham had sparked a debate about director Oliver Stone's film *Natural Born Killers,* which is reputedly linked to more copycat assaults and murders than any other movie to date. Grisham wrote in protest against the film after learning that a friend of his, Bill Savage, had been killed by nineteen-year-old Sarah Edmondson and her boyfriend Benjamin Darras, eighteen: after repeated viewings of Stone's film on video, the two had gone on a killing spree with the film's murderous, gleeful heroes expressly in mind. Characterizing the film as "a horrific movie that glamorized casual mayhem and bloodlust," Grisham proposed legal action:

> Think of a film as a product, something created and brought to market, not too dissimilar from breast implants. Though the law has yet to declare movies to be products, it is only a small step away. If something goes wrong with the product, either by design or defect, and injury ensues, then its makers are held responsible. . . . It will take only one large verdict against the like of Oliver Stone, and his production company, and perhaps the screenwriter, and the studio itself, and then the party will be over. The verdict will come from the heartland, far away from Southern California, in some small courtroom with no cameras. A jury will finally say enough is enough; that the demons placed in Sarah Edmondson's mind were not solely of her own making.

4   As a producer of books made into lucrative movies—themselves hardly devoid of violence—and as a veteran of contract negotiations within the entertainment industry, Grisham may have become accustomed to thinking of films in industry terms as "products." As a seasoned courtroom lawyer, he may have found the analogy between such products and breast implants useful for invoking product liability to pin personal responsibility on movie producers and directors for the lethal consequences that their work might help unleash.

Oliver Stone retorted that Grisham was drawing "upon the superstition about the magical power of pictures to conjure up the undead spectre of censorship." In dismissing concerns about the "magical power of pictures" as merely superstitious, Stone sidestepped the larger question of responsibility fully as much as Grisham had sidestepped that of causation when he attributed liability to filmmakers for anything that "goes wrong" with their products so that "injury ensues."

Because aggression is the most prominent effect associated with media violence in the public's mind, it is natural that it should also remain the primary focus of scholars in the field. The "aggressor effect" has been studied both to identify the short-term, immediate impact on viewers after exposure to TV violence, and the long-term influences. . . . There is near-unanimity by now among investigators that exposure to media violence contributes to lowering barriers to aggression among some viewers. This lowering of barriers may be assisted by the failure of empathy that comes with growing desensitization, and intensified to the extent that viewers develop an appetite for violence—something that may lead to still greater desire for violent programs and, in turn, even greater desensitization.

When it comes to viewing violent pornography, levels of aggression toward women have been shown to go up among male subjects who view sexualized violence against women. "In explicit depictions of sexual violence," a report by the American Psychological Association's Commission on Youth and Violence concludes after surveying available research data, "it is the message about violence more than the sexual nature of the materials that appears to affect the attitudes of adolescents about rape and violence toward women." Psychologist Edward Donnerstein and colleagues have shown that if investigators tell subjects that aggression is legitimate, then show them violent pornography, their aggression toward women increases. In slasher films, the speed and ease with which "one's feelings can be transformed from sensuality into viciousness may surprise even those quite conversant with the links between sexual and violent urges."

8   Viewers who become accustomed to seeing violence as an acceptable, common, attractive way of dealing with problems find it easier to identify with aggressors and to suppress any sense of pity or respect for victims of violence. Media violence has been found to have stronger effects of this kind when carried out by heroic, impressive, or otherwise exciting figures, especially when they are shown as invulnerable and are rewarded or not punished for what they do. The same is true when the violence is shown as justifiable, when viewers identify with the aggressors rather than with their victims, when violence is routinely resorted to, and when the programs have links to how viewers perceive their own environment.

While the consensus that such influences exist grows among investigators as research accumulates, there is no consensus whatsoever about the size of the correlations involved. Most investigators agree that it will always be difficult to disentangle the precise effects of exposure to media violence from the many other factors contributing to societal violence. No reputable scholar accepts the view expressed by 21 percent of the American public in 1995, blaming television more than any other factor for teenage violence. Such tentative estimates as have been made suggest that the media account for between 5 and 15 percent of societal violence. Even these estimates are rarely specific enough to indicate whether what is at issue is all violent crime, or such crimes along with bullying and aggression more generally.

One frequently cited investigator proposes a dramatically higher and more specific estimate than others. Psychiatrist Brandon S. Centerwall has concluded from large-scale epidemiological studies of "white homicide" in the United States, Canada, and South Africa in the period from 1945 to 1974, that it escalated in these societies within ten to fifteen years of the introduction of television, and that one can therefore deduce that television has brought a doubling of violent societal crime:

> Of course, there are many factors other than television that influence the amount of violent crime. Every violent act is the result of a variety of forces coming together—poverty, crime, alcohol and drug abuse, stress—of which childhood TV exposure is just one. Nevertheless, the evidence indicates that if hypothetically, television technology had never been developed, there would today be 10,000 fewer homicides each year in the United States, 70,000 fewer rapes, and 700,000 fewer injurious assaults. Violent crime would be half of what it now is.

Centerwall's study, published in 1989, includes controls for such variables as firearm possession and economic growth. But his conclusions have been criticized for not taking into account other factors, such as population changes during the time period studied, that might also play a role in changing crime rates. Shifts in policy and length of prison terms clearly affect these levels as well. By now, the decline in levels of violent crime in the United States since Centerwall's study was conducted, even though television viewing did not decline ten to fifteen years before, does not square with his extrapolations. As for "white homicide" in South Africa under apartheid, each year brings more severe challenges to official statistics from that period.

12   Even the lower estimates, however, of around 5 to 10 percent of violence as correlated with television exposure, point to substantial numbers of violent crimes in a population as large as America's. But if such estimates are to be used in discussions of policy decisions, more research will be needed to distinguish between the effects of television in general and those of particular types of violent programming, and to indicate specifically what sorts of images increase the aggressor effect and by what means; and throughout to be clearer about the nature of the aggressive acts studied.

Media representatives naturally request proof of such effects before they are asked to undertake substantial changes in programming. In considering possible remedies for a problem, inquiring into the reasons for claims about risks is entirely appropriate. It is clearly valid to scrutinize the research designs, sampling methods, and possible biases of studies supporting such claims, and to ask about the reasoning leading from particular research findings to conclusions. But to ask for some demonstrable pinpointing of just when and how exposure to media violence affects levels of aggression sets a dangerously high threshold for establishing risk factors.

We may never be able to trace, retrospectively, the specific set of television programs that contributed to a particular person's aggressive conduct. The same is true when it comes to the links between tobacco smoking and cancer, between drunk driving and automobile accidents, and many other risk factors presenting public health hazards. Only recently have scientists identified the specific channels through which tobacco generates its carcinogenic effects. Both precise causative mechanisms and documented occurrences in individuals remain elusive. Too often, media representatives formulate their requests in what appear to be strictly polemical terms, raising dismissive questions familiar from debates over the effects of tobacco: "How can anyone definitively pinpoint the link between media violence and acts of real-life violence? If not, how can we know if exposure to media violence constitutes a risk factor in the first place?"

Yet the difficulty in carrying out such pinpointing has not stood in the way of discussing and promoting efforts to curtail cigarette smoking and drunk driving. It is not clear, therefore, why a similar difficulty should block such efforts when it comes to media violence. The perspective of "probabilistic causation". . . is crucial to public debate about the risk factors in media violence. The television industry has already been persuaded to curtail the glamorization of smoking and drunk driving on its programs, despite the lack of conclusive documentation of the correlation between TV viewing and higher incidence of such conduct. Why should the industry not take analogous precautions with respect to violent programming?

16   Americans have special reasons to inquire into the causes of societal violence. While we are in no sense uniquely violent, we need to ask about all possible reasons why our levels of violent crime are higher than in all other stable industrialized democracies. Our homicide rate would be higher still if we did not imprison more of our citizens than any society in the world, and if emergency medical care had not improved so greatly in recent decades that a larger proportion of shooting victims survive than in the past. Even so, we have seen an unprecedented rise not only in child and adolescent violence, but in levels of rape, child abuse, domestic violence, and every other form of assault.

Although America's homicide rate has declined in the 1990s, the rates for suicide, rape, and murder involving children and adolescents in many regions have too rarely followed suit. For Americans aged 15 to 35 years, homicide is the second leading cause of death, and for young African Americans, 15 to 24 years, it is *the* leading cause of death. In the decade following the mid-1980s, the rate of murder committed by teenagers 14 to 17 more than doubled. The rates of injury suffered by small children are skyrocketing, with the number of seriously injured children nearly quadrupling from 1986 to 1993; and a proportion of these injuries are inflicted by children upon one another. Even homicides by children, once next to unknown, have escalated in recent decades.

America may be the only society on earth to have experienced what has been called an "epidemic of children killing children," which is ravaging some of its communities today. As in any epidemic, it is urgent to ask what it is that makes so many capable of such violence, victimizes so many others, and causes countless more to live in fear. Whatever role the media are found to play in this respect, to be sure, is but part of the problem. Obviously, not even the total elimination of media violence would wipe out the problem of violence in the United States or any other society. The same can be said for the proliferation and easy access to guns, or for poverty, drug addiction, and other risk factors. As Dr. Deborah Prothrow-Stith puts it, "It's not an either or. It's not guns or media or parents or poverty."

We have all witnessed the four effects that I have discussed . . . —fearfulness, numbing, appetite, and aggressive impulses—in the context of many influences apart from the media. Maturing involves learning to resist the dominion that these effects can gain over us; and to strive, instead, for greater resilience, empathy, self-control, and respect for self and others. The process of maturation and growth in these respects is never completed for any of us; but it is most easily thwarted in childhood, before it has had chance to take root. Such learning calls for nurturing and education at first; then for increasing autonomy in making personal decisions about how best to confront the realities of violence.

20   Today, the sights and sounds of violence on the screen affect this learning process from infancy on, in many homes. The television screen is the lens through which most children learn about violence. Through the magnifying power of this lens, their everyday life becomes suffused by images of shootings, family violence, gang warfare, kidnappings, and everything else that contributes to violence in our society. It shapes their experiences long before they have had the opportunity to consent to such shaping or developed the ability to cope adequately with this knowledge. The basic nurturing and protection to prevent the impairment of this ability ought to be the birthright of every child.

Personal Response

Has this essay in any way changed your views on the impact of media violence on young people? Select a statement or passage that especially interests you, either positively or negatively, and discuss your response to it.

Questions for Class or Small-Group Discussion

1. Bok summarizes the viewpoints of both John Grisham and Oliver Stone on the matter of "copycat" killings. Summarize the opinions of both Grisham and Stone. What does Bok think both men sidestep in their arguments? What do you think of Grisham's and Stone's arguments? Do you agree with either one? Do you think Bok is correct in her comments on their arguments?

2. Explain what you understand Bok to mean by the term " 'aggressor effect' " (paragraph 6). What do investigators have to say about violent pornography and the aggressor effect?

3. What is your response to this statement: "No reputable scholar accepts the view expressed by 21 percent of the American public in 1995, blaming television more than any other factor for teenage violence" (paragraph 9)? What does Bok have to say about the studies conducted by Brandon S. Centerwall?

4. Bok notes the difficulty of showing the precise causal relationships between tobacco smoking and cancer and between drunken driving and automobile accidents,

even though most people seem to accept that smoking causes cancer and that drunk driving is a chief cause of automobile accidents. What do you think of her application of the " 'probabilistic causation' " factor to the matter of media violence? That is, how valid do you find her logic? Are you convinced that even though we cannot precisely pinpoint the direct causes of societal violence, we can still discuss and propose "efforts to curtail" the "risk factors in media violence" (paragraph 15)?

5. What, according to Bok, might be the effects on children of early and ongoing exposure to media violence? Are you persuaded by her argument that research on the causal links between exposure to media violence and violent behavior must continue?

TOUGH TALK ON ENTERTAINMENT

Andrea Sachs and Susanne Washburn

This forum, compiled by Andrea Sachs and Susanne Washburn, appeared in conjunction with the June 12, 1995, Time *magazine cover story on the entertainment industry. It represents the voices of many people, as each expresses a different opinion on the topic.*

De gustibus non est disputandum was the way the ancient Romans put it: There is no point arguing about matters of taste. But that was easy for the Romans to say; they—and their children—weren't awash in a tide of explicit films, TV programs, and recorded music. We are. And the consequences of this condition—even the question whether there *are* any consequences—have spurred arguments that grow more intense as mass entertainment becomes more pervasive. In the aftermath of Bob Dole's latest attack on Hollywood, *Time* asked some prominent people who produce or comment on the arts for their reactions:

Lynne Cheney

Fellow, American Enterprise Institute.   In one scene of Oliver Stone's film *Natural Born Killers* the hero drowns his girlfriend's father in a fish tank and kills her mother by tying her down on her bed, pouring gasoline on her, and burning her alive. Meanwhile, a raucous, laugh-filled sound track tells the audience to regard this slaughter as the funniest thing in the world. Is it any wonder that millions of Americans are concerned about kids growing up in a culture that sends such messages—or that someone who wants to be our president would talk about it?

A lot of the commentary about Bob Dole's remarks on Hollywood has focused on whether he has gained political advantage from them, and I think there is no question but that he has. Not so much because he has positioned himself better with the cultural right, but because, as Americans across the political spectrum realize, he is right—just as President Clinton was right a few years ago when he castigated rap singer Sister Souljah for saying that blacks have killed one another long enough and that it was time for them to start killing whites. When you glamorize murder, as *Natural Born Killers* does; or glorify violence against women, as does 2 Live Crew; when lyrics are anti-Semitic, as Public Enemy's are, or advocate hatred of gays and immigrants, as those of Guns n' Roses do, it's not just conservatives who know something has gone wrong; any thinking liberal does too.

4   Those producing this garbage tell us we're naive. *Natural Born Killers* isn't an attempt to profit from murder and mayhem, says Oliver Stone. It's a send-up of the way the tabloid press exploits violence—a claim that would be a lot more convincing if Stone would contribute to charity the multimillion-dollar profits the movie earned last year. Time Warner CEO Gerald Levin, whose company produced *Natural Born Killers* and has put out much of the most offensive music, says that rappers like Ice-T are misunderstood: when Ice-T chants "Die, die, die, pig, die," he is not really advocating cop killing, but trying to put us in touch with the "anguished" mind of someone who feels this way.

This is nonsense—rationalization of the most obvious sort. What we need to do, each of us as individuals, is let those who are polluting the culture know that we are going to embarrass them and shame them until they stop, until they use their vast talents and resources to put us in touch with our best selves—instead of with the worst parts of our nature.

John Edgar Wideman

Author and Professor.   Which is more threatening to America—the violence, obscenity, sexism, and racism of movies and records, or the stark reality these movies and music reflect? If a messenger, even one who happens to be black and a rapper, arrives bearing news of a terrible disaster, what do we accomplish by killing the messenger?

I wasn't around when black people were barred from playing drums. But I know the objections to African drumming weren't aesthetic; Southern legislators feared the drums' power to signal a general slave revolt. I was around when finding black music on the radio was a problem. Growing up in Pittsburgh, Pennsylvania, the only way to hear the latest rhythm-and-blues sounds after dark was searching the scratchy hyperspace for *Randy's Record Shack* beaming up from Nashville, Tennessee.

8   Banning, ignoring, exploiting, damning black art has a long history. Protecting black freedom of expression and participation at all levels of society began just yesterday. So it's not accidental that politicians reaffirm the doublespeak and hypocrisy of America's pretensions to democracy. Let's deregulate everything; let the marketplace rule. Except when rap music captures a lion's share of the multibillion-dollar music market. Then, in the name of decency and family values, we're duty bound to regulate it. On the other hand, in areas of the economy where black people are appallingly underrepresented—the good jobs, for instance, that enable folks to maintain families—we should abhor intervention because it's not fair.

The best art interrogates and explodes consensus. Recall how traditional African American gospel music, transformed in the 1960s to freedom songs, the oratory of Martin Luther King, and the essays of James Baldwin inspired and guided us. But we can't have the best art unless we are willing to risk living with the rest, the second rate and fifteenth rate, the stuff that eventually Xs itself because its worthlessness teaches us not to buy or listen.

We must not lose patience and stop paying attention. We must not mistake jingoism or propaganda or sensationalism for art. We must not fear change, fear the shock and disruption true art inflicts. We must not smother what we don't want to hear with the drone of morally bankrupt, politically self-serving Muzak.

Donna Britt

Syndicated Columnist.   As a columnist who often writes about how American parents of every color, income, and political stripe feel they're engaged in a losing war with cultural swill, I was glad to hear Bob Dole lambaste the entertainment industry. Every parent I know feels bombardment; who cares who thrusts it under the microscope?

12   Sure, it's hypocritical. Dole, who long ignored the issue, is playing politics by reducing a complex and unwieldy problem to too-easy sound bites. But who isn't? People who excoriate Dole for hypocrisy in blasting movies in which fictional characters use the same assault weapons he supports in real life ignore that his most passionate attackers make fortunes off the depravity they're protecting. Free speech invokers who say only parents are responsible for policing what their children hear and see overlook that even good parents—who've never been busier or had a more pervasive pop culture to contend with—are sometimes too overwhelmed to fight. Bad parents—and there are millions—aren't even trying. But we all must share the planet with the kids they're raising badly.

Paul Schrader

Screenwriter and Director.   I don't know which is more appalling—the conservatives' hypocrisy or the entertainment industry's sanctimony.

There are solid arguments here, both Dole's and the libertarian response. You'll never know it from what you hear or read. That's because the debate, as framed by Dole and the entertainment industry, is not about values or freedom. It's about popularity. Hollywood calls popularity money; politicians call it votes.

The entertainment conglomerates are fond of invoking the First Amendment. That's because there's precious little excuse for what they've been up to the past twenty years. We've worked so long and hard at making audiences dumber, they have actually become dumber.

16   Is Dole up to anything different? Several years ago, I was involved in a public debate over a film I adapted from Nikos Kazantzakis' *The Last Temptation of Christ.* It

was assailed as blasphemous by religious conservatives, most of whom had not seen the film. I realized at the time it didn't matter whether they had seen it. This was not a debate about the spiritual values of *Last Temptation;* this was a fight about who controls the culture. *Last Temptation,* like other cultural totems—flag burning, Robert Mapplethorpe, gun control, NEA, abortion—had become a symbol of cultural hegemony.

Yes, the entertainment industry is an empty, soulless empire. I can't bring myself to defend many of the films now made; I can't even defend those Dole approves of. Hollywood must examine itself. Its greed is sickening. It must judge the social impact, not just the popularity impact, of what it does. So must politicians who seek to exploit cultural values.

Katha Pollitt

Poet, Writer, and Social Critic.   People like pop culture—that's what makes it popular. Movies drenched in sex and gore, gangsta rap, even outright pornography are not some sort of alien interstellar dust malevolently drifting down on us, but products actively sought out and beloved by millions. When fighting to abolish the NEA and other government support for the arts, conservatives are quick to condemn "cultural elitism" and exalt the majority tastes served by the marketplace. So how can they turn around and blame entertainment corporations for following the money and giving mass audiences what they want? Talk about elitism!

I too dislike many pop-culture products, although probably not the ones that bother Senator Dole. But the fact is, no system of regulation or voluntary restraint is going to have much effect on mass entertainment. And I'd like to hear how Dole squares his antiviolence stand with his ardent support for the N.R.A. and the overturning of the assault-weapons ban. Guns don't kill people; rap music kills people? Oliver Stone movies kill people? Please.

20   Ultimately, culture reflects society—for a violent nation, violent amusements. But if Senator Dole and his fellow conservatives are serious about elevating American tastes, they'd do better to encourage greater variety in culture than to seek to homogenize it even further. Let them increase the NEA budget until it at least equals that for military bands. Let them restore to the public schools the art and music and performance programs that have been cut in the name of "getting back to basics." Let them support public radio and television—or not complain when the kids watch *Beavis and Butthead* and their parents watch *Married . . . with Children,* a show whose raw humor at the expense of family values enriches not some Hollywood liberal, by the way, but Newt Gingrich's publisher, Rupert Murdoch.

That Dole and other cultural conservatives claim to speak out of concern for women is particularly galling. What have they ever done for women? These are the same people who were silent when Republican congressmen compared poor single mothers to mules and alligators, who want to ban abortion. If these men want to do something about entertainment that insults women, why not start with Rush

Limbaugh and his references to pro-choice women as "feminazis"? Oh, but I forgot. Criticizing gangsta rap for demeaning women is defending "American values." Criticizing right-wing talk radio for doing the same is "politically correct."

Danyel Smith

Music Editor, *VIBE* Magazine.   Senator Bob Dole's recent attacks on hip-hop music and violent films are as ugly and transparent as some of the so-called gangsta rappers he wants to huff and puff and blow away. Like those of the worst rappers, Dole's views sound tinny and half-desperate. Like the lamest films, Dole goes for the spectacular (guns, violence, melodrama) rather than the substantive (love, sex, race, class). The main thing Dole, weak rappers, and weak movies share is an ultimate goal: money. Staten Island hip-hoppers Wu-Tang Clan said it best with their 1994 hit single, *C.R.E.A.M. (Cash Rules Everything around Me)*.

The mass of folks going to the movies and buying records are in their teens, twenties, and early thirties. The optimism of *Forrest Gump* rang false for a lot of us. *The Lion King* offered moments of uplift that faded when the lights came up. But hip-hop songs such as KRS-One's *Build & Destroy,* Gang Starr's *Just to Get a Rep* and Tupac Shakur's *Holler If Ya Hear Me* sound fierce and true, reflecting in mood and content the real world around me and many hundreds of thousand of fans.

24   Yes, sexism runs rampant through hip-hop. But it, like the violence in the music, runs rampant through the world, and needs to be protested and dealt with—not just silenced on the whim of an ambitious politician. The assumption that simply because the Notorious B.I.G. raps around gunfire in a song, people are going to run out and shoot stuff up is insulting and tired. We are trying to make sense of the world—just like every generation has had to do. Forgive us if our salve is your sandpaper, but we are not you—and we're not sure we want to be.

Bill Bradley

Democratic Senator from New Jersey.   I applaud Senator Dole. Almost by any measure, the airwaves have become the pathways for too much trash. Violence without context and sex without attachment come into our homes too frequently in ways that we cannot control unless we are monitoring the television constantly.

Studies show that by the time a kid reaches eighteen, he's seen 26,000 murders on TV. That has implications. It creates a sense of unreality about the finality, pain, suffering, and inhumanity of brutal violence. The question really is, What is government's role? The answer has got to be more citizenship in the boardroom, not censorship. The public has got to hold boards of directors, executives, and corporations accountable for making money out of trash.

For example, if you see something that offends you, find out who the sponsor is, find out who's on its board of directors, find out where they live, who their neighbors are, their local clubs, churches, and synagogues. Send a letter to the members of the board at their homes and ask whether they realize they are making huge profits from the brutal degradation of other human beings. Then send a copy of that letter to all of their neighbors and friends. You can also begin to put economic pressure on a corporation. Because the market that the economic conservative champions undermines the moral character that the social conservative desires, you have to try to introduce into the functioning of the market a moral sensibility that is usually absent.

David Mamet

28 **Playwright.** Politics seems to me much like the practice of stage magic. The magician is rewarded for appearing to perform that which we know to be impossible. We onlookers agree to endorse his claims and applaud his accomplishments if he can complete his performance before getting caught out. Similarly, we know, in our hearts, that politicians running for office are, in the main, mountebanks. They promise us an impossible future, or in the case of Senator Dole, a return to an imaginary pristine past.

It is in our nature to credit the ridiculous for the sake of the momentary enjoyment it affords. We do so at the magic show, at the car showroom, and during the electoral process. It has long been the favored trick of the Republican Party to seek support through the creation of a villain. This imaginary being, whose presence stands between us and a Perfect World, this pornographer, this purveyor of filth, this destroyer of the family is he or she who used to be known by the name of communist, fellow traveler, labor agitator. Other historical names include nigger lover, papist, Yellow Peril, faggot, and Jew.

It is the pleasure of the demagogue to turn otherwise sane people one against the other by this ancient trick, in order to further his or her own personal ends.

Yes, popular culture, in the main, is garbage. Perhaps it always has been, I don't know. I know we have a legitimate human desire for leadership, and Senator Dole's demagoguery corrupts this desire into a search for a victim and a longing for revenge. Whether as entertainment or politics, I find such actions objectionable.

Stanley Crouch

32 **Critic.** Regardless of the political opportunism that may propel the rising attack on the entertainment industry, the attention is more than a good thing because our mass popular culture is the most influential in the world. But when questions are raised about that industry's irresponsible promotion of certain material, the industry's executives tell us it has no influence. Everyone has to know that is a steaming pile of shuck. At its best, popular art has been part of our ongoing redefinition of American life, moving us to question our prejudices and our political policies, our social fears and the ways in which we live our personal lives.

But what we are faced with now is the panting exploitation of all our worst inclinations. We see the cult of slut chic in which Madonna has been such an influence across all lines of race and style that video after video looks like a combination of film-school virtuosity and bimbo routines with a backbeat. We see films in which dramatic intensity is replaced by the shock of gore that takes place in a ruthless universe of amoral one-liners derived from James Bond.

Narcissism and anarchic resentment are promoted in such a calculated fashion that numskull pop stars pretend to be rebels while adhering to the most obvious trends. The executives who promote these performers say that the issue is one of "freedom of expression," while others claim that we are getting "reports from the streets." But the rapper Ice Cube told an interviewer that his work was for young people and that if his audience wanted something else he would give it to them. That is not the statement of a rebel.

These people are not about breaking taboos, they are about making money, and they know where to draw the line. A few years ago, there was an understandable controversy about the anti-Semitic statements of Professor Griff when he was a member of the rap group Public Enemy. He was soon gone from the group. That is a perfect example of how responsibly the industry can work. We will hear no "reports from the streets" that give voice to the mad ravings of Khalid Muhammad or Louis Farrakhan, regardless of the young black people who cheer them at rallies. We have no idea how often the words *nigger, bitch,* and *ho* have been recorded in gangsta rap, but we can be comfortably sure that no rap group will ever be signed and promoted if it uses the word *kike* as frequently. Nor should it be.

36   Why is this? Because the Third Reich proved beyond all reasonable doubt what the constant pumping of hate-filled images and inflammatory statements can do to a culture. I do not believe censorship is the answer. But I have no doubt good taste and responsibility will not limit the entertainment industry's ability to provide mature work that attacks our corruption, challenges our paranoia, and pulls the covers off the shortcomings that Balkanize us. What we need is simply the same sense of responsibility and dire consequences that we bring to the issue of anti-Semitism.

Personal Response

Whose opinions among those expressed in this forum come closest to your own? Explain why you agree with those opinions.

Questions for Class or Small-Group Discussion

1. Discuss the opinions of the people participating in this forum. With whom do you and your classmates find yourselves siding? Why? Does much disagreement surface among the members of your class on these opinions?

2. The issue under discussion here is to some degree a political issue. How does that consideration add to your understanding of the public debate over violence in the media? Do you feel that either major political party has recommended a wholly satisfactory solution to the problem?

3. Discuss the merits of a controversial film, such as Oliver Stone's *Natural Born Killers* or Quentin Tarantino's *Pulp Fiction.* Choose a film most of you have seen, or

rent the video version and watch it together. What appeals to you about it? What shocks or angers you? What makes it a good or bad film?

PERSPECTIVES ON MUSIC, FILM, AND MEDIA STUDIES

Suggestions for Synthesis

1. Write a paper in which you draw on the comments of Isabelle Leymarie and any of the commentators in "Tough Talk on Entertainment" as you argue for or against the power of the media to influence violent behavior in individuals.

2. Drawing on at least two of the readings in this chapter, write an essay on the subject of the sexual and/or violent content of Hollywood films. Explore whether you think anything should be done about such films and if so, what can or should be done.

3. Drawing on at least two of the readings in this chapter, write an essay on the subject of the morality of Hollywood films, including your own position on the subject.

Additional Writing Topics

1. In paragraph 1 of "Rock 'n' Revolt," Isabelle Leymarie refers to a claim by John Philips "that any rock group can whip a crowd into a hysterical frenzy by carefully controlling a sequence of rhythms." If you have ever seen such a phenomenon, where a crowd became hysterically frenzied, describe what happened and explore why you think music has that kind of control over people's emotions.

2. In paragraph 2 of "Hollywood Poison Factory," Michael Medved reports that many Americans in 1992, when the article was written, believed that "movies [then were] worse than ever." Write a paper in which you argue either in support of or against that statement as it applies to today's films. Support your argument with specific examples of movies.

3. Discuss the extent to which you agree with Michael Medved ("Hollywood Poison Factory") that Hollywood films of the 1990s were "morally and spiritually empty," using specific examples to support your generalizations. Alternatively, consider that statement as it applies to films today. Could Medved still make the same assertion about today's films?

4. With the observations of Louise Bernikow in "Cinderella: Saturday Afternoon at the Movies" in mind, do your own analysis of any fairy tale or children's film for its depiction of female and male sex roles. Do you find stereotyped assumptions about masculinity and femininity? In what ways do you think the fairy tale or film reinforces or shapes cultural definitions of masculinity and femininity?

5. Explain why you agree or disagree with the opinion expressed by any of the writers in this chapter: Isabelle Leymarie, Leonard Pitts, Michael Medved, Louise Bernikow, or Sissela Bok.

6. Select a recent, popular film and do a close analysis of the values you think the film endorses.

7. Write a position paper on the topic of sexually explicit and graphically violent Hollywood films by selecting one film for close analysis and two or three others to use as examples to support your position.

8. Explore the effects on you, either positive or negative, of a movie or movies you saw when you were growing up.

9. With Peter H. Gibbon's "The End of Admiration: The Media and the Loss of Heroes" in mind, argue either in support of or against the statement that America no longer has heroes.

Research Topics

1. In the opening paragraph of "Rock 'n' Revolt," Isabelle Leymarie gives examples of rock musicians and groups whose music and/or lives have been "fraught with violence." Research one, two, or several of the performers or groups that Leymarie names, and argue in support of or against the view that they are violent or menaces to society.

2. Isabelle Leymarie refers to "certain physiological and psychological effects [of music] which have been scientifically documented" ("Rock 'n' Revolt," paragraph 8). Research the phenomenon of the physiological and psychological effects of music. Look not only for information about scientific research on the subject but also for the comments or criticisms of people skeptical of such research. Weigh the evidence and arrive at your own opinion on the subject.

3. Research a particular musician, musical group, or entertainer from the 1950s, 1960s, or 1970s. For instance, Leonard Pitts mentions Elvis Presley, Little Richard, Lenny Bruce, the Beatles, and the Smothers Brothers. Find out the performer's history, the audience he or she appealed to, what distinguished him or her from others, and what his or her influence seems to have been on popular culture. Formulate your own assessment of the entertainer's significance and make that your thesis or central idea.

4. Research a particular kind of music, such as "grunge," alternative, blues, jazz, or salsa for the purpose of identifying its chief characteristics, the way in which it differs from and is influenced by other kinds of music, and its artistic merit or social significance. Include opposing viewpoints and argue your own position on its merits or significance.

5. Select a particular genre of film, such as comedy, western, romance, fantasy, or action, and research observations of various film historians, film critics, and other film commentators about the films in that genre. One approach is to assess the historical development of the genre and its current state: Consider, for instance, whether the genre has already had a "golden age," or whether filmmakers are still perfecting the genre. As you do your preliminary reading, look for a controversial issue on which to focus your research. Then draw your own conclusions after you thoroughly research your subject.

6. Much has been written about certain images in films, such as the portrayal of women, of minorities, and of class issues. Select a particular image or theme to

research for its representation in films. Choose a particular period (films from this year or last year, or films from a previous decade, for instance) and narrow your focus as much as possible. This task will become more manageable once you begin searching for sources and discover the nature of articles, books, and other materials on the general subject.

7. Research any of the issues raised by Sissela Bok's article, perhaps including her book, *Mayhem: Violence as Public Entertainment,* as one of your sources. For instance, you may want to read more about the effects of violent entertainment on children's moral and psychological development, the debate between protecting children and preserving First Amendment rights, or the measures taken by other nations to control media violence without censorship. Formulate your own position on the issue, and support it with references from your source materials.

CHAPTER 10

TELEVISION

A welcome innovation to many people when it first appeared, television has nevertheless been the target of suspicion, attack, and ridicule from the time it was invented. At first, people thought "the tube" would never replace the radio, especially when its early live-only broadcasts included inevitable comical errors. Once the problems were resolved, and television broadcasting became increasingly sophisticated in both technology and programming, television became a commonplace medium. Television programs now number in the thousands, with not only cable access but also computer-controlled satellite dishes bringing a dizzying array of viewing choices into people's homes. Many families own not only two or three (or more) televisions but also at least one VCR. With the seemingly endless demand for television shows from viewers, network producers and local station managers are always looking for programs that will attract viewers and draw sponsors.

One of the criticisms of television is that people, especially children, spend too much time watching it and doing nothing else. In fact, because so many people do spend so much of their time sitting and watching, we now have the term *couch potato* in our vocabulary. Pete Hamill is highly critical of the power of television on viewers. In his essay, "Crack and the Box," Hamill makes the unusual comparison of television addiction to drug addiction. He believes that mindlessly watching vapid programs on television is analogous to the mind-numbing effects of drugs on addicts. See if you agree with his view on the tremendous hold television has on many people's lives.

Next, Mike Males, in "Stop Blaming Kids and TV," offers a vastly different viewpoint on the power of television to affect young people. He cites numerous studies as well as his own personal observations from working with youths to support his firm belief that critics are wrongheaded to blame teens and mass media for problems such as youth violence, excessive teenaged drinking, and increased rates of smoking among teenagers. Rather, he argues, the real causes of these problems are alcoholic or drug-addicted parents, abusive parents or caregivers, and poverty.

The final two essays articulate opposing views on the subject of television and violence. Susan R. Lamson, in "TV Violence: Does

It Cause Real-Life Mayhem?" and William F. Buckley Jr., in "Don't Blame Violence on the Tube," express opposing opinions on whether television violence causes violent and criminal behavior. Lamson writes from the perspective of her official position in the National Rifle Association, and Buckley writes as a long-time host of a television show. As a further indication of the positions from which these authors are writing, consider the publications where their pieces were first published: Lamson's appeared in *American Hunter* and Buckley's in *TV Guide*. As you might guess from this information and the titles of their essays, Lamson argues that television violence has enormous influence on children and bears large responsibility for the high U.S. homicide rate, whereas Buckley argues that television does not cause violent behavior. Although the articles were published a decade ago, the arguments both writers use are still relevant today. Where do you stand on this issue?

CRACK AND THE BOX

Pete Hamill

Pete Hamill is a New York journalist, essayist, novelist, and biographer. He has also served as editor-in-chief of both the New York Post *and the* New York Daily News. *Among his many works are the novels* Loving Women *(1989) and* Snow in August *(1997); his memoir,* A Drinking Life *(1994); and the biographies* Why Sinatra Matters *(1998) and* Diego Rivera *(1999). Hamill first published "Crack and the Box" in* Esquire *magazine in 1990. It later appeared in* Piecework: Writings on Men and Women, Fools and Heroes, Lost Cities, Vanished Friends, Small Pleasures, Large Calamities, and How the Weather Was *(1996), a collection of Hamill's essays.*

One sad, rainy morning last winter I talked to a woman who was addicted to crack cocaine. She was twenty-two, stiletto-thin, with eyes as old as tombs. She was living in two rooms in a welfare hotel with her children, who were two, three, and five years of age. Her story was the usual tangle of human woe: early pregnancy, dropping out of school, vanished men, smack and then crack, tricks with johns in parked cars to pay for the dope. I asked her why she did drugs. She shrugged in an empty way and couldn't really answer beyond "makes me feel good." While we talked and she told her tale of squalor, the children ignored us. They were watching television.

Walking back to my office in the rain, I brooded about the woman, her zombie-like children, and my own callous indifference. I'd heard so many versions of the same story that I almost never wrote them anymore; the sons of similar women, glimpsed a dozen years ago, are now in Dannemora or Soledad or Joliet; in a hundred cities, their daughters are moving into the same loveless rooms. As I walked, a series of homeless men approached me for change, most of them junkies. Others sat in doorways, staring at nothing. They were additional casualties of our time of plague, demoralized reminders that although this country holds only two percent of the world's population, it consumes 65 percent of the world's supply of hard drugs.

Why, for God's sake? Why do so many millions of Americans of all ages, races, and classes choose to spend all or part of their lives stupefied? I've talked to hundreds of addicts over the years; some were my friends. But none could give sensible answers. They stutter about the pain of the world, about despair or boredom, the urgent need for magic or pleasure in a society empty of both. But then they just shrug. Americans have the money to buy drugs; the supply is plentiful. But almost nobody in power asks, *Why?* Least of all, George Bush and his drug warriors.

4   In the last Nielsen survey of American viewers, the average family was watching television seven hours a day. This has never happened before in history. No people has ever been entertained for seven hours a *day.* The Elizabethans didn't go to the theater seven hours a day. The pre-TV generation did not go to the movies seven hours a day. Common sense tells us that this all-pervasive diet of instant imagery, sustained now for forty years, must have changed us in profound ways.

Television, like drugs, dominates the lives of its addicts. And though some lonely Americans leave their sets on without watching them, using them as electronic companions, television usually absorbs its viewers the way drugs absorb their users. Viewers can't work or play while watching television; they can't read; they can't be out on the streets, falling in love with the wrong people, learning how to quarrel and compromise with other human beings. In short, they are asocial. So are drug addicts.

One Michigan State University study in the early eighties offered a group of four- and five-year-olds the choice of giving up television or giving up their fathers. Fully one-third said they would give up Daddy. Given a similar choice (between cocaine or heroin and father, mother, brother, sister, wife, husband, children, job), almost every stone junkie would do the same.

There are other disturbing similarities. Television itself is a consciousness-altering instrument. With the touch of a button, it takes you out of the "real" world in which you reside and can place you at a basketball game, the back alleys of Miami, the streets of Bucharest, or the cartoony living rooms of Sitcom Land. Each move from channel to channel alters mood, usually with music or a laugh track. On any given evening, you can laugh, be frightened, feel tension, thump with excitement. You can even tune in *MacNeil/Lehrer* and feel sober.

8   But none of these abrupt shifts in mood is *earned.* They are attained as easily as popping a pill. Getting news from television, for example, is simply not the same experience as reading it in a newspaper. Reading is *active.* The reader must decode little symbols called *words,* then create images or ideas and make them connect; at its most basic level, reading is an act of the imagination. But the television viewer doesn't go through that process. The words are spoken to him or her by Dan Rather

or Tom Brokaw or Peter Jennings. There isn't much decoding to do when watching television, no time to think or ponder before the next set of images and spoken words appears to displace the present one. The reader, being active, works at his or her own pace; the viewer, being passive, proceeds at a pace determined by the show. Except at the highest levels, television never demands that its audience take part in an act of imagination. Reading always does.

In short, television works on the same imaginative and intellectual level as psychoactive drugs. If prolonged television viewing makes the young passive (dozens of studies indicate that it does), then moving to drugs has a certain coherence. Drugs provide an unearned high (in contrast to the earned rush that comes from a feat accomplished, a human breakthrough earned by sweat or thought or love).

And because the television addict and the drug addict are alienated from the hard and scary world, they also feel they make no difference in its complicated events. For the junkie, the world is reduced to him or her and the needle, pipe, or vial; the self is absolutely isolated, with no desire for choice. The television addict lives the same way. Many Americans who fail to vote in presidential elections must believe they have no more control over such a choice than they do over the casting of *L.A. Law.*

The drug plague also coincides with the unspoken assumption of most television shows: Life should be *easy.* The most complicated events are summarized on TV news in a minute or less. Cops confront murder, chase the criminals, and bring them to justice (usually violently) within an hour. In commercials, you drink the right beer and you get the girl. *Easy!* So why should real life be a grind? Why should any American have to spend years mastering a skill or craft, or work eight hours a day at an unpleasant job, or endure the compromises and crises of a marriage?

12   The doper always whines about how he or she *feels;* drugs are used to enhance feelings or obliterate them, and in this the doper is very American. No other people on earth spend so much time talking about their feelings; hundreds of thousands go to shrinks, they buy self-help books by the millions, they pour out intimate confessions to virtual strangers in bars or discos. Our political campaigns are about emotional issues now, stated in the simplicities of adolescence. Even alleged statesmen can start a sentence, "I feel that the Sandinistas should . . ." when they once might have said, "I *think* . . ." I'm convinced that this exaltation of cheap emotions over logic and reason is one by-product of hundreds of thousands of hours of television.

Most Americans under the age of fifty have now spent their lives absorbing television; that is, they've had the structures of drama pounded into them. Drama is always about conflict. So news shows, politics, and advertising are now all shaped by those structures. Nobody will pay attention to anything as complicated as the part played by Third World debt in the expanding production of cocaine; it's much easier to focus on Manuel Noriega, a character right out of *Miami Vice,* and believe that even in real life there's a Mister Big.

What is to be done? Television is certainly not going away, but its addictive qualities can be controlled. It's a lot easier to "just say no" to television than to heroin or crack. As a beginning, parents must take immediate control of the sets, teaching children to watch specific television *programs,* not "television," to get out of the house and play with other kids. Elementary and high schools must begin teaching television as a subject, the way literature is taught, showing children how shows are made, how to distinguish between the true and the false, how to recognize cheap emotional manipulation. All Americans should spend more time reading. And thinking.

For years, the defenders of television have argued that the networks are only giving the people what they want. That might be true. But so is the Medellin Cartel.

Personal Response

Have you ever been addicted to television? If so, explain why you found it so appealing. If not, explain why you think you were never "hooked" on television viewing.

Questions for Class or Small-Group Discussion

1. Discuss whether you think Hamill is exaggerating when he says that television addiction is like drug addiction. Outline Hamill's major points of comparison between the two, and then consider whether you think the comparison holds on all points.

2. What do you think of Hamill's argument, in paragraph 3, that the government is asking the wrong questions in its war on drugs? Do you agree with him?

3. Do you agree with Hamill that television viewing is an entirely passive activity (paragraphs 8–9)? Can you give examples of television programs that prove him wrong?

4. Discuss your own television viewing habits. Do your own experiences bear out Hamill's views on the deadening effects of television?

5. Discuss Hamill's contention that because television is drama, and so many people watch television, "nobody will pay any attention to anything [. . .] complicated" (paragraph 13). Do you agree with him? Why or why not?

STOP BLAMING KIDS AND TV

Mike Males

Mike Males, senior researcher for the Justice Policy Institute and sociology instructor at the University of California, Santa Cruz, is author of several books: The Scapegoat Generation: America's War on Adolescents *(1996),* Framing Youth: Ten Myths About the Next Generation *(1998),* Smoked: Why Joe Camel is Still Smiling *(1999),* Juvenile Injustice: America's "Youth Violence" Hoax *(2000), and* Kids & Guns: How Politicians, Experts and the Press

Fabricate Fear of Youth *(2001). This essay first appeared in the October 1997 issue of* The Progressive.

"Children have never been very good at listening to their elders," James Baldwin wrote in *Nobody Knows My Name.* "But they have never failed to imitate them." This basic truth has all but disappeared as the public increasingly treats teenagers as a robot-like population under sway of an exploitative media. White House officials lecture film, music, Internet, fashion, and pop-culture moguls and accuse them of programming kids to smoke, drink, shoot up, have sex, and kill.

So do conservatives, led by William Bennett and Dan Quayle. Professional organizations are also into media-bashing. In its famous report on youth risks, the Carnegie Corporation devoted a full chapter to media influences.

Progressives are no exception. *Mother Jones* claims it has "proof that TV makes kids violent." And the Institute of Alternative Media emphasizes, "the average American child will witness . . . 200,000 acts of (TV) violence" by the time that child graduates from high school.

4   None of these varied interests note that during the eighteen years between a child's birth and graduation from high school, there will be fifteen million cases of *real* violence in American homes grave enough to require hospital emergency treatment. These assaults will cause ten million serious injuries and 40,000 deaths to children. In October 1996, the Department of Health and Human Services reported 565,000 serious injuries that abusive parents inflicted on children and youths in 1993. The number is up four-fold since 1986.

The Department of Health report disappeared from the news in one day. It elicited virtually no comment from the White House, Republicans, or law-enforcement officials. Nor from Carnegie scholars, whose 150-page study, "Great Transitions: Preparing Adolescents for a New Century," devotes two sentences to household violence. The left press took no particular interest in the story, either.

All sides seem to agree that fictional violence, sex on the screen, Joe Camel, beer-drinking frogs, or naked bodies on the Internet pose a bigger threat to children than do actual beatings, rape, or parental addictions. This, in turn, upholds the Clinton doctrine that youth behavior is the problem, and curbing young people's rights the answer.

Claims that TV causes violence bear little relation to real behavior. Japanese and European kids behold media as graphically brutal as that which appears on American screens, but seventeen-year-olds in those countries commit murder at rates lower than those of American seventy-year-olds.

8   Likewise, youths in different parts of the United States are exposed to the same media but display drastically different violence levels. TV violence does not account for the fact that the murder rate among black teens in Washington, D.C., is twenty-five times higher than that of white teens living a few Metro stops away. It doesn't explain why, nationally, murder doubled among nonwhite and Latino youth over the last decade, but declined among white Anglo teens. Furthermore, contrary to the TV

brainwashing theory, Anglo sixteen-year-olds have lower violent-crime rates than black sixty-year-olds, Latino forty-year-olds, and Anglo thirty-year-olds. Men, women, whites, Latino, blacks, Asians, teens, young adults, middle-agers, and senior citizens in Fresno County—California's poorest urban area—display murder and violent-crime rates double those of their counterparts in Ventura County, the state's richest.

Confounding every theory, America's biggest explosion in felony violent crime is not street crime among minorities or teens of any color, but domestic violence among aging, mostly white baby boomers. Should we arm Junior with a V-chip to protect him from Mom and Dad?

In practical terms, media-violence theories are not about kids, but about race and class: If TV accounts for any meaningful fraction of murder levels among poorer, nonwhite youth, why doesn't it have the same effect on white kids? Are minorities inherently programmable?

The newest target is Channel One, legitimately criticized by the Unplug Campaign—a watchdog sponsored by the Center for Commercial-Free Public Education—as a corporate marketing ploy packaged as educational TV. But then the Unplug Campaign gives credence to claims that "commercials control kids" by "harvesting minds," as Roy Fox of the University of Missouri says. These claims imply that teens are uniquely open to media brainwashing.

12   Other misleading claims come from Johns Hopkins University media analyst Mark Crispin Miller. In his critique of Channel One in the May edition of *Extra!*, Miller invoked such hackneyed phrases as the "inevitable rebelliousness of adolescent boys," the "hormones raging," and the "defiant boorish behavior" of "young men." Despite the popularity of these stereotypes, there is no basis in fact for such anti-youth bias.

A 1988 study in the *Journal of Youth and Adolescence* by psychology professors Grayson Holmbeck and John Hill concluded: "Adolescents are *not* in turmoil, *not* deeply disturbed, *not* at the mercy of their impulses, *not* resistant to parental values, and *not* rebellious."

In the November 1992 *Journal of the American Academy of Child and Adolescent Psychiatry,* Northwestern University psychiatry professor Daniel Offer reviewed 150 studies and concluded, in his article "Debunking the Myths of Adolescence," that "the effects of pubertal hormones are neither potent nor pervasive."

If anything, Channel One and other mainstream media reinforce young people's conformity to—not defiance of—adult values. Miller's unsubstantiated claims that student consumerism, bad behaviors, and mental or biological imbalances are compelled by media ads and images could be made with equal force about the behaviors of his own age group. Binge drinking, drug abuse, and violence against children by adults over the age of thirty are rising rapidly.

16   The barrage of sexually seductive liquor ads, fashion images, and anti-youth rhetoric, by conventional logic, must be influencing those hormonally unstable middle-agers.

I worked for a dozen years in youth programs in Montana and California. When problems arose, they usually crossed generations. I saw violent kids with dads or uncles in jail for assault. I saw middle-schoolers molested in childhood by mom's boyfriend. I saw budding teen alcoholics hoisting forty-ouncers alongside forty-year-old sots. I also saw again and again how kids start to smoke. In countless trailers and small apartments dense with blue haze, children roamed the rugs as grownups puffed. Mom and seventh-grade daughter swapped Dorals while bemoaning the evils of men. A junior-high basketball center slept outside before a big game because a dozen elders—from her non-inhaling sixteen-year-old brother to her grandma—were all chain smokers. Two years later, she'd given up and joined the party.

As a rule, teen smoking mimicked adult smoking by gender, race, locale, era, and household. I could discern no pop-culture puppetry. My survey of 400 Los Angeles middle-schoolers for a 1994 *Journal of School Health* article found children of smoking parents three times more likely to smoke by age fifteen than children of nonsmokers. Parents were the most influential but not the only adults kids emulated. Nor did youngsters copy elders slavishly. Youths often picked slightly different habits (like chewing tobacco, or their own brands).

In 1989, the Centers for Disease Control lamented, "75 percent of all teenage smokers come from homes where parents smoke." You don't hear such candor from today's put-politics-first health agencies. Centers for Disease Control tobacco chieftain Michael Eriksen informed me that his agency doesn't make an issue of parental smoking. Nor do anti-smoking groups. Asked Kathy Mulvey, research director of INFACT: "Why make enemies of fifty million adult smokers" when advertising creates the real "appeal of tobacco to youth?"

20   Do ads hook kids on cigarettes? Studies of the effects of the Joe Camel logo show only that a larger fraction of teen smokers than veteran adult smokers choose the Camel brand. When asked, some researchers admit they cannot demonstrate that advertising causes kids to smoke who would not otherwise. And that's the real issue. In fact, surveys found smoking declining among teens (especially the youngest) during Joe's advent from 1985 to 1990.

The University of California's Stanton Glantz, whose exposure of 10,000 tobacco documents enraged the industry, found corporate perfidy far shrewder than camels and cowboys.   → Treachery

"As the tobacco industry knows well," Glantz reported, "kids want to be like adults." An industry marketing document advises: "To reach young smokers, present the cigarette as one of the initiations into adult life . . . the basic symbols of growing up."

The biggest predictor of whether a teen will become a smoker, a drunk, or a druggie is whether or not the child grows up amid adult addicts. Three-fourths of murdered kids are killed by adults. Suicide and murder rates among white teenagers resemble those of white adults, and suicide and murder rates among black teens track those of black adults. And as far as teen pregnancy goes, for minor mothers, four-fifths of the fathers are adults over eighteen, and half are adults over twenty.

24   The inescapable conclusion is this: If you want to change juvenile behavior, change adult behavior. But instead of focusing on adults, almost everyone points a finger at kids—and at the TV culture that supposedly addicts them.

Groups like Mothers Against Drunk Driving charge, for instance, that Budweiser's frogs entice teens to drink. Yet the 1995 National Household Survey found teen alcohol use declining. "Youths aren't buying the cute and flashy beer images," an in-depth *USA Today* survey found. Most teens found the ads amusing, but they did not consume Bud as a result.

By squabbling over frogs, political interests can sidestep the impolitic tragedy that adults over the age of twenty-one cause 90 percent of America's 16,000 alcohol-related traffic deaths every year. Clinton and drug-policy chief Barry McCaffrey ignore federal reports that show a skyrocketing toll of booze and drug-related casualties among adults in their thirties and forties—the age group that is parenting most American teens. But both officials get favorable press attention by blaming alcohol ads and heroin chic for corrupting our kids.

Progressive reformers who insist kids are so malleable that beer frogs and Joe Camel and Ace Ventura push them to evil are not so different from those on the Christian right who claim that *Our Bodies, Ourselves* promotes teen sex and that the group Rage Against the Machine persuades pubescents to roll down Rodeo Drive with a shotgun.

28   America's increasingly marginalized young deserve better than grownup escapism. Millions of children and teenagers face real destitution, drug abuse, and violence in their homes. Yet these profound menaces continue to lurk in the background, even as the frogs, V-chips, and Mighty Morphins take center stage.

Personal Response

What is your immediate response to this essay? Are you surprised at Males's defense of young people? Have you heard similar arguments before, or is his approach different from what you are used to hearing about television and its influence on young people?

Questions for Class or Small-Group Discussion

1. Comment on this statement, which refers to the quotation that opens the essay: "This basic truth has all but disappeared as the public increasingly treats teenagers as a robot-like population under sway of an exploitative media" (paragraph 1). State the "basic truth" that Males believes the quotation suggests. Then consider what Males seems to mean when he says that teenagers are treated "as a robot-like population." Do you agree with him on that point?

2. Discuss this statement: "In practical terms, media-violence theories are not about kids, but about race and class" (paragraph 10). Are you persuaded by the evidence Males presents to support this assertion? Can you add further proof or offer a counterargument?

3. Respond to this statement in paragraph 24: "If you want to change juvenile behavior, change adult behavior."

4. How persuaded are you by Males's argument? Do you think that his personal observations strengthen or weaken his argument? What do you think about his use of loaded language and sarcasm? How would you assess the strengths and weaknesses of his argument overall?

TV VIOLENCE: DOES IT CAUSE REAL-LIFE MAYHEM?

Susan R. Lamson

Susan R. Lamson, former director of national affairs for the National Rifle Association, now directs the Conservation, Wildlife and Natural Resources Institute for Legislative Action, National Rifle Association. At a congressional hearing on television violence in 1993, which she refers to in this article, Lamson explained the position of the National Rifle Association on the role of television violence. She continues to represent the NRA before congressional hearings. In this July 1993 American Hunter *article, Lamson answers the question posed by her title.*

Turn on your TV virtually any time of any day and you can bring a carnival of murder, mayhem, and bloodshed right into your living room. Maybe, like many Americans, you've grown accustomed to it and even expect it. But step back and look at this kaleidoscope of killing through the eyes of a child—and consider what role it's played for America's new generation of ultraviolent killers—and you see what a menace TV violence really is.

Televised mayhem is seen as a leading cause of America's epidemic of violent crime. It was the subject of May 12 hearings before the House Energy and Commerce Committee's Telecommunications and Finance subcommittee and the Senate Judiciary Committee's Constitution subcommittee. I represented NRA at the hearings and was joined by the nation's leading experts on human behavior and psychology to call for an end—or at least a reduction—of the broadcast brutality that's taking such a vicious toll on society.

As Dr. Brandon S. Centerwall, professor of epidemiology at the University of Washington, explained: "The U.S. national homicide rate has doubled since the 1950s. As a member of the Centers for Disease Control violence research team, my task was to determine why. A wide array of possible causes was examined—the 'baby boom' effect, trends in urbanization, economic trends, trends in alcohol abuse, the role of capital punishment, the effects of civil unrest, the availability of firearms, exposure to television."

4   "Over the course of seven years of investigation," Dr. Centerwall continued, "each of these purported causes was tested in a variety of ways to see whether it could be eliminated as a credible contributor to the doubling of rates of violence in the United States. And, one by one, each of them was invalidated, except for television."

If that's frightening to you, consider this: In his landmark 1989 study, Centerwall concluded, "it is estimated that exposure to television is etiologically [causally] related to approximately one-half of the homicides committed in the United States, or approximately 10,000 homicides annually, and to a major proportion—perhaps one-half—of rapes, assaults, and other forms of interpersonal violence in the United States."

While not all agree with Centerwall's assessment of the problem's severity, few challenge his claim that Hollywood bloodshed *does* spill out from the screen and into our lives. As the American Psychological Association testified, the cause-and-effect link between TV violence and human aggression has been well-established for nearly twenty years. But until recently the TV networks have been reluctant to change. That's why in 1990 Congress passed the Television Violence Act, that allowed the networks to cooperate and develop programming standards with which they and the public could live.

The problem is, violence sells. Media executives know it and profit from it. More viewers means higher ratings, which add up to more advertising dollars. So, as the National Institute of Mental Health has found, 80 percent of all television programs contain violent acts. But the violence is like a drug: Viewers develop a tolerance for it, so media "pushers" give them steadily more.

8   Typically, prime-time programming has averaged eight to twelve violent acts per hour. A recent study by the Annenberg School of Communications found violence in children's programming at an historic high—thirty-two violent acts per hour. And a recent *TV Guide* study counted 1,845 acts of violence in eighteen hours of viewing time, an average of 100 violent acts per hour, or one every thirty-six seconds.

While adults may see all this TV mayhem as just the latest "action entertainment," children don't get it. Psychologists agree that up to ages three and four, children can't distinguish fact from fantasy on TV. For them, TV is a reflection of the world, and it's not a friendly place. Still, juvenile viewership is high. Children average nearly four hours of TV per day, and in the inner cities that increases to as many as eleven hours. Which means that in many cases, TV is the reality.

And this TV violence "addiction" is taking an increasingly grisly toll. FBI and census data show the homicide arrest rate for seventeen-year-olds more than doubled between 1985 and 1991, and the rate for fifteen- and sixteen-year-olds increased even faster. Psychologists point to several effects of televised mayhem: Children are taught that society is normally violent. They become disproportionately frightened of being victimized and become less likely to help victims of crime. They also grow more aggressive and violent themselves.

Through the Television Violence Act, the major networks have agreed on a set of standards to reduce the level of gratuitous violence in their programs. But so far, there's been little change; network executives promise better for the fall 1993 season.

12   Ironically, this year's congressional hearings on TV violence were in May— "sweeps month,"—when the networks compete for the viewership ratings that determine their advertising profits for the year to come. Some critics are calling May 1993 one of the most violent sweeps months in TV history.

Whereas in years past, entertainment executives flatly refuted the dangers of TV violence, the network heads who testified during the May hearings were more receptive of change—or so they said. Still, their words somehow ring hollow, especially given the brutality of their "sweeps month" programming.

Howard Stringer, president of CBS, Warren Littlefield of NBC, and Thomas S. Murphy of ABC all spoke at the congressional hearings. Stringer talked of his network's "principles," "seriousness," "responsibility," and "careful and extensive discussion"—yet there seems to be no end to the bloodshed. Then, in a *Washington Post* story days later, Stringer blamed firearms: "There are 200 million guns, 66 million handguns in America. That has a lot to do with violence." (Readers will remember that the Washington, DC, affiliate of Stringer's network recently rejected NRA's new commercial on the failings of the criminal justice system. The remarkable excuse given by CBS's affiliate was that the commercial "tends to inflame or incite.")

Barring legislation, congressional hearings can't accomplish much without unified grassroots pressure from citizens. Ultimately, your letters, phone calls, and faxes are the best ammunition in the fight to cut televised brutality and thus curb crime and safeguard your Second Amendment rights. When you see examples of pointless, gratuitous violence in your TV programming, write to the network executives and let them know how you feel. The appropriate names and addresses are as follows:

(IE: Send Junkmail to rich people!)

Chairman of the Board
Capital Cities/ABC, Inc.
77 W. 66th St.
New York, NY 10023-6201

President
CBS Broadcast Group
524 W. 57th St.
New York, NY 10019-2902

President
NBC Entertainment
30 Rockefeller Plaza
New York, NY 10012-0002

16   Better yet, make a note of what products or services are advertised during violent programs, and voice your outrage to the leaders of those companies. You can get the proper names and addresses through your library's reference section. Excellent resources include *Standard & Poor's Register of Corporations, Directors, and Executives*, Dun & Bradstreet's *Million Dollar Directory*, and *Moody's Manuals*.

In the end, only you—as a consumer, TV viewer, and voter—can demand an end to the televised violence that's bloodying our society. If all NRA members and gun owners do their part in this fight, we *can* cut into the TV destruction that so gravely threatens both our children and our Bill of Rights.

Personal Response

Do you agree with Lamson that television shows entirely too much violence? If so, does such violence bother you? Explain your answer.

Questions for Class or Small-Group Discussion

1. Lamson asks readers to consider the role that television has played "for America's new generation of ultraviolent killers" (paragraph 1). Discuss whether you think Lamson offers conclusive proof to support her belief in the causal relationship between television violence and real-life violence.

2. Lamson says in paragraph 2 that "televised mayhem is seen as a leading cause of America's epidemic of violent crime." Discuss other causes that may also account for the epidemic of crime.

3. Watch prime-time television for one evening or children's programs for one Saturday morning, and record the number of violent acts you see. Decide beforehand exactly what will be considered a violent act. (For instance, will you include verbal assaults?) If several of your classmates do the same, on different evenings or different channels, you should get a good indication of whether the figures Lamson cites in paragraph 8 are still accurate today. Do a follow-up discussion of your observations.

4. Evaluate the argument Lamson makes here. Do you think her interest in the National Rifle Association in any way influences her argument? Does it influence your evaluation of the argument?

DON'T BLAME VIOLENCE ON THE TUBE

William F. Buckley, Jr.

William F. Buckley Jr. is founder of The National Review *and host of the long-running television show* Firing Line. *He has written several books of nonfiction, including* Up from Liberalism *(1959, 1984) and* The Unmaking of a Mayor *(1966). His novels, most of which feature international intrigue, include* Saving the Queen *(1976),* Stained Glass *(1978),* Who's on First *(1980),* Marco Polo, If You Can *(1981),* Atlantic High *(1983),* See You Later, Alligator *(1985), and* High Jinx *(1986). Buckley's other books include* Racing Through Paradise *(1987),* On the Firing Line *(1989),* The Culture of Liberty *(1993), and* Brothers No More *(1995). This essay first appeared in* TV Guide *in 1994.*

There's something about violence that—abstractly—appeals. Children reflect this most directly. Children don't lie: They haven't reached the age of guile, so when they gravitate to toy guns, and gory comics, and movies with arrows through chests, and boiling oil, and exploding turrets, the eyes marvel with fascination, and the nickels pour out for more. One needs to reflect on the phenomenon, and apply it not to children, but to their parents.

The chestnut about how if you kill one person you're a murderer, if you kill a million you are a great general, applies, if indirectly, to the uproar about TV. What hurts is the *particularization* of violence. When what you see on the screen is machine guns or artillery blazing forth and dozens, even hundreds, of people—Indians, or Nazis, or Japanese—dropping in their tracks, that's stuff you look at without ever disturbing the rhythm of your hand passing from the popcorn to your mouth. It's when the screen focuses on an individual that one's emotional attention is arrested.

And then it's what happens to the victim that makes the difference. If he is merely going to be shot, that doesn't, in most cases, bother people or even grip their imagination. Especially if he is the fifth or fifteenth person shot in that television hour. It is when the act of violence causes the viewer to fasten his attention not so much on the capacity of so many people to kill, but on the capacity of some people to engage in individuated cruelty—that's when you feel the impulse to close your eyes, and when the memory is haunting. These are distinctions Attorney General Reno didn't make when she yakked about how the TV world has to clean up its act, or she will report it to Congress.

4   Consider the elementary distinction: We are viewing *Roots,* the story of slavery in the United States. A mean white master sets out to punish the unruly or insolent or courageous slave, and somebody steps up with a big long whip. The first stroke brings out an instant diagonal welt on the slave's back, and as you see it, you hear his grunt of pain. What then does the camera do?

What it ought to do is what it generally does—turn to look in on the faces of the bystanders; or of the slavemaster's wife, mistress, children; whatever. And what you hear is the repeated slash of the whip and the yelps of pain.

That is violence going on, no question about it, but it is a violence that at least has the grace to blush. It is the lady's fan lifted up to conceal the view of the bull's horn that has got the matador in the groin and is tossing him skyward, the shuttered eyes of the man viewing the same scene. It is what distinguishes the sadist from the viewer who wants realism and excitement and drama but doesn't want that element of violence that indulges instincts it is the purpose of civilization to quieten.

The six-year-old who takes pleasure in seeing his brother disciplined will, if all goes well with his moral development, want to avoid seeing any such scene by the time he is sixteen. What he has learned in the interval is that pain is something we seek to avoid. Pain—violence—is what is done by people who aren't socialized, and are insensible to the pain of others. When pain is unavoidable, the doctors are there with narcotics. When it is unnecessary—as with the crime that surrounds us—it is nevertheless the stuff of real life, and we learn about real life primarily, these days, from television.

8   ‾The statistic is that by the time the average child finishes elementary school, he will have seen some 8,000 people "killed" on TV. And the fuss seems to be about the impact that viewing has on the young American growing up. It is tempting to postulate a correlation: (1) We live in a society in which crime is rampant and generally increasing. And (2) we live in a society in which crime-on-TV is increasing. There are, granted, little oscillations in both generalities: Crime has slightly decreased this year, in several categories. And violence is less frequent on network television, but it is nevertheless all over the place, on TV as in city streets. (3) Therefore: Television is responsible for the proliferation of crime.

We do not in fact know whether this is so. As has been pointed out by critics of television critics, the same stuff we see here on TV is seen in Great Britain and Japan, yet we have more than three times as much crime as Great Britain, and nine times as much as Japan: So why didn't all that violence corrupt the Brits and the Japanese?

It isn't easy to answer that objection, not if your design is like that of Sen. Hollings of South Carolina. He seems to want to hold television responsible for national violence. And of course it springs quickly to mind that if a politician denounces somebody or something for the crime wave, people will get the impression that he is *doing something* about crime, which is generally not the case. It can't be established that crime on the screen has zero connection with crime on the street. No one can tell us how much crime we would have in America, or in England or Japan, if there were *no* crime on television. Perhaps less. Certainly a little less, because we know that specific acts of violence depicted on television have been imitated.

We can't know what it is in the nature of some individuals that causes them to take insane risks. We can't know why early in December a jilted ensign shot his girlfriend and one of his Annapolis classmates and then himself, instead of behaving like however many other jilted ensigns who *don't* slaughter the girl who draws away from them. And we cannot establish that he was attracted to violence because of all the killings he saw on television. The Hutus and Tutsis twice in thirty years have killed each other in tribal warfare on a scale that dwarfs American murder (23,750 per year) into insignificance. During most of that time there was no television in Burundi.

12   Our problem is this insensibility to others' feelings, to their rights, to their person. The Christian religion, like most others, teaches us that it is sinful to cause pain, except as civil punishment. We develop in such a way as to cultivate this moral sense that tells us violence is wrong. And if our education succeeds, we feel a progressive distaste for any lascivious treatment of pain. If that moral development isn't cultivated, we are callous. To the extent that we are that, we indulge ourselves in gross forms of realism, and involve ourselves in bloody spectacles that seemed routine to the Romans, who enjoyed witnessing the torture of Christians by lions. It wasn't

television that moved the crowds to shout out their joy at seeing men and women torn limb from limb, or that caused Elizabethan society to devise excruciating ways in which to end the lives of heretics. These were the fruit of different, and undeveloped, moral perspectives.

Roots, I have heard it said, caused many Americans to realize just what it was that Americans were capable of doing to other human beings during the days of slavery. I don't doubt that the horror we feel for the Holocaust is significantly the responsibility of such scenes as Herman Wouk gave us in the miniseries based on his great *Winds of War* novels. The thing to keep your eyes on, surely, is just that one detail: the barring of the entirely redundant detail.

Good Fellas told us a story of life in the Mafia. It is as violent as violence gets. But there was a single scene in it that startled the viewer. Or put it this way: One hopes not to encounter anyone who saw it and *wasn't* startled when one of the protagonists opened the trunk of the car where the wounded antagonist lay and plunged a kitchen knife borrowed from his mother into his whimpering prisoner. The viewer saw it—almost all. There was no closeup of the blade entering the stomach and chest—that much was left to the imagination. And such are the critical distinctions in a society that affirms some threshold in matters of taste.

That taste can never be generated by acts of Congress or claps of thunder issuing from the Attorney General. We suffer from many ailments in America, and a whole lot can be said about the insufficiencies of TV, but not that it is responsible for original sin, whose harvest in every human being varies from season to season, leaving us only to know that here and there, there will always be sin. Don't blame it on the tube. Television violence can do as much to enhance our inclination to oppose violence as to reinforce any inclination to engage in it.

Personal Response

Do you agree with the critics who say television is too violent, or do you agree with Buckley?

Questions for Class or Small-Group Discussion

1. How convincing do you find Buckley's argument? Where do you see weaknesses, if any, in his reasoning?

2. What do you think of Buckley's observation that people were violent long before television was invented? Does that fact necessarily mean that television does not cause violence?

3. Comment on Buckley's concluding statement: "Television violence can do as much to enhance our inclination to oppose violence as to reinforce any inclination to engage in it."

4. As Buckley concedes, it is true that some people commit violent acts after watching a television show (paragraph 10). However, most people do not commit violent acts. What do you think keeps people from committing crimes, and how do you

account for the extreme cruelty and violence of a few? What role, if any, do you think violent media play in such violence?

PERSPECTIVES ON TELEVISION

Suggestions for Synthesis

1. Compare and contrast Susan R. Lamson's argument in "TV Violence: Does It Cause Real-Life Mayhem?" with William F. Buckley's in "Don't Blame Violence on the Tube." State whose argument you prefer and why.

2. Compare and contrast Pete Hamill's "Crack and the Box" with Mike Males's "Stop Blaming Kids and TV."

3. Drawing on two or more of the essays in this chapter, explore the positive and negative aspects of a particular type of television programming, such as situation comedies, medical dramas, or soap operas.

4. Drawing on two or more of the essays in this chapter, write an opinion paper on the role of television in American popular culture.

Additional Writing Topics

1. Write a paper in which you either defend or challenge the position of Pete Hamill ("Crack and the Box"), Mike Males ("Stop Blaming Kids and TV"), Susan R. Lamson ("TV Violence: Does It Cause Real-Life Mayhem?"), or William F. Buckley Jr. ("Don't Blame Violence on the Tube").

2. Write a letter to the president of one of the major television networks in which you express your views on the nature and quality of its programming for children.

3. Write a letter to either or both the sponsors and the producer of a television program you find particularly violent, mindless, or vulgar, explaining your complaint and what you would like to see changed.

4. Write a letter to the sponsors or producer of a television program you find intellectually stimulating, educational, or informative, praising the program and pointing out its best features.

5. Discuss examples of current television programs for children that you think are either potentially beneficial or potentially harmful to them.

6. Respond to the comment by Pete Hamill that although America makes up only "two percent of the world's population, it consumes 65 percent of the world's supply of hard drugs" ("Crack and the Box").

7. Write an analysis of a popular television show. Your analysis can be either positive or negative, depending on your own feelings about the show. You may criticize a ridiculous, boring, or poorly acted show, for instance, or you may praise a brilliant, hilarious, or wonderfully acted one.

Research Topics

1. Susan R. Lamson states in "TV Violence: Does It Cause Real-Life Mayhem?" that "the cause-and-effect link between TV violence and human aggression has been well-established for nearly twenty years" (paragraph 6). Research the causal connection between television violence and human aggression and either support or refute her statement.

2. Research the Television Violence Act. Find out what it is and what critics, behaviorists, and media experts say about its potential effectiveness. Then explain your own opinion of the effectiveness of such an act.

3. In 1961, Newton N. Minow coined the term *vast wasteland* for what he saw as television's empty content and anti-intellectualism. Argue either that television remains a vast wasteland or that the phrase is unfair to television. Base your position on research into the views of experts or others who have published opinions on the subject. Include the results of studies or any other relevant data you find.

4. Research any of the topics suggested by the writers in this chapter.

5. Research any of the subjects relevant to this chapter that are suggested by the titles of books that Mike Males has written: *The Scapegoat Generation: America's War on Adolescents* (1996), *Framing Youth: Ten Myths About the Next Generation* (1998), *Smoked: Why Joe Camel is Still Smiling* (1999), *Juvenile Injustice: America's "Youth Violence" Hoax* (2000), or *Kids & Guns: How Politicians, Experts and the Press Fabricate Fear of Youth* (2001). Refer to one or more of these books in your paper.

CHAPTER 11

ADVERTISING

Advertising is big business. A company may spend millions of dollars promoting a product in a single ad campaign. Advertising spots on spectacular televised events, such as the Super Bowl or the Olympics, can cost advertisers dearly, as does space in magazines and newspapers with wide circulation. Clearly, advertising has an effect on the success of sales, or advertising space and time would not cost what they do, and companies would not commit so many dollars to print and television ads. Because of its potential to influence consumers, the advertising industry has always been the object of criticism from a number of quarters. Analysts protest the potentially harmful images of some ads, consumer advocate groups object to advertisements for certain products, and government regulatory committees create guidelines ensuring fairness in advertising. The essays in this chapter address some of these issues surrounding the advertising industry.

Jean Kilbourne, in "Advertising's Influence on Media Content," argues that advertising has a big influence not only on audiences but also on the media itself. She explains two major ways in which that influence is exerted and gives examples to support her allegations. As you read her examples and her analyses of the influence of advertisers on various kinds of media, see if you can think of other examples to either support or refute what she claims. In an essay that also acknowledges the influence of advertising but that sees its influence in a different light, Richard Wolkomir and Joyce Wolkomir, in "You Are What You Buy," profile James B. Twitchell, author of *Lead Us Into Temptation: The Triumph of American Materialism.* Their article provides a historical overview of mass marketing, using many examples of successful advertising campaigns as they follow Twitchell through a Wal-Mart.

William Lutz, in "With These Words I Can Sell You Anything," analyzes the way advertisers use words to manipulate consumers. In particular, he is concerned about imprecise and essentially meaningless "weasel" words. As you read his analysis and consider his examples, think about how often you see and read those words in advertisements and on products themselves. Think about the extent to which you are influenced by such words as you make decisions about what brands or products to buy.

The chapter ends with a defense of advertising. Attacking consumer advocates and government regulators who are critical of the manipulative power of advertising, John O'Toole, in "What Advertising Isn't," insists that advertisers use fair and legitimate strategies to sell their products. As you read O'Toole's opposing opinion, consider whether you think that he offers a reasonable counterargument to the arguments of the other writers in this chapter.

ADVERTISING'S INFLUENCE ON MEDIA CONTENT

Jean Kilbourne

Jean Kilbourne has lectured for many years on advertising images of women and on alcohol and liquor advertisements. A widely published writer and speaker who has twice been named Lecturer of the Year by the National Association of Campus Activities, she is perhaps best known for her award-winning documentaries on advertising images, Killing Us Softly, Slim Hopes, *and* Pack of Lies. *This piece is an excerpt from chapter 1 of Kilbourne's latest book,* Can't Buy My Love: How Advertising Changes the Way We Think and Feel *(2000) (hard cover title:* Deadly Persuasion: Why Women and Girls Must Fight the Addictive Power and Advertising). *You can find additional resources and other information at Kilbourne's Web site: <www.jeankilbourne.com>.*

Advertising's influence on media content is exerted in two major ways: via the suppression of information that would harm or "offend the sponsor" and via the inclusion of editorial content that is advertiser-friendly, that creates an environment in which the ads look good. The line between advertising and editorial content is blurred by "advertorials" (advertising disguised as editorial copy) "product placement" in television programs and feature films, and the widespread use of "video news releases," corporate public-relations puff pieces aired by local television stations as genuine news. Up to 85 percent of the news we get is bought and paid for by corporations eager to gain positive publicity.

Although people have become used to news reporters popping up in commercials and movies (as Joan Lunden and Linda Ellerbee did in television commercials for Vaseline and Maxwell House coffee, respectively, and as almost everyone at CNN did in the movie *Contact*), many were shocked in late 1997 when retired newsman David Brinkley became the pitchman for agribusiness giant Archer Daniels Midland, a company that has been convicted of price fixing on an international scale.

In 1998 Nike's sponsorship of CBS's Olympic coverage was rewarded when the correspondents delivered the news wearing jackets emblazoned with Nike's symbolic swoosh. The president of CBS News vehemently denied that this sponsorship had anything to do with the thwarting of a follow-up to a hard-hitting investigative piece on Nike for *48 Hours*. The editor of *The San Francisco Examiner* likewise denied that Nike's cosponsorship of their big annual promotion was in any way related to the decision to kill a column by a reporter that was highly critical of Nike.

4   In 1996 Chrysler Corporation set off a furor by demanding in writing that magazines notify it in advance about "any and all editorial content that encompasses sexual, political, social issues or any editorial that might be construed as provocative or offensive." According to Chrysler spokesman Mike Aberlich, placing an ad is like buying a house: "You decide the neighborhood you want to be in." Fear of losing the lucrative Chrysler account led *Esquire* to kill a long story with a gay theme, already in page proofs, by accomplished author David Leavitt. Will Blythe, the magazine's literary editor, promptly quit, saying in his letter of resignation that "in effect, we're taking marching orders (albeit, indirectly) from advertisers." Of course, had Blythe not gone public, the public would never have known what happened. When we don't get the story, we don't know what we're missing.

In reaction to the Chrysler letter, the American Society of Magazine Editors and Magazine Publishers of America issued a joint statement in the fall of 1997 calling for editorial integrity and barring magazines from giving advertisers a preview of stories, photos, or tables of contents for upcoming issues. This is to their credit, of course, but it won't protect us from similar phenomena occurring: According to an article in the *Columbia Journalism Review*, in 1997 a major advertiser (unnamed in the article) warned all three newsweeklies—*Time, Newsweek,* and *U.S. News & World Report*—that it would award all of its advertising to the magazine that portrayed its company's industry in the most favorable light during the upcoming quarter.

More often than not, self-censorship by magazine editors and television producers makes such overt pressure by corporations unnecessary. According to Kurt Andersen, the former editor of *New York* magazine, "Because I worked closely and happily with the publisher at *New York*, I was aware who the big advertisers were. My antennae were turned on, and I read copy thinking, 'Is this going to cause Calvin Klein or Bergdorf big problems.'" No doubt this is what ran through the minds of the CBS executives who canceled Ed Asner's series after two large corporate advertisers—Vidal Sassoon and Kimberly-Clark—withdrew their sponsorship because of Asner's association with Medical Aid for El Salvador.

Sometimes the self-censorship involves an entire industry rather than a specific company or corporation. For example, several radio stations in the Midwest not only refused to play a commercial advocating vegetarianism in which country singer k.d. lang appeared as a spokesperson, but also banned lang's songs from the air. Clearly this kind of thinking has more serious consequences than an occasional editorial omission or favorable mention—it warps a worldview and distorts the editorial content we read and the programs we listen to and watch.

8   Nowhere is this more obvious than in most women's and girls' magazines, where there is a very fine line, if any, between advertising and editorial content. Most of these magazines gladly provide a climate in which ads for diet and beauty products

will be looked at with interest, even with desperation. And they suffer consequences from advertisers if they fail to provide such a climate.

Gloria Steinem provides a striking example of this in her article "Sex, Lies & Advertising," in which she discusses an award-winning story on Soviet women that was featured on the cover of the November 1980 issue of *Ms.* In those days, *Ms.,* like every other woman's magazine, depended on advertising. Following that story, *Ms.* lost all hope of ever getting Revlon ads. Why? Because the Soviet women on the cover weren't wearing makeup.

More recently, the editor of *New Woman* magazine in Australia resigned after advertisers complained about the publication's use of a heavyset cover girl, even though letters had poured in from grateful readers. According to *Advertising Age International,* her departure "made clear the influence wielded by advertisers who remain convinced that only thin models spur sales of beauty products." One prevalent form of censorship in the mass media is the almost complete invisibility, the eradication, of real women's faces and bodies.

No wonder women's magazines so often have covers that feature luscious cakes and pies juxtaposed with articles about diets. "85 Ways to Lose Weight," *Woman's Day* tells us—but probably one of them isn't the "10-minute ice cream pie" on the cover. This is an invitation to pathology, fueling the paradoxical obsession with food and weight control that is one of the hallmarks of eating disorders.

12 It can be shocking to look at the front and back covers of magazines. Often there are ironic juxtapositions. A typical woman's magazine has a photo of some rich food on the front cover, a cheesecake covered with luscious cherries or a huge slice of apple pie with ice cream melting on top. On the back cover, there is usually a cigarette ad, often one implying that smoking will keep women thin. Inside the magazine are recipes, more photos of fattening foods, articles about dieting—and lots of advertising featuring very thin models. There usually also is at least one article about an uncommon disease or trivial health hazard, which can seem very ironic in light of the truly dangerous product being glamorized on the back cover.

In February 1999, *Family Circle* featured on its front cover a luscious photo of "gingham mini-cakes," while promoting articles entitled "New! Lose-Weight, Stay-Young Diet," "Super Foods That Act Like Medicine," and "The Healing Power of Love." On the back cover was an ad for Virginia Slims cigarettes. The same week, *For Women First* featured a chocolate cake on its cover along with one article entitled "Accelerate Fat Loss" and another promising "Breakthrough Cures" for varicose veins, cellulite, PMS, stress, tiredness, and dry skin. On the back cover, an ad for Doral cigarettes said, "Imagine getting more." *The Ladies' Home Journal* that same month offered on its cover "The Best Chocolate Cake You Ever Ate," along with its antidote, "Want to Lose 10 lbs? Re-program Your Body." Concern for their readers' health was reflected in two articles highlighted on the cover, "12 Symptoms You Must Not Ignore" and "De-Stressors for Really Crazy Workdays"—and then undermined by the ad for Basic cigarettes on the back cover (which added to the general confusion by picturing the pack surrounded by chocolate candies).

The diseases and health hazards warned about in the women's magazines are often ridiculous. *Woman's Day* once offered a "Special Report on Deadly Appliances," which warned us about how our appliances, such as toasters, coffeemakers, baby monitors, and nightlights, can suddenly burst into flame. Lest we think this is not a serious problem, the article tells us that in 1993, the last year for which figures were available, 80 people died and 370 were injured by these killer appliances. I don't wish to minimize any death or injury. However, on the back cover of this issue of *Woman's Day* is an advertisement for cigarettes, a product that kills over four hundred thousand people, year in and year out.

The January 1995 issue of *Redbook* warns us on the cover about all sorts of pressing problems from frizzy hair to "erotic accidents" and promotes an article entitled "If Only They'd Caught It Sooner: The Tests Even Healthy Women Need." On the back cover, as always, an ad for Virginia Slims. Needless to say, being set afire from smoking in bed (one of the leading causes of fire deaths) does not make it into the "erotic accidents" article.

16   An informal survey of popular women's magazines in 1996 found cover stories on some of the following health issues: skin cancer, Pap smears, leukemia, how breast cancer can be fought with a positive attitude, how breast cancer can be held off with aspirin, and the possibility that dry-cleaned clothes can cause cancer. There were cigarette ads on the back covers of all these magazines—and not a single mention inside of lung cancer and heart disease caused by smoking. In spite of increasing coverage of tobacco issues in the late 1990s, the silence in women's magazines has continued, in America and throughout the world. In my own research, I continue to find scanty coverage of smoking dangers, no feature stories on lung cancer or on smoking's role in causing many other cancers and heart disease . . . and hundreds of cigarette ads.

Dr. Holly Atkinson, a health writer for *New Woman* between 1985 and 1990, recalled that she was barred from covering smoking-related issues, and that her editor struck any reference to cigarettes in articles on topics ranging from wrinkles to cancer. When Atkinson confronted the editor, a shouting match ensued. "Holly, who do you think supports this magazine?" demanded the editor. As Helen Gurley Brown, former editor of *Cosmopolitan,* said: "Having come from the advertising world myself, I think, 'Who needs somebody you're paying millions of dollars a year to come back and bite you on the ankle?' "

It is not just women's magazines that tailor their articles to match their ads. The July 1995 issue of *Life* magazine warns us of the dangers our children face, including drugs, and asks, "How can we keep our children safe?" On the back cover is a Marlboro ad. Our children are far more likely to die from tobacco-related diseases than from any other cause, but cigarettes are not mentioned in the article.

Americans rely on the media for our health information. But this information is altered, distorted, even censored on behalf of the advertisers—advertisers for alcohol, cigarettes, junk food, diet products. We get most of our information from people who are likely to be thinking, "Is this going to cause Philip Morris or Anheuser-Busch big problems?" Of course, in recent years there has been front-page coverage of the liability suits against the tobacco industry and much discussion about antismoking legislation. However, there is still very little information about the health conse-quences of smoking, especially in women's magazines. The Partnership for a Drug-Free America, made up primarily of media companies dependent on advertising, basically refuses to warn children against the dangers of alcohol and tobacco. The government is spending $195 million in 1999 on a national media campaign to dis-suade adolescents from using illicit drugs, but not a penny of the appropriated tax dollars is going to warn about the dangers of smoking or drinking.

20   No wonder most people still don't understand that these heavily advertised drugs pose a much greater threat to our young people and kill far more Americans than all illicit drugs combined. Thirty percent of Americans still don't know that smoking shortens life expectancy, and almost 60 percent don't know it causes emphysema. There is still so much ignorance that, when I was invited recently to give a talk on to-bacco advertising to students at a progressive private school outside Boston, the per-son extending the invitation said she was also going to invite someone from the tobacco industry to represent "the other side." I was tempted to ask her if she felt equally compelled to have a batterer on hand during a discussion of domestic violence.

The influence of these huge and powerful corporations on the media leads to a pernicious kind of censorship. The problem is exacerbated by the fact that many of these corporations own and control the media. In 1996 the Seagram Company ran a whiskey ad on an NBC affiliate in Texas, thus breaking the decades-old tradition of liquor ads not being carried on television. Although network television is leery of run-ning liquor ads for fear of offending their beer advertisers, *Advertising Age* reported that Seagram might have a "winning card to play," since the company owns 50 per-cent of both the USA Network and the Sci-Fi Channel. Although both have a ban on hard-liquor advertising, a top executive for USA Network said, "If Seagram came to us with a hard-liquor ad, we'd have to look at it."

Today, Time Warner, Sony, Viacom, Disney, Bertelsmann, and News Corporation together control most publishing, music, television, film, and theme-park entertain-ment throughout the developed world. It is estimated that by the end of the millen-nium these companies will own 90 percent of the world's information, from newspapers to computer software to film to television to popular music. We may be able to change the channel, but we won't be able to change the message.

Almost everywhere we look these days, anywhere in the world, there is a message from one of these conglomerates. An ad in *Advertising Age* shows a huge picture of the earth and the headline, "Do you see the trillion dollar market?" The triumph of democracy is becoming the triumph of consumerism, as the global village is reduced to a "trillion dollar market."

24   "Why 6,000,000 women who used to carry a little red book now carry a little red lipstick," says an ad for *Allure,* an American beauty magazine, featuring a Chinese woman in a military uniform wearing bright red lipstick. The copy continues, "When nail polish becomes political, and fashion becomes philosophy, *Allure* magazine will

be there." In the world of advertising the political is only personal. Six million women carrying a book of political ideas might be a movement, even a revolution. The same women, carrying lipstick, are simply red-lipped consumers. Advertisers are adept at appropriating dissent and rebellion, slickly packaging it, and then selling it right back to us.

Although the conglomerates are transnational, the culture they sell is American. Not the American culture of the past, which exported writers like Ernest Hemingway and Edgar Allan Poe, musical greats like Louis Armstrong and Marian Anderson, plays by Eugene O'Neill and Tennessee Williams, and Broadway musicals like *West Side Story*. These exports celebrated democracy, freedom, and vitality as the American way of life.

Today we export a popular culture that promotes escapism, consumerism, violence, and greed. Half the planet lusts for Cindy Crawford, lines up for blockbuster films like *Die Hard 2* with a minimum of dialogue and a maximum of violence (which travels well, needing no translation), and dances to the monotonous beat of the Backstreet Boys. *Baywatch,* a moronic television series starring Ken and Barbie, has been seen by more people in the world than any other television show in history. And at the heart of all this "entertainment" is advertising. As Simon Anholt, an English consultant specializing in global brand development, said, "The world's most powerful brand is the U.S. This is because it has Hollywood, the world's best advertising agency. For nearly a century, Hollywood has been pumping out two-hour cinema ads for Brand U.S.A., which audiences around the world flock to see." When a group of German advertising agencies placed an ad in *Advertising Age* that said, "Let's make America great again," they left no doubt about what they had in mind. The ad featured cola, jeans, burgers, cigarettes, and alcohol—an advertiser's idea of what makes America great.

Some people might wonder what's wrong with this. On the most obvious level, as multinational chains replace local stores, local products, and local character, we end up in a world in which everything looks the same and everyone is Gapped and Starbucked. Shopping malls kill vibrant downtown centers locally and create a universe of uniformity internationally. Worse, we end up in a world ruled by, in John Maynard Keynes's phrase, the values of the casino. On this deeper level, rampant commercialism undermines our physical and psychological health, our environment, and our civic life and creates a toxic society. Advertising corrupts us and, I will argue, promotes a dissociative state that exploits trauma and can lead to addiction. To add insult to injury, it then co-opts our attempts at resistance and rebellion.

28   Although it is virtually impossible to measure the influence of advertising on a culture, we can learn something by looking at cultures only recently exposed to it. In 1980 the Gwich'in tribe of Alaska got television, and therefore massive advertising, for the first time. Satellite dishes, video games, and VCRs were not far behind. Before this, the Gwich'in lived much the way their ancestors had for a thousand generations. Within ten years, the young members of the tribe were so drawn by television they no longer had time to learn ancient hunting methods, their parents' language, or their oral history. Legends told around campfires could not compete with *Beverly Hills*

90210. Beaded moccasins gave way to Nike sneakers, sled dogs to gas-powered ski-mobiles, and "tundra tea" to Folger's instant coffee.

Human beings used to be influenced primarily by the stories of our particular tribe or community, not by stories that are mass-produced and market-driven. As George Gerbner, one of the world's most respected researchers on the influence of the media, said, "For the first time in human history, most of the stories about people, life, and values are told not by parents, schools, churches, or others in the community who have something to tell, but by a group of distant conglomerates that have something to sell." The stories that most influence our children these days are the stories told by advertisers.

Personal Response

What is your initial response to what Kilbourne tells us that she will argue in the rest of her book: "Advertising corrupts us and, I will argue, promotes a dissociative state that exploits trauma and can lead to addiction. To add insult to injury, it then co-opts our attempts at resistance and rebellion" (paragraph 21)? Are you skeptical or intrigued? Without having read her book, are you inclined to think she's right, or do you find her argument in this excerpt unconvincing?

Questions for Class or Small-Group Discussion

1. What is your opinion on the matter of whether corporations should have the right to review editorial content of publications they advertise in and whether magazines should practice self-censorship? Is it just good business, or is it more than that, as Kilbourne claims? Do you think Kilbourne overreacts when she writes that this practice "warps a worldview and distorts the editorial content we read and the programs we listen to and watch" (paragraph 7)?

2. State in your own words the issues that Kilbourne is most concerned about in her allegations against women's and girls' magazines. To what extent do you agree with her? Although she cites many examples, can you provide others that either support or refute her arguments?

3. Summarize Kilbourne's point about alcohol and tobacco advertising. Is her argument valid? To what extent do you agree with her?

4. Kilbourne alleges that America exports "a popular culture that promotes escapism, consumerism, violence, and greed" (paragraph 26). To what extent do you agree with her? Can you provide examples that either support or refute this view?

YOU ARE WHAT YOU BUY

Richard Wolkomir and Joyce Wolkomir

Richard Wolkomir and Joyce Wolkomir are writers whose work appears often in Smithsonian *magazine. They are authors of* Junkyard

Bandicoots and Other Tales of the World's Endangered Species
(1992). This article was published in the October 2000 issue of
Smithsonian. See a related article, James B. Twitchell's "In Praise of
Consumerism," in chapter 22.

Along with two friends who need a new plastic dish drainer, James Twitchell, a professor of 19th-century poetry at the University of Florida in Gainesville, is visiting a
Wal-Mart. Twitchell gazes raptly upon the aisles stacked with TV sets in boxes, and
picnic baskets and T-shirts and beach balls. So much mass-produced stuff! Twitchell
is energized—as any dedicated scholar would be upon entering an archive packed
with new material.

"Look at this wire shopping cart—it's the equivalent of the Las Vegas poker
chip," he says. "In a casino, instead of gambling with your real money, you use little
colored plastic disks, so it seems OK. This huge cart is something like that: it's so
roomy you don't feel you're buying too much. Marketers fooled around with the size
of these carts, getting them just right."

Twitchell loves this stuff. He loves it so much that he has switched from teaching
and writing solely about Romantic-era poetry to buzzier issues, such as adolescents
wearing dungarees slung low to reveal their Joe Boxers, and whether the Jolly Green
Giant is an avatar of Zeus. And now, reveling in all these bedspreads and CD players
and croquet sets and yellow raincoats, Twitchell tells his friends that one reason he
began studying such fine points of mass marketing is that his parents, long ago, denied him Wonder Bread.

4   Twitchell's father, a Vermont physician, dismissed Wonder Bread as "air and water." His mother warned that Coca-Cola was sugar water that would "rot your teeth."
Now he keeps a cellophane-wrapped loaf of Wonder Bread and an aluminum can of
Coke—icons among American consumables—atop his computer monitor. In one of
Twitchell's recent books, *Lead Us Into Temptation: The Triumph of American Materialism,* he wrote that everything he loved as a youth was from the forbidden mass
culture: "It was mass produced, mass marketed and consumed en masse." And if he
wanted to savor Pepsi and Whoppers and Dairy Queen sundaes, he had to do it on the
sly, "for we would not countenance them inside the family circle."

Twitchell—who is now in his 50s, trim and urbane—says his study of mass culture, especially advertising, began 15 years ago, when he was teaching a class on the
Romantic poets. "I suddenly realized my students had no interest in what I had to
say." He asked them to complete a line from Wordsworth: "My heart leaps up when I
behold a ———— in the sky." Nobody could supply the missing "rainbow," but his students could flawlessly recite the contents of a Big Mac: two all-beef patties, special
sauce, lettuce, cheese, pickles and onions on a sesame-seed bun.

"It was an epiphany," he says.

At the time, the much-discussed book by E. D. Hirsch, et al., *Cultural Literacy:
What Every American Needs To Know,* argued that cultures need the glue of shared
knowledge, like who Napoleon was or where Beirut is. "I realized he was right, we do
need a body of information," explains Twitchell. "But he was wrong about what body

of information we share, because it isn't from high culture—it's from pop culture, the world my students knew so well." His students knew little about Dickens or Keats. "But they could recite the 'Mmm, mmm good' Campbell's Soup jingle," he says. "They didn't know Rembrandt, but they could tell you Ben's and Jerry's last names." Twitchell was stunned. "I wanted to know why the stuff they knew was so powerful it pushed my stuff out of the way."

8   Since then, he has been observing himself, his law professor wife, his two daughters, now grown, his colleagues, students, neighbors. He has invited himself into advertising agencies as an academic gadfly on the wall. He has explored advertising's history. And he has learned the average adult now encounters some 3,000 advertisements every day, from bus flanks to messages over the telephone as the caller waits on hold. He has probed the impact of all that mass marketing in such works as *ADCULTUSA* and his latest book, *Twenty Ads That Shook the World.*

Academics usually excoriate modern materialism as spiritually deadening and socially corrupting, he observes. "My own take is that humans love things, and we've always been materialistic, but until the Industrial Revolution only the wealthy had things—now the rest of us are having a go at arranging our lives around things." Especially in the past 20 years, young people have had lots more money to spend. "Now they're driving the market for mass-produced objects." And especially for youths, Twitchell maintains, advertising has become our social studies text. "Ask 18-year-olds what freedom means, and they'll tell you, 'It means being able to buy whatever I want!'"

But advertising's job is not just urging, "Buy this!" Twitchell cites 1950s ad ace Rosser Reeves, who created a television commercial in which a hammer clangs an anvil to remind viewers how a headache feels (or maybe to induce one) while reporting good news: Anacin is "for fast, Fast, FAST relief. . . ." Reeves would hold up two quarters. It was advertising's task, he said, to make you believe those two quarters were different. Even more important, the ad had to persuade you that one of those quarters was worth more.

To illustrate the process, Twitchell points to 1930s ads claiming Schlitz steam-cleaned its beer bottles. What the ads omitted was that all brewers steam-cleaned their bottles. Thus, through advertising, the company achieved "ownership" of product purity—it created for itself what the ad industry calls a USP (Unique Selling Proposition).

12   According to Twitchell, it was in the Victorian era that mass culture reared up, driven by the steam-powered printing press, which spewed out text and images and notions for the "mob." Victorians invented the word "mob," he says, by shortening the Latin mobile vulgus, "rabble on the move." Victorian education strove to differentiate literature from pulp novels, to show classical music's superiority to dance-hall tunes, to instill "art appreciation." But with the machine age churning out cheap goods, consumerism was erupting all over, and so was advertising.

Thomas J. Barratt, the 19th-century manufacturer of Pears' Soap, noted: "Any fool can make soap. It takes a clever man to sell it." And Barratt was just that man.

"The manufacture of soap is a turning point in civilization," says Twitchell. Originally, farmers boiled animal fats with wood ashes and molded the result into soap balls, which soon stank. With the machine age came soap concocted from caustic soda and vegetable fats, pressed into bars that lasted forever. But one soap was much like another.

In 1881, at James Gamble's soap factory in Cincinnati, a worker forgot to turn off the mixing machinery, inadvertently producing a batch of soap so air-filled it floated. Gamble claimed his new soap, Ivory, floated because it was pure—in fact, 99 44/100 percent pure.

Earlier, England's Andrew Pears—the father-in-law of Thomas J. Barratt—had developed a translucent soap. It seemed a natural to appeal to the class-conscious Briton's desire for whiter skin, versus a laborer's weathered tan. Barratt got the message across in such ways as plastering his company's new slogan, an early version of Nike's "Just Do It," on walls all over the British Empire: "Good Morning! Have You Used Your Pears' Soap?"

16   But Barratt's greatest coup was co-opting Bubbles, a John Everett Millais painting of the artist's angelic grandson watching a just-blown soap bubble waft upward. Barratt sold Millais on the notion that, distributed as a free poster, his painting would reach thousands upon thousands of potential new art lovers, for their edification. For their further edification, Barratt had a cake of the soap lying in the painting's foreground, inscribed "Pears'."

Branding made advertising possible. In the early 1800s, soap was just soap. Like biscuits or nails, it came in barrels, and to get some, you told the store clerk, "Two bars of soap, please." By the late 1800s—nudged by Barratt's advertising—you might specify Pears' Soap.

Twitchell says Barratt's hijacking of art to sell soap "blurred, for the first time and forevermore, the bright line between art and advertising, between high culture and the vulgar, between pristine and corrupt." Today, art co-opted by advertising is so commonplace we do not blink at Michelangelo's David wearing Levi's cutoffs.

Back in the Wal-Mart, Twitchell veers toward a barrel displaying kitchen floor mats. "Two for five dollars!" he says, reading a sign. It is clearly tempting. Two floor mats, one price. But he pulls himself away from the alluring floor mats to ruminate about literature. "I'm supposed to teach English Romantic poetry," he says. "That period, the beginning of the 19th century, is where many of our views on materialism came from, because that was when the Industrial Revolution began producing the surfeit of things that will cause the trouble."

20   Surpluses produced by the new technologies, like steam power, were particularly apt to pile up after wars, and that was especially true in the aftermath of the Civil War. "What it takes to win a war is the ability to produce more war materials than your opponent, but when the war ends you have too many blankets, boots, rifles, and too much patent medicine—which was the subject of the first real advertising." he explains. "In the 1870s we had the rise of advertising, along with the rise of newspapers, and now we start talking about two nostrums or two pairs of boots as if they were different, when we know they are the same."

Modern advertising, Twitchell insists, learned its stuff from religion. "I grew up a Vermont Congregationalist. My father was a doctor in our town, and his father had been a doctor in our town, and my mother's family had lived around there since the Revolution." His was, except for Wonder Bread denial, a stable life. "In the world where I grew up, you knew who you were by a series of time-tested anchors—ancestry, land, religion, where you went to school, your accent, your job—but we've been rapidly losing those anchors," he argues. "One marriage out of two ends in divorce, the average person changes jobs seven or eight times during a lifetime." With the old determinants of social position shifting or gone, he says, "we're starting to build our identity around driving a Lexus or displaying Ralph Lauren's polo player on our shirt."

He notes that many of modern advertising's founders had religious backgrounds. A Baptist minister's son, Bruce Barton, cofounded the large ad agency Batten, Barton, Durstine & Osborne (which comedian Fred Allen suggested sounded like "a trunk falling downstairs"). Artemus Ward, who wrote psalms to Sapolio Soap, was the son of an Episcopal minister. John Wanamaker, whose marketing genius helped create the modern department store, once considered becoming a Presbyterian minister. Rosser Reeves, creator of the Anacin anvils, was the son of a Methodist minister.

Twitchell contends that these founders of modern advertising, and others like them, modeled their messages on parables they heard in church. He sketches a typical TV commercial in which someone is distressed. Perhaps it is a young woman, if the product is a dish detergent. Perhaps it is a middle-aged man, if the product is a cold remedy. The heroine or hero consults another person who gives witness: a certain product "works miracles." The product is tried. Relief! Ads create and then promise to absolve you of secular sins, such as halitosis or dandruff, or "ring around the collar" or "dishpan hands."

24   But Twitchell says that advertising also reaches back to paganism. Instead of Zeus in the clouds and dryads in trees, we have televisions that are inhabited by the Jolly Green Giant, the Michelin Man, the Man from Glad, Mother Nature, Aunt Jemima, the White Knight, the Energizer Bunny and Speedy Alka-Seltzer with his magical chant: "Plop, plop, fizz, fizz. . . ."

Commercial culture is so potent, Twitchell believes, that it has "colonized" society. For instance, Christmas was low-key until the 1800s, when stores reinvented the holiday to sell off their surpluses. On December 24, 1867, R. H. Macy kept his Manhattan store open until midnight, setting a one-day sales record of more than $6,000.

Santa started as "a weird conflation of St. Nicholas (a down-on-his-luck nobleman who helped young women turn away from prostitution) and Kriss Kringle (perhaps a corruption of the German Christkindl, a gift giver)." Today's familiar Santa, Twitchell continues, originated in the 1930s, because Coca-Cola's sales slumped in winter. Ads began showing Santa—in his modern persona—relaxing in a living room after toy delivery, quaffing a Coke apparently left for him by the home's children. "Coke's Santa was elbowing aside other Santas—Coke's Santa was starting to own Christmas." Rudolph the Red-Nosed Reindeer was a 1930s creation of a Montgomery Ward copywriter. And Twitchell says Kodak ads universalized the tradition of blowing out birthday-cake candles and other "Kodak Moments" to "show what you can do with fast Kodak film and the Kodak Flashmatic attachment on your Kodak camera."

Ads have even changed our attitude toward debt, which once could lead to prison. "Think only of how consumer debt was merchandised until it became an accepted habit, not an abhorred practice," observes Twitchell. "Think only of how the concept of shine and 'new and improved' replaced the previous value of patina and heirloom." Twitchell says politics hit its modern ad-driven stride starting with the 1952 "Eisenhower Answers America" Presidential campaign, designed by Rosser Reeves. Regarding his own ads, Ike said ruefully: "To think an old soldier should come to this."

28   Athletes have become logo-bedecked living billboards. But Twitchell argues that commercial culture has affected us all. Cereal, for example, is now synonymous with breakfast. "Before Messrs. Post and Kellogg, this meal consisted of breaking fast by finishing last night's dinner," he says, adding that leftovers went to the family dog. Dog food was a creation of Ralston Purina's ad agency. Twitchell says that some marketing ploys fizzled, of course, citing an old ad headlined: "Sunday is Puffed Grain Day."

Mother's Day began in the early 1900s when Philadelphia merchandiser John Wanamaker elevated to stardom a local woman mourning for her mother. He ran full-page ads in the Philadelphia Inquirer. Soon only a blackguard would fail to buy Mom a present on her newly special day. Wanamaker reportedly gloated that he would rather be the founder of Mother's Day than the king of England.

Twitchell is no longer amazed that his students, inundated with commercial messages, display their status with manufacturers' logos on their shirt pockets or on their sunglasses. "At a Palm Beach store a woman explained to me that the more expensive the sunglasses, the smaller the logo, so that with Cartier you can barely see the Cy." His students derogatorily refer to certain classmates as "Gaps," after the retail chain where they buy their clothes. In the 19th century, people learned manners from novels and magazines; in the 20th from sitcoms and ads. When his daughter was a teenager, he heard her telling friends, after watching a teen TV show, *90210,* "Can you believe how cool Kelly looked in Dylan's Porsche!" Twitchell shrugs: "That's all they have for Trollope."

Economist Thorstein Veblen coined the term "conspicuous consumption": displaying possessions to impress others. "Between ages 15 and 25, we males consume the most as a percentage of our disposable income because we're displaying our feathers to potential mates," says Twitchell. "Now it's more complicated because females are working and they can display too." But the urge wanes. "After about age 45, many people start moving away from acquisition. Thus, ads, TV shows, and movies, which are studded with paid-for product placements, concentrate ferociously on youths, who seem to get the message.

32   But not all analysts agree with Madison Avenue's youth fixation. In fact, according to Beth Barnes, an associate professor at Syracuse University and chair of the advertising department at the S. I. Newhouse School of Public Communications,

advertisers are increasingly recognizing that the over-45 age-group is growing fast. And older Americans often have the magic ingredient: disposable income. "I think the change is slow, but inevitable," Barnes says. For one thing, she notes, advertising is increasingly segmented, exploiting today's highly segmented media to aim fine-tuned messages at specific subcultures, including age-groups. "Advertising for soft drinks may stay aimed at youth," she says. "But the trick is to go after older people with products in which they are not set in their ways—computers, for instance, or travel and tourism, or financial services, or new products, like Chrysler's PT Cruiser."

About a year ago, marketing circles buzzed over the surprising number of over-45 on-line shoppers. "It makes sense. They're amazingly machine savvy—my mother just got a new computer because her old one was too slow."

It is true, Barnes continues, that younger people may be less loyal to brands, and easier to woo away. But she adds: "There's a flip side to that—young people are lot more skeptical too!"

Perhaps. "Why," asks James Twitchell, "are my daughters willing to buy a bottle of water worth two cents and pay $1.50?" They aren't buying the product itself; they're buying the values that advertising has attached to the product, such as being hip. He cites a Madison Avenue adage: "You don't drink the beer; you drink the advertising."

36   Many of today's ads leave the average reader or viewer totally confused about what is being sold. For instance, in one current TV commercial, a cool young couple is driving down a city street, their car's windshield wipers clacking. They are so tuned in, they notice that the passing scene is rife with tempos, such as a boy bouncing a basketball, all in perfect sync with the rhythmic clack of their windshield wipers. What is going on?

"Often advertising is not about keeping up with the Joneses, but about separating you from them," Twitchell points out. "That's especially true of advertising directed at a particular group, such as adolescents or young-adult males—it's called 'dog-whistle' advertising because it goes out at frequencies only dogs can hear." In this case, the "dogs" are the commercial's target group of young adults. The young couple is hip enough to be driving their model of Volkswagen. "The idea is, your parents can't understand this, but you can." He cites a recent advertisement for a new sport utility vehicle that actually has the headline: "Ditch the Joneses!"

The most egregious example of this oblique marketing ploy was, of course, Benetton's spate of ads that employed the force of shock in order to create product recognition. The image of a nun and a priest, locked in a passionate kiss, was offensive to many people. But the pieces de resistance were Benetton's portraits of 25 death row inmates in America's prisons. This ad campaign cost Benetton its lucrative contract with Sears, Roebuck & Company and ended Oliviero Toscani's 18-year career as Benetton's creative director.

Such an ad may look senseless to a 50-year-old, Twitchell says, "but it's being properly decoded by a 23-year-old." It works. Today's average American consumes twice as many goods and services as in 1950, and the average home is twice as large as a post-World War II average home. A decade ago, most grocery stores stocked about 9,000 items; today's stores carry some 24,000.

40   Twitchell says he does not believe for a minute that our commercial society is a better world. "But it might be a safer world, oddly enough, if we value machine-made objects about which lies are told, rather than feuding over how to save souls," he says. "And we may be moving into a quieter world as people who were never able to consume before begin getting and spending."

He points upward, to the Wal-Mart's ceiling, with its exposed girders, pipes, wires and ducts, painted industrial gray. "That's to give you the illusion that you're buying stuff as close to the factory as possible," he says. His eyes fix upon Kraft Macaroni & Cheese boxes, each inscribed "The Cheesiest." He says, "It looks like a cornucopia, and the message is, 'Take one!' And see, the stack still sits on its freight pallet, to give you the idea there aren't many middlemen between you and the factory price."

Everything in the store is a brand-name product. "See, a stack of Fedders' air conditioners in their boxes. It was Wal-Mart founder Sam Walton's great insight that if he sold only branded items and negotiated lower prices, the manufacturers would do all the advertising for him."

Twitchell wanders back to the alluring display of floor mats that had first attracted his eye. He stares, transfixed. "Two for five dollars! I came in here meaning to buy one. That idea of two seemingly for the price of one took hold in the 1940s, especially with Alka-Seltzer, which you originally took as only one tablet until they halved the dosage so you'd take two: 'Plop, plop. . . .' " A few steps farther, he eyes a display of bottled mineral water. "This one is made by Pepsi. When they studied its marketing in Wichita, they were astonished to find out that buyers of these lower-priced mineral waters didn't care if it came from underground springs or runoff from Alpine glaciers—they bought the water because they liked the name and the feel of the bottle in their hand."

44   He pauses at a rack of greeting cards. "It's how we exchange emotions now, the commercializing of expression. The most touching are the cards to send to kids, offering your sympathy because their parents just got divorced." Such cards perform a useful service. "They're facilitators of difficulty, and they help us handle emotionally fraught events quickly and efficiently."

As his friends prepare to leave the Wal-Mart, without the dish drainer they had sought, Twitchell stops. "I'm going to go buy those two floor mats, but after you leave, because I'm ashamed to be seen succumbing to that two-for-the-price-of-one deal," he says.

Even so, Twitchell—deprived as a boy of Wonder Bread and Coke—believes the stuff cramming our stores, which advertisements strain to get us to buy, is not necessarily invidious to our cultural health. "After all," he says, "we don't call them 'bads'—we call them 'goods!' "

Personal Response

Respond to James B. Twitchell's comments on students wearing manufacturers' logos (paragraph 30). Do you wear such logos with pride, or do you avoid wearing them? Explore your viewpoint on this very popular practice.

Questions for Class or Small-Group Discussion

1. Wolkomir and Wolkomir conducted their interview of James B. Twitchell in a Wal-Mart store. Discuss the appropriateness of that store as a site for the interview. What is your impression of Twitchell as a result of this interview?

2. Discuss this comment: "[E]specially for youths [. . .] advertising has become our social studies text" (paragraph 9). What do you understand Twitchell to mean by that? To what extent do you agree with him?

3. In response to Thomas J. Barratt's observation, "Any fool can make soap. It takes a clever man to sell it" (paragraph 13), discuss advertising campaigns that you think are particularly clever, like the Pears' Soap campaign that Wolkomir and Wolkomir describe.

4. State in your own words what advertisers do to sell their products, commenting on some of the techniques to which Wolkomir and Wolkomir refer. How does the placing of manufacturers' logos on their products help sell the products? Why do you think that young people especially like those products?

WITH THESE WORDS I CAN SELL YOU ANYTHING

William Lutz

William Lutz has become nationally known for his analyses of language in advertisements and other public statements. A professor of English at Rutgers University, Lutz is former chair of the Committee on Public Doublespeak of the National Council of Teachers of English and former editor of the Quarterly Review of Doublespeak. *His books are* Beyond Nineteen Eighty-Four *(1984),* Doublespeak: From "Revenue Enhancement" to "Terminal Living": How Government, Business, Advertisers, and Others Use Language to Deceive *(1990),* The New Doublespeak: Why No One Knows What Anyone's Saying Anymore *(1997), and* Doublespeak Defined: Cut Through the Bull**** and Get the Point *(1999). This essay is from* Doublespeak.

One problem advertisers have when they try to convince you that the product they are pushing is really different from other, similar products is that their claims are subject to some laws. Not a lot of laws, but there are some designed to prevent fraudulent or untruthful claims in advertising. Even during the happy years of nonregulation under President Ronald Reagan, the FTC did crack down on the more blatant abuses in advertising claims. Generally speaking, advertisers have to be careful in what they say in their ads, in the claims they make for the products they advertise. Parity claims are safe because they are legal and supported by a number of court decisions. But beyond parity claims there are weasel words.

Advertisers use weasel words to appear to be making a claim for a product when in fact they are making no claim at all. Weasel words get their name from the way weasels eat the eggs they find in the nests of other animals. A weasel will make a small hole in the egg, suck out the insides, then place the egg back in the nest. Only when the egg is examined closely is it found to be hollow. That's the way it is with weasel words in advertising: Examine weasel words closely and you'll find that they're as hollow as any egg sucked by a weasel. Weasel words appear to say one thing when in fact they say the opposite, or nothing at all.

Help—The Number One Weasel Word

The biggest weasel word used in advertising doublespeak is *help.* Now *help* only means to aid or assist, nothing more. It does not mean to conquer, stop, eliminate, end, solve, heal, cure, or anything else. But once the ad says *help,* it can say just about anything after that because *help* qualifies everything coming after it. The trick is that the claim that comes after the weasel word is usually so strong and so dramatic that you forget the word *help* and concentrate only on the dramatic claim. You read into the ad a message that the ad does not contain. More importantly, the advertiser is not responsible for the claim that you read into the ad, even though the advertiser wrote the ad so you would read that claim into it.

4   The next time you see an ad for a cold medicine that promises that it "helps relieve cold symptoms fast," don't rush out to buy it. Ask yourself what this claim is really saying. Remember, *helps* means only that the medicine will aid or assist. What will it aid or assist in doing? Why, "relieve" your cold "symptoms." *Relieve* only means to ease, alleviate, or mitigate, not to stop, end, or cure. Nor does the claim say how much relieving this medicine will do. Nowhere does this ad claim it will cure anything. In fact, the ad doesn't even claim it will *do* anything at all. The ad only claims that it will aid in relieving (not curing) your cold symptoms, which are probably a runny nose, watery eyes, and a headache. In other words, this medicine probably contains a standard decongestant and some aspirin. By the way, what does *fast* mean? Ten minutes, 1 hour, 1 day? What is fast to one person can be very slow to another. *Fast* is another weasel word.

Ad claims using *help* are among the most popular ads. One says, "Helps keep you young looking," but then a lot of things will help keep you young looking, including exercise, rest, good nutrition, and a facelift. More importantly, this ad doesn't say the product will keep you young, only "young *looking.*" Someone may look young to one person and old to another.

A toothpaste ad says, "Helps prevent cavities," but it doesn't say it will actually prevent cavities. Brushing your teeth regularly, avoiding sugars in food, and flossing daily will also help prevent cavities. A liquid cleaner ad says, "Helps keep your home germ free," but it doesn't say it actually kills germs, nor does it even specify which germs it might kill.

Help is such a useful weasel word that it is often combined with other action-verb weasel words such as *fight* and *control.* Consider the claim, "Helps control dandruff symptoms with regular use." What does it really say? It will assist in controlling (not eliminating, stopping, ending, or curing) the *symptoms* of dandruff, not the cause of dandruff nor the dandruff itself. What are the symptoms of dandruff? The ad deliberately leaves that undefined, but assume that the symptoms referred to in the ad are the flaking and itching commonly associated with dandruff. But just shampooing with *any* shampoo will temporarily eliminate these symptoms, so this shampoo isn't any different from any other. Finally, in order to benefit from this product, you must use it regularly. What is "regular use"—daily, weekly, hourly? Using another shampoo "regularly" will have the same effect. Nowhere does this advertising claim say this particular shampoo stops, eliminates, or cures dandruff. In fact, this claim says nothing at all, thanks to all the weasel words.

8   Look at ads in magazines and newspapers, listen to ads on radio and television, and you'll find the word *help* in ads for all kinds of products. How often do you read or hear such phrases as "helps stop . . . ," "helps overcome . . . ," "helps eliminate . . . ," "helps you feel . . . ," or "helps you look . . ."? If you start looking for this weasel word in advertising, you'll be amazed at how often it occurs. Analyze the claims in the ads using *help,* and you will discover that these ads are really saying nothing.

There are plenty of other weasel words used in advertising. In fact, there are so many that to list them all would fill the rest of this book. But, in order to identify the doublespeak of advertising and understand the real meaning of an ad, you have to be aware of the most popular weasel words in advertising today.

Virtually Spotless

One of the most powerful weasel words is *virtually,* a word so innocent that most people don't pay any attention to it when it is used in an advertising claim. But watch out. *Virtually* is used in advertising claims that appear to make specific, definite promises when there is no promise. After all, what does *virtually* mean? It means "in essence or effect, although not in fact." Look at that definition again. *Virtually* means *not in fact.* It does *not* mean "almost" or "just about the same as," or anything else. And before you dismiss all this concern over such a small word, remember that small words can have big consequences.

In 1971, a federal court rendered its decision on a case brought by a woman who became pregnant while taking birth control pills. She sued the manufacturer, Eli Lilly and Company, for breach of warranty. The woman lost her case. Basing its ruling on a statement in the pamphlet accompanying the pills, which stated that, "When taken as directed, the tablets offer virtually 100 percent protection," the court ruled that there was no warranty, expressed or implied, that the pills were absolutely effective. In its ruling, the court pointed out that, according to *Webster's Third New International Dictionary, virtually* means "almost entirely" and clearly does not mean "absolute" (*Whittington* v. *Eli Lilly and Company,* 333 F. Supp. 98). In other words, the Eli Lilly company was really saying that its birth control pill, even when taken as directed, *did not in fact* provide 100 percent protection against pregnancy. But Eli Lilly didn't want to put it that way because then many women might not have bought Lilly's birth control pills.

12   The next time you see the ad that says that this dishwasher detergent "leaves dishes virtually spotless," just remember how advertisers twist the meaning of the weasel word *virtually.* You can have lots of spots on your dishes after using this detergent and the ad claim will still be true, because what this claim really means is that this detergent does not *in fact* leave your dishes spotless. Whenever you see or hear an ad claim that uses the word *virtually,* just translate that claim into its real meaning. So the television set that is "virtually trouble free" becomes the television set that is not in fact trouble free, the *virtually foolproof operation* of any appliance becomes an operation that is in fact not foolproof, and the product that "virtually never needs service" becomes the product that is not in fact service free.

New and Improved

If *new* is the most frequently used word on a product package, *improved* is the second most frequent. In fact, the two words are almost always used together. It seems just about everything sold these days is "new and improved." The next time you're in the supermarket, try counting the number of times you see these words on products. But you'd better do it while you're walking down just one aisle, otherwise you'll need a calculator to keep track of your counting.

Just what do these words mean? The use of the word *new* is restricted by regulations, so an advertiser can't just use the word on a product or in an ad without meeting certain requirements. For example, a product is considered new for about six months during a national advertising campaign. If the product is being advertised only in a limited test market area, the word can be used longer, and in some instances has been used for as long as two years.

What makes a product "new"? Some products have been around for a long time, yet every once in a while you discover that they are being advertised as "new." Well, an advertiser can call a product new if there has been "a material functional change" in the product. What is "a material functional change"? you ask. Good question. In fact it's such a good question it's being asked all the time. It's up to the manufacturer to prove that the product has undergone such a change. And if the manufacturer isn't challenged on the claim, then there's no one to stop it. Moreover, the change does not have to be an improvement in the product. One manufacturer added an artificial lemon scent to a cleaning product and called it "new and improved," even though the product did not clean any better than without the lemon scent. The manufacturer defended the use of the word new on the grounds that the artificial scent changed the chemical formula of the product and therefore constituted "a material functional change."

16   Which brings up the word *improved.* When used in advertising, *improved* does not mean "made better." It only means "changed" or "different from before." So, if the detergent maker puts a plastic pour spout on the box of detergent, the product has been "improved," and away we go with a whole new advertising campaign. Or, if the

cereal maker adds more fruit or a different kind of fruit to the cereal, there's an improved product. Now you know why manufacturers are constantly making little changes in their products. Whole new advertising campaigns, designed to convince you that the product has been changed for the better, are based on small changes in superficial aspects of a product. The next time you see an ad for an "improved" product, ask yourself what was wrong with the old one. Ask yourself just how "improved" the product is. Finally, you might check to see whether the "improved" version costs more than the unimproved one. After all, someone has to pay for the millions of dollars spent advertising the improved product.

Of course, advertisers really like to run ads that claim a product is "new and improved." While what constitutes a "new" product may be subject to some regulation, "improved" is a subjective judgment. A manufacturer changes the shape of its stick deodorant, but the shape doesn't improve the function of the deodorant. That is, changing the shape doesn't affect the deodorizing ability of the deodorant, so the manufacturer calls it "improved." Another manufacturer adds ammonia to its liquid cleaner and calls it "new and improved." Since adding ammonia does affect the cleaning ability of the product, there has been a "material functional change" in the product, and the manufacturer can now call its cleaner "new," and "improved" as well. Now the weasel words *new and improved* are plastered all over the package and are the basis for a multimillion-dollar ad campaign. But after six months the word *new* will have to go, until someone can dream up another change in the product. Perhaps it will be adding color to the liquid, or changing the shape of the package, or maybe adding a new dripless pour spout, or perhaps a ————. The "improvements" are endless, and so are the new advertising claims and campaigns.

New is just too useful and powerful a word in advertising for advertisers to pass it up easily. So they use weasel words that say "new" without really saying it. One of their favorites is *introducing,* as in, "Introducing improved Tide," or "Introducing the stain remover." The first is simply saying, here's our improved soap; the second, here's our new advertising campaign for our detergent. Another favorite is *now,* as in, "Now there's Sinex," which simply means that Sinex is available. Then there are phrases like "Today's Chevrolet," "Presenting Dristan," and "A fresh way to start the day." The list is really endless because advertisers are always finding new ways to say *new* without really saying it. If there is a second edition of this book, I'll just call it the "new and improved" edition. Wouldn't you really rather have a "new and improved" edition of this book rather than a "second" edition?

Acts Fast

Acts and *works* are two popular weasel words in advertising because they bring action to the product and to the advertising claim. When you see the ad for the cough syrup that "Acts on the cough control center," ask yourself what this cough syrup is claiming to do. Well, it's just claiming to "act," to do something, to perform an action. What is it that the cough syrup does? The ad doesn't say. It only claims to perform an action or do something on your "cough control center." By the way, what and where is your "cough control center"? I don't remember learning about that part of the body in human biology class.

20   Ads that use such phrases as "acts fast," "acts against," "acts to prevent," and the like are saying essentially nothing, because *act* is a word empty of any specific meaning. The ads are always careful not to specify exactly what "act" the product performs. Just because a brand of aspirin claims to "act fast" for headache relief doesn't mean this aspirin is any better than any other aspirin. What is the "act" that this aspirin performs? You're never told. Maybe it just dissolves quickly. Since aspirin is a parity product, all aspirin is the same and therefore functions the same.

Works Like Anything Else

If you don't find the word *acts* in an ad, you will probably find the weasel word *works.* In fact, the two words are almost interchangeable in advertising. Watch out for ads that say a product "works against," "works like," "works for," or "works longer." As with *acts, works* is the same meaningless verb used to make you think that this product really does something, and maybe even something special or unique. But *works,* like *acts,* is basically a word empty of any specific meaning.

Like Magic

Whenever advertisers want you to stop thinking about the product and start thinking about something bigger, better, or more attractive than the product, they use that very popular weasel word, *like.* The word *like* is the advertiser's equivalent of a magician's use of misdirection. *Like* gets you to ignore the product and concentrate on the claim the advertiser is making about it. "For skin like peaches and cream" claims the ad for a skin cream. What is this ad really claiming? It doesn't say this cream will give you peaches-and-cream skin. There is no verb in this claim, so it doesn't even mention using the product. How is skin ever like "peaches and cream"? Remember, ads must be read literally and exactly, according to the dictionary definition of words. (Remember *virtually* in the Eli Lilly case.) The ad is making absolutely no promise or claim whatsoever for this skin cream. If you think this cream will give you soft, smooth, youthful-looking skin, you are the one who has read that meaning into the ad.

The wine that claims "It's like taking a trip to France" wants you to think about a romantic evening in Paris as you walk along the boulevard after a wonderful meal in an intimate little bistro. Of course, you don't really believe that a wine can take you to France, but the goal of the ad is to get you to think pleasant, romantic thoughts about France and not about how the wine tastes or how expensive it may be. That little word *like* has taken you away from crushed grapes into a world of your own imaginative making. Who knows, maybe the next time you buy wine, you'll think those pleasant thoughts when you see this brand of wine, and you'll buy it. Or, maybe you weren't even thinking about buying wine at all, but now you just might pick up a bottle the next time you're shopping. Ah, the power of *like* in advertising.

24   How about the most famous "like" claim of all, "Winston tastes good like a cigarette should"? Ignoring the grammatical error here, you might want to know what

this claim is saying. Whether a cigarette tastes good or bad is a subjective judgment because what tastes good to one person may well taste horrible to another. Not everyone likes fried snails, even if they are called *escargot*. (*De gustibus non est disputandum*, which was probably the Roman rule for advertising as well as for defending the games in the Colosseum.) There are many people who say all cigarettes taste terrible, other people who say only some cigarettes taste all right, and still others who say all cigarettes taste good. Who's right? Everyone, because taste is a matter of personal judgment.

Moreover, note the use of the conditional, *should*. The complete claim is, "Winston tastes good like a cigarette should taste." But should cigarettes taste good? Again, this is a matter of personal judgment and probably depends most on one's experiences with smoking. So, the Winston ad is simply saying that Winston cigarettes are just like any other cigarette: Some people like them and some people don't. On that statement R. J. Reynolds conducted a very successful multimillion-dollar advertising campaign that helped keep Winston the number-two-selling cigarette in the United States, close behind number one, Marlboro.

Can It Be Up to the Claim?

Analyzing ads for doublespeak requires that you pay attention to every word in the ad and determine what each word really means. Advertisers try to wrap their claims in language that sounds concrete, specific, and objective, when in fact the language of advertising is anything but. Your job is to read carefully and listen critically so that when the announcer says that "Crest can be of significant value . . ." you know immediately that this claim says absolutely nothing. Where is the doublespeak in this ad? Start with the second word.

Once again, you have to look at what words really mean, not what you think they mean or what the advertiser wants you to think they mean. The ad for Crest only says that using Crest "can be" of "significant value." What really throws you off in this ad is the brilliant use of *significant*. It draws your attention to the word *value* and makes you forget that the ad only claims that Crest "can be." The ad doesn't say that Crest *is* of value, only that it is "able" or "possible" to be of value, because that's all that *can* means.

It's so easy to miss the importance of those little words, *can be*. Almost as easy as missing the importance of the words *up to* in an ad. These words are very popular in sale ads. You know, the ones that say, "Up to 50 percent Off!" Now, what does that claim mean? Not much, because the store or manufacturer has to reduce the price of only a few items by 50 percent. Everything else can be reduced a lot less, or not even reduced. Moreover, don't you want to know 50 percent off of what? Is it 50 percent off the "manufacturer's suggested list price," which is the highest possible price? Was the price artificially inflated and then reduced? In other ads, *up to* expresses an ideal situation. The medicine that works "up to ten times faster," the battery that lasts "up to twice as long," and the soap that gets you "up to twice as clean" all are based on ideal situations for using those products, situations in which you can be sure you will never find yourself.

Unfinished Words

Unfinished words are a kind of "up to" claim in advertising. The claim that a battery lasts "up to twice as long" usually doesn't finish the comparison—twice as long as what? A birthday candle? A tank of gas? A cheap battery made in a country not noted for its technological achievements? The implication is that the battery lasts twice as long as batteries made by other battery makers, or twice as long as earlier model batteries made by the advertiser, but the ad doesn't really make these claims. You read these claims into the ad, aided by the visual images the advertiser so carefully provides.

Unfinished words depend on you to finish them, to provide the words the advertisers so thoughtfully left out of the ad. Pall Mall cigarettes were once advertised as "A longer finer and milder smoke." The question is, longer, finer, and milder than what? The aspirin that claims it contains "Twice as much of the pain reliever doctors recommend most" doesn't tell you what pain reliever it contains twice as much of. (By the way, it's aspirin. That's right; it just contains twice the amount of aspirin. And how much is twice the amount? Twice of what amount?) Panadol boasts that "nobody reduces fever faster," but, since Panadol is a parity product, this claim simply means that Panadol isn't any better than any other product in its parity class. "You can be sure if it's Westinghouse," you're told, but just exactly what it is you can be sure of is never mentioned. "Magnavox gives you more" doesn't tell you what you get more of. More value? More television? More than they gave you before? It sounds nice, but it means nothing, until you fill in the claim with your own words, the words the advertiser didn't use. Since each of us fills in the claim differently, the ad and the product can become all things to all people, and not promise a single thing.

Unfinished words abound in advertising because they appear to promise so much. More importantly, they can be joined with powerful visual images on television to appear to be making significant promises about a product's effectiveness without really making any promises. In a television ad, the aspirin product that claims fast relief can show a person with a headache taking the product and then, in what appears to be a matter of minutes, claiming complete relief. This visual image is far more powerful than any claim made in unfinished words. Indeed, the visual image completes the unfinished words for you, filling in with pictures what the words leave out. And you thought that ads didn't affect you. What brand of aspirin do you use?

32 Some years ago, Ford's advertisements proclaimed "Ford LTD—700 percent quieter." Now, what do you think Ford was claiming with these unfinished words? What was the Ford LTD quieter than? A Cadillac? A Mercedes Benz? A BMW? Well, when the FTC asked Ford to substantiate this unfinished claim, Ford replied that it meant that the inside of the LTD was 700 percent quieter than the outside. How did you finish those unfinished words when you first read them? Did you even come close to Ford's meaning?

Combining Weasel Words

A lot of ads don't fall neatly into one category or another because they use a variety of different devices and words. Different weasel words are often combined to make an ad claim. The claim, "Coffee-Mate gives coffee more body, more flavor," uses unfinished words (*more* than what?) and also uses words that have no specific meaning (*body* and *flavor*). Along with *taste* (remember the Winston ad and its claim to taste good), *body* and *flavor* mean nothing because their meaning is entirely subjective. To you, *body* in coffee might mean thick, black, almost bitter coffee, while I might take it to mean a light brown, delicate coffee. Now, if you think you understood that last sentence, read it again, because it said nothing of objective value; it was filled with weasel words of no specific meaning: *thick, black, bitter, light brown,* and *delicate.* Each of those words has no specific, objective meaning, because each of us can interpret them differently.

Try this slogan: "Looks, smells, tastes like ground-roast coffee." So, are you now going to buy Taster's Choice instant coffee because of this ad? *Looks, smells,* and *tastes* are all words with no specific meaning and depend on your interpretation of them for any meaning. Then there's that great weasel word *like,* which simply suggests a comparison but does not make the actual connection between the product and the quality. Besides, do you know what "ground-roast" coffee is? I don't, but it sure sounds good. So, out of seven words in this ad, four are definite weasel words, two are quite meaningless, and only one has any clear meaning.

Remember the Anacin ad—"Twice as much of the pain reliever doctors recommend most"? There's a whole lot of weaseling going on in this ad. First, what's the pain reliever they're talking about in this ad? Aspirin, of course. In fact, any time you see or hear an ad using those words *pain reliever,* you can automatically substitute the word *aspirin* for them. (Makers of acetaminophen and ibuprofen pain relievers are careful in their advertising to identify their products as nonaspirin products.) So, now we know that Anacin has aspirin in it. Moreover, we know that Anacin has twice as much aspirin in it, but we don't know twice as much as what. Does it have twice as much aspirin as an ordinary aspirin tablet? If so, what is an ordinary aspirin tablet, and how much aspirin does it contain? Twice as much as Excedrin or Bufferin? Twice as much as a chocolate chip cookie? Remember those Unfinished Words and how they lead you on without saying anything.

Finally, what about those doctors who are doing all that recommending? Who are they? How many of them are there? What kind of doctors are they? What are their qualifications? Who asked them about recommending pain relievers? What other pain relievers did they recommend? And there are a whole lot more questions about this "poll" of doctors to which I'd like to know the answers, but you get the point. Sometimes, when I call my doctor, she tells me to take two aspirin and call her office in the morning. Is that where Anacin got this ad?

Read the Label, or the Brochure

Weasel words aren't just found on television, on the radio, or in newspaper and magazine ads. Just about any language associated with a product will contain the doublespeak of advertising. Remember the Eli Lilly case and the doublespeak on the information sheet that came with the birth control pills. Here's another example.

In 1983, the Estée Lauder cosmetics company announced a new product called "Night Repair." A small brochure distributed with the product stated that "Night Repair was scientifically formulated in Estée Lauder's U.S. laboratories as part of the Swiss Age-Controlling Skincare Program. Although only nature controls the aging process, this program helps control the signs of aging and encourages skin to look and feel younger." You might want to read these two sentences again, because they sound great but say nothing.

First, note that the product was "scientifically formulated" in the company's laboratories. What does that mean? What constitutes a scientific formulation? You wouldn't expect the company to say that the product was casually, mechanically, or carelessly formulated, or just thrown together one day when the people in the white coats didn't have anything better to do. But the word *scientifically* lends an air of precision and promise that just isn't there.

40   It is the second sentence, however, that's really weasely, both syntactically and semantically. The only factual part of this sentence is the introductory dependent clause—"only nature controls the aging process." Thus, the only fact in the ad is relegated to a dependent clause, a clause dependent on the main clause, which contains no factual or definite information at all and indeed purports to contradict the independent clause. The new "skincare program" (notice it's not a skin cream but a "program") does not claim to stop or even retard the aging process. What, then, does Night Repair, at a price of over $35 (in 1983 dollars) for a .87-ounce bottle do? According to this brochure, nothing. It only "helps," and the brochure does not say how much it helps. Moreover, it only "helps control," and then it only helps control the "*signs* of aging," not the aging itself. Also, it "encourages" skin not to *be* younger but only to "look and feel" younger. The brochure does not say younger than what. Of the sixteen words in the main clause of this second sentence, nine are weasel words. So, before you spend all that money for Night Repair, or any other cosmetic product, read the words carefully, and then decide if you're getting what you think you're paying for.

Other Tricks of the Trade

Advertisers' use of doublespeak is endless. Rosser Reeves has explained advertising's function this way: to make something out of nothing. The best way advertisers can make something out of nothing is through words. Although there are a lot of visual images used on television and in magazines and newspapers, every advertiser wants to create that memorable line that will stick in the public consciousness. I am sure pure joy reigned in one advertising agency when a study found that children who were asked to spell the word *relief* promptly and proudly responded "r-o-l-a-i-d-s."

The variations, combinations, and permutations of doublespeak used in advertising go on and on, running from the use of rhetorical questions ("Wouldn't you really rather have a Buick?" "If you can't trust Prestone, who can you trust?") to flattering you with compliments ("The lady has taste." "We think a cigar smoker is someone special." "You've come a long way, baby."). You know, of course, how you're *supposed* to answer those questions, and you know that those compliments are just leading up to the sales pitches for the products. Before you dismiss such tricks of the trade as obvious, however, just remember that all of these statements and questions were part of very successful advertising campaigns.

A more subtle approach is the ad that proclaims a supposedly unique quality for a product, a quality that really isn't unique. "If it doesn't say Goodyear, it can't be polyglas." Sounds good, doesn't it? Polyglas is available only from Goodyear because Goodyear copyrighted that trade name. Any other tire manufacturer could make exactly the same tire but could not call it *polyglas,* because that would be copyright infringement. *Polyglas* is simply Goodyear's name for its fiberglass-reinforced tire.

44   Since we like to think of ourselves as living in a technologically advanced country, science and technology have a great appeal in selling products. Advertisers are quick to use scientific doublespeak to push their products. There are all kinds of elixirs, additives, scientific potions, and mysterious mixtures added to all kinds of products. Gasoline contains "HTA," "F-310," "Platformate," and other chemical-sounding additives, but nowhere does an advertisement give any real information about the additive.

Shampoo, deodorant, mouthwash, cold medicine, sleeping pills, and any number of other products all seem to contain some special chemical ingredient that allows them to work wonders. "Certs contains a sparkling drop of Retsyn." So what? What's "Retsyn"? What's it do? What's so special about it? When they don't have a secret ingredient in their product, advertisers still find a way to claim scientific validity. There's "Sinarest. Created by a research scientist who actually gets sinus headaches." Sounds nice, but what kind of research does this scientist do? How do you know if she is any kind of expert on sinus medicine? Besides, this ad doesn't tell you a thing about the medicine itself and what it does.

Advertising Doublespeak Quick Quiz

Now it's time to test your awareness of advertising doublespeak. (You didn't think I would just let you read this and forget it, did you?) The following is a list of statements from some recent ads. Your job is to figure out what each of these ads really says.

Domino's Pizza:	"Because nobody delivers better."
Sinutab:	"It can stop the pain."
Tums:	"The stronger acid neutralizer."
Maximum Strength Dristan:	"Strong medicine for tough sinus colds."
Listermint:	"Making your mouth a cleaner place."
Cascade:	"For virtually spotless dishes nothing beats Cascade."
Nuprin:	"Little. Yellow. Different. Better."
Anacin:	"Better relief."
Sudafed:	"Fast sinus relief that won't put you fast asleep."
Advil:	"Advanced medicine for pain."
Ponds Cold Cream:	"Ponds cleans like no soap can."
Miller Lite Beer:	"Tastes great. Less filling."

Philips Milk of Magnesia:	"Nobody treats you better than MOM (Philips Milk of Magnesia)."
Bayer:	"The wonder drug that works wonders."
Cracker Barrel:	"Judged to be the best."
Knorr:	"Where taste is everything."
Anusol:	"Anusol is the word to remember for relief."
Dimetapp:	"It relieves kids as well as colds."
Liquid Drāno:	"The liquid strong enough to be called Drāno."
Johnson & Johnson Baby Powder:	"Like magic for your skin."
Puritan:	"Make it your oil for life."
Pam:	"Pam, because how you cook is as important as what you cook."
Ivory Shampoo and Conditioner:	"Leave your hair feeling Ivory clean."
Tylenol Gel-Caps:	"It's not a capsule. It's better."
Alka-Seltzer Plus:	"Fast, effective relief for winter colds."

The World of Advertising

In the world of advertising, people wear "dentures," not false teeth; they suffer from "occasional irregularity," not constipation; they need deodorants for their "nervous wetness," not for sweat; they use "bathroom tissue," not toilet paper; and they don't dye their hair, they "tint" or "rinse" it. Advertisements offer "real counterfeit diamonds" without the slightest hint of embarrassment, or boast of goods made out of "genuine imitation leather" or "virgin vinyl."

48   In the world of advertising, the girdle becomes a "body shaper," "form persuader," "control garment," "controller," "outerwear enhancer," "body garment," or "anti-gravity panties," and is sold with such trade names as "The Instead," "The Free Spirit," and "The Body Briefer."

A study some years ago found the following words to be among the most popular used in U.S. television advertisements: *new, improved, better, extra, fresh, clean, beautiful, free, good, great,* and *light.* At the same time, the following words were found to be among the most frequent on British television: *new, good-better-best, free, fresh, delicious, full, sure, clean, wonderful,* and *special.* While these words may occur most frequently in ads, and while ads may be filled with weasel words, you have to watch out for all the words used in advertising, not just the words mentioned here.

Every word in an ad is there for a reason; no word is wasted. Your job is to figure out exactly what each word is doing in an ad—what each word really means, not what the advertiser wants you to think it means. Remember, the ad is trying to get you to buy a product, so it will put the product in the best possible light, using any device, trick, or means legally allowed. Your only defense against advertising (besides taking up permanent residence on the moon) is to develop and use a strong critical reading, listening, and looking ability. Always ask yourself what the ad is *really* saying. When you see ads on television, don't be misled by the pictures, the visual images. What does the ad *say* about the product? What does the ad *not* say? What information is missing from the ad? Only by becoming an active, critical consumer of the doublespeak of advertising will you ever be able to cut through the doublespeak and discover what the ad is really saying.

Professor Del Kehl of Arizona State University has updated the Twenty-Third Psalm to reflect the power of advertising to meet our needs and solve our problems. It seems fitting that this chapter close with this new Psalm.

THE ADMAN'S 23RD

The Adman is my shepherd;
I shall ever want.
He maketh me to walk a mile for a Camel;
He leadeth me beside Crystal Waters
    In the High Country of Coors;
He restoreth my soul with Perrier.
He guideth me in Marlboro Country
For Mammon's sake.
Yea, though I walk through the Valley of the Jolly Green Giant,
In the shadow of B.O., halitosis, indigestion, headache pain, and
    hemorrhoidal tissue,
I will fear no evil,
For I am in Good Hands with Allstate;
Thy Arid, Scope, Tums, Tylenol, and Preparation H—
They comfort me.
Stouffer's preparest a table before the TV
In the presence of all my appetites;
Thou anointest my head with Brylcream;
My Decaffeinated Cup runneth over.
Surely surfeit and security shall follow me
All the days of Metropolitan Life,
And I shall dwell in a Continental Home
With a mortgage forever and ever.

Amen.

Personal Response

Make a list of the brand name products you have used today. Which, if any, did you buy because of claims made in their advertisements?

Questions for Class or Small-Group Discussion

1. Bring copies of magazine or newspaper advertisements to class and do a careful analysis of their language and the way in which they manipulate consumers. What "weasel" words do you find in the ads? What unfinished words or words with no special meaning do you find?

2. Play the role of an advertiser who must sell a new product. (You make up the product.) Write an advertisement that uses "weasel" words, unfinished words, or words

with no special meaning. Then write an advertisement for the same product without using any of those words. Share your advertisements with classmates and discuss which was easier to write and why.

3. Listen to ads on radio and television, look at ads in magazines and newspapers, or walk down a supermarket aisle, as Lutz suggests, and notice the use of the words *help, virtually, new,* and *improved.* How often do you see those words used? Do you agree with Lutz that the ads "are really saying nothing" (paragraph 8)?

4. Complete the advertising doublespeak quick quiz (paragraph 46).

5. Discuss the extent to which you think it matters that advertisements use meaningless, empty words. That is, do you think the use of "weasel" words in advertisements is a fair practice? Is anyone harmed by such words? Why should consumers care "what the ad is *really* saying" (paragraph 50)?

WHAT ADVERTISING ISN'T

John O'Toole

John O'Toole is president of the American Association of Advertising Agencies. Before that, he served as chairman of the board of Foote, Cone, and Belding Communications, Inc., one of the world's largest advertising agencies. In this essay, reprinted from his book The Trouble with Advertising, *Second Edition (1985), O'Toole defends the practices advertisers use to sell products.*

Advertising . . . is salesmanship functioning in the paid space and time of mass media. To criticize it for being that, for being true to its nature, is to question whether it should be permitted—a position taken by only the most rabid, none of whom has come up with a reasonable substitute for its role in the economy. And to criticize it for not being something else—something it might resemble but by definition can never be—is equally fruitless. Yet much of the professional criticism I spoke of has its feet planted solidly on those two pieces of shaky ground.

As a format for conveying information, advertising shares certain characteristics with journalism, education, entertainment, and other modes of communication. But it cannot be judged by the same standards, because it is essentially something else. This point is missed by many in government, both the regulators and the elected representatives who oversee the regulators.

The Federal Trade Commission was pushing not too long ago for one of those quasi-laws they call a Trade Regulation Ruling (when they were empowered to write the law of the land, I don't know; but that's another argument). This particular TRR would have required an ad or commercial for any product claiming to be nutritious to list all its nutritive elements. For two reasons advertising cannot comply with such a requirement and still end up as advertising.

4   One, advertising is salesmanship, and good salesmanship does not countenance boring the prospect into glassy-eyed semiconsciousness. Yet I am sure—and consumers on whom sample ads and commercials were tested agreed—that a lengthy litany of niacin, riboflavin, ascorbic acid, and so on is as interesting as watching paint dry.

Less subjective is the fact that such a listing can't be given for many good, wholesome products within the confines of a thirty-second commercial. Since that's the standard length today, the end result of the proposed TRR would have been to ban those products from television advertising. The FTC staff did not consider that advertising necessarily functions in the paid space and time of mass media. Adding twenty or more seconds of Latin makes that impossible.

This example illustrates the problems that can arise when regulators try to dictate what must go into advertising. An FTC attorney named Donald F. Turner was quoted by Professor Raymond Bauer in a piece for the *Harvard Business Review* as saying, "There are three steps to informed choice. (1) The consumer must know the product exists. (2) The consumer must know how the product performs. (3) He must know how it performs compared to other products. If advertising only performs step one and appeals on other than a performance basis, informed choice cannot be made."

This is probably true in an ad for a new floor wax from S. C. Johnson or an antiperspirant from Bristol-Myers. But what about a new fragrance from Max Factor? How do you describe how Halston performs compared to other products? Is it important for anyone to know? Is it salesmanship to make the attempt? Or suppose you're advertising Coca-Cola. There can't be many people left in the world who don't know Coke exists or how it performs. Granted, there may be a few monks or aborigines who don't know how it performs in relation to other products, but you can't reach them through advertising. So why waste the time or space?

8   The reason Coca-Cola advertises is to maintain or increase a level of awareness about itself among people who know full well it exists and what it tastes like, people whom other beverage makers are contacting with similar messages about their products. Simple information about its existence and its popularity—information that triggers residual knowledge in the recipient about its taste and other characteristics—is legitimate and sufficient. It does what a salesman would do.

On the other hand, advertising for a big-ticket item—an automobile, for instance—would seemingly have to include a lot of information in order to achieve its end. But the advertising is not attempting to sell the car. It is an advance salesman trying to persuade the prospect to visit a showroom. Only there can the principal salesman do the complete job. Turner's definition is neither pertinent nor possible in the case of automobiles. In such cases mass communications media cannot convey the kind of information one needs in order to "know how the product performs" or to "know how it performs compared to other products." You have to see it, kick the tires, ask the salesman questions about it, let the kids try out the windshield wipers. And surely you have to drive it.

In the paid space and time of mass media, the purpose of automobile advertising is to select the prospect for a particular car and, on the basis of its appeal to his income, life-style, or basic attitudes, to persuade him he's the person the designers and engineers had in mind when they created this model. If the information is properly chosen and skillfully presented, it will point out the relevance of the car to his needs and self-image sufficiently to get him into the showroom. Then it's up to the salesman to sell him the car—but with a different package of information, including the tactile and experiential, than could be provided in the ad.

From time to time some government regulator will suggest that advertising information should be limited to price and function. But consider how paleolithic that kind of thinking is. Restricting advertising to a discussion of price and function would eliminate, among other things, an equally essential piece of information: what kind of people make and market this product or provide this service.

12   The reputation, quality standards, taste, and responsibility of the people who put out a product is information that's not only important to the consumer but is increasingly demanded by the consumer. It's information that can often outweigh price and function as these differences narrow among products within the same category. It's information that is critical to the advertising my agency prepares for clients like Johnson's Wax, Sunkist Growers, Hallmark, Sears, and many others. Advertising would not be salesmanship without it. Put it this way: If surgeons advertised and you had a hot appendix, would you want the ads to be limited to price and function information?

The government regulators, and the consumer advocates dedicated to influencing them, do not understand what advertising is and how it is perceived by the consumer. And their overwhelming fear that the one is always trying to deceive the other leads them to demand from advertising the kind of product information that characterizes *Consumer Reports.* They expect advertising to be journalism, and they evaluate it by journalistic standards. Since it is not, advertising, like the ugly duckling, is found wanting.

It is not in the nature of advertising to be journalistic, to present both sides, to include information that shows the product negatively in comparison with other entries in the category (unless, of course, the exclusion of such information would make the ad misleading or product usage hazardous). For example, advertising for Sunkist lemons, which might point out the flavor advantages of fresh lemons over bottled juice, should not be expected to remind people that fresh lemons can't be kept as long as a bottle of concentrate. Information is selected for journalism—or should be—to provide the recipient with as complete and objective an account as possible. Information is selected for advertising to persuade the recipient to go to a showroom or make a mental pledge to find the product on a store shelf.

Advertising, like the personal salesman, unabashedly presents products in their most favorable light. I doubt that there's a consumer around who doesn't understand that. For instance, would you, in a classified ad offering your house for sale, mention the toilet on the second floor that doesn't flush? I doubt that even a conscience as rigorous as Ralph Nader's would insist, in an ad to sell his own used car, on information about that worn fan belt or leaky gasket. No reader would expect it. Nor does anyone expect it from our clients.

16   Information, as far as advertising is concerned, is anything that helps a genuine prospect to perceive the applicability of a product to his or her individual life, to understand how the product will solve a problem, make life easier or better, or in some way provide a benefit. When the knowledge can't safely be assumed, it also explains how to get the product. In other words, it's salesmanship.

It is not witchcraft, another craft government regulators and otherwise responsible writers are forever confusing with mine. For the same reasons people like to believe that someone is poisoning our water supply or, as in the Joseph McCarthy era, that pinkos proliferate in our government and are trying to bring it down, someone is always rejuvenating the idea of subliminal advertising.

Subliminal advertising is defined as advertising that employs stimuli operating below the threshold of consciousness. It is supposed to influence the recipient's behavior without his being aware of any communication taking place. The most frequently cited example, never fully verified, involved a movie theater where the words *Drink Coke* were flashed on the screen so briefly that while the mind recorded the message, it was not conscious of receiving it. The result was said to be greatly increased sales of Coca-Cola at the vending counter.

I don't like to destroy cherished illusions, but I must state unequivocally that there is no such thing as subliminal advertising. I have never seen an example of it, nor have I ever heard it seriously discussed as a technique by advertising people. Salesmanship is persuasion involving rational and emotional tools that must be employed on a conscious level in order to effect a conscious decision in favor of one product over its competitive counterparts, and in order to have that decision remembered and acted upon at a later time. Furthermore, it's demeaning to assume that the human mind is so easily controlled that anyone can be made to act against his will or better judgment by peremptory commands he doesn't realize are present.

20   Even more absurd is the theory proposed by Wilson Bryan Key in a sleazy book entitled *Subliminal Seduction.* From whatever dark motivations, Key finds sexual symbolism in every ad and commercial. He points it out to his readers with no little relish, explaining how, after reducing the prospect to a pliant mass of sexual arousal, advertising can get him to buy anything. There are some who might envy Mr. Key his ability to get turned on by a photograph of a Sunkist orange.

Most professional critics are much less bizarre in their condemnations. Uninformed about the real nature of advertising, perhaps, but not mad. For instance, they often ascribe recondite powers to advertising—powers that it does not have and that they cannot adequately define—because it is not solely verbal. Being for the most part lawyers and academics, they are uncomfortable with information conveyed by means other than words. They want things spelled out, even in television commercials, despite the fact that television is primarily a visual medium. They do not trust graphic and musical information because they aren't sure that the meaning they receive is the same one the consumer is receiving. And since they consider the consumer much more gullible and much less astute than they, they sound the alarm and then charge to the rescue. Sorcery is afoot.

Well, from time immemorial, graphics and music have been with us. I suspect each has been part of the salesman's tool kit for as long as there have been salesmen. The songs of medieval street vendors and Toulouse-Lautrec's Jane Avril attest.

A mouth-watering cake presented photographically as the end benefit of Betty Crocker Cake Mix is just as legitimate as and more effective than a verbal description. The mysteriously exuberant musical communication "I Love New York" honestly conveys the variety of experiences offered by New York State; it is not witchcraft. It is not to be feared unless you fear yourself. But perhaps that is the cradle that spawns consumer advocates and government regulators. There is something murky in that psyche, some kink in the mentality of those who feel others are incapable of making mundane decisions for themselves, something Kafka-like in the need to take over the personal lives of Americans in order to protect them from themselves.

24　　　I read with growing disquiet a document put out by the staff of the Federal Trade Commission in 1979 entitled *Consumer Information Remedies*. In discussing how to evaluate consumer information, they wrote,

> The Task Force members struggled long and hard to come up with a universally satisfactory definition of the *value* of consumer information. Should the Commission consider a mandatory disclosure to be a valuable piece of information, for instance, if it were later shown that although consumers understood the information, they did not use it when making purchase decisions? Is there a value in improving the *quality* of market decisions through the provision of relevant information, or is it necessary for the information to change behavior to have value?

The ensuing "remedies" make it clear that the staff really judges the value of a mandatory disclaimer by the degree to which it changes consumer behavior in the direction they are seeking.

But wait a minute. I'm a consumer, too. Who are they to be wondering what to do with me next if I understand but choose to ignore some dumb disclaimer they've forced an advertiser to put in his ad? It's my God-given right to ignore any information any salesman presents me with—and an ad, remember, is a salesman. And what's this about changing behavior? Well, mine is going to change if the employees of a government I'm paying for start talking like that out loud. It's going to get violent.

Later in the same document, the staff addresses "Sub-Optional Purchases." While I have no quarrel with their intent, I find my hackles rising as they define the problem in terms of people "misallocating resources," consumers wasting their dollars on "products that do not best satisfy their needs." Listen, fellows, those are *my* resources you're talking about. Those are *my* dollars, what there is of them after you guys in Washington have had your way with my paycheck. I'm going to allocate them as I damn well please. And if I want to waste a few on products that do not best satisfy my needs—an unnutritious but thoroughly delicious hotdog at the ball park, for example—try to stop me.

Perhaps I, in turn, am seeking evidence of conspiracy. Perhaps I'm looking under beds. But I think I understand the true nature of government bureaucrats. They, on the other hand, do not understand that of advertising. They and other professional critics—the journalists, consumerists, academicians—don't understand that it's not journalism or education and cannot be judged on the basis of objectivity and exhaustive, in-depth treatment. Thorough knowledge of a subject cannot be derived from an advertisement but only from a synthesis of all relevant sources: the advertising of competitors, the opinions of others, the more impartial reports in newspapers, magazines and, increasingly, television.

28   The critics also don't understand that advertising isn't witchcraft, that it cannot wash the brain or coerce someone to buy what he doesn't want. It shouldn't be castigated for what it cannot and does not purport to do. And it isn't entertainment, either. A commercial should offer some reward to the viewer in return for his time, but that reward need not always take the form of entertainment. Sometimes the tone should be serious, even about seemingly frivolous subjects. Hemorrhoids are not funny to those who have them.

Advertising sometimes resembles other fields, just as an elephant resembles a snake to the blind man who feels its trunk, and a tree to another who feels its leg. But advertising is really salesmanship functioning in the paid space and time of mass media. . . . We can find enough reasons to criticize advertising without flailing it for not being what it isn't.

Personal Response

What do you think of O'Toole's defense of advertisements? Are you persuaded by him, especially after reading some of the attacks against advertising in the rest of this chapter? Explain your answer.

Questions for Class or Small-Group Discussion

1. Analyze O'Toole's argument and discuss the points on which you either agree or disagree with him. What do you find persuasive about it? What weaknesses do you find?

2. O'Toole is highly critical of consumer advocates and government regulators. Do you agree with his opinion of those groups? Do you see a need for such groups? What might happen if such groups did not exist?

3. Respond to O'Toole's statement that advertising "isn't entertainment." Do you agree? Can you give examples of advertisements that do attempt to entertain?

4. Are you surprised by O'Toole's stating "unequivocally that there is no such thing as subliminal advertising" (paragraph 19)? Explain your answer.

PERSPECTIVES ON ADVERTISING

Suggestions for Synthesis

1. Advertisers, like producers of music, movies, and television shows, contend that they do not create problems but simply reflect the values of society. Drawing on at least two of the readings in this chapter, write an essay in which you explore the subject of how much responsibility advertisers should bear for the images they produce in their advertisements.

2. Write an essay on the ethics of advertising, drawing on at least two of the essays in this chapter.

3. Compare and contrast any two essays in this chapter.

4. Conduct a panel discussion on advertising in which members of your class play the roles of the authors whose essays appear in this section. The rest of the students in the audience should ask questions from their perspectives as consumers. For a writing assignment, do an analysis of the panel discussion.

Additional Writing Topics

1. Write a paper in response to the central argument of any of the essays in this chapter.

2. Survey a selection of magazines aimed at a specific audience—girls, women, boys, men—in terms of the kind of analysis Jean Kilbourne does in "Advertising's Influence on Media Content." Explain what you find and whether your conclusions agree with or differ from hers.

3. Use examples of well-known advertisements to explore the question of whether advertisers underestimate the intelligence of consumers.

4. Explain why you agree or disagree with the following remark by James B. Twitchell in Richard Wolkomir and Joyce Wolkomir's "You Are What You Buy." Referring to his daughters' willingness to spend $1.50 on a bottle of water worth two cents, Twitchell says, " 'They aren't buying the product itself; they're buying the values that advertising has attached to the product' " (paragraph 35).

5. Write a letter to the head of a major corporation whose product poses a serious threat to the environment. In the letter, express your views on the product's advertisements.

6. Analyze a recent advertising campaign of a major corporation whose product poses a threat to the environment or to human health and well-being.

Research Topics

1. Research the subject of advertising ethics by locating articles and books representing the opinions of both those who are critical of advertisements and those who defend them. Argue your own position on the subject, supporting it with relevant source materials.

2. Research images of a specific group in advertising. For instance, you could focus on images of women, as Jean Kilbourne has done in "Advertising's Influence on Media Content," and locate additional research and opposing viewpoints. Consider, also, the topics of advertising images of men, advertisements that encourage destructive behavior, or advertisements aimed at children.

3. Take as your starting point any of the accusations Jean Kilbourne makes in "Advertising's Influence on Media Content" about corporate sponsors, self-censorship, alcohol or tobacco advertisements, or conflicting messages in women's magazines. Locate sources, do some preliminary reading, and narrow your focus on one aspect of the broader topic.

4. Research the rise of advertising in Britain and America.

5. Research the history of a particular advertising campaign, perhaps taking as your starting point some of the products whose histories Richard Wolkomir and Joyce Wolkomir refer to in "You Are What You Buy."

PART 3

SOCIAL AND BEHAVIORAL SCIENCES

CHAPTER 12

EDUCATION

Education is a complex and crucially important subject. Without education, people face obstacles to participating fully in society. Because of its importance, education is also the subject of controversy. People are divided on issues such as what material is appropriate for the classroom, what methods of delivering material work best, how much homework ought to be required of students, and what skills and knowledge students must demonstrate to go on to subsequent educational levels. Periodically, philosophies of education change, curricula are restructured, classrooms are transformed, and instructors learn new approaches to teaching their subject matter.

As a student who has gone through many years of education, beginning in the primary grades, you are uniquely positioned to comment on this subject. You have been immersed in education and are presumably currently enrolled in at least one class, the course for which you are using this textbook. In the essays in this chapter, writers express their strong opinions on the subject of education. All criticize certain aspects of the educational system in America, so you are likely to find yourself either nodding your head in agreement or shaking your head in disagreement with what they say.

The first essay, Marianne M. Jennings's "The Real Generation Gap," is bound to evoke strong responses from many readers. She is particularly disturbed by what she sees schools teaching young people today. Jennings describes a generation of ignorant, unskilled, and unthinking young people being indoctrinated into a condition of passivity and what she refers to as "amoral darkness." She calls for outspoken criticism of the curricula in elementary and secondary schools to bring attention to the plight of America's young people.

Next is a 1999 *Time* magazine cover story on homework. Author Romesh Ratnesar reports on the state of homework in America's middle- and upper-class elementary and middle schools. Ratnesar interviewed students, parents, educators, and researchers for his story and concludes that the issue of how much and what kinds of homework teachers assign needs to be revisited for the good of all parties concerned. Related to Rantesar's cover story and published in the same issue of *Time* is Howard Gardner's "A Prescription for Peace." Gardner writes from the point of view of the parent, albeit a parent well qualified to write on this topic: He is also a child psychologist and an educational theorist whose work on multiple intelligences has made many people rethink the way our educational systems are structured. Gardner offers some basic, practical advice for families grappling with the effects of homework on their lives.

Finally, in a short but pointed essay by a well-known historian, public television host, and biographer, "No Time to Read?" reminds us of the importance of reading books. David McCullough urgently and fervently advises his audience to "read for pleasure. Read what you like and all that you like. Read literally to your heart's content." For him, books are our most important source of education.

As you read these selections, think about your own education, the courses you have taken, the homework you have had to do, and the teachers who have taught you. Where do you find yourself agreeing with the authors, and where do you disagree? Are your experiences similar to or different from what they describe? What is your own philosophy of education? How important do you believe education is to your well-being and sense of self?

THE REAL GENERATION GAP

Marianne M. Jennings

Marianne M. Jennings has taught legal and ethical studies and business at Arizona State University since 1977. Author of more than one hundred articles and six books, she is also a columnist for the Arizona Republic, and her articles have appeared in the Wall Street Journal, *the* Chicago Tribune, *and numerous other U.S. newspapers. A collection of her essays,* Nobody Fixes Real Carrot Sticks Anymore, *was published in 1994. "The Real Generation Gap" was delivered at a Shavano Institute for National Leadership seminar sponsored by Hillsdale College, "Heroes for a New Generation and a New Century." The text of this talk was reprinted in the August 1998 edition of* Imprimis, *a monthly publication of Hillsdale College.*

Born in 1980, today's college freshmen are part of "Generation X." They came into the world long after Vietnam, Richard Nixon, and Watergate. They never saw Senator Sam

Ervin's eyebrows. Can you imagine? They were also born after *Saturday Night Fever*. They do not know John Travolta has had two movie careers. Nor do they know what it is like to live in a society in which marriage is the predominant social institution. Unfortunately, they do know about broken homes and "single-parent families." And they know what it is like to be the children of child care because 67 percent of them have mothers working outside their homes.

The members of Generation X know a lot about Madonna, Princess Diana, G.I. Jane, Michael Jackson, Michael Jordan, and Mike Tyson. They know nothing at all about Kate Smith, Mother Teresa, Rosie the Riveter, John Wayne, Babe Ruth, and Audie Murphy. Almost without exception, their favorite role models are the type of celebrities seen on MTV, ESPN, and the cover of *People*.

One disturbing poll reveals that nearly 100 percent of today's youth can name the "Three Stooges," but not even 1 percent can name three justices on the U.S. Supreme Court. Seventy-three percent want to start their own businesses, but 53 percent voted for small business foe Bill Clinton. Only 19 percent attend church regularly. Only 1 percent include a member of the clergy on their lists of most admired individuals.

4   What all these statistics tell us is that the gap between generations is wider than ever before. There are five areas in which the gap is most pronounced: skills, knowledge, critical thinking, work, and morality.

The Skills Gap

Iowa test scores have been a standard measurement of academic achievement for many decades. And what they have been measuring lately is frightening. Students who should be scoring at the ninetieth percentile are barely scoring at the seventieth; those who should be at the seventieth are hovering between the thirtieth and fortieth. Between 70 and 90 percent of all students entering the California State University system have to take some form of remedial course work in basic subjects like English and math. Eighty-seven percent of students entering New York community colleges flunk the placement test—they can't even pass the test that would put them into remedial courses! As New York Mayor Rudolph Guiliani observed several years ago, if skills actually determined entrance into the New York system of higher education, three of every four students would probably be denied admission. (The state has recently begun to administer such tests, and it appears that Guiliani was right.) It is also a matter of public record that national ACT and SAT college entrance test scores are steadily declining despite "adjustments" designed to boost them artificially.

Yet one-third of many high schools' students maintain 4.0 (straight A) grade point averages. Why? Because grade inflation, which occurs at every level of education, is rampant. My daughter Sarah has been in the public school system since the third grade, and she is living proof. She has consistently received good grades without the benefit of a good education.

When she enrolled in an algebra class in the eighth grade, I offered to help her with her homework. She took me up on this offer one evening when we were sitting together at the kitchen table. The first problem was: "What is 10 percent of 470?"

I was stunned to discover that Sarah couldn't solve it without the aid of a calculator. Another problem involved determining 25 percent of a given figure. She not only didn't know the answer, but she didn't know that this percentage could be expressed as "one-quarter" or "one-fourth."

8   Here was my own flesh and blood—my straight-A student! I couldn't help asking, "Are the other kids this dumb?" Without missing a beat, Sarah replied, "Oh, they're much dumber." She may be right. On the most recent International Math and Science Survey, which tests students from forty-two countries, one-third of all American high school seniors could not compute the price of a $1,250 stereo that was discounted by 20 percent.

The Knowledge Gap

Algebra is not the only area where today's students have trouble. Hillsdale College President George Roche writes, "Tens of thousands of students do not know when Columbus sailed to the New World, who wrote the Declaration of Independence, or why the Civil War was fought." Part of the problem is that most parents don't realize that what is being taught in modern public schools is actually widening the knowledge gap between them and their children.

One of the most popular history textbooks, produced as a result of the campaign for national education standards in the late 1980s, disparages the "Father of Our Country." George Washington was not, the authors of *The United States: In the Course of Human Events* contend, really successful as a soldier, as a politician, or as a human being. Much is made of Thomas Jefferson's subjective observation that Washington was possessed of "a heart that was not warm in its affections."

How is Generation X ever going to find out that Washington the general did more than any individual to win the war that established our nation? Or that Washington the president risked his reputation and his career to ensure that we would have limited government, a sound economy, and a virtuous citizenry? Or that Washington the man constantly performed acts of kindness and charity for others, including Jefferson? It certainly isn't going to learn such important lessons from a textbook that claims Washington was not much of a man because he did not, in modern lingo, "feel our pain."

12   Special sections in each chapter feature biographies of people who have made a difference in history. Almost all are politically correct minorities and/or females. One, for example, is a female astronaut. The authors allege that she was unfairly excluded from Project Mercury because she had no flight experience. This, of course, is characterized as an insufficient reason to deny her the "right" to participate.

The seventeenth-century English philosopher John Locke is not mentioned—there is no room, evidently, to discuss his significant role in bringing about the Enlightenment or the American Revolution. Famous religious leaders are also ignored, although the authors do bow to the ancient gods of primitive peoples. Pre-Columbian cultures like the Toltecs are praised for their lavishly decorated temples, their calendars, their games—so what if they practiced human sacrifice?

This best-selling textbook reveals a glimpse of the version of history—or rather, non-history—Generation X is being taught. I should know. Last summer, I took Sarah, then fourteen years old, on a tour of Boston, Massachusetts. I carefully explained the historic significance of each site to her. After several hours, she said, "Now, Mom, what war was this?" While I was still in a state of shock we arrived at the Old North Church and listened to a tour guide tell the story of Paul Revere. Sarah's question this time was, "What side was he on?" I asked incredulously, "What exactly did you do in the advanced placement U.S. history class you just completed?" Her response was, "I made a great many charts, and I did a lot of little projects with painting."

I do not mean to pick on Sarah. She and her peers are victims of a pernicious system that has turned traditional liberal arts education on its head. The situation is no better in higher education. At some colleges and universities, professors deliver lectures on the "the Apostle Paul as a Homosexual" and "Jesus Acted Up: A Gay and Lesbian Manifesto." Stanford University achieved notoriety a decade ago for its course, "Black Hair as Culture and History." A current survey on American religion at another school fails to mention Catholicism. One new cutting-edge psychology course is titled, "Gender Discrepancies and Pizza Consumption."

16   Before long, the loss of knowledge may even make simple conversation impossible. In my classroom, I cannot say, "Never look a gift horse in the mouth," or my students will give me a blank stare. I cannot say, "Me thinks thou dost protest too much," or at least one will inevitably respond, "Excuse me, Professor Jennings, shouldn't that be, 'I thinks?' " The literary shorthand of our culture is being lost. This is no small loss either, for words are symbols of important ideas.

The Critical Thinking Gap

Indoctrination is partly to blame for the knowledge gap. This is not a new trend in education. When I was in school, I was taught about "global cooling," and my teachers predicted that the earth was going to be frozen over in a new ice age. Today, my children are told that global warming is going to bring on an ecological apocalypse. But the level of indoctrination has risen sharply. Environmentalism has become an obsession with the teachers of Generation X. They constantly bombard students with dire warnings about pollution, scarce resources, and weather-related disasters. A recent cartoon sums up the attitude the students typically develop. It shows a little girl declaring to her mother that her day in school was a bust: "We didn't do anything to save mankind or the environment. We wasted the whole day on reading and math."

Indoctrination makes students passive receivers of information. As such docile participants, most public school students are incapable of independent thought—of drawing logical inferences or exhibiting other critical thinking skills. They are also incapable of looking at a statement and determining its validity. I refer to this as the "frou-frou head" problem, because students are so lacking in skills and knowledge and are so indoctrinated by politically correct thinking that they are not able to think clearly or make sound, well-informed judgments.

High school freshman Nathan Zohmer of Idaho recently conducted an experiment in science class that reveals the serious nature of this problem. He told classmates and teachers that they should sign his petition to ban a dangerous substance, "dihydrogen monoxide," which causes excessive vomiting and sweating. He informed them that dihydrogen monoxide is a component in acid rain. In its gaseous state, it can cause serious burns. Accidental inhalation can kill. To make matters worse, it contributes to soil erosion, decreases the effectiveness of automobile brakes, and its presence has been detected in some terminal cancer tumors.

20   Forty-seven of the fifty students and teachers signed the petition with no questions asked. Not one thought to inquire, "Just what *is* dihydrogen monoxide?" If they had, they would have discovered they had signed a petition calling for a ban on H_2O—water.

The Work Ethic Gap

Then there is the work ethic gap. In a recent survey, 80 percent of Generation X respondents said they want an active social life, while only 37 percent admit success at work is important. More adult males are living at home with their parents than at any time in our country's history. Why this staggering statistic? Moms and dads provide comfortable room and board while salaries can be used for fun. The desire for independence is missing along with the drive for achieving that independence.

There is no longer a stigma attached to joining the welfare rolls or reneging on financial obligations. Personal bankruptcies are at an all-time high. What is unique about these bankruptcies is the fact that the majority are not the result of the loss of a job or health problems; they involve one or two wage earners who have simply overextended themselves. Credit card debt, which has skyrocketed in recent years, is mainly held by those whose annual income exceeds $50,000. Evidently, the willingness to save and to delay gratification, the drive for success, and the concern for reputation are fast disappearing in a culture that condones irresponsible spending.

The average time for completion of a bachelor's degree is 5.5 years, so most students are not on a fast track. And they have developed some bad habits by the time they get into college. One is whining. As long as there have been students there has been whining—about workload, about subjects, about grades. But now there is *preemptive whining.* Even before the semester begins, even before papers and tests are handed back, students come into my office at Arizona State University with a laundry list of complaints.

24   Last year, one-third of my students protested their grades. In my first twenty years of teaching, not a single student questioned my judgment, but I expect half of my students to do so in the next ten. They are infected with an entitlement mentality. Good grades are not earned by hard work and subject mastery but by signing up to take the class.

I once counseled a graduate student who was doing poorly by saying: "Look, the problem is that you have a lack of depth when it comes to your studies. You have no knowledge base on which you can draw. You are going to have to start reading." He said with some surprise, "What do you mean? Books?"

A recent study analyzing the habits of elementary school children revealed that the average time spent on homework is ten minutes. Worse yet, the same study found that schools are increasingly adopting a "no homework" policy. Perhaps the saddest aspect of this situation is the reason more assignments are not given: Parents complain about the work their children are given.

Following last spring's final exams, a student came to my office and said, "You made us stretch to the maximum. It wasn't a bad feeling." Unfortunately, most students do not understand the pride that comes with conquering what seems to be impossible. Generation X is filled with self-esteem but bereft of knowledge.

28   In the math survey mentioned earlier, students from around the world were asked how they felt they had done upon completion of the exam. While the scores proved that the United States finished in the bottom third of all countries participating, it did finish first in terms of students' perception of personal performance. Americans exhibited the highest self-esteem while students from Japan and Singapore, who finished in the top two slots, were the least arrogant about their performance.

The Morality Gap

The most grievous problem is the morality gap. Sarah is a basketball player and a devoted fan of *Sports Illustrated.* Recently, she shared with me one of the magazine's top stories, which summarized a poll of 1,000 Olympic athletes. One of the questions posed was, "If we could give you a drug that would guarantee your victory at the Olympic Games but would also guarantee your death in five years, would you take it?" Fifty-four percent said yes.

Another survey conducted by the Lutheran Brotherhood asked, "Are there absolute standards for morals and ethics or does everything depend on the situation?" Seventy-nine percent of the respondents in the eighteen to thirty-four age group said that standards did not exist and that the situation should always dictate behavior. Three percent said they were not sure.

If this poll is correct, 82 percent of all students believe that right and wrong are relative terms and that morality is a ridiculous concept. This is the den of lions into which I walk every day. It is called the modern American classroom.

32   When I finish teaching a course, I ask my students to fill out a written evaluation form. Many of them comment, "This business ethics class was really fascinating. I had never heard these ideas before." Mind you, I am not teaching quantum physics—I am presenting simple, basic ideas and principles that should be followed in the marketplace: Be honest. Treat other people the way that you want to be treated. Work hard. Live up to your obligations.

Comedian Jay Leno revealed during one of his street interviews on the *Tonight Show* that the same young people don't seem to know the Ten Commandments. What they do know about morality is what they have picked up in scattered, disconnected bits from parents, friends, television, and magazines. And a good deal of this is immoral rather than moral. As a result, Generation X lacks a solid moral foundation for its views on school, work, marriage, family, and community.

Closing the Generation Gap

Are there ways to close the yawning generation gap, which is really the sum of all these smaller gaps? Of course there are. We live in a miraculous age. Great changes have revolutionized the way we live. I started law school with an electric type-writer—state-of-the-art back then. Now I have a computer, a fax machine, and electronic mail. The tools of high technology allow for improved education, wider access to knowledge, more work productivity, and greater freedom to make moral decisions. But these same tools also demand greater personal responsibility.

Is Generation X ready? I don't know. Remember the 1986 disaster at the Chernobyl nuclear plant in Ukraine? The world's worst nuclear accident did not happen because nuclear power is a flawed technology. It happened because a handful of young, cocky engineers chose to disregard established safety parameters while performing a routine test of equipment. Ironically, the test was designed to provide power to operate the reactor core cooling system in the event of an emergency. The engineers' carelessness and arrogance, which caused the release of large quantities of radioactive substances into the atmosphere, has since caused the death, pain, and suffering of innocent victims in Belarus, Ukraine, and Russia.

36   Look at what happened to Barings Bank, the venerable institution that financed the Napoleonic wars. It went bankrupt in 1995 because one trader, twenty-eight-year-old Nick Leeson, was able to sit in front of his computer and violate the prime ethical rule of banking: You don't take other people's money and recklessly gamble with it. He made a $27 billion bet that the Japanese stock market would rally after the Kobe earthquake. The marked dropped instead, and Barings's losses reached a staggering $1.3 billion.

At the end of 1997, twenty-nine-year-old Marisa Baridis entered a guilty plea when she was charged with selling inside information. For $2,000 to $10,000 a tip, she and her friends made a dramatic impact on the stock market by using nonpublic information to take advantage of others. Ms. Baridis, who profited handsomely from such cheating, was the compliance officer for the investment bank and brokerage house of Morgan Stanley. She enjoyed a great deal of technological access to confidential information and a great deal of unilateral authority. In a tape-recorded conversation, she referred to insider trading as the "illegalist [sic] thing you can do," but, lacking the basic values of fairness and honesty, she easily dismissed the law she was responsible for enforcing. She also cost shareholders and companies millions of dollars.

High technology demands *more* individual judgment and *more* moral accountability. Generation X boasts thousands of techno-wise youth. But it is missing real wisdom, informed by a strong education and a strong spiritual ethic. When I point this out to some of my students and colleagues, they say, "Hey, don't shove that Judeo-Christian stuff down our throats! We don't want that." Then I remind them that this "stuff" exists everywhere, and that it has been considered vital to civil society for centuries. I challenge them to name one country in the world where bribery and cheating are legal and approved by the populace. I tell them to examine the most basic ethical principles of Moses and Jesus and compare them to those of Aristotle, Confucius, and Mohammed. The major religions of the world are in agreement on certain universals that have stood the test of time.

One such standard of university morality is what is referred to by Christians as the "Golden Rule": Do unto others as you would have them do unto you. The same notion of fairness can be found in the basic tenets of Buddhism, Judaism, Hinduism, and even in philosophy in the form of Kant's "categorical imperative." Throughout time, this simple test of ethics has been recognized in various cultures as a means of preserving civility, decency, and morality. Its beauty lies in its simplicity. Its profundity lies in its universal recognition and adherence.

Parents as Teachers

40   As parents we have to stand up and be counted. When our children come home from school, as my daughter did one day, spinning yarns about Ethan Allen and the "Green Mountain Persons," we have to set the record straight. Truth matters. It was Ethan Allen and the "Green Mountain Boys," and this fact is not a slight to women. When preschoolers are exposed to storybooks on "alternative" lifestyles and early sex education (endorsed by the National Education Association, by the way), we must sound our objections loudly and clearly. We must exert pressure on superintendents, principals, and teachers. We must take the initiative and run for positions on school boards and city councils.

We must also seize moments of morality with our children to teach them the difference between right and wrong and impose punishments when they stray from moral principles. Most important, we must restore the twin notions that being judgmental is not the same as being narrow-minded and that expressing moral outrage is not a form of "hate speech." What a different world we would have if choosing right and rejecting wrong were not considered fanatical!

When I graduated from law school, a speaker offered nine words I have never forgotten: "Truth is violated by falsehood but outraged by silence." The past twenty-five years have been filled with falsehoods about our history and our culture. Generation X has never lived in a time of truth. Condemning immorality has become virtually the only sin, so it has not even witnessed the courage of conviction. We have been silent as an entire generation has seen truth repeatedly violated.

There is a difference between holding beliefs and being valiant in defending beliefs. As parents, struggling to close the generation gap, we must be valiant in defending our beliefs. Indeed, this is a call to action for all who guide our youth and offer them instruction. When immorality and adultery are described as "private" and therefore "irrelevant" in the public square, with no impact on character and leadership, we must shout from the rooftops, "Personal conduct *is* character! Character does matter!" When the lessons of history, literature, science, and religion are distorted, attacked, or lost in the shuffle, we must rescue them. It is time to break our silence and confront those who have perpetrated so many myths, so much fraud, and so little substance for so long.

44   It is still possible to reclaim Generation X from the hopelessly flawed indoctrination it has experienced. But reclaiming our children will require the type of introspection that results in moral courage and is followed by the expression of moral outrage. One of my students commented to me at the end of a semester, "You've dispelled so many myths. Now I know morality in business is not a crime." And I responded, "It's even better, son. Neither is the moral life a sin." Breaking our silence will allow truth to emerge, and its rare and illuminating quality will attract the attention and devotion of a generation trained and raised in amoral darkness.

Personal Response

Explore your immediate response to Jennings's criticism of the educational backgrounds of today's college freshmen. How do you respond to her opening paragraphs about Generation X, their role models, and their failure to recognize the names of people who served as role models for her generation?

Questions for Class or Small-Group Discussion

1. Jennings identifies five areas where she believes "the gap between generations is wider than ever before" (paragraph 4). Summarize her central point about each of those five areas and then discuss them in turn. Do you think her remarks accurately reflect your own educational experience? Do you agree with her generalizations?

2. In paragraphs 1, 2, 3, and 9, Jennings names people and events that she claims today's generation of young people do not know. Is her claim right in your case? How many of them do you recognize or know? Do you agree with her implication that not knowing who those people are, or certain facts about the historical events she names, is a mark of ignorance?

3. Jennings maintains that "political correctness" is "a pernicious system that has turned traditional liberal arts education on its head" (paragraph 15). What is your opinion of that statement?

4. Respond to this statement: "Generation X is filled with self-esteem but bereft of knowledge" (paragraph 27).

THE HOMEWORK ATE MY FAMILY

Romesh Ratnesar

Romesh Ratnesar, who has been a staff writer for Time *magazine since 1997, admits to not having taken his homework very seriously when he was in school. This article appeared as the cover story on homework in the January 25, 1999, issue of* Time.

It's a typical Tuesday afternoon in early January for 11-year-old Molly Benedict, a sixth-grader at Presidio Middle School in San Francisco. When she gets home from school at 3:30, she heads straight for the basement of her family's two-story house, flips on her computer and bangs out a one-page book report on J. K. Rowling's *Harry Potter and the Sorcerer's Stone.* After half an hour of work, Molly takes the paper upstairs and gives it to her mother Libby for proofreading. As Molly nibbles a snack of a bagel and orange-spice tea, Mom jots some corrections. "Why don't you say, 'This is the best book I ever read,' " Libby suggests. "Teachers really like strong opinions like that."

Time to kick back, call a few friends and get ready for *Felicity,* right? Not even close. Next Molly pulls out her math assignment: more than 100 fraction and long-division problems. Once she slogs through those, Molly labels all the countries and bodies of water on a map of the Middle East. And she's not through yet: she then reviews a semester's worth of science, including the ins and outs of the circulatory system.

By 5:30, after doing two hours of homework, Molly sits down at the piano and practices for an hour. She'll barely have enough time to eat dinner and touch up that book report before crashing. "With less work I think we could learn what we're learning now," Molly says. "But I don't think it's too overwhelming." The strain of homework weighs more heavily on her mother. "I didn't feel [stressed] until I was in my 30s," says Libby, 43. "It hurts my feelings that my daughter feels that way at 11."

4   Most of us remember homework, if we remember it at all, as one of the minor annoyances of growing up. Sure, we dreaded the multiplication tables and those ridiculous shoe-box dioramas. But let's admit it: we finished most of our assignments on the bus ride to school—and who even bothered with the stuff until after the requisite hours had been spent alphabetizing baseball cards, gabbing on the phone or watching reruns of *Gilligan's Island?*

Kids today have scant time for such indulgences. Saddled with an out-of-school curriculum chock-full of Taekwondo lessons, ceramics workshops and bassoon practice, America's youngsters barely have time to check their e-mail before hunkering down with homework. On the whole, U.S. students come home with more schoolwork than ever before—and at a younger age. According to researchers at the University of Michigan, 6-to-9-year-olds in 1981 spent 44 min. a week on homework; in 1997 they did more than two hours' worth. The amount of time that 9-to-11-year-olds devoted to homework each week increased from 2 hr. 49 min. to more than 3½ hr.

After some historical ups and downs, homework in this country is at a high-water mark. In the early decades of the century progressive educators in many school districts banned homework in primary school in an effort to discourage rote learning. The cold war—specifically, the launch of Sputnik in 1957—put an end to that, as lawmakers scrambled to bolster math and science education in the U.S. to counter the threat of Soviet whiz kids. Students frolicked in the late 1960s and '70s, as homework declined to near World War II levels. But fears about U.S. economic competitiveness and the publication of *A Nation at Risk,* the 1983 government report that focused attention on the failings of American schools, ratcheted up the pressure to get tough again. Other forces have kept the trend heading upward: increasing competition to get into the best colleges and the batteries of statewide standardized tests—starting in grade school in a growing number of states—for which teachers must prepare their pupils.

The homework crunch is heard loudest in the country's better middle-class school districts, where parents push their kids hard and demand that teachers deliver enough academic rigor to get students into top secondary schools and colleges. Now there's a blowback: the sheer quantity of nightly homework and the difficulty of the assignments can turn ordinary weeknights into four-hour library-research excursions, leave kids in tears and parents with migraines, and generally transform the placid refuge of home life into a tense war zone. "The atmosphere in the house gets very frustrated," says Lynne O'Callaghan, a mom in Portland, Ore., whose daughter Maeve, 8, does two hours of homework a night. "Some days it's just a struggle. Who wants it that way?" Laura Mandel, a mother of three in Warren, N.J., feels similarly embattled. "It's ironic that politicians talk so much about family values," says Mandel, "when you can't have any family time anymore because the kids are so busy keeping their nose to the grindstone."

8   While kids grow more frazzled, parents are increasingly torn. Just how involved should they be? Should they help a son or daughter finish that geography assignment, or stay aloof and risk having a frustrated, sleep-deprived child? Should they complain to teachers about the heavy workload or be thankful that their kids are being pushed toward higher achievement? Battles over homework have become so intense that some school districts have decided to formally prescribe the amount of homework kids at each grade level should receive. All of which leaves open the questions of just how much and what kind of homework is best. Though there's evidence that homework does improve academic performance, at least in the junior high and high school years, its true value may be more subtle. It encourages good study habits and acclimates students to self-directed work—but only when it's not so oppressive that it turns them off school altogether.

The war over homework is about even larger issues. Schools in the 1990s are expected to fill so many roles—and do so with often paltry resources and ill-qualified teachers—that it's no surprise more work gets sent home. For baby-boomer parents homework has become both a status gauge—the nightly load indicates the toughness of their child's school—and an outlet for nervy overbearance so that each homework assignment is practically theirs to complete too. Yet the growth in dual-income families means less energy and shorter fuses for assisting the kids. And all the swirling arguments over homework underscore the bigger questions that confound American teachers, parents and policymakers: What should we expect from our children? What do we want them to learn? How much is enough?

Erica Astrove is pretty sure she knows. She's just seven—a loquacious, blue-eyed second-grader at the public Hunnewell School in Wellesley, Mass. She plays the piano, takes skating lessons and plans to add pottery and chorus. For fun Erica reads almanacs; her parents gave her a book on world maps and flags for Christmas. "My little researcher," her mother Christina says. There's not much Erica shies away from—except homework. Recently, she told her mother she doesn't want to go to middle school, high school or college because of homework. Asked if she might have a bit more tolerance for homework once she enters third grade, Erica shakes her head. "I'm going to keep on crying," she says.

Erica's mom has experience drying tears. Her homework agonies began when her eldest daughter Kate was in second grade. In addition to nightly spelling and reading assignments, Kate sometimes came home with math problems so vexing that Christina wondered whether algebra was required to solve them. Mother and daughter pored over some problems for two hours. They once scattered 200 pennies on the kitchen table in a vain attempt to get a solution. "The [problems] would be so hard," Christina says, "that I would leave them for my husband to solve when he got home from work late." Those were not happy times. "It made all our time together negative," Christina says. "It was painful for all of us."

12   The pain caused by homework isn't just emotional. Carl Glassman, father of two girls who attend public school in New York City, reports that last year his eldest daughter missed much of her first semester in sixth grade because of pneumonia, "due to the fact that she was doing homework until 11 every night." Laura Mandel, the New Jersey mother of three, found her son Jeffrey, 6, suffering homework-related nightmares this month when she tried gently to rouse him for school. "Oh, Mom," he pleaded, half asleep, "don't tell me there's another homework sheet."

The steady flood of homework can cause chronic weariness. Holly Manges, a high-achieving fifth-grader at the public Eastern elementary school in Lexington, Ohio, approached her mother earlier this school year close to tears. "Is it O.K. if I don't get all A's?" she asked. "I don't care anymore. I'm just too tired." Over time, that homework fatigue can pull at the fabric of families. As early as third grade, Rachel Heckelman, now 11, came home every day from her elementary school in Houston with three hours' worth of homework. The assignments were often so dizzyingly complex—one asked her to design an entire magazine—that Rachel looked for any way to procrastinate. Her mother Lissa tried banning TV for the night. When that didn't work, Lissa pleaded with increasing impatience. "I would get red in the face, and she would get defensive," Lissa says. Rachel's father typically removed himself from the fracas by repairing to the bedroom and shutting the door.

The frustrations that homework visits upon kids can irk their parents to the point of revolt. David Kooyman, of Covina, Calif., was so incensed about his three grade-schoolers' homework load that he exacted a pledge from their teachers not to lower his kids' grades if they didn't do assignments. When the kids found themselves lost in class discussions, Kooyman reluctantly allowed them to do the homework, but he is planning to sue the school district for violating his civil rights. "They have us hostage to homework," he grumbles. "I'm 47, and I have 25-year-old teachers telling me what to do with my home life."

Other parents are ambivalent. Many resent teachers for piling on projects that cut into unstructured family time. And yet the drive of middle- and upper-middle-class Americans to keep their children at the head of the class has never been more intense. The teachers who assign mountains of homework often believe they are bowing to the wishes of demanding parents. Says Jeana Considine, a fifth-grade teacher at Elm Elementary School in Hinsdale, Ill.: "The same parents who are complaining that they don't have enough family time would be really upset if their child didn't score well." Pepperdine University president David Davenport, father of a fourth-grader who clocks two hours of homework a night, sees a chain reaction: "The pressure to get into highly selective colleges and universities backs up into high school advanced-placement courses, which backs up to elementary schools." Anxious parents can rail about what teachers do in the classroom, but homework is still one area where parents can directly improve their child's chances.

16   So even those determined to remain passive observers while their kids labor over essays and science-fair projects can find themselves getting sucked in. "It's something I never wanted to do. I hated doing homework when I was a kid," says Lizanne Merrill, a New York City artist whose daughter Gracie is in second grade. But Gracie often trudges home with elaborate assignments that all but demand Merrill's involvement. A research paper assigned to be done over Christmas vacation required Gracie, 8, to do some fieldwork on sea turtles at the American Museum of Natural History. Mom went along: "I just tell myself, if I don't help out on her homework, what kind of deadbeat mother would I be?"

It's hard to blame parents like Alexis Rasley of Oak Park, Ill., if they occasionally get too involved. Last fall a homework assignment for fifth-graders at the public Horace Mann School was to build a mini–space station that accounted for food, water, waste treatment, radiation shielding and zero gravity. Rasley's son Taylor, 10, spent countless maddening hours toiling at a basement countertop surrounded by cut-open soda bottles. "He just kept sitting there saying, 'I don't know what to do,'" Rasley says. "When the frustration level gets that high, you say, 'O.K., I'm going to help,' because the situation has become so hurtful."

Being an attentive, empathetic parent is one thing; acting as a surrogate student is another. But when pressures mount, the line can get blurred. When Susan Solomon of San Francisco saw her son bogged down last year with a language-arts paper that would help his application to an élite high school, she took matters into her own hands: she did his math homework. He later copied his mother's calculations in his own handwriting. "He knew how to do it," Solomon shrugs. "It was just busywork." In the affluent Boston suburb of Sherborn, Mass., parents at the public Pine Hill School tend to talk about homework in the first-person plural; and they sometimes become more than equal partners in carrying out such third-grade projects as writing up the ownership history of their house, complete with a sketch of the floor plan. Homework has been known to arrive at school two hours after the child does.

"So much of this is about parents wanting their kids to look good," admits psychologist Kim Gatof, mother of third-grader Jake. For an "invention convention," members of Jake's class are building contraptions of their devising. Jake wants to build a better mousetrap. "I can say, 'Just build it yourself,'" says Kim. "Or we can help with it, and it can be on the same level as the others." Jake may have a hard time topping Tucker Carter, another third-grader, who has already made his presentation. Tucker whipped up a fully functioning battery-operated alarm clock that uses a windshield pump to squirt cold water at the sleeper. The kids whooped at this bit of ingenuity, but even they were suspicious. Either Tucker is a prodigiously gifted engineer, or his dad built the clock for him. Sighed David Nihill, the school's principal: "It looks like Alexander Graham Bell made it himself."

20   Is all this homework really doing any good? Julian Betts, an associate professor of economics at the University of California, San Diego, examined surveys on the homework habits of 6,000 students over five years and found that students who did an extra 30 min. of nightly math homework beginning in seventh grade would, by 11th grade, see their achievement level soar by the equivalent of two grades. Betts argues that the amount of homework is a better indicator of how students perform than the size of class or the quality of teachers. But his study was limited to students in junior high and high school. What about younger children? In 1989 University of Missouri psychology professor Harris Cooper reviewed more than 100 studies on homework and concluded that while benefits from homework can be measured starting in junior high, the effect of home assignments on standardized test scores in the lower grades is negligible or nonexistent. "Piling on massive amounts of homework will not lead to gains," Cooper says, "and may be detrimental by leading children to question their abilities."

Still, some researchers make a case for elementary school homework. Carol Huntsinger, an education professor at the College of Lake County, near Chicago, compared the academic performance of local Chinese-American children with that of European-American kids. In the early grades, the Chinese-American students outperformed their white counterparts in math and mastery of vocabulary words. After examining a host of other factors, Huntsinger concluded that homework made the critical difference. In first grade the Chinese-American children were doing more than 20 min. of math homework a night, some of it formally assigned by their parents, while their white classmates averaged just 5 min.

It may be unwise to make too much of Huntsinger's study, which focused on a small group of families. All experts agree that weighing second-graders down with hours of homework is pointless and probably damaging to their self-esteem and desire to learn. But in reasonable amounts, homework has value for students at all grade levels. "Homework has benefits that go well beyond its immediate direct impact on what's going on in school," says Cooper. Doing homework is important for honing organizational skills, learning how to manage time and developing the ability to learn autonomously.

The question of the day, of course, is what is the right amount? Cooper recommends 10 to 20 min. nightly in first grade and an increase of 10 min. a night for each grade after that. But the point is not simply to fill up a set amount of time. For preoccupied teachers, admits Michelann Ortloff, a Portland school official and former elementary school teacher, "it's always easy to pull a few things out of the workbook, give them to students and say, 'This is your homework.'" Too many teachers send kids home with mind-numbing math worksheets that are not even reviewed the next day. Too many are enamored of those unwieldy "projects" that seem to exasperate kids more than they instruct them and that lead to excessive parent involvement. For young students, the optimal arrangement would mix skill-building drills with creative tasks closely tied to what's being taught in the classroom—such as interviewing grandparents as a social-studies lesson or using soccer standings to teach rudimentary statistics.

24   Educators agree that parents should be vigilant about making sure such a healthy blend is maintained. Everyone frowns on parents' doing homework for their kids, but most agree that parents should monitor homework; offer guidance, not answers, when asked for help; and give teachers regular reports on how their kids are handling it all. Gail Block, a fifth-grade language-arts instructor in San Francisco who feels that homework helps overcome the limits of time in the classroom, was nonetheless surprised to hear that her student Molly Benedict takes close to three hours a night to finish. Pepperdine president Davenport notes the amount of time his daughter spends on each assignment at the bottom of her work sheet. "Sometimes," he says, "teachers are not aware of how much time is being spent."

Parents could benefit from a little perspective too. American students on the whole still work less, play more and perform worse than many of their counterparts around the world. As Harold Stevenson and James Stigler point out in their book *The Learning Gap,* Japanese and Chinese elementary school students spend significantly more time on homework than do children in the U.S. A first-grader in Taipei does seven times as much homework as a first-grader in Minneapolis—and scores higher on tests of knowledge and skills.

But American parents should worry less about the precise number of minutes their students devote to homework and more about the uneven and poorly conceived way in which it is assigned. "What defines the homework problem in the U.S. today is variation," Cooper says. Less than one-third of U.S. school districts provide any guidelines to parents and teachers on how much homework children should receive and what purpose it's supposed to serve. In places that have instituted formal homework policies, a semblance of sanity has arrived. In Hinsdale, Ill., parents often complained that their children got too much homework from some teachers and too little from others. So a committee of teachers, parents and administrators spent several months devising a formal policy that requires "meaningful and purposeful" homework at all grade levels but limits the load according to age and mandates that some of it be optional. Besides helping students build their homework appetite over time, the policy aims to persuade the academically more eager parents that it's safe to back off.

The need for a more rational approach to homework may be one argument for establishing national standards for what all U.S. students should know. If such standards existed, teachers might assign homework with a more precise goal in mind, and parents might spend fewer nights agonizing about whether their children were overburdened or understimulated by homework. Of course, the debate over national standards is a complex one, and cramming for a national test could mean more mindless at-home drudgery for kids. But not necessarily. When Taylor Hoss, 10, of Vancouver, Wash., came home last year with packets of extra homework assigned in preparation for the state's new mandatory assessment exams, his parents shuddered. But as they worked through the test-prep material, the Hosses were pleased with the degree of critical thinking the questions required. "I was very impressed," says Taylor's dad Schuyler. "It makes you connect the dots."

28   There are other ways of soothing nerves. Both parents and students must be willing to embrace the "work" component of homework—to recognize the quiet satisfaction that comes from practice and drill, the steady application of concepts and the mastery of skills. It's a tough thing to ask of many American parents. "You want your children to be happy, and you pray for their success in the future," says Laura Mandel. "But does homework bring either of those goals? I don't think more homework will make a more successful adult." Maybe not, but wisely assigned homework may help make a more successful, well, child. "It is all about learning responsibility," says Janine Bempechat, an assistant professor at Harvard's Graduate School of Education. "When you have homework on a regular basis, you learn persistence, diligence and delayed gratification."

Molly Benedict, for one, seems to be swallowing the bad medicine with surprising equanimity. "I don't have a lot of time to do just whatever," she admits. "My friends and I think it's a lot of work. But we've adapted well." Kids like Molly have learned it's a rough world, and homework is only part of it. But who knows? If teachers and parents start approaching homework with a little less heat and a little more care, kids may still have time left to be kids. Or whatever.

Personal Response

Write for a few minutes on your own experiences with homework in your elementary and secondary education.

Questions for Class or Small-Group Discussion

1. Discuss your views on the subject of "just how much and what kind of homework is best" (paragraph 8). How would you answer these questions facing teachers, parents, and policymakers: "What should we expect from our children? What do we want them to learn? How much is enough?" (paragraph 9)?

2. Summarize the advantages and disadvantages of homework, according to Ratnesar. Do you think the benefits outweigh the disadvantages? Do you support the suggestion that more schools institute formal homework policies (paragraph 26)?

3. What do you think of the fact that American students generally perform far worse than students in many other countries (paragraph 25)? Do you think that we need national standards for what students should know (paragraph 27)?

4. This article addresses the subject of homework for primarily middle- and upper-middle-class students. How do you think the issues shift, if at all, when discussing homework for students in other socioeconomic classes?

A PRESCRIPTION FOR PEACE
Howard Gardner

Howard Gardner is a professor at the Harvard Graduate School of Education. He has been awarded eighteen honorary degrees and is the author of eighteen books and several hundred articles. His most recent books are the following: Good Work: When Excellence and Ethics Meet (2001), The Disciplined Mind: Beyond Facts and Standardized Tests (2000), The K–12 Education That Every Child Deserves (1999), Intelligence Reframed (1997), and Extraordinary Minds: Portraits of Exceptional Individuals and an Examination of our Extraordinariness (1996). Gardner is best known in educational circles for his theory of multiple intelligences, a critique of the notion that there exists but a single human intelligence that can be assessed by standard psychometric instruments. This essay appeared in the January 25, 1999, issue of Time magazine to accompany that week's cover story on homework.

The English and French met memorably on the battlefield of Agincourt. During the Civil War, the North and South shed fraternal blood at Gettysburg. For many parents and children, the encounter over homework bears the mark of a similar armed struggle: Who is in control? What weapons should be used? What are the spoils of victory, the costs of loss? And the ultimate question of warfare: What is it all for?

I've had to ponder these questions as a child psychologist, an educational reformer and a father of four. I've got the battle scars to prove it. Perhaps the chief lesson I've learned is that homework is but one chapter in the lengthy book of parenting. The tensions can be reduced if the family's approach to homework echoes the broader relationship between child and parents that has unfolded over many years. Moreover, if families see homework as an occasion for energized action rather than angry reaction, homework can become a far more productive and even enjoyable activity.

We have many desires and expectations for our children, some explicit, some tacit. I hope my children will become responsible people who meet commitments; are generous to others; and are knowledgeable about the world, their heritage, the beautiful objects and experiences of life, the discoveries of today, the challenges of tomorrow. It's important to be clear about such goals. It is equally important to lead lives that embody these goals. I can hardly expect my children to want to study, to love music, to be responsible and helpful if those around them don't model such behavior.

4   In short, education is not just what happens in school; it takes place at home, on the street, in the wider community and especially nowadays as a result of daily exposure to the mass media. And yet, of course, we allocate certain facets of education to

schools. We expect teachers to foster the basic literacies; to convey important insights and practices from our own society; to introduce youngsters to crucial bodies of knowledge and to the ways in which scholars have approached them—the "mental habits" of the historian, the mathematician, the scientist. We hope as well that teachers will serve as role models. As the longtime East Harlem school principal Deborah Meier, now in Boston, has declared with respect to teachers and students, "We need to be their Joe DiMaggios."

Enter homework. While much education takes place from 8 a.m. to 3 p.m., it's valuable for students to do additional work at home—perhaps an hour or so in the elementary years, two to three hours at the secondary level. There's so much to be mastered that most students can't do it all in school. Practice is best done in the hours after school. Some projects need the reflective periods that can't be provided in the classroom. And of course it is valuable for youngsters to learn to work on their own, to monitor their own learning, to be able to use guidance and suggestions from parents and peers.

I believe the major problem surrounding homework is that it is seen as an intrusion from outside, to which parents and children must react. Youngsters value their "out of school" time; they would rather be playing with friends or watching TV than sitting alone at a desk. Parents are afraid that unless their children do homework, they will not get into a good college or will not develop good work habits. So at the first sign that the youngster is not performing well, homework becomes the central battleground of the after-school hours.

Let's say instead that homework were seen not as an intrusion but rather as a daily occasion where major tasks and opportunities of growing up could be worked through. Homework can serve as an occasion where one acquires a sense of responsibility. We should *act*—not react. And let me propose a meaning for each of these three key letters:

Amplification

8   Homework can amplify what one already values as a parent or child. If one wants to know more about what a tax is, or how to read a poem, or how steady practice with conjugations can allow one to be understood in a faraway country, homework provides a wonderful means to reinforce these endeavors. Homework seems less problematic in Asian societies because families and schools are already in accord on the need for home study. Indeed, when Asians move to America, parents often purchase their own copies of textbooks so they can learn along with their children.

Countering

Not every aspect of homework is wondrous. Some homework is boring drill. As a parent, I tried not to criticize the homework, since that causes tension. Instead I tried to complement it by providing alternative experiences or encounters. If the school insists on having students memorize mountains of information about, say, Central Asia without giving them a sense of the place, I would bring out a book or rent a movie that brings the region to life. If the school requires a lesson on rocks, one can spend an afternoon at a science museum, or for that matter on a neighboring lot or hill.

Finally, as my work on multiple intelligences has taught me, individuals have distinctly different kinds of minds—even and sometimes especially when they are members of the same family. Unfortunately, this fact has not been seriously confronted in schools. Parents have a special responsibility when their youngsters do not learn in the traditional ways. It is up to us to find ways to help children use *their kinds of minds* both to understand the work of school and to exhibit their understanding to others. Suppose that the assignment is to learn about evolution by reading a chapter and answering some factual questions. The parent of a youngster with strong "naturalistic" intelligence might accompany the child to a natural-history museum and trace the antecedents of *Homo sapiens*. Siblings with other profiles of intelligence might benefit instead from viewing a drama about Darwin's life or creating a new form of "virtual life" on the computer.

Teaching

Even the best schools can't teach everything. In fact, I think the best schools do not even try to cover all fronts. Rather than complaining about this, parents should try to make a virtue of necessity. We should bone up on (or remember) the knowledge we value and teach it to our children. Sometimes it will be academic subject matter, but just as often it will be a value or an attitude. Perhaps the greatest gift my mother gave me when I was young was her commitment to sit just behind me each day when I practiced the piano. She said little, though she would occasionally make a comment or suggest that we listen to a record or go to a concert. I learned to love music. Even more important, I learned that—no matter how much or how little talent one has—one can steadily improve by working regularly at something. Now every day I sit slightly behind my 13-year-old son Benjamin while he practices piano, hoping he will love music throughout his life and learn the value of systematic honing of one's skills.

12

I've dwelled here on my family and my values. But each family must identify its own values. Some will highlight competition, others cooperation; some will stress mastery of technology, others the cultivation of an art or craft or the achievement of athletic prowess; some will seek a curriculum that emphasizes facts and figures, others a curriculum that encourages youngsters to be creative or even iconoclastic.

We cannot all find schools that meet these goals. I urge that we view school as one of several educational experiences. And when the dreaded *H* word looms, we should take an active stance: amplifying when we are in agreement, countering when we feel there is a lack and teaching—always teaching—what we feel is sacred.

The Duke of Wellington is said to have observed, "The battle of Waterloo was won on the playing fields of Eton." This statement reflects a recognition that teaching and learning can occur in many places and that *work* need not be contrasted with *play*. The ultimate test is whether youngsters grow up to be decent human beings and whether, when it is their turn, they can successfully transmit values and practices to their offspring. Recent talk that parents do not matter is highly misleading. We do matter, especially when it comes to inculcating discipline, respect, responsibility, core values. Perhaps we cannot turn battlegrounds into playing fields, but at least we should attempt to make work at home part of the larger tapestry of success in life.

Personal Response

Gardner mentions the values that his mother instilled in him and that he wishes to instill in his own children (paragraph 11). He adds: "But each family must identify its own values" (paragraph 12). What values have you learned from your family? What would you hope to pass on to your own children?

Questions for Class or Small-Group Discussion

1. What do you think of Gardner's proposal to make homework a productive and enjoyable activity? Do you think he is being realistic? To what extent do you agree with him that education occurs in many places in addition to school (paragraph 4)?

2. Discuss each of the three components of Gardner's plan for parents to make homework an opportunity for families rather than disagreeable tasks for children.

3. Respond to this statement in the concluding paragraph: "Recent talk that parents do not matter is highly misleading. We do matter. . . ." To what degree do you agree with Gardner that parents do matter in how their children turn out?

NO TIME TO READ?

David McCullough

David McCullough is a biographer, historian, lecturer, and teacher. He holds twenty-one honorary degrees and has received many awards for his writing, including the Pulitzer Prize for his widely acclaimed biography, Truman *(1992). His other books include* The Path Between the Seas *(1977), chronicling the building of the Panama Canal;* Mornings on Horseback *(1981), on the life of the young Theodore Roosevelt; and* Brave Companions *(1992), essays on heroic figures of the past and present. His most recent biography is* John Adams *(2001). McCullough is also well known to viewers of PBS as the host of* The American Experience *and numerous PBS documentaries. "No Time to Read?" appeared in the April 18, 2000, issue of* Family Circle.

Once upon a time in the dead of winter in the Dakota territory, Theodore Roosevelt took off in a makeshift boat down the Little Missouri River in pursuit of a couple of thieves who had stolen his prized rowboat. After several days on the river, he caught up and got the draw on them with his trusty Winchester, at which point they surrendered. Then Roosevelt set off in a borrowed wagon to haul the thieves cross-country to justice. They headed across the snow-covered wastes of the Badlands to the railhead at Dickinson, and Roosevelt walked the whole way, the entire 40 miles. It was an astonishing feat, what might be called a defining moment in Roosevelt's eventful life. But what makes it especially memorable is that during that time, he managed to read all of *Anna Karenina*.

I often think of that when I hear people say that they haven't time to read.

Reportedly, the average American does have time to watch 28 hours of television every week, or approximately four hours a day. The average person, I'm told, reads at a rate of 250 words per minute. So, based on these statistics, were the average American to spend those four hours a day with a book instead of watching television, he or she could, in a week, read: the complete poems of T. S. Eliot; two plays by Thornton Wilder, including *Our Town;* the complete poems of Maya Angelou; Faulkner's *The Sound and the Fury; The Great Gatsby;* and The Book of Psalms.

4   That's all in one week.

But a week is a long time by today's standards, when information is available at the touch of a finger. Information has become an industry, a commodity to be packaged, promoted and marketed incessantly. The tools for "accessing" data grow ever more wondrous and ubiquitous and essential if we're to keep in step, we've come to believe. All hail the Web, the Internet, the Information Highway.

We're being sold the idea that information is learning, and we're being sold a bill of goods.

Information isn't learning. It isn't wisdom. It isn't common sense necessarily. It isn't kindness. Or good judgment. Or imagination. Or a sense of humor. Or courage. Information doesn't tell us right from wrong.

8   Knowing the area of the state of Connecticut in square miles, or the date on which the United Nations Charter was signed, or the jumping capacity of a flea may be useful, but it isn't learning of itself.

The greatest of all avenues to learning—to wisdom, adventure, pleasure, insight, to understanding human nature, understanding ourselves and our world and our place in it—is in reading books.

Read for life, all your life. Nothing ever invented provides such sustenance, such infinite reward for time spent, as a good book.

Read for pleasure. Read what you like, and all you like. Read literally to your heart's content. Let one book lead to another. They nearly always do.

12   Take up a great author, new or old, and read everything he or she has written. Read about places you've never been. Read biography, history. Read books that changed history: Tom Paine's *Common Sense;* the autobiography of Frederick Douglass; Rachel Carson's *Silent Spring.*

Read those books you know you're supposed to have read and imagine as dreary. A classic may be defined as a book that stays long in print, and a book stays long in print only because it is exceptional. Why exclude the exceptional from your experience?

Go back and read again the books written supposedly for children, especially if you think they are only for children. My first choice would be *The Wind in the Willows*. There's much, very much, you can learn in the company of Toad, Rat and Mole.

And when you read a book you love—a book you feel has enlarged the experience of being alive, a book that "lights the fire"—then spread the word.

16   To carry a book with you wherever you go is old advice and good advice. John Adams urged his son, John Quincy, to carry a volume of poetry. "You'll never be alone," he said, "with a poet in your pocket."

Personal Response

Do you read books for pleasure during your leisure time? If so, what do you like to read? If not, why not?

Questions for Class or Small-Group Discussion

1. How effective do you find McCullough's opening anecdote about Theodore Roosevelt?

2. Do you agree with McCullough that, on the "idea that information is learning, [. . .] we're being sold a bill of goods" (paragraph 6)? Do you agree with him that "[i]nformation isn't learning" (paragraph 7)?

3. Discuss the extent to which you agree with McCullough's implication that people would have time to read books if they just took the time.

4. Have you read any of the books or any works by the authors that McCullough names? What authors have you heard about whose books you would like to read (paragraph 12)? What books do you "know you're supposed to have read and imagine as dreary" (paragraph 13)? Which of the books for children, besides *The Wind in the Willows,* do you think McCullough may have in mind when he says to read the "books written supposedly for children" (paragraph 14)?

PERSPECTIVES ON EDUCATION

Suggestions for Synthesis

1. Write an essay on the subject of homework, drawing on Romesh Ratnesar's "The Homework Ate My Family," Howard Gardner's "A Prescription for Peace," and Marianne M. Jennings's "The Real Generation Gap."

2. Taking into consideration two or more of the essays in this chapter, write a paper defining *education*.

3. Drawing on two or more essays in this chapter, write a paper on the role of parents in children's education.

Additional Writing Topics

1. Keeping in mind Romesh Ratnesar's discussion of homework for middle-class children in "The Homework Ate My Family," explore the subject of the connection between socioeconomic level and quality of education.

2. Taking into consideration Howard Gardner's "A Prescription for Peace," write an essay from the point of view of either a student feeling pressured by homework or a parent of a child feeling pressured by homework.

3. Assume the role of a student member of the curriculum task force for a department or unit at your university such as business, foreign languages, education, mathematics, computer science, history, music, physics, or your major area, if you have declared one. Your committee has been asked to consider adding a multicultural component to the required courses for the major without dropping any of the courses already required. What recommendations for or against such an addition would you make? In your recommendations, take into consideration the viewpoint of Marianne M. Jennings in "The Real Generation Gap."

4. Select a statement from Marianne M. Jennings's "The Real Generation Gap" with which you strongly agree or disagree. You may want to pick one of the five areas she discusses and respond to her on the general issue, or you may want to select a specific statement and respond to it. Consider, for instance, her allegations that today's young people have been "indoctrinated," that "political correctness" is "a pernicious system," or that today's young people are "a generation trained and raised in amoral darkness."

5. Argue in support of or against this statement from David McCullough's "No Time to Read?":"The greatest of all avenues to learning [. . .] is in reading books" (paragraph 9)

6. Some people argue that not everyone deserves to go to college and that admitting average or mediocre students into colleges has debased American higher education. Argue in support of or against that position.

7. Describe a teacher who made an impact on you. What made that teacher so important to you? Try to explain not only physical characteristics but, more importantly, personality features and admirable qualities. If a particular incident was especially significant in your relationship, narrate what happened.

8. Imagine that the number of students admitted to college directly after high school has been limited to the upper 33 percent of all graduating seniors and that you do not meet the requirements for admission to college. Under special circumstances, students who fall below the 33 percent mark may be admitted. In a letter to the admissions officer at the college of your choice, argue that you should be admitted despite your class ranking and give reasons why you would make a good student.

Research Topics

1. Research the conflict of traditional versus revisionist curriculum. Interview educators and read periodical articles from the last several years on *political correctness,* defenses for or against *the canon,* or related topics.

2. Rearch the tracking systems used in many schools. Find opinions supporting and opposing such systems, consider their advantages and disadvantages, and arrive at your own conclusion based on your reading.

3. Research the subject of homework, perhaps starting with some of the studies Romesh Ratnesar mentions in "The Homework Ate My Family" (paragraphs 20–22).

4. Spend some time searching the Internet or going through your library's catalog of books and periodicals on the subject of education. You will find a very large number of subtopics under that broad heading. Select a seemingly controversial subtopic that interests you. Keep searching until you have narrowed your focus to one specific aspect of the subject that is suitable for your research project.

CHAPTER 13

POVERTY AND HOMELESSNESS

Once largely ignored, the issues of poverty, homelessness, and welfare have often inspired increasingly heated discussion in recent years. At the community level, social workers and staff members at shelters for the homeless and impoverished struggle to meet the needs of desperate people, whereas at the state and federal levels, legislators argue over whether to cut welfare funding. The numbers of people in poverty, especially women and children, continue to rise. Many families whose incomes provide just enough for basic necessities, such as shelter and food, are only a paycheck or two away from living on the streets. Worse, a growing number of the nation's poor actually work full-time. Compounding the difficulty of these issues are certain attitudes toward or stereotyped beliefs about people on welfare or suffering homelessness. Charges of laziness and fraud are often leveled at welfare recipients, despite studies that demonstrate the vast majority of people on welfare want to work and live independent lives.

The essays in this chapter examine some of the issues associated with poverty and homelessness. First, Anna Quindlen in "Our Tired, Our Poor, Our Kids" looks at the plight of homeless mothers and children in America. She points out some of the effects of homelessness on children, emphasizes the importance of affordable housing, and touches on the effects of welfare reform on homelessness. Closely related to Quindlen's opinion piece is an editorial published in *America* magazine, a publication whose primary audience is Catholics. "Still Hungry, Still Homeless" comments on the rise of poverty and homelessness in the United States, notes the increase in requests for emergency housing and food, and like Quindlen, mentions the effect of welfare reform on this serious social problem.

Melanie Scheller's highly personal essay, "On the Meaning of Plumbing and Poverty," makes concrete and vivid some of the generalizations of Quindlen's essay and the *America* editorial. By presenting graphic, painful details, Scheller conveys a very real sense not only of the experience of a child living in poverty but also of the shame and diminished self-esteem she carried with her as a result of living in homes without indoor plumbing.

Finally, Peter Singer broadens his focus to world poverty while addressing his essay to the American middle class. Using the logic of his training as a utilitarian philosopher, Singer offers a hypothetical ethical scenario to raise readers' awareness of what he sees as their moral responsibility to donate to world aid funds for poor and starving children.

As you read these essays, think about your own attitudes toward welfare, homelessness, and poverty. Do the Quindlen essay and the *America* editorial in any way reinforce or change your attitudes? Are you moved by Scheller's personal essay? Does Singer persuade you to donate to charities?

OUR TIRED, OUR POOR, OUR KIDS
Anna Quindlen

Anna Quindlen began her journalism career at the New York Post *and then became deputy metropolitan editor of the* New York Times. *In 1986, she began her syndicated column "Life in the Thirties" and a few years later "Public and Private," for which she won a Pulitzer Prize in 1992. Currently she contributes* Newsweek's *prestigious back page column,* The Last Word, *every other week. Her columns are collected in* Living Out Loud *(1988) and* Thinking Out Loud *(1992). She has written three best-selling novels,* Object Lessons *(1991),* One True Thing *(1994), and* Black and Blue *(1998), and an advice book,* A Short Guide to a Happy Life *(2000). This essay appeared in the March 12, 2001, issue of* Newsweek.

Six people live here, in a room the size of the master bedroom in a modest suburban house. Trundles, bunk beds, dressers side by side stacked with toys, clothes, boxes, in tidy claustrophobic clutter. One woman, five children. The baby was born in a shelter. The older kids can't wait to get out of this one. Everyone gets up at 6 A.M., the little ones to go to day care, the others to school. Their mother goes out to look for an apartment when she's not going to drug-treatment meetings. "For what they pay for me to stay in a shelter I could have lived in the Hamptons," Sharanda says.

Here is the parallel universe that has flourished while the more fortunate were rewarding themselves for the stock split with SUVs and home additions. There is a boom market in homelessness. But these are not the men on the streets of San Francisco holding out cardboard signs to the tourists. They are children, hundreds of thousands of them, twice as likely to repeat a grade or be hospitalized and four times as likely to go hungry as the kids with a roof over their heads. Twenty years ago New York City provided emergency shelter for just under a thousand families a day; last month it had to find spaces for 10,000 children on a given night. Not since the Great Depression have this many babies, toddlers and kids had no place like home.

Three mothers sit in the living room of a temporary residence called Casa Rita in the Bronx and speak of this in the argot of poverty. "The landlord don't call back when they hear you got EARP," says Rosie, EARP being the Emergency Assistance Rehousing Program. "You get priority for Section 8 if you're in a shelter," says Edna, which means federal housing programs will put you higher on the list. Edna has four kids, three in foster care; she arrived at Casa Rita, she says, "with two bags and a baby." Rosie has three; they share a bathroom down the hall with two other families. Sharanda's five range in age from 13 to just over a year. Her eldest was put in the wrong grade when he changed schools. "He's humiliated, living here," his mother says.

4   All three women are anxious to move on, although they appreciate this place, where they can get shelter, get sober and keep their kids at the same time. They remember the Emergency Assistance Unit, the city office that is the gateway to the system, where hundreds of families sit every day surrounded by their bags, where children sleep on benches until they are shuffled off dull-eyed for one night in a shelter or a motel, only to return as supplicants again the next day.

In another world middle-class Americans have embraced new-home starts, the stock market and the Gap. But in the world of these displaced families, problems ignored or fumbled or unforeseen during this great period of prosperity have dovetailed into an enormous subculture of children who think that only rich people have their own bedrooms. Twenty years ago, when the story of the homeless in America became a staple of news reporting, the solution was presented as a simple one: affordable housing. That's still true, now more than ever. Two years ago the National Low Income Housing Coalition calculated that the hourly income necessary to afford the average two-bedroom apartment was around $12. That's more than twice the minimum wage.

The result is that in many cities police officers and teachers cannot afford to live where they work, that in Las Vegas old motels provide housing for casino employees, that in shelters now there is a contingent of working poor who get up off their cots and go off to their jobs. The result is that if you are evicted for falling behind on your rent, if there is a bureaucratic foul-up in your welfare check or the factory in which you work shuts down, the chances of finding another place to live are very small indeed. You're one understanding relative, one paycheck, one second chance from the street. And so are your kids.

So-called welfare reform, which emphasizes cutbacks and make-work, has played a part in all this. A study done in San Diego in 1998 found that a third of homeless families had recently had benefits terminated or reduced, and that most said that was how they had wound up on the street. Drugs, alcohol and domestic abuse also land mothers with kids in the shelter system or lead them to hand their children over to relatives or foster homes. Today the average homeless woman is younger than ever before, may have been in foster care or in shelters herself and so considers a chaotic childhood the norm. Many never finished high school, and have never held a job.

8   Ralph Nunez, who runs the organization Homes for the Homeless, says that all this calls for new attitudes. "People don't like to hear it, but shelters are going to be

the low-income housing of the future," he says. "So how do we enrich the experience and use the system to provide job training and education?" Bonnie Stone of Women in Need, which has eight other residences along with Casa Rita, says, "We're pouring everything we've got into the nine months most of them are here—nutrition, treatment, budgeting. By the time they leave, they have a subsidized apartment, day care and, hopefully, some life skills they didn't have before."

But these organizations are rafts in a rising river of need that has roared through this country without most of us ever even knowing. So now you know. There are hundreds of thousands of little nomads in America, sleeping in the back of cars, on floors in welfare offices or in shelters five to a room. What would it mean, to spend your childhood drifting from one strange bed to another, waking in the morning to try to figure out where you'd landed today, without those things that confer security and happiness: a familiar picture on the wall, a certain slant of light through a curtained window? "Give me your tired, your poor," it says on the base of the Statue of Liberty, to welcome foreigners. Oh, but they are already here, the small refugees from the ruin of the American dream, even if you cannot see them.

Personal Response

What image of the homeless did you have before reading this essay? Has your understanding of them changed in any way now that you have read it? If so, in what way has it changed? If not, explain why.

Questions for Class or Small-Group Discussion

1. Comment on this statement: "Not since the Great Depression have this many babies, toddlers and kids had no place like home" (paragraph 2). Were you surprised by it? What effect do you think Quindlen hopes to achieve by mentioning the Great Depression?

2. Explain why, according to Quindlen, there are so many homeless women and children in America. What is the effect of homelessness on children? Are you persuaded of the seriousness of the problem?

3. What does Quindlen mean by the term *working poor* (paragraph 6)?

4. Quindlen uses the term *so-called* to describe welfare reform (paragraph 7). Why do you think she does that? What fault does she find with welfare reform? Do you agree with her?

STILL HUNGRY, STILL HOMELESS

America magazine editorial

America *magazine describes itself as a journal of opinion on current events, historical events, spiritual events, family, books, film, and television for Catholic people. This editorial appeared in the magazine's February 5, 2001, issue.*

One might think that last year's particularly strong economy would have led to a reduction in the number of requests for emergency food and shelter. In fact, however, the year 2000 actually saw a rise in both areas. This was among the sad findings of the United States Conference of Mayors' annual survey of 25 cities around the country, which was released in late December.

Officials in the survey cities estimated that requests for emergency food assistance jumped by 17 percent—the second highest rate of increase since 1992. Over half of the people seeking help were children and their parents: a particularly disturbing finding, given the need for parents to be able to provide adequate and nutritious food for their children. A third of the adults, moreover, were employed. This reflects the fact that minimum wage jobs at $5.50 an hour cannot cover the cost of living for most Americans. Mirroring the conclusions of the mayors' report, Catholic Charities USA found in its own year-end survey that its agencies had seen what it termed "a startling 22 percent increase in the use of their emergency services."

How could this be, in the face of what many politicians have trumpeted as our unprecedented level of prosperity? Ironically, the mayors' report points out that the very strength of the economy has been partly to blame. Seeing that the earnings of middle-class Americans have risen, landlords have been quick to realize that they can charge much higher rents. But for families at the bottom of the economic ladder, whose earnings did not increase, the consequence has been an ever more desperate search for housing within their income range; it is a search that has sometimes ended in homelessness. Even those lucky enough to have Section 8 vouchers have discovered that apartment owners often refuse to accept them, knowing that they can command higher prices than the government's reimbursement rate for the vouchers. Thus, in nearly half the survey cities, the report cites housing costs as a primary reason for the increase in requests for emergency food and shelter.

4   Welfare reform has played its part in this bleak scenario. People leaving Temporary Assistance for Needy Families (T.A.N.F.) may indeed have full-time jobs that pay above the minimum wage and yet still not be making enough to lift them above the poverty line. And all too frequently, they are unaware that despite being employed, they may still be eligible for the food stamps (and Medicaid) that could tide them over from one month to the next. Government agencies are not as aggressive as they should be in promoting these programs among the working poor. True, the number of food assistance facilities has increased, but the strain on their limited resources is so great that half the cities report that these facilities must either send people away or reduce the amount of what they can provide.

The same situation applies to emergency housing requests. Nearly a quarter of them, says the mayors' report, went unmet. Turned-away families in San Antonio, for instance, found themselves obliged to sleep in cars or parks, under bridges or in already doubled- or tripled-up substandard housing. Even when they can be accommodated, in 52 percent of the cities homeless families may have to break up, with older male youths and fathers sent elsewhere.

The outlook for the future is not bright. Almost three-fourths of the survey cities expect a rise in the demand for emergency food. As the officials in Boston put it, "the number of pantries increases every year, and [yet] the requests for assistance have increased by as much as 40 percent." Nor, they add, do they "see any relief in the near future." Again, there as elsewhere, high housing costs, along with low-paying jobs, lead the list of causes for more hunger and homelessness. The answer is implied in the comments of the respondents from Burlington, Vt.: "Without a significant commitment to building a significant number of new and affordable housing units, homelessness will continue to rise." The new secretary-designate of the Department of Housing and Urban Development, Mel Martinez, said at his Senate confirmation hearing that he would try to make more housing available to low-income Americans. We hope that he will act on his words. For many years, however, Congress has shown little interest in this neglected area of American life.

In releasing its annual report in December, Fred Kammer, S.J., president of Catholic Charities USA, spoke of its findings as "a story about . . . escalating need in a land of skyrocketing wealth." He recalled Bill Clinton's promise to "end welfare as we know it." That has happened, but the rise in requests for emergency food and housing calls into question the effectiveness of welfare reform. The real goal, Father Kammer concluded, should be to "end poverty as we know it." Now is the time for Congress to take the strong measures needed to assist the most vulnerable members of society.

Personal Response

Are you surprised that the numbers of hungry and homeless people in America are rising? Write for a few minutes on your reaction to that fact or to any other part of the essay that caught your attention as you read it.

Questions for Class or Small-Group Discussion

1. How does the editorial account for the fact that requests for emergency food and shelter continue to rise despite a strong economy (paragraph 1)? That is, what factors account for the high numbers of children and their parents, including employed adults, seeking emergency aid?

2. The editorial comments that "the rise in requests for emergency food and housing calls into question the effectiveness of welfare reform" (paragraph 7). Why has the welfare reform program not worked, according to the editorial? What do you know about the welfare reform program? Do you think it is a good plan, or do you find fault with it, too?

3. Are you persuaded that "now is the time for Congress to take the strong measures needed to assist the most vulnerable members of society" (paragraph 7)? What measures does the editorial suggest would be appropriate? How effective do you think those measures would be? Can you offer any other solutions to the problem of homelessness and poverty in America?

ON THE MEANING OF PLUMBING
AND POVERTY

Melanie Scheller

Melanie Scheller writes books. "On the Meaning of Plumbing and Poverty" first appeared in the North Carolina Independent Weekly *in 1990.*

Several years ago I spent some time as a volunteer on the geriatric ward of a psychiatric hospital. I was fascinated by the behavior of one of the patients, an elderly woman who shuffled at regular intervals to the bathroom, where she methodically flushed the toilet. Again and again she carried out her sacred mission as if summoned by some supernatural force, until the flush of the toilet became a rhythmic counterpoint for the ward's activity. If someone blocked her path or if, God forbid, the bathroom was in use when she reached it, she became agitated and confused.

Obviously, that elderly patient was a sick woman. And yet I felt a certain kinship with her, for I too have suffered from an obsession with toilets. I spent much of my childhood living in houses without indoor plumbing and, while I don't feel compelled to flush a toilet at regular intervals, I sometimes feel that toilets, or the lack thereof, have shaped my identity in ways that are painful to admit.

I'm not a child of the Depression, but I grew up in an area of the South that had changed little since the days of the New Deal. My mother was a widow with six children to support, not an easy task under any circumstances, but especially difficult in rural North Carolina during the 1960s. To her credit, we were never seriously in danger of going hungry. Our vegetable garden kept us stocked with tomatoes and string beans. We kept a few chickens and sometimes a cow. Blackberries were free for the picking in the fields nearby. Neighbors did their good Christian duty by bringing us donations of fresh fruit and candy at Christmastime. But a roof over our heads—that wasn't so easily improvised.

4   Like rural Southern gypsies, we moved from one dilapidated Southern farmhouse to another in a constant search for a decent place to live. Sometimes we moved when the rent increased beyond the $30 or $40 my mother could afford. Or the house burned down, not an unusual occurrence in substandard housing. One year, when we were gathered together for Thanksgiving dinner, a stranger walked in without knocking and announced that we were being evicted. The house had been sold without our knowledge and the new owner wanted to start remodeling immediately. We tried to finish our meal with an attitude of thanksgiving while he worked around us with his tape measure.

Usually, we rented from farm families who'd moved from the old home place to one of the brick boxes that are now the standard in rural Southern architecture. The old farmhouse wasn't worth fixing up with a septic tank and flush toilet, but it was good enough to rent for a few dollars a month to families like mine. The idea of tenants' rights hadn't trickled down yet from the far reaches of the liberal North. It never occurred to us to demand improvements in the facilities. The ethic of the land said we should take what we could get and be grateful for it.

Without indoor plumbing, getting clean is a tiring and time-consuming ritual. At one point, I lived in a five-room house with six or more people, all of whom congregated in the one heated room to eat, do homework, watch television, dress and undress, argue, wash dishes. During cold weather we dragged mattresses from the unheated rooms and slept huddled together on the floor by the woodstove. For my bathing routine, I first pinned a sheet to a piece of twine strung across the kitchen. That gave me some degree of privacy from the six other people in the room. At that time, our house had an indoor cold-water faucet, from which I filled a pot of water to heat on the kitchen stove. It took several pots of hot water to fill the metal washtub we used.

Since I was a teenager and prone to sulkiness if I didn't get special treatment, I got to take the first bath while the water was still clean. The others used the water I left behind, freshened up with hot water from the pot on the stove. Then the tub had to be dragged to the door and the bath water dumped outside. I longed to be like the woman in the Calgon bath oil commercials, luxuriating in a marble tub full of scented water with bubbles piled high and stacks of thick, clean towels nearby.

8   People raised in the land of the bath-and-a-half may wonder why I make such a fuss about plumbing. Maybe they spent a year in the Peace Corps, or they backpacked across India, or they worked at a summer camp and, gosh, using a latrine isn't all that bad. And of course it's *not* that bad. Not when you can catch the next plane out of the country, or pick up your duffel bag and head for home, or call mom and dad to come and get you when things get too tedious. A sojourn in a Third World country, where everyone shares the same primitive facilities may cause some temporary discomfort, but the experience is soon converted into amusing anecdotes for cocktail-party conversation. It doesn't corrode your self-esteem with a sense of shame the way a childhood spent in chronic, unrelenting poverty can.

In the South of my childhood, not having indoor plumbing was the indelible mark of poor white trash. The phrase "so poor they didn't have a pot to piss in" said it all. Poor white trash were viciously stereotyped, and never more viciously than on the playground. White-trash children had cooties—everybody knew that. They had ringworm and pink-eye—don't get near them or you might catch it. They picked their noses. They messed in their pants. If a white-trash child made the mistake of catching a softball during recess, the other children made an elaborate show of wiping it clean before they would touch it.

Once a story circulated at school about a family whose infant daughter had fallen into the "slop jar" and drowned. When I saw the smirks and heard the laughter with which the story was told, I felt sick and afraid in the pit of my stomach. A little girl had died, but people were laughing. What had she done to deserve that laughter? I could only assume that using a chamber pot was something so disgusting, so shameful, that it made a person less than human.

My family was visibly and undeniably poor. My clothes were obviously hand-me-downs. I got free lunches at school. I went to the health department for immunizations. Surely it was equally obvious that we didn't have a flush toilet. But, like an alcoholic who believes no one will know he has a problem as long as he doesn't drink in public, I convinced myself that no one knew my family's little secret. It was a form of denial that would color my relationships with the outside world for years to come.

12   Having a friend from school spend the night at my house was out of the question. Better to be friendless than to have my classmates know my shameful secret. Home visits from teachers or ministers left me in a dither of anticipatory anxiety. As they chattered on and on with Southern small talk about tomato plants and relish recipes, I sat on the edge of my seat, tensed against the dreaded words, "May I use your bathroom, please?" When I began dating in high school, I'd lie in wait behind the front door, ready to dash out as soon as my date pulled in the driveway, never giving him a chance to hear the call of nature while on our property.

With the help of a scholarship I was able to go away to college, where I could choose from dozens of dormitory toilets and take as many hot showers as I wanted, but I could never openly express my joy in using the facilities. My roommates, each a pampered only child from a well-to-do family, whined and complained about having to share a bathroom. I knew that if I expressed delight in simply having a bathroom, I would immediately be labeled as a hick. The need to conceal my real self by stifling my emotions created a barrier around me and I spent my college years in a vacuum of isolation.

Almost twenty years have passed since I first tried to leave my family's chamber pot behind. For many of those years, it followed behind me—the ghost of chamber pots past—clanging and banging and threatening to spill its humiliating contents at any moment. I was convinced that everyone could see it, could smell it even. No college degree or job title seemed capable of banishing it.

If finances had permitted, I might have become an Elvis Presley or a Tammy Faye Bakker, easing the pain of remembered poverty with gold-plated bathtub fixtures and leopard-skinned toilet seats. I feel blessed that gradually, ever so gradually, the shame of poverty has begun to fade. The pleasures of the present now take priority over where a long-ago bowel movement did or did not take place. But, for many Southerners, chamber pots and outhouses are more than just memories.

16   In North Carolina alone, 200,000 people still live without indoor plumbing. People who haul their drinking water home from a neighbor's house or catch rainwater in barrels. People who can't wash their hands before handling food, the way restaurant employees are required by state law to do. People who sneak into public restrooms every day to wash, shave, and brush their teeth before going to work or to school. People who sacrifice their dignity and self-respect when forced to choose between going homeless and going to an outhouse. People whose children think they deserve the conditions in which they live and hold their heads low to hide the shame. But they're not the ones who should feel ashamed. No, they're not the ones who should feel ashamed.

Personal Response

What do you think of Scheller's experiences growing up in poverty? Can you sympathize with her? Do you recall a particular period or occasion in your life when you felt a similar sense of shame or acute awareness of yourself in relation to others?

Questions for Class or Small-Group Discussion

1. Summarize in your own words the effects of poverty on Scheller, and then discuss your own reactions to what she describes.

2. In paragraph 8, Scheller says that people wonder why she "make[s] such a fuss about plumbing." Indeed, she writes about a subject that people seldom discuss in either conversation or writing. How well do you think she has handled her subject? Does she convince you of her reasons for making the fuss?

3. Scheller concludes by repeating "they're not the ones who should feel ashamed" (paragraph 16). Who do you think should feel ashamed, according to Scheller?

THE SINGER SOLUTION TO WORLD POVERTY

Peter Singer

Peter Singer, an Australian-born philosopher and bioethicist, is author of the highly influential book Animal Liberation *(1975). He has served as president of the International Association of Bioethics and as editor of its official journal,* Bioethics. *His other books include* How Are We to Live?: Ethics in an Age of Self Interest *(1993),* Rethinking Life and Death: The Collapse of Our Traditional Ethics *(1995), and* Writings on an Ethical Life *(2000). Singer is on the faculty at the Center for Human Values at Princeton University. This essay appeared in the September 4, 1999, issue of* New York Times Magazine.

In the Brazilian film *Central Station,* Dora is a retired schoolteacher who makes ends meet by sitting at the station writing letters for illiterate people. Suddenly she has an opportunity to pocket $1,000. All she has to do is persuade a homeless nine-year-old boy to follow her to an address she has been given. (She is told he will be adopted by wealthy foreigners.) She delivers the boy, gets the money, spends some of it on a television set, and settles down to enjoy her new acquisition. Her neighbor spoils the fun, however, by telling her that the boy was too old to be adopted—he will be killed and his organs sold for transplantation. Perhaps Dora knew this all along, but after her neighbor's plain speaking, she spends a troubled night. In the morning Dora resolves to take the boy back.

Suppose Dora had told her neighbor that it is a tough world, other people have nice new TVs too, and if selling the kid is the only way she can get one, well, he was only a street kid. She would then have become, in the eyes of the audience, a monster. She redeems herself only by being prepared to bear considerable risks to save the boy.

At the end of the movie, in cinemas in the affluent nations of the world, people who would have been quick to condemn Dora if she had not rescued the boy go home to places far more comfortable than her apartment. In fact, the average family in the United States spends almost one-third of its income on things that are no more necessary to them than Dora's new TV was to her. Going out to nice restaurants, buying new clothes because the old ones are no longer stylish, vacationing at beach resorts—so much of our income is spent on things not essential to the preservation of our lives and health. Donated to one of a number of charitable agencies, that money could mean the difference between life and death for children in need.

4   All of which raises a question: In the end, what is the ethical distinction between a Brazilian who sells a homeless child to organ peddlers and an American who already has a TV and upgrades to a better one—knowing that the money could be donated to an organization that would use it to save the lives of kids in need?

Of course, there are several differences between the two situations that could support different moral judgments about them. For one thing, to be able to consign a child to death when he is standing right in front of you takes a chilling kind of heartlessness; it is much easier to ignore an appeal for money to help children you will never meet. Yet for a utilitarian philosopher like myself—that is, one who judges whether acts are right or wrong by their consequences—if the upshot of the American's failure to donate the money is that one more kid dies on the streets of a Brazilian city, then it is, in some sense, just as bad as selling the kid to the organ peddlers. But one doesn't need to embrace my utilitarian ethic to see that, at the very least, there is a troubling incongruity in being so quick to condemn Dora for taking the child to the organ peddlers while, at the same time, not regarding the American consumer's behavior as raising a serious moral issue.

In his 1996 book, *Living High and Letting Die,* the New York University philosopher Peter Unger presented an ingenious series of imaginary examples designed to probe our intuitions about whether it is wrong to live well without giving substantial amounts of money to help people who are hungry, malnourished, or dying from easily treatable illnesses like diarrhea. Here's my paraphrase of one of these examples:

Bob is close to retirement. He has invested most of his savings in a very rare and valuable old car, a Bugatti, which he has not been able to insure. The Bugatti is his pride and joy. In addition to the pleasure he gets from driving and caring for his car, Bob knows that its rising market value means that he will always be able to sell it and live comfortably after retirement. One day when Bob is out for a drive, he parks the Bugatti near the end of a railway siding and goes for a walk up the track. As he does so, he sees that a runaway train, with no one aboard, is running down the railway track. Looking farther down the track, he sees the small figure of a child very likely to be killed by the runaway train. He can't stop the train and the child is too far away to warn of the danger, but he can throw a switch that will divert the train down the siding where his Bugatti is parked. Then nobody will be killed—but the train will destroy his Bugatti. Thinking of his joy in owning the car and the financial security it represents, Bob decides not to throw the switch. The child is killed. For many years to come, Bob enjoys owning his Bugatti and the financial security it represents.

8   Bob's conduct, most of us will immediately respond, was gravely wrong. Unger agrees. But then he reminds us that we, too, have opportunities to save the lives of children. We can give to organizations like Unicef or Oxfam America. How much would we have to give one of these organizations to have a high probability of saving the life of a child threatened by easily preventable diseases? (I do not believe that children are more worth saving than adults, but since no one can argue that children have brought their poverty on themselves, focusing on them simplifies the issues.) Unger called up some experts and used the information they provided to offer some plausible estimates that include the cost of raising money, administrative expenses, and the cost of delivering aid where it is most needed. By his calculation, $200 in donations would help a sickly two-year-old transform into a healthy six-year-old— offering safe passage through childhood's most dangerous years. To show how practical philosophical argument can be, Unger even tells his readers that they can easily donate funds by using their credit card and calling one of these toll-free numbers: (800) 367-5437 for Unicef; (800) 693-2687 for Oxfam America.

Now you, too, have the information you need to save a child's life. How should you judge yourself if you don't do it? Think again about Bob and his Bugatti. Unlike Dora, Bob did not have to look into the eyes of the child he was sacrificing for his own material comfort. The child was a complete stranger to him and too far away to relate to in an intimate, personal way. Unlike Dora, too, he did not mislead the child or initiate the chain of events imperiling him. In all these respects, Bob's situation resembles that of people able but unwilling to donate to overseas aid and differs from Dora's situation.

If you still think that it was very wrong of Bob not to throw the switch that would have diverted the train and saved the child's life, then it is hard to see how you could deny that it is also very wrong not to send money to one of the organizations listed above. Unless, that is, there is some morally important difference between the two situations that I have overlooked.

Is it the practical uncertainties about whether aid will really reach the people who need it? Nobody who knows the world of overseas aid can doubt that such uncertainties exist. But Unger's figure of $200 to save a child's life was reached after he had made conservative assumptions about the proportion of the money donated that will actually reach its target.

12   One genuine difference between Bob and those who can afford to donate to overseas aid organizations but don't is that only Bob can save the child on the tracks, whereas there are hundreds of millions of people who can give $200 to overseas aid organizations. The problem is that most of them aren't doing it. Does this mean that it is all right for you not to do it?

Suppose that there were more owners of priceless vintage cars—Carol, Dave, Emma, Fred and so on, down to Ziggy—all in exactly the same situation as Bob, with their own siding and their own switch, all sacrificing the child in order to preserve their own cherished car. Would that make it all right for Bob to do the same? To answer this question affirmatively is to endorse follow-the-crowd ethics—the kind of ethics that led many Germans to look away when the Nazi atrocities were being committed. We do not excuse them because others were behaving no better.

We seem to lack a sound basis for drawing a clear moral line between Bob's situation and that of any reader of this article with $200 to spare who does not donate it to an overseas aid agency. These readers seem to be acting at least as badly as Bob was acting when he chose to let the runaway train hurtle toward the unsuspecting child. In the light of this conclusion, I trust that many readers will reach for the phone and donate that $200. Perhaps you should do it before reading further.

Now that you have distinguished yourself morally from people who put their vintage cars ahead of a child's life, how about treating yourself and your partner to dinner at your favorite restaurant? But wait. The money you will spend at the restaurant could also help save the lives of children overseas! True, you weren't planning to blow $200 tonight, but if you were to give up dining out just for one month, you would easily save that amount. And what is one month's dining out, compared to a child's life? There's the rub. Since there are a lot of desperately needy children in the world, there will always be another child whose life you could save for another $200. Are you therefore obliged to keep giving until you have nothing left? At what point can you stop?

16   Hypothetical examples can easily become farcical. Consider Bob. How far past losing the Bugatti should he go? Imagine that Bob had got his foot stuck in the track of the siding, and if he diverted the train, then before it rammed the car it would also amputate his big toe. Should he still throw the switch? What if it would amputate his foot? His entire leg?

As absurd as the Bugatti scenario gets when pushed to extremes, the point it raises is a serious one: Only when the sacrifices become very significant indeed would most people be prepared to say that Bob does nothing wrong when he decides not to throw the switch. Of course, most people could be wrong; we can't decide moral issues by taking opinion polls. But consider for yourself the level of sacrifice that you would demand of Bob, and then think about how much money you would have to give away in order to make a sacrifice that is roughly equal to that. It's almost certainly much, much more than $200. For most middle-class Americans, it could easily be more like $200,000.

Isn't it counterproductive to ask people to do so much? Don't we run the risk that many will shrug their shoulders and say that mortality, so conceived, is fine for saints but not for them? I accept that we are unlikely to see, in the near or even medium-term future, a world in which it is normal for wealthy Americans to give the bulk of their wealth to strangers. When it comes to praising or blaming people for what they do, we tend to use a standard that is relative to some conception of normal behavior. Comfortably off Americans who give, say, 10 percent of their income to overseas aid organizations are so far ahead of most of their equally comfortable fellow citizens that I wouldn't go out of my way to chastise them for not doing more. Nevertheless, they should be doing much more, and they are in no position to criticize Bob for failing to make the much greater sacrifice of his Bugatti.

At this point various objections may crop up. Someone may say: "If every citizen living in the affluent nations contributed his or her share I wouldn't have to make such a drastic sacrifice, because long before such levels were reached, the resources would have been there to save the lives of all those children dying from lack of food or medical care. So why should I give more than my fair share?" Another, related objection is that the government ought to increase its overseas aid allocations, since that would spread the burden more equitably across all taxpayers.

20   Yet the question of how much we ought to give is a matter to be decided in the real world—and that, sadly, is a world in which we know that most people do not, and in the immediate future will not, give substantial amounts to overseas aid agencies. We know, too, that at least in the next year, the United States government is not going to meet even the very modest United Nations–recommended target of 0.7 percent of gross national product; at a moment it lags far below that, at 0.09 percent, not even half of Japan's 0.22 percent or a tenth of Denmark's 0.97 percent. Thus, we know that the money we can give beyond that theoretical "fair share" is still going to save lives that would otherwise be lost. While the idea that no one need do more than his or her fair share is a powerful one, should it prevail if we know that others are not doing their fair share and that children will die preventable deaths unless we do more than our fair share? That would be taking fairness too far.

Thus, this ground for limiting how much we ought to give also fails. In the world as it is now, I can see no escape from the conclusion that each one of us with wealth surplus to his or her essential needs should be giving most of it to help people suffering from poverty so dire as to be life-threatening. That's right: I'm saying that you shouldn't buy that new car, take that cruise, redecorate the house, or get that pricey new suit. After all, a $1,000 suit could save five children's lives.

So how does my philosophy break down in dollars and cents? An American household with an income of $50,000 spends around $30,000 annually on necessities, according to the Conference Board, a nonprofit economic research organization. Therefore, for a household bringing in $50,000 a year, donations to help the world's poor should be as close as possible to $20,000. The $30,000 required for necessities holds for higher incomes as well. So a household making $100,000 could cut a yearly check for $70,000. Again, the formula is simple: Whatever money you're spending on luxuries, not necessities, should be given away.

Now, evolutionary psychologists tell us that human nature just isn't sufficiently altruistic to make it plausible that many people will sacrifice so much for strangers. On the facts of human nature, they might be right, but they would be wrong to draw a moral conclusion from those facts. If it is the case that we ought to do things that, predictably, most of us won't do, then let's face that fact head-on. Then, if we value the life of a child more than going to fancy restaurants, the next time we dine out we will know that we could have done something better with our money. If that makes living a morally decent life extremely arduous, well, then that is the way things are. If we don't do it, then we should at least know that we are failing to live a morally decent life—not because it is good to wallow in guilt but because knowing where we should be going is the first step toward heading in that direction.

24   When Bob first grasped the dilemma that faced him as he stood by that railway switch, he must have thought how extraordinarily unlucky he was to be placed in a situation in which he must choose between the life of an innocent child and the sacrifice of most of his savings. But he was not unlucky at all. We are all in that situation.

Personal Response

Do you contribute to charities? If not, are you moved to start doing so after reading this essay? Why do you think more people do not contribute to charities, especially if they could, as Singer argues, help improve life for the world's impoverished children?

Questions for Class or Small-Group Discussion

1. How effective do you find the opening example from the film *Central Station?* Does it help clarify for you the thesis of Singer's essay? Do you agree with Singer that the failure to donate money to a charity that would save a Brazilian child from starvation is "just as bad as selling the kid to organ peddlers" (paragraph 5)?

2. Comment on the hypothetical scenario from Peter Unger's book that Singer paraphrases in paragraph 7. Do you agree that "Bob's conduct . . . was gravely wrong" and that failure to donate money to charities that would save children's lives is equally wrong (paragraph 8)? How persuasive do you find Singer's discussion of the ethical implications of failing to donate to charities?

3. Discuss your answer to this question: "While the idea that no one need to do more than his or her fair share is a powerful one, should it prevail if we know that others are not doing their fair share and that children will die preventable deaths unless we do more than our fair share?" (paragraph 20).

4. To what extent do you agree with Singer that "we ought to do things that, predictably, most of us won't do" (paragraph 23)? How persuasive do you find Singer's argument to be?

PERSPECTIVES ON POVERTY AND HOMELESSNESS

Suggestions for Synthesis

1. Taking into consideration Anna Quindlen's "Our Tired, Our Poor, Our Children," the editorial "Still Hungry, Still Homeless," and Melanie Scheller's "On the Meaning of Plumbing and Poverty," explore the effects of poverty on self-esteem or other aspects of the well-being of children.

2. Drawing on the readings in this chapter, consider the problems associated with meeting the needs of welfare recipients, impoverished families, or homeless people.

What possible solutions are there to the problems? Can you propose additional suggestions for reducing the large numbers of people in poverty or without homes?

3. Taking into consideration two or more of the essays in this chapter, what conclusions can you draw about women, children, and poverty?

4. Working in small groups and drawing on the essays in this chapter, create a scenario involving one or more of the following people: a welfare recipient or a homeless person, a welfare caseworker or a staff member at a homeless shelter, a police officer, and either or both a wealthy person and a working-class person with a regular income and a home. Provide a situation, create dialogue, and role-play in an effort to understand the varying perspectives of different people on the issue of welfare or homelessness. Then present your scenario to the rest of your classmates. For an individual writing project, do an analysis of the scenario or fully develop the viewpoint of the person whose role you played.

Additional Writing Topics

1. With Anna Quindlen's "Our Tired, Our Poor, Our Children" and the editorial "Still Hungry, Still Homeless" in mind, write your own opinion piece on the subject of poverty and homelessness in America.

2. Write a letter to Melanie Scheller in response to her essay "On the Meaning of Plumbing and Poverty."

3. Describe in detail a particular period in your life or an occasion when you felt a sense of shame or an acute awareness of yourself in relation to others.

4. If you have ever experienced the effects of poverty, too little income, not enough work, or a need to juggle child care with the demands of a job, write an essay describing that experience, how you felt about it, and how you handled it.

5. Create a different hypothetical situation similar to Peter Unger's scenario of Bob and his Bugatti in "The Singer Solution to World Poverty." Detail the moral dilemma of your own scenario and discuss the ethical implications of various responses to the dilemma.

Research Topics

1. Research your state's policy on welfare, including residency requirements, eligibility for payments, monitoring of recipients, and related issues. Then write a paper outlining your opinion of your state's welfare policy, including any recommendations you would make for changing it.

2. From time to time, politicians propose establishing orphanages that would house not only orphaned children but also the children of single parents on welfare or parents deemed unfit to raise their children. Research this subject, and then write a paper in which you argue for or against the establishment of such orphanages. Make sure you consider as many perspectives as possible on this complex issue, including the welfare of the child, the rights of the parent or parents, and society's responsibility to protect children.

3. Research the subject of poverty in America. Focus your research on a particular group, such as children, women, two-parent families, or single-parent families, or target a particular aspect of the subject such as the effects of race, parental education, or employment on poverty.

4. Research an area of public policy on welfare reform, child welfare, homelessness, family welfare, food stamps, job training, or any other issue related to any reading in this chapter.

CHAPTER 14

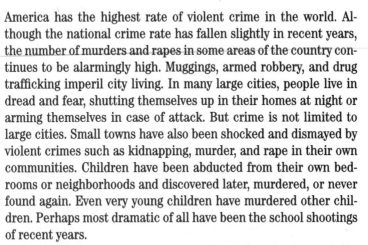

CRIMINAL BEHAVIOR

America has the highest rate of violent crime in the world. Although the national crime rate has fallen slightly in recent years, the number of murders and rapes in some areas of the country continues to be alarmingly high. Muggings, armed robbery, and drug trafficking imperil city living. In many large cities, people live in dread and fear, shutting themselves up in their homes at night or arming themselves in case of attack. But crime is not limited to large cities. Small towns have also been shocked and dismayed by violent crimes such as kidnapping, murder, and rape in their own communities. Children have been abducted from their own bedrooms or neighborhoods and discovered later, murdered, or never found again. Even very young children have murdered other children. Perhaps most dramatic of all have been the school shootings of recent years.

Because they have drawn so much media attention and discussion among families, school officials, community members, and national leaders, school shootings are the subject of the first three essays in this chapter. Lou Prato, in "How Much Is Too Much?" offers differing opinions on television coverage of the shooting in Littleton, Colorado. He presents the views of both those who criticize media coverage and those who defend it. Next, William S. Pollack, in "The Columbine Syndrome," explores the subject of teenage boys and violence, particularly the effect of the school shootings on how people view boys and how boys respond to such views. Third in the series is Gary Kleck's "There Are No Lessons to Be Learned from Littleton." Kleck looks at possible causes of school violence in the United States, examines potential consequences of such acts, and considers what lessons, if any, can be learned from them.

Broadening the focus of this chapter, "What's Wrong with America and Can Anything Be Done about It?" by Wayne M. Barrett and Bernard Rowe traces the antecedents of a host of social problems, including crime and violence, to a decline in decency and discipline. They suggest a number of remedies that seem controversial to many readers. As you read what these authors say, consider whether you agree or disagree with them. If you disagree, what do you think are causes and possible solutions for the nation's serious social problems?

In the final reading, "Maintaining the Crime Supply," Barbara Ehrenreich uses irony to convey her views on the problem of crime in America. She humorously treats crime as a commodity and suggests that the American people have an insatiable appetite for crime and punishment. In the course of her ironic mock argument, she not only implies her criticism of the criminal justice system's actions but also gets at the root causes of crime. As you read her essay, consider how much you agree with her on the issues she raises.

HOW MUCH IS TOO MUCH?

Lou Prato

A former radio and television news director, Lou Prato operates a writing and consulting business in State College, Pennsylvania. He is author of Covering the Environmental Beat: An Overview for Radio and TV Journalists *(1991) and* The Penn State Football Encyclopedia *(1998; 2nd ed. 2001). This piece first appeared in the June 1999 issue of the* American Journalism Review, *a publication of the College of Journalism at the University of Maryland. The* Review *features articles, commentaries, and book reviews on the subjects of communications and media. Its audience is largely composed of editors, columnists, reporters, and correspondents for all types of media.*

The shocking high school shootings that left 14 students and a teacher dead in Littleton, Colorado, in April have once again brought broadcast journalists under scrutiny for how they respond to a crisis. Critics continue to be disturbed by what they call excessive coverage of violence. They also are upset by what they see on the air in these live situations, and they wonder about the ethics and accountability of TV news.

"I'm distressed by this pattern of wall-to-wall coverage of violent events to the exclusion of any other news and by the need to do it live," says Paul Klite, founder of Rocky Mountain Media Watch, a Denver-based group that monitors newscasts throughout the nation. "What you get now in live coverage is a lot of speculation and a lot of incomplete information and repetition. It may be dramatic and sensational, but it's not very substantive."

What gave the incident in suburban Denver more impact and made it seem even more horrific was that it was still evolving in the first few hours—and it involved teenagers. Millions watched over the cable news networks as students ran for their lives and police swarmed school grounds. That early video came from local stations, which were providing feeds to CNN, Fox News Channel and MSNBC, as well as to the networks. Viewers saw the movements of police SWAT teams, the dramatic rescue of a bloodied student from a second-floor window and emotional interviews with parents and surviving students.

4   Meg Moritz, associate dean at the University of Colorado's School of Journalism, says most of her students didn't like what they saw. "They were offended by the reporters who they said were insensitive and put mikes in the faces of kids who were clearly distraught," Moritz says. "They also brought up the age of some reporters. Some reporters are not quite 30 and maybe never covered a story like this before. . . . One student complained about a young female reporter who smiled throughout her live shot—maybe out of nervousness. But he thought it was very inappropriate.

"Personally, I thought there was a lot of good coverage. I think the problem TV reporters face in comparison to newspapers is that during live situations, you are never in total control; there is no professional editing process as in print and, thus, some things get on the air that shouldn't."

Denver's TV columnists were generally satisfied with how the local broadcast media covered the shootings. But Joanne Ostrow of the *Denver Post,* who praised KUSA-TV for most of its coverage, criticized the NBC affiliate for broadcasting a cell phone conversation with a terrified student who pinpointed the location of a friend still hiding from the gunmen. At the time there was some fear that the killers were monitoring the local stations. There were multiple TV sets in the school. KUSA also had urged other students inside the school to call the station but then realized its mistake and broadcast an apology, telling students who were watching not to call but to continue hiding. Later, in attempting to identify one of the gunmen, the same station ran the wrong school yearbook photograph twice, on air and on the Web.

"The news media's goal is to cover tragedies like this with discretion, without allowing tactical details or misinformation to spill out," Ostrow wrote in a piece published April 21. But, she added, "For the most part, Denver's broadcast media delivered."

8   Massive coverage continued for days. The three broadcast networks even sent their prime-time anchors and morning show hosts to do on-the-scene reports.

Serious, responsible reporting was integrated with second-guessing and speculating about the causes of the shootings. The *Los Angeles Times'* TV critic, Howard Rosenberg, may have summed this up best when he wrote April 26: "From the hysterical tone of some of the coverage . . . you might get an impression that Littleton represents a national epidemic, that heavily armed homicidal kids are marching on classrooms everywhere like killer ants. That does not appear to be the case even when other schoolhouse shootings are taken into account."

Klite blames TV news for some of the hysteria. It's "more than just a mirror of . . . what's going on out there. There is a fixation on reporting on violence because it's good for the ratings." Of course, Denver's working news folks disagree. "Local TV news is certainly vulnerable to justified criticism, but those who say that we reported on this just because it's good for the ratings are terribly wrong," says Rick Sallinger, who covered the story for KCNC-TV, the CBS affiliate in Denver. "It is absolutely impossible to turn your back on something like this. . . . Not only is this affecting the entire community, but the people directly involved are depending on us for information. And they got it."

Personal Response

If you recall details of the live television coverage of the Littleton, Colorado, school shooting, write about your impressions of that coverage. If you do not recall that particular event, select another, more recent event that was covered live and comment on it.

Questions for Class or Small-Group Discussion

1. Prato mentions that critics of broadcast journalists find fault with their "excessive coverage of violence" (paragraph 1). To what extent do you agree that television coverage of violence is excessive? Do you think that television has a "fixation on reporting violence" (paragraph 10)?

2. Meg Moritz defends the news coverage of the Littleton, Colorado, shooting but acknowledges that during live situations, reporters "'are never in total control'" (paragraph 5). Comment on the examples that she gives of how live coverage of the Littleton situation was potentially dangerous. What is your position on the issue of live coverage of breaking news?

3. On the matter of the accountability of broadcast journalists, Prato notes that responsible "reporting was integrated with second-guessing and speculating" and then quotes Howard Rosenberg as perhaps having summed up this complaint the best (paragraph 9). What is Rosenberg's point and how would you respond to him on that point?

 ——————————————————————————

THE COLUMBINE SYNDROME: BOYS AND THE FEAR OF VIOLENCE

William S. Pollack

William S. Pollack is Assistant Clinical Professor in the Department of Psychiatry at Harvard Medical School. A clinical psychologist, he directs the Center for Men and Young Men at McLean Hospital in Belmont, Massachusetts. He is the author of Real Boys: Rescuing Our Sons from the Myths of Masculinity *(1999),* Real Boys' Voices *(2000), and* Real Boys Workbook *(2001). Pollack serves as an advisor to the President's National Campaign against Youth Violence. This essay appeared in the fall 2000 issue of* National Forum.

"I don't want to be that type of kid who comes to school and just takes out a gun and starts shooting."—Bobby, age 12, from a city in the West

"The other day I walked into school and a girl was carrying balloons and one of them popped. Everyone in the whole school got really terrified."—Errol, age 17, from a suburb in the West

"I think there are people at my school who have the potential for doing something similar."—Jules, age 17, from a suburb in the South

"People were coming up to me and begging me not to kill them. I felt like telling them: 'Cut it out; I'm not going to do anything.' "—Cody, age 14, from a suburb in New England

"You can't say 'them' or 'you.' You have to say 'us.' "—Jimmy, age 16, from a small town in the West

Probably no risk other than violence has made America more afraid of boys and made boys more afraid of being male and living in this country. Though it has been understood for decades that the perpetrators of most violence crimes in our nation are male, the recent spate of school shootings, culminating in the heinous massacre of teachers and students recently carried out in suburban Littleton, Colorado, has made the public ever more frightened and confused about the threat of extreme violence and its connection, in particular, with boys. Boys of adolescent age, boys just like the ones who have contributed to my research, are the ones pulling the triggers and injuring, sometimes killing, their peers and school teachers. What many people do not realize—and what the media following as well as they might—is that most of the victims of teenage violence, indeed the vast majority, are also boys.

Consequences of the Columbine Syndrome

In my travels across our country, listening to boys and doing research for my latest book, *Real Boys' Voices* (Random House, 2000), I have come to see that the effect of these terrifying crimes has been immense. It has led to the "Columbine Syndrome": across our nation students, parents, and teachers are absolutely terrified—sometimes to an extreme degree—about which boys amongst them are violent, who the next perpetrators might be, and who their victims will become. Paranoia is rampant. School children and the adults around them are constantly canvassing the student body and worrying, often inappropriately, that particular students may be murderous. Grady, age seventeen, from a school in the South says, "When a kid's wearing a trenchcoat and he's going for something in his jacket, you learn from watching the news that more than likely he might have a gun."

The consequence is that boys themselves are becoming increasingly afraid. They are frightened not only of being victimized by the rage and violence of other boys, but also of being accused, or falsely accused, of having the disposition it takes to snap into hyper-violent action and embark on a murderous rampage. Boys fear that despite their true nature, they will automatically, because they are boys, be seen as somehow toxic, dangerous, and culpable. As one young preadolescent boy said, "I think women like small kids. Girls like newborn babies. They don't like big people. We bigger guys scare everybody, and then we get blamed even when we've done nothing wrong."

4   Boys are also afraid of the violence they may feel inside themselves and of whether it is safe to talk with us about it. As they internalize this fear of being

misunderstood—and of being charged with having a violent temperament they genuinely do not have—boys themselves are beginning to worry if maybe, just maybe, the demon is within, if lurking underneath their conscious understanding of themselves, are uncontrollable urges to do depraved violent acts. The Columbine Syndrome means that America's boys today are as confused about violence as they are afraid of it. They fear each other and they fear their own selves.

The "Boy Code"

While the statistics indicate that teenage boys not only commit a considerable percentage of the nation's violent juvenile crimes but also become the frequent victims of those crimes, in reality there seems to be no inherent biological factor that makes boys more violent than their female counterparts. Violence committed by and acted out upon boys seems to stem, more often than not, from what we teach (or do not teach) boys about the behavior we expect from them. It comes from society's set of rules about masculinity, the Boy Code that says, "To be a man, you must show your strength and your power. You must show that you can hold your own if challenged by another male. You can show your rage, but you must not show any other emotions. You must protect your honor and fight off shame at all costs."

Think of it yourself. A boy gets slightly angry as a way to express his pain, and there will be mixed emotions. Some of us may show some fear, but if the anger is in control, we are unlikely to respond in a drastic manner. So long as it is "within bounds," society tends to approve of, if not encourage, aggression by and among boys. Violence in boys is widely (although, as I have said, incorrectly) seen an inevitable, if not biologically pre-ordained. As long as nobody is seriously hurt, no lethal weapons are employed, and especially within the framework of sports and games—football, soccer, boxing, wrestling—aggression and violence are widely accepted and even encouraged in boys. Boys are constantly trying to prove their masculinity through aggression, and society is complicit; winning a game, or even a fight, helps many boys gain society's respect.

The corollary to this message, simply enough, is that soft, gentle, non-violent boys, are "feminine" and therefore losers. While we often pay lip service to helping boys "put feelings into words" and even create multi-million educational programs to address this, if you're "a big guy" and start to express your vulnerable emotions too openly, people crawl back in fear. Or imagine the boy who misses a goal and bursts into tears on the soccer field. He is not considered masculine. Peers call him a "girl," "sissy" or "fag." Parents cringe. It is precisely in this environment that even the most hearty boy soon learns to avoid showing his pain in public. He may want to cry, he may wish he could speak of his fear, sadness, or shame, but he holds it back. He resists. Instead, the boy displays anger, aggression, and violence.

8   Perhaps it should not shock us, then, when we hear from the boys who say that while they overwhelmingly condemn extreme violence, and to a large extent do not engage in it, they can understand, empathize, with the boys who hit, hurt, and even kill. They tell us about what the teasing and razzing "can do to your head," how alone

and isolated some boys can become, and how rage is indeed often the only sanctioned emotion that does not bring further ridicule to them. We are all afraid of boys and violence, but boys, it turns out, are the most in fear. Gun detectors, violence screening tools or "profiles," armed guards, and "zero tolerance" only goad our sons into the very aggression we, and they, are afraid of; by expecting boys to be angry, rambunctious, and dangerous, we push boys to fulfill these prophecies. This is the essence, I believe, of the Columbine Syndrome. By living in fear and expecting danger, that is exactly what we produce.

To compound the risk to all of us, society is now giving boys another complex and confusing message, what I call the "No Black Shirts" response. Because the Columbine killers were outcast boys, spiteful nonconforming boys who wore dark clothing and were estranged from their peers, society has now rushed to the conclusion that adolescent boys who seem "different," especially ones who seem quiet, distant, and in pain, are the likely perpetrators of the next ghastly Columbine-like crime. Sadly, what the huge majority of outcast boys needs most—in fact what many so-called "popular" boys, boys on the "inside" often desperately need as well—is not to have their pain suppressed and disregarded, but rather to have it listened to and understood.

Curbing the Syndrome

Boys in pain require immediate intervention. As soon as we detect that a boy is experiencing emotional distress, we need to stop what we are doing, turn towards him, and hear him out. Whether he is wearing a black hood or Brooks Brothers sweater, whether he is well-liked or an outcast, he needs us to come toward him, embrace and affirm him, and assuage his hurt feelings before they push him to the edge. Boys are simply not inherently violent or dangerous, and the emotional distress that they may feel, in the first instance, does not make them any more so. But if we continue to give boys the message that expressing their distress is forbidden, that we will ignore their vulnerable feelings when we see them, and that we actually expect them to act out angrily and violently, we should not be surprised that the world becomes, for all of us, a mighty frightful place.

As the voices I heard (sampled in brief above) and published in detail in *Real Boys' Voices* exemplify only a tiny percentage of boys are capable of egregious acts of violence. In truth, as aggressive as they can perhaps be pushed to become, most boys are quite anxious about and revolted by the prevalence of violence in society. They feel powerless to do anything about it, though, because they simply feel too much shame, too concerned about how other people will respond to their confessions of fear.

12   The solution, I believe, is for society to commit to a whole new way of seeing boys and violence. First, as a society we need to decide, unequivocally, that as much as we will not exalt boys who fight, we also will not punish or ostracize those who show their vulnerability. By defending and actually providing positive reinforcement to boys who openly exhibit their moments of fear, longing, anxiety, and despair, by telling these

boys and men that they are fully "masculine" no matter what emotions they share with us, we can help them avoid the repression and resistance that may make them bottle up their emotions and then spill them out in irrational acts. Second, because society may not change overnight, we need to be on the lookout for the signs of sadness and depression that in boys and men so often seem harder to see, or more difficult to believe and accept. In my book, I outlined these many signs. If we are attentive to them, and if we help boys overcome the pain and disaffection that gives rise to them, much of the aggression and violence we now see will evaporate, or be directed towards safe, appropriate channels.

Finally, we must simply decide, as a society, that most boys, as angry or aggressive as they may become, are highly unlikely to become dangerous in any way. The boys' voices quoted at the beginning of this piece are overwhelming proof that most of our sons have a non-violent nature and that, in reality, their greater struggle is with sadness and the fear of violence rather than with violence itself. Together we must create prophecies that their gentle nature will triumph over old pressures to act tough and lash out. Perhaps if we hear boys' fears about violence in a new light, read their stories with a new empathy, we may be able to reach across the boundaries of fear and create a new dialogue of peace. For boys and for the rest of us, the only cure for the Columbine Syndrome, in the end, is to develop safe spaces that are friendly to boys and thereby create genuine security. The time is now!

Personal Response

Write for a few minutes in response to Pollack's assessment of the climate of fear associated with boys and violence.

Questions for Class or Small-Group Discussion

1. In your own words, explain what you understand the term "Columbine Syndrome" to mean.

2. According to Pollack, in what ways do boys experience "the fear of violence"? On the basis of your own experiences and observations, to what extent do you agree with him on this point?

3. What does Pollack mean by the term *boy code?* Discuss your response to his explanation of that term. In particular, comment on these statements: "[A]ggression and violence are widely accepted and even encouraged in boys" (paragraph 6) and "The corollary to this message . . . is that soft, gentle, non-violent boys are 'feminine' " paragraph 7).

4. Summarize the several courses of action Pollack urges as a solution for curbing the Columbine Syndrome. Then discuss his proposed solution in terms of its practicality, the likelihood of its success, the ability of American society to act on it, and any other relevant considerations.

THERE ARE NO LESSONS TO BE LEARNED FROM LITTLETON

Gary Kleck

Gary Kleck, author of Point Blank: Guns and Violence in America *(1991) and* Targeting Guns: Firearms and Their Control *(1997), is a professor in the School of Criminology and Criminal Justice at Florida State University. He is coauthor, with Don B. Kates Jr., of* The Great American Gun Debate: Essays on Firearms and Violence *(1997) and* Armed: New Perspectives on Gun Control *(2001). This essay was first published in the winter/spring 1999 issue of* Criminal Justice Ethics.

On April 21, 1999, two young men armed with guns and explosives murdered 13 people, wounded 31 others, and then committed suicide in a high school in Littleton, Colorado. This mass shooting had been preceded by three other highly publicized mass shootings in schools involving adolescent boys in the preceding year-and-a-half in Pearl, Mississippi; West Paducah, Kentucky; and Jonesboro, Arkansas (and there had been at least seven other multi-victim school shootings in the six years before that), and was followed by two more occurring within a month in Springfield, Oregon, and Conyers, Georgia.

In the aftermath of this spate of murders, a wave of commentary followed, in which journalists and other writers of every ideological stripe explained to their readers what lessons were to be learned from Littleton or, more broadly, from this cluster of massacres. In a typical commentary, a writer would diagnose one or more key problems that supposedly contributed to the killings, and then prescribe one or more solutions. The diagnoses and solutions generally fitted remarkably well with preexisting news media themes, reflecting either an impressive ability of news providers to identify causes and solutions in advance or a tendency to exclude the solutions that do not easily fit the themes.

A partial list of the problems that have been blamed for the recent mass killings in schools would include: guns, "assault weapons," large-capacity ammunition magazines, lax regulation of gun shows; the failure of parents to secure guns, school cliques, and the exclusion of "outsiders"; bullying and taunting in schools, especially by high school athletes; inadequate school security, especially a lack of metal detectors, armed guards, locker searches, and so forth; excessively large high schools; inadequate monitoring of potentially violent students by schools; lazy, uninvolved Baby Boomer parents and correspondingly inadequate supervision of their children; young killers not being eligible for the death penalty; a lack of religion, especially in schools; violent movies and television; violent video games; violent material and communications on the World Wide Web/Internet (including bomb-making instructions); anti-Semitism, neo-Nazi sentiments, and Hitler worship; "Industrial" music, Marilyn Manson's music, and other "dark" variants of rock music; Satanism; "Goth" culture among adolescents; and Southern culture.

4   The purpose of this essay is not to sort out which diagnoses are correct. Many of them are plausible, and some are probably even accurate. Likewise, some of the proposed preventive measures may well be effective. Rather, my main point is that it is generally a mistake to diagnose the causes of violence and crime, or to identify effective ways to reduce violence and crime, via a focus on unusual, heavily publicized violent events, because diagnoses and prescriptions developed or promoted in the immediate aftermath of such events are especially likely to be irrelevant or even counterproductive.

A casual consumer of the flood of news coverage of these shootings could easily draw the conclusion that violence in schools is a growing problem or that youth violence, gun violence, or violence in general has been increasing. In fact, these are the recent trends in violence:

- the homicide rate dropped by a third from 1991 to 1998,

- the juvenile share of arrests for violent crime has been declining since 1992,

- gun violence, and the gun share of violent crimes, has been declining since 1993,

- the lethality of gun crime (the share ending in death) has been declining since the mid-1970s,

- mass murder has been declining for decades (the share of homicide victims killed in incidents with four or more victims dropped in half between 1976 and 1994), and

- school gun violence has generally declined since national statistics were first gathered for the 1992–1993 school year.

In sum, the cluster of mass shootings in schools that occurred in the late 1990s may well be one of the few forms of violence that have been increasing in recent years. Even gun homicides in schools have generally been declining in recent years, despite the massacres. Indeed, excluding the Littleton killings, U.S. schools experienced just two gun homicides during the 1998–1999 school year, which would have been the lowest total since national statistics were first compiled. While some of these facts were mentioned occasionally in news stories about these events, many writers nevertheless offered explanations for the nonexistent "trend" in youth/school/gun violence.

Misdescription of the phenomenon to be explained leads to misdiagnosis of its causes. If there is no increase in youth/school/gun violence, it is fruitless to search for contributing factors that have been increasing in recent years. The only kind of violence that did increase was mass shootings in schools, (so far) only for a very short period of time. Thus, long-term or significant social trends may be irrelevant to these murders, however relevant some of them may be to more commonplace forms of violence. Rather, this short-term clustering may largely reflect an endogenous process by which each new act is triggered by news media accounts of the previous ones. Adolescent boys, faced with powerlessness and anonymity, and otherwise unhappy for a multitude of diverse reasons, recognize that fame, importance, and a sort of immortality have been the rewards for previous mass killers and realistically anticipate the same rewards for themselves if they copy their actions. This process can perpetuate itself until the news media loses interest or competing stories push schoolyard massacres off the front pages.

8   A tragedy that has already occurred obviously cannot be prevented by any actions taken now. Therefore, actions will prevent harm only to the extent that the events they can effectively head off are likely to be repeated in the future. Yet, the more bizarre an event, the less likely it is to be repeated. Thus, because bizarre events are unlikely to be repeated in quite the same way in the future, the more narrowly a preventive measure is tailored to the specifics of such events, the less likely it is to save lives.

One might argue that while commentary on these media-heavy tragedies might not successfully identify measures that could prevent such events in the future, analysis of the extraordinary events might identify measures that could prevent more commonplace kinds of violence. This might make sense if the heavily publicized events closely resembled more ordinary acts of violence, but in many important ways they do not.

Particular violent events are heavily covered by the news media precisely because they are unusual and thus unrepresentative of broader categories of crime and violence. For example, violent incidents with many victims are the ones most likely to be covered heavily. Yet less than one percent of Americans who are murdered are killed in incidents with four or more dead victims (often regarded by experts as the admittedly arbitrary cutoff between mass killings and "ordinary" homicides). Only two percent are killed in incidents with more than two victims, and these are most commonly killings within families. Their high body count itself makes mass killings unusual and unrepresentative of murder or violence in general.

This would not be problematic if the causes of, and likely solutions to, mass killings matched closely with likely causes and solutions to "ordinary" violence, but mass killings differ from ordinary violence in crucial ways. For example, mass killings are almost invariably planned, while other homicides and assaults are rarely planned. Likewise, firearms are virtually a necessity to killing large numbers of people in a single incident, but far less essential for killing a single person. Further, mass killers often come from middle-class backgrounds and have little prior record of criminal behavior, while these things are rarely true of "ordinary" killers.

12   A particularly worrisome implication is that a focus on mass murders tends to distract attention from the role of underclass poverty in generating the "ordinary" violence that accounts for almost all of its casualties. There really was a recent increase in juvenile violence, especially with guns, but it was confined to the period from 1985 to 1991, and it had little to do with middle class-linked causes, and everything to do with the collapse of the legitimate economy in America's inner city ghettoes and the resultant rise of the crack economy to fill the vacuum.

Just as few homicides involve large numbers of victims, very few occur in schools. Schools continue to be the safe havens that they were traditionally perceived to be, however much media coverage of these killings has eroded that perception. While there is serious violence in a few schools, and considerable gun violence outside of schools, gun violence in schools is extremely rare. In the 1996–97 school year, 90 percent of public schools did not experience a single serious violent crime (murder, rape, sexual battery, robbery, or attack with a weapon) regardless of gun involvement, and over 99.99 percent have never had a homicide. The violence that does occur in schools is mostly unarmed fighting (including a good deal of bullying), while gun violence, even among adolescents, is almost entirely confined to places other than schools. Less than one in 400 adolescent gun homicides in 1994 occurred in a school or on school grounds.

The school shootings triggered a barrage of transparently irrelevant proposed solutions, tossed out without regard to their relevance to the events that supposedly occasioned the proposals. Mississippi responded to the Pearl shootings by making murder on school property a capital offense, even though premeditated murder, regardless of location, was already a capital offense in Mississippi. The killers in this incident, moreover, were ineligible for the death penalty because of their ages, eleven and thirteen; the minimum age for the death penalty was left unchanged.

Following the first four of these shootings, members of Congress were pushing a bill that would "crack down" on dealers who sell firearms to children even though none of these cases involved a dealer selling a gun to a child. After the shooting in West Paducah, in which the killer was armed with five firearms and shot eight different people in the school lobby, newspapers reported that the school system was considering installing metal detectors. The stories did not explain how metal detectors could prevent attacks by those willing to shoot their way into a school.

16   After it was found that such transfers were involved in the Littleton case, some analysts proposed restricting sales at gun shows. Gun show sales, however, had nothing at all to do with any of the other high-profile school shootings. The most common modes of acquisition of guns by shooters were theft (the West Paducah, Jonesboro, and Conyers shootings, as well as a somewhat less prominent case in Edinboro, Pennsylvania), while the Springfield shooter was given his guns by his father. Further, even in the Littleton case the three longguns that accounted for all of the deaths were purchased on the killers' behalf by the eighteen-year-old girlfriend of one of the shooters. Under both Colorado and federal law, she would have been eligible to purchase the same guns from any gun store. Further, one of the two killers turned eighteen before the shootings and was likewise eligible to buy longguns from any gun store.

Consequently, regulation of gun shows was totally irrelevant to preventing any of these massacres. One irony of addressing such proposals in the context of mass killings, however, is that some of them make sense, but not in connection with mass killings. As a result, some people will reject the value of a measure with regard to ordinary violence because it is irrelevant to the unusual events at hand. A prime example is extending background checks to private gun transfers at gun shows. The

Littleton and other mass shootings are the worst possible examples of cases in which the background checks could succeed since determined killers who plan their murders over a long period of time are the people least likely to be blocked from getting a gun by background checks. As a long-time advocate of extending background checks to all private transfers of guns, not just the few that take place at gun shows, I worry that the real merits of such a step will be obscured by the inane debate over the nonexistent link between gun shows and the Littleton massacre. More broadly, mass killings and other premeditated murders are the very worst examples for buttressing a case in favor of gun control because they involve the perpetrators most strongly motivated and able to evade the controls.

Even under the best of circumstances, the lessons one could derive from the examination of individual violent events are inherently ambiguous. The fact that violence did occur necessarily means that all existing preventive measures failed. This can lead to any of a number of very different conclusions: (1) we need different preventive measures, (2) we need more of the existing measures, or (3) nothing can be done. The ongoing issue most frequently linked to the school shootings was gun control, and reactions by those on both sides of that issue were predictable. Pro-gun people concluded that despite the existence of laws completely prohibiting the purchase and carrying of guns by minors, youthful killers got guns anyway; therefore gun control is ineffective. Meanwhile, pro-control people concluded that if existing gun controls failed, it showed that stronger measures were called for—anything from tougher controls over gun shows and laws requiring guns to be kept locked to lawsuits against gun companies supposedly marketing guns to juveniles.

Assessments of preventive measures based on a narrow focus on violent events that did occur, however, are inherently misleading because they necessarily focus only on the failures of preventive efforts. One cannot infer how much success a policy has had by counting its failures. Successes of preventive measures, unlike failures, usually cannot be observed directly. Instead, they can be detected only indirectly through careful comparison of persons, places, and times subject to the preventive measures with those not subject to them.

Diagnosis of the causes of violence is similarly distorted by a narrow focus on the attributes of a few violent actors, distracting attention from violent actors who lacked the attributes, and from the even larger number of people who had the attributes but were not violent.

Those who propose preventive measures in the context of these mass shootings can plausibly assert that the irrelevance of their proposals to these incidents does not matter because the proposals are meritorious with respect to more common sorts of violence. If that is the case, however, honest advocates should show why their proposals are relevant to more ordinary violence and not coast dishonestly on the emotional momentum created by extraordinary violent events that their policies could not prevent. It would, however, be naive to expect those playing hard-ball politics to follow the intellectually honest path since they will be loathe to forego exploiting the emotional power that comes from tying their recommendations to the most horrific and frightening crimes.

One might justify drawing lessons from high-profile tragedies by arguing that one should make use of the temporarily elevated level of concern about violence to advance worthy solutions that might not prevent unusual events like those that just occurred, but would be effective in the long run with more mundane crimes.

This argument, however, would seem to depend on the dubious premise that people make wise choices in times of fear and hysteria (sometimes euphemistically referred to as "intense public concern"). Unfortunately, frightened people often favor actions that make them feel better over those that would actually make them safer, if the actions can be implemented quickly and easily and are touted as producing results immediately.

24   People are less likely to be in a logical or critical frame of mind in the aftermath of the most ghastly crimes, a situation that smart advocates exploit. In such a context, people are more willing to believe that "something must be done," and not look too closely at the details and full set of consequences of proposed solutions. Decisions about serious matters should not be made in the sort of overheated aftermath in which demagoguery flourishes. Such an atmosphere is more conducive to lynch mob justice and empty, politically easy gestures than to wise public policy.

Littleton and the other school shootings do raise serious issues, some largely ignored by the news media, and others only briefly mentioned and obscured by the noisy debates over the irrelevancies. These issues might include school bullying and taunting, male-on-female teen dating violence, and violence-saturated entertainment disseminated by profit-hungry corporations. But we will be best able to separate the issues that matter from the ones that do not if we learn our lessons from careful analysis of "ordinary" crime and violence rather than from the freakish events chosen for our attention by the news media.

Personal Response

Are you convinced that "there are no lessons to be learned from Littleton"? If not, what lessons do you think we can learn from the Littleton, Colorado, shooting in particular or from school shootings in general?

Questions for Class or Small-Group Discussion

1. Locate Kleck's thesis and consider how effectively he supports that thesis as you discuss the essay. To what extent did/do you believe that "violence in schools is a growing problem or that youth violence, gun violence, or violence in general has been increasing"? Were you surprised by the statistics that Kleck cites in paragraphs 5, 6, 10, and 13? Are you persuaded that there is no " 'trend' in youth/school/gun violence"?

2. How convinced are you by Kleck's argument against the position that "commentary on these media-heavy tragedies [. . .] could prevent such events in the future" (paragraph 9)? What differences does Kleck see between "mass killings" and " 'ordinary' violence"?

3. According to Kleck, what are the "transparently irrelevant proposed solutions" to the problem of school shootings (paragraph 14)? Discuss your views on his evidence. To what extent do you agree with him that the proposed solutions are irrelevant to the problem?

4. In paragraphs 18–24, Kleck states some of the lessons people say we could learn from the school shootings and then rejects each in turn. Summarize what those lessons are and why he rejects them. To what extent do you agree with his arguments on these points?

WHAT'S WRONG WITH AMERICA AND CAN ANYTHING BE DONE ABOUT IT?

Wayne M. Barrett and Bernard Rowe

Wayne M. Barrett is Managing Editor of USA Today *magazine and writes often of sports, especially hockey and baseball. Bernard Rowe, a British citizen, is a retired chartered accountant (the British term for what Americans call a CPA or Certified Public Accountant) and a textile industry consultant who lives in Valley Stream, New York. They wrote this essay for* USA Today *in 1994.*

It is a clichéd tale as old as the hills. The elder generation looks at society's youngsters and shakes its head in disappointed wonder and disgust. "When I was a kid . . . ," the admonishment inevitably begins. Today, however, the Establishment is in no position to criticize anyone or anything. If American youth is poisoned with skewed values and a lack of respect, one doesn't have to look very far to see where such behavior originates. Consider the following incidents:

- Unmarried pregnant teenage girls, no longer outcasts among their high school peers, instead are made cheerleaders and crowned homecoming queens by court order.

- The Chief Council for the President of the United States commits suicide and, before the body is even cold, Clinton administration officials rifle through his office to remove all "incriminating" paperwork that related to the chief executive and first lady.

- In 1993, New York Mets outfielder Vince Coleman threw an M-80 firecracker into a crowd of fans outside Dodger Stadium in Los Angeles. A handful of people, including a little girl, were injured in the explosion. In response to the heat the Mets took following this ugly and unforgivable occurrence, the club's vice president of baseball operations, Gary Hunsicker, stated: "This incident didn't happen during working hours. It didn't happen in the clubhouse. It only involves the Mets because he is an employee of the Mets. This is Vince Coleman's incident. This is Vince Coleman's problem."

- *The Program*, a Disney movie about a college football team, contained a scene in which a drunken player lies on a busy highway's dividing line, with traffic zooming past. A New Jersey man and Pennsylvania teenager, imitating the dangerous stunt, were killed, while a New York teenager was paralyzed. The film's producers and distributors were blamed. (The scene subsequently was removed from the film and videotape version.)

- A New York City mugger was awarded $4,300,000 by the state's Court of Appeals, which ruled that the arresting officer used too much force by shooting him. The U.S. Supreme Court refused to overturn the decision.

- A 1993 survey released by Who's Who among American High School Students found that the nation's top secondary school pupils get their good grades the old-fashioned way—they cheat. Eighty percent said cheating was common at their schools, and 78 percent admitted to doing so themselves.

- The handshake, long the symbol of sportsmanship and good will, has been banned at the closing of school sporting events in California's Ventura County. It seems that some players were spitting in their hands before shaking or slapping opponents in the face during the post-game ritual.

- Madison Square Garden Network announcer John Andariese has covered the National Basketball Association since 1972. Recently, he compared the "old days" to contemporary times, where players "diss" each other with trash talk. Bench-clearing brawls often are the result. "It wasn't that long ago when respect came from winning the game; a series; a championship. Self-respect was about being part of the game; now it's a reason to be thrown out of the game.

   "Today, self-respect is so misplaced," he told the *New York Post.* "It's about putting your own feelings above all else. The individual's interests, including commercial interests, come before the team. . . . We've made heroes out of guys who do bad things; selfish things. The attention they receive is often equated with their ability to be entertaining, and that's when commercial opportunities present themselves."

- Fox Television, in a live update on the New York Rangers' fifty-four-year quest for the Stanley Cup, cut to a reporter outside Madison Square Garden just before the opening faceoff of Game 5 of the finals. No sooner did the camera go on than a bunch of Big Apple rooters standing behind the reporter started chanting: "Let's Go Rangers! F— Vancouver!" Loudly, over and over again. Did Fox switch back to the studio? Of course not. Instead, the obscene chant came cascading right into the viewer's living room, over and over.

- Fallen football hero O. J. Simpson, wanted by the Los Angeles Police on a double-murder charge, took cops on a cross-county highway chase, captured live by news helicopter cameras. As O. J.'s car passed under an overpass, a group of revelers cheered him on, apparently delighted to be part of the action.

It all comes down to a breakdown in discipline and the advent of liberalism. The general idea is of total *laissez-faire*—the concept that everyone has a personal right to do whatever he or she wants. America has institutionalized selfishness.

People need not look out for anyone but themselves. My interest then becomes myself. I no longer have to worry about anyone else. When there is the understanding that people just live for themselves, when that attitude permeates a society, individuals attempt to protect themselves without regard for others. If they can't protect their rights in a civilized way, they're prepared to carry it through using a violent route, oftentimes with little or no regard for right and wrong, or how that action will impact upon themselves or those around them. After all, that person reasons, I'm free and have my own rights.

4   One can track this growth in liberalism with the breakdown of the great religions. The church taught a certain level of morals. "Thou shalt not steal" didn't come from the schools. Parents taught that. They took their kids to church, synagogue, or the mosque, and the youngsters were taught there that you mustn't kill; you mustn't do certain things. Along came liberalism, and no one bothered to teach those things anymore. This effectively has led to a bankrupt society. True, there are numerous social welfare programs, but, because Americans have let go of all other moral values, much of the good that these programs could have generated or produced has been lost.

There used to be corporal punishment in the schools. If teachers tried that today, they would be sued. If parents do it, they risk having the state take away their offspring. Accordingly, such discipline wasn't only given up in school, but in the home as well.

Everywhere, there is unbridled freedom bordering on license. Children are allowed to watch any television program, no matter what it is. By allowing kids unrestricted access to TV, the movies, and new computer information systems, they not only are being exposed to greater knowledge, they are being exposed to all of the world's ills without countervailing criticism. No one comes on at the end to say, "This is wrong; this should not have happened." No one tries to utilize the media to show youngsters a piece of news that might be startling and use it as a lesson, asking them: "What happens if . . . ?"

Not surprisingly, then, the nation's work ethic has suffered as well. Today, employees have rights against their employer, oftentimes out of balance with what rights should be. True, there was a time when employers exploited individuals, and the unions had to right major wrongs. People were made to work in a certain way that was beyond what was reasonable. The unions have come full circle and introduced a system whereby the employees almost control what they will do, what rights they have, and how much they will work.

8   Within the workplace, certain individuals may be motivated, but they often are held back by the others, who complain, "What are you doing? Why are you being so productive? If management sees this, it will want more from us." They then will use whatever means are at their disposal—violence not excepted—to stop the more productive workers. While the advent of unions brought back a certain sense of balance, it took away the decency of the individual, which no longer counts.

When individuals are institutionalized, it effectively removes a lot of their creativity and motivation. There is a tremendous loss, especially in the aspect of discipline. Doing what management wants is only one facet of discipline. The other is fulfilling your moral obligation when you take on a job or assignment.

That the work ethic has been weakened by Western society becomes particularly noticeable in considering newcomers to our shores. Immigrant labor has not been subject to generations of this kind of influence, so they come to this country willing to work, willing to give it their best. They feel they owe it. They have a job. They're determined to achieve for themselves, their families, and the relatives back home. They are willing to work hard, sacrificing and doing without for years.

These people never remove the yoke from their shoulders. They were born into societies where children, parents, and grandparents lived in one community. Children knew that, as they grew up, they had an obligation to take care of their parents. Today, as youngsters grow up and go to college, their main concern is for themselves and their own well-being.

12   Marriage is another dying institution. Today, many people decide to live together to see if they're compatible. Does that produce the best results? Obviously not. "If we live together," the attitude goes, "why should I commit myself? Why should I assume responsibility? Indeed, why should I give of myself more than I need to so that I can still have the physical contact my desires require without having to give a financial or moral commitment to just one person or to the children who may come from this relationship? I can come and go as I please. If someone better arrives on the scene, I can go with him or her."

Such an attitude inevitably leads to a lack of discipline and responsibility for another. If children see their parents act this way, why should they be any different? When they go to school, why should they care about their friends? Why do they have to worry that other kids may be hurt? To take it a step further, why would it worry them if they hurt other youngsters?

Meanwhile, lawsuit mania has gripped America. The phenomenon goes back to the same issue: I have a right! I'm entitled to sue for anything and everything that may impinge upon that right, no matter what society's needs.

Take the Rodney King case. This is a man who everyone agrees required force to be subdued after a high-speed auto chase, but excessive force was used by the Los Angeles police. There was a wrong committed here, but remember, King was in the wrong, too. Conceding that he had inflicted upon him a certain amount of pain, he did deserve something for his suffering. He should have been given a small amount of financial compensation, but not a seven-digit settlement.

16   This is a man who in his lifetime never dreamed of earning that kind of money or had been deprived of anything resembling that sort of income. He probably is way better off having been subjected to physical abuse at the hands of the police. That doesn't justify the wrong, but neither does it justify a multimillion-dollar lawsuit. It's not an issue of civil rights. The system has been made to look stupid. The courts and lawyers should be viewed with a certain amount of integrity. Once respect has disappeared, so has the sense of honesty.

Now, consider the impact of the legal system on physicians. Much of what the medical profession does today simply is to avoid lawsuits, because it's a "cover yourself just in case" kind of world. This is the price society pays for allowing malpractice lawyers to reach for the moon. The measure of compensation should be related to what is right and what is wrong. Instead, the dollar amounts are astronomical. In the end, society pays. When individuals who have observed the system at work find themselves with the potential for a claim, however spurious, they say, "Well, it's my turn to exploit it now." There are bumper stickers that sum it up quite succinctly: "Hit me; I need the cash." That's not what society should be all about.

The Drug Scourge

The drug problem in America also can be traced back to a lack of discipline, lack of education, and lack of knowledge between right and wrong. Again there is the attitude: I have rights. I want to take drugs. Meanwhile, the government says they must be outlawed. A tremendous amount of resources have been sunk into the war on drugs, with no victory in sight. As a result of interdictment efforts, however, drugs are becoming more and more expensive, and more and more people are turning to crime to finance their drug habits. One way of looking at it is the government has made criminals out of noncriminals.

When addicts kill for drug money, people act perplexed and ask, "How on Earth did this happen?" Actually, the surprise is that it doesn't happen more often. As the situation worsens, society does what it absolutely shouldn't—legislate against its own people.

20   In a society pervasive with so many freedoms, government simply can't say, with regard to drugs, "No, you can't do what you want." It hasn't worked and won't work. The easy solution is to legalize drugs. There's a strong case for that. Fundamentally, the price of drugs would drop to next to nothing. Sell it like alcohol and cigarettes, with a label: "Warning—this stuff may kill you." The criminals peddling it will be out of business overnight. The people addicted to it no longer will have to commit crimes to obtain it. If they want to rot their bodies and minds, or even kill themselves, let them.

Making drugs illegal recalls an old Hebrew saying: "Stolen waters are sweet." If you tell people they can't have drugs, especially in a *laissez-faire* society such as ours, the response will be, "I'll show you what I can have." Yet, if you were to say, "Take this poison," people would respond, "Are you crazy?"

Here is where education can be so valuable. Morality can be introduced into many subjects. So can the concepts of quality, decency, right, and wrong. Programs can be designed so that almost every teacher and every subject can introduce moral values.

In the old days, a child was told, "Sit here and pay attention." If a student dozed off or talked during lessons, there was instant retribution. To some extent, such a system was shown to have been very successful, though many children failed to achieve their full potential. Nevertheless, it certainly gave kids a better education than they're getting today.

24   Contemporary students, as they grow older and become more mature, discover that much of school has been a waste of time. They didn't learn very much, and thus have very little respect for teachers. Think what's going to happen when they have children to send to school. Can they convincingly tell their kids, "You must respect your teacher"? Absolutely not. Yet, the system doesn't change, except to give children more rights and greater freedom, and only in the negative form.

What is the price society pays?—criminals in the classroom. Never before did children come to school armed in order to protect themselves. Walk the streets of New York and you will see thousands of kids there on a normal school day. These youngsters have grown up with zero discipline. What happens when they get older?

In the past, the military system, while far from perfect, accomplished two things: It made people live a disciplined life and took them off the streets. American society has abandoned another of the fortresses of discipline. For whatever bad or good influence it had, the military at least showed people they couldn't do whatever they wanted. It also often gave them a vocation.

Discipline and decency are disappearing from the family as well. So much used to take place within the network of the family, including the education of the children. Parents sat down with them and went through their homework, helped them with assignments, and saw to it that they were progressing. Today, too many parents are jealous of their time. Watching a favorite TV show becomes more important than helping with their offspring's homework.

28   Children today seem to be kept only out of a grudging obligation. Parents will send their kids off to a private high school if they can afford it, or, in the summer, to camp. Look at it from the youngsters' viewpoint. They no longer see the constant cohesive unit of the family. On the contrary, they remember that their father sent them money and took care of their economic needs. The child comes to regard the economic thread as what is important. "My father was busy chasing the dollar. He gave me food. He sent me to camp. But other than that, I didn't really need him. I didn't need my mother, either." When there's a substitute for everything and children don't see the need for the family unit, it is an unreasonable expectation that they, in turn, will grow up and create a proper family unit.

Children very quickly perceive the way adults are. Parents who have no time for their kids and show no interest in them, who don't give up their time to help others, can't expect their children to grow up and do that. As a result, society winds up with a next generation whose main interests are themselves. They are liberated, free, have rights they are entitled to, and only have to make sure they will have means to provide for themselves. In their old age, they will not be able to depend on their children, anymore than their parents can depend on them.

A Revolution Is Needed

There has to be a total revolution in this country in attitudes and outlook. If we don't come up with a quick, solid remedy, some very serious unwanted changes will take place, almost as great as what happened in the Soviet Union. When the American dream bursts, there's no predicting exactly where the pieces will fall.

Most of the standard remedies already have been tried. We have raised and lowered taxes, adjusted interest rates, added police officers in an effort to promote law and order, poured more money into the educational system, and interdicted the traffic of narcotics, even attempting to impede their flow at the source by shipping drug enforcement agents overseas. The net effect has been minor.

32   Some success stories can be demonstrated, but, overall, it's hard to dispute that the United States is a nation in decline. Fundamentally, there's a perception by most Americans that we are worse off than we were, and our hopes for the future are dim. Gone are the days when we looked to the future and saw the Great American Promise.

The basic ingredient for a happy society is that anyone who wishes to work should be able to find a job. In the United States today, unemployment is rampant, layoffs are all too common, and jobs flow overseas. One problem is lack of productivity by American workers.

Industry, struggling to survive in the face of cheap foreign competition, has changed its methods. Massive layoffs have resulted, and a healthier type of American company is emerging. "Leaner and meaner" is the cliché. Industry can look forward to reduced costs, and therefore be more competitive.

Government, meanwhile, remains extremely wasteful, maintaining multiple employees for each one required in industry. The numbers range all the way from twenty-five to fifty, depending on which survey one chooses to read or believe. Even in the face of all the cuts in the private sector, there's been virtually no drastic actions by the federal, state, or city government. They all remain overbloated. Elected officials are afraid to antagonize the army of civil servants and refuse to reduce their own staffs.

36   The public does not have confidence in the government or in the economy. People don't have the confidence that the future will be brighter. The key to reversing this malaise is that good jobs must be provided. How this can be accomplished is no secret. Too much of the employment in this country has been lost to foreigners. The United States exported many of its jobs through various government policies, often in the name of helping developing countries. At the same time, it allowed tremendous amounts of imports, often undercutting American companies.

America has a great history of charity, and many countries of the world are grateful, but the United States is in a time of crisis. The way to ensure that America will be here tomorrow to continue its tradition of decency and kindness is to make sure that many of those jobs exported overseas are returned home.

How can that be accomplished? The simplest way, one guaranteed to produce an almost immediate effect, is by imposing strict import controls. The United States should turn to its major trading partners—Taiwan, Korea, Japan, and China, which account for a very large part of the trade deficit—and say to them, "You may export into the United States, dollar for dollar, what you purchase from America." It is ludicrous to think that the United States should allow a two- or three-to-one ratio of imports to exports. Under the dollar-for-dollar proposal, there would be an immediate shortage of many products and some short-term price increases. However, people can survive without a new camera this month or maintain their cars for another six months—or purchase an American car—until things stabilize.

The United States would have to maintain this policy for a minimum of three years, then ease off in increments of no greater than 10 percent. Then, the manufacturers and entrepreneurs will feel secure in the knowledge that, if they produce goods in this country, they will have a local market and potential for export. They will be willing to invest in the necessary plant and machinery—almost immediately—to manufacture goods. Meanwhile, foreign companies should be encouraged with incentives to introduce more and more production in the United States. A new flow of jobs will be created within an extremely short period of time.

40   One important side effect may be a reduction in crime. American youths—especially minorities—face high rates of unemployment, poor prospects, and a lack of interest in life. Providing them with reasonably paying productive jobs can help make them feel they are valued members of society.

Next is the issue of taxation. Practically speaking, Americans don't like paying taxes and, above all, feel that much of what they pay is wasted. So long as there's mismanagement in government, there is resentment on the part of taxpayers. People recognize the need to finance national and local services, so they are prepared to pay, but there's the general sense out there—and not without justification—that the U.S. taxpayer isn't getting value for the buck.

Another major irritant is that the burden of taxation does not seem to be shared by all. There is massive avoidance of taxation in many industries, and the government doesn't even want to admit the scale of avoidance because it's embarrassingly large. People accept the idea of being taxed if everyone shares the burden. One way is to generate a taxation system that virtually encompasses the entire country. Take certain industries and tax them at source. This is not a value-added tax, which runs through all the multiple stages of production and becomes very expensive to collect. The United States has to look for something that is simple, efficient, and easy to collect.

For example, the utility companies could be taxed very highly. Abolish income tax altogether and corporation taxes because they require massive administration, massive collection systems, massive policing and effectively turn the nation into a country of crooks. Under the new plan, every electric bill would be taxed heavily. Oil, if it's imported, would be taxed at the ports; domestic oil wells, at the source. There's no reason Americans can't pay up to $4 a gallon for gas as they do in many European countries. Everyone would be caught up in the net because nobody can avoid electricity or phone bills. Among the benefits would be a very simple method of collection. A far smaller IRS would emerge.

44   Right now, America is a nation in crisis, so all the old rules are off. An enormous number of government employees no longer would be necessary. Within industry, a tremendous amount of money is spent to assist in the collection of taxes. There would be substantial savings there. As government expenses go down, revenues could be rebudgeted.

As for the poor, government now pays out a substantial amount in welfare and other social programs. Instead of money, services should be provided. It would be a cleaner system, with much less fraud. A lot of the people on such programs have been shown to take the money and use it in ways that don't necessarily benefit their welfare.

Undoubtedly, a system that sucks in the needy, while failing to show them a way out, is inherently flawed. Temporary and short-term help must be axiomatic to the system. All who enter must be encouraged to leave as soon as possible. Life within the system can not be made more comfortable than outside it. There must be an end to the credo: "We are better off on welfare than at work." To achieve this, all citizens—on welfare and off—should be issued identity cards with photos. Such a card would be required in all dealings with officialdom as well as the maintenance of bank accounts, financial securities, homes, and other assets and liabilities. In order to secure welfare benefits, a potential recipient would have to submit to a means test to be verified by the identity card. If, and while, assets remain below established criteria, appropriate benefits would be granted, and only for that period.

These benefits would be distributed on community campuses, as it is vitally important to establish appropriate homes to house welfare recipients. All beneficiaries would be required to live on campus and to participate in maintaining it based on their abilities. The campus would be sparsely, yet adequately, furnished and would provide food prepared in a communal kitchen. The cash allowance would be extremely limited, sufficient for only the barest of necessities (which, for the most part, already would be supplied on campus). There would be counselors available to assist with interviews and appropriately sponsored job training. Travel to and from such locations would be arranged by the counselor social workers using vouchers instead of cash.

48   This system would be managed by appropriate community boards. Its members—all volunteers—would be drawn from the community, industry, local government, clergy, and the judiciary. The government would pay 50 percent of the cost, the balance to be covered by regional utilities and local donations.

It's Time to Bring Back the Draft

What should be done about the military? The first thing to do is forget about the idea of a volunteer army. The United States must reintroduce the draft. The purpose of conscription is two-fold. There is an immediate problem with a generation that has grown up without discipline. The best thing America can do about it is to draft youths aged seventeen to twenty-one for a period of eighteen months to two years. Run them through military training and teach them what they didn't learn in school. The military could be used to handle works projects. After a certain number of months in initial basic training, a schedule could be set up allocating perhaps two days a week for military training, four days for production, and one day off.

The military also could be used for policing. If an area is out of control, like Los Angeles during the Rodney King riots, call in the Army. In New York, for example, the police don't have the numbers to cope with street crime. Hire the military. Have a soldier on every corner twenty-four hours a day. See how anxious street thugs are to mug someone when they see an armed soldier standing on the corner.

Congress has passed numerous law enforcement bills, many calling for more prisons, which already are draining too much revenue. Obviously, there is a great need to put away people who are dangerous to society. The numbers being seen now, though, in terms of percentage of the general population in prison, is very high, and they are costing society a fortune.

52   America's criminal justice system has several significant flaws. It fails to convey the impression that justice is done, that it is swift, and that it acts as a deterrent to potential perpetrators. Speed is essential to an effective system of justice. "Delay defeats equity" is a long-held maxim of law. It also is vital to remember the victim. At present, virtually no effort is made to compensate the victim. Adoption of the following will improve the situation:

- Abolish the jury system. It is time-consuming, expensive, allows for clever manipulation of jurors by attorneys, and suggests that, having heard and understood the evidence, judges are incapable of rendering a fair verdict.

- Establish a court of petty/small crimes that can deal swiftly with many of the lesser cases in a manner similar to small claims court.

- Require mandatory sentencing for violent crimes without parole.

- Institute capital punishment for all deliberate murders. A death sentence should be subject to immediate priority appeals and then followed right away by execution. Keeping inmates on death row for years is immoral, cruel, and wasteful.

- Enact caning or birching for thieves. Besides being a just punishment, it will avoid clogging up the prison system.

- Make prison labor tougher. Prisoners should be made to work long and hard as part of their sentence. The soft and easy jobs presently offered do not make jail a place to avoid at any cost. The proceeds from this labor should pay for prisoner upkeep, and the balance should be turned over to crime victims as partial compensation.

- Community service sentences need to be stricter. Whenever criminals today are sentenced to community service, it usually means some cushy job with the Red Cross or similar agency. Let community service provide meaningful work for a city or state agency, such as sanitation, road repair, graffiti scrubbing, etc. Any wages earned would help compensate victims.

- Lower the age for adult crime. Anyone fourteen years old and up should be treated as an adult. Children below that age should be limited to a flogging (under appropriate medical supervision).

America needs a better way to educate the nation's youth; a revamped military system; vastly altered social services; a slimmed down, more efficient bureaucracy; a stronger, more caring family unit; and a revitalized economy with no income taxes that nevertheless generates enough revenue to erase the deficit almost overnight. Will any of it happen, and, if it did, would society's ills be cured? If America is to be saved, we must try.

Personal Response

What is your response to Barrett and Rowe's assertion in their first paragraph that "American youth is poisoned with skewed values and a lack of respect"?

Questions for Class or Small-Group Discussion

1. Discuss the authors' contention that America's abandonment of decency and discipline and its adoption of liberalism have led to an "institutionalized selfishness" (paragraph 2). Do you think their examples in the opening section are ample evidence of "skewed values and a lack of respect"? Do you agree that Americans are, in general, a selfish people? How do Barrett and Rowe connect this allegation with the gun-control issue?

2. Summarize the complaints Barrett and Rowe lodge against American society. Which ones do you support? Which ones do you question? Explain your answers.

3. What do you think of the solution Barrett and Rowe propose for the drug problem in America? Do you favor legalization of drugs? If so, would you legalize all or just some drugs? Explore the pros and cons of this issue.

4. Do you agree with Barrett and Rowe that "there has to be a total revolution in this country in attitudes and outlook" (paragraph 30)? Explain why or why not. Do you agree with the changes they call for, or would you suggest others?

5. How do you feel about Barrett and Rowe's proposal that America bring back the draft and the uses to which they propose putting the military?

6. What do you think of the solutions Barrett and Rowe propose for the high crime rate in this country? Which would you favor? Do any seem extreme to you?

MAINTAINING THE CRIME SUPPLY

Barbara Ehrenreich

Barbara Ehrenreich's articles appear in a variety of popular magazines and newspapers, including Time *magazine,* Ms. *magazine, and the* New York Times, *among many others. Her books include* Witches, Midwives, and Nurses: A History of Women Healers *(with Deirdre English) (1973),* Hearts of Men: American Dreams and the Flight from Commitment *(1984),* For Her Own Good: 150 Years of the Experts' Advice to Women *(with Deirdre English) (1989),* Blood Rites: Origins and History of the Passions

of War (1997), Fear of Falling: The Inner Life of the Middle
Class *(2000), and* Nickel and Dimed: Or, (Not) Getting by in
America *(2001).This essay is included in the 1995 collection of her
essays and columns,* The Snarling Citizen.

It's impossible to address the problem of crime without beginning to worry about the law of supply and demand. Not that many people go around breaking that particular law, but you can be sure we'd get them if they did. Thanks to tough new legislation, we will soon have the most massive and splendid Punishment Industry on earth today: shiny new prisons for every state, harsh new sentences for every infringement, lethal injections more readily available than measles vaccine! Already the United States has a larger proportion of its population locked up than any other nation, South Africa included, so the only worry is—what if we run out of crime?

If punishment actually worked, a crime shortage would develop in no time at all. Would-be criminals would study the available sentences, do a careful cost-benefit analysis, and conclude that armed robbery or, say, aggravated assault just wasn't their cup of tea. Yes, if deterrence worked, as our leaders seem to think it does, we would soon have a vast oversupply of electric chairs and unattractive, heavily walled, rural real estate.

And if crime frightens you, try to imagine a world without crime. It would be unthinkable: Nothing on TV except *Sesame Street* and *Jeopardy* reruns. Chuck Norris reduced to panhandling. No execution tailgate parties, no Court Channel or *NYPD Blue.* Because—let us be honest about it—crime is our favorite entertainment spectacle, crime and punishment, that is. Think how many happy hours the average family spends watching the bad guys get perforated by bullets or menaced by Nazi-biker fiends in the pen.

4   This is nothing to be ashamed of. Historically, people have long demanded the pleasure of seeing others punished, and usually in live, nonfiction form. Executions were public as a matter of course, providing a festive occasion for the masses. Participatory punishment, in the form of lynchings and stonings, offered the average citizen a vivid, hands-on experience. In fact, historically speaking, the problem has been not to "stop crime" but to keep the local Punishment Industry supplied with victims. When the Romans ran out of criminals to feed to the lions, they scoured the world for edible prisoners of war. The Athenians used to designate some poor vagrant every year, drive him out of town, and subject him to a ritual stoning-to-death.

We think of ourselves as far more enlightened because our victims must be genuine criminals as certified by a court of law. The only exception is in the case of death-row inmates who turn out, at the very last moment, not to be guilty at all. In some cases the courts have ruled that they should fry anyway—because the facilities are ready and waiting and everyone is in the mood.

Other than that, we are restricted to criminals, as the word is generally defined, and the supply is by no means unlimited. One line of criminological reasoning, which might be called the "liberal" theory, holds that there is nothing wrong with our present approach to maintaining the crime supply. Just take a quarter of the child population, raise them in desperate poverty (with racial discrimination thrown in where applicable), and subject them to commercials, night and day, advising that life without $100 footwear is not worth living. As an added measure, make sure none of the available jobs pay more than about $5 an hour, and presto—little muggers are born, and in numbers sufficient to stock the Punishment Industry for years to come!

Conservatives naturally question the liberal theory. They point to the occasional person who grows up poor and virtuous, or, alternatively, affluent and twisted. Deprivation and temptation are not enough, they say—a good supply of crime requires technology too. Hence the Republicans' understandable reluctance to get behind gun control. Why make it even marginally more difficult for a teenager to get his hands on a gun just as we are about to beef up the Punishment Industry with new legislation? As even the National Rifle Association is too modest to point out, there is no way we would lead the world in the business of crime and punishment if it were not for our wide-open supply of guns.

8   The other tried-and-true approach is to simply broaden the definition of crime. This is the function of drug prohibition. A few decades ago, a person who smoked marijuana was a degenerate rake or a dashing bohemian, depending on your point of view. Now he or she is a criminal, qualifying for years in the slammer. Some states have gone further, making possession of rolling papers an equally dastardly crime. Similarly the "crime" of graffiti writing could be broadened to include possession of a Magic Marker, or crossing state lines with intent to buy one. The possibilities are endless once you realize that there is no crime, no matter how seemingly minor, that cannot be federalized, subjected to mandatory minimum sentencing, or transformed into a capital offense.

But a growing number of experts, including many criminal judges, assure us that there is nothing to worry about. No matter how fiercely Draconian it becomes, the Punishment Industry will never diminish the supply of crime. On the contrary, there is evidence that a few years in the pen serves to season a criminal and make him more productive at his work. So as long as we do nothing to disturb the marvelous synergy of poverty and temptation, guns on the street and gun-fun on the tube, the supply of crime will never fall below the widespread demand for punishment.

Or we could decide, all of us law-abiding citizens, to cut off crime at the source, where poverty intersects with weaponry, and to satisfy the public appetite for cruelty with something other than the Punishment Industry. Bearbaiting has been proposed; also cockfighting and the public torment of stray dogs.

Personal Response

Do you believe that Americans are as fascinated by crime and punishment as Ehrenreich implies in paragraph 3, where she says that "crime is our favorite entertainment spectacle"? Can you imagine, as she suggests, a television or film world without crime? Do you personally enjoy movies and television programs about crime and punishment?

Questions for Class or Small-Group Discussion

1. What does Ehrenreich mean by "the law of supply and demand" (paragraph 1)? What do *Draconian* and *synergy* (paragraph 9) mean?

2. Analyze Ehrenreich's writing strategy by discussing her use of irony. Consider how you know—or at what point you realize—that she means the opposite of what she says. How well do you think her use of common terms from economics works to further her ironic intent? What position is Ehrenreich really arguing?

3. Summarize the ideas that Ehrenreich mockingly describes as "liberal" and "conservative" theories of crime production. Would you place her in the "liberal" or the "conservative" camp? What position, for instance, would you take on gun control? What does she imply are the real root causes of crime in America?

4. Why do you think Ehrenreich encloses *crime* in quotation marks when referring to graffiti writing in paragraph 8? What position do you infer from that paragraph on decriminalizing marijuana use?

PERSPECTIVES ON CRIMINAL BEHAVIOR

Suggestions for Synthesis

1. Write an essay on any aspect of school shootings covered by at least two of the essays on that subject. Consider, for instance, what the articles by Lou Prato and Gary Kleck say about the effects of news media in reporting school violence or what William S. Pollack and Gary Kleck say about adolescent boys and violence.

2. Conduct a classroom forum on the problem of inner-city violence. In preparation, decide what aspects of the problem you want to address in the forum and from which perspectives you will examine the problem. Consider including the perspectives of law enforcement officers, sociologists, behavioral scientists, educators, and social workers. For a writing assignment, examine one aspect of the problem of inner-city violence and offer solutions for it, taking into consideration two or more of the essays in this chapter.

3. Compare Barbara Ehrenreich's views on America's criminal justice system in "Maintaining the Crime Supply" with those of Wayne M. Barrett and Bernard Rowe in "What's Wrong with America and Can Anything be Done about It?"

4. Select one specific aspect of the problem of crime and violence in America, as addressed in two or more of the essays in this chapter. Write a paper assessing the seriousness of the problem you choose and offering possible solutions, to the degree that you can identify possible solutions.

Additional Writing Topics

1. Select any of the readings on school shootings and write a critique of or response to it.

2. Argue for or against the legalization of certain drugs, such as marijuana.

3. Argue for or against reinstating the draft in America.

4. Argue for or against stricter gun control laws, taking into consideration what Gary Kleck says about that subject.

5. Drawing on Lou Prato's "How Much Is Too Much?" argue your position on the subject of television coverage of violent incidents such as school shootings.

6. Respond to the allegation by Wayne M. Barrett and Bernard Rowe in "What's Wrong with America?" that American young people are disrespectful and lack values.

7. Select any of the complaints about America that Wayne M. Barrett and Bernard Rowe make in "What's Wrong with America?" and respond by explaining the extent to which you agree with them. For instance, consider any of these statements: "America has institutionalized selfishness" (paragraph 3); "Everywhere there is unbridled freedom bordering on license" (paragraph 6); "[America's] work ethic has suffered" (paragraph 7); "[L]awsuit mania has gripped America" (paragraph 14); America's drug problem "can be traced back to a lack of discipline, lack of education, lack of knowledge between right and wrong" (paragraph 18).

8. In the manner of Barbara Ehrenreich in "Maintaining the Crime Supply," write your own ironic proposal to resolve any of the issues raised in this chapter.

Research Topics

1. In paragraph 3 of "There Are No Lessons to Be Learned from Littleton," Gary Kleck catalogues a list of problems that are often mentioned when looking for something to blame for school shootings. These include the availability and ease of accessing guns, school cliques, lax parental supervision, bullying in schools, lax school security, lack of religion in schools, the Internet, neo-Naziism, and Satanism, among others. Select one of those subjects as a beginning point for research, framing your questions and narrowing your focus as you read and discover more about your subject.

2. Research recent statistics on serious crimes such as armed robbery, rape, murder, and assault with a deadly weapon and argue ways to reduce the rates of these violent crimes in America.

3. Expand any of the writing topics mentioned in the end-of-chapter exercises to include library and Internet research. For instance, any of the following, properly focused, could be subjects of research projects: gun control, legalization of marijuana, social conditions at the root of crime in America, the efficacy of capital punishment or life in prison as deterrents, or calls for reform in the penal system.

CHAPTER 15

GENDER AND SEX ROLES

Many people use the word *gender* interchangeably with the word *sex,* but the two have different meanings. Sex is a biological category; a person's sex—whether male or female—is genetically determined. On the other hand, gender refers to the socially constructed set of expectations for behavior based on one's sex. Masculinity and femininity are gender constructs whose definitions vary and change over time and with different cultures or groups within cultures. What is considered appropriate and even desirable behavior for men and women in one culture may be strongly inappropriate in another. Within American culture, definitions of masculinity and femininity have changed over time, but they continue to be shaped by a number of influences, such as parental expectations, peer pressure, and media images. We are born either male or female, and most of us learn to behave in ways consistent with a specific society's expectations for a particular sex.

First, in "You Can Never Have Too Many," best-selling author Jane Smiley muses on the presence of Barbie dolls in her household as her daughters were growing up. Far from criticizing them for setting up an impossible model of femininity for impressionable young girls, Smiley sees Barbie dolls as aids to helping girls figure out who they are and what they want to be. "Barbies are all right with me," she says.

Next, Joan DeGuire North, in "Strangers in a Strange Land: Women in Higher Education Administration," identifies what she sees as four differences between the ways that women and men conduct themselves in meetings. She believes these differences have real effects on the level of success that men and women achieve as leaders and administrators. As a longtime administrator herself, North draws on years of her own observations, but she also bases her conclusions on extensive reading of the literature on this topic.

Continuing the theme of gender differences, Ana Veciana-Suarez writes in "Thank Heaven for Little Boys" from a perspective different from those of North and another author in this chapter, Lois Gould. Those authors discuss the disadvantages for females of certain feminine behavioral traits, whereas Veciana-Suarez argues that males suffer unfair treatment. The time has come, she argues, to stop seeing males as fatally awed and to recognize the value of masculine traits.

Finally, Lois Gould creates her own modern fairy tale in "X: A Fabulous Child's Story," which plays on many of the traditional sex-role expectations about appropriate behavior for boys and girls. Her story about what happens when one set of parents refuses to reveal the sex of their child delightfully highlights the wide acceptance of very clear assumptions about what a child can or cannot do in terms of behavior, dress, talent, and potential solely on the basis of the child's sex. Before you read Gould's essay, jot down a list of characteristics you associate with males and do the same for females. Try to recall your early childhood, the toys you played with, the games you played, and your playmates. Then see how many of the sex-role stereotypes that Gould identifies in her fantasy are true to your own experiences.

YOU CAN NEVER HAVE TOO MANY

Jane Smiley

Jane Smiley is the author of many novels, including The Greenlanders *(1988),* A Thousand Acres *(1991),* Moo *(1995),* The All-True Travels and Adventures of Lidie Newton *(1998), and* Horse Heaven *(2000). This essay was first published in a collection of essays entitled* The Barbie Chronicles, *edited by Yona Zeldis McDonough (1999).*

For my daughter's sixteenth birthday, my six-year-old son wanted to give her a Barbie. I greatly guided him toward the Rapunzel Barbie, whose hair was so long that her head was cocked backward on her neck, or the Birthday Wishes Barbie, in a massive organdy skirt. The one he finally chose was Baywatch Barbie. Okay, she had a dolphin with her. I am willing to admit that that might have been the draw. But you know, Barbies are all right with me. I may have had more Barbies pass through my house than anyone. I like to think so.

I was slightly too old for Barbie myself when they first came out in 1959—I was more of a stuffed-animal girl, anyway—so my first real Barbie experience came when my now–twenty-year-old daughter was three. My First Barbie came home, and was disrobed. The clothes were lost. I spent the required amount of time deploring Barbie's proportions and coloring and the fact that her feet can wear only high heels. Barbie could not have been shaped more differently from me, or have a more different *weltanschauung* from mine, but, hey, here she came with all her stuff.

The one I still remember most fondly was Twirly Curls Barbie. Like Rapunzel Barbie, Twirly Curls Barbie had a serious neck problem because of the weight of her hair. But she came with an intriguing pink-and-cream machine that attached to the ends of a couple of hanks of hair and twisted them together in a chignon. The catch was that the hair had to be neatly combed for the machine to work, an impossible task for a four-year-old, so I spent a lot of time combing the doll until I gave up. My daughters were not in the habit of shaving their Barbies' heads, but they could have. It's a good idea.

4   Both my girls went through periods where they would wear only pink and purple. I chalk this up to the Barbie influence. Both of them learned how to put on makeup before kindergarten. Lucy could apply lipstick with her eyes closed by the time she was five.

I don't wear makeup. Nor do I have any gowns, bikinis, pink high heels, floral accessories or feminine furniture (like a dressing table or a pink chaise longue). There are no blonds in my family. I could never wear short shorts or feather boas or halter tops. In other words, if my daughters were to learn certain Hollywood-inspired essentials of American womanhood, it wasn't going to be from me, but from Barbie.

And so the Barbies came through the house in a flood. And I am here to tell you that Doctor Barbie was not one of them. Frilly, sexy, pink, purple, bedizened and bejeweled were the preferred Barbies at my house, the more rhinestones the better. We had dozens, because, frankly, Barbies are cheap in more ways than one. My daughters had three mothers: me; their stepmother, who was not unlike me stylistically; and Barbie.

A friend of mine (male) maintains that Barbies have such staying power because they are the only anatomically adult dolls available, and children can manipulate and control them as they cannot the other adults in their lives. But I think girls like Barbie because through her they can try on a no-holds-barred, all-stops-out model of femininity, and that is something they need to do, especially if their own mothers are more androgynous-looking and sober-dressing than Barbie can be. The more a girl is drawn to Barbie, the less she should be deprived of her, no matter what the child's mother's own values are. Longing is more likely to breed attachment than satisfaction is.

8   Finally, after seventeen years, the Barbies in my house went the way of all flesh. In their last year with us, they were subject to any number of tragic narratives, at least partly inspired by that disguised Barbie literature, *Sweet Valley High*. I discovered the older girls showing the younger girls how to bandage the Barbies with toilet paper (gruesomely decorated with red nail polish) when they happened to get into alcohol-related car crashes with Ken.

My older daughter wandered in the land of Barbie for many years—after all, Nancy Drew is a Barbie; Elizabeth and Jessica, the *Sweet Valley High* twins, are Barbies; Cinderella, Sleeping Beauty, and Beauty of *Beauty and the Beast* all are Barbies. The prettiest girl in school, always a blond, or so it seems, is a Barbie, too. All the blonds on TV and in the movies are Barbies. A girl has to have a Barbie doll in order to decide whether she herself wants to be a Barbie.

On one hand, she has the ever-present mom, who is wearing jeans, cutting her hair ever shorter, getting glasses at forty if not sooner, driving a dark-colored sedan, going to work or cleaning the house, or, worse, espousing all kinds of selfless values of hard work, charity, civic virtue, environmental responsibility.

On the other hand, she has the ever-present Barbie, a tireless consumer whose favorite color is pink, whose jeans are much harder to get on her than her ballet tutu, whose hair requires constant care, and who has more high heels than any First Lady of the Philippines who ever lived. Barbie represents, in every way, getting what you want when you want it, no matter who objects.

12   Just after she stopped reading *Sweet Valley High* and passed her Barbies down to her younger sister, my older daughter changed her views on her future. No longer did she plan to be a fashion consultant or a Hollywood movie star. No longer did beauty school attract her. She began to read authors like Sandra Cisneros and books like *Our Bodies, Ourselves*. She began her collection of all the works of U2, a band Barbie would never understand. She became socially conscious. She got to be the editor of her high-school newspaper, not because it was a status position, but because she had views she wanted to air on homophobia, the environment and women's rights.

Now she is planning to go to graduate school and law school and become an expert on women's health issues, perhaps adolescent health issues like anorexia and bulimia. She can go on for hours about women's problems with appearance and self-image. Barbie should be proud. My daughter wouldn't have gotten here without her.

Have we ever known a Barbie who, in the end, was cherished? I don't think so. More than all the other dolls in the toy box, perhaps because she isn't cuddly or sweet, Barbie is meant to be fiddled with, thought about, manipulated, done to. All of this aids in a girl's making up her mind about who she is and what she wants. That Barbie is a genius.

Personal Response

What is your opinion of Barbie dolls?

Questions for Class or Small-Group Discussion

1. Explain what Smiley seems to be referring to when she writes: "I spent the required amount of time deploring Barbie's proportions and coloring and the fact that her feet can wear only high heels" (paragraph 2).

2. Respond to this statement: "The more a girl is drawn to Barbie the less she should be deprived of her, no matter what the child's mother's own values are" (paragraph 7).

3. Discuss your understanding of this statement: "A girl has to have a Barbie doll in order to decide whether she herself wants to be a Barbie" (paragraph 9). To what extent do you agree with Smiley?

STRANGERS IN A STRANGE LAND: WOMEN IN HIGHER EDUCATION ADMINISTRATION

Joan DeGuire North

Joan DeGuire North is Dean of the College of Professional Studies at the University of Wisconsin—Stevens Point. She has served in administrative positions at the University of Alabama and at several private colleges. She consults and writes on a variety of topics, including management styles, group decisions, stress management, faculty vitality, and wellness. This article was first published in the summer 1991 issue of Initiatives, *a publication of the National Association for Women in Education, and revised in 2001.*

My mother died in September 1990, only a few years after her retirement from a professional position which caused her considerable stress over the years. The grieving process has provided me with opportunities to consider my mother's situation and fueled my own confusion about difficulties many women seem to have in higher education management. It is with this background that I began this research, not as a scholar, but as a practitioner, a woman administrator trying to understand what is the truth about women's styles in administration.

Until recently, I would not have spoken about many of these things. In twenty-plus years of administrative roles at state universities and private colleges, I seldom thought about my gender as a factor in my job performance. Like some other women in visible, leadership positions (Bell, 1991), I did not want others to think of me as a woman or a WOMAN administrator, so I tried to keep gender out of my frames of reference. Only when faced with overwhelming evidence of being treated differently than the men who surrounded me did I deal, briefly, with the notion that I was different in gender-related ways from my male colleagues.

For most of my career, women have argued against the proposition that women are different; we wanted equal treatment and guaranteed our employers equal behavior. And our scholars backed us up: "The desire to affirm that women are equal has made some scholars reluctant to show they are different, because differences can be used to justify unequal treatment and opportunity" (Tannen, 1990, p. 17).

4   In recent years greater emphasis seems to have been given by writers and researchers to the notion that women may indeed be different from men in a number of ways, including how they lead and manage. This shift comes in part because of the emerging notion that "pretending that women and men are the same hurts women, because the ways they are treated are based on the norms for men" (Tannen, 1990, p. 16). Or, as another writer described male-oriented management cultures: "For the majority of women, it is still an alien culture where enormous trade-offs are required to achieve even moderate success" (Loden, 1985, p. 70).

And so, thanks to my mother and to my getting old enough to be bold, I decided to focus on my perceptions of how differences between men and women might affect women's success and satisfaction in higher education administration or other corporate structures. Admittedly, there is no absolute canon which describes and predicts the behavior and motivation of men or women. But the number of studies in a variety of settings attempting to understand the age-old questions about how men and women differ continues to grow. And while it is almost impossible not to appear to overgeneralize when one discusses such broad categories, many of the studies I identify acknowledge, as I do, that there is great variability among women and among men and that there are men with considerable "female" characteristics and vice versa. Despite all these caveats, there remains a notion that there are things inherently different about being a woman rather than a man and that some of these differences spill over into the workplace.

Some Differences

How do men and women operate in organizations? Do they approach their jobs differently, as some writers are suggesting (Hegelsen, 1990; Statham, 1987)? My observation is that they do, and that the differences may not work favorably for some women in our current organizations. The behaviors exhibited by some men and women in meetings support my contention.

Effectiveness in leading and participating in meetings is an essential skill in organizations, whether they operate with old-line bureaucratic rules or some new version of modern management. Meetings can serve as a microcosm within which to study differences between male and female leadership. I would like to suggest four dynamics that may affect differentially the "success" of women and men in meetings—success meaning the extent to which one is able to persuade others to certain points of view or to get support for actions one advances.

8   The first concerns group norms about what constitutes fair talking time, listening practices, and certain meeting behaviors. The second explores gender differences in language patterns. The third focuses on two different ways of approaching decisions, based on a feeling versus a thinking orientation. The fourth explores two different approaches to the group tasks: from an inductive or deductive modality.

Talking, Listening, and Meeting Behaviors.   In seeking to discover if there is a unique female "voice" in conversations, the linguistic researcher Dale Spender concluded that women consistently speak less frequently than men and listen more. After tape-recording conversations between men and women in different settings, Spender remarked:

> After weeks—indeed months—of making tapes and listening to them with the aim of identifying the characteristics of women's speech and the differences in the speech of men, I began to suspect that as a linguistic researcher, I was a distinct failure. Although I had hours of tapes of conversations between women and men it did not seem to me that I had enough data from women to draw any

conclusions. . . . I almost despaired of ever being able to record sufficient sustained speech to identify any possible features specific to women. Of course it took some time for me to appreciate that the salient characteristic of women's talk in conversation with men was *silence* (1989, p. 8).

Her basic premise is that over the years, women have been expected to be more quiet than men. She goes on to show that in general, women are allowed about one-third of the air time in conversations with men; any amount beyond that is perceived by both the men and the women as domineering.

She reports an experiment with a group of academic feminists who were quite certain that the one-third/two-thirds rule would not characterize their conversations with males. The tape recorder found otherwise: "Fourteen feminists who believed that they had a fair share of the conversation spoke between 8 percent and 38 percent of the time" (p. 9). Spender reacts:

> In my own case I have found it difficult—and impossible—to discover what happens if women aim, not for what feels like a *fair* share, but for *half* the conversation time. Difficult because a woman has to break every rule in the polite conversation book if she tries to talk for half the time: It *feels* unfair, rude, and objectionably overbearing. For me it has also been impossible to talk for 50 percent of the time because no man has stayed "conversing" with me for the mandatory three minutes—the time I set for the minimal unit of interaction. The highest score I have ever attained (in conversation with a male colleague) was 44 percent and this was accompanied by angry assertions on his part that I was being "impossible," "unreasonable," that I "didn't listen to a word that was being said." At the time—before the tape had been analyzed—I felt he was probably right (p. 10).

12   Let's consider this prospect. Imagine that you are a female dean among several other deans, all male. Imagine that the topic for the deans' meeting is the distribution of $129,000 worth of lab modernization funds coming to your campus. Imagine that each of you has a turn to speak on behalf of your own labs and then there is a general discussion during which the group attempts to come to conclusions about that $129,000. If each man present talks his share of two-thirds of the time and if the lone female in attendance talks her share of one-third of the time, whose labs do you think will get funded?

Spender does acknowledge that some contexts do permit women to speak 50 percent or more of the time, contexts in which women are the authority figures, such as classroom teachers. She speculates: "No doubt a comparable pattern would also emerge were tapes to be made of Mrs. Thatcher addressing her all-male cabinet. And what this implies is that it is not the sex, but the power and authority which determines the right to talk: It is interesting that so many men still possess such power and authority vis-à-vis women" (p. 10). Spender also notes that she analyzed no ethnically mixed conversations, so she can't speculate about talk among black or white women and black men.

Let's take another look at these dynamics. One of the reasons that women speak less is that they are listening more. So not only are women in meetings speaking less often than their male counterparts, but even when they do talk, they will be speaking to a group who are not listening as intently as women generally do.

Perhaps this contrast between speaking and listening is better understood by looking at the research about the early development of boys and girls. McClelland (1975) tells us that boys and girls differ in early aggressiveness behavior through some combination of hormones and cultural upbringing. Boys typically display aggressive behaviors—shoving, taunting, and so forth—as a way to identify their presence and identity. Unsure about whether or not they are heard, they seem to be speaking to the world loudly, making sure they make their mark: I am here! I'm a Boy! Pay attention to me! I talk, I act, therefore I am (McClelland, 1975, p. 84).

16   Girls on the other hand seem to "pay more attention to what goes on around them and modify their behavior accordingly. They are more about relationships. They are more interdependent" (McClelland, 1975, p. 84). They don't have to shout to make themselves known; they know others are listening. They attend to the weaving of relationships with others and practice their interpersonal skills. Sensitive to others, they learn to develop a good antenna for sensing things in others and in the environment. They hone their listening skills.

We should not be surprised that researchers are finding that when women do get the opportunity to speak, they spend part of their time acknowledging those who have preceded them:

> A number of studies have documented that in verbal discourse, women are more likely than men to express courtesy, gratitude, respect, and appreciation . . . through echoing, summarizing, polite speech, and nonantagonistic responses (Shakeshaft, 1989, p. 181).

From an organizational viewpoint, it is also important to note that the "talker" is perceived as more important than the "listener":

> The act of giving information by definition frames one in a position of higher status, while the act of listening frames one as lower. Children instinctively sense this—as do most men. But when women listen to men, they are not thinking in terms of status. Unfortunately, their attempts to reinforce connections and establish rapport, when interpreted through the [men's] lens of status, can be misinterpreted as casting them in a subordinate position (Tannen, 1990, p. 139).

Let's review this scenario. Not only is the female dean advocating her point of view a third less often than the males, but she is devoting part of her air time to dovetailing with the other points of view. And all along, the men are listening to her one-third less time and likely believing that their views are dominating, since the woman is so "quiet."

20   So what's a woman to do? In my experience, what some of us do is monitor the flow of conversation in meetings and attempt to make our points more frequently. I remember in my early years in administration literally forcing myself to speak up at least twice during meetings. Sensing the importance of adequate air time to the achievement of results, some of us try to be just as verbal as our male counterparts. But, both the literature and my experience suggest that this approach has its

difficulties. The more verbal woman in the meeting may be perceived as overbearing and pushy, because cultural norms do not prepare us for women speaking their fair share of the time (Sandler, 1986; Carli, 1990; Spender, 1989). Again, speaking personally, I believe that these scenarios describe choices many women administrators must consciously make every day, even every meeting: Shall I risk the possibility of my views being overlooked or shall I risk the possibility of being viewed as domineering?

Other meeting-related behaviors may also affect communication patterns. Have you ever noticed, for instance, that women frequently sit together, seldom at the power positions at the end of tables? I have begun to diagram seating patterns in large meetings I attend. I discovered that women cluster together even though there are usually so few that they could be easily dispersed among the men. Spatial arrangements influence relationships, perceptions of affiliations, and deference (Filley, 1975). People who sit together are perceived to be friendly with one another and to have similar viewpoints. Women who habitually sit with other women may be perceived to be separating themselves from the other members of the team and not affiliating with the male members. Such behavior makes it easier for the men to see the women as "other" and as a potential threat to their interests.

Another set of meeting-related behaviors suggests greater or lesser ownership of the meeting. Men seem freer to stand up and move around, make more extraneous sounds and jokes than women do. Women seem to stay in their place more and stick to the serious agenda, seldom initiating kidding or joking, perhaps fearful of starting a round of off-color joking. I have also noticed that junior people and women carry more papers and background materials into meetings, which visually suggests that they are not as confident in their first-hand grasp of the issues. And the women appear to take more notes on the meeting, again reinforcing the notion that they need help with the details. Unfortunately, this does not go unnoticed; women are often asked to take meeting minutes.

Language Patterns.   The notion that men and women speak different languages has been at the heart of many jokes and stories about the frustrations of marriage and relationships. Tannen (1990) highlights some of these misunderstandings between men and women, pointing out that conversation is a way males establish their status in the group and preserve their independence. Females, on the other hand, use conversation for establishing relationships. Tannen suggests that males use information to maintain a "one-up" position, withholding enough information so that others still have to rely on them.

24   Similarly, men view giving advice as a special role for the superior one, a belief that may explain situations in which the male does not seem to listen but jumps at the opportunity to suggest solutions. This behavior may well make women feel they have not been heard and, further, that they are kept in an inferior position when they did not actually ask for advice.

Although Tannen's approach concentrates on the personal side of male–female relationships, women in professional meetings with men may also find themselves at a disadvantage because they are unaware of the subtle motivation behind male language. It's hard to compete in the "one-up" game if you don't know you are playing. And the males who are playing clearly win and operate as though the females are subordinate.

This scenario becomes even worse in situations wherein the female is in a position to ask a male to accomplish some task. Tannen points out that in the framework of competitive conversation the man may think he is being told what to do and interpret this as a subordination of his role, while the woman may regard it as just a request of a colleague to accomplish a goal. Trouble brews.

Other gender differences in language patterns might also influence women's success in meetings. The Lakoff study (1975) identified several patterns of women's language which suggest hesitancy and lack of forcefulness: tag questions ("I think we ought to evaluate all majors, don't you?"); rising intonation at the end of statements ("When will your report be finished? Early next week?"); hedges, such as "kinda," "I guess," "I think" (Lakoff, 1975).

28   While one may argue about how widespread these patterns of speech are among today's women this research does suggest that certain deferential speaking patterns associated with women may make them seem less knowledgeable in group decision-making situations. One can speculate that the debate over the lab modernization funds is unlikely to be won by anyone who seems so unsure about her position. To further complicate this issue, recent research involving college students suggests that although both men and women listeners view women who use tentative speech as less knowledgeable and competent, the male listeners reported being more influenced by females with tentative speech than with assertive speech, because they were less threatened (Carli, 1990).

And what happens if women try to talk more like the men? Tannen notes: "Apart from the repugnance of women having to do all the changing, this doesn't work either, because women who talk like men are judged differently—and harshly" (p. 18).

Marshall (1987) summarizes the "clashing of two cultures" in language patterns of men and women:

> Men and women have different styles and fail to appreciate the other's style because of differences in links, topic shifts, self-disclosure, aggressiveness, interruption, and listening (Coates, 1986). Women typically link their talk with what the previous speaker said; men are more likely to ignore it. In women's talk, self-disclosure is an opportunity for sharing experience; for men, self-disclosure is viewed as a request for advice. Women avoid verbal aggressiveness and view it as unpleasant interruption; for men, loud and aggressive argument is expected ritual display. When women interrupt, it is often with encouraging comment and active listening prods; men's interruptions are seen as attempts to seize a turn, and may ultimately silence the speaker. Women encourage others to speak; men compete for the role of speaker. . . . [T]hese fundamental differences lead to miscommunication between men and women, resentment by women toward men, and men's denigration of women's ability to compete and speak up (p. 10).

To return to our hypothetical deans' meeting, one might expect that misunderstanding between the female dean's message and the men's understanding of her message could easily occur. Multiply this situation by all the meetings and negotiations which take place by all the years a woman works in administration and one can begin to speculate about a kind of quiet desperation which I believe can characterize some women in higher education administration, women who may secretly think that it's their fault that they are not more influential.

32   **Feeling or Thinking Interpretations.**   One of the most widely used measures of differences in personality, the Myers-Briggs Type Indicator, consistently shows only one gender-related difference in personality orientation: the feeling versus thinking patterns:

> More men than women (six out of ten) report that they prefer to make decisions on the basis of principles, that is, logically and objectively. Thus more men prefer the thinking and more women feeling. . . . The T–F dimension is the only pair of preferences which shows a sex trend and is distributed equally in the general population (Keirsey & Bates, 1978, p. 20).

While the proportion is not overwhelming and there is no evidence that the feeling or thinking approach makes better meetings, it is nonetheless worth noting that in hypothetical meetings, 60 percent of the women would be approaching decisions from a point of view very different from that of 60 percent of the men.

These women will be more likely to argue from passion, favor situational solutions, and use feelings in their discourse. The men in the thinking mode will be more likely to argue from logic and precedent, favor laws and fairness, and attempt to preserve objectivity. Let's go over that again: argue from passion versus argue from logic, favor situational solutions versus favor laws and fairness, use feelings in discourse versus use objectivity.

Sound like a fair fight? Perhaps in theory, but in practice, this discussion occurs within a "masculine wilderness" (Sanford, 1980) which is heavily dominated by the masculine in organizational practices. Our male-dominant society has defined active use of feelings in management as taboo (Miller, 1986). From the beginning, in accord with the early principles of scientific management, our organizations have been characterized by hierarchies, rules, regulations, high standards of fairness, attempts at clarity, handbooks, grievance systems, administrative roles and structures, and Robert's Rules of Order. Clearly, the thinking and rational approach dominates. And the stranger in a strange land, more often the woman, learns the new language or risks failure. For the women and the 40 percent of men who are "feeling," is this a little like conducting business in an alien tongue?

36   The feeling–thinking dimension also presents other opportunities for misunderstanding or failure in group and interpersonal settings. In every administrator's life, there are times when people argue against one's strongly held views, when actions one deeply desires do not occur, when the budget gets cut, when one is surrounded by coldness and callousness, when one's faculty and colleagues appear to deeply misunderstand. Those administrators with less dominant feeling orientation—mostly men—may be better equipped to handle such disappointments. They are still an arm's length away; they can be viewed as illogical, disappointing, a loss, fodder for a

new fight. But for those whose feeling orientation dominates, these disappointments are felt, not simply acknowledged.

For the feeler, such events can seem like personal failures that suggest the shattering of a relationship ("How could he do that to me?") or signal a sense of personal inadequacy ("I'm just no good at this; someone else should be dean"). For the thinking person, failure is losing a rook; for the feeling person, it is checkmate. The thinking person can bounce back on subsequent issues and continue to work well with those associated with the bad news. The feeling person may take some time to return to a sense of optimism about dealing with new challenges and may find difficulty working with people associated with the defeat.

I find it strangely ironic that women (and men for whom the feeling orientation is dominant) may actually be perceived as getting along less well with others than do those with the thinking orientation. Aren't we the ones who supposedly value relationships above all? Yes and no. Males with a thinking orientation seem to value maintaining a large number of smooth, though not especially intimate, relationships as a means to an end—filling out a football team, getting a good evaluation. Women seem to prefer maintaining a smaller number of close, intimate relationships that do not necessarily serve any further purpose. As Hennig and Jardim (1977) put it: "Boys learn how to put up with each other, to tolerate each other, and to use each other to a degree that girls hardly ever find necessary" (p. 52).

With their tendency toward more easily accessible feelings, women may be less able to subordinate those feelings just to get along with others. Dr. Elizabeth Corday and Dr. Mark Green, characters on the popular TV program *ER,* are good examples. She acts with passion, from her true feelings; we know when she is angry with others. Dr. Green attempts to maintain outwardly smooth, though distant, relationships with everyone. As Hennig and Jardim point out:

> Relationships for women tend to be ends in themselves.... As a result, and without even knowing it, women tend to fall into the great trap of overemotionalism: intolerance—"I don't like him or her and I can't work with either of them"—or a painful vulnerability to criticism (1977, p. 53).

40   The feeling person has much to offer a group but may be at a disadvantage in meetings and interpersonal situations of thinking-oriented organizations. The feeling person may be more comfortable approaching issues from different viewpoints and values than the majority thinkers, but those differences may not be understood or accepted by the majority. And so these feelers may have less success winning arguments or persuading the group. They may feel failure more painfully and may be less than fully enthusiastic group members for a time after a loss, and less able or willing to maintain smooth and friendly relationships with all group members. And yet, I have also heard criticism of women administrators who operate from a logical, thinking style that they should be more nurturing, more "female."

Inductive or Deductive World View.   On an old television program *Thirtysomething,* when Ellen asked Gary for his impressions about a guy she was going to date, he replied matter of factly, "Women form impressions; men shake hands." Gary put his finger on another characteristic of what I associate with women's world view.

I would like to suggest that preferences between two ways of finding meaning—deductively and inductively—may be somewhat gender related. As Toor (1990) notes,

> The masculine way of knowing is logical, methodical, fact oriented. The feminine way of knowing, however, involves plunging headlong into the senses and temporarily releasing the idea of goals and performance (p. 61).

The deductive way, which I associate with the masculine, is the way of goal setting and planning; it defines the outcome and pushes to its reality. The inductive way, which I associate with the feminine, examines the reality, its context and pieces, and then makes meaning of the whole. Clearly, these two approaches can be employed by both men and women, but I suggest that they may tend to break along gender lines.

44   Let's consider for a moment girls' and boys' early experiences which suggest that, on their path toward independence, boys display analytic and manipulative patterns. They push reality; they test taking charge of the pieces. According to McClelland (1975),

> Boys start early assertively moving things about in the environment (trucks, toys, stones, etc.) . . . [becoming better able to] abstract common elements out of changing situations. . . . In short, men spend more time actively inspecting the environment, pulling things apart, taking things out of context, and putting them back together in a new way (pp. 87–88).

Girls on the other hand seem to have a greater grasp for the context, the whole, the gestalt, and they adjust to their environment, suggesting a responsiveness to reality:

> They have a more complex interdependent relationship with the world than men do. They are more "open" to influence, where men are "closed." . . . [Men] show a preference for the simple, the closed, the direct. In contrast, women are more interested in the complex, the open, the less defined. . . . Women are concerned with the context; men are forever trying to ignore it for the sake of something they can abstract from it (pp. 88–89).

I think there are commonalities among the notions of the inductive, the female, eastern, and Type B personality. All are characterized by a certain patience and calm in order to fully understand the environment and forge a productive relationship with it. They are all approaches without pushing, all concentrating more on the flow. Our former chancellor tells of advice he got from a Tennessee fishing guide who, in my terms, captures the inductive approach: "I take what the river gives me. When the water is low, I go to the deep holes; when the water is high I skirt the shores; when there is no bass, I look for trout; when there is no trout, I look for carp; when there is no carp, I look for catfish." The fishing guide knows to watch for reality and then choose it.

The alternative approaches—the deductive, masculine, western, Type A—suggest that we take a stand, make a decision, a plan, or direction; and then we push, motivate, nudge until we have been successful in turning our intentions into reality.

48   What are the implications of this dichotomy for men and women in meetings? The inductive approach further suggests a listening, "tentative," conversational style, that permits the whole picture to become clear—perhaps another reason why women talk less. And, yet, while an inductive woman is methodically putting the whole picture together, others in a meeting may perceive her as slow or indecisive compared to the deductive (men?), who have obvious and strong viewpoints. The inductive may see arguments from a less parochial viewpoint in a group dominated by narrow interests and therefore, lose her advocacy role. Pursuing a more holistic approach may cause women to be "caught between contending interest groups and power centers" (Gender and leadership, 1989, p. 2). But the inductive style can also be quite helpful in meetings where many points of view are conflicting, because the inductive approach is more likely to pull the pieces together into consensus.

The deductive approach suggests beginning with the premise, the rule, or the direction and then filling in the implications or implementations. This approach suggests being prepared before meetings, knowing what principles should govern decisions, wanting discussion to go certain directions, and being willing to lobby beforehand to assure certain outcomes. This is the "can do" approach that can dominate discussion and conclusions but can also get a group moving to speedy finish. If this approach dominates a meeting, there is usually little tolerance for time spent trying to fully involve quieter members or assure that the members "feel good" about the direction or listen to whole new ways of viewing the situation. The approach seems well-suited to a "male" approach to meetings and may be at loggerheads with a different approach brought by many women.

Conclusions

We are hearing from some quarters that a new era in management in the new century will see more women in upper levels of corporations and higher education to handle the challenges of the new millennium (Naisbitt & Aburdene, 1990). Others note that "the recognition of the need for greater balance between the traditional masculine approach to managing and the feminine approach isn't an idea that appeals only to women" (Loden, 1985, p. 76).

I do believe that we could be witnessing a powerful paradigm shift toward identifying the special and unique contributions women can bring to organizations and away from assuming that male and female administrators operate pretty much the same way—the male way (Gordon, 1991; Helgesen, 1990). The *Harvard Business Review* calls this "the second wave of women . . . drawing on the skills and attitudes they developed from their shared experience as women" (Rosener, 1990, p. 119).

52   That sage futurist, Marilyn Ferguson, told us ten years ago that "as women enlarge their influence in policymaking and government, their yin perspective will push out the boundaries of the old yang paradigm" (Ferguson, 1980, p. 226). But I must

admit that I found it none too reassuring that she identified earlier writers who predicted the same, one as early as 1890. We have been waiting a long time.

And while I continue to keep a candle in my window, I fear that the four gender differences I have suggested will work to discourage women from administrative positions. I fear that organizations will not recognize the creative power of combining a female approach with the traditional male ones. I fear that success for women in "foreign" administrative structures will be dearly bought and that some veteran women administrators will in their inevitable mid-life crises choose work alternatives more compatible with their deepest values or, at least, less of a hassle. And think where that would leave us.

Coming at a time when campuses are expanding their notions of the status quo to accommodate cultural diversity, the idea that women may offer alternative approaches to administration and communication may be more easily accepted today than perhaps at any other time in our history. Clearly more research is needed, as well as wider discussions of these topics. My recent experience with these issues suggests that simply knowing about this kind of research helps people—men and women—learn to understand each other, respect each others' styles, and slowly modify opinions and behaviors to accommodate different approaches to getting work done.

References

Bell, C. (1991). If I weren't involved with school, I might be a radical: An analysis of women superintendents' gender consciousness. Paper presented at the Annual Meeting of the American Educational Research Association, Chicago.

Carli, L. (1990). Gender, language, and influence. *Journal of Personality and Social Psychology* 59(5), 941–951.

Coates, J. (1986). *Women, men and language: A sociolinguistic account of sex differences in language.* New York: Longman.

Ferguson, M. (1980). *The Aquarian conspiracy: Personal and social transformation in the 1980s.* Los Angeles: J. P. Tarcher.

Filley, A. C. (1975). *Interpersonal conflict resolution.* Glenview, IL: Scott, Foresman.

Gender and leadership. (1989, February). *Academic Leader* 5(2), 1–2.

Gilligan, C. (1982). *In a different voice.* Cambridge: Harvard.

Gordon, S. (1991). *Prisoners of men's dreams: Striking out for a new feminine future.* Boston: Little, Brown.

Helgesen, S. (1990). *The female advantage: Women's ways of leadership.* New York: Doubleday/Currency.

Hennig, M., & Jardim, A. (1977). *The managerial woman.* New York: Pocket Books.

Keirsey, D., & Bates, M. (1978). *Please understand me.* Del Mar, CA: Prometheus Nemesis Books.

Lakoff, R. (1975). *Language and woman's place.* New York: Harper and Row.

Loden, M. (1985). *Feminine leadership or how to succeed in business without being one of the boys.* New York: Times Books.

Marshall, C. (1987, November). Using sociolinguistics for exploring gender and culture issues in educational administration. Paper presented at the annual meeting of American Educational Research Association Special Interest Group, Research on Women in Education, Portland, OR.

McClelland, D. C. (1975). *Power: The inner experience.* New York: John Wiley and Sons.

Miller, J. B. (1986). *Toward a new psychology of women.* Boston: Beacon Press.

Naisbitt, J., & Aburdene, P. (1990). *Megatrends 2000.* New York: William Morrow.

Rosener, J. (1990). Ways women lead. *Harvard Business Review,* November–December, pp. 119–125.

Sanford, N. (1980). *Learning after college.* Orinda, CA: Montaigne.

Sandler, B. (1986). The campus climate revisited: Chilly for women faculty, administrators, and graduate students. Washington, D.C.: Association of American Colleges.

Shakeshaft, C. (1989). *Women in educational administration.* Newbury Park, CA: Sage Publications.

Spender, D. (1989). *The writing or the sex?* New York: Pergamon.

Statham, A. (1987). The gender model revisited: Differences in the management styles of men and women. *Sex Roles* 16(7/8).

Tannen, D. (1990). *You just don't understand me.* New York: William Morrow.

Toor, D. (1990). *The road by the river.* New York: Harper and Row.

Personal Response

To what extent do your own informal observations of men and women in positions of authority support or refute North's observations?

Questions for Class or Small-Group Discussion

1. Comment on the opening section of the essay. How successful do you consider North's strategy of appealing to personal experience to introduce her topic?

2. North identifies "four dynamics that may affect differentially the 'success' of women and men in meetings" (paragraph 7). Summarize the main points North makes about each of those four areas.

3. North cites references to a great many works by researchers and scholars to support her own generalizations and observations about gender differences. Select quotations or paraphrases from her secondary sources that you find most fruitful for comments or responses in class or small-group discussion.

4. Discuss the extent to which you agree with the conclusions North draws in her final section.

THANK HEAVEN FOR LITTLE BOYS

Ana Veciana-Suarez

Ana Veciana-Suarez is a Miami Herald *columnist and author of the novel* The Chin Kiss King *(1997) and* Birthday Parties in Heaven: Thoughts on Love, Life, Grief, and Other Matters of the Heart *(2000). This essay appeared in the* Back Talk *section of the June 23, 1998, issue of* Woman's Day. Back Talk, *a regular feature of the magazine, provides a forum for guest writers to express their opinions on timely or controversial topics.*

sexist

I am the mother of sons. I say this with both pride and temerity.

Pride because my four boys are wonderful, responsible, conscientious human beings. Temerity because these days, no matter what their characters, all men are targets for bashing.

"Four boys!" exclaimed a woman I met at a party. "Sure hope they'll be different from the batch of men we've got out now."

4   Whoa! Since when did masculinity become synonymous with macho? How did we come to view males as a fatally flawed gender?

I wish I could say my fleeting party conversation was unusual. It wasn't. I hear similar complaints from many other women. You know what I mean: Men are insensitive brutes. Men manipulate women and subjugate them in marriage. Men are deadbeat fathers. They can't commit to relationships. Men are angry Peter Pans, perpetuallly boyish and often irresponsible. On and on go the diatribes.

Too bad, since in our attempt to harness our sons, to "feminize" them, we're the losers. The truth is, my boys, and most of the men I know, are wonderful, appealing, endearing—in their own ways. They are natural competitors but not ruthless in this pursuit. Their hearts are in the right place, even though they may not always be able to articulate all that those caring hearts hold.

I've thought about this a lot since my husband died three years ago. Before that, it seemed only natural that our sons emulate him. I didn't worry much about what it took to be a boy and, consequently, a man. Now, because I have to be both father and mother to them, I feel a responsibility to teach them what it means to be a family provider and protector. I want them to learn to become the men of the house. It's a pretty hard lesson to teach when the world is taking cheap shots at their gender, and in an era when manliness is mistaken for destructiveness.

8   I used to believe that little boys' behavior was determined more by societal demands than by biology and hormones. Not any more.

Though I've tried to raise my children equally (my eldest is a girl), the fact is that boys—my boys and their friends—are like cubs at play, pawing, smacking, rolling, bumping, ramming, twirling, elbowing. This, I realize, is the way they bond, the equivalent of girls braiding each other's hair or chattily trading secrets on the phone.

Boys are hard-wired to be more physical, to take more risks, to be competitive and aggressive and performance-oriented. This isn't necessarily bad; it just *is*.

I was reminded of the difference between girls' and boys' behavior not too long ago, while visiting a friend with three daughters who played so quietly I hardly noticed them. "Girls," my friend observed, "tend to be calmer than boys. Boys like to play rough. They always have to be top dog."

12   I remembered then the soft charm of my daughter's girlhood, the genteel way she so naturally related to her playmates. She loved sports and could wrestle with the best of her brothers, but her attitude was different from theirs, as were the dynamics of her relationships with her friends. While her group tended toward consensus and cooperation, her brothers turned anything—even putting away laundry—into a form of competition.

The ability to reach a consensus and the desire to cooperate are excellent qualities. So are competition and the dogged pursuit of the top.

Isn't it time we celebrated these traits, instead of treating masculinity as some kind of fatal flaw? I've learned much from my sons: how to be assertive, when tact is not necessarily the best tool, how not to flinch from confrontation. From me I hope they are learning openness, compassion, gentleness, and a general aptitude for nurturing.

I encourage these things in all my children—encourage them to leaven one set of traits with another, because both are needed to thrive in this world.

Personal Response

Explore your response to Veciana-Suarez's question: "Isn't it time we celebrated [men's abilities], instead of treating masculinity as some kind of fatal flaw?" (paragraph 14).

Questions for Class or Small-Group Discussion

1. What do you understand Veciana-Suarez to mean when she writes that "men are targets for bashing" and viewed "as a fatally flawed gender"? Do you agree with her statements on this point?

2. Veciana-Suarez implies that "attempts to harness our sons" are attempts to "'feminize'" them. Discuss what you think she means by that statement and whether you agree with her.

3. What gender-based distinctions does Veciana-Suarez draw between boys' and girls' behavior? Are you convinced from her evidence that behavioral differences between males and females are biologically, not socially, determined? How do your own observations of male and female behavior compare with or differ from hers?

X: A FABULOUS CHILD'S STORY

Lois Gould

Lois Gould is a writer and a journalist. In addition to short stories and newspaper articles, she has written several novels: Such Good

Friends (1970), Necessary Objects (1972), and La Presidenta *(1981). This story first appeared as a "Story for Free Children" in* Ms. *magazine in 1972 and has since been reprinted countless times.*

Once upon a time, a baby named X was born. This baby was named X so that nobody could tell whether it was a boy or a girl. Its parents could tell, of course, but they couldn't tell anybody else. They couldn't even tell Baby X, at first.

You see, it was all part of a very important Secret Scientific Xperiment, known officially as Project Baby X. The smartest scientists had set up this Xperiment at a cost of Xactly 23 billion dollars and 72 cents, which might seem like a lot for just one baby, even a very important Xperimental baby. But when you remember the prices of things like strained carrots and stuffed bunnies, and popcorn for the movies and booster shots for camp, let alone twenty-eight shiny quarters from the tooth fairy, you begin to see how it adds up.

Also, long before Baby X was born, all those scientists had to be paid to work out the details of the Xperiment, and to write the *Official Instruction Manual* for Baby X's parents and, most important of all, to find the right set of parents to bring up Baby X. These parents had to be selected very carefully. Thousands of volunteers had to take thousands of tests and answer thousands of tricky questions. Almost everybody failed because, it turned out, almost everybody really wanted either a baby boy or a baby girl, and not Baby X at all. Also, almost everybody was afraid that a Baby X would be a lot more trouble than a boy or a girl. (They were probably right, the scientists admitted, but Baby X needed parents who wouldn't *mind* the Xtra trouble.)

4   There were families with grandparents named Milton and Agatha, who didn't see why the baby couldn't be named Milton or Agatha instead of X, even if it *was* an X. There were families with aunts who insisted on knitting tiny dresses and uncles who insisted on sending tiny baseball mitts. Worst of all, there were families that already had other children who couldn't be trusted to keep the secret. Certainly not if they knew the secret was worth 23 billion dollars and 72 cents—and all you had to do was take one little peek at Baby X in the bathtub to know if it was a boy or a girl.

But, finally, the scientists found the Joneses, who really wanted to raise an X more than any other kind of baby—no matter how much trouble it would be. Ms. and Mr. Jones had to promise they would take equal turns caring for X, and feeding it, and singing it lullabies. And they had to promise never to hire any baby-sitters. The government scientists knew perfectly well that a baby-sitter would probably peek at X in the bathtub, too.

The day the Joneses brought their baby home, lots of friends and relatives came over to see it. None of them knew about the secret Xperiment, though. So the first thing they asked was what kind of a baby X was. When the Joneses smiled and said, "It's an X!" nobody knew what to say. They couldn't say, "Look at her cute little dimples!" And they couldn't say, "Look at his husky little biceps!" And they couldn't even say just plain "kitchy-coo." In fact, they all thought the Joneses were playing some kind of rude joke.

But, of course, the Joneses were not joking. "It's an X" was absolutely all they would say. And that made the friends and relatives very angry. The relatives all felt embarrassed about having an X in the family. "People will think there's something wrong with it!" some of them whispered. "There *is* something wrong with it!" others whispered back.

8   "Nonsense!" the Joneses told them all cheerfully. "What could possibly be wrong with this perfectly adorable X?"

Nobody could answer that, except Baby X, who had just finished its bottle. Baby X's answer was a loud, satisfied burp.

Clearly, nothing at all was wrong. Nevertheless, none of the relatives felt comfortable about buying a present for a Baby X. The cousins who sent the baby a tiny football helmet would not come and visit any more. And the neighbors who sent a pink-flowered romper suit pulled their shades down when the Joneses passed their house.

The *Official Instruction Manual* had warned the new parents that this would happen, so they didn't fret about it. Besides, they were too busy with Baby X and the hundreds of different Xercises for treating it properly.

12   Ms. and Mr. Jones had to be Xtra careful about how they played with little X. They knew if they kept bouncing it up in the air and saying how *strong* and *active* it was, they'd be treating it more like a boy than an X. But if all they did was cuddle it and kiss it and tell it how *sweet* and *dainty* it was, they'd be treating it more like a girl than an X.

On page 1,654 of the *Official Instruction Manual,* the scientists prescribed: "plenty of bouncing and plenty of cuddling, *both.* X ought to be strong and sweet and active. Forget about *dainty* altogether."

Meanwhile, the Joneses were worrying about other problems. Toys, for instance. And clothes. On his first shopping trip, Mr. Jones told the store clerk, "I need some clothes and toys for my new baby." The clerk smiled and said, "Well, now, is it a boy or a girl?" "It's an X," Mr. Jones said, smiling back. But the clerk got all red in the face and said huffily, "In *that* case, I'm afraid I can't help you, sir." So Mr. Jones wandered helplessly up and down the aisles trying to find what X needed. But everything in the store was piled up in sections marked "Boys" or "Girls." There were "Boys' Pajamas" and "Girls' Underwear" and "Boys' Fire Engines" and "Girls' Housekeeping Sets." Mr. Jones went home without buying anything for X. That night he and Ms. Jones consulted page 2,326 of the *Official Instruction Manual.* "Buy plenty of everything!" it said firmly.

So they bought plenty of sturdy blue pajamas in the Boys' Department and cheerful flowered underwear in the Girls' Department. And they bought all kinds of toys. A boy doll that made pee-pee and cried, "Pa-pa." And a girl doll that talked in three languages and said, "I am the Pres-i-dent of Gen-er-al Mo-tors." They also bought a storybook about a brave princess who rescued a handsome prince from his ivory tower, and another one about a sister and brother who grew up to be a baseball star and a ballet star, and you had to guess which was which.

16   The head scientists of Project Baby X checked all their purchases and told them to keep up the good work. They also reminded the Joneses to see page 4,629 of the *Manual,* where it said, "Never make Baby X feel *embarrassed* or *ashamed* about what it wants to play with. And if X gets dirty climbing rocks, never say 'Nice little Xes don't get dirty climbing rocks.'"

Likewise, it said, "If X falls down and cries, never say 'Brave little Xes don't cry.' Because, of course, nice little Xes *do* get dirty, and brave little Xes *do* cry. No matter how dirty X gets, or how hard it cries, don't worry. It's all part of the Xperiment."

Whenever the Joneses pushed Baby X's stroller in the park, smiling strangers would come over and coo: "Is that a boy or a girl?" The Joneses would smile back and say, "It's an X." The strangers would stop smiling then, and often snarl something nasty—as if the Joneses had snarled at *them.*

By the time X grew big enough to play with other children, the Joneses' troubles had grown bigger, too. Once a little girl grabbed X's shovel in the sandbox, and zonked X on the head with it. "Now, now, Tracy," the little girl's mother began to scold, "little girls mustn't hit little . . ." and she turned to ask X, "Are you a little boy or a little girl, dear?"

20   Mr. Jones who was sitting near the sandbox, held his breath and crossed his fingers.

X smiled politely at the lady, even though X's head had never been zonked so hard in its life, "I'm a little X," X replied.

"You're a *what?*" the lady exclaimed angrily. "You're a little b-r-a-t, you mean!"

"But little girls mustn't hit little Xes, either!" said X, retrieving the shovel with another polite smile. "What good does hitting do, anyway?"

24   X's father, who was still holding his breath, finally let it out, uncrossed his fingers, and grinned back at X.

And at their next secret Project Baby X meeting, the scientists grinned, too. Baby X was doing fine.

But then it was time for X to start school. The Joneses were really worried about this, because school was even more full of rules for boys and girls, and there were no rules for Xes. The teacher would tell boys to form one line, and girls to form another line. There would be boys' games and girls' games, and boys' secrets and girls' secrets. The school library would have a list of recommended books for girls, and a different list of recommended books for boys. There would even be a bathroom marked BOYS and another one marked GIRLS. Pretty soon boys and girls would hardly talk to each other. What would happen to poor little X?

The Joneses spent weeks consulting their *Instruction Manual* (there were 249½ pages of advice under "First Day of School"), and attending urgent special conferences with the smart scientists of Project Baby X.

28   The scientists had to make sure that X's mother had taught X how to throw and catch a ball properly, and that X's father had been sure to teach X what to serve at a doll's tea party. X had to know how to shoot marbles and how to jump rope and, most of all, what to say when the Other Children asked whether X was a Boy or a Girl.

Finally, X was ready. The Joneses helped X button on a nice new pair of red-and-white checked overalls, and sharpened six pencils for X's nice new pencilbox, and marked X's name clearly on all the books in its nice new bookbag. X brushed its teeth and combed its hair, which just about covered its ears, and remembered to put a napkin in its lunchbox.

The Joneses had asked X's teacher if the class could line up alphabetically, instead of forming separate lines for boys and girls. And they had asked if X could use the principal's bathroom, because it wasn't marked anything except BATHROOM. X's teacher promised to take care of all those problems. But nobody could help X with the biggest problem of all—Other Children.

Nobody in X's class had ever known an X before. What would they think? How would X make friends?

32   You couldn't tell what X was by studying its clothes—overalls don't even button right-to-left, like girls' clothes, or left-to-right, like boys' clothes. And you couldn't guess whether X had a girl's short haircut or a boy's long haircut. And it was very hard to tell by the games X liked to play. Either X played ball very well for a girl, or else X played house very well for a boy.

Some of the children tried to find out by asking X tricky questions, like "Who's your favorite sports star?" That was easy. X had two favorite sports stars: a girl jockey named Robyn Smith and a boy archery champion named Robin Hood. Then they asked, "What's your favorite TV program?" And that was even easier. X's favorite TV program was "Lassie," which stars a girl dog played by a boy dog.

When X said that its favorite toy was a doll, everyone decided that X must be a girl. But then X said that the doll was really a robot, and that X had computerized it, and that it was programmed to bake fudge brownies and then clean up the kitchen. After X told them that, the other children gave up guessing what X was. All they knew was they'd sure like to see X's doll.

After school, X wanted to play with the other children. "How about shooting some baskets in the gym?" X asked the girls. But all they did was make faces and giggle behind X's back.

36   "How about weaving some baskets in the arts and crafts room?" X asked the boys. But they all made faces and giggled behind X's back too.

That night, Ms. and Mr. Jones asked X how things had gone at school. X told them sadly that the lessons were okay, but otherwise school was a terrible place for an X. It seemed as if Other Children would never want an X for a friend.

Once more, the Joneses reached for their *Instruction Manual.* Under "Other Children," they found the following message: "What did you Xpect? *Other Children* have to obey all the silly boy—girl rules, because their parents taught them to. Lucky X—you don't have to stick to the rules at all! All you have to do is be yourself. P.S. We're not saying it'll be easy."

X liked being itself. But X cried a lot that night, partly because it felt afraid. So X's father held X tight, and cuddled it, and couldn't help crying a little, too. And X's mother cheered them both up by reading an Xciting story about an enchanted prince called Sleeping Handsome, who woke up when Princess Charming kissed him.

40   The next morning, they all felt much better, and little X went back to school with a brave smile and a clean pair of red-and-white checked overalls.

There was a seven-letter-word spelling bee in class that day. And a seven-lap boys' relay race in the gym. And a seven-layer-cake baking contest in the girls' kitchen corner. X won the spelling bee. X also won the relay race. And X almost won the baking contest, except it forgot to light the oven. Which only proves that nobody's perfect.

One of the Other Children noticed something else, too. He said, "Winning or losing doesn't seem to count to X. X seems to have fun being good at boys' skills *and* girls' skills."

"Come to think of it," said another one of the Other Children, "maybe X is having twice as much fun as we are!"

44   So after school that day, the girl who beat X at the baking contest gave X a big slice of her prizewinning cake. And the boy X beat in the relay race asked X to race him home.

From then on, some really funny things began to happen. Susie, who sat next to X in class, suddenly refused to wear pink dresses to school any more. She insisted on wearing red-and-white checked overalls—just like X's. Overalls, she told her parents, were much better for climbing monkey bars.

Then Jim, the class football nut, started wheeling his little sister's doll carriage around the football field. He'd put on his entire football uniform, except for the helmet. Then he'd put the helmet *in* the carriage, lovingly tucked under an old set of shoulder pads. Then he'd start jogging around the field, pushing the carriage and singing "Rock-a-bye Baby" to his football helmet. He told his family that X did the same thing, so it must be okay. After all X was now the team's star quarterback.

Susie's parents were horrified by her behavior, and Jim's parents were worried sick about his. But the worst came when the twins, Joe and Peggy, decided to share everything with each other. Peggy used Joe's hockey skates, and his microscope, and took half his newspaper route. Joe used Peggy's needlepoint kit, and her cookbooks, and took two of her three baby-sitting jobs. Peggy started running the lawn mower, and Joe started running the vacuum cleaner.

48   Their parents weren't one bit pleased with Peggy's wonderful biology experiments, or with Joe's terrific needlepoint pillows. They didn't care that Peggy mowed the lawn better, and that Joe vacuumed the carpet better. In fact, they were furious. It's all that little X's fault, they agreed. Just because X doesn't know what it is, or what it's supposed to be, it wants to get everybody *else* mixed up, too!

Peggy and Joe were forbidden to play with X any more. So was Susie, and then Jim, and then *all* the Other Children. But it was too late; the Other Children stayed mixed up and happy and free, and refused to go back to the way they'd been before X.

Finally, Joe and Peggy's parents decided to call an emergency meeting of the school's Parents' Association, to discuss "The X Problem." They sent a report to the principal stating that X was a "disruptive influence." They demanded immediate action. The Joneses, they said, should be *forced* to tell whether X was a boy or a girl. And then X should be *forced* to behave like whichever it was. If the Joneses refused to tell, the Parents' Association said, then X must take an Xamination. The school psychiatrist must Xamine it physically and mentally, and issue a full report. If X's test showed it was a boy, it would have to obey all the boys' rules. If it proved to be a girl, X would have to obey all the girls' rules.

And if X turned out to be some kind of mixed-up misfit, then X should be Xpelled from the school. Immediately!

52   The principal was very upset. Disruptive influence? Mixed-up misfit? But X was an Xcellent student. All the teachers said it was a delight to have X in their classes. X was president of the student council. X had won first prize in the talent show, and second prize in the art show, and honorable mention in the science fair, and six athletic events on field day, including the potato race.

Nevertheless, insisted the Parents' Association, X is a Problem Child. X is the Biggest Problem Child we have ever seen!

So the principal reluctantly notified X's parents that numerous complaints about X's behavior had come to the school's attention. And that after the psychiatrist's Xamination, the school would decide what to do about X.

The Joneses reported this at once to the scientists, who referred them to page 85,759 of the *Instruction Manual.* "Sooner or later," it said, "X will have to be Xamined by a psychiatrist. This may be the only way any of us will know for sure whether X is mixed up—or whether everyone else is."

56   The night before X was to be Xamined, the Joneses tried not to let X see how worried they were. "What if . . . ?" Mr. Jones would say. And Ms. Jones would reply, "No use worrying." Then a few minutes later, Ms. Jones would say, "What if . . . ?" and Mr. Jones would reply, "No use worrying."

X just smiled at them both, and hugged them hard and didn't say much of anything. X was thinking. What if . . . ? And then X thought: No use worrying.

At Xactly nine o'clock the next day, X reported to the school psychiatrist's office. The principal, along with a committee from the Parents' Association, X's teacher, X's classmates, and Ms. and Mr. Jones, waited in the hall outside. Nobody knew the details of the tests X was to be given, but everybody knew they'd be *very* hard, and that they'd reveal Xactly what everyone wanted to know about X, but were afraid to ask.

It was terribly quiet in the hall. Almost spooky. Once in a while, they would hear a strange noise inside the room. There were buzzes. And a beep or two. And several bells. An occasional light would flash under the door. The Joneses thought it was a white light, but the principal thought it was blue. Two or three children swore it was either yellow or green. And the Parents' Committee missed it completely.

60   Through it all, you could hear the psychiatrist's low voice, asking hundreds of questions, and X's higher voice, answering hundreds of answers.

The whole thing took so long that everyone knew it must be the most complete Xamination anyone had ever had to take. Poor X, the Joneses thought. Serves X right, the Parents' Committee thought. I wouldn't like to be in X's overalls right now, the children thought.

At last, the door opened. Everyone crowded around to hear the results. X didn't look any different; in fact, X was smiling. But the psychiatrist looked terrible. He looked as if he was crying! "What happened?" everyone began shouting. Had X done something disgraceful? "I wouldn't be a bit surprised!" muttered Peggy and Joe's parents. "Did X flunk the *whole* test?" cried Susie's parents. "Or just the most important part?" yelled Jim's parents.

"Oh, dear," sighed Mr. Jones.

64   "Oh, dear," sighed Ms. Jones.

"*Sssh,*" ssshed the principal. "The psychiatrist is trying to speak."

Wiping his eyes and clearing his throat, the psychiatrist began, in a hoarse whisper. "In my opinion," he whispered—you could tell he must be very upset—"in my opinion, young X here . . ."

"Yes? Yes?" shouted a parent impatiently.

68   "*Sssh!*" ssshed the principal.

"Young *Sssh* here, I mean young X," said the doctor, frowning, "is just about . . ."

"Just about *what?* Let's have it!" shouted another parent.

". . . just about the *least* mixed-up child I've ever Xamined!" said the psychiatrist.

72   "Yay for X!" yelled one of the children. And then the others began yelling, too. Clapping and cheering and jumping up and down.

"*SSSH!*" SSShed the principal, but nobody did.

The Parents' Committee was angry and bewildered. How *could* X have passed the whole Xamination? Didn't X have an *identity* problem? Wasn't X mixed up at *all?* Wasn't X *any* kind of a misfit? How could it *not* be, when it didn't even *know* what it was? And why was the psychiatrist crying?

Actually, he had stopped crying and was smiling politely through his tears. "Don't you see?" he said, "I'm crying because it's wonderful! X has absolutely no identity problem! X isn't one bit mixed up! As for being a misfit—ridiculous! X knows perfectly well what it is! Don't you, X?" The doctor winked, X winked back.

76   "But what *is* X?" shrieked Peggy and Joe's parents. "We still want to know what it is!"

"Ah, yes," said the doctor, winking again. "Well, don't worry. You'll all know one of these days. And you won't need me to tell you."

"What? What does he mean?" some of the parents grumbled suspiciously.

Susie and Peggy and Joe all answered at once. "He means that by the time X's sex matters, it won't be a secret any more!"

80   With that, the doctor began to push through the crowd toward X's parents. "How do you do," he said, somewhat stiffly. And then he reached out to hug them both. "If I ever have an X of my own," he whispered, "I sure hope you'll lend me your instruction manual."

Needless to say, the Joneses were very happy. The Project Baby X scientists were rather pleased, too. So were Susie, Jim, Peggy, Joe, and all the Other Children. The Parents' Association wasn't, but they had promised to accept the psychiatrist's report, and not make any more trouble. They even invited Ms. and Mr. Jones to become honorary members, which they did.

Later that day, all X's friends put on their red-and-white checked overalls and went over to see X. They found X in the back yard, playing with a very tiny baby that none of them had ever seen before. The baby was wearing very tiny red-and-white checked overalls.

"How do you like our new baby?" X asked the Other Children proudly.

84   "It's got cute dimples," said Jim.

"It's got husky biceps, too," said Susie.

"What kind of baby is it?" asked Joe and Peggy.

X frowned at them. "Can't you tell?" Then X broke into a big, mischievous grin. *"It's a Y!"*

Personal Response

Explore your reaction to this fable. Did you enjoy it? Why or why not? Did the experiences of X seem familiar to you and, if so, in what ways?

Questions for Class or Small-Group Discussion

1. Identify the traditional sex-role expectations or assumptions about gender differences that the story explores or exposes.

2. Select a passage of several paragraphs and read it aloud, using masculine pronouns for all references to X. Then do to the same using feminine pronouns. Discuss the effects of substituting sex-specific pronouns for the indefinite *X*.

3. Discuss whether you think that society will some day be "genderless." How possible do you think it would be to raise a child not to be conscious of gender? What advantages and disadvantages do you see in having a "genderless" society?

4. Discuss your own experiences growing up. Did your parents treat you differently on the basis of your sex? Did teachers? Other children? How, if at all, do you think television and other media influence your feelings about being male or female?

PERSPECTIVES ON GENDER

Suggestions for Synthesis

1. Drawing on two or more of the essays in this chapter, write a reflective essay in which you explore your own concepts of masculinity and femininity (and perhaps androgyny) and the way in which that concept has shaped the way you are today. Consider to what degree you think that sex determines destiny.

2. Compare and/or contrast the views on gender differences expressed by Joan North in "Strangers in a Strange Land: Women in Higher Education Administration," Ana Veciana-Suarez in "Thank Heaven for Little Boys," and Lois Gould in "X: A Fabulous Child's Story."

3. Write an essay explaining how you think at least one other author in this chapter would respond to Jane Smiley's opinion of Barbie dolls in "You Can Never Have Too Many."

Additional Writing Topics

1. With the observations of Lois Gould in "X: A Fabulous Child's Story" in mind, conduct your own investigative analysis of any of the following for their depiction of female and male sex roles: fairy tales, children's stories, advertising images, music videos, television programs, or film. Do you find stereotyped assumptions about masculinity and femininity? In what ways do you think the subject of your analysis reinforces or shapes cultural definitions of masculinity and femininity?

2. Examine media images for the ways in which gays and lesbians are portrayed. Focus on a particular medium, such as print advertisements, television situation comedies, or film.

3. Explore ways in which you would like to see definitions of masculinity and femininity changed. How do you think relationships between the sexes would be affected if those changes were made?

4. Write a personal narrative recounting an experience in which you felt you were being treated unfairly or differently from persons of the other sex. What was the situation, how did you feel, and what did you do about it?

5. Explain the degree to which you consider gender issues to be important. Do you think too much is made of gender? Does it matter whether definitions of masculinity and femininity are rigid?

6. Explain why you agree or disagree with the opinions in Jane Smiley's "You Can Never Have Too Many" or Ana Veciana-Suarez's "Thank Heaven for Little Boys."

7. Select a statement, example, or reference from any of the essays in this chapter that particularly impressed you, either favorably or unfavorably, and respond to or explore it.

8. Do your own informal research on leadership styles of men and women by observing them in meetings, in the classroom, and in any other situation in which men and women conduct business, make decisions, or otherwise relate to each other in a professional or semiprofessional way. What conclusions can you draw? How do your conclusions compare to those of Joan DeGuire North in "Strangers in a Strange Land: Women in Higher Education Administration"?

Research Topics

1. Research the history of the contemporary women's movement, the men's movement, or the gay rights movement in America and report on its origins, goals, and influence. You will have to either extend or narrow your scope, depending on the time you have for the project and the nature of your purpose.

2. Research the subject of bisexuality, making sure to include differing viewpoints, and then explain your own viewpoint on the topic, supporting your position with relevant source materials.

3. Through research and interviews, write a paper on some aspect of the gay and lesbian experience in America.

4. Expand topic number 1 under "Additional Writing Topics" to include library research of articles and books by people who have done their own studies or have expressed opinions on the subject of sex-role stereotyping in books, movies, or other media.

5. Look at Joan DeGuire North's list of references following her article "Strangers in a Strange Land: Women in Higher Education Administration" for possible references for your own research on a topic suggested by the list. For instance, you could research gender differences in communication styles, worldviews, or leadership styles.

CHAPTER 16

RACE AND ETHNICITY

Racial or ethnic heritage is as important to shaping identity as are sex and social class. One's race or ethnicity can also influence quality of life, educational opportunity, and advancement in employment. American society has a long history of struggling to confront and overcome racism and discrimination on the basis of ethnic heritage. Beginning well before the Civil War, American antislavery groups protested the enslavement of African Americans and worked to abolish slavery in all parts of the country. Other groups besides African Americans have experienced harsh treatment and discrimination solely because of their color or ethnic heritage. These groups include Chinese men brought to America to help construct a cross-country railroad in the nineteenth century, European immigrants who came to America in large numbers near the end of the nineteenth century in search of better lives than they could expect in their homelands, Japanese men who came in the twentieth century to work at hard labor for money to send home, and Latinos/Latinas and Hispanics migrating north to America. As a result of the heightened awareness of the interplay of race, class, and gender, schools at all levels, from elementary through postgraduate, have incorporated course materials on race, class, and/or gender or created whole courses devoted to those important components of individual identities and histories.

The chapter begins with George Henderson's "Race in America," which provides a succinct historical overview of immigration to America. Henderson maintains that America has never truly been a melting pot and that its history has always been composed of migrants, immigrants, and slaves. Observing that America is "at a crossroads in its race relations," Henderson reviews several options for where we can go from here. Next is the first article in a series by the *Washington Post* on the effects of recent increases in the numbers of immigrants on American life today and in the future. William Booth in "One Nation, Indivisible: Is It History?" contrasts the effects of the first great wave of immigration to America in the period between 1890 and 1920 with the recent second great wave of immigration, as he explores the question of whether America is truly a "melting pot." As you read his article, keep in mind the question posed by its title and consider whether you think, as the writer implies, that the concept of America as a single, indivisible nation is soon to be a matter of history, not fact.

The next two essays take as their subjects specific American groups, Hispanics and blacks, and the difficulties they encounter living in a predominantly white society. In "Hispanics and the American Dream," Linda Chavez writes fervently of the particular strengths of Hispanics in America. She argues that "policy prescriptions offered by many Hispanic advocacy organizations and most politicians seem oddly out of sync," charging that current policies perpetuate demeaning stereotypes. Alex Kotlowitz, in "Colorblind," focuses on two towns across the river from one another, "whose only connections are two bridges and a powerful undertow of contrasts." As he researched the circumstances surrounding the death of a black teenager, Kotlowitz discovered a history of racial hostility between the two towns. His interviews with both blacks and whites led him to conclude that only when the members of both groups question their own perspectives can they learn to understand each other. "It's all about perspective," he insists.

RACE IN AMERICA

George Henderson

George Henderson is Dean of the College of Liberal Arts at the University of Oklahoma, where he is also a professor of human relations, education, and sociology. Henderson has served as a race-relations consultant to many national and international organizations. He is author of Our Souls to Keep: Black/White Relations in America *(1999) and co-editor with Grace Xuequin Ma of* Rethinking Ethnicity and Health Care: A Sociocultural Perspective *(1999). This essay appeared in a special issue on race in America in the spring 2000 issue of* National Forum.

Because of intermarriage, most Americans have multiple ethnic and racial identities. Some persons of mixed lineage prefer to assume culturally nondescript identities. For example, they have become "white people," "black people," "Indians," "Latinos," "Asians," or just plain "Americans" in order to somehow deflect from themselves any connection with their ancestors. The task of tracing their families has become too taxing or too insignificant. Even so, the effects of ethnicity and race are pervasive: disparate patterns of community relationships and economic opportunities haunt us. At some time in their history, all ethnic groups in the United States have been the underclass. Also, at different times, all ethnic groups have been both the oppressed and the oppressors.

Ethnicity is the most distinguishing characteristic of Americans, where we are sorted primarily on the basis of our cultural identities or nationalities. An ethnic group is a culturally distinct population whose members share a collective identity and a common heritage. Historically, the overwhelming majority of ethnic groups emerged in the United States as a result of one of several responses to the following processes: (1) migration, (2) consolidation of group forces in the face of an impending threat from an aggressor, (3) annexation or changes in political boundary lines, or (4) schisms within a church. Hence, "ethnic minority" presupposes people different from the mainstream or dominant cultured persons.

But it is the erroneous belief that people who come to America can be placed in categories based on their unique gene pools that has resulted in the most blatant instances of discrimination. Races, however defined, do not correspond to genetic reality because inbreeding world populations share a common gene pool. A much more practical dictum, and one that has often been ignored throughout American history, is that all people belong to the same species. Unfortunately, too few individuals believe that the only race of any significance is the human race.

A Brief History

4   At the time of the American Revolution, the American population was largely composed of English Protestants who had absorbed a substantial number of German and Scotch-Irish settlers and a smaller number of French, Dutch, Swedes, Poles, Swiss, Irish, and other immigrants. The colonies had a modest number of Catholics, and a smaller number of Jews. Excluding Quakers and Swedes, the colonists treated Native Americans with contempt and hostility, and engaged in wars against them that bordered on genocide. They drove natives from the coastal plains in order to make way for a massive white movement to the West. Although Africans, most of whom were slaves, comprised one-fifth of the American population during the Revolution, they, similar to Indians, were not perceived by most white colonists as being worthy of assimilation.

The white peoples of the new nation had long since crossed Caucasian lines to create a conglomerate but culturally homogeneous society. People of different ethnic groups—English, Irish, German, Huguenot, Dutch, Swedish—mingled and intermarried. English settlers and peoples from western and northern Europe had begun a process of ethnic assimilation that caused some writers to incorrectly describe the nation as melted into one ethnic group: American. In reality, nonCaucasian Americans were not included in the Eurocentric cultural pot.

During the 150 years immediately following the Revolution, large numbers of immigrants came to the United States from eastern European countries. They were the so-called "new immigrants." During the latter part of that period, slaves were emancipated, numerous Indian tribes were conquered and forced to relocate to reservations, portions of Mexico's land were taken, and Asians began emigrating to the United States. The English language and English-oriented cultural patterns grew even more dominant. Despite a proliferation of cultural diversity within the growing ethnic enclaves, Anglo-conformity ideology spawned racist notions about Nordic and Aryan racial superiority. This ideology gave rise to nativist political agendas and exclusionist immigration policies favoring western and northern European immigrants.

Non-English-speaking western Europeans and northern Europeans were also discriminated against. The slowness of some of those immigrants, particularly Germans, to learn English, their tendency to live in enclaves, and their establishment of ethnic-language newspapers were friction points. Such ethnic-oriented lifestyles prompted many Americanized people to chide: "If they don't like it here, they can go back to where they came from." But that solution was too simplistic. Immigrants from all countries and cultures, even those who were deemed socially and religiously undesirable, were needed to help build a nation—to work the farms, dig the ore, build the railroads and canals, settle the prairies, and otherwise provide human resources.

8   Beginning in the 1890s, immigrants from eastern and southern Europe were numerically dominant. That set the stage for racist statements about inferior, darker people threatening the purity of blond, blue-eyed Nordics or Aryans through miscegenation. Intermixture was perceived as a deadly plague. Although the immigrants from eastern and southern Europe were not suitable marriage partners, their critics stated, they could be properly assimilated and amalgamated. This kind of ethnocentrism prevented large numbers of other immigrants and indigenous peoples of color from becoming fully functioning citizens. And the legacy for the children of people denied equal opportunities was second-class citizenship. We can easily document the negative effects of second-class citizenship: abhorrent inequalities, unwarranted exclusions, and atmospheres of rejection.

Immigrants who lived in remote, isolated areas were able to maintain some semblance of being ethnic nations within America. But the growth of cities brought about the decline of farming populations and ethnic colonies. A short time was required for the white immigrants who settled in cities to discard their native languages and cultures. But it is erroneous to think of any ethnic group as melting away without leaving a trace of its cultural heritage. All ethnic groups have infused portions of their cultures into the tapestry of American history.

Early twentieth-century eastern European immigrants were a very disparate mixture of peoples. They came from nations that were trying to become states—Poland, Czechoslovakia, Lithuania, and Yugoslavia; from states trying to become nations—Italy, Turkey, and Greece; and from areas outside the Western concept of either state or nation. All of them included people such as Jews who did not easily fit into any of those categories. Through social and educational movements, laws, and superordinate goals such as winning wars and establishing economic world superiority, eastern Europeans and other white ethnic groups were able to enter mainstream America.

The cultures and colors of Third World ethnic groups were in stark contrast to European immigrants. Those differences became obstacles to assimilation and, more importantly, to people of color achieving equal opportunities. Nonwhite groups in the United States occupied specific low-status niches in the workplace, which in turn resulted in similarities among their members in such things as occupations, standard of living, level of education, place of residence, access to political power, and quality of health care. Likenesses within those groups facilitated the formation of stereotypes and prejudices that inhibited the full citizenship of nonwhite minorities.

12   Immigrants who held highly esteemed occupations—lawyers, artists, engineers, scientists, and physicians—became Americanized much faster than those who held less esteemed positions—unskilled laborers, farm workers, coal miners, and stock clerks. But even in those instances there were pro-European biases and stereotypes. For example, French chefs, Italian opera singers, Polish teachers, German conductors, and Russian scientists were more highly recruited than Africans, Hispanics, and Asians who had the same skills. Racial and quasi-racial groups—including American Indians, Mexican Americans, Asian Americans, African Americans, and Puerto Ricans—were not nearly so readily absorbed as various Caucasian ethnic groups. And that is generally the situation today. Despite numerous and impressive gains during the past century, a disproportionate number of peoples of color are still treated like pariahs.

What Does the Future Hold?

If U.S. Census Bureau population projections are correct, our nation is undergoing mind-boggling demographic changes: Hispanics will triple in numbers, from 31.4 million in 1999 to 98.2 million in 2050; blacks will increase 70 percent, from 34.9 million to 59.2 million; Asians and Pacific Islanders will triple, from 10.9 million to 37.6 million; Native Americans and Alaska Natives will increase from approximately 2.2 million to 2.6 million. During the same period, the non-Hispanic white population will increase from 196.1 million to 213 million. Also, the foreign-born population, most of them coming from Asia and Latin America, will increase from 26 million to 53.8 million. The non-Hispanic white population will decrease from 72 percent of the total population in 1999 to 52 percent in 2050, and the nation's workforce will be composed of over 50 percent racial and ethnic minorities and immigrants. Who then will be the pariahs?

Without equal opportunities, the melting pot will continue to be an unreachable mirage, a dream of equality deferred, for too many people of color. This does not in any way detract from the significance of the things minorities have achieved. Ethnic-group histories and lists of cultural contributions support the contention that each group is an integral part of a whole nation. Although all American ethnic minority groups have experienced continuous socioeconomic gains, the so-called "playing field" that includes white participants is not yet level. Simply stated, the rising tide of economic prosperity has not yet lifted the masses of people of color. Whatever our life circumstances, the citizens of the United States are bound together not as separate ethnic groups but as members of different ethnic groups united in spirit and behavior and locked into a common destiny.

There is little doubt that our nation is at a crossroads in its race relations. Where we go from here is up to all of us. We can try segregation again, continuance of the status quo, silence in the face of prejudice and discriminatory practices, or activism. The choice is ours.

16   Segregation of ethnic minorities is not a redeeming choice for the United States. It did not work during earlier times, and it will not work now. There have never been separate but equal majority-group and minority-group communities in the United States. And the pretense of such a condition would once again be a particularly pernicious injustice to all citizens. Racial segregation diminishes both the perpetrators and their victims. Preserving the status quo in education, employment, health care, and housing, which so often is little more than codified racial discrimination, is not justice for minorities either.

Inaction by people who witness oppressive acts is equally unacceptable. Even though they may be shocked and frustrated by the problems, standing in wide-eyed horror is not an adequate posture to assume. While they may be legally absolved of any wrongdoing, these silent people must come to terms with what others believe to be their moral culpability. Of course, silence may be prudent. Usually, there is a high price to be paid by those who would challenge racism in community institutions. Friends, jobs, promotions, and prestige may be lost. Furthermore, few victories come easily, and most of the victors are unsung heroes.

Individuals who choose to challenge purveyors of bigotry and unequal opportunities must also take care that in their actions to redress racial injustices, they do not emulate the oppressors whom they deplore. That might makes right, that blood washes out injustices—these too are false strategies for achieving justice. "It does not matter much to a slave what the color of his master is," a wise black janitor once said. We, the descendants of migrants, immigrants, and slaves, can build a better nation—a place where all people have safe housing, get a top-quality education, do meaningful work for adequate wages, are treated fairly in criminal-justice systems, have their medical needs met, and in the end die a timely death unhurried by bigots. This is the kind of history that should be made.

Personal Response

Noting that America is "at a crossroads in its race relations," Henderson identifies four options for "where we can go from here" (paragraph 15). Explain which option you think you will choose and why.

Questions for Class or Small-Group Discussion

1. State in your own words what you understand Henderson to mean when he says that "all ethnic groups [in America] have been both the oppressed and the oppressors" (paragraph 1). What examples does he give? Can you provide other examples that either support or refute that statement?

2. Comment on this statement: "But it is the erroneous belief that people who come to America can be placed in categories based on their unique gene pools that has resulted in the most blatant instances of discrimination" (paragraph 3). Do you agree with Henderson on this point?

3. State in your own words why America is not, according to Henderson, a true melting pot. To what extent do you agree with him? In preparation for your answer to this question, make sure you understand what these words and terms mean: *ethnic enclave, nativist,* and *exclusionist* (paragraph 6); *miscegenation, ethnocentrism,* and *second-class citizenship* (paragraph 8).

4. In his discussion of options for where we can go from here, Henderson says of those who choose activisim: "Individuals who choose to challenge purveyors of bigotry and unequal opportunities must also take care that in their actions to redress racial injustices, they do not emulate the oppressors whom they deplore" (paragraph 18). What do you understand him to mean by that statement? Why might people working against oppression become oppressors themselves?

ONE NATION, INDIVISIBLE: IS IT HISTORY?

William Booth

William Booth is a Washington Post *staff writer. This article was the first in a series examining the effects of changing demographics on American life. It appeared in the Sunday, February 22, 1998, issue of the* Washington Post.

At the beginning of this century, as steamers poured into American ports, their steerages filled with European immigrants, a Jew from England named Israel Zangwill penned a play whose story line has long been forgotten, but whose central theme has not. His production was entitled "The Melting Pot" and its message still holds a tremendous power on the national imagination—the promise that all immigrants can be transformed into Americans, a new alloy forged in a crucible of democracy, freedom, and civic responsibility. In 1908, when the play opened in Washington, the United States was in the middle of absorbing the largest influx of immigrants in its history—Irish and Germans, followed by Italians and East Europeans, Catholics and Jews—some eighteen million new citizens between 1890 and 1920.

Today, the United States is experiencing its second great wave of immigration, a movement of people that has profound implications for a society that by tradition pays homage to its immigrant roots at the same time it confronts complex and deeply ingrained ethnic and racial divisions. The immigrants of today come not from Europe but overwhelmingly from the still developing world of Asia and Latin America. They are driving a demographic shift so rapid that within the lifetimes of today's teenagers, no one ethnic group—including whites of European descent—will comprise a majority of the nation's population.

This shift, according to social historians, demographers, and others studying the trends, will severely test the premise of the fabled melting pot, the idea, so central to national identity, that this country can transform people of every color and background into "one America." Just as possible, they say, is that the nation will continue to fracture into many separate, disconnected communities with no shared sense of commonality or purpose. Or perhaps it will evolve into something in between, a pluralistic society that will hold onto some core ideas about citizenship and capitalism, but with little meaningful interaction among groups.

4   The demographic changes raise other questions about political and economic power. Will that power, now held disproportionately by whites, be shared in the new America? What will happen when Hispanics overtake blacks as the nation's single largest minority? "I do not think that most Americans really understand the historic changes happening before their very eyes," said Peter Salins, an immigration scholar who is provost of the State Universities of New York. "What are we going to become? Who are we? How do the newcomers fit in—and how do the natives handle it—this is the great unknown."

Fear of strangers, of course, is nothing new in American history. The last great immigration wave produced a bitter backlash, epitomized by the Chinese Exclusion Act of 1882 and the return, in the 1920s, of the Ku Klux Klan, which not only targeted blacks, but Catholics, Jews, and immigrants, as well. But despite this strife, many historians argue that there was a greater consensus in the past on what it meant to be an American, a yearning for a common language and culture, and a desire—encouraged, if not coerced by members of the dominant white Protestant culture—to assimilate. Today, they say, there is more emphasis on preserving one's ethnic identity, of finding ways to highlight and defend one's cultural roots.

Difficult to Measure

More often than not, the neighborhoods where Americans live, the politicians and propositions they vote for, the cultures they immerse themselves in, the friends and spouses they have, the churches and schools they attend, and the way they view themselves are defined by ethnicity. The question is whether, in the midst of such change, there is also enough glue to hold Americans together. Black community activist Nathaniel J. Wilcox in Miami says, "Hispanics don't want some of the power, they want all the power." "As we become more and more diverse, there is all this potential to make that reality work for us," said Angela Oh, a Korean American activist who emerged as a powerful voice for Asian immigrants after the Los Angeles riots in 1992. "But yet, you witness this persistence of segregation, the fragmentation, all these fights over resources, this finger-pointing. You would have to be blind not to see it."

It is a phenomenon sometimes difficult to measure, but not observe. Houses of worship remain, as the Rev. Martin Luther King Jr. described it three decades ago, among the most segregated institutions in America, not just by race but also ethnicity. At high school cafeterias, the second and third generation children of immigrants clump together in cliques defined by where their parents or grandparents were born. There are television sit-coms, talk shows, and movies that are considered black or white, Latino or Asian. At a place like the law school of the University of California at Los Angeles, which has about one thousand students, there are separate student associations for blacks, Latinos, and Asians with their own law review journals.

8   It almost goes without saying that today's new arrivals are a source of vitality and energy, especially in the big cities to which many are attracted. Diversity, almost everyone agrees, is good; choice is good; exposure to different cultures and ideas is good. But many scholars worry about the loss of community and shared sense of reality among Americans, what Todd Gitlin, a professor of culture and communications at New York University, calls "the twilight of common dreams." The concern is echoed by many on both the left and the right, and of all ethnicities, but no one seems to know exactly what to do about it.

Academics who examine the census data and probe for meaning in the numbers already speak of a new "demographic balkanization," not only of residential segregation, forced or chosen, but also of a powerful preference to see ourselves through a racial prism, wary of others, and, in many instances, hostile. At a recent school board meeting in East Palo Alto, California, police had to break up a fight between Latinos and blacks, who were arguing over the merits and expense of bilingual education in a school district that has shifted over the past few years from majority African American to majority Hispanic. One parent told reporters that if the Hispanics wanted to learn Spanish they should stay in Mexico.

The demographic shifts are smudging the old lines demarcating two historical, often distinct societies, one black and one white. Reshaped by three decades of rapidly rising immigration, the national story is now far more complicated. Whites currently account for 74 percent of the population, blacks 12 percent, Hispanics 10 percent, and Asians 3 percent. Yet according to data and predictions generated by the U.S. Census Bureau and social scientists poring over the numbers, Hispanics will likely surpass blacks early in the next century. And by the year 2050, demographers predict, Hispanics will account for 25 percent of the population, blacks 14 percent, Asians 8 percent, with whites hovering somewhere around 53 percent. As early as next year, whites will no longer be the majority in California; in Hawaii and New Mexico this is already the case. Soon after, Nevada, Texas, Maryland, and New Jersey are also predicted to become "majority minority" states, entities where no one ethnic group remains the majority.

Effects of 1965 Law

The overwhelming majority of immigrants come from Asia and Latin America—Mexico, the Central American countries, the Philippines, Korea, and Southeast Asia. What triggered this great transformation was a change to immigration law in 1965, when Congress made family reunification the primary criterion for admittance. That new policy, a response to charges that the law favored white Europeans, allowed immigrants already in the United States to bring over their relatives, who in turn could bring over more relatives. As a result, America has been absorbing as many as one million newcomers a year, to the point that now almost one in every ten residents is foreign born. These numbers, relative to the overall population, were slightly higher at the beginning of this century, but the current immigration wave is in many ways very different, and its context inexorably altered, from the last great wave.

12   This time around tensions are sharpened by the changing profile of those who are entering America's borders. Not only are their racial and ethnic backgrounds more varied than in decades past, their place in a modern postindustrial economy has been recast. The newly arrived today can be roughly divided into two camps: those with college degrees and highly specialized skills, and those with almost no education or job training. Some 12 percent of immigrants have graduate degrees, compared to 8 percent of native Americans. But more than one-third of the immigrants have no high school diploma, double the rate for those born in the United States. Before 1970, immigrants were actually doing better than natives overall, as measured by education, rate of home ownership, and average income. But those arriving after 1970 are younger, more likely to be underemployed, and live below the poverty level. As a group, they are doing worse than natives. About 6 percent of new arrivals receive some form of welfare, double the rate for U.S.-born citizens. Among some newcomers—Cambodians and Salvadorans, for example—the numbers are even higher.

With large numbers of immigrants arriving from Latin America, and segregating in barrios, there is also evidence of lingering language problems. Consider that in Miami, three-quarters of residents speak a language other than English at home, and 67 percent of those say that they are not fluent in English. In New York City, four of every ten residents speak a language other than English at home, and of these, half said they do not speak English well.

It is clear that not all of America is experiencing the impact of immigration equally. Although even small midwestern cities have seen sharp changes in their racial and ethnic mix in the past two decades, most immigrants continue to cluster into a handful of large, mostly coastal metropolitan areas: Los Angeles, New York, San Francisco, Chicago, Miami, Washington, D.C., and Houston. They are home to more than a quarter of the total U.S. population and more than 60 percent of all foreign-born residents. But as the immigrants arrive, many American-born citizens pour out of these cities in search of new homes in more homogeneous locales. New York and Los Angeles each lost more than one million native-born residents between 1990 and 1995, even as their populations increased by roughly the same numbers with immigrants. To oversimplify, said University of Michigan demographer William Frey, "For every Mexican who comes to Los Angeles, a white native-born leaves."

Most of the people leaving the big cities are white, and they tend to be working class. This is an entirely new kind of "white flight," whereby whites are not just fleeing the city centers for the suburbs but also are leaving the region and often the state. "The Ozzies and Harriets of the 1990s are skipping the suburbs of the big cities and moving to more homogeneous, mostly white smaller towns and smaller cities and rural areas," Frey said. They're headed to Atlanta, Las Vegas, Phoenix, Portland, Denver, Austin, and Orlando, as well as smaller cities in Nevada, Idaho, Colorado, and Washington. Frey and other demographers believe the domestic migrants—black and white—are being "pushed" out, at least in part, by competition with immigrants for jobs and neighborhoods, political clout and lifestyle. Frey sees in this pattern "the emergence of separate Americas, one white and middle-aged, less urban and another intensely urban, young, multicultural, and multiethnic. One America will care deeply about English as the official language and about preserving social security. The other will care about things like retaining affirmative action and bilingual education."

Ethnic Segregation

16   Even within gateway cities that give the outward appearance of being multicultural, there are sharp lines of ethnic segregation. When describing the ethnic diversity of a bellwether megacity such as Los Angeles, many residents speak roaringly of the great mosaic of many peoples. But the social scientists who look at the hard census data see something more complex. James P. Allen, a cultural geographer at California State University–Northridge, suggests that while Los Angeles, as seen from an airplane, is a tremendously mixed society, on the ground, racial homogeneity and segregation are common. This is not a new phenomenon; there have always been immigrant neighborhoods. Ben Franklin, an early proponent of making English the official language, worried about close-knit German communities. Sen. Daniel Patrick Moynihan (D–N.Y.) described the lingering clannishness of Irish and other immigrant populations in New York in *Beyond the Melting Pot*, a benchmark work from the 1960s that he wrote with Nathan Glazer.

But the persistence of ethnic enclaves and identification does not appear to be going away and may not in a country that is now home to not a few distinct ethnic groups, but to dozens. Hispanics in Los Angeles, to take the dominant group in the nation's second largest city, are more segregated residentially in 1990 than they were ten or twenty years ago, the census tracts show. Moreover, it is possible that what mixing of groups that does occur is only a temporary phenomenon as one ethnic group supplants another in the neighborhood.

If there is deep-seated ethnic segregation, it clearly extends to the American workplace. In many cities, researchers find sustained "ethnic niches" in the labor market. Because jobs are often a matter of whom one knows, the niches were enduring and remarkably resistant to outsiders. In California, for example, Mexican immigrants are employed overwhelmingly as gardeners and domestics, in apparel and furniture manufacturing, and as cooks and food preparers. Koreans open small businesses. Filipinos become nurses and medical technicians. African Americans work in government jobs, an important niche that is increasingly being challenged by Hispanics who want in.

UCLA's Roger Waldinger and others have pointed to the creation, in cities of high immigration, of "dual economies." For the affluent, which includes a disproportionate number of whites, the large labor pool provides them with a ready supply of gardeners, maids, and nannies. For businesses in need of cheap manpower, the same is true. Yet there are fewer "transitional" jobs—the blue-collar work that helped Italian and Irish immigrants move up the economic ladder—to help newcomers or their children on their way to the jobs requiring advanced technical or professional skills that now dominate the upper tier of the economy.

A Rung at a Time

20   Traditionally, immigration scholars have seen the phenomenon of assimilation as a relentless economic progression. The hard-working new arrivals struggle along with a new language and at low-paying jobs in order for their sons and daughters to climb the economic ladder, each generation advancing a rung. There are many cases where this is true. More recently, there is evidence to suggest that economic movement is erratic and that some groups—particularly in high immigration cities—can get "stuck." Among African Americans, for instance, there emerge two distinct patterns. The black middle class is doing demonstrably better—in income, home ownership rates, education—than it was when the demographic transformation (and the civil rights movement) began three decades ago. But for African Americans at the bottom, research indicates that immigration, particularly of Latinos with limited education, has increased joblessness and frustration.

In Miami, where Cuban immigrants dominate the political landscape, tensions are high between Hispanics and blacks, said Nathaniel J. Wilcox, a community activist there. "The perception in the black community, the reality, is that Hispanics don't want some of the power, they want all the power," Wilcox said. "At least when we were going through this with the whites during the Jim Crow era, at least they'd hire us. But Hispanics won't allow African Americans to even compete. They have this feeling that their community is the only community that counts."

Yet many Hispanics too find themselves in an economic "mobility trap." While the new immigrants are willing to work in low-end jobs, their sons and daughters, growing up in the barrios but exposed to the relentless consumerism of popular culture, have greater expectations, but are disadvantaged because of their impoverished settings, particularly the overwhelmed inner-city schools most immigrant children attend. "One doubts that a truck-driving future will satisfy today's servants and assemblers. And this scenario gets a good deal more pessimistic if the region's economy fails to deliver or simply throws up more bad jobs," writes Waldinger, a professor of sociology and director of center for regional policy studies at the University of California–Los Angeles.

Though there are calls to revive efforts to encourage "Americanization" of the newcomers, many researchers now express doubt that the old assimilation model works. For one thing, there is less of a dominant mainstream to enter. Instead, there are a dozen streams, despite the best efforts by the dominant white society to lump groups together by ethnicity. It is a particularly American phenomenon, many say, to label citizens by their ethnicity. When they lived in El Salvador, for example, they saw themselves as a nationality. When they arrive in the United States, they become Hispanic or Latino. So too with Asians. Koreans and Cambodians find little in common, but when they arrive here they become "Asian," and are counted and courted, encouraged or discriminated against as such. "My family has had trouble understanding that we are now Asians, and not Koreans, or people from Korea or Korean Americans, or just plain Americans," said Arthur Lee, who owns a dry cleaning store in Los Angeles. "Sometimes, we laugh about it. Oh, the Asian students are so smart! The Asians have no interest in politics! Whatever. But we don't know what people are talking about. Who are the Asians?"

24 Many immigrant parents say that while they want their children to advance economically in their new country, they do not want them to become "too American." A common concern among Haitians in South Florida is that their children will adopt the attitudes of the inner city's underclass. Vietnamese parents in New Orleans often try to keep their children immersed in their ethnic enclave and try not to let them assimilate too fast.

Hyphenated Americans

One study of the children of immigrants, conducted six years ago among young Haitians, Cubans, West Indians, Mexicans, and Vietnamese in South Florida and southern California, suggests the parents are not alone in their concerns. Asked by researchers Alejandro Portes and Ruben Rumbauthow how they identified themselves, most chose categories of hyphenated Americans. Few choose "American" as their identity. Then there was this—asked if they believe the United States is the best country in the world, most of the youngsters answered: no.

Personal Response

Does the fact that many immigrant parents say "they do not want [their children] to become 'too American'" (paragraph 24) surprise you? How important do you consider your race or ethnicity to your identity? Is the neighborhood where you grew up largely composed of a particular racial or ethnic group, or does it have a mixed population?

Questions for Class or Small-Group Discussion

1. State in your own words what is meant by the terms *melting pot* (paragraphs 1 and 3) and *pluralistic society* (paragraph 3). What does *demographic balkanization* (paragraph 9) mean?

2. State in your own words how, according to Booth, the second great wave of immigration differs from the first great wave. What possible effect do social historians and demographers see in this second wave?

3. How has the 1965 immigration law affected American demographics?

4. In what ways, according to Booth, is America still a highly segregated country? Explain whether your own observations and/or experiences support his assertions.

5. Summarize Booth's discussion of terminology for various racial or ethnic groups (paragraphs 23 through 25). What impact do you think labels or identity markers have on members of those groups?

HISPANICS AND THE AMERICAN DREAM

Linda Chavez

Linda Chavez is president of the Center for Equal Opportunity in Washington, D.C., and writes a weekly column for USA Today. *She regularly appears on* The McLaughlin Group, CNN & Co., *and* The NewsHour with Jim Lehrer. *Her books include* Out of the Barrio: Toward a New Politics of Hispanic Assimilation *(1992) and* From Sugar Daddies to Uncle Sam *(1999). This essay was first published in* Imprimis *in 1996.*

The more than twenty-one million Hispanics now living in the United States are fast becoming the nation's largest minority group. Some demographers can already see the day when one of three Americans will be of Hispanic descent. Will this mean a divided nation with millions of unassimilated, Spanish-speaking, poor, uneducated Hispanics living in the barrios? Well, here is one reply:

> Each decade offered us hope, but our hopes evaporated into smoke. We became the poorest of the poor, the most segregated minority in schools, the lowest paid group in America, and the least educated minority in this nation.

This pessimistic view of Hispanics' progress—offered in 1990 by the president of the National Council of La Raza, one of the country's leading Hispanic civil rights groups—is the prevalent one among Hispanic leaders and is shared by many outside the Hispanic community as well. Hispanics are widely perceived as the dregs of society with little hope of participating in the American Dream.

The trouble with this perception is that it is wrong. The success of Hispanics in the United States has been tremendous. They represent an emerging middle class that is a valuable addition to our culture and our economy. However, their story has been effectively suppressed by Hispanic advocates whose only apparent interest is in spreading the notion that Latinos cannot make it in this society. This has been an easy task since the Hispanic poor, who, although they only constitute about one-fourth of the Hispanic population, are visible to all. These are the Hispanics most likely to be studied, analyzed, and reported on, and certainly they are the ones most likely to be read about. A recent computer search of stories about Hispanics in major newspapers and magazines over a twelve-month period turned up more than eighteen hundred stories in which the words *Hispanic* or *Latino* occurred in close connection with the word *poverty.* In most people's minds, the expression "poor Hispanic" is almost redundant.

Has Hispanics' Progress Stalled?

4   Most Hispanics, rather than being poor, lead solidly lower middle- or middle-class lives, but finding evidence to support this thesis is sometimes difficult. Of course,

Hispanic groups vary one from another, as do individuals within any group. Most analysts acknowledge, for example, that Cubans are highly successful. Within one generation, they have virtually closed the earnings and education gap with other Americans. Although some analysts claim their success is due exclusively to their higher socioeconomic status when they arrived, many Cuban refugees—especially those who came after the first wave in the 1960s—were in fact skilled or semiskilled workers with relatively little education. Their accomplishments in the United States mainly are attributable to diligence and hard work.

Cubans have tended to establish enclave economies, in the traditional immigrant mode, opening restaurants, stores, and other émigré-oriented services. Some Cubans have even formed banks, specializing in international transactions attuned to Latin American as well as local customers, and others have made major investments in real estate development in South Florida. These ventures have provided not only big profits for a few Cubans but jobs for many more. By 1980, there were eighteen thousand Cuban-owned businesses in Miami, and about 70 percent of all Cubans there owned their own homes.

But Cubans are, as a rule, dismissed as the exception among Hispanics. What about other Hispanic groups? Why has there been no "progress" among them? The largest and most important group is the Mexican American population. Its leaders have driven much of the policy agenda affecting all Hispanics, but the importance of Mexican Americans also stems from the fact that they have had a longer history in the United States than any other Hispanic group. If Mexican Americans whose families have lived in the United States for generations are not yet making it in this society, they may have a legitimate claim to consider themselves a more or less permanently disadvantaged group.

That is precisely what Mexican American leaders suggest is happening. Their "proof" is that statistical measures of Mexican American achievement in education, earnings, poverty rates, and other social and economic indicators have remained largely unchanged for decades. If Mexican Americans had made progress, it would show up in these areas, so the argument goes. Since it doesn't, progress must be stalled. In the post–civil rights era, it is also assumed that the failure of a minority to close the social and economic gap with whites is the result of persistent discrimination. Progress is perceived not in absolute but in relative terms. The poor may become less poor over time, but so long as those on the upper rungs of the economic ladder are climbing even faster, the poor are believed to have suffered some harm, even if they have made absolute gains and their lives are much improved. But in order for Hispanics (or any group on the lower rungs) to close the gap, they would have to progress at an even greater rate than non-Hispanic whites.

8   Is this a fair way to judge Hispanics' progress? No. It makes almost no sense to apply this test today (if it ever did) because the Hispanic population itself is changing so rapidly. In 1959, 85 percent of all persons of Mexican origin living in the United States were native-born. Today, only about two-thirds of the people of Mexican origin were born in the United States, and among adults barely one in two was born here.

Increasingly, the Hispanic population, including that of Mexican origin, is made up of new immigrants, who, like immigrants of every era, start off at the bottom of the economic ladder. This infusion of new immigrants is bound to distort our image of progress in the Hispanic population if, each time we measure the group, we include people who have just arrived and have yet to make their way in this society.

In 1980, there were about 14.6 million Hispanics living in the United States; in 1990, there were nearly twenty-one million, representing an increase of 44 percent in one decade. At least one-half of this increase was the result of immigration, legal and illegal. Not surprisingly, when these Hispanics—often poorly educated with minimal or no ability to speak English—are added to the pool being measured, the achievement level of the whole group falls. Yet no major Hispanic organization will acknowledge the validity of this reasonable assumption. Instead, Hispanic leaders complain, "Hispanics are the population that has benefited least from the American economy."

In fact, a careful examination of the voluminous data on the Hispanic population gathered by the Census Bureau and other federal agencies shows that, as a group, Hispanics have made significant progress and that most of them have moved into the social and economic mainstream. In most respects, Hispanics—particularly those born here—are very much like other Americans: They work hard, support their own families without outside assistance, have more education and higher earnings than their parents, and own their own homes. In short, they are pursuing the American Dream with increasing success.

The Hispanic Family

No institution is more important to the success of Hispanics (or any group) than the family. Studies published in the early 1990s reported that 73 percent of all Mexican-origin families and 77 percent of all Cuban-origin families consist of married couples. Only 20 percent of the Mexican-origin and 19 percent of the Cuban-origin families are headed by women with no husband present. While out-of-wedlock births to Mexican-origin women are higher than those to white women generally, they fall considerably short of the number of such births to black women, and Hispanic children born out of wedlock are still likely to grow up in families with two parents.

12   The babies of Mexican-origin women, even those who have received little or no prenatal care, are generally quite healthy. There is also a lower infant mortality rate and smaller incidence of low birth weight, a common predictor of health problems, than among blacks and whites. While researchers are not sure what accounts for the apparent health of even poor Mexican babies, one reason may be that their mothers are less likely to drink, smoke, or use drugs, and they place special emphasis on good nutrition while pregnant.

In general, Hispanic families are somewhat more traditional than non-Hispanic families: Men are expected to work to support their families and women to care for children. Hispanic families tend to be child-centered, which increases the importance of women's role as child bearers. Hispanics are also more likely than other Americans to believe that the demands and needs of the family should take precedence over those of the individual. In an earlier age this attitude was common among other ethnic groups—Italians, for example. Today, however, it runs counter to the dominant culture of individualism characteristic of American life and may even impede individual success. This perhaps explains why so many young Hispanics are starting to drop out of school to take jobs, a decision that has some immediate financial benefits for the family but is detrimental to the individual in the long run. Nonetheless, Hispanics' attachment to family is one of their most positive cultural attributes. Family members are expected to help each other in times of financial or other need, which some analysts believe explains why so many Mexican-origin families shun welfare even when their poverty makes them eligible for assistance.

Hispanics and Public Policy

For most Hispanics, especially those born in the United States, the last few decades have brought greater economic opportunity and social mobility. They are building solid lower middle- and middle-class lives that include two-parent households, with a male head who works full-time and earns a wage commensurate with his education and training. Their educational level has been steadily rising, their earnings no longer reflect wide disparities with those of non-Hispanics, and their occupational distribution is coming to resemble more closely that of the general population. They are buying homes—42 percent of all Hispanics owned or were purchasing their homes in 1989, including 47 percent of all Mexican Americans—and moving away from inner cities. Even in areas with very high concentrations of Hispanics, like Los Angeles, the sociologist Douglas Massey reports, "segregation [is] low or moderate on all dimensions." And, in what is perhaps the ultimate test of assimilation, about one-third of all U.S.-born Hispanics under the age of thirty-five are marrying non-Hispanics.

In light of these facts, the policy prescriptions offered by many Hispanic advocacy organizations and by most politicians seem oddly out of sync. They rely too much on government programs of doubtful efficacy like affirmative action, welfare, and bilingual public education. And they perpetuate demeaning stereotypes of the very people they claim they are championing. What they should be doing instead is promoting tax reform, deregulation, enterprise zones, English instruction, and private education—all of which will help Hispanics help themselves.

16   Groups do not all advance at precisely the same rate in this society—sometimes because of discrimination, sometimes because of other factors. As Thomas Sowell and others have pointed out, no multiethnic society in the world exhibits utopian equality of income, education, and occupational status for every one of its ethnic groups. What is important is that opportunities be made available to all persons, regardless of race or ethnicity. Ultimately, however, it will be up to individuals to take advantage of those opportunities. Increasing numbers of Hispanics are doing just that. And no government action can replace the motivation and will to succeed that propels genuine individual achievement.

Personal Response

Are you convinced by Linda Chavez's argument? Has your understanding of Hispanics changed or been reinforced as a result of reading this essay? Explain your answer. If you are Hispanic, describe your feelings as you read the essay.

Questions for Class or Small-Group Discussion

1. How does Linda Chavez answer the question she poses in paragraph 1: "Will this [the possibility that one day one of three Americans will be of Hispanic descent] mean a divided nation with millions of unassimilated, Spanish-speaking, poor, uneducated Hispanics living in the barrios?"

2. Chavez notes in paragraph 3 that a recent search of stories in periodicals over a one-year period "turned up more than eighteen hundred stories in which the words *Hispanic* or *Latino* occurred in close connection with the word *poverty.*" Discuss the implications of this statement. What Hispanic group does Chavez use as an outstanding example of an exception to the popular perception of Hispanics? In what other ways are stereotypes of any racial or ethnic group reinforced, consciously or unconsciously, by the media?

COLORBLIND

Alex Kotlowitz

Alex Kotlowitz's investigative articles appear regularly in such national magazines as the New Yorker *and the* New York Times Sunday Magazine. *Formerly a staff writer for the* Wall Street Journal, *he is the author of* There are No Children Here: The Story of Two Boys Growing up in the Other America *(1992) and* The Other Side of the River: A Story of Two Towns, a Death and America's Dilemma *(1998). This essay appeared in the January 11, 1998, issue of the* New York Times *Magazine.*

One Christmas day seven years ago, I'd gone over to the Henry Horner Homes in Chicago to visit with Lafeyette and Pharoah, the subjects of my book *There Are No Children Here.* I had brought presents for the boys, as well as a gift for their friend Rickey, who lived on the other side of the housing complex, an area controlled by a rival gang. Lafeyette and Pharoah insisted on walking over with me. It was eerily quiet, since most everyone was inside, and so, bundled from the cold, we strolled toward the other end in silence. As we neared Damen Avenue, a kind of demilitarized zone, a uniformed police officer, a white woman, approached us. She looked first at the two boys, neither of whom reached my shoulder, and then directly at me. "Are you O.K.?" she asked.

About a year later, I was with Pharoah on the city's North Side, shopping for high-tops. We were walking down the busy street, my hand on Pharoah's shoulder, when a middle-aged black man approached. He looked at me, and then at Pharoah. "Son," he asked, "are you O.K.?"

Both this white police officer and middle-aged black man seemed certain of what they witnessed. The white woman saw a white man possibly in trouble; the black man saw a black boy possibly in trouble. It's all about perspective—which has everything to do with our personal and collective experiences, which are consistently informed by race. From those experiences, from our histories, we build myths, legends that both guide us and constrain us, legends that include both fact and fiction. This is not to say the truth doesn't matter. It does, in a big way. It's just that getting there may not be easy, in part because everyone is so quick to choose sides, to refute the other's myths and to pass on their own.

4   We'd do well to keep this in mind as we enter the yearlong dialogue on race convened by President Clinton. Yes, conversation is critical, but not without self-reflection, both individually and communally. While myths help us make sense of the incomprehensible, they can also confine us, confuse us, and leave us prey to historical laziness. Moreover, truth is not always easily discernible—and even when it is, the prism, depending on which side of the river you reside on, may create a wholly different illusion. Many whites were quick to believe Susan Smith, the South Carolina mother who claimed that a black man had killed her children. And with the reawakening of the Tawana Brawley case, we learn that, although a grand jury has determined otherwise, many blacks still believe she was brutally raped by a group of white men. We—blacks and whites—need to examine and question our own perspectives. Only then can we grasp each other's myths and grapple with the truths.

In 1992, I came across the story of a sixteen-year-old black boy, Eric McGinnis, whose body had been found a year earlier floating in the St. Joseph River in southwestern Michigan. The river flows between Benton Harbor and St. Joseph, two small towns whose only connections are two bridges and a powerful undertow of contrasts.

St. Joseph is a town of nine thousand and, with its quaint downtown and brick-paved streets, resembles a New England tourist haunt. But for those in Benton Harbor, St. Joseph's most defining characteristic is its racial makeup: It is 95 percent white. Benton Harbor, a town of twelve thousand on the other side of the river, is 92 percent black and dirt poor. For years, the municipality so hurt for money that it could not afford to raze abandoned buildings.

Eric, a high-school sophomore whose passion was dancing, was last seen at the Club, a teenage nightspot in St. Joseph, where weeks earlier he had met and started dating a white girl. The night Eric disappeared, a white man said he caught the boy trying to break into his car and chased him—away from the river, past an off-duty white deputy sheriff. That was the last known moment he was seen alive, and it was then that the myths began.

8   I became obsessed with Eric's death, and so for five years moved in and out of these two communities, searching for answers to both Eric's disappearance and to matters of race. People would often ask which side of the river I was staying on, wanting to gauge my allegiance. And they would often ask about the secrets of those across the way or, looking for affirmation, repeat myths passed on from one generation to the next.

Once, during an unusually bitter effort by white school-board members to fire Benton Harbor's black superintendent, one black woman asked me: "How do you know how to do this? Do you take lessons? How do you all stick together the way you do?" Of course, we don't. Neither community is as unified or monolithic as the other believes. Indeed, contrary to the impression of those in St. Joseph, the black community itself was deeply divided in its support for the superintendent, who was eventually fired.

On occasion, whites in St. Joseph would regale me with tales of families migrating to Benton Harbor from nearby states for the high welfare benefits. It is, they would tell me, the reason for the town's economic decline. While some single mothers indeed moved to Benton Harbor and other Michigan cities in the early eighties to receive public assistance, the truth is that in the thirties and forties factories recruited blacks from the South, and when those factories shut down, unemployment, particularly among blacks, skyrocketed.

But the question most often asked was: "Why us? Why write about St. Joseph and Benton Harbor?" I would tell them that while the contrasts between the towns seem unusually stark, they are, I believe, typical of how most of us live: physically and spiritually isolated from one another.

12   It's not that I didn't find individuals who crossed the river to spend time with their neighbors. One St. Joseph woman, Amy Johnson, devotes her waking hours to a Benton Harbor community center. And Eric McGinnis himself was among a handful of black teenagers who spent weekend nights at the Club in St. Joseph. Nor is it that I didn't find racial animosity. One St. Joseph resident informed me that Eric got what he deserved: "That nigger came on the wrong side of the bridge," he said. And Benton Harbor's former school superintendent, Sherwin Allen, made no effort to hide his contempt for the white power structure.

What I found in the main, though, were people who would like to do right but don't know where to begin. As was said of the South's politicians during Jim Crow, race diminishes us. It incites us to act as we wouldn't in other arenas: clumsily, cowardly, and sometimes cruelly. We circle the wagons, watching out for our own.

That's what happened in the response to Eric's death. Most everyone in St. Joseph came to believe that Eric, knowing the police were looking for him, tried to swim the river to get home and drowned. Most everyone in Benton Harbor, with equal certitude, believes that Eric was killed—most likely by whites, most likely because he dated a white girl. I was struck by the disparity in perspective, the competing realities, but I was equally taken aback by the distance between the two towns—which, of course, accounts for the myths. Jim Reeves, the police lieutenant, who headed the investigation into Eric's death, once confided that this teenager he'd never met had more impact on him than any other black person.

I'm often asked by whites, with some wonderment, how it is that I'm able to spend so much time in black communities without feeling misunderstood or unwelcomed or threatened. I find it much easier to talk with blacks about race than with fellow whites. While blacks often brave slights silently for fear that if they complain they won't be believed, when asked, they welcome the chance to relate their experiences. Among whites, there's a reluctance—or a lack of opportunity—to engage.

Race for them poses no urgency; it does not impose on their daily routines. I once asked Ben Butzbaugh, a St. Joseph commissioner, how he felt the two towns got along. "I think we're pretty fair in this community," he said. "I don't know that I can say I know of any out-and-out racial-type things that occur. I just think people like their own better than others. I think that's pretty universal. Don't you? . . . We're not a bunch of racists. We're not anything America isn't." Butzbaugh proudly pointed to his friendship with Renée Williams, Benton Harbor's new school superintendent. "Renée was in our home three, four, five days a week," he noted. "Nice gal. Put herself through school. We'd talk all the time." Williams used to clean for Butzbaugh's family.

16   As I learned during the years in and out of these towns, the room for day-to-day dialogue doesn't present itself. We become buried in our myths, certain of our truths—and refuse to acknowledge what the historian Allan Nevins calls "the grains of stony reality" embedded in most legends. A quarter-century ago, race was part of everyday public discourse; today it haunts us quietly, though on occasion—the Rodney King beating or the Simpson trial or Eric McGinnis's death—it erupts with jarring urgency. At these moments of crisis, during these squalls, we flail about, trying to find moral ballast. By then it is usually too late. The lines are drawn. Accusations are hurled across the river like cannon fire. And the cease-fires, when they occur, are just that, cease-fires, temporary and fragile. Even the best of people have already chosen sides.

Personal Response

If you are black or white, describe your feelings as you read this essay and your perspective of the tension between the two groups. If you are neither black nor white, explain your perspective of the tension between whites and blacks.

Questions for Class or Small-Group Discussion

1. Locate Kotlowitz's central idea or thesis, and then summarize his viewpoint on that issue. What is your opinion of his viewpoint? Do you agree or disagree with him? To what extent do your own observations or experiences support his conclusions?

2. Discuss your understanding of this statement: "It's all about perspective—which has everything to do with our personal and collective experiences, which are consistently informed by race. From those experiences, from our histories, we build myths, legends that both guide us and constrain us, legends that include both fact and fiction" (paragraph 3). Then explain the extent to which you agree with Kotlowitz.

3. Explain the reference to Jim Crow in paragraph 13, and then respond to Kotlowitz's statement that "race diminishes us. It incites us to act as we wouldn't in other arenas: clumsily, cowardly, and sometimes cruelly."

4. Are you surprised by Kotlowitz's comment in paragraph 15 that he finds it "much easier to talk with blacks about race than with fellow whites"? Does his explanation

seem plausible to you? To what extent is your own experience or observation similar to his?

PERSPECTIVES ON RACE AND ETHNICITY

Suggestions for Synthesis

1. Compare what Linda Chavez, in "Hispanics and the American Dream," says about Hispanics and assimilation into American society with the developments that William Booth discusses in "One Nation, Indivisible: Is It History?"

2. Refer to the comments of at least two writers in this chapter as you discuss the subject of stereotypes and prejudice. As you plan your essay, consider the following questions: Where do people get prejudices? What aspects of American culture reinforce and/or perpetuate stereotypes? How can you personally work against stereotyping and prejudice?

3. Conduct a class workshop on prejudice in America. The entire class should agree on the topics to cover and the format for the workshop. Individual students may volunteer to write papers or speak from notes for presentation to the class, or you may want to invite guest speakers such as the affirmative action officer from your campus or the director of your campus minority studies program, if you have one.

4. Explore your position on the issue of a "melting pot" (a society in which minorities are assimilated into the dominant culture) versus pluralism (a society in which ethnic and racial groups maintain separate identities, with no dominant culture). Take into consideration the views of two or more authors in this chapter.

5. Several of the authors in this chapter touch on the issue of labels. Synthesize their discussions into your own analysis of the role labels play in one's identity, self-esteem, and/or self-concept.

6. Interview at least one other person whose racial or ethnic heritage is different from yours about some of the points raised in at least two of the essays in this chapter. Then write an essay explaining what you learned and how the interview has in any way changed your own views on the issue of racism.

Additional Writing Topics

1. Write a reflective essay on your own cultural heritage, explaining your family's background and how you feel about that heritage.

2. Explain the importance of race or ethnicity to your own self-identity. Is it as important as your gender, your job, your socioeconomic level, or your educational level?

3. Alex Kotlowitz writes in "Colorblind": "We—blacks and whites—need to examine and question our own perspectives. Only then can we grasp each other's myths and grapple with the truths" (paragraph 4). Write an essay responding to that statement in which you try to sort out the two perspectives and offer some possible ways for the two groups to begin understanding one another.

4. Write a letter to the editor of the *New York Times Magazine* in which you explain your response to Alex Kotlowitz's viewpoint in "Colorblind."

5. Write an essay exploring the role of racial and ethnic diversity in your educational experiences in high school and college. Consider these questions: How diverse are the student populations of schools you have attended? How large a component did multiculturalism play in the curricula of courses you have taken? Have you been satisfied with that aspect of your education?

6. Referring to Alex Kotlowitz's "Colorblind" where relevant, explain your own theory on the conditions that prevent blacks and whites in America from understanding one another's perspectives.

7. Respond to this statement: "It's all about perspective—which has everything to do with our personal and collective experiences, which are consistently informed by race. From those experiences, from our histories, we build myths, legends that both guide us and constrain us, legends that include both fact and fiction" (Alex Kotlowitz's "Colorblind," paragraph 3).

8. Respond to Linda Chavez's claim, in "Hispanics and the American Dream," that public policies like affirmative action, welfare, and bilingual public education are ineffective and, worse, "perpetuate demeaning stereotypes of the very people they claim they are championing" (paragraph 15).

9. Narrate your first experience with prejudice, discrimination, or bigotry, as either a witness or a victim. Describe in detail the incident and how it made you feel.

10. Explain the effects of racial prejudice on a person or a group of people familiar to you.

11. Write an essay in which you set forth starting points for countering prejudice or ethnic and racial hatred in the United States.

Research Topics

1. As a starting point for a research project, read Linda Chavez's *Out of the Barrio: Toward a New Politics of Hispanic Assimilation* or Alex Kotlowitz's *There Are No Children Here: The Story of Two Boys Growing Up in the Other America* or *The Other Side of the River: A Story of Two Towns, a Death, and America's Dilemma.* You may decide to find out more about a major point the author makes, or something the author mentions may lead you to a suitable topic. If the book has a bibliography, you have an excellent list of potential resources for your project.

2. Research one aspect of the subject of immigration raised by William Booth in "One Nation, Indivisible: Is It History?" or Linda Chavez in "Hispanics and the American Dream."

3. Research and write a paper on one of the following topics related to some of the essays in this chapter: Jim Crow; the influx of Chinese immigrants to America in the nineteenth century; the Chinese Exclusion Act of 1882 and its implications for Japanese immigrants; the Japanese religion Shinto; the internment of people of

Japanese ancestry in America during World War II; or the economic, political, or historical relationship of the United States with Puerto Rico, Cuba, Central America, or Mexico.

4. Research the subject of multiculturalism in American education by reading expressions of differing opinions on the subject.

5. Select a topic from any of the writing topics in Suggestions for Synthesis or Additional Writing Topics, and expand it to include library research, Internet research, and/or interviews.

CHAPTER 17

TERRORISM

Terrorism is a sinister and reprehensible expression of hatred or vengeance. Terrorists, whether individuals or groups, target specific enemies and contrive to cause destruction, create havoc, and in general make a spectacular and grisly statement. Acts of terrorism are not new to this century nor the last, but they do seem to have grown more deadly, more widespread, and increasingly more difficult to combat. Nations, religions, and groups of assorted allegiances and identities have all been victims of numerous violent acts over time.

America is one nation that has experienced terrorism both abroad and at home. For instance, in 1979, militant students in Tehran stormed the U.S. Embassy there and held 52 hostages for 444 days. In 1983, a suicide-bomb attack destroyed the U.S. Embassy in Beirut, killing 63. That same year, also in Beirut, Hezbollah suicide bombers claimed responsibility for blowing up U.S. and French military headquarters, killing 241 U.S. and 58 French servicemen. In 1988, Pan Am flight 103, on its way to the United States, exploded over Lockerbie, Scotland, killing 270 people. On American soil, in 1993 a bomb in the underground garage of the World Trade Center killed six and injured more than 1,000 people; in 1995, a truck bomb destroyed a federal building in Oklahoma City, killing 168 and injuring more than 600.

By far the largest acts of terrorism in terms of lives lost and effects on the economy, the way people live, and American society in countless ways have been the September 11, 2001, attacks on the World Trade Center in New York City and the Pentagon in Washington, D.C. Those attacks have had profound effects on America and both its allies and foes. Many countries around the world expressed not only their shock and outrage at the terrorism on American soil but also their deep sympathy for the families, friends, and loved ones of those who lost their lives or were injured in the attacks. The essays in this chapter represent some perspectives on that tragic day and its aftereffects. All were written within weeks, some just days, of September 11.

First, Fareed Zakaria in "The End of the End of History" writes on the end of the post–Cold War period. Zakaria takes as his starting point a reference to a 1990 essay (and later book) by Francis

Fukuyama called "The End of History." Fukuyama argues that, in a sense, History (with a capital "H") ended—or approached its end—with the end of the Cold War, the end of communism, and the end of dictatorships. These oppressive forms of government have been replaced by the principles of liberal democracy, Fukuyama believes, and the world has evolved into a kind of ideal civilization. Zakaria, then, suggests that, with the September 11 terrorist attacks, "[t]his is surely the End of the End of History." He calls for countries that have benefited from free trade and American democracy to support the United States in its fight against terrorism. As if in reply, Zakaria's article is followed by a *Times* of London editorial entitled "With One Voice: Washington, Westminister and the World," published just three days after the attacks. Like major newspapers around the world, *The Times* called for unified support of America's fight against terrorism.

Lance Morrow's opinion piece, "The Case for Rage and Retribution," discusses the response of Americans to terrorist attacks on the World Trade Center in New York City and the Pentagon in Washington, D.C., on September 11, 2001. Morrow argues that Americans need to express rage and ruthless indignation over the attacks and suggests that those behind the attacks need to be found and killed. Reshma Memon Yaqub, in "I'm Not the Enemy," does not disagree with Morrow but offers a desperate caution. She describes her panicked reaction to the news of the September 11 attacks and then makes a plea to her fellow Americans not to mistake the actions of a few extremist Muslims as representing the beliefs of all Muslims. Speaking as an American who is Muslim as well as a mother, a wife, and a sister, she expresses her pain for the suffering of victims of the attacks and her fear for the safety of her family and friends.

Finally, David Pryce-Jones, in "Why They Hate Us," offers his observations on the sources of anti-American sentiment in the international Arab community. He explains the division between extremist Muslims and moderate Muslims and addresses the need for military retaliation against those who were responsible for the September 11 terrorist attacks in America.

THE END OF THE END OF HISTORY

Fareed Zakaria

Fareed Zakaria was born in Chicago and grew up in New York City. He taught in Harvard University's Department of Government and

> *ran the Project on the Changing Security Environment and American*
> *National Interests. Zakaria was managing editor of* Foreign Affairs
> *from 1993–2000 and became editor of* Newsweek *magazine's*
> *overseas editions in October 2000. He writes on international affairs*
> *for a variety of periodicals, including the* New York Times, *the* Wall
> Street Journal, *and the* New Republic. *Zakaria was named "one*
> *of the 21 most important people of the 21st century" by* Esquire
> *magazine in 1999. This essay appeared in the September 24, 2001,*
> *issue of* Newsweek.

Historians will surely say, "This was the week that America changed." In the midst of jagged emotions of the moment—horror, rage, grief—we can all sense that the country has crossed a watershed. But we don't quite know what that means. Accustomed as we are to whipping up a froth of hysteria about trivia, we are struck silent by honest-to-goodness history.

Or History. This is surely the End of the End of History—the notion that after the cold war, ideological or political tussles were dead and life would be spent managing the economy and worrying about consumerism. In his brilliant essay, Francis Fukuyama actually considered the threat of radical Islam but pointed out correctly that, unlike communism, it has no ideological appeal beyond the borders of the Muslim world. Radical Islam as an ideology, in other words, posed no threat to the West. But we pose a threat to it, one its followers feel with blinding intensity. It turns out it takes only one side to restart History.

This is also the end of the triumph of economics. That's not to say that the economy will not remain central to our society. But the idea that politics was unimportant and that government didn't matter seems almost absurd in the light of last week's events. (And not just government and the highest levels. Who can look at the extraordinary sacrifices made by the firefighters and policemen of New York City and still believe that making a million dollars is the meaning of life?) When asked whether the administration's $40 billion request to rebuild New York and combat terrorism would bust the budget, the president's spokesman brushed it off, saying simply, "National security comes first."

4   Around the world we will see governments become more powerful, more intrusive and more important. This may not please civil libertarians and human-rights activists, but it will not matter. The state is back, and for the oldest Hobbesian reason in the book—the provision of security.

For Americans, security has seemed a birthright. As a result, for much of the past century America has felt that foreign policy was a matter of choice, not necessity. We have been deeply involved in the world, but we have also withdrawn from it when we wished. In our diplomacy and alliances, we assumed that the world needed us more than we needed them.

No more. Of course we should and will strike alone when necessary. Well-placed sources have told me that the administration is convinced that the Afghan government knows where Osama bin Laden is. He may even be under its protection. We should make clear to the governments of Afghanistan and Pakistan that unless they hand him over they will pay a terrible price. But that price would be greater still if we get NATO and Russia to join with us.

Even more importantly, the real war against terrorism is going to be a war of police work, intelligence and covert actions. We cannot do this alone. We will need the active support of other governments to cooperate, share information, close down safe houses, confiscate assets and make arrests. For the first time, we need them as much as they need us.

8   Some have said that this is also, finally, the end of the cold war. Our military, for example, will now properly refocus itself around this new threat. Yes, but in another sense, the cold war is back. The long twilight struggle we face, like that against communism, is both military and political. The first is crucial: just as the nuclear buildup and proxy battles were at the center of the cold war, so military strikes and covert operations will be at the core of this one. But as important was the political struggle we waged across the world. From the start, America realized one of its chief missions was to discredit communism and lessen its appeal around the world. Our task now is to make sure that radical Islam is not seen as an attractive option around the Muslim world. We can do this in various ways but most significantly by supporting Muslim moderates and secularists. No matter how successful the military strategy, ultimately this war will be won or lost on these political grounds.

For America, this is the end of unilateralism. And for the rest of the world it is the end of the free ride. People are now going to realize just how much they enjoyed the benefits of globalization; the peace and prosperity; the ease of trade and travel, the information and entertainment. They watched the movies, listened to the music, read the magazines, vacationed in America and sent their children to college here. But none of this required them actively to support the United States or affirm its values. They could denounce America by day and consume its bounties by night.

But all these countries—in Europe and Asia and Latin America—must recognize that the world they have gotten used to will not survive if America is crippled. The United States is the pivot that makes today's globalization go round. If other countries believe in individual liberty, in free enterprise and free trade, in religious freedom, in democracy, then they are eating the fruits of the American order. And this order can be truly secure only when all those who benefit from it stand in its defense. Those abroad who love liberty cannot watch this war as if it were a horror movie, wondering how it will end. This is your struggle, too.

Personal Response

In what ways, if any, did the September 11, 2001, terrorist attacks change you?

Questions for Class or Small-Group Discussion

1. In what ways do you think America has changed since the September 11 terrorist attacks? Do you think that Zackaria is right in calling the week of those events "a watershed" (paragraph 1)? Explain your answer.

2. What do you understand Zackaria to mean when he says that "we are struck silent by honest-to-goodness history. Or History" (paragraphs 1–2). What distinction does he draw between *history* and *History?* What do you think Zackaria means when he says, "This is also the end of the triumph of economics" (paragraph 3)?

3. Zakaria predicts that "we will see governments become more powerful, more intrusive and more important." He goes on to say, "This may not please civil libertarians and human-rights activists but it will not matter. The state is back ..." (paragraph 4). How far do you think the government should be allowed to go in order to protect the nation? Are there any limits beyond which it should not go to protect national security? Is there a point at which individual liberty becomes more important, or is the common good always of higher importance?

4. Discuss the point Zakaria makes in paragraph 8 by contrasting the beliefs and actions of radical Islam with Muslim moderates and secularists.

5. In what way had America been unilateralist before September 11, and how were the terrorist attacks responsible for "the end of unilateralism" for America (paragraph 9)?

WITH ONE VOICE: WASHINGTON, WESTMINSTER AND THE WORLD

The Times of London

Following the September 11 terrorist attacks on the World Trade Center and the Pentagon, this article appeared in September 14, 2001, issue of The Times of London.

Soon the dead will be counted—in many thousands. It is a miracle that the living are still being rescued by the masked and dust-caked, bone tired, devoted crews sifting the rubble mountain on the still unstable streets of Lower Manhattan. By now, each survivor is a reminder of how very many have been crushed or burnt to death. There are companies which had hundreds working in the twin towers and still have no news from or about a single employee. The final toll could exceed that of the bloodiest day's fighting ever recorded. Anger and anguish is more likely to mount than subside in the coming days.

The World Trade Centre will soon be shown, too, to have been as international as its name boasted. The roll of the dead will contain names from dozens of nations from every continent, names of colleagues and competitors in towers that were the very opposite of Babel, names of those who worked together with the most sophisticated modern communications. Many hundreds of them, more than most people in this country can at first have imagined, will be young and British.

This was never an American catastrophe but always the world's. It is the world's literally as well as metaphorically. The silent dead of many lands will speak to that truth; their countrymen must hear them. We are all counter-terrorists now. That cannot be repeated too often by the politicians we trust to defend our freedoms. And they will need to muster all their eloquence because this will be a war of attrition, costly, long and full of risk, against fanatics within the gates.

4   Nothing is harder for democracies than eternal vigilance and constraints on cherished liberties. Tolerance is small for high casualties in unconventional military operations. President Bush called this yesterday the first war of the 21st century; but support can leech rapidly away from wars that cannot securely be said to be over—as wars against terrorism by definition cannot be. In this war of attrition, the coalition that must be built is for the long term; it is useless if it is not wide; and yet it must be held together without sacrificing flexibility. It is essential to preserve the freedom to act of the United States and its close allies.

In this world-spanning task of persuasion, George W. Bush will need help. A newcomer, to the international scene but also to Washington, he lacks experience; but he has people about him who can meet that need. What has been more important over the past few days, though, is another lack: the President uses words like pieces of wood. Time and again he has striven to match the occasion, to comfort, inspire, to intimidate. Like his father before him, he has fallen flat. For the world beyond his homelands, his language poses a genuine problem of leadership.

It is part of the burden of being the leader of the free world that an American President is expected to be possessed of Hobbes's "common power to keep men in awe." The White House aura alone is not enough to project it. Speechwriters do not yet seem able to supply it.

No one else can speak for a President. But Britain could be of huge help in the task of coalition-building. Tony Blair did that job magnificently over Kosovo; after his inexplicable failures to explain what Britain's purposes are in Macedonia, he has once again shown this week how well he can raise his game in emergencies. His decision to recall Parliament for today's emergency debate provides an opportunity to show what quantities of goodwill and determination Britain has and how much Washington can expect by way of backing.

8   This debate will also be the debut of Iain Duncan Smith as Leader of the Opposition. It so happens that the Conservatives have voted, and voted decisively, for a politician who is better known in Washington, where his standing could hardly be higher, than he as yet is in his own country. As a former serving officer, Mr Duncan Smith could have been tempted to do the political equivalent of pulling rank, outbidding the Government and demanding tougher military action whatever was decided. In his acknowledgement speech yesterday, he showed no such inclination. Rightly judging that this emergency cannot permit of politics as usual, he made a point of his determination to stand four-square with the Government. In combination, these two could be a formidable team putting the counter-terrorist case to the world and, in Europe, ensuring that there are no transatlantic misunderstandings either now or as plans of action are developed in concert.

Much will be expected of America's friends—and not only of its friends. The world divides after this tremendous event into two camps, with no possibility of neutrality, no middle way, between them.

In the first camp stand those governments and peoples ready to do everything possible, quite possibly at considerable risk to themselves, to search out the conspirators behind these monstrous acts and, more generally, to declare war on terrorism wherever it is found. In the second camp are those who harbour terrorism—and also those who tolerate it, since in practice if not morally that comes to much the same thing. A safe house is a safe house, regardless of motive or political circumstance.

The tolerators have been tolerated until now, where it was known that clandestine cells were powerful enough to destabilise the government that challenged them. There has even been acceptance that some societies attempt, as some Japanese commentators have pusillanimously been urging even in this dreadful week, to avoid being involved for fear that their citizens and country may then become a target for terrorists too.

12 That tolerance is now at an end; it was never realistic. The world's sole superpower will always be terrorism's prime target, but as Lord Robertson of Port Ellen, Nato's Secretary-General, remarked after Nato governments invoked Article 5 of its Charter for the first time in the Alliance's 52-year history, what happened in the United States could have happened to any Nato member.

To have declared this attack to be an attack on all—thus entitling the United States to material as well as moral support in the military actions on which it decides—is thus to acknowledge reality as well as to fulfil the duty of solidarity. It was unfortunate that a British Foreign Secretary should have chosen, as Jack Straw did yesterday, to give the impression that Article 5 could also, because of the requirements for consultation that Nato co-ordination implies, act as a constraint on America. In strict legal terms that may be true; this decision in no way gives the Pentagon a blank cheque. But reining Washington in is the last thing America's closest ally should be suggesting. There will be fierce arguments enough ahead; any caveats should be reserved for operational questions.

Nato will not be the only, perhaps not even the main, actor in the drama whose first act is unfolding. The Bush Administration has been widely suspected of unilateralist leanings, but it has given no hint of that this week. On the contrary, there is every reason to believe that when Mr Bush says he is out to "rally the world," he means precisely that. America, Colin Powell said yesterday, "has a right to expect everybody to take sides. . . . We will judge accordingly. It is time for people to say what they are and to act like it." The US is working particularly closely with Russia, where President Putin has shown himself anxious to respond positively; and Mr Powell has been emphatic about including Muslim nations in the grand coalition. They have, as he says and as Egypt, Jordan and others know from their own experience, "just as much to fear from terrorism that strikes at innocent civilians."

This will, however, pose difficult political and diplomatic challenges. If the Afghanistan-based Saudi terrorist Osama bin Laden is the target, the most critical allies for operational purposes will be the states that border Afghanistan. Those to the country's north have solid motives to offer facilities, and little to fear from doing so.

16   Pakistan, however, which is politically and strategically vital to any operation aimed at bin Laden and his networks, is an entirely different matter. Not only is it home to two and a half million Afghan refugees, in camps which have become hotbeds of militancy, but its support for Taleban has had monstrous consequences for Pakistan itself. The country has become progressively Talebanised; and the agent of this Islamist radicalisation is Pakistan's own military intelligence, which acts much like a state within a state and which, as promoter, armourer and technical adviser, has been hand in mailed fist with Taleban and still is.

It is this radicalisation, quite as much as the country's corrosive political corruption, that led to the crisis that brought President Pervez Musharraf to power in a "temporary" military custodianship. America strongly condemned that coup but may now be thankful for it. Mr Musharraf has given very strong undertakings of cooperation; and he may be assumed to be sincere since it is strongly in Pakistan's interest to shed its deserved image of being soft on terrorism.

He has also stopped saying that his Government has no influence with Taleban and sent emissaries to press them to yield up bin Laden. But the loyalty of his commanders cannot be relied on.

For the West, therefore, an essential part of the task ahead is to do what it can to help and reassure vulnerable governments which want to do the right thing but are with reason fearful that they may not survive in power if they do. That was true in the Gulf War; and the lesson then, which should be remembered now, is that the best defence is attack. So long as the Western allies were understood to be absolutely determined to deal with Saddam Hussein, they had Arab support. When they wavered, so did Iraq's neighbours. That lesson should be applied to Pakistan now.

20   The West, and this applies in particular to Britain itself, needs to lead in another respect by force of example. In this confrontation, the democracies occupy the moral high ground. But they must clean their own houses of terrorist taint. Out of misplaced tolerance, Britain has harboured far too many who describe themselves as Muslim clerics but who are cheerleaders and fundraisers for bin Laden and his kind. Today in Parliament, Mr Blair must tell the country as much as discretion permits about how Britain intends to strike back against terrorism. But he must tell the country in plain English how he proposes, in addition, to purge supporters of terror such as these, who have no claim to be considered political refugees, from Britain's streets.

Personal Response

Which statements in this article do you especially like? Are there any statements that you take exception to? Explain your answer.

Questions for Class or Small-Group Discussion

1. Summarize *The Times'* view of America and its willingness to help in America's fight against terrorism. What do you think are the implications of this statement: "We are all counter-terrorists now" (paragraph 3).

2. Discuss this statement in paragraph 3: "This was never an American catastrophe but always the world's. It is the world's literally as well as metaphorically." To what extent do you agree with it?

3. Explain what you understand by this statement: "[T]his will be a war of attrition, costly, long and full of risk, against fanatics within the gates" (paragraph 3). What is "a war of attrition"? Who are the "fanatics within the gates"?

4. This article asserts that the coalition against terrorism will "pose difficult political and diplomatic challenges" (paragraph 15). Discuss what challenges *The Times* foresaw and what political and diplomatic challenges have been faced since the article was published.

THE CASE FOR RAGE AND RETRIBUTION

Lance Morrow

Lance Morrow joined Time *magazine in 1965 as a writer covering national affairs. In 1976, he became an essayist at* Time *and has written hundreds of pieces on everything from politics to culture to international affairs, including more than 150 Time cover stories. He won the National Magazine Award in 1981 in Essay and Criticism for a series of essays about America. Morrow is the author of five books, including two collections of essays,* Fishing in the Tiber *(1988) and* America: A Rediscovery *(1987), and two memoirs,* The Chief: A Memoir of Fathers and Sons *(1984) and* The Heart *(1995). He has been University Professor at Boston University since 1996. This essay appeared in a* Time *Special Edition, which was published within days of the September 11, 2001, terrorist attacks in New York and Washington.*

For once, let's have no "grief counselors" standing by with banal consolations, as if the purpose, in the midst of all this, were merely to make everyone feel better as quickly as possible. We shouldn't feel better.

For once, let's have no fatuous rhetoric about "healing." Healing is inappropriate now, and dangerous. There will be time later for the tears of sorrow.

A day cannot live in infamy without the nourishment of rage. Let's have rage.

4   What's needed is a unified, unifying, Pearl Harbor sort of purple American fury—a ruthless indignation that doesn't leak away in a week or two, wandering off into Prozac-induced forgetfulness or into the next media sensation (O.J. . . . Elián . . . Chandra . . .) or into a corruptly thoughtful relativism (as has happened in the recent past, when, for example, you might hear someone say, "Terrible what he did, of course, but, you know, the Unabomber does have a point, doesn't he, about modern technology?").

Let America explore the rich reciprocal possibilities of the *fatwa*. A policy of focused brutality does not come easily to a self-conscious, self-indulgent, contradictory, diverse, humane nation with a short attention span. America needs to relearn a lost discipline, self-confident relentlessness—and to relearn why human nature has equipped us all with a weapon (abhorred in decent peacetime societies) called hatred.

As the bodies are counted, into the thousands and thousands, hatred will not, I think, be a difficult emotion to summon. Is the medicine too strong? Call it, rather, a wholesome and intelligent enmity—the sort that impels even such a prosperous, messily tolerant organism as America to act. Anyone who does not loathe the people who did these things, and the people who cheer them on, is too philosophical for decent company.

It's a practical matter, anyway. In war, enemies are enemies. You find them and put them out of business, on the sound principle that that's what they are trying to do to you. If what happened on Tuesday does not give Americans the political will needed to exterminate men like Osama bin Laden and those who conspire with them in evil mischief, then nothing ever will and we are in for a procession of black Tuesdays.

8   This was terrorism brought to near perfection as a dramatic form. Never has the evil business had such production values. Normally, the audience sees only the smoking aftermath—the blown-up embassy, the ruined barracks, the ship with a blackened hole at the waterline. This time the first plane striking the first tower acted as a shill. It alerted the media, brought cameras to the scene so that they might be set up to record the vivid surreal bloom of the second strike ("Am I seeing this?") and then—could they be such engineering geniuses, so deft at demolition?—the catastrophic collapse of the two towers, one after the other, and a sequence of panic in the streets that might have been shot for a remake of *The War of the Worlds* or for *Independence Day*. Evil possesses an instinct for theater, which is why, in an era of gaudy and gifted media, evil may vastly magnify its damage by the power of horrific images.

It is important not to be transfixed. The police screamed to the people running from the towers, "Don't look back!"—a biblical warning against the power of the image. Terrorism is sometimes described (in a frustrated, oh-the-burdens-of-great-power tone of voice) as "asymmetrical warfare." So what? Most of history is a pageant of asymmetries. It is mostly the asymmetries that cause history to happen—an obscure Schickelgruber nearly destroys Europe; a mere atom, artfully diddled, incinerates a city. Elegant perplexity puts too much emphasis on the "asymmetrical" side of the phrase and not enough on the fact that it is, indeed, real warfare. Asymmetry is a concept. War is, as we see, blood and death.

It is not a bad idea to repeat a line from the 19th century French anarchist thinker Pierre-Joseph Proudhon: "The fecundity of the unexpected far exceeds the prudence of statesmen." America, in the spasms of a few hours, became a changed country. It turned the corner, at last, out of the 1990s. The menu of American priorities was rearranged. The presidency of George W. Bush begins now. What seemed important a few days ago (in the media, at least) became instantly trivial. If Gary Condit is mentioned once in the next six months on cable television, I will be astonished.

During World War II, John Kennedy wrote home to his parents from the Pacific. He remarked that Americans are at their best during very good times or very bad times; the inbetween periods, he thought, causes them trouble. I'm not sure that is true. Good times sometimes have a tendency to make Americans squalid.

12   The worst times, as we see, separate the civilized of the world from the uncivilized. This is the moment of clarity. Let the civilized toughen up, and let the uncivilized take their chances in the game they started.

Personal Response

Letters to the editor of *Time* in the weeks following the publication of Morrow's essay expressed mixed opinions. Although some people agreed with him absolutely, others agreed in part and some vehemently disagreed with him. What is your opinion?

Questions for Class or Small-Group Discussion

1. Examine Morrow's use of language. In what ways does he convey his personal rage?

2. What do you think of Morrow's opening paragraphs, in which he suggests that grief counselors offer "banal consolation" and that the notion of healing is "fatuous rhetoric" and "inappropriate"? Do you agree with him?

3. In paragraph 9, Morrow notes that terrorism is sometimes defined as " 'asymmetrical warfare,' " and then he observes: "It is mostly the asymmetries that cause history to happen—an obscure Schickelgruber nearly destroys Europe; a mere atom, artfully diddled, incinerates a city." The latter reference is obviously to the atom bombs dropped on Japan during World War II, but you may not know the reference to Schickelgruber. Adolf Hitler's father, Alois, was born to an unmarried woman named Schickelgruber. Years later, he asked his stepfather, Johann Georg Hiedler, to falsify his birth certificate by claiming that Alois was his legitimate son. Hiedler agreed to do so, but a clerical error recorded the name as Hitler, not Hiedler. Thereafter, Adolf's father called himself Alois Hitler. What is Morrow's point in this paragraph?

4. Morrow argues that hatred is "a wholesome and intelligent" response to the terrorist attacks. He calls for America to "explore the rich reciprocal possibilities of the *fatwa*" (paragraph 5) and to "exterminate men like bin Laden and those who conspire with them in evil mischief" (paragraph 7). To what extent do you agree with Morrow?

I'M NOT THE ENEMY

Reshma Memon Yaqub

Reshma Memon Yaqub, a staff reporter for Worth *magazine, writes on a variety of subjects, including Muslim-related topics and business. Her work has also appeared in* Rolling Stone, Glamour, *and* Good Housekeeping. *In 1999 she completed her Hajj, the journey to Mecca that Muslims take for spiritual cleansing and forgiveness. Her diary, one of the few first-person accounts of the journey to be published, appeared in* Worth *magazine in March 2000. Yaqub lives outside Washington, D.C., with her family. This piece was published in the September 13, 2001, edition of the* Washington Post. *You may e-mail her directly at <ReshmaYaqub@hotmail.com>.*

The horror is unspeakable. Like every American, I am paralyzed by the carnage on the news, on our streets. My head pounds, thinking of the grief engulfing thousands of families whose loved ones were killed or injured Tuesday. When I close my eyes, I see bodies tumbling from the windows of skyscrapers.

As the attack unfolded, I panicked, racing through what until this moment had felt like a safe, suburban neighborhood to find my son and his babysitter, who were playing, as usual, at a nearby park. I begged my husband, who was at work in a prominent Washington building, to come home. With the phone lines going in and out, I felt sure that it just wasn't over.

Like every American, I am afraid. Wondering what this means for us. Wondering whether it's over, or when and where the next attack will take place. It's the first time I've felt the kind of fear I imagine that people in other countries feel when they are at war.

4 Like every American, I am outraged. And I want justice. But perhaps unlike many other Americans, I'm feeling something else, too. A different kind of fear. I'm feeling what my 6 million fellow American Muslims are feeling—the fear that we too will be considered guilty in the eyes of America, if it turns out that the madmen behind this terrorism were Muslim.

I feel as though I've suddenly become the enemy of two groups—those who wish to hurt Americans, and those Americans who wish to strike back. It's a frightening corner to be in. In the past, when lone Muslims have committed acts of terrorism—or have been mistakenly assumed to be guilty, as in Oklahoma City—hate crimes have abounded against American Muslims who look like they're from "that part of the world," against American mosques, against American children in Muslim schools who pray to the same peace-loving God as Jews and Christians.

I am now not just afraid, as we all are, for our safety as Americans. I am also afraid for the safety of my sisters-in-law, who wear head scarves in public, and I implore them not to walk alone in the streets of our hometown. I am afraid for my brother, a civil rights lawyer who defends Muslims in high-profile discrimination cases. I am afraid to hear people openly state that Muslim blood is worthless and deserves to be spilled, as I heard when I was in college during the Persian Gulf War.

I am afraid that my son won't understand why strangers aren't smiling at him the way they used to. I am afraid that we will be dehumanized because of our skin color, or features, or clothing. My heart aches each time a friend or relative calls, CNN blaring in the background, and sadly reminds me, "It's over for us now. Muslims are done for."

8   I was briefly heartened to hear author Tom Clancy, interviewed on CNN, explaining that Islam is a peaceful religion and that we as Americans must not let go of our ideals of religious tolerance, because it's the way our country behaves when it's been hurt that really reflects who we are.

Still, I'm afraid that Americans might view the televised images of a few misguided and deeply wounded people overseas celebrating the pain that America is now feeling, and will assume that I too must share that anti-American sentiment, that I, or my family, or my community, or my religion, could be part of the problem. In fact, every major American Muslim organization has decried this violence against us all. In fact, Islam forbids such acts of violence. In fact, all the Muslims I know cringe at the idea of our faith being used, abused, in the name of political agendas.

And though I, like other Americans, want the perpetrators brought to justice, I shudder to think of the innocent lives that may be unnecessarily lost overseas in that pursuit. Children like ours. Mothers like us.

Every time I hear of an act of terrorism, I have two prayers. My first is for the victims and their families. My second is, please don't let it be a Muslim. Because unlike when an act of terrorism is committed by a Christian or a Jew, when it is a Muslim, it's not considered an isolated act perpetrated by an isolated group of madmen. The entire faith is characterized as barbaric, as inhuman. And, my fellow Americans, I stand before you, as broken as you are, to tell you that it's not. That we are not. That we Muslims love our country as you do, and that we are bleeding and grieving alongside you.

Personal Response

What Yaqub fears is racial profiling. Have you ever been the victim of racial profiling? If so, write about that experience. If not, write about an experience in which you were afraid or were faced with danger.

Questions for Class or Small-Group Discussion

1. Summarize the two fears that Yaqub says she has and discuss what you understand her to mean by this statement: "I feel as though I've suddenly become the enemy of two groups—those who wish to hurt Americans, and those Americans who wish to strike back" (paragraph 5). Based on your experience and observations, do you think she is justified in feeling this way?

2. State in your own words what Yaqub says are the facts about her religion and why she fears it is misunderstood. How is that misunderstanding related to her fear for her family and her fellow Muslims?

3. What is the effect of Yaqub's repetition of the phrase "Like every American" in her first three paragraphs and her direct address to her "fellow Americans" in the last paragraph?

4. Discuss this statement: "[U]nlike when an act of terrorism is committed by a Christian or a Jew, when it is a Muslim, it's not considered an isolated act perpetrated by an isolated group of madmen. The entire faith is characterized as barbaric, as inhuman" (paragraph 11). To what extent do you think she is correct?

WHY THEY HATE US

David Pryce-Jones

Vienna-born David Pryce-Jones is a senior editor at National Review *and a political analyst who has published in dozens of international magazines and newspapers. He is author of nine novels and twelve nonfiction books, including* The Closed Circle: An Interpretation of the Arabs *(1989),* The Strange Death of the Soviet Empire *(1995), and* The War that Never Was *(2001). This article was published in the October 1, 2001, issue of* National Review.

They danced in the streets of the West Bank towns and in Gaza when they heard the news. They danced in parts of Lebanon. In Baghdad, state television played a song called "Down with America" as the World Trade Center towers collapsed. To these and their kind, the fact that many innocent people far away were killed is cause for rejoicing. They are possessed by hate, a simple thing that reduces everything and everybody to a simple perspective. Our tribe good, destined for victory—their tribe bad, destined for destruction. Us or Them.

There are of course many millions of Arabs and Muslims, including Iraqis and Palestinians, who do not rejoice, who repudiate this horror committed in their name, and who hope against hope that it is not as it seems, that Arabs and Muslims are not responsible. These are educated people, often secular in outlook, at home in Western culture as well as their own. They are as threatened as the rest of the civilized world by Islamic fanaticism. Only the bravest of them, though, will dare to say what they think, for fear of persecution and assassination. Now and again, the fanatics threaten to overthrow the local rulers. There follow such ghastly tests of strength as the flattening of the two of Hama by the late Syrian dictator Hafiz Assad, and the ongoing civil wars in Algeria and Sudan. Here too are cases of Us or Them, though both sides are Muslim.

Democracy is essentially a process of compromise between conflicting interests according to mutually agreed rules. This arises from an understanding that the alternative is a test of strength in which the strong will send the weak to the wall with no justice. Democracy means Us and Them. Yet nothing in the history or the culture of Arabs and Muslims allows them to put this into any form of political practice. From long ago they have inherited a cast-iron absolute system, in which the ruler does as he pleases, and the rest have no redress, indeed going to the wall. In the absence of inherent processes of compromise at any level of society, it is not a coincidence that absolute Muslim rulers are engaged in tests of strength everywhere with people of other religious persuasions: Hindus in Kashmir, Christians and animists in Africa, Buddhists in China and Indonesia, Jews in Israel.

4   Hate begins here, in the flagrant injustice and violence of daily life, in the corruption of the rich and the mindless poverty of the poor, in the absence of proper

social mechanisms to do anything about it. And who is responsible for this? It requires a rather special character to be able to lay the blame for social failure where it properly belongs, on the people who comprise one's own society. Much easier, more satisfying, to blame everybody except oneself. And haven't Westerners themselves been putting their shoulders to that wheel by reiterating for many years that the plight of Arabs and Muslims has nothing to do with their own conduct or culture, but only with colonialism, imperialism, capitalism, Zionism, globalization? And that we are, therefore, guilty for whatever they may do?

It is of course impossible to fight so many powerful and conspiratorial isms all at once. A sense grows in the man on the street of his utter hopelessness and weakness in the face of this hydra of Them. He feels ashamed of his impotence, deprived of his manhood and dignity, unable to treat others on the equal footing to which all mankind has a right. There is no point telling a man that his shame is unwarranted and likely to injure him first and foremost: He feels how it burns. Shame is the explosive fuel of his hate.

The terrorists took care in the selection of their targets. The World Trade Center stood as a symbol of American success, just as the Pentagon symbolizes American military might. These buildings serve as a projection of the U.S. presence. The terrorists cannot make aircraft, but in their attack on these buildings they also took care to convert American technology into an instrument against America. You boast that you are rich and successful, their actions declare, but we are able to turn your vaunted superiority against you. Now it is time for Americans to suffer in the eyes of all the shame and humiliation oppressing Us.

They are dancing in the West Bank towns and elsewhere because at last they feel that America too knows the inferiority that comes from not being master of one's own destiny. They are dancing because at last they perceive themselves on an equal footing with the tribal Them.

8   Compromise is inconceivable, even if there were some mechanism for it, which there isn't. The usual range of liberal Westerners are already urging caution and restraint, arguing that retaliation Israeli-style only engenders more attacks. But that is to concede that we and the terrorists are on an unequal footing, and that they really are inferiors, children who must be humored and allowed their ways, however harmful. The truth is that they are, and always have been, on an equal footing. Now that they have committed an act of war, they need to be met accordingly. A test of strength is what they demand, and a test of strength is therefore what they must have. Anything less will encourage them to believe that they are destined to be victorious and to destroy the democratic tribe.

Anything less will also condemn to civil war and worse the many Arabs and Muslims who are certain to be victims, if ever Islamic terrorists were to become absolute rulers in yet more countries than Iran and Afghanistan. Democracy alone is able to supplant that sort of sterile hate and transform Us or Them into the Us and Them that we all deserve.

Personal Response

In what way, if any, has this article helped you understand how the beliefs and actions of Muslim extremists are at odds with the Islamic ideals held by hundreds of millions or even a billion people around the world?

Questions for Class or Small-Group Discussion

1. State in your own words the explanation Pryce-Jones gives for "why they hate us" (title). That is, what is the source of anti-American sentiment in the international Arab community?

2. Comment on Pryce-Jones's use of the words *Us* and *Them* and of the phrases "Us or Them" and "Us and Them." How effective do you find their use? Do they help you understand "why they hate us"?

3. Explain what Pryce-Jones means by "this hydra of Them" in paragraph 5. How appropriate do you find that metaphor?

4. Discuss your response to Pryce-Jones's closing remarks in paragraphs 8 and 9. Why is compromise inconceivable? What would be the effects of not retaliating against Islamic terrorists for the attacks of September 11? What repercussions would not retaliating have on both America and the Arab and Muslim worlds?

PERSPECTIVES ON TERRORISM

Suggestions for Synthesis

1. Fareed Zakaria in "The End of the End of History," Reshma Memon Yaqub in "I'm Not the Enemy," and David Pryce-Jones in "Why They Hate Us" all bring up the subject of the contrast between the beliefs and actions of radical Islam with Muslim moderates and secularists. Drawing on those three essays and any others in this chapter that are relevant, write an essay contrasting extremist Muslims with moderate and secularist Muslims.

2. Taking into account at least two of the readings in this chapter, write an essay exploring the effects of the September 11, 2001, terrorist attacks on Americans, or analyze the responses of people in other nations to those attacks.

3. Taking into account at least two essays in this chapter, explain the effect that America's wealth, power, commercialism, or any other aspect of its culture has on the way America is perceived by people in other nations.

4. Explore the nature and effects of hatred, taking into account what at least two of the authors in this chapter say about hatred.

Additional Writing Topics

1. Fareed Zakaria mentions the "extraordinary sacrifices made by the firefighters and policemen of New York City" ("The End of the End of History," paragraph 3). Write a reflective essay on the nature of heroism and extraordinary sacrifice as demonstrated during the September 11 terrorist attacks or after them.

2. Fareed Zakaria in "The End of the End of History" predicts that "we will see governments become more powerful, more intrusive and more important. This may not please civil libertarians and human-rights activists but it will not matter. The state is back . . ." (paragraph 4). Write an essay explaining your viewpoint on the issue of how far the state should be allowed to restrict civil liberties for the sake of national security.

3. Write an essay in response to this statement in "With One Voice: Washington, Westminster and the World" by *The Times of London:* "This was never an American catastrophe but always the world's. It is the world's literally as well as metaphorically."

4. Write an opinion essay in response to Lance Morrow's "The Case for Rage and Retribution."

5. Write a letter to Reshma Memon Yaqub in reply to "I'm Not the Enemy."

6. Respond to David Pryce-Jones in "Why They Hate Us." Consider, among other things, your thoughts on this statement in paragraph 8: "Compromise is inconceivable. . . . Anything less [than a test of strength] will encourage [terrorists] to believe that they are destined to be victorious."

7. Write a personal essay explaining your feelings about the September 11 terrorist attacks and/or how you see them affecting you or your generation in the years to come.

8. Write an essay explaining how you think the September 11 terrorist attacks have changed America.

Research Topics

1. Research the effects of the September 11 terrorist attacks in New York and Washington on the American economy, the American image abroad, or America's role in international politics. All of these topics are broad, so after selecting one, narrow it down further. For instance, you might begin by asking what the economic effects of the attacks were on the airline industry, investment firms, or the Stock Exchange, and then further narrow your focus as you begin reading on the subject.

2. *The Times of London* article, "With One Voice," suggests that the war against terrorism will be a costly one (paragraph 3). Research the costs of that war and do an analysis of the economics of such a war.

3. *The Times of London* article, "With One Voice," asserts that "Britain could be of huge help in the task of coalition-building" (paragraph 7). Research the role Britain played in coalition building following the terrorist attacks in New York and Washington.

4. Following the terrorist attacks against New York and Washington, the North Atlantic Treaty Organization (NATO) invoked article 5 of its mutual defense treaty. Research the purpose of NATO and assess its role in the aftermath of the September 11 attacks.

5. Research the practice of racial profiling, particularly as a reaction to the September 11, 2001, terrorist attacks in New York and Washington, D.C.

PART 4
SCIENCE AND TECHNOLOGY

CHAPTER 18

COMPUTERS AND CYBERSPACE

The field of computer science is constantly changing, with new, ever-faster programs emerging more frequently than most people can fathom. Although early researchers recognized the potential of computers, few of them probably envisioned the staggering capabilities of computers today or the extent to which computers would be so closely and inextricably linked with people's everyday lives. Increasingly sophisticated computers make child's play of activities that just a few years ago were challenging or impossible tasks. Young children today learn skills—sometimes before they enter school—that many of their grandparents will never even try to learn. Indeed, computer technology has advanced at such a rapid rate that its powers seem unlimited, a prospect that fills some with eager anticipation and leaves others feeling intimidated and frightened.

The first piece in this chapter, Lori Gottlieb's "Is There a Geek in the House?" focuses on the subject of "techno gadgets," more specifically the PalmPilot. Medical student Gottlieb explains her difficulty in learning to use the tool and wonders why half of her classmates had the same trouble she did with the device. In a light-hearted way, she describes the experiences of many people faced with new technology. Similarly, Seth Shostak in "You Call this Progress?" laments another facet of the new technology, in this case, e-mail. Cataloguing what he sees as a long list of faults with e-mail, he argues that, although he welcomes most new technology, e-mail is just too pernicious and invasive for his comfort. Do Gottlieb's and Shostak's complaints strike a sympathetic chord in you, or are you completely comfortable with all the latest gadgets and happy corresponding via e-mail? In contrast to Gottlieb and Shostak, Joe Saltzman in "Dick Tracy Never Had It So Good" is thrilled with the technological advances since his youth that have made his life so much better. He almost seems to be responding to the complaints of Gottlieb and Shostak, as he offers a definite opposing view.

Many young people apparently have none of the trouble that Gottlieb and Shostak describe. "The Generation Lap" is an excerpt from Don Tapscott's book *Growing Up Digital,* which chronicles how the new generation, raised on digital technology, is engineering an inescapable revolution. Tapscott calls this Net generation

"N-Gen" and draws on the opinions, experiences, and insights of over three hundred N-Geners to give a fact-filled profile of the new youth culture. This excerpt recasts the concept of a "generation gap" as a "generation lap" because of the way children are overtaking adults, lapping them as it were, in many technological areas of daily life.

Amy Bruckman drafted the final essay in this chapter, "Christmas Unplugged," with a pencil, she says, because she made the difficult decision to leave her laptop computer behind during a visit to her parents for Christmas. Bruckman, one of the new generation of young people who grew up with computers, now teaches computing, specializing in virtual communities. Her essay reveals her deep dependence on the Internet as well as her satisfaction in occasionally disconnecting from all things electronic. As you read this and the Tapscott piece, consider your own use of the Internet: Do you use it to communicate, to shop, to research topics of interest? Just how reliant are you on your computer?

Your responses to the readings in this chapter will undoubtably be influenced by your own familiarity with and skill or lack of it in using computers. You may well know far more about them than some of the authors represented here, or you may have no background or interest in the subject at all. However, these four perspectives are varied enough that they should provide plenty of material for fruitful class discussion or writing about computers and cyberspace.

IS THERE A GEEK IN THE HOUSE?

Lori Gottlieb

Lori Gottlieb, a medical student at Stanford University, is a former Hollywood executive. Her work has appeared in the New York Times, Salon, *and* Slate, *among other publications. She is author of* Stick Figure: A Diary of My Former Self *(2000), a memoir. Gottlieb wrote this piece for the January/February 2001 issue of* Time Digital Magazine.

I'm always the last person to buy new techno gadgets and the last to figure out how they work. I just got my first cell phone in March, and I still don't know how to use speed dial. So when I heard that Stanford Medical School would be handing out Palm Vxs to each of us preclinical students, I panicked. Sure, it's natural to feel inadequate in a class full of Rhodes scholars, but what if I turned out to be the only medical student too stupid to use a Palm?

It didn't help that I overheard some classmates complaining about the Palm training-session requirement. "What are they gonna do, show us how to use a stylus?" someone asked sarcastically, and the entire group laughed like hyenas.

I felt hopeful when the training session began not with the dreaded high-tech gadgets but with good, old-fashioned paperwork: a human-subjects release form. Our usage would be tracked, the student coordinator told us, but our identities would remain anonymous. "So," she assured us, "you can download all the porn you want." From the sighs of relief that followed, I assumed that 1) my classmates weren't getting enough sex; 2) they were way ahead of me and already knew how to download. I didn't know which was worse. I felt a lot better when Liz, a recent Harvard graduate, peeled the protective plastic sticker off the display, held it up and asked, "Do we need this for anything?" Cluelessness loves company.

4   Still, the rest of the tutorial was a disaster. The only parts I halfway understood were setting the clock and writing practice memos to ourselves. I scrawled in, "Check out movie times for *Almost Famous.*" Then we were instructed to beam our memos to each other. I struggled through the Palm-specific alphabet to change mine to something more intelligent sounding. "Get *JAMA* article on viral gastroenteritis," I slowly scribbled, which I had no intention of doing, but by then it didn't matter because the class had moved on to hot synching. Whatever that was.

It turned out that several other Future Doctors of America were completely stymied by this device too. I ran into Lauren, who was looking for the location of a new lecture. "It's in your Palm," I suggested, but she said the Palm was too complicated; she'd rather just ask someone. Then another classmate admitted, "This thing gives me a headache. I'm always forgetting to bring my cell phone with me. How will I remember to bring my Palm too?"

Suddenly the class was divided into the Techies and the Technophobes, and the Techies were greatly outnumbered. Everywhere I went, I overheard students anxiously crowded around a Palm: "Where's tonight's reading list?" "Oh, my God, I think I deleted my contact file!" "Can someone please tell me how to access the drug database?"

I wondered how an entire class of medical students could be so incompetent. After all, we had aced our MCATs, earned near-perfect GPAs, gone through rigorous undergraduate programs, and somehow been admitted to a highly competitive medical program. Could we really be that stupid? I got my answer when I saw a classmate's Palm plastered with yellow Post-it notes. "Why don't you enter these into your Palm?" I asked, but she explained that even if she could figure that out, she doubted she'd know how to retrieve the information when she needed it. It was far more efficient to write everything on Post-its, and if she stuck them on her Palm, they'd be consolidated in one place instead of scattered loosely in her bag. Hmmm, I thought. Finally, a smart idea.

Personal Response

What are your favorite "techno gadgets"? If you share Gottlieb's discomfort with them, explain why.

Questions for Class or Small-Group Discussion

1. What seems to be Gottlieb's difficulty with technological gadgets? Are your own experiences similar to or different from hers? If you are experienced with technological gadgets, do you have any sympathy for her?

2. Gottlieb observes that her "class was divided into the Techies and the Technophobes, and the Techies were greatly outnumbered" and wonders "how an entire class of medical students could be so incompetent" (paragraphs 6–7). Does she offer a satisfactory answer to her question? Can you suggest any other answers to explain the difficulty she and her classmates had?

3. Discuss your experience with technological gadgets. Are you comfortable with them? What gadgets do you own? How do you think such gadgets enhance people's lives?

YOU CALL THIS PROGRESS?

SETH SHOSTAK

Seth Shostak is an astronomer at the Search for Extraterrestrial Intelligence (SETI) Institute in California. For much of his career, he has conducted radio astronomy research on galaxies. He has published dozens of papers in professional journals and written several hundred popular articles on various topics in astronomy, technology, film, and television. This essay appeared in the "My Turn" column of the January 18, 1999, issue of Newsweek.

It's as ubiquitous as winter damp, a pernicious miasma that brings rot and ruin to society's delicate underpinnings. I speak of e-mail, the greatest threat to civilization since lead dinnerware addled the brains of the Roman aristocracy.

A technical byproduct of the Internet, e-mail lets 10 million Americans pound out correspondence faster than you can say QWERTY. One twitch of the finger is all it takes to dispatch missives to the next continent or the next cubicle at light speed. The result is a flood of what is loosely called communication, a tsunami of bytes that is threatening to drown white-collar workers everywhere. Masquerading as a better way to put everyone in touch, e-mail has become an incessant distraction, a nonstop obligation and a sure source of stress and anxiety. I expect that a public statement by the surgeon general is in the offing.

Mind you, e-mail started out cute and cuddly, an inoffensive spinoff from a government defense project. The technically inclined used it to send personal messages to colleagues without the need for a stamp or a wait. Only a small group of folks—mostly at universities—were plugged in to this select network. The amount of traffic was manageable. E-mail was something to be checked every week or so. But technology marches on. Today access to the Internet is widespread, as common and accessible as a cheap motel. Everyone's wired, and everyone has something to say.

4   Unfortunately, this is not polite correspondence, the gentle art of letter writing in electronic form. E-mail is aggressive. It has a built-in, insistent arrogance. Because it arrives more or less instantaneously, the assumption is that you will deal with it quickly. "Quickly" might mean minutes, or possibly hours. Certainly not days. Failure to respond directly usually produces a second missive sporting the mildly critical plaint, "Didn't you get my last e-mail?" This imperative for the immediate makes me yearn for old-style written communication, in which a week might lapse between inquiry and response. Questions and discussion could be considered in depth. A reply could be considered (or mentally shelved, depending on circumstance). Today, however, all is knee-jerk reaction.

In addition, there is the dismaying fact that electronically generated mail, despite being easy to edit, is usually prose at its worst. Of every 10 e-mails I read, nine suffer from major spelling faults, convoluted grammar and a stunning lack of logical organization. ASCII graffiti. For years I assumed this was an inevitable byproduct of the low student test scores so regularly lamented in newspaper editorials. Johnny can't read, so it's not surprising that he can't write either. But now I believe that the reason for all this unimpressive prose is something else: e-mail has made correspondents of folks who would otherwise never compose a text. It encourages messaging because it is relatively anonymous. The shy, the introverted and the socially inept can all hunker down before a glowing computer and whisper to the world. This is not the telephone, with its brutally personal, audible contact. It's not the post, for which an actual sheet of paper, touched by the writer and displaying his imperfect calligraphic skills, will end up under the nose of the recipient. E-mails are surreptitiously thrown over an electronic transom in the dead of night, packaged in plain manila envelopes.

Still, it is not these esthetic debilities that make e-mail such a threat. Rather, it's the unstoppable proliferation. Like the brooms unleashed by the sorcerer's apprentice, e-mails are beginning to overwhelm those who use them. Electronic correspondence is not one to one. It is one to many, and that's bad news on the receiving end. The ease with which copies of any correspondence can be dispensed to the world ensures that I am "kept informed" of my co-workers' every move. Such bureaucratic banter was once held in check by the technical limitations of carbon paper. Now my colleagues just punch a plastic mouse to ensure my exposure to their thoughts, their plans and the endless missives that supposedly prove that they're doing their jobs.

Because of e-mail's many-tentacled reach, its practitioners hardly care whether I'm around or not. I'm just another address in a list. So the deluge of digital correspondence continues irrespective of whether I'm sitting in my cubicle doing the boss's business or lying on the Côte d'Azur squeezing sand through my toes. Either way the e-mail, like a horde of motivated Mongolians, just keeps a-comin'. Vacations have lost their allure, and I hesitate to leave town. Consider: if I disappear for two weeks of rest and recreation, I can be sure of confronting screenfuls of e-mail upon my return. It's enough to make a grown man groan. The alternative is to take a laptop computer along, in the desperate hope of keeping up with e-mail's steady drip, drip, drip. Needless to say, there's something unholy about answering e-mails from your holiday suite. A friend recently told me that he can't afford to die: the e-mail would pile up and nobody could handle it.

8   Today I will receive 50 electronic messages. Of that number, at least half require a reply. (Many of the others consist of jokes, irrelevant bulletins and important announcements about secret cookie recipes. I actually like getting such junk e-mails, as they allow the pleasure of a quick delete without guilt.) If I spend five minutes considering and composing a response to each correspondence, then two hours of my day are busied with e-mail, even if I don't initiate a single one. Since the number of Internet users is doubling about once a year, I expect that by the start of the new millennium, I—and millions like me—will be doing nothing but writing e-mails. The collapse of commerce and polite society will quickly follow.

I'm as much in favor of technology as the next guy. Personally, I think the Luddites should have welcomed the steam looms. But if you insist on telling me that e-mail is an advance, do me a favor and use the phone.

Personal Response

How frequently do you use e-mail? Do you share Shostak's distaste for it, or do you find it a good way to communicate?

Questions for Class or Small-Group Discussion

1. State in your own words what Shostak's complaints about e-mail are and discuss your viewpoint on those complaints. Do you agree with him on all points, some of them, or none of them?

2. How would you answer the question posed by Shostak in his title?

3. Could any of the things that Shostak complains about be seen as positive points rather than negative ones? Explain your answer.

DICK TRACY NEVER HAD IT THIS GOOD!

Joe Saltzman

Joe Saltzman is Associate Mass Media Editor of USA Today. He is a professor of journalism in the University of Southern California Annenberg School of Journalism in Los Angeles and associate dean of the Annenberg School for Communication. This essay appeared on the "Words & Images" page of the April 2000 issue of USA Today magazine.

When I was a kid, my friends and I were in awe of a comic strip detective named Dick Tracy who had a miniature two-way radio watch on his wrist that he used to talk to his colleagues. It was all fantasy 50 years ago, but today it seems everyone has a cell phone and a Palm Pilot doing things that Detective Tracy only dreamed about. The idea of a stranger on a train passing information in a split second via the infrared port on her Palm Pilot to another stranger on another train aiming his Palm Pilot at hers is proof enough we're living in the early 21st century.

Other dreams have become startling reality. Lugging around many pounds of 78 rpm records that housed Richard Wagner's "Ring," one swooned at the idea of carrying all of that music in the palm of one's hand. Now, that is possible with CDs. Watching movies at the local cinema, one barely could imagine what it would be like to have copies of cherished films and play them at home in a miniature theater. Now, DVD and HDTV make all of this possible.

The idea of a video phone has been with us for decades, but now, with the computer and digital cameras, we can send live pictures to relatives and friends, and the old photo album is an electronic smorgasbord. The electronic equivalent of the oversized leather address book and appointment calendar now fits in a pocket. Portable TVs, MP3 players, and the old favorite boom box reconfigured in smaller yet louder packages let us take entertainment anywhere we want to be.

4   One company that always offered watches that did a lot more than tell time, Casio, offers a wrist audio player, which holds 16 megabytes of music (about half an hour at CD-level sound quality) that connects to your PC through a USB port so you can transfer music files from your hard drive. Another one of its products is called PCUnite, a personal-digital assistant watch that holds addresses, phone numbers, and appointments. It can swap data with your PC or Palm Pilot through its infrared port. Or there's a Wrist Cam watch that not only tells time, but is a digital camera that stores about 100 pictures in its memory banks. And the Global Positioning System watch tells you exactly where you are via satellite and tracks you as you move about. If you punch in where you want to go, the watch will tell you how to get there and how long it will take you. If your kids ask, "When will we get there?," you can give them an answer within a moment.

The real question is: How do all of these 21st-century gizmos improve a life? Most of us don't know how we managed before copy machines and computers. Some of us feel naked without our Palm Pilots to tell us what to do and when to do it during a busy day. Once you've bought a cell or car phone, you can't imagine what life was like before you had one. Instant communication. For this worried husband, the car phone has saved many an ulcer or possible heart attack by keeping constant track of a wife driving alone. Those of us with long commutes find such a phone invaluable in making use of what otherwise would be wasted time. And e-mail has made it possible to keep in touch at our pace and on our time schedule. Crumpled photographs in wallets were never as effective as digitized pictures sent over the Internet in seconds to happy parents and grandparents. And seeing a sick friend on a computer video phone thousands of miles away makes the conversation even more personal and satisfying.

There are some out there who still long for purple carbon paper, manual typewriters, and rotary telephones. There are some out there who worry that all of these infrared and microwave devices are going to give us brain tumors and other horrible illnesses. There are some out there who think the computer and all of its handheld derivations are dangerous toys destroying true knowledge and privacy. There are some out there who believe the glut of music and movies will destroy the written word, resulting in a world of self-satisfied ignoramuses.

These are the same pessimists who have complained about every new invention that has become popular. Their 20th-century ancestors insisted that the mass-produced penny press was corrupting civilization and rotting the brains and eyesight of working people; that radios were destroying the peace and sanctity of the home—giving women strange and dangerous ideas; and that TV was downsizing the brains of all who watched it, damaging fragile eyes, and even causing cancer.

8   What all of these inventions so damned by other generations have in common is that they opened up new worlds to millions of people without discrimination as to wealth, power, or geography. These inventions make democracy viable in the 21st century. Today, the World Wide Web and Internet, for example, even with all of their indiscriminate information and trivia, are giving more people the opportunity to learn and discover than any invention in history. If knowledge is power, these inventions have given the power to most of the people—at least until those who control governments and businesses harness the inventions to their own profit.

The idea that anyone, regardless of race, color, creed, or status, can listen to Beethoven, watch "Citizen Kane," or have a conversation with anyone in the world is a wondrous concept that overwhelms the petty criticisms of the elite who simply do not like anyone but themselves to enjoy the art, culture, and knowledge available in the 21st century.

The more things change, the more they stay the same.

Personal Response

Of the many devices Saltzman names in paragraphs 1 to 4, which do you own? Of those you do not have, which one would you most like to have? Why?

Questions for Class or Small-Group Discussion

1. Although Saltzman's list of technological devices that have been developed since his youth is pretty long, are there any others that he might have named? Are there any devices not yet invented that you would like to see developed?

2. How would you answer Saltzman's question in paragraph 5: "How do all of these 21st-century gizmos improve a life?"

3. What is your response to the way in which Saltzman dismisses the complaints of people both now and in the past to every new technological advance? That is, is he being fair to them? Are there any legitimate reasons for resisting each new technological "gizmo"?

THE GENERATION LAP

Don Tapscott

Don Tapscott is chairman of the Alliance for Converging Technologies, a research think tank funded by many of the world's leading

*technology, manufacturing, retail, financial, and government organi-
zations, and president of New Paradigm Learning Corporation. His
books include* The Digital Economy: Promise and Peril in the Age
of Networked Intelligence *(1995),* Paradigm Shift: The New
Promise of Information Technology *(coauthored) (1992),* Blueprint to the Digital Economy: Creating Wealth in the Era of
E-Business *(coedited) (1998). "The Generation Lap" is an excerpt
from a chapter of his book* Growing Up Digital: The Rise of the
Net Generation *(1997), in which he coins the term* N-Gen *to refer to technologically fluent youth.*

I love troubleshooting computer problems for teachers, and it's quite unfortunate that some of them see me as a negative. Outside of school I help out my
mom with computer-related projects. I think I am a little less patient with her
than with my teachers (it's a normal family thing I guess). My mom used to ask
me why I was always on the Internet or playing with the computer, then I started
to involve her and show her what I had been doing and she got interested. Now
she has a computer on her desk at school (she's a teacher) and uses it all the
time. She even sent me a "Virtual Bouquet" this past Christmas!

—Andy Putschoegl, seventeen,
Oakdale, Minnesota

When it comes to understanding and using the new media and technology, many parents are falling woefully behind their children. We've shifted from a generation gap
to a *generation lap*—kids outpacing and overtaking adults on the technology track,
lapping them in many areas of daily life. Austin Locke, fifteen, sums it up perfectly:
"For once in our civilization, children are educating older people. Children are more
adept at using computers. Parents, teachers, and other adults are looking to children
for information and help with computers and other computer-related stuff."

Society has never before experienced this phenomenon of the knowledge hierarchy being so effectively flipped on its head. But it is definitely happening and the
situation is magnified with each new technology. University students in their twenties share childhood memories of having to explain to their parents what a mouse or
CD player was. The challenge in these episodes was not only how to explain the new
technology, but how to convince their parents they needed something they'd never
even heard of.

Children—Authorities for the First Time

Most kids love the new technology. In a 1995 study on home computing conducted by
Carnegie Mellon University, researchers introduced computers and the Internet into
forty-eight demographically diverse families. In forty-one of the forty-eight families,
the heaviest user was a child. They concluded, "Teenagers are central to Internet use
at home. They often provide the motivation for parents to invest in a computer, . . .
become sources of expertise within the household, and catalyze Internet use by other
family members."

4   Stories about six-year-olds programming new VCRs after their parents' unsuccessful efforts are now cliché. A newer version is the fourteen-year-old girl whose parents recently asked her to install Net Nanny software on the family computer to keep Internet pornography out of the house. Of course, her parents are oblivious to the fact that if she sets up the system, she then controls it.

Two-thirds of the kids in the *Growing Up Digital* survey on FreeZone said they were more proficient at the computer than their parents.

"This is a unique period in history in that the role of the child in the home is changing," states John Seely Brown, chief scientist at Xerox PARC. He explains that in the past the parents were the authority figures in terms of anything of particular value. The notion of the child being able to do anything new, novel, or really useful for the parent was bogus. Parents traditionally have known more than children in virtually every conceivable domain—with the one exception of immigrant children learning a new culture and language more quickly and acting as translators for their parents.

"So, for the first time there are things that parents want to be able to know about and do, where the kids are, in fact, the authority," he says. "This means that now you have a different conversation happening around the dinner table." On certain subjects, the parents are the authority, and on other subjects of value, the kids are the authority.

8   The implications are huge. Family members begin to respect each other for what their authorities actually are. This creates more of a peer dynamic within families and if managed well by the parents can create a more open, consensual, and effective family unit.

This insight can be extended to other social institutions, as well. For example, imagine the changing relationship between students and teachers in Finland. The government has chosen five thousand N-Geners to train the country's teachers on how to use computers. For the first time ever, in one domain, the students will be the teachers and the teachers will be the students. The power dynamic between students and teachers will be forever altered.

The same is true as N-Geners enter universities and the workforce. Managers around the world still make very limited personal use of the new technology. In the developed world, this is especially true in Europe (lesser so in Scandinavia) and Japan. Imagine the impact of this wave of technologically fluent youth, each one commanding power and respect through his or her knowledge of something crucial to the companies' success. Further, being an authority in at least one domain (in their families, schools, and other settings), will N-Geners be satisfied with the old hierarchical model of the enterprise?

Successful companies will be those recognizing that networked structures work more effectively. As Seely Brown puts it: "What you find in leading organizations today is that each one of us is, in some way, an authority in some domains and a student in other domains. We must be prepared to learn major things from our subordinates and vice versa." Peer interaction in homes and schools is setting the stage for the kind of experiences that prepare us to move into the postmodern world.

12   Seventeen-year-old Andy Putschoegl speaks wistfully of the Apple IIgs of his early childhood, much like his grandparents probably spoke of their favorite stuffed toys. Andy experiences the generation lap every day in his high school classes where he lends a hand to his fellow students and rescues his teachers. During one episode last year, this so-called *rescuing* entailed hacking the school's computer system. "I suppose you might call it hacking," Andy explained. "What I did was start up the computer from an alternate disk and bypass a lot of the security features. And that was because the media personnel hadn't told the teachers what their passwords were and the teachers couldn't use their computers—not just the Internet—but the regular computers."

Barbara Harr, who runs the Lakeforest Library Connection (LLC) in a Rockville, Maryland, shopping mall, has firsthand experience with the generation lap. One day a child and his mother came to the library to do a homework assignment that required use of an encyclopedia. The child headed for the computer equipped with a CD-ROM encyclopedia and the mother went to the reference shelf. The mother insisted that they use the book since it seemed to have the appropriate information and was easily photocopied. The child couldn't persuade his mom that the computer version was at least as good, if not better. He said, "Mom, it's the same thing. It's right here. Don't you get it?"

Harr notes that parents who are not threatened by the lap can benefit. "Kids are totally surrounded by a multimedia environment, virtually from the day they are born. It is a totally different experience, and there is a comfort level that is established early on. Parents today with young children probably have an advantage compared to other adults because they can learn this new technology with their kids."

Needless to say, some adults have difficulty accepting the generation lap and seeing the potential for growth. Mike Uttech, thirteen, of Paris, Texas, describes this well: "I have some teachers who won't accept the fact that a student knows more about something than they do. Some of my teachers love me to help out with tasks—whether it is saving files to disks, printing, or other tasks. But other teachers think I'm being rude knowing more than they do. I also find it funny when a teacher won't let me help and then gets the computer specialist at the school to do it. I think that the teachers and adults should listen to us more and maybe even learn something from us."

Personal Response

Explain the degree to which your experience is similar to that of university students Tapscott mentions in paragraph 2 when he writes: "The challenge [. . .] was not only how to explain the new technology, but how to convince their parents they needed something they'd never even heard of."

Questions for Class or Small-Group Discussion

1. How does the opening quotation relate to the discussion that follows?

2. What implications does Tapscott see in the situations where children know more than their parents about new technology?

3. What are the implications for other social institutions besides the family when young people know more about technology than older people know?

4. How does Tapscott illustrate his statement that "some adults have difficulty accepting the generation lap and seeing the potential for growth"? To what extent does your own experience support that statement?

CHRISTMAS UNPLUGGED
Amy Bruckman

Amy Bruckman is an assistant professor in the College of Computing at the Georgia Institute of Technology. She and her students in the Electronic Learning Communities (ELC) research group study online communities and education. Bruckman is the founder of Media-MOO, a text-based virtual reality environment or MUD (multiuser dimension) designed to be a professional community for media researchers and MOOSE Crossing (a MUD designed to be a constructivist learning environment for kids). MOOSE Crossing includes a new programming language, MOOSE, designed to help kids learn programming. Bruckman received her Ph.D. in 1997 from MIT, where she studied in the MIT Media Lab's Epistemology and Learning group. She received her master's degree for work in the Media Lab's Interactive Cinema Group in 1991 and her bachelor's degree in physics from Harvard University in 1987. More information about her work is available at http://www.cc.gatech.edu/~asb/.

If I had a network link, I'd be home now.

From my chaise lounge on the terrace of my parents' Miami Beach apartment, I see a grid of four-lane roads with palm-treed median strips, yachts moored on the inland waterway, a golf course, and a dozen tall, white condominiums. The hum of traffic is punctuated by the soft white thunk of racquets striking tennis balls somewhere below. The temperature is in the seventies and a breeze blows through my toes. I am a long way from Boston. If I had a net link, I'd know exactly how far.

I'd know the weather forecast for Miami, and, if I cared, for Boston too. Just about anything you might like to know is out there on the worldwide computer network—the Net—if you know where to look.

4   It's Christmas day in Miami, but I'm not sure it would really be Christmas or I would really be in Miami if I were plugged into the Net. I would be in my virtual office, a "room" in the text-based virtual reality environment where I do most of my work. I have a desk there, piled with things to do, and a fish tank—just like my "real" office. Except that the virtual fish don't need to be fed—they're just a program I created one day while procrastinating from real work. My virtual office is just some data

on a computer housed at MIT that I can tap into from anywhere, but it is a place to me. When I log onto the network, I am there.

And I would be there right now, if not for a difficult choice I made two days ago. I was packed for my trip south and had called a cab. I had the important things: airline ticket, wallet, bathing suit. I stood in the hall staring at a padded gray bag, the one containing my Macintosh PowerBook computer. I grabbed the bag, double-locked the door, and started to walk down the hall. I stopped. I went back, opened the door, and put down the gray bag. I stood in the doorway, feeling foolish. The taxi honked. The honk gave me courage: I locked up again, leaving my computer—my office—behind.

A vacation should be about escaping from routines: going somewhere else provides a new perspective. But when I travel with my PowerBook, I bring many of my routines with me. I can readily gain access to all my familiar tools for finding information. It's as if I never left. And that's the problem. Had I brought my computer, I would not have written this essay (for which I am using a pencil). Instead, I would have logged onto the network and entered its seductive, engrossing world. By now I would have read the newswire and Miss Manners's column, answered a dozen questions from friends and colleagues, and possibly posted my thoughts on a movie I saw last night to a public discussion group. It would be as if I never left home.

The network destroys a sense of time as well as place. Daily and seasonal rhythms are subtle at best. As morning turns to evening, I am more likely to bump into my friends in Hawaii, less likely to encounter my friends in England. In the summer, things quiet down. April 1st is the only real network holiday—don't believe anything you read that day! Beyond that, life on the Net proceeds at an even, unpunctuated pace. There are no holiday decorations on the Net.

8   On my flight down here I saw a young boy carrying a sleek black bag on his shoulder. He held it naturally, but with a hint of importance. It took me a moment to see the logo: it contained his Nintendo Game Boy. His generation sees nothing remarkable about traveling at all times with a computer. It is already possible to connect to the network from a palm-sized computer with a cellular link. As computers get smaller and cheaper, we will lose even the excuse of the weight of that black bag or the cost of losing it.

The Net is becoming an important part of the lives of a broader segment of the population. Its spread presents a worrisome challenge: Is it ever possible for us to take uninterrupted time off any more? The new technologies of connectedness are pushing people to blend their many roles into one: Personal mail is mixed with professional correspondence, and work crises arrive on a cellular phone during leisure time. If our coworkers and competitors have made themselves perpetually available, we feel all the more pressure to do the same, lest we be left behind. One of my colleagues deliberately vacations in places so remote that getting a Net connection is almost impossible—it's the only way she can get a real break, and, for a little while at least, be a carefree newlywed instead of a world-renowned researcher. But such exotic locales are getting harder and harder to find.

I love the network and the people and places I find there. But sometimes I find it important to disconnect—to leave the cellular phone and the beeper in a desk drawer, leave that padded gray bag at home. To be out of touch, not for hours but for days. To leave behind routines, both virtual and real.

Personal Response

Does the computer play as important a role in your life as it does in Amy Bruckman's? Can you enjoy leisure time and vacations without the interruption of such devices as fax machines, voice mail, answering machines, and cellular phones?

Questions for Class or Small-Group Discussion

1. Why does Bruckman describe the decision to leave her computer at home when she visited her parents for Christmas (paragraph 5) as a difficult choice? How does she convey that sense of difficulty?

2. According to Bruckman, in what way does "the network [destroy] a sense of time as well as place"?

3. According to Bruckman, how do computers and other technologies such as fax machines, voice mail, and telephone answering machines affect people's private lives?

4. Discuss the extent to which you agree with Bruckman that sometimes it is "important to disconnect" (paragraph 10).

PERSPECTIVES ON COMPUTERS AND CYBERSPACE

Suggestions for Synthesis

1. Drawing on two or more essays in this chapter, explore the impact of technology on contemporary culture.

2. Compare and contrast Joe Saltzman's "Dick Tracy Never Had It This Good!" with either Lori Gottlieb in "Is There a Geek in the House?" or Seth Shostak in "You Call This Progress?"

3. Write a paper in which you create a hypothetical response from either Don Tapscott in "The Generation Lap" or Amy Bruckman in "Christmas Unplugged" to either Lori Gottlieb in "Is There a Geek in the House?" or Seth Shostak in "You Call This Progress?"

4. Explain what you see as both the positive and negative aspects of the recent advances in technology, incorporating the views of at least two of the writers in this chapter.

Additional Writing Topics

1. Write an essay in response to any of the writers in this chapter.

2. Explain the importance of high-tech systems such as computers, cellular phones, voice mail, and telephone answering machines in your life.

3. Write an essay explaining what you see as the benefits and/or dangers of the Internet.

4. Narrate your own experience with what Don Tapscott calls "the generation lap."

5. Explain the direction you see computer technology going in over the next decade or two.

Research Topics

1. Research an area of computer technology that is still in the experimental stages or still being refined, such as virtual reality or artificial intelligence.

2. Interview instructors in the humanities and in the sciences about their views on the potential uses and dangers of computer technology. Summarize your findings in a formal paper, and explain conclusions you have reached after these interviews. Supplement your interviews with library research.

3. Research the impact of technology in one of the following areas: marketing, shopping, entertainment, scholarship/research, American culture, education, or government and politics.

4. Research a problem associated with the Internet such as the availability of pornography for children, the potential dangers of e-mail, or privacy issues.

CHAPTER 19

NATURAL SCIENCES

The natural sciences include such disciplines as biology, physics, astronomy, and chemistry. Their inquiry focuses on the workings and phenomena of the natural world, from the ocean floor to the farthest galaxies of the universe. Two essays in this chapter cover that range and hint at the enormous possibility for increasing human knowledge of the world we inhabit; the other two comment on the subject of people's readiness to accept anything offered as "science" and the ways to counter that gullibility. The authors reprinted here share a belief in the wonders and joy of science and in the close relationship of science and creative imagination.

For instance, Jacob Bronowski, in "The Reach of the Imagination," emphasizes the imaginative component of scientific thinking as he explains the workings of the imagination and why he believes it marks the chief difference between humans and other animals. Consider whether you agree with him on this point. Do other differences of equal importance distinguish humans' superiority over other animals? To what extent do you agree with him about the imaginative and creative components of science and its link with the humanities?

"The Chemist" is written by a scientist who works to popularize science and enhance its accessibility to the public. In this brief chapter from his book celebrating the truly interdisciplinary nature of life today, chemist Roald Hoffmann explores the metaphor of discovery used by scientists from historical, psychological, philosophical, and sociological perspectives. As you read the essay, think about the broader issue raised by Hoffmann, that is, the interconnectedness of the disciplines. Do you see such a connection in the courses you are now taking?

Another writer who is excited about science is Matt Ridley. In his article, "The Year of the Genome," he celebrates the results of both the public and the private research into the human genome, gives a brief history of the history of discoveries in genetics, and suggests that we are now at "the beginning of a whole new way of understanding human biology."

The final two writers represented in this chapter, one a scientist herself and the other a science journalist, address the issue of the general public's being too willing to accept what they call "junk science" or "pseudoscience." Lee Ann Fisher Baron in "The Influence of 'Junk Science' and the Role of Science Education" discusses some of the unfounded scientific claims that too many people believe. Her examples of how "junk science" claims persuade people to buy certain products include some very popular items such as fat-free foods and herbal supplements. The examples cited by the other writer, Boyce Rensberger in "The Nature of Evidence," also have widespread followers: parapsychology and UFOs. Baron and Rensberger both suggest reasons to account for the general public's "gullibility" and offer steps that educators, scientists, and journalists can take to better inform people about the nature of evidence.

THE REACH OF THE IMAGINATION

Jacob Bronowski

Jacob Bronowski (1908–1974) was a Polish-born American scientist whose television series Ascent of Man *(1974) combined art, philosophy, and science to explain the connections between science and the humanities. His books include* The Common Sense of Science *(1951),* Science and Human Values *(1959), and* William Blake, a Man with a Mask *(1965). This essay was originally delivered as the Blashfield Address at a meeting of the American Academy of Arts and Letters and the National Institute of Arts and Letters in May 1966. It was reprinted in the spring 1990 issue of* American Scholar.

For three thousand years, poets have been enchanted and moved and perplexed by the power of their own imagination. In a short and summary essay I can hope at most to lift one small corner of that mystery; and yet it is a critical corner. I shall ask, What goes on in the mind when we imagine? You will hear from me that one answer to this question is fairly specific: which is to say, that we can describe the working of the imagination. And when we describe it as I shall do, it becomes plain that imagination is a specifically *human* gift. To imagine is the characteristic act, not of the poet's mind, or the painter's, or the scientist's, but of the mind of man.

My stress here on the word *human* implies that there is a clear difference in this between the actions of men and those of other animals. Let me then start with a classical experiment with animals and children which Walter Hunter thought out in Chicago about 1910. That was the time when scientists were agog with the success of Ivan Pavlov in forming and changing the reflex actions of dogs, which Pavlov had first announced in 1903. Pavlov had been given a Nobel Prize the next year, in 1904; although in fairness I should say that the award did not cite his work on the conditioned reflex, but on the digestive gland.

Hunter duly trained some dogs and other animals on Pavlov's lines. They were taught that when a light came on over one of three tunnels out of their cage, that tunnel would be open; they could escape down it, and were rewarded with food if they did. But once he had fixed that conditioned reflex, Hunter added to it a deeper idea: He gave the mechanical experiment a new dimension, literally—the dimension of time. Now he no longer let the dog go to the lighted tunnel at once; instead, he put out the light, and then kept the dog waiting a little while before he let him go. In this way Hunter timed how long an animal can remember where he has last seen the signal light to his escape route.

4   The results were and are staggering. A dog or a rat forgets which one of three tunnels has been lit up within a matter of seconds—in Hunter's experiment, ten seconds at most. If you want such an animal to do much better than this, you must make the task much simpler: You must face him with only two tunnels to choose from. Even so, the best that Hunter could do was to have a dog remember for five minutes which one of two tunnels had been lit up.

I am not quoting these times as if they were exact and universal: They surely are not. Hunter's experiment, more than fifty years old now, had many faults of detail. For example, there were too few animals, they were oddly picked, and they did not all behave consistently. It may be unfair to test a dog for what he *saw*, when he commonly follows his nose rather than his eyes. It may be unfair to test any animal in the unnatural setting of a laboratory cage. And there are higher animals, such as chimpanzees and other primates, which certainly have longer memories than the animals that Hunter tried.

Yet when all these provisos have been made (and met, by more modern experiments) the facts are still startling and characteristic. An animal cannot recall a signal from the past for even a short fraction of the time that a man can—for even a short fraction of the time that a child can. Hunter made comparable tests with six-year-old children, and found, of course, that they were incomparably better than the best of his animals. There is a striking and basic difference between a man's ability to imagine something that he saw or experienced, and an animal's failure.

Animals make up for this by other and extraordinary gifts. The salmon and the carrier pigeon can find their way home as we cannot: They have, as it were, a practical memory that man cannot match. But their actions always depend on some form of habit: on instinct or on learning, which reproduce by rote a train of known responses. They do not depend, as human memory does, on calling to mind the recollection of absent things.

8   Where is it that the animal falls short? We get a clue to the answer, I think, when Hunter tells us how the animals in his experiment tried to fix their recollection. They most often pointed themselves at the light before it went out, as some gun dogs point rigidly at the game they scent—and get the name *pointer* from the posture. The animal makes ready to act by building the signal into its action. There is a primitive imagery in its stance, it seems to me; it is as if the animal were trying to fix the light on its mind by fixing it in its body. And indeed, how else can a dog mark and (as it were)

name one of the three tunnels, when he has no such words as *left* and *right,* and no such numbers as *one, two, three?* The directed gesture of attention and readiness is perhaps the only symbolic device that the dog commands to hold on to the past, and thereby to guide himself into the future.

I used the verb *to imagine* a moment ago, and now I have some ground for giving it a meaning. *To imagine* means to make images and to move them about inside one's head in new arrangements. When you and I recall the past, we imagine it in this direct and homely sense. The tool that puts the human mind ahead of the animal is imagery. For us, memory does not demand the preoccupation that it demands in animals, and it lasts immensely longer, because we fix it in images or other substitute symbols. With the same symbolic vocabulary we spell out the future—not one but many futures, which we weigh one against another.

I am using the word *image* in a wide meaning, which does not restrict it to the mind's eye as a visual organ. An image in my usage is what Charles Peirce called a *sign,* without regard for its sensory quality. Peirce distinguished between different forms of signs, but there is no reason to make his distinction here, for the imagination works equally with them all, and that is why I call them all *images.*

Indeed, the most important images for human beings are simply words, which are abstract symbols. Animals do not have words, in our sense: There is no specific center for language in the brain of any animal, as there is in the human being. In this respect at least we know that the human imagination depends on a configuration in the brain that has only evolved in the last one or two million years. In the same period, evolution has greatly enlarged the front lobes in the human brain, which govern the sense of the past and the future; and it is a fair guess that they are probably the seat of our other images. (Part of the evidence for this guess is that damage to the front lobes in primates reduces them to the state of Hunter's animals.) If the guess turns out to be right, we shall know why man has come to look like a highbrow or an egghead: because otherwise there would not be room in his head for his imagination.

12   The images play out for us events which are not present to our senses, and thereby guard the past and create the future—a future that does not yet exist, and may never come to exist in that form. By contrast, the lack of symbolic ideas, or their rudimentary poverty, cuts off an animal from the past and the future alike, and imprisons him in the present. Of all the distinctions between man and animal, the characteristic gift which makes us human is the power to work with symbolic images: the gift of imagination.

This is really a remarkable finding. When Philip Sidney in 1580 defended poets (and all unconventional thinkers) from the Puritan charge that they were liars, he said that a maker must imagine things that are not. Halfway between Sidney and us, William Blake said, "What is now proved was once only imagined." About the same time, in 1796, Samuel Taylor Coleridge for the first time distinguished between the passive fancy and the active imagination, "the living Power and prime Agent of all human Perception." Now we see that they were right, and precisely right: The human gift is the gift of imagination—and that is not just a literary phrase.

Nor is it just a literary gift; it is, I repeat, characteristically human. Almost everything that we do that is worth doing is done in the first place in the mind's eye. The richness of human life is that we have many lives; we live the events that do not happen (and some that cannot) as vividly as those that do; and if thereby we die a thousand deaths, that is the price we pay for living a thousand lives. (A cat, of course, has only nine.) Literature is alive to us because we live its images, but so is any play of the mind—so is chess: The lines of play that we foresee and try in our heads and dismiss are as much a part of the game as the moves that we make. John Keats said that the unheard melodies are sweeter, and all chess players sadly recall that the combinations that they planned and which never came to be played were the best.

I make this point to remind you, insistently, that imagination is the manipulation of images in one's head; and that the rational manipulation belongs to that, as well as the literary and artistic manipulation. When a child begins to play games with things that stand for other things, with chairs or chessmen, he enters the gateway to reason and imagination together. For the human reason discovers new relations between things not by deduction, but by that unpredictable blend of speculation and insight that scientists call *induction*, which—like other forms of imagination—cannot be formalized. We see it at work when Walter Hunter inquires into a child's memory, as much as when Blake and Coleridge do. Only a restless and original mind would have asked Hunter's questions and could have conceived his experiments, in a science that was dominated by Pavlov's reflex arcs and was heading toward the behaviorism of John Watson.

16   Let me find a spectacular example for you from history. What is the most famous experiment that you had described to you as a child? I will hazard that it is the experiment that Galileo is said to have made in Sidney's age, in Pisa about 1590, by dropping two unequal balls from the Leaning Tower. There, we say, is a man in the modern mold, a man after our own hearts: He insisted on questioning the authority of Aristotle and St. Thomas Aquinas, and seeing with his own eyes whether (as they did) the heavy ball would reach the ground before the light one. Seeing is believing.

Yet seeing is also imagining. Galileo did challenge the authority of Aristotle, and he did look at his mechanics. But the eye that Galileo used was the mind's eye. He did not drop balls from the Leaning Tower of Pisa—and if he had, he would have got a very doubtful answer. Instead, Galileo made an imaginary experiment in his head, which I will describe as he did years later in the book he wrote after the Holy Office silenced him: *Discorsi . . . intorno a due nuove scienze,* which was smuggled out to be printed in the Netherlands in 1638.

Suppose, said Galileo, that you drop two unequal balls from the tower at the same time. And suppose that Aristotle is right—suppose that the heavy ball falls faster, so that it steadily gains on the light ball, and hits the ground first. Very well. Now imagine the same experiment done again, with only one difference: This time the two unequal balls are joined by a string between them. The heavy ball will again move ahead, but now the light ball holds it back and acts as a drag or brake. So the light ball will be speeded up and the heavy ball will be slowed down; they must reach the ground together because they are tied together, but they cannot reach the ground as quickly as the heavy ball alone. Yet the string between them has turned the two balls into a single mass which is heavier than either ball—and surely (according to Aristotle) this mass should therefore move faster than either ball? Galileo's imaginary experiment has uncovered a contradiction; he says trenchantly, "You see how, from your assumption that a heavier body falls more rapidly than a lighter one, I infer that a (still) heavier body falls more slowly." There is only one way out of the contradiction: The heavy ball and the light ball must fall at the same rate, so that they go on falling at the same rate when they are tied together.

This argument is not conclusive, for nature might be more subtle (when the two balls are joined) than Galileo has allowed. And yet it is something more important: It is suggestive, it is stimulating, it opens a new view—in a word, it is imaginative. It cannot be settled without an actual experiment, because nothing that we imagine can become knowledge until we have translated it into, and backed it by, real experience. The test of imagination is experience. But then, that is as true of literature and the arts as it is of science. In science, the imaginary experiment is tested by confronting it with physical experience; and in literature, the imaginative conception is tested by confronting it with human experience. The superficial speculation in science is dismissed because it is found to falsify nature; and the shallow work of art is discarded because it is found to be untrue to our own nature. So when Ella Wheeler Wilcox died in 1919, more people were reading her verses than Shakespeare's; yet in a few years her work was dead. It had been buried by its poverty of emotion and its trivialness of thought: which is to say that it had been proved to be as false to the nature of man as, say, Jean Baptiste Lamarck and Trofim Lysenko were false to the nature of inheritance. The strength of the imagination, its enriching power and excitement, lies in its interplay with reality—physical and emotional.

20   I doubt if there is much to choose here between science and the arts: The imagination is not much more free, and not much less free, in one than in the other. All great scientists have used their imagination freely, and let it ride them to outrageous conclusions without crying "Halt!" Albert Einstein fiddled with imaginary experiments from boyhood, and was wonderfully ignorant of the facts that they were supposed to bear on. When he wrote the first of his beautiful papers on the random movement of atoms, he did not know that the Brownian motion which it predicted could be seen in any laboratory. He was sixteen when he invented the paradox that he resolved ten years later, in 1905, in the theory of relativity, and it bulked much larger in his mind than the experiment of Albert Michelson and Edward Morley which had upset every other physicist since 1881. All his life Einstein loved to make up teasing puzzles like Galileo's, about falling lifts and the detection of gravity; and they carry the nub of the problems of general relativity on which he was working.

Indeed, it could not be otherwise. The power that man has over nature and himself, and that a dog lacks, lies in his command of imaginary experience. He alone has the symbols which fix the past and play with the future, possible and impossible. In the Renaissance, the symbolism of memory was thought to be mystical, and devices that were invented as mnemonics (by Giordano Bruno, for example, and by Robert Fludd) were interpreted as magic signs. The symbol is the tool which gives man his power, and it is the same tool whether the symbols are images or words, mathematical signs or mesons. And the symbols have a reach and a roundness that goes beyond their literal and practical meaning. They are the rich concepts under which the mind gathers many particulars into one name, and many instances into one general induction. When a man says *left* and *right,* he is outdistancing the dog not only in looking for a light; he is setting in train all the shifts of meaning, the overtones and the ambiguities, between *gauche* and *adroit* and *dexterous,* between *sinister* and the sense of right. When a man counts *one, two, three,* he is not only doing mathematics; he is on the path to the mysticism of numbers in Pythagoras and Vitruvius and Kepler, to the Trinity and the signs of the Zodiac.

I have described imagination as the ability to make images and to move them about inside one's head in new arrangements. This is the faculty that is specifically human, and it is the common root from which science and literature both spring and grow and flourish together. For they do flourish (and languish) together; the great ages of science are the great ages of all the arts, because in them powerful minds have taken fire from one another breathless and higgledy-piggledy, without asking too nicely whether they ought to tie their imagination to falling balls or a haunted island. Galileo and Shakespeare, who were born in the same year, grew into greatness in the same age; when Galileo was looking through his telescope at the moon, Shakespeare was writing *The Tempest* and all Europe was in ferment, from Johannes Kepler to Peter Paul Rubens, and from the first table of logarithms by John Napier to the Authorized Version of the Bible.

Let me end with a last and spirited example of the common inspiration of literature and science, because it is as much alive today as it was three hundred years ago. What I have in mind is man's ageless fantasy, to fly to the moon. I do not display this to you as a high scientific enterprise; on the contrary, I think we have more important discoveries to make here on earth than wait for us, beckoning, at the horned surface of the moon. Yet I cannot belittle the fascination which that ice-blue journey has had for the imagination of men, long before it drew us to our television screens to watch the tumbling astronauts. Plutarch and Lucian, Ariosto and Ben Jonson wrote about it, before the days of Jules Verne and H. G. Wells and science fiction. The seventeenth century was heady with new dreams and fables about voyages to the moon. Kepler wrote one full of deep scientific ideas, which (alas) simply got his mother accused of witchcraft. In England, Francis Godwin wrote a wild and splendid work, *The Man in the Moone,* and the astronomer John Wilkins wrote a wild and learned one, *The Discovery of a New World.* They did not draw a line between science and fancy; for example, they all tried to guess just where in the journey the earth's gravity would stop. Only Kepler understood that gravity has no boundary, and put a law to it—which happened to be the wrong law.

24   All this was a few years before Isaac Newton was born, and it was all in his head that day in 1666 when he sat in his mother's garden, a young man of twenty-three, and thought about the reach of gravity. This was how he came to conceive his brilliant image, that the moon is like a ball which has been thrown so hard that it falls exactly as fast as the horizon, all the way round the earth. The image will do for any satellite, and Newton modestly calculated how long therefore an astronaut would take to fall round the earth once. He made it ninety minutes, and we have all seen now that he was right; but Newton had no way to check that. Instead he went on to calculate how long in that case the distant moon would take to round the earth, if indeed it behaves like a thrown ball that falls in the earth's gravity, and if gravity obeyed a law of inverse squares. He found that the answer would be twenty-eight days.

In that telling figure, the imagination that day chimed with nature, and made a harmony. We shall hear an echo of that harmony on the day when we land on the moon, because it will be not a technical but an imaginative triumph, that reaches back to the beginning of modern science and literature both. All great acts of imagination are like this, in the arts and in science, and convince us because they fill out reality with a deeper sense of rightness. We start with the simplest vocabulary of images, with *left* and *right* and *one, two, three,* and before we know how it happened the words and the numbers have conspired to make a match with nature: We catch in them the pattern of mind and matter as one.

Personal Response

Discuss the aspects of this essay you find especially intriguing and why. If you do not find any aspect of this essay intriguing, explain why.

Questions for Class or Small-Group Discussion

1. Elaborate on Bronowski's statement that imagination "is the faculty that is specifically human, and it is the common root from which science and literature both spring and grow and flourish together" (paragraph 22). What do you think he means, and why?

2. Discuss the ways in which scientists you know about were imaginative, making sure you explain why you think so.

3. Bronowski's essay was written before the first moon landing (see paragraphs 23–25). If Bronowski were writing today, what example do you think he would use in his closing paragraphs to demonstrate that scientific achievement is the result of both technology and imagination? What examples would you use? Why?

4. Working with members of a small group, interview a scientist about the importance of the imagination in his or her work. Before the interview, work in your group to draw up a list of appropriate questions. Select one member to set up the appointment, one to ask the questions, one to record the answers, and one to report to the rest of the class the results of your interview.

THE CHEMIST
Roald Hoffmann

Roald Hoffmann is professor of chemistry at Cornell University. He was responsible for a twenty-six part PBS television series designed to explain chemistry to high school and junior college students and has worked actively to popularize chemistry. He is author, with Vivian Torrence as artistic collaborator, of Chemistry Imagined: Reflections on Science *(1993), from which this essay is taken.*

In describing what they do, scientists have by and large bought the metaphor of discovery and artists that of creation. The cliché "uncovering the secrets of nature" has set, like good cement, in our minds. But I think that the metaphor of discovery is effective in describing only part of the activity of scientists, and a smaller piece still of the work of chemists. The historical, psychological, philosophical, and sociological reasons for the ready acceptance of the metaphor deserve a closer look.

History and Psychology
The rise of modern science in Europe coincided with the age of geographical exploration. Men set foot on distant shores, explored *terra incognita*. Even in our century, a man I was named after first sailed the Northwest passage and reached the South Pole. Voyages of discovery, maps filled in—those are powerful images indeed. So is penetration into a royal tomb full of glistening gold vessels. It's no surprise that these metaphors were and are accepted by (predominantly male) scientists as appropriate descriptors of their generally laboratory-bound activity. Is there some vicarious sharing of imagined adventures at work here?

Philosophy
The French rationalist tradition, and the systematization of astronomy and physics before the other sciences, have left science with a reductionist philosophy at its core. There is supposed to exist a logical hierarchy of the sciences, and understanding is to be defined solely in vertical terms as reduction to the more basic science. The more mathematical, the better. So biological phenomena are to be explained by chemistry, chemistry by physics, and so on. The logic of a reductionist philosophy fits the discovery metaphor—one digs deeper and discovers the truth.

4   But reductionism is only one face of understanding. We have been made not only to disassemble, disconnect, and analyze but also to build. There is no more stringent test of passive understanding than active creation. Perhaps *test* is not the word here, for building or creation differ inherently from reductionist analysis. I want to claim a greater role in science for the forward, constructive mode.

Sociology

Those philosophers of science who started out as practicing scientists have generally, I believe, come from physics and mathematics. The education of professional philosophers is likely to favor the same fields; quite understandably, there is a special role for logic in philosophy. No wonder that the prevailing ideology of reasoning in the underlying scientific areas of expertise of philosophers of science has been extended by them, unrealistically I believe, to all science.

What is strange is that chemists should accept the metaphor of discovery. Chemistry is the science of molecules (up to a hundred years ago one would have said *substances* or *compounds*) and their transformations. Some of the molecules are indeed *there,* just waiting to be "known" by us, their static properties—what atoms are in them, how the atoms are connected, the shapes of molecules, their splendid colors—and in their dynamic characteristics—the molecules' internal motions, their reactivity. The molecules are those of the earth—for instance, simple water and complex malachite. Or of life—relatively simple cholesterol and more complicated hemoglobin. The discovery paradigm certainly applies to the study of these molecules.

But so many more molecules of chemistry are made by us, in the laboratory. We're awfully prolific. A registry of known, well-characterized compounds now numbers nearly ten million. These were not on earth before. It is true that their constitution follows underlying rules, and if Chemist A had not made such-and-such a molecule on a certain day, then it is likely to have been synthesized a few days or decades later by Chemist B. But it is a human being, a chemist, who chooses the molecule to be made and a distinct way to make it. This work is not so different from that of the artist who, constrained by the physics of pigment and canvas, shaped by his or her training, nevertheless creates the new.

8 Even when one is clearly operating in the discovery mode in chemistry, elucidating the structure or dynamics of a known, naturally occurring molecule, one usually has to intervene with created molecules. I recently heard a beautiful lecture by Alan Battersby, an outstanding British organic chemist, on the biosynthesis of uroporphyrinogen-III. (Even in the trade, the name of this molecule is abbreviated as uro'gen-III.) It's not a glamorous molecule, but it should be: for from this precursor plants make chlorophyll, the basis of all photosynthetic activity. All cells use another uro'gen-III derivative in cytochromes for electron transport. And the crucial iron-containing, oxygen-carrier piece of hemoglobin derives from this small disk-shaped molecule.

Uro'gen-III, pictured on the next page, is made from four rings, called *pyrroles,* themselves tied into a larger ring. Note the markers A and P in each ring. They're in the same order as one goes around the ring (from about 10 o'clock), except for the last set, which are "reverse." So the markers read A, P, A, P, A, P, P, A.

How this natural molecule is assembled, within us, is clearly a discovery question. In fact, the four pyrrole rings are connected up, with the aid of an enzyme, into a chain, then cyclized. But the last ring is first put in "incorrectly," that is, with the

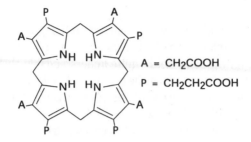

same order of the A, P labels as in the other rings: A, P, A, P, A, P, A, P. Then, in a fantastic separate reaction sequence, just that last ring, with its attached labels, is flipped into position.

This incredible but true story was deduced by Battersby and his coworkers using a sequence of synthetic molecules, not natural ones, which were made slightly different from the natural ones. Each was designed to test some critical part of the natural process in the living system. Each was then treated under the physiological conditions to allow the sequence of the natural events to be traced out. Using molecules we've made, we've learned how nature builds a molecule that makes life possible.

12   The synthesis of molecules puts chemistry very close to the arts. We create the objects that we or others then study or appreciate. That's exactly what writers, composers, visual artists, all working within their areas, working perhaps closer to the soul, do. I believe that, in fact, this creative capacity is exceptionally strong in chemistry. Mathematicians also study the objects of their own creation, but those objects, not to take anything away from their uniqueness, are mental concepts rather than real structures. Some branches of engineering are actually close to chemistry in this matter of synthesis. Perhaps this is a factor in the kinship the chemist–narrator feels for the builder Faussone, who is the main character in Primo Levi's novel *The Monkey's Wrench*.

In the building of theories and hypotheses, even more than in synthesis, the act is a creative one. One has to imagine, to conjure up a model that fits often irregular observations. There are rules; the model should be consistent with previously received reliable knowledge. There are hints of what to do; one sees what was done in related problems. But what one seeks is an explanation that was not there before, a connection between two worlds. Often, actually, it's a metaphor that serves as the clue: "Two interacting systems, hmm . . . , let's model them with a resonating pair of harmonic oscillators, or . . . a barrier penetration problem." The world out there is moderately chaotic, frighteningly so, in the parts we do not understand. We want to see a pattern in it. We're clever, we "connoisseurs of chaos," so we find/create one. Had more philosophers of science been trained in chemistry, I'm sure we would have a very different paradigm of science before us.

Is art all creation? I don't think so. In substantial measure it is discovery, of the deep truths of what is also around us, often overlapping, but more often reaching outside the set of problems that science has set for itself to try to understand. Art aspires to discover, explore, unravel—whatever metaphor you please—the nonunique, chanced, irreducible world within us.

Personal Response

How much do you know about chemistry? Was chemistry required in your high school? If so, describe your experience with the class. Did you like it or not? Why?

Questions for Class or Small-Group Discussion

1. Discuss this statement: "There is no more stringent test of passive understanding than active creation" (paragraph 4). Give an example from your own experiences to illustrate the statement.

2. What connections do you see between what chemists do and what artists do? Do you think the metaphors of discovery and of creation are appropriate for both, as Hoffmann suggests? Why or why not?

3. In class, list all of the things you can think of that are in some way touched by chemistry. After you have written for a few minutes, stop and compare your list with that of a classmate before writing for a few more minutes. Then volunteer to read your list aloud, having classmates check off identical items.

4. Despite the widespread influence of chemistry in almost every aspect of our lives, most people know very little about it. Discuss what difference it makes that few of us have any serious understanding of chemistry. Do you think it ought to be a required subject in high school? Why or why not?

THE YEAR OF THE GENOME

Matt Ridley

Matt Ridley holds a Ph.D. in zoology and is a former science editor, Washington correspondent, and U.S. editor for the Economist. *He is author of* The Red Queen: Sex and the Evolution of Human Nature *(1994),* The Origins of Virtue: Human Instincts and the Evolution of Cooperation *(1997), and* Genome: The Autobiography of a Species in 23 Chapters *(2000). This article was published in the January 2001 issue of* Discover.

Imagine that one day there lands upon earth an alien spacecraft stuffed with a million crumpled pieces of paper, each covered in text written in an unknown script. The best brains in the world are put to the task of deciphering the code, which takes 10 years. But it takes another 40 years to smooth out all of the pages, translate them in English, sort them, and publish them as a vast book. Then, at long last, the task is done, and we sit down to read the book from beginning to end. It contains thousands of stories about the past, the present, and the future of humankind, from the origin of life to the recipe for curing cancer.

What an extraordinary and unlikely tale. And yet that is essentially what happened this year. After 50 years of preparation, we have suddenly been placed in the position of being able to read the entire genetic story of human beings—the genome.

On June 26 Francis Collins, head of the Human Genome Project, and Craig Venter, head of Celera Genomics, jointly announced that they had completed the reading of a "rough draft" of the human genome—the complete set of human DNA. The announcement came at least two years earlier than expected and marked a dead heat in a fiercely contested scientific marathon.

4   The researchers on the Human Genome Project had been working toward a complete human sequence since the late 1980s. In early 1998, with less than 10 percent of the job done, scientists were predicting that it would take seven more years. Then Venter announced that he would undertake to do the job by 2001, using private funds.

Twice before he had delivered on equally dramatic promises. In 1991 he invented a quick way to find human genes, using expressed sequence tags, after the senior scientists at the Human Genome Project had said it wouldn't work. In 1995, he invented a new "shotgun" technique for sequencing DNA and read the full genome of a bacterium while the establishment was still dismissing the technique as unworkable.

So Venter's threat was serious. The Human Genome Project reorganized its efforts, and the race was on. In the end, both projects announced together that they had finished a rough draft last June. A rough draft is a sequence with 91 percent of the letters in the right place, each letter having been read and reread between five and seven times. Plenty of gaps remain, but they amount to less than 10 percent of the text.

This announcement was the beginning of a whole new way of understanding human biology. Everything we have laboriously discovered hitherto about how our bodies work will be dwarfed by the knowledge tumbling from the genome.

8   It was also the end to a great detective story. In 1860, Gregor Mendel made the bizarre discovery that inheritance comes in tiny particles called genes that do not decay with age, or blend with one another. In 1953, James Watson and Francis Crick made the even more unexpected discovery that those particles are actually digital messages written along strands of DNA in code, using a four-letter chemical alphabet. In 1961, Marshall Nirenberg and Johann Matthaei cracked the first "word" in that code, revealing exactly how DNA instructs the cell to build proteins. It was then inevitable—if mind-boggling—that one day we would read all the genetic messages that a human body inherits. Now we have.

But, of course, the genome announcement is just a beginning. For the document that has been produced—a 3.3-billion-letter book, as long as 900 Bibles—is almost entirely mysterious. We do not know even the basic facts about it, such as how many genes it contains—although the guesses are converging on a figure of 38,000—let alone what each gene is and how genes interact with one another. We do not know why the genes are hidden in great stretches of apparently meaningless text, or so-called junk DNA. We stand on the brink of a continent of new knowledge.

Most people do not see the genome in such romantic terms. They want to know how it will help cure cancer; they speculate about customized medicine, with drugs designed for the individual, not the population. They worry that it will lead to designer babies for the rich or to a lessening of respect for the disabled; they fear the patenting of genes by private corporations; they predict that medical insurance may cease to be offered by insurance companies to those whose risks are known and high.

All these are real issues. The medical possibilities and ethical fears that dominate the debate are by no means trivial. But there is a larger philosophical truth missed. The genome represents an unprecedented draft of self-knowledge for humankind with implications that stretch far beyond medicine. It promises to tell us new things about our past as a species, and it promises new insights into philosophical conundrums, not least of which is the puzzle of free will.

12   We have been misled into thinking that genetics is all about disorders. Geneticists have so far concentrated on genes that are linked to disease: first the simple but rare inherited diseases like cystic fibrosis (the gene for which is on chromosome 7) or Huntington's (chromosome 4), then the environmental diseases for which different people inherit different susceptibilities, such as Alzheimer's (chromosome 19) or breast cancer (chromosomes 13 and 17). More recently, they have begun to seek genes that affect our behavior, prompting us to be dyslexic (chromosome 6), homosexual (perhaps on the X chromosome), adventurous (chromosome 11), or even highly religious (no map location yet).

A well-studied example of a human gene is the ACE gene on chromosome 17, which seems to predict physical performance. According to a group of scientists at University College, London, possessing one version of this gene rather than another dramatically improves the ability to increase muscle strength with training and increases the mechanical efficiency of trained muscle. Mountain climbers, rowers, and other athletes tend to have this high-performance version of the gene. Likewise, one version of the APOE gene on chromosome 19 predicts the likelihood of a boxer suffering from premature Alzheimer's disease. A person with the "wrong" versions of both these genes would be well advised not to become an athlete in a contact sport.

But that word "wrong" is all wrong, is it not? There is still too much tendency to think in terms of genetic divergence from the presumed norm. Back in the Stone Age, the low-performance version of the ACE gene might have resisted starvation better, and the risky version of the APOE gene might have had some other advantage. Besides, to define a gene as an "Alzheimer's gene" or a "dyslexia gene" is a bit like defining the heart as a "heart-attack organ." This is misleading. Neither blue nor brown eyes (a gene somewhere on chromosome 15) are normal. With the genome in hand, we can see genes in better context. We can study how and why all human beings inherit a musical sense, rather than why some people are more musical than others.

Genes are windows on the past. Some reflect the history of infectious disease in different tribes. The A and B blood groups (chromosome 9) protect against cholera; the cystic fibrosis and Tag-Sachs (15) mutations may protect against tuberculosis;

the sickle-cell (11) and thalassemia (16) mutations protect against malaria. Hence the prevalence of these particular mutations in certain peoples.

16   Other genes tell a story of responses to culture. The fact that adult Europeans are twice as likely as Asians to tolerate lactose in milk (no location yet) reflects a much longer history of dairy farming in the West; the ability to dehydrogenate alcohol (chromosome 4) is more common in people with a history of drinking fermented fluids; the prevalence of the blond-hair gene in young northern Europeans (perhaps on chromosome 15?) may reflect a sexual preference for youthful mates.

Still others tell of events long before recorded history. The unusual genes of the Basque people mirror the unique nature of their language and suggest that they are descendants of preagricultural Europeans. The astonishing similarity between embryonic-development genes called Hox genes in fruit flies and people (chromosomes 2, 7, 9, 12, and 17) tells us that the common ancestor of people and insects was a segmented animal; yet this animal lived more than 600 million years ago and left no fossils. The genome is going to be a treasure trove of such stories.

Science has a habit of addressing problems raised by philosophy. It may not be too much to claim that the mystery of free will has been recast by recent discoveries in genetics, which have exposed the myth that genes are puppet masters and we are their puppets. Take, as an example, the various learning mutations that have been discovered in fruit flies and subsequently in mice and people (chromosomes 2 and 16). These are found in genes that are central to memory and learning, many of them part of the CREB (cyclic-AMP response elements binding protein) system in the brain. The mutations reveal that every time a person learns something, he has to switch on some of these genes in order to lay down new connections between brain cells.

That sounds like dull molecular plumbing. But actually it is revolutionary philosophy. In attempting to answer the question of whether we possess free will, the Scottish philosopher David Hume impaled himself on the following dilemma: Either our actions are determined, in which case we are not responsible for them, or they are the result of random events, in which case we are also not responsible for them. But the CREB genes show how to escape this fix. If genes are at the mercy of behavior, but behavior is also at the mercy of genes, then our actions can be determined by forces that originate within us as well as by outside influences. The will is therefore a mixture of instincts and outside influences. This makes it deterministic and responsible, but not predictable.

20   Curiously, the free will story brings us to cancer, which is where the whole genome project started. Cancer researchers first suggested sequencing the human genome in the mid-1980s. They were just beginning to realize that cancer was a wholly genetic process. Genetic, but not hereditary. Most cancer is not inherited—though there are well-known mutations that increase susceptibility to cancer, such as BRCA1 and BRCA2, both of which are associated with breast cancer.

Yet cancer is a disease of the genes. Like free will, it is a process mediated by the genes but not caused by them. Like the CREB genes of memory, changes in cancer genes are the consequence, not the cause, of environmental effects. Cigarette smoke, for example, causes cancer by mutating genes inside human cells called oncogenes, which encourage cells to multiply, and tumor-suppressor genes, which prevent them from multiplying. To turn malignant, a tumor must evolve with at least one oncogene jammed in the "on" position and at least one tumor-suppressor gene jammed in the "off" position.

Little wonder that President Clinton, announcing the genome last June, mused that one day people may know cancer only as a star sign, not a disease. That was going much too far, because cancer is also a disease of aging: Its incidence increases steadily with age. Rendering it easily curable will only increase its incidence. Nonetheless, by identifying all oncogenes and tumor-suppressor genes and understanding how they work, the Human Genome Project will transform cancer therapy. Already, drugs based on the most famous of the tumor-suppressors, p53 (chromosome 17), are in early clinical trials.

The human genome opens a world of medical opportunity, of commercial promise, of ethical danger, and of social challenge. It is also a cornucopia of scientific possibilities that ranks alongside the revolutions wrought by Euclid, Copernicus, Newton, Darwin, and Einstein. It is a fitting bang with which to start a new millennium.

Personal Response

Questions for Class and Small-Group Discussion

1. Explain the opening analogy. How does it represent scientific discoveries leading to the completion of the genome's "rough draft" (paragraphs 1–2)?

2. Discuss what Ridley has to say about the larger implications of the genome, beyond medical possibilities. To what extent do you agree with him that those things are larger in implication than either "the medical possibilities or ethical issues fears" (paragraph 11).

3. Discuss this statement: "We have been misled into thinking that genetics is all about disorders" (paragraph 12).

THE INFLUENCE OF "JUNK SCIENCE" AND THE ROLE OF SCIENCE EDUCATION

Lee Ann Fisher Baron

Lee Ann Fisher Baron is Professor of Natural Science at Hillsdale College, where she has taught since 1989. Recipient of many awards for her teaching and work in science education, Baron has developed

*programs to interest middle-school girls in scientific careers and writ-
ten laboratory study guides for high school summer science camps,
among other things. This essay is based on a presentation Baron
did for a seminar on "junk science" held at Hillsdale College, and it
was published in* Imprimis *in February 2001.*

Science is exciting partly because single discoveries can change the course of history.
Think of the effects on human health and longevity of the discovery of antibiotics, the
multi-faceted impact on our lives of the discovery of polymers, or the far-reaching importance of the Human Genome Project. Unfortunately, however, most of the "revolutionary discoveries" made throughout history have turned out to be wrong.

Error is a regular part of science. That is why reports of new findings or discoveries, no matter where or how widely they are reported, should be regarded with
healthy skepticism. The proper scientific approach to such claims involves a set of
procedures called the scientific method. This method requires the design of tests or
experiments that can be repeated with the same results by anyone. These tests must
also contain controls to ensure that the results are statistically significant.

Let me illustrate the importance of controls by describing briefly an experiment
in which my daughter participated as a subject some years ago at the University of
Michigan Medical School. Its purpose was to determine whether the vaccine for tuberculosis could lengthen the interval during which newly-diagnosed type 1 diabet-
ics do not experience severe high or low blood sugar. The subjects were divided into
a group of those who received the vaccine and a control group of those who received
a placebo. The subjects did not know who got the vaccine and, just as importantly,
neither did the researchers—a type of control referred to as a "double-blind." By using two groups, the researchers were able to measure the "placebo effect"—a phenomenon in which patients improve because they falsely believe that they are
receiving medicine. And by keeping themselves ignorant of the breakdown of the
groups, the researchers were prevented from reading their hypotheses into the
results.

"Junk Science"

4   Most erroneous conclusions by scientists are discovered during the process of publishing their research. Other scientists review submitted articles, often repeating any
relevant tests or experiments and always evaluating the conclusions that have been
drawn from them. So-called "junk science" bypasses this system of peer review. Presented directly to the public by people variously described as "experts" or "activists,"
often with little or no supporting evidence, this "junk science" undermines the ability of elected representatives, jurists, and others—including everyday consumers—
to make rational decisions.

An example of "junk science" I like to use with my students is the myth of
"fat-free foods" invented by the food industry with the help of federal regulators. By
regulatory definition, these foods may contain monoglycerides and diglycerides, but
not triglycerides. From the point of view of solid science this definition makes no

In these data, I believe, lies the reason for the popularity of pseudoscience. Without a grasp of scientific ways of thinking, the average person cannot tell the difference between science based on real data and something that resembles science—at least in their eyes—but is based on uncontrolled experiments, anecdotal evidence, and passionate assertions. They like it all.

The claim, for example, that brains can transmit information telepathically, strikes them as no less believable than the claim that whole stars can collapse into infinitesimal points. Many among the public have not yet learned that what makes science special is that evidence has to meet certain standards.

My own encounters with believers in pseudoscience—based on anecdotal evidence, to be sure—are consistent with the view that many adults are fascinated by claims that the world is filled with wonders and that some of them remain inexplicable. No problem there. But instead of dismissing such people as hopelessly beyond the pale, both scientists and journalists need to find ways of teaching them how to think more rigorously.

12   First, I suggest, journalists need to learn more about scientific methods and thinking. Most full-time science writers are already up on this, but nonspecialist journalists seldom are, and it is increasingly common that they cover stories with science content. It is important that we educate these nonspecialist journalists.

Second, when scientists talk to journalists, they ought to move beyond the highlights of their findings and wade into the methods, taking the initiative to ensure that the reporter understands why the results may be believed. Journalists, then, must make it a point to explain in their stories, somehow, that the new finding is founded on a plausible base of evidence.

Personal Response

Rensberger writes: "Americans are overwhelmingly interested in science but don't understand it and know even less about how it is done" (paragraph 8). To what extent does this statement describe you?

Questions for Class or Small-Group Discussion

1. Rensberger says that "the weakness in the public's understanding of science lies in an area not often addressed between scientists and journalists—*the nature of evidence*" (paragraph 5). What do you understand him to mean by that term?

2. Rensberger mentions parapsychology and UFOs as examples of "pseudoscience." Discuss what you know about those subjects and your understanding of why they are considered "pseudoscience." What other examples of pseudoscientific subjects or beliefs can you name?

3. Renseberger offers two ways that he thinks scientists and journalists can teach the general public "how to think more rigorously" (paragraph 11). Discuss his suggestions and the likelihood you think his plan has of succeeding.

PERSPECTIVES ON NATURAL SCIENCES

Suggestions for Synthesis

1. Explore the connections between two essays in this chapter by comparing and contrasting them. Consider what ideas their authors have in common, how they differ, and what their observations have taught you about the natural sciences.

2. The writers in this chapter share a firm belief in the importance of science. Argue either in support of or against the positions that at least two of them take on the value of science by first summarizing their position and then explaining why you do or do not support that viewpoint.

3. Write an essay on the subject of "junk science" and/or "pseudoscience," drawing on both Lee Ann Fisher Baron's "The Influence of 'Junk Science' and the Role of Science Education" and Boyce Rensberger's "The Nature of Evidence."

Additional Writing Topics

1. Define the abstract term *imagination,* using examples from both science and the humanities to illustrate what you mean.

2. Support or argue against Roald Hoffmann's assertion that art is not all creation but "in substantial measure it is discovery" ("The Chemist," paragraph 14).

3. Write a personal essay in which you explore your own interest in and involvement with science.

4. Write an essay explaining how just one scientific discipline has an impact on your everyday life and reasons why you believe it has that impact.

Research Topics

1. Select one of the many scientific discoveries that have "change[d] the course of human history" (Lee Ann Fisher Baron, "The Influence of 'Junk Science' and the Role of Science Education," paragraph 1) and research its discovery and how it changed humans' lives.

2. Research the history of important discoveries that led to the genome project, especially those of people mentioned in paragraph 8 of Matt Ridley's "The Year of the Genome": Gregor Mendel, James Watson and Francis Crick, and/or Marshall Nirenberg and Johann Matthaei.

3. Read about research into how the brain works or the results of neurological damage, and write a paper that not only reports your findings but that also takes a position on some aspect of the subject. For example, Oliver Sacks's *The Man Who Mistook His Wife for a Hat* is a fascinating account of Sacks's work with people who have suffered damage to parts of their brains. To make this subject suitable for a research paper, you might begin by finding out what controversies surround treatment for neurological damage and then reading opposing opinions on the controversy. Once you have read enough opposing viewpoints to form your own opinion, take a side and explain why you have chosen that position.

4. Scientists know much more about how the brain works now than they did when Jacob Bronowski wrote "The Reach of the Imagination." Research the latest thinking about the way the brain works, for example in relation to Bronowski's conjecture about the importance of the frontal lobe in imaginative thinking. Explore differing theories, take a position, and explain why you believe as you do.

5. Jacob Bronowski, Roald Hoffmann, and Boyce Rensberger were all involved in television series intended to popularize science for laypeople. Research the life and efforts of one of these men, or do a comparative analysis of two or all three of them. In addition to reading about their television work, locate contemporary reviews of the programs. Then draw your own conclusions about their success or failure.

6. Read about the efforts of schools to encourage students to take math and science classes. Find out the rationale for such programs and what steps they have taken to increase interest in the subjects. Then draw your own conclusions about the relative importance of increasing enrollment in math and science courses and in improving test scores in those subjects.

CHAPTER 20

BIOETHICS

Research into the complex structure of the human body since James D. Watson and Francis Crick discovered in 1953 that deoxyribonucleic acid (DNA) molecules arrange themselves in a double helix has made enormous advances. The discovery of this pattern in DNA, a substance that transmits the genetic characteristics from one generation to the next, earned Watson and Crick a Nobel Prize in 1962. Their work led other scientists to work on such things as recombinant DNA and gene splicing in the 1970s and eventually to the Human Genome Project, whose goal was to map the entire sequence of human DNA. A genome is the complete set of instructions for making a human being. Each nucleus of the one hundred trillion cells that make up the human body contains this set of instructions, which are written in the language of DNA. This major undertaking by scientists around the world promises to provide medical doctors with the tools to predict the development of human diseases. When the project began in 1988, scientists thought that it would take fifteen years to complete, but the project progressed faster than first predicted and is now finished well ahead of schedule.

Now that the human code has been mapped, scientists can begin to better understand how humans grow, what causes human diseases, and what new drugs would combat those diseases by either preventing or curing them. Scientists already are able to identify variations or defects in the genetic makeup of certain cells in human bodies that may result in diseases with genetic origins. Eventually, they will be able to develop tests of an individual's likelihood of developing one of thousands of inherited diseases such as sickle-cell anemia, cystic fibrosis, or muscular dystrophy, and even heart disease or cancer. Because there are more than 30,000 genes that make up the "instruction manual" for the human body, it will take some time before all of them are codified and their functions known. The Human Genome Project raised a number of difficult ethical questions, however, as the essays in this chapter indicate. One of the most controversial steps forward in the potential of scientists to manipulate genes is the capacity to clone living creatures, though there are other potential uses of gene therapy.

The first two essays, by James D. Watson and Ian Wilmut, respectively, were written for a special *Time* magazine issue on the future of medicine. Wilmut is the Scottish embryologist who cloned the first mammal, the famous sheep Dolly. Watson and Wilmut hold different opinions on just what should and what should not be done with research into human cloning. Next, Jeff Lyon's "Playing God: Has Science Gone Too Far?" looks at the ethical and moral issues of human cloning, gene therapy, and stem cell research. His article reports the opinions of many people, including representatives of several major religions, in answer to this question: "Is it right for scientists to assume powers that many people believe should belong only to God?"

The last two essays in this chapter offer opposing viewpoints on the bioethical issue of human cloning. Ruth Macklin, in "Human Cloning? Don't Just Say No," defends the position that, lacking evidence for harmful effects of new technology that enables scientists to clone animals and possibly humans, government need not ban experimentation. In contrast, Charles Krauthammer, in "Of Headless Mice . . . and Men," warns of potentially horrific results if cloning is not immediately prohibited. As you read what each writer says about the subject, consider how convincing you find that reasoning.

ALL FOR THE GOOD

James D. Watson

James D. Watson, with Francis Crick, discovered in 1953 that DNA molecules arrange themselves in a double helix. In 1962, Watson, Crick, and a British biophysicist, Maurice Wilkins, shared the Nobel Prize in physiology or medicine for their work on DNA. In 1968 Watson became director of the Cold Springs Harbor Laboratory of Quantitative Biology, in New York State. He published The Double Helix, *his best-selling story of the discovery of the structure of DNA, in 1968. A recipient of the Presidential Medal of Freedom and author of many scientific papers, Watson directed the Human Genome Project from 1988 to 1992. He wrote this piece for* Time *magazine's January 11, 1999, issue on the future of medicine.*

There is lots of zip in DNA-based biology today. With each passing year it incorporates an ever increasing fraction of the life sciences, ranging from single-cell organisms, like bacteria and yeast, to the complexities of the human brain. All this wonderful biological frenzy was unimaginable when I first entered the world of genetics. In 1948, biology was an all too descriptive discipline near the bottom of science's totem pole, with physics at its top. By then Einstein's turn-of-the-century ideas about the interconversion of matter and energy had been transformed into the powers of the atom. If not held in check, the weapons they made possible might well destroy the very fabric of civilized human life. So physicists of the late 1940s were simultaneously revered for making atoms relevant to society and feared for what their toys could do if they were to fall into the hands of evil.

Such ambivalent feelings are now widely held toward biology. The double-helical structure of DNA, initially admired for its intellectual simplicity, today represents to many a double-edged sword that can be used for evil as well as good. No sooner had scientists at Stanford University in 1973 begun rearranging DNA molecules in test tubes (and, equally important, reinserting the novel DNA segments back into living cells) than critics began likening these "recombinant" DNA procedures to the physicist's power to break apart atoms. Might not some of the test-tube-rearranged DNA molecules impart to their host cells disease-causing capacities that, like nuclear weapons, are capable of seriously disrupting human civilization? Soon there were cries from both scientists and nonscientists that such research might best be ruled by stringent regulations—if not laws.

As a result, several years were to pass before the full power of recombinant-DNA technology got into the hands of working scientists, who by then were itching to explore previously unattainable secrets of life. Happily, the proposals to control recombinant-DNA research through legislation never got close to enactment. And when anti-DNA doomsday scenarios failed to materialize, even the modestly restrictive governmental regulations began to wither away. In retrospect, recombinant-DNA may rank as the safest revolutionary technology ever developed. To my knowledge, not one fatality, much less illness, has been caused by a genetically manipulated organism.

4   The moral I draw from this painful episode is this: Never postpone experiments that have clearly defined future benefits for fear of dangers that can't be quantified. Though it may sound at first uncaring, we can react rationally only to real (as opposed to hypothetical) risks. Yet for several years we postponed important experiments on the genetic basis of cancer, for example, because we took much too seriously spurious arguments that the genes at the root of human cancer might themselves be dangerous to work with.

Though most forms of DNA manipulation are now effectively unregulated, one important potential goal remains blocked. Experiments aimed at learning how to insert functional genetic material into human germ cells—sperm and eggs—remain off limits to most of the world's scientists. No governmental body wants to take responsibility for initiating steps that might help redirect the course of future human evolution. These decisions reflect widespread concerns that we, as humans, may not have the wisdom to modify the most precious of all human treasures—our chromosomal "instruction books." Dare we be entrusted with improving upon the results of the several million years of Darwinian natural selection? Are human germ cells Rubicons that geneticists may never cross?

Unlike many of my peers, I'm reluctant to accept such reasoning, again using the argument that you should never put off doing something useful for fear of evil that may never arrive. The first germ-line gene manipulations are unlikely to be attempted for frivolous reasons. Nor does the state of today's science provide the knowledge that would be needed to generate "superpersons" whose far-ranging talents would make those who are genetically unmodified feel redundant and unwanted. Such creations will remain denizens of science fiction, not the real world, far into the future. When they are finally attempted, germ-line genetic manipulations will probably be done to change a death sentence into a life verdict—by creating children who are resistant to a deadly virus, for example, much the way we can already protect plants from viruses by inserting antiviral DNA segments into their genomes.

If appropriate go-ahead signals come, the first resulting gene-bettered children will in no sense threaten human civilization. They will be seen as special only by those in their immediate circles, and are likely to pass as unnoticed in later life as the now grownup "test-tube baby" Louise Brown does today. If they grow up healthily gene-bettered, more such children will follow, and they and those whose lives are enriched by their existence will rejoice that science has again improved human life. If, however, the added genetic material fails to work, better procedures must be developed before more couples commit their psyches toward such inherently unsettling pathways to producing healthy children.

8   Moving forward will not be for the faint of heart. But if the next century witnesses failure, let it be because our science is not yet up to the job, not because we don't have the courage to make less random the sometimes most unfair courses of human evolution.

Personal Response

Are you as comfortable with the possibility that something might go wrong in "gene-bettered children" as Watson seems to be (paragraph 7)? What is your opinion on that point?

Questions for Class or Small-Group Discussion

1. What do you think of the comparison Watson makes between the potential of human cloning and the public response to physicists' learning how to make the atomic bomb in the 1940s and biologists' ability to do recombinant DNA procedures in the 1970s? Are you persuaded that the issues are the same? How? If not, how do they differ?

2. Discuss your response to this statement: "Never postpone experiments that have clearly defined future benefits for fear of dangers that can't be quantified" (paragraph 4).

3. Comment on Watson's response to those who believe that humans "may not have the wisdom to modify the most precious of all human treasures—our chromosomal 'instruction book' " (paragraph 5). Do you share his view on this point?

4. State in your own words what Watson's position on genetic engineering is. Where do you position yourself on that subject?

DOLLY'S FALSE LEGACY

Ian Wilmut

Ian Wilmut is the Scottish embryologist whose team of researchers, in 1996, was the first to clone a mammal from fully differentiated adult mammary cells. Wilmut holds a Ph.D. in animal genetic engineering from Darwin College, University of Cambridge, and has been a researcher at the Animal Research Breeding Station (now known as the Roslin Institute) in Edinburgh, Scotland, since 1974. He is coauthor of The Second Creation: Dolly and the Age of Biological Control *(2000). This essay appeared in the January 11, 1999, issue of* Time *magazine.*

Overlooked in the arguments about the mortality of artificially reproducing life is the fact that, at present, cloning is a very inefficient procedure. The incidence of death among fetuses and offspring produced by cloning is much higher than it is through natural reproduction—roughly 10 times as high as normal before birth and three times as high after birth in our studies at Roslin. Distressing enough for those working with animals, these failure rates surely render unthinkable the notion of applying such treatment to humans.

Even if the technique were perfected, however, we must ask ourselves what practical value whole-being cloning might have. What exactly would be the difference between a "cloned" baby and a child born naturally—and why would we want one?

The cloned child would be a genetically identical twin of the original, and thus physically very similar—far more similar than a natural parent and child. Human personality, however, emerges from both the effects of the genes we inherit (nature) and environmental factors (nurture). The two clones would develop distinct personalities, just as twins develop unique identities. And because the copy would often be born in a different family, cloned twins would be less alike in personality than natural identical twins.

4   Why "copy" people in the first place? Couples unable to have children might choose to have a copy of one of them rather than accept the intrusion of genes from a donor. My wife and I have two children of our own and an adopted child, but I find it helpful to consider what might have happened in my own marriage if a copy of me

had been made to overcome infertility. My wife and I met in high school. How would she react to a physical copy of the young man she fell in love with? How would any of us find living with ourselves? Surely the older clone—I, in this case—would believe that he understood how the copy should behave and so be even more likely than the average father to impose expectations upon his child. Above all, how would a teenager cope with looking at me, a balding, aging man, and seeing the physical future ahead of him?

Each of us can imagine hypothetical families created by the introduction of a cloned child—a copy of one partner in a homosexual relationship or of a single parent, for example. What is missing in all this is consideration of what's in the interests of the cloned child. Because there is no form of infertility that could be overcome only by cloning, I do not find these proposals acceptable. My concerns are not on religious grounds or on the basis of a perceived intrinsic ethical principle. Rather, my judgment is that it would be difficult for families created in this way to provide an appropriate environment for the child.

Cloning is also suggested as a means of bringing back a relative, usually a child, killed tragically. Any parent can understand that wish, but it must first be recognized that the copy would be a new baby and not the lost child. Herein lies the difficulty, for the grieving parents are seeking not a new baby but a return of the dead one. Since the original would be fondly remembered as having particular talents and interests, would not the parent expect the copy to be the same? It is possible, however, that the copy would develop quite differently. Is it fair to the new child to place it in a family with such unnatural expectations?

What if the lost child was very young? The shorter the life, the fewer the expectations parents might place on the substitute, right? If a baby dies within a few days of birth and there is no reason to think that death was caused by an inherited defect, would it then be acceptable to make a copy? Is it practical to frame legislation that would prevent copying of adults or older children, but allow copying of infants? At what age would a child be too old to be copied in the event of death?

8   Copying is also suggested as a means by which parents can have the child of their dreams. Couples might choose to have a copy of a film star, baseball player or scientist, depending on their interests. But because personality is only partly the result of genetic inheritance, conflict would be sure to arise if the cloned child failed to develop the same interests as the original. What if the copy of Einstein shows no interest in science? Or the football player turns to acting? Success also depends upon fortune. What of the child who does not live up to the hopes and dreams of the parent simply because of bad luck?

Every child should be wanted for itself, as an individual. In making a copy of oneself or some famous person, a parent is deliberately specifying the way he or she wishes that child to develop. In recent years, particularly in the U.S., much importance has been placed on the right of individuals to reproduce in ways that they wish. I suggest that there is a greater need to consider the interests of the child and to reject these proposed uses of cloning.

By contrast, human cloning could, in theory, be used to obtain tissues needed to treat disorders such as Parkinson's disease and diabetes. These diseases are associated with cell types that do not repair or replace themselves, but suitable cells will one day be grown in culture. These uses cannot be justified now; nor are they likely to be in the near future.

Moreover, there is a lot we do not know about the effects of cloning, especially in terms of aging. As we grow older, changes occur in our cells that reduce the number of times they can reproduce. This clock of age is reset by normal reproduction during the production of sperm and eggs; that is why children of each new generation have a full life span. It is not yet known whether aging is reversed during cloning or if the clone's natural life is shortened by the years its parent has already lived. Then there is the problem of the genetic errors that accumulate in our cells. There are systems to seek out and correct such errors during normal reproduction; it is not known if that can occur during cloning. Research with animals is urgently required to measure the life span and determine the cause of death of animals produced by cloning.

12   Important questions also remain on the most appropriate means of controlling the development and use of these techniques. It is taken for granted that the production and sale of drugs will be regulated by governments, but this was not always the case. A hundred years ago, the production and sale of drugs in the U.S. was unregulated. Unscrupulous companies took the opportunity to include in their products substances, like cocaine, that were likely to make the patients feel better even if they offered no treatment for the original condition. After public protest, championed by publications such as the *Ladies' Home Journal,* a federal act was passed in 1906. An enforcement agency, known now as the FDA, was established in 1927. An independent body similar to the FDA is now required to assess all the research on cloning.

There is much still to be learned about the biology associated with cloning. The time required for this research, however, will also provide an opportunity for each society to decide how it wishes the technique to be used. At some point in the future, cloning will have much to contribute to human medicine, but we must use it cautiously.

Personal Response

Does it surprise you that the man who cloned the first mammal is so cautious about the possibility of cloning humans? What do you think of his caution?

Questions for Class or Small-Group Discussion

1. What point does Wilmut believe is largely overlooked in the debate over human cloning? What do you have to say about the issues he raises on that point?

2. State the reasons Wilmut cites for why people might want to clone themselves or their children, and comment on each of those reasons. Can you think of other reasons why people would want to clone humans? Do any of the possible reasons seem more valid to you than others?

3. Wilmut suggests certain ways that human cloning might be used besides cloning entire humans. What do you think of those uses of the technology?

4. Wilmut states that there are important questions that need to be considered before proceeding with the technology to clone humans. What are those questions? To what extent do you agree with him that these questions are weighty enough to postpone research until they are answered?

PLAYING GOD: HAS SCIENCE GONE TOO FAR?

Jeff Lyon

Jeff Lyon, with Peter Gorner, wrote Altered Fates: Gene Therapy and the Retooling of Human Life *(1995). He and Gorner won a Pulitzer Prize for journalism in 1987 for the stories on which this book was based. Lyon is a science writer for the* Chicago Tribune *and writes extensively on genetic engineering. This article was published in* Woman's Day *in July 2001.*

Until recently, human cloning wasn't something most adults expected to see in their lifetimes. Even five years ago, many scientists believed it would still be another 20 years or more before they figured out how to clone any species of mammal—that is, how to get a single cell from an adult animal to generate a whole new animal. But that assumption was demolished in February 1997, when British embryologist Ian Wilmut, Ph.D., announced that he and colleagues at the Roslin Institute in Edinburgh, Scotland, had successfully cloned a sheep: the now world-famous Dolly.

Since then the floodgates have opened, and cattle, goats, mice and pigs have all been cloned. Dogs haven't been cloned yet, but researchers at Texas A & M University are working on it. And now it seems it may not be long before the ultimate line is crossed.

Last January Panos Zavos, Ph.D., then professor of reproductive physiology at the University of Kentucky, announced that he was leaving his position to team up with Severino Antinori, M.D., an Italian fertility specialist, to try to clone a human by 2003. Their purpose, he said, is to help infertile couples who want a genetically related child.

4   And last fall a sect called the Raelians, based in Montreal, announced that an American couple had paid the sect $500,000 to clone their deceased baby girl and that Brigitte Boisselier, Ph.D., the sect's scientific director, had agreed to attempt it. The Raelians believe all life on earth was created by aliens through genetic engineering. They endorse cloning and claim to have the scientific know-how and enough potential surrogate mothers to achieve their goal.

Welcome to the future, where science fiction becomes science fact and researchers and ordinary citizens alike must wrestle with a question that has profound meaning for humankind: Should scientists be allowed to pursue research that may one day enable them to shape and even create life? Or to put it another way: Is it right for scientists to assume powers that many people believe should belong only to God?

Less than a decade ago, this question would have prompted an automatic answer from most people: No, it shouldn't be allowed—not that it is likely to happen any time soon. But in a swift and startling turnabout, the answer to that question has become less clear, even as scientists are taking baby steps toward making such things happen.

Last March, Dr. Boisselier and Dr. Zavos both appeared before a congressional panel investigating whether to draft a law banning human-cloning experiments in the United States—a measure President Bush has said he would sign. The U.S. Food and Drug Administration prohibits these experiments, but a federal law would carry more weight and be a stronger deterrent against conducting this work. Of course, scientists would still be free to work in countries that look upon this research more favorably.

8   "Those that say ban it, those would not be the Neil Armstrongs that would fly us to the moon," Dr. Zavos said, adding that it would be difficult, if not impossible, to stop the science of cloning now. "The genie's out of the bottle," he said. And as if to prove his point, last January Britain became the first nation to legalize cloning human embryos for limited research purposes.

Yet, even as the likelihood of human cloning becomes more real, the science is still rudimentary. Most cloned animals die in the womb, and even those that initially seem healthy often develop fatal defects of the heart, lungs, kidney, brain and immune system down the road. Something about cloning seems to disrupt normal gene activation in the developing fetus. This could prove catastrophic if an attempt is made to clone a human. Dr. Wilmut has said that trying it now would be "criminally irresponsible."

Nor is cloning the only sign that humans are assuming powers once relegated to the Almighty. Last September six-year-old Molly Nash of Englewood, Colorado, was given a blood transfusion that doctors hoped would help cure her of Fanconi's anemia. This rare, often fatal, hereditary disease causes the bone marrow to fail to produce blood cells and platelets. The transfused blood came from her baby brother, Adam. It had been collected from his umbilical cord at the time of his birth. Adam had been conceived in a laboratory dish with other embryos produced by his parents' eggs and sperm. He had been implanted in his mother's womb because he was disease free and because his tissue and blood type matched his sister's—in other words, so he could be her donor. The other embryos were discarded. Cord blood is rich in stem cells, the mother cells found in various organs that generate the functional cells of those organs. It was hoped that Adam's stem cells would generate functioning bone marrow and a healthy new blood supply for Molly.

The procedure seems to have worked. Tests done in January found that almost all of Molly's bone marrow came from Adam. "While we will continue to monitor Molly, especially over this first critical year, her prognosis looks great," said John

Wagner, M.D., a transplant specialist at the University of Minnesota Medical School, who performed the transfusion. The Nashes did not doubt they had done the right thing. "You could say it was an added benefit to have Adam be the right bone-marrow type, which would not hurt him in the least and would save Molly's life," Lisa, their mother, said in September. "We didn't have to think twice about it." But some ethicists were concerned. Would children now be bred for their biological usefulness?

12   Stem cells, meanwhile, are the focus of another scientific endeavor that rivals cloning in its potential to bestow Godlike powers on human beings. Researchers hope someday to be able to direct a person's stem cells to grow new organs and tissue for that person in a lab. The cells could be told to grow a liver for someone who needs a transplant, for example, or brain cells for someone with Alzheimer's disease. And because the cells would contain the person's own DNA, there would be no problem with tissue rejection.

Advances in genetic engineering and gene therapy are also transforming the nature of life and the way we live. Researchers have already created genetically altered seeds and grains designed to produce hardier plants and bigger harvests—and American consumers are already eating some of this altered produce without knowing it. And despite a tragic setback in September 1999, when 18-year-old Jesse Gelsinger of Tucson, Arizona, died during a gene-therapy experiment at the University of Pennsylvania, research is also moving forward in developing safer, more effective ways to deliver healthy new genes into a patient's cells.

Thanks to the Human Genome Project, the ongoing effort to codify and learn the function of the more than 30,000 genes that make up the instruction manual for the human body, researchers are also zeroing in on which genes cause and can cure various diseases. In a few years it may be possible for people to go to a doctor's office and, in the time it takes to read this article, get a full lab report detailing their genetic predisposition to various diseases. If the report noted a susceptibility to lung cancer, for example, they would then be counseled not to smoke. In the not-too-distant future, scientists could also have the power to design smarter, more attractive and athletic offspring by tinkering with a child's genetic makeup before or after birth. Such powers would enable them to change the course of human evolution, and to do it in a matter of generations.

And then there is the ultimate quest: to create life itself. In 1953 researchers at the University of Chicago mixed methane, ammonia, hydrogen and water—the ingredients of the so-called "primordial soup" that existed on the young earth—and passed an electric current through it to simulate lightning. To their amazement, they found traces of amino acids—the chemical building blocks of life—in the residue. Now, a team of scientists headed by a brilliant maverick named J. Craig Venter, Ph.D., director of the Institute for Genomic Research in Rockville, Maryland, is conducting another experiment.

16   Working with a harmless species of bacteria called Mycoplasma genitalium that has only 517 genes—the fewest of any known organism—Dr. Venter and his

colleagues disrupted the microbe's genes one by one to see which it needed to survive. In a paper published in the December 1999 issue of *Science* they estimated that M. genitalium needs 265 to 350 of its genes to stay alive. The next task, they wrote, is to narrow down that number as a "first step" toward "engineering" a cell with "a minimum genome" in the lab: in other words, manufacturing a living microbe.

That's as far as Dr. Venter has taken the research. The question is whether anyone should take it any further. In the issue of *Science* containing his paper, a panel of bioethicists—thinkers who specialize in weighing the thorny issues raised by modern medicine and biology—addressed this point at his request. They did not give a thumbs-down to the experiment. Instead, they gave it a conditional thumbs-up. The prospect of humans creating a life form "does not violate any fundamental moral precepts," the authors wrote. But they did raise questions they felt needed to be considered, such as whether the new technology would "be used for the benefit of all" and the possibility that it could be misused to create new biological weapons.

It must be said that even if scientists do pursue this goal, achieving it is probably years off. The genes essential to sustain *M. genitalium,* for example, include at least 100 whose function is unknown. If science cannot yet understand the workings of a cell with a paltry 500 genes—even a fruit fly has more than 10,000—it can hardly claim mastery of biology. The task would also require an expertise in the workings of cells and gene activation that is still beyond us. But most people thought cloning a mammal was decades away when Dolly was cloned. And even if the breakthrough is far off, the seeming lack of opposition to it is striking.

"A couple of years ago I'd have opposed this experiment," says Arthur Caplan, Ph.D., director of the University of Pennsylvania Center for Bioethics, who co-headed the panel that evaluated Dr. Venter's experiment. "I think society's becoming used to genetic tinkering. Despite all our religious grounding, we are becoming increasingly secular in thinking that life is not a mystery beyond our understanding. I have been told that creating life violates God's will and that it's unnatural. But I've heard no persuasive arguments for banning these experiments. There are certainly issues that demand attention if the research is to proceed. But they are safety questions. For example, you could make things that get out of the containment facility or that pose a threat because they have properties we don't understand. There is also the possibility of misapplication in the weapons and terrorism area. It needs comment and oversight to make sure no one does anything nasty or dangerous. But those risks aren't so great that you can't proceed."

20   Different people simply have different beliefs about how life came to exist and where humans fit in the grand design. "I see life as a process of chemistry," says Norman Pace, Ph.D., a professor of molecular, cellular and developmental biology at the University of Colorado who is involved in his own quest to isolate the minimal components of life in the lab. "I see life as chemicals talking to one another in sophisticated ways developed through natural selection. Much of it we don't yet understand, but that doesn't mean it's a spiritual matter. These spiritual issues are human inventions."

Even if God exists, say others, we can't call these pursuits "playing God" because they don't reflect how God operates. "In nature, chance determines things," says R. Alta Charo, J.D., professor of law and medical ethics at the University of Wisconsin Law School. "I believe that the essence of God is to let the odds play out." In contrast, she says, "It is the essential attribute of being human to make choices, to exercise control, to have dominion over the natural world." She sees these quests as "completely consistent with what it means to be humans on this planet. I believe knowledge is an intrinsic good and that until it is shown to cause harm, it should be encouraged. I believe we should have eaten the apple."

Not everyone shares these views. Lori Andrews, Ph.D., a professor of law at the Chicago-Kent College of Law in Chicago and a legal specialist in new reproductive technologies, thinks ethicists have become too accepting of a whole laundry list of unsettling scientific quests. "It's like we've become deadened to the ethical dimensions of this," she says. "We're viewing biology as playing with Tinker Toys. There seems to be less resistance to the whole idea of tampering with life."

Dr. Andrews cites the news last January that researchers at Oregon Health Sciences University in Portland had produced a genetically altered rhesus monkey—one of humankind's closest relatives—by inserting a jellyfish gene into a monkey egg before it was fertilized. ANDi, as the monkey was named, is the first "transgenic" primate: the first to have genes of another species in every cell of his body. Lead researcher Gerald Schatten, Ph.D., said the long-term goal is to create monkeys that have been modified to develop disease traits for use in studying new treatments. Is that a good goal? Does it justify creating ANDi? An ethicist at the university acknowledged that some people think "maybe we shouldn't do this on nonhuman primates." Dr. Andrews is more outspoken. "The day you start doing genetic engineering on monkeys," she says, "humans can't be far behind."

24   Richard Hayes, former assistant political director of the Sierra Club, finds the lack of loud public debate about these technologies "chilling" and holds bioethicists partly to blame. "Many of these academics have become almost apologists for genetic engineering and cloning," says Hayes, now executive director of the Exploratory Initiative on the New Human Genetic Technologies, a network of professionals and activists interested in stimulating that debate. "You rarely find a bioethicist who thinks there's anything fundamentally wrong with these technologies. In Europe it's very different, because they had the Nazi Holocaust. But here we have consumer-driven markets."

Not all bioethicists fit this mold, of course. Leon Kass, M.D., Ph.D., the Addie Clark Harding professor in the Committee on Social Thought at the University of Chicago, is one who doesn't. It worries him, he says, "that the scientists' view of what they're doing could rapidly become the public's view, and that kind of shrunken understanding of what life is—that it's nothing but chemicals—could spread even further in the culture than it already has. It seems to support the materialist view of life—which, even though I'm a trained scientist, I regard as false and inadequate."

Dr. Kass argues further that making a microbe in a lab is not really creating life. "It's a gross exaggeration. It's like reproducing a Mozart symphony. You haven't written the score; you are merely recopying it. I'm bothered that we are coming under the illusion that because we know how to reproduce a few things, we are absolutely in charge. It's a form of hubris and folly." Besides, he says, even if a scientist could create a human from scratch, "would he really be the author or just the instrument of God's handiwork?"

Lisa Sowle Cahill, Ph.D., J. Donald Monan chair of theology at Boston College and former president of the Catholic Theological Society of America, wonders about this, too. "The Bible says we are created in the image of God and God is the Creator," she says. "Does that mean only God creates? Or does it mean that because we are made in God's image we share that ability?" If so, who is to say which of our efforts do and don't cross the line? "Are we playing God when we wipe out smallpox or cure cancer? Why is it wrong to put a jellyfish gene in a monkey?" It makes us uncomfortable for many reasons, she says, "but defining why it is wrong is more difficult—for me, anyway."

28   Like many religions, the Catholic Church "doesn't have a final position on a lot of these questions," says Dr. Cahill. "It cautiously welcomes new genetic therapies, but it is concerned about protecting human life and has ruled out research using human embryos. Other things are not settled."

But religion can guide and prod people to think in ways they otherwise might not. "It is the nature of religion to be conservative," says Harold S. Kushner, Rabbi Laureate of Temple Israel in Natick, Massachusetts, and author of the forthcoming *Living a Life That Matters: Resolving the Conflict between Conscience and Success.* "Religion says, 'Wait a minute, there are time-tested values here which we should be very slow to disregard.' I'd hope our experience with polluted air and toxic and nuclear waste would have taught us not to go where we can just because we can. I'd hope for a self-imposed moratorium on doing what's possible until we figure out whether we really want to do it."

"In vitro fertilization is wonderful," says Rabbi Kushner. "DNA repair is good. My wife and I had a son who died of a genetic disease, and the idea of fixing what's missing and giving an innocent child life is exciting. But it is one thing to repair, and another to let parents make sure they have perfect children. My concern is we will lose the knack of loving children who are less than perfect. And my concern with cloning is less ambivalent. I mind very much if we clone people. The whole idea of God's plan for humanity, which calls for people to have children and die, means that one generation, scarred and wearied by its experience, gives way to another that's born fresh and innocent and full of promise. Once you start fooling with that, I think you undermine what God had in mind for the human race. As for creating life artificially, there is something special about humans being created out of an act of love, not chemistry."

Dr. Kass agrees. There is a difference between using new technologies to cure disease and "using them to engineer so-called improvements," he says. "As a species we don't have the wisdom to know what an improvement would be. The better path

is caution and humility before these awesome powers we may never fully understand." Indeed, says Rabbi Kushner, "A scientist ought to stand in awe of the things
modern science can do and realize that he has seen the face of God, he hasn't become
God."

32   One thing is clear. These technologies are here to stay, and it's up to all of us to
decide what to do with them. "We want to support the most creative and compassionate science possible," says Laurie Zoloth, Ph.D., head of the Jewish Studies department at San Francisco State University. "The bold scientific approach allowed
Pasteur and Salk to take leaps that advanced the cause of humankind. But the human capacity for error is enormous. And the human capacity for terrible moral
choices is also great. We live in a society in which some 44 million people have too
little access to health care. And now we're developing technologies that may give
enormous life-shaping power to people who have the money to control it. So there is
a lot to be cautious about."

Hayes is more blunt. "What's at stake is our common human future. Genetic modification could lead to the creation of separate genetic castes and social division beyond anything in history. There's no reason to go down this road. We need to summon
the maturity to use our technology in ways that affirm rather than degrade humanity.
We have to decide which uses we approve of and which we oppose."

The only way we can do that, says Dr. Zoloth, is through an "enormous national
conversation. All we have is the ability to keep talking and raising fears and hopes
and encouraging scientists to stop and reflect." History shows we can achieve great
things if we keep talking. "When we wanted to think about race, we had a transfor-
mative national conversation. The civil-rights movement was America at its best. The
Vietnam war sparked such a conversation. Now we need to have one about genetics.
This is exactly the moment when we must decide who controls this technology and
on behalf of whom. The need cannot be overestimated. This is far too important to
leave in the hands of market forces alone."

Personal Response

Write for a few minutes in answer to the question posed by the title of this article.

Questions for Class or Small-Group Discussion

1. Lyon reports that a panel of bioethicists did not give "thumbs down" to Dr. J. Craig
Venter's question about whether he should continue his experiments on creating life
in the laboratory. What is your response to the panel's opinion? Do you agree that
"the prospect of humans creating a life form 'does not violate any fundamental
moral precepts' " (paragraph 17)?

2. In your own words, summarize what representatives from various religious bodies
have to say in answer to Lyon's overarching question about whether humans should
be trying to do those things that many people believe only God should do.

3. Discuss this remark by R. Alta Charo: " 'I believe knowledge is an intrinsic good and that until it is shown to cause harm, it should be encouraged. I believe we should have eaten the apple' " (paragraph 21).

4. What do you think about continuing research similar to that done with ANDi, the first " 'transgenic' " monkey (paragraph 23)? Why do you think there is "a lack of loud public debate about" this and other technologies mentioned in the article (paragraph 24)?

5. Discuss your position on the subject of stem cell research, which Lyon mentions in paragraph 9, after first explaining just where the controversy lies, what benefits the research would have, and what problems might result from it.

HUMAN CLONING? DON'T JUST SAY NO
Ruth Macklin

Ruth Macklin is professor of bioethics at Albert Einstein College of Medicine. She is author of the following books: Man, Mind, and Morality: The Ethics of Behavior Control *(1982),* Mortal Choices: Bioethics in Today's World *(1987),* Enemies of Patients *(1993),* Surrogates & Other Mothers: The Debates over Assisted Reproduction *(1993), and* Against Relativism: Cultural Diversity and the Search for Ethical Universals in Medicine *(1999). Macklin wrote this essay for the "Commentary" section of the March 10, 1997, issue of* U.S. News & World Report.

Last week's news that scientists had cloned a sheep sent academics and the public into a panic at the prospect that humans might be next. That's an understandable reaction. Cloning is a radical challenge to the most fundamental laws of biology, so it's not unreasonable to be concerned that it might threaten human society and dignity. Yet much of the ethical opposition seems also to grow out of an unthinking disgust— a sort of "yuk factor." And that makes it hard for even trained scientists and ethicists to see the matter clearly. While human cloning might not offer great benefits to humanity, no one has yet made a persuasive case that it would do any real harm, either.

Theologians contend that to clone a human would violate human dignity. That would surely be true if a cloned individual were treated as a lesser being, with fewer rights or lower stature. But why suppose that cloned persons wouldn't share the same rights and dignity as the rest of us? A leading lawyer–ethicist has suggested that cloning would violate the "right to genetic identity." Where did he come up with such a right? It makes perfect sense to say that adult persons have a right not to be cloned without their voluntary, informed consent. But if such consent is given, whose "right" to genetic identity would be violated?

Many of the science-fiction scenarios prompted by the prospect of human cloning turn out, upon reflection, to be absurdly improbable. There's the fear, for instance, that parents might clone a child to have "spare parts" in case the original child needs an organ transplant. But parents of identical twins don't view one child as an organ farm for the other. Why should cloned children's parents be any different?

Vast Difference

4   Another disturbing thought is that cloning will lead to efforts to breed individuals with genetic qualities perceived as exceptional (math geniuses, basketball players). Such ideas are repulsive, not only because of the "yuk factor" but also because of the horrors perpetrated by the Nazis in the name of eugenics. But there's a vast difference between "selective breeding" as practiced by totalitarian regimes (where the urge to propagate certain types of people leads to efforts to eradicate other types) and the immeasurably more benign forms already practiced in democratic societies (where, say, lawyers freely choose to marry other lawyers). Banks stocked with the frozen sperm of geniuses already exist. They haven't created a master race because only a tiny number of women have wanted to impregnate themselves this way. Why think it will be different if human cloning becomes available?

So who will likely take advantage of cloning? Perhaps a grieving couple whose child is dying. This might seem psychologically twisted. But a cloned child born to such dubious parents stands no greater or lesser chance of being loved, or rejected, or warped than a child normally conceived. Infertile couples are also likely to seek out cloning. That such couples have other options (in vitro fertilization or adoption) is not an argument for denying them the right to clone. Or consider an example raised by Judge Richard Posner: a couple in which the husband has some tragic genetic defect. Currently, if this couple wants a genetically related child, they have four not altogether pleasant options. They can reproduce naturally and risk passing on the disease to the child. They can go to a sperm bank and take a chance on unknown genes. They can try in vitro fertilization and dispose of any afflicted embryo—though that might be objectionable, too. Or they can get a male relative of the father to donate sperm, if such a relative exists. This is one case where even people unnerved by cloning might see it as not the worst option.

Even if human cloning offers no obvious benefits to humanity, why ban it? In a democratic society we don't usually pass laws outlawing something before there is actual or probable evidence of harm. A moratorium on further research into human cloning might make sense, in order to consider calmly the grave questions it raises. If the moratorium is then lifted, human cloning should remain a research activity for an extended period. And if it is ever attempted, it should—and no doubt will—take place only with careful scrutiny and layers of legal oversight. Most important, human cloning should be governed by the same laws that now protect human rights. A world not safe for cloned humans would be a world not safe for the rest of us.

Personal Response

How convincing do you find Macklin's argument? Do you think she makes a sensible point, or is she underestimating the potential negative implications of cloning?

Questions for Class or Small-Group Discussion

1. Locate the places in the article where Macklin summarizes the ethical opposition to cloning. How does she counter those objections? To what extent do you agree with either Macklin or her opponents in the debate?

2. Discuss whether you are persuaded that "many of the science-fiction scenarios prompted by the prospect of human cloning [. . . are] absurdly improbable" (paragraph 3).

3. Explain the reference to the Nazis and eugenics in paragraph 4. Do you find Macklin's comparison of Nazi eugenics programs with lawyers choosing to marry other lawyers a fair one?

4. What do you think of Macklin's suggestion that a moratorium, not an outright ban, on research into human cloning is the most sensible approach to take (paragraph 6)?

OF HEADLESS MICE . . . AND MEN

Charles Krauthammer

Charles Krauthammer is a contributing editor to the New Republic *and writes a weekly syndicated column for the* Washington Post. *A political scientist, psychiatrist, journalist, and speech writer, Krauthammer won a Pulitzer Prize in 1981 for his commentary on politics and society. He has published a book,* Cutting Edges: Making Sense of the Eighties *(1985). Krauthammer also contributes to* Time *magazine, where the following essay appeared in January 1998.*

Last year Dolly the cloned sheep was received with wonder, titters, and some vague apprehension. Last week the announcement by a Chicago physicist that he is assembling a team to produce the first human clone occasioned yet another wave of Brave New World anxiety. But the scariest news of all—and largely overlooked—comes from two obscure labs, at the University of Texas and at the University of Bath. During the past four years, one group created headless mice; the other, headless tadpoles.

For sheer Frankenstein wattage, the purposeful creation of these animal monsters has no equal. Take the mice. Researchers found the gene that tells the embryo to produce the head. They deleted it. They did this in a thousand mice embryos, four of which were born. I use the term loosely. Having no way to breathe, the mice died instantly.

Why then create them? The Texas researchers want to learn how genes determine embryo development. But you don't have to be a genius to see the true utility of manufacturing headless creatures: for their organs—fully formed, perfectly useful, ripe for plundering.

4   Why should you be panicked? Because humans are next. "It would almost certainly be possible to produce humans without a forebrain," Princeton biologist Lee Silver told the London *Sunday Times*. "These human bodies without any semblance of consciousness would not be considered persons, and thus it would be perfectly legal to keep them 'alive' as a future source of organs."

"Alive." Never have a pair of quotation marks loomed so ominously. Take the mouse–frog technology, apply it to humans, combine it with cloning, and you become a god: With a single cell taken from, say, your finger, you produce a headless replica of yourself, a mutant twin, arguably lifeless, that becomes your own personal, precisely tissue-matched organ farm.

There are, of course, technical hurdles along the way. Suppressing the equivalent "head" gene in man. Incubating tiny infant organs to grow into larger ones that adults could use. And creating artificial wombs (as per Aldous Huxley), given that it might be difficult to recruit sane women to carry headless fetuses to their birth/death.

It won't be long, however, before these technical barriers are breached. The ethical barriers are already cracking. Lewis Wolpert, professor of biology at University College, London, finds producing headless humans "personally distasteful" but, given the shortage of organs, does not think distaste is sufficient reason not to go ahead with something that would save lives. And Professor Silver not only sees "nothing wrong, philosophically or rationally," with producing headless humans for organ harvesting; he wants to convince a skeptical public that it is perfectly O.K.

8   When prominent scientists are prepared to acquiesce in—or indeed encourage—the deliberate creation of deformed and dying quasi-human life, you know we are facing a bioethical abyss. Human beings are ends, not means. There is no grosser corruption of biotechnology than creating a human mutant and disemboweling it at our pleasure for spare parts.

The prospect of headless human clones should put the whole debate about "normal" cloning in a new light. Normal cloning is less a treatment for infertility than a treatment for vanity. It is a way to produce an exact genetic replica of yourself that will walk the earth years after you're gone.

But there is a problem with a clone. It is not really you. It is but a twin, a perfect John Doe Jr., but still a junior. With its own independent consciousness, it is, alas, just a facsimile of you.

The headless clone solves the facsimile problem. It is a gateway to the ultimate vanity: immortality. If you create a real clone, you cannot transfer your consciousness into it to truly live on. But if you create a headless clone of just your body, you have created a ready source of replacement parts to keep you—your consciousness—going indefinitely.

12   Which is why one form of cloning will inevitably lead to the other. Cloning is the technology of narcissism, and nothing satisfies narcissism like immortality. Headlessness will be cloning's crowning achievement.

The time to put a stop to this is now. Dolly moved President Clinton to create a commission that recommended a temporary ban on human cloning. But with physicist Richard Seed threatening to clone humans, and with headless animals already here, we are past the time for toothless commissions and meaningless bans.

Clinton banned federal funding of human-cloning research, of which there is none anyway. He then proposed a five-year ban on cloning. This is not enough. Congress should ban human cloning now. Totally. And regarding one particular form, it should be draconian: The deliberate creation of headless humans must be made a crime, indeed a capital crime. If we flinch in the face of this high-tech barbarity, we'll deserve to live in the hell it heralds.

Personal Response

Explain your response to Krauthammer's vision of the future of mankind if the law does not prohibit cloning of headless animals, including humans.

Questions for Class or Small-Group Discussion

1. Krauthammer begins by describing examples of the successful cloning of headless mice and tadpoles that died as soon as they were born. "Why then create them?" he asks. How does he answer that question?

2. Paragraph 4 begins with the question, "Why should you be panicked?" Summarize Krauthammer's answer to that question. Are you persuaded that you should panic?

3. Do you agree with Krauthammer that "cloning is the technology of narcissism" (paragraph 12)?

4. Comment on Krauthammer's concluding paragraphs. To what extent do you agree with him?

5. Explain these references: Brave New World (paragraph 1); Frankenstein (paragraph 2); Aldous Huxley (paragraph 6). What does *draconian* mean (paragraph 14)?

PERSPECTIVES ON BIOETHICS

Suggestions for Synthesis

1. Compare and contrast the views of James D. Watson in "All for the Good" and Ian Wilmut in "Dolly's False Legacy" on the subject of human cloning. Whom do you find more persuasive?

2. Compare and contrast Ruth Macklin's "Human Cloning? Don't Just Say No" and Charles Krauthammer's "Of Headless Mice . . . and Men." Whom do you find more persuasive?

3. Drawing on at least two of the essays in this chapter, explain where you stand on one of the questions raised in the readings in this chapter about the implications and dangers of genetics research.

4. Conduct a class forum on the ethical, social, and/or legal problems that are associated with the Human Genome Project, human cloning, stem cell research, and/or other genetics research. For a writing project, summarize the views of your classmates, and state your own position on the subject.

5. Invite professionals to speak to your class on the ethical, social, and legal problems associated with the Human Genome Project or stem cell research. For instance, you might invite a molecular biologist, an ethics professor, or someone else familiar with genetics research or the Human Genome Project to speak. An alternative is to interview such a person. For a writing project, draw on the views of the professionals who visit your class or whom you interview as you explain your own position on the subject.

Additional Writing Topics

1. Write a response to James D. Watson ("All for the Good"), Ian Wilmut ("Dolly's False Legacy"), Ruth Macklin ("Human Cloning? Don't Just Say No"), Charles Krauthammer ("Of Headless Mice . . . and Men"), or any of the people quoted in Jeff Lyon's "Playing God: Has Science Gone Too Far?" Explain where you agree, where you disagree, and where you have real concerns about what the person says. Be sure to state why you believe as you do

2. Write an essay in which you explain what other issues, besides the ones identified by the authors of articles in this chapter, need to be looked at closely. For instance, do you think care must be taken to make the results of genetic research available to everyone while protecting the rights of both researchers who make the discoveries and companies that want to profit from them?

3. Write a reflective essay in response to this statement from Charles Krauthammer's "Of Headless Mice . . . and Men": "When prominent scientists are prepared to acquiesce in—or indeed encourage—the deliberate creation of deformed and dying quasi-human life, you know we are facing a bioethical abyss. [. . .] There is no grosser corruption of biotechnology than creating a human mutant and disemboweling it at our pleasure for spare parts" (paragraph 8).

4. Argue your position on one of these issues or any other raised by the essays in this chapter: stem cell research, physician-assisted suicide, universal health care, access to expensive treatments for self-induced health problems, embryo research, mandatory testing for HIV diseases, and compulsory genetic screening for certain risk groups or during premarital examinations.

Research Topics

1. Research one of the issues suggested by any of the Additional Writing Topics. Other topics you might consider are the gene and its changing meaning, the status of genetic disease and genetic therapy, or the process of social negotiation of scientific knowledge.

2. Research the Human Genome Project, and write a paper in which you elaborate on its main objectives, provide representative views on the controversy surrounding it, and explain your own position and why you believe as you do.

3. Jeff Lyon in "Playing God: Has Science Gone Too Far?" refers to a special issue of *Science* in which a panel of bioethicists considered whether Dr. J. Craig Venter should continue his research on engineering a living microbe. Read the opinions of that panel as a starting point for your thinking and then conduct further research on the debate over whether humans should attempt to create life.

4. Research some aspect of the history and/or practice of eugenics, such as the program of Nazi Germany under Hitler or in the U.S. programs for forced sterilization for mentally ill patients.

CHAPTER 21
PUBLIC HEALTH

Epidemics, pandemics, and plagues have been much dreaded realities from the very beginning of human existence. Consider such major outbreaks of disease as the bubonic plague in thirteenth- and fourteenth-century Europe; cholera epidemics in various parts of the world from time to time, up to the present; the smallpox epidemic that swept Sweden in 1764; the typhus epidemic that killed more than three million Russians during World War I; or the influenza plague of 1918 to 1919 that killed more than 20 million people around the world. More recently, untreatable, deadly viruses have infected populations in certain areas of the world, worrying health officials that they may spread elsewhere. The Ebola virus in Africa, for instance, produces acute suffering in its victims, most of whom die within days of being infected. Viruses are particularly difficult to contain, because they live inside body cells, where antibiotics cannot reach them. Worse, once a person is infected with a virus, it can continue to live in the body's cells, waiting to strike again many years later.

Even such previously treatable diseases as herpes, hepatitis, and chicken pox are becoming resistant to treatment and causing deaths in increasingly higher numbers. Cases of deaths caused by herpes simplex 1 (HSV1) and related members of the herpes family, such as cytomegalovirus (CVM), chicken pox, and genital herpes (HSV2), have been reported. Although certain groups such as pregnant women are particularly vulnerable to these diseases, these and other viruses pose a considerable threat to the general population. More than three million Americans are believed to harbor the mysterious and deadly hepatitis C virus, for instance, with even more people harboring the less-mysterious but potentially life-threatening hepatitis A and hepatitis B viruses.

This chapter focuses on one particular public health problem, AIDS/HIV. First, Johanna McGeary's "Death Stalks a Continent" gives a detailed look at the AIDS epidemic in Africa and explains how the region's social dynamics "colluded to spread the disease and help block effective intervention." Her article tells the personal stories of disease victims and reports the viewpoints of both caretakers and those who may be responsible for spreading the disease. Related to McGeary's article, especially her plea for the West to help, is Faith McLellan's report on the United Nations General Assembly Special Session on HIV/AIDS in New York in July 2001. In "Human Rights: A Critical Framework for the Response to HIV/AIDS," McLellan reports that the primary human rights concern of the three-day conference was on the status of women and children. She notes that the aim of the conference was to draft a political Declaration of Commitment and to gain support for a global AIDS fund.

The last two articles in the chapter take up the issue of the high cost of AIDS drugs for developing countries or countries whose HIV/AIDS rates are extremely high. *The Economist* cover story, "Science and Profit," looks at the relationship between scientific research and the profit motive and addresses the allegation that "the ignoble search for profit distorts and corrupts." Although acknowledging that the question of drugs for developing countries is a difficult one, the article comes down on the side of drug companies. In contrast, Tom Fiedler, in "AIDS Fight Boils Down to Dollars vs. Lives," argues that the U.S. government has deliberately sided against those who have means to stop the growth of AIDS and calls for U.S. drug companies to allow Brazilian pharmaceuticals to produce cheaper generic versions of their drugs. As you read two sides of this issue, consider which you find more persuasive. Should drug companies bear the financial burden of sending life-saving drugs to developing countries? What are the implications if they do lower their prices for those countries or let other companies make generic versions? Does the morality issue supersede the profit motive in this instance?

DEATH STALKS A CONTINENT

Johanna McGeary

Johanna McGeary, a Time *magazine reporter, spent a month traveling through South Africa, Botswana, and Zimbabwe doing research for this February 12, 2001, cover story.*

Imagine your life this way. You get up in the morning and breakfast with your three kids. One is already doomed to die in infancy. Your husband works 200 miles away, comes home twice a year and sleeps around in between. You risk your life in every act of sexual intercourse. You go to work past a house where a teenager lives alone tending young siblings without any source of income. At another house, the wife was branded a whore when she asked her husband to use a condom, beaten silly and thrown into the streets. Over there lies a man desperately sick without access to a doctor or clinic or medicine or food or blankets or even a kind word. At work you eat with colleagues, and every third one is already fatally ill. You whisper about a friend who admitted she had the plague and whose neighbors stoned her to death. Your leisure is occupied by the funerals you attend every Saturday. You go to bed fearing adults your age will not live into their 40s. You and your neighbors and your political and popular leaders act as if nothing is happening.

Across the southern quadrant of Africa, this nightmare is real. The word not spoken is AIDS, and here at ground zero of humanity's deadliest cataclysm, the ultimate tragedy is that so many people don't know—or don't want to know—what is happening.

As the HIV virus sweeps mercilessly through these lands—the fiercest trial Africa has yet endured—a few try to address the terrible depredation. The rest of society looks away. Flesh and muscle melt from the bones of the sick in packed hospital wards and lonely bush kraals. Corpses stack up in morgues until those on top crush the identity from the faces underneath. Raw earth mounds scar the landscape, grave after grave without name or number. Bereft children grieve for parents lost in their prime, for siblings scattered to the winds.

4   The victims don't cry out. Doctors and obituaries do not give the killer its name. Families recoil in shame. Leaders shirk responsibility. The stubborn silence heralds victory for the disease: denial cannot keep the virus at bay.

The developed world is largely silent too. AIDS in Africa has never commanded the full-bore response the West has brought to other, sometimes lesser, travails. We pay sporadic attention, turning on the spotlight when an international conference occurs, then turning it off. Good-hearted donors donate; governments acknowledge that more needs to be done. But think how different the effort would be if what is happening here were happening in the West.

By now you've seen pictures of the sick, the dead, the orphans. You've heard appalling numbers: the number of new infections, the number of the dead, the number who are sick without care, the number walking around already fated to die.

But to comprehend the full horror AIDS has visited on Africa, listen to the woman we have dubbed Laetitia Hambahlane in Durban or the boy Tsepho Phale in Francistown or the woman who calls herself Thandiwe in Bulawayo or Louis Chikoka, a long-distance trucker. You begin to understand how AIDS has struck Africa—with a biblical virulence that will claim tens of millions of lives—when you hear about shame and stigma and ignorance and poverty and sexual violence and migrant labor and promiscuity and political paralysis and the terrible silence that surrounds all this dying. It is a measure of the silence that some asked us not to print their real names to protect their privacy.

8   Theirs is a story about what happens when a disease leaps the confines of medicine to invade the body politic, infecting not just individuals but an entire society. As AIDS migrated to man in Africa, it mutated into a complex plague with confounding social, economic and political mechanics that locked together to accelerate the

virus' progress. The region's social dynamics colluded to spread the disease and help block effective intervention.

We have come to three countries abutting one another at the bottom of Africa—Botswana, South Africa, Zimbabwe—the heart of the heart of the epidemic. For nearly a decade, these nations suffered a hidden invasion of infection that concealed the dimension of the coming calamity. Now the omni-present dying reveals the shocking scale of the devastation.

AIDS in Africa bears little resemblance to the American epidemic, limited to specific high-risk groups and brought under control through intensive education, vigorous political action and expensive drug therapy. Here the disease has bred a Darwinian perversion. Society's fittest, not its frailest, are the ones who die—adults spirited away, leaving the old and the children behind. You cannot define risk groups: everyone who is sexually active is at risk. Babies too, unwittingly infected by mothers. Barely a single family remains untouched. Most do not know how or when they caught the virus, many never know they have it, many who do know don't tell anyone as they lie dying. Africa can provide no treatment for those with AIDS.

They will all die, of tuberculosis, pneumonia, meningitis, diarrhea, whatever overcomes their ruined immune systems first. And the statistics, grim as they are, may be too low. There is no broad-scale AIDS testing: infection rates are calculated mainly from the presence of HIV in pregnant women. Death certificates in these countries do not record AIDS as the cause. "Whatever stats we have are not reliable," warns Mary Crewe of the University of Pretoria's Center for the Study of AIDS. "Everybody's guessing."

The TB Patient

12   Case No. 309 in the Tugela Ferry Home-Care Program shivers violently on the wooden planks someone has knocked into a bed, a frayed blanklet pulled right up to his nose. He has the flushed skin, overbright eyes and careful breathing of the tubercular. He is alone, and it is chilly within the crumbling mud walls of his hut at Msinga Top, a windswept outcrop high above the Tugela River in South Africa's KwaZulu-Natal province. The spectacular view of hills and veld would gladden a well man, but the 22-year-old we will call Fundisi Khumalo, though he does not know it, has AIDS, and his eyes seem to focus inward on his simple fear.

Before he can speak, his throat clutches in gasping spasms. Sharp pains rack his chest; his breath comes in shallow gasps. The vomiting is better today. But constipation has doubled up his knees, and he is too weak to go outside to relieve himself. He can't remember when he last ate. He can't remember how long he's been sick—"a long time, maybe since six months ago." Khumalo knows he has TB, and he believes it is just TB. "I am only thinking of that," he answers when we ask why he is so ill.

But the fear never leaves his eyes. He worked in a hair salon in Johannesburg, lived in a men's hostel in one of the cheap townships, had "a few" girlfriends. He knew other young men in the hostel who were on-and-off sick. When they fell too ill to work anymore, like him, they straggled home to rural villages like Msinga Top. But where

Khumalo would not go is the hospital. "Why?" he says. "You are sick there, you die there."

"He's right, you know," says Dr. Tony Moll, who has driven us up the dirt track from the 350-bed hospital he heads in Tugela Ferry. "We have no medicines for AIDS. So many hospitals tell them, 'You've got AIDS. We can't help you. Go home and die.' " No one wants to be tested either, he adds, unless treatment is available. "If the choice is to know and get nothing," he says, "they don't want to know."

16   Here and in scattered homesteads all over rural Africa, the dying people say the sickness afflicting their families and neighbors is just the familiar consequence of their eternal poverty. Or it is the work of witchcraft. You have done something bad and have been bewitched. Your neighbor's jealously has invaded you. You have not appeased the spirits of your ancestors, and they have cursed you. Some in South Africa believe the disease was introduced by the white population as a way to control black Africans after the end of apartheid.

Ignorance about AIDS remains profound. But because of the funerals, southern Africans can't help seeing that something more systematic and sinister lurks out there. Every Saturday and often Sundays too, neighbors trudge to the cemeteries for costly burial rites for the young and the middle-aged who are suddenly dying so much faster than the old. Families say it was pneumonia, TB, malaria that killed their son, their wife, their baby. "But you starting to hear the truth," says Durban home-care volunteer Busi Magwazi. "In the church, in the graveyard, they saying, 'Yes, she died of AIDS.' Oh, people talking about it even if the families don't admit it."

Ignorance is the crucial reason the epidemic has run out of control. Surveys say many Africans here are becoming aware there is a sexually transmitted disease called AIDS that is incurable. But they don't think the risk applies to them. And their vague knowledge does not translate into changes in their sexual behavior. It's easy to see why so many don't yet sense the danger when few talk openly about the disease. And Africans are beset by so plentiful a roster of perils—famine, war, the violence of desperation or ethnic hatred, the regular illnesses of poverty, the dangers inside mines or on the roads—that the delayed risk of AIDS ranks low.

The Outcast

To acknowledge AIDS in yourself is to be branded as monstrous. Laetitia Hambahlane (not her real name) is 51 and sick with AIDS. So is her brother. She admits it; he doesn't. In her mother's broken-down house in the mean streets of Umlazi township, though, Laetitia's mother hovers over her son, nursing him, protecting him, resolutely denying he has anything but TB, though his sister claims the sure symptoms of AIDS mark him. Laetitia is the outcast, first from her family, then from her society.

20   For years Laetitia worked as a domestic servant in Durban and dutifully sent all her wages home to her mother. She fell in love a number of times and bore four children. "I loved that last man," she recalls. "After he left, I had no one, no sex." That was 1992, but Laetitia already had HIV.

She fell sick in 1996, and her employers sent her to a private doctor who couldn't diagnose an illness. He tested her blood and found she was HIV positive. "I wish I'd died right then," she says, as tears spill down her sunken cheeks. "I asked the doctor, 'Have you got medicine?' He said no. I said, 'Can't you keep me alive?' " The doctor could do nothing and sent her away. "I couldn't face the word," she says. "I couldn't sleep at night. I sat on my bed, thinking, praying. I did not see anyone day or night. I ask God, Why?"

Laetitia's employers fired her without asking her exact diagnosis. For weeks she could not muster the courage to tell anyone. Then she told her children, and they were ashamed and frightened. Then, harder still, she told her mother. Her mother raged about the loss of money if Laetitia could not work again. She was so angry she ordered Laetitia out of the house. When her daughter wouldn't leave, the mother threatened to sell the house to get rid of her daughter. Then she walled off her daughter's room with plywood partitions, leaving the daughter a pariah, alone in a cramped, dark space without windows and only a flimsy door opening into the alley. Laetitia must earn the pennies to feed herself and her children by peddling beer, cigarettes and candy from a shopping cart in her room, when people are brave enough to stop by her door. "Sometimes they buy, sometimes not," she says. "That is how I'm surviving."

Her mother will not talk to her. "If you are not even accepted by your own family," says Magwazi, the volunteer home-care giver from Durban's Sinoziso project who visits Laetitia, "then others will not accept you." When Laetitia ventures outdoors, neighbors snub her, tough boys snatch her purse, children taunt her. Her own kids are tired of the sickness and don't like to help her anymore. "When I can't get up, they don't bring me food," she laments. One day local youths barged into her room, cursed her as a witch and a whore and beat her. When she told the police, the youths returned, threatening to burn down the house.

24   But it is her mother's rejection that wounds Laetitia most. "She is hiding it about my brother," she cries. "Why will she do nothing for me?" Her hands pick restlessly at the quilt covering her paper-thin frame. "I know my mother will not bury me properly. I know she will not take care of my kids when I am gone."

Jabulani Syabusi would use his real name, but he needs to protect his brother. He teaches school in a red, dusty district of KwaZulu-Natal. People here know the disease is all around them, but no one speaks of it. He eyes the scattered huts that make up his little settlement on an arid bluff. "We can count 20 who died just here as far as we can see. I personally don't remember any family that told it was AIDS," he says. "They hide it if they do know."

Syabusi's own family is no different. His younger brother is also a teacher who has just come home from Durban too sick to work anymore. He says he has tuberculosis, but after six months the tablets he is taking have done nothing to cure him. Syabusi's wife Nomsange, a nurse, is concerned that her 36-year-old brother-in-law may have something worse. Syabusi finally asked the doctor tending his brother what is wrong. The doctor said the information is confidential and will not tell him. Neither will his brother. "My brother is not brave enough to tell me," says Syabusi, as he stares sadly toward the house next door, where his only sibling lies ill. "And I am not brave enough to ask him."

Kennedy Fugewane, a cheerful, elderly volunteer counselor, sits in an empty U.S.-funded clinic that offers fast, pinprick blood tests in Francistown, Botswana, pondering how to break through the silence. This city suffers one of the world's highest infection rates, but people deny the disease because HIV is linked with sex. "We don't reveal anything," he says. "But people are so stigmatized even if they walk in the door." Africans feel they must keep private anything to do with sex. "If a man comes here, people will say he is running around," says Fugewane, though he acknowledges that men never do come. "If a woman comes, people will say she is loose. If anyone says they got HIV, they will be despised."

28   Pretoria University's Mary Crewe says, "It is presumed if you get AIDS, you have done something wrong." HIV labels you as living an immoral life. Embarrassment about sexuality looms more important than future health risks. "We have no language to talk candidly about sex," she says, "so we have no civil language to talk about AIDS." Volunteers like Fugewane try to reach out with flyers, workshops, youth meetings and free condoms, but they are frustrated by a culture that values its dignity over saving lives. "People here don't have the courage to come forward and say, 'Let me know my HIV status,'" he sighs, much less the courage to do something about it. "Maybe one day . . ."

Doctors bow to social pressure and legal strictures not to record AIDS on death certificates. "I write TB or meningitis or diarrhea but never AIDS," says South Africa's Dr. Moll. "It's a public document, and families would hate it if anyone knew." Several years ago, doctors were barred even from recording compromised immunity or HIV status on a medical file; now they can record the results of blood tests for AIDS on patient charts to protect other health workers. Doctors like Moll have long agitated to apply the same openness to death certificates.

The Truck Driver

Here, men have to migrate to work, inside their countries or across borders. All that mobility sows HIV far and wide, as Louis Chikoka is the first to recognize. He regularly drives the highway that is Botswana's economic lifeline and its curse. The road runs for 350 miles through desolate bush that is the Texas-size country's sole strip of habitable land, home to a large majority of its 1.5 million people. It once brought prospectors to Botswana's rich diamond reefs. Now it's the link for transcontinental truckers like Chikoka who haul goods from South Africa to markets in the continent's center. And now the road brings AIDS.

Chikoka brakes his dusty, diesel-belching Kabwe Transport 18-wheeler to a stop at the dark roadside rest on the edge of Francistown, where the international trade routes converge and at least 43% of adults are HIV-positive. He is a cheerful man even after 12 hard hours behind the wheel freighting rice from Durban. He's been on the road for two weeks and will reach his destination in Congo next Thursday. At 39, he is married, the father of three and a long-haul trucker for 12 years. He's used to it.

32   Lighting up a cigarette, the jaunty driver is unusually loquacious about sex as he eyes the dim figures circling the rest stop. Chikoka has parked here for a quickie. See

that one over there, he points with his cigarette. "Those local ones we call bitches. They always waiting here for short service." Short service? "It's according to how long it takes you to ejaculate," he explains. "We go to the 'bush bedroom' over there [waving at a clump of trees 100 yds. away] or sometimes in the truck. Short service, that costs you 20 rands [$2.84]. They know we drivers always got money."

Chikoka nods his head toward another woman sitting beside a stack of cardboard cartons. "We like better to go to them," he says. They are the "businesswomen," smugglers with gray-market cases of fruit and toilet paper and toys that they need to transport somewhere up the road. "They come to us, and we negotiate privately about carrying their goods." It's a no-cash deal, he says. "They pay their bodies to us." Chikoka shrugs at a suggestion that the practice may be unhealthy. "I been away two weeks, madam. I'm human. I'm a man. I have to have sex."

What he likes best is dry sex. In parts of sub-Saharan Africa, to please men, women sit in basins of bleach or saltwater or stuff astringent herbs, tobacco or fertilizer inside their vagina. The tissue of the lining swells up and natural lubricants dry out. The resulting dry sex is painful and dangerous for women. The drying agents suppress natural bacteria, and friction easily lacerates the tender walls of the vagina. Dry sex increases the risk of HIV infection for women, already two times as likely as men to contract the virus from a single encounter. The women, adds Chikoka, can charge more for dry sex, 50 to 60 rands ($6.46 to $7.75), enough to pay a child's school fees or to eat for a week.

Chikoka knows his predilection for commercial sex spreads AIDS; he knows his promiscuity could carry the disease home to his wife; he knows people die if they get it. "Yes, HIV is terrible, madam," he says as he crooks a finger toward the businesswoman whose favors he will enjoy that night. "But, madam, sex is natural. Sex is not like beer or smoking. You can stop them. But unless you castrate the men, you can't stop sex—and then we all die anyway."

36   Millions of men share Chikoka's sexually active lifestyle, fostered by the region's dependence on migrant labor. Men desperate to earn a few dollars leave their women at hardscrabble rural homesteads to go where the work is: the mines, the cities, the road. They're housed together in isolated males-only hostels but have easy access to prostitutes or a "town wife" with whom they soon pick up a second family and an ordinary STD and HIV. Then they go home to wives and girlfriends a few times a year, carrying the virus they do not know they have. The pattern is so dominant that rates of infection in many rural areas across the southern cone match urban numbers.

If HIV zeros in disproportionally on poor migrants, it does not skip over the educated or the well paid. Soldiers, doctors, policemen, teachers, district administrators are also routinely separated from families by a civil-service system that sends them alone to remote rural posts, where they have money and women have no men. A regular paycheck procures more access to extramarital sex. Result: the vital professions are being devastated.

Schoolmaster Syabusi is afraid there will soon be no more teachers in his rural zone. He has just come home from a memorial for six colleagues who died over the past few months, though no one spoke the word AIDS at the service. "The rate here—they're so many," he says, shaking his head. "They keep on passing it at school." Teachers in southern Africa have one of the highest group infection rates, but they hide their status until the telltale symptoms find them out.

Before then, the men—teachers are mostly men here—can take their pick of sexual partners. Plenty of women in bush villages need extra cash, often to pay school fees, and female students know they can profit from a teacher's favor. So the schoolmasters buy a bit of sex with lonely wives and trade a bit of sex with willing pupils for A's. Some students consider it an honor to sleep with the teacher, a badge of superiority. The girls brag about it to their peers, preening in their ability to snag an older man. "The teachers are the worst," says Jabulani Siwela, an AIDS worker in Zimbabwe who saw frequent teacher-student sex in his Bulawayo high school. They see a girl they like; they ask her to stay after class; they have a nice time. "It's dead easy," he says. "These are men who know better, but they still do it all the time."

The Prostitute

40   The working woman we meet directs our car to a reedy field fringing the gritty eastern townships of Bulawayo, Zimbabwe. She doesn't want neighbors to see her being interviewed. She is afraid her family will find out she is a prostitute, so we will call her Thandiwe. She looked quite prim and proper in her green calf-length dress as she waited for johns outside 109 Tongogaro Street in the center of downtown. So, for that matter, do the dozens of other women cruising the city's dim street corners: not a mini or bustier or bared navel in sight. Zimbabwe is in many ways a prim and proper society that frowns on commercial sex work and the public display of too much skin.

That doesn't stop Thandiwe from earning a better living turning tricks than she ever could doing honest work. Desperate for a job, she slipped illegally into South Africa in 1992. She cleaned floors in a Johannesburg restaurant, where she met a cook from back home who was also illegal. They had two daughters, and they got married; he was gunned down one night at work.

She brought his body home for burial and was sent to her in-laws to be "cleansed." This common practice gives a dead husband's brother the right, even the duty, to sleep with the widow. Thandiwe tested negative for HIV in 1998, but if she were positive, the ritual cleansing would have served only to pass on the disease. Then her in-laws wanted to keep her two daughters because their own children had died, and marry her off to an old uncle who lived far out in the bush. She fled.

Alone, Thandiwe grew desperate. "I couldn't let my babies starve." One day she met a friend from school. "She told me she was a sex worker. She said, 'Why you suffer? Let's go to a place where we can get quick bucks.' " Thandiwe hangs her head. "I went. I was afraid. But now I go every night."

44   She goes to Tongogaro Street, where the rich clients are, tucking a few condoms in her handbag every evening as the sun sets and returning home strictly by 10 so that she won't have to service a taxi-van driver to get a ride back. Thandiwe tells her family she works an evening shift, just not at what. "I get 200 zim [$5] for sex," she says,

more for special services. She uses two condoms per client, sometimes three. "If they say no, I say no." But then sometimes resentful johns hit her. It's pay-and-go until she has pocketed 1,000 or 1,500 Zimbabwe dollars and can go home—with more cash than her impoverished neighbors ever see in their roughneck shantytown, flush enough to buy a TV and fleece jammies for her girls and meat for their supper.

"I am ashamed," she murmurs. She has stopped going to church. "Every day I ask myself, 'When will I stop this business?' The answer is, 'If I could get a job' . . ." Her voice trails off hopelessly. "At the present moment, I have no option, no other option." As trucker Chikoka bluntly puts it, "They give sex to eat. They got no man; they got no work; but they got kids, and they got to eat." Two of Thandiwe's friends in the sex trade are dying of AIDS, but what can she do? "I just hope I won't get it."

In fact, causal sex of every kind is commonplace here. Prostitutes are just the ones who admit they do it for cash. Everywhere there's premarital sex, sex as recreation. Obligatory sex and its abusive counterpart, coercive sex. Transactional sex: sex as a gift, sugar-daddy sex. Extramarital sex, second families, multiple partners. The nature of AIDS is to feast on promiscuity.

Rare is the man who even knows his HIV status: males widely refuse testing even when they fall ill. And many men who suspect they are HIV positive embrace a flawed logic: if I'm already infected, I can sleep around because I can't get it again. But women are the ones who progress to full-blown AIDS first and die fastest, and the underlying cause is not just sex but power. Wives and girlfriends and even prostitutes in this part of the world can't easily say no to sex on a man's terms. It matters little what comes into play, whether it is culture or tradition or the pathology of violence or issues of male identity or the subservient status of women.

48   Beneath a translucent scalp, the plates of Gertrude Dhlamini's cranium etch a geography of pain. Her illness is obvious in the thin, stretched skin under which veins throb with the shingles that have blinded her left eye and scarred that side of her face. At 39, she looks 70. The agonizing thrush, a kind of fungus, that paralyzed her throat has ebbed enough to enable her to swallow a spoon or two of warm gruel, but most of the nourishment flows away in constant diarrhea. She struggles to keep her hand from scratching restlessly at the scaly rash flushing her other cheek. She is not ashamed to proclaim her illness to the world. "It must be told," she says.

Gertrude is thrice rejected. At 19 she bore a son to a boyfriend who soon left her, taking away the child. A second boyfriend got her pregnant in 1994 but disappeared in anger when their daughter was born sickly with HIV. A doctor told Gertrude it was her fault, so she blamed herself that little Noluthando was never well in the two years she survived. Gertrude never told the doctor the baby's father had slept with other women. "I was afraid to," she says, "though I sincerely believe he gave the sickness to me." Now, she says, "I have rent him from my heart. And I will never have another man in my life."

Gertrude begged her relatives to take her in, but when she revealed the name of her illness, they berated her. They made her the household drudge, telling her never to touch their food or their cooking pots. They gave her a bowl and a spoon strictly for her own use. After a few months, they threw her out.

Gertrude sits upright on a donated bed in a cardboard shack in a rough Durban township that is now the compass of her world. Perhaps 10 ft. square, the little windowless room contains a bed, one sheet and blanket, a change of clothes and a tiny cooking ring, but she has no money for paraffin to heat the food that a home-care worker brings. She must fetch water and use a toilet down the hill. "Everything I have," she says, "is a gift." Now the school that owns the land under her hut wants to turn it into a playground and she worries about where she will go. Gertrude rubs and rubs at her raw cheek. "I pray and pray to God," she says, "not to take my soul while I am alone in this room."

52   Women like Gertrude were brought up to be subservient to men. Especially in matters of sex, the man is always in charge. Women feel powerless to change sexual behavior. Even when a woman wants to protect herself, she usually can't: it is not uncommon for men to beat partners who refuse intercourse or request a condom. "Real men" don't use them, so women who want their partners to must fight deeply ingrained taboos. Talk to him about donning a rubber sheath and be prepared for accusations, abuse or abandonment.

A nurse in Durban, coming home from an AIDS training class, suggested that her mate should put on a condom, as a kind of homework exercise. He grabbed a pot and banged loudly on it with a knife, calling all the neighbors into his house. He pointed the knife at his wife and demanded: "Where was she between 4 p.m. and now? Why is she suddenly suggesting this? What has changed after 20 years that she wants a condom?"

Schoolteacher Syabusi is an educated man, fully cognizant of the AIDS threat. Yet even he bristles when asked if he uses a condom. "Humph," he says with a fine snort. "That question is nonnegotiable." So despite extensive distribution of free condoms, they often go unused. Astonishing myths have sprung up. If you don one, your erection can't grow. Free condoms must be too cheap to be safe: they have been stored too long, kept too hot, kept too cold. Condoms fill up with germs, so they spread AIDS. Condoms from overseas bring the disease with them. Foreign governments that donate condoms put holes in them so that Africans will die. Education programs find it hard to compete with the power of the grapevine.

The Child in No. 17

In crib No. 17 of the spartan but crowded children's ward at the Church of Scotland Hospital in KwaZulu-Natal, a tiny, staring child lies dying. She is three and has hardly known a day of good health. Now her skin wrinkles around her body like an oversize suit, and her twigsize bones can barely hold her vertical as nurses search for a vein to take blood. In the frail arms hooked up to transfusion tubes, her veins have collapsed. The nurses palpate a threadlike vessel on the child's forehead. She mews like a wounded animal as one tightens a rubber band around her head to raise the vein. Tears pour unnoticed from her mother's eyes as she watches the needle tap-tap at her daughter's temple. Each time the whimpering child lifts a wan hand to brush away the pain, her mother gently lowers it. Drop by drop, the nurses manage to collect 1 cc of blood in five minutes.

56   The child in crib No. 17 has had TB, oral thrush, chronic diarrhea, malnutrition, severe vomiting. The vial of blood reveals her real ailment, AIDS, but the disease is not listed on her chart, and her mother says she has no idea why her child is so ill. She breastfed her for two years, but once the little girl was weaned, she could not keep solid food down. For a long time, her mother thought something was wrong with the food. Now the child is afflicted with so many symptoms that her mother had to bring her to the hospital, from which sick babies rarely return.

She hopes, she prays her child will get better, and like all the mothers who stay with their children at the hospital, she tends her lovingly, constantly changing filthy diapers, smoothing sheets, pressing a little nourishment between listless lips, trying to tease a smile from the vacant, staring face. Her husband works in Johannesburg, where he lives in a men's squatter camp. He comes home twice a year. She is 25. She has heard of AIDS but does not know it is transmitted by sex, does not know if she or her husband has it. She is afraid this child will die soon, and she is afraid to have more babies. But she is afraid too to raise the subject with her husband. "He would not agree to that," she says shyly. "He would never agree to have no more babies."

Dr. Annick DeBaets, 32, is a volunteer from Belgium. In the two years she has spent here in Tugela Ferry, she has learned all about how hard it is to break the cycle of HIV transmission from mother to infant. The door to this 48-cot ward is literally a revolving one: sick babies come in, receive doses of rudimentary antibiotics, vitamins, food; go home for a week or a month; then come back as ill as ever. Most, she says, die in the first or second year. If she could just follow up with really intensive care, believes Dr. DeBaets, many of the wizened infants crowding three to a crib could live longer, healthier lives. "But it's very discouraging. We simply don't have the time, money or facilities for anything but minimal care."

Much has been written about what South African Judge Edwin Cameron, himself HIV positive, calls his country's "grievous ineptitude" in the face of the burgeoning epidemic. Nowhere has that been more evident than in the government's failure to provide drugs that could prevent pregnant women from passing HIV to their babies. The government has said it can't afford the 300-rand-per-dose, 28-dose regimen of AZT that neighboring nations like Botswana dole out, using funds and drugs from foreign donors. The late South African presidential spokesman Parks Mankahlana even suggested publicly that it was not cost effective to save these children when their mothers were already doomed to die: "We don't want a generation of orphans."

60   Yet these children—70,000 are born HIV positive in South Africa alone every year—could be protected from the disease for about $4 each with another simple, cheap drug called nevirapine. Until last month, the South African government steadfastly refused to license or finance the use of nevirapine despite the manufacturer's promise to donate the drug for five years, claiming that its "toxic" side effects are not yet known. This spring, however, the drug will finally be distributed to leading public hospitals in the country, though only on a limited basis at first.

The mother at crib No. 17 is not concerned with potential side effects. She sits on the floor cradling her daughter, crooning over and over, "Get well, my child, get well." The baby stares back without blinking. "It's sad, so sad, so sad," the mother says. The child died three days later.

The children who are left when parents die only add another complex dimension to Africa's epidemic. At 17, Tsepho Phale has been head of an indigent household of three young boys in the dusty township of Monarch, outside Francistown, for two years. He never met his father, his mother died of AIDS, and the grieving children possess only a raw concrete shell of a house. The doorways have no doors; the window frames no glass. There is not a stick of furniture. The boys sleep on piled-up blankets, their few clothes dangling from nails. In the room that passes for a kitchen, two paraffin burners sit on the dirt floor alongside the month's food: four cabbages, a bag of oranges and one of potatoes, three sacks of flour, some yeast, two jars of oil and two cartons of milk. Next to a dirty stack of plastic pans lies the mealy meal and rice that will provide their main sustenance for the month. A couple of bars of soap and two rolls of toilet paper also have to last the month. Tsepho has just brought these rations home from the social-service center where the "orphan grants" are doled out.

Tsepho has been robbed of a childhood that was grim even before his mother fell sick. She supported the family by "buying and selling things," he says, but she never earned more than a pittance. When his middle brother was knocked down by a car and left physically and mentally disabled, Tsepho's mother used the insurance money to build this house, so she would have one thing of value to leave her children. As the walls went up, she fell sick. Tsepho had to nurse her, bathe her, attend to her bodily functions, try to feed her. Her one fear as she lay dying was that her rural relatives would try to steal the house. She wrote a letter bequeathing it to her sons and bade Tsepho hide it.

64 As her body lay on the concrete floor awaiting burial, the relatives argued openly about how they would divide up the profits when they sold her dwelling. Tsepho gave the district commissioner's office the letter, preventing his mother's family from grabbing the house. Fine, said his relations; if you think you're a man, you look after your brothers. They have contributed nothing to the boys' welfare since. "It's as if we don't exist anymore either," says Tsepho. Now he struggles to keep house for the others, doing the cooking, cleaning, laundry and shopping.

The boys look at the future with despair. "It is very bleak," says Tsepho, kicking aimlessly at a bare wall. He had to quite school, has no job, will probably never get one. "I've given up my dreams. I have no hope."

Orphans have traditionally been cared for the African way: relatives absorb the children of the dead into their extended families. Some still try, but communities like Tsepho's are becoming saturated with orphans, and families can't afford to take on another kid, leaving thousands alone.

Now many must fend for themselves, struggling to survive. The trauma of losing parents is compounded by the burden of becoming a breadwinner. Most orphans sink into penury, drop out of school, suffer malnutrition, ostracism, psychic distress. Their makeshift households scramble to live on pitiful handouts—from overstretched relatives, a kind neighbor, a state grant—or they beg and steal in the streets. The orphans' present desperation forecloses a brighter future. "They hardly ever succeed in having a life," says Siphelile Kaseke, 22, a counselor at an AIDS orphans' camp near Bulawayo. Without education, girls falls into prostitution, and older boys migrate illegally to South Africa, leaving the younger ones to go on the streets.

68   Every day spent in this part of Africa is acutely depressing: there is so little countervailing hope to all the stories of the dead and the doomed. "More than anywhere else in the world, AIDS in Africa was met with apathy," says Suzanne LeClerc-Madlala, a lecturer at the University of Natal. The consequences of the silence march on: infection soars, stigma hardens, denial hastens death, and the chasm between knowledge and behavior widens. The present disaster could be dwarfed by the woes that loom if Africa's epidemic rages on. The human losses could wreck the region's frail economies, break down civil societies and incite political instability.

In the face of that, every day good people are doing good things. Like Dr. Moll, who uses his after-job time and his own fund raising to run an extensive volunteer home-care program in KwaZulu-Natal. And Busi Magwazi, who, along with dozens of others, tends the sick for nothing in the Durban-based Sinoziso project. And Patricia Bakwinya, who started her Shining Stars orphan-care program in Francistown with her own zeal and no money, to help youngsters like Tsepho Phale. And countless individuals who give their time and devotion to ease southern Africa's plight.

But these efforts can help only thousands; they cannot turn the tide. The region is caught in a double bind. Without treatment, those with HIV will sicken and die; without prevention, the spread of infection cannot be checked. Southern Africa has no other means available to break the vicious cycle, except to change everyone's sexual behavior—and that isn't happening.

The essential missing ingredient is leadership. Neither the countries of the region nor those of the wealthy world have been able or willing to provide it.

72   South Africa, comparatively well off, comparatively well educated, has blundered tragically for years. AIDS invaded just when apartheid ended, and a government absorbed in massive transition relegated the disease to a back page. An attempt at a national education campaign wasted millions on a farcical musical. The premature release of a local wonder drug ended in scandal when the drug turned out to be made of industrial solvent. Those fiascoes left the government skittish about embracing expensive programs, inspiring a 1998 decision not to provide AZT to HIV-positive pregnant women. Zimbabwe too suffers savagely from feckless leadership. Even in Botswana, where the will to act is gathering strength, the resources to follow through have to come from foreign hands.

AIDS' grip here is so pervasive and so complex that all societies—theirs and ours—must rally round to break it. These countries are too poor to doctor themselves. The drugs that could begin to break the cycle will not be available here until global pharmaceutical companies find ways to provide them inexpensively. The health-care systems required to prescribe and monitor complicated triple-cocktail regimens won't exist unless rich countries help foot the bill. If there is ever to be a vaccine, the West will have to finance its discovery and provide it to the poor. The cure for this epidemic is not national but international.

The deep silence that makes African leaders and societies want to deny the problem, the corruption and incompetence that render them helpless is something the West cannot fix. But the fact that they are poor is not. The wealthy world must help with its zeal and its cash if southern Africa is ever to be freed of the AIDS plague.

Personal Response

McGeary says that "every day spent in this part of Africa is acutely depressing" (paragraph 68), and most would agree that just reading about what she has witnessed could be depressing as well. What is the effect of this article on you personally?

Questions for Class or Small-Group Discussion

1. McGeary writes that AIDs in Africa is "a complex plague with confounding social, economic and political mechanics that locked together to accelerate the virus' progress" (paragraph 8). Why do you understand the specifics of those "mechanics" to be?

2. McGeary remarks that "[t]he region's social dynamics colluded to spread the disease and help block effective intervention" (paragraph 8). Explain what she means by that statement.

3. In paragraph 5, McGeary makes this comment: "Think how different the effort would be if what is happening [in the southern quadrant of South Africa] were happening in the West." How different do you think the effort would be?

4. McGeary ends her article by asserting that "the West will have to finance [a vaccine] and provide it to the poor" (paragraph 73). Are you persuaded that developed countries must help Africa fight its epidemic?

HUMAN RIGHTS: A CRITICAL FRAMEWORK FOR THE RESPONSE TO HIV/AIDS

Faith McLellan

Faith McLellan is North American Senior Editor of Lancet *in New York City. A graduate of Wake Forest University and the University of Texas Medical Branch, she earned a doctorate in the medical humanities. This article appeared in the July 14, 2001, issue of* Lancet, *which features articles of interest to the medical world, with heavy emphasis on research techniques.*

A lack of respect for human rights is driving the spread of the AIDS epidemic, according to panelists in a round table discussion on HIV and human rights at the

United Nations General Assembly Special Session on HIV/AIDS in New York this month (see Lancet 2001; 357: 2073, 2107, 2112). As part of a 3-day UN conference, the first of its kind to be devoted to a public health issue, the primary human rights concern was the status of women and children. Strengthening the status of women and increasing their participation in decision making, and protecting children orphaned by the disease are central to effective intervention.

Chaired by Poland's Minister for Health, Grzegorza Opala, the session began with statements by the heads of several UN organisations who emphasised that HIV/AIDS is a human rights violation that intensifies other rights violations, especially those affecting women and children. The significant impact on children, more than 4.3 million of whom have so far died, and thousands orphaned, urgently needs to be addressed. Children are being forced into work as a result of the social and economic effect of AIDS, with one child prostitute in Africa noting the futility of the choices confronting her: "It is better to die of disease than starvation." The aim of the conference was to draft a political Declaration of Commitment and gain support for a global AIDS fund to help tackle the epidemic. The draft declaration endorses the empowerment of women as critical to controlling the epidemic.

Carol Bellamy, Executive Director of the United Nations Children's Fund (UNICEF) and others stressed the need to focus on education. More than half of all teenage girls who took part in a UNICEF survey in South Africa believed that a person who appears healthy cannot be infected with HIV. A right to education about the disease is a fundamental human right, and the panel urged governments throughout the world to ensure that at least 90% of all young people aged 15 to 24 years have access to youth-specific AIDS education by 2005. These targets are set out in the UNAIDS draft Declaration of Commitment.

4   Mary Robinson, the UN High Commissioner for Human Rights, argued that there is no greater human rights problem in the world today than HIV/AIDS. She said that the human rights dimension, with its emphasis on education, and freedom of association and expression, causes more hesitancy and resistance than any other aspect of the disease, which has also had a devastating impact on the right to development, an issue of critical importance to many UN member states. International human rights law is the framework on which response to HIV/AIDS needs to be built. Countries that take steps to address the pandemic are actually investing in sustainable development, as a comprehensive approach to address poverty, and provide basic social and economic services, among other issues. Robinson urged governments—or, where governments refuse to address the issues, civil society—to take the lead in forcing discussion about the epidemic. Although access to prevention, treatment, and care should not depend on geography, at present it does.

HIV/AIDS places a disproportionate burden on women and girls, a pandemic that is yet to be fully realised. Respect for the human rights of women is not simply a matter of justice or fairness, but one, literally, of life and death. Because of the imbalance of power between men and women that exists in many parts of the world, some women are unable to say no to unwanted or unprotected sex. Further, although women are the primary caregivers of those infected with HIV, their own care has become a secondary concern. Women often go untreated and uncared for: although more men than women are infected with HIV, more women than men have died of AIDS.

According to Noeleen Heyzer, Executive Director of the UN Development Fund for Women (UNIFEM) we need to make gender equality a guiding principle in the global community's response to the epidemic. She suggested three areas of focus: first, women and young people need an equal say in the design of interventions and must participate fully in decision making in order to obtain an equal benefit. Second, all actions must be targeted to take into account the special needs of women and girls. Gender-specific data are needed, as the crisis is clearly different for women and men, but are often in short supply. Finally, violence, an unfortunately important aspect of the HIV/AIDS experience for women, must be addressed directly. "Gender equality is a key response to the crisis of HIV," she concluded.

Personal Response

Are you surprised that the AIDS crisis is viewed as a human rights problem? What do you think of the suggestion that empowering women would go a long way toward addressing the HIV/AIDS crisis?

Questions for Class or Small-Group Discussion

1. Comment on this statement by Mary Robinson: "[T]here is no greater human rights problem in the world today than HIV/AIDS" (paragraph 4). In what ways is HIV/AIDS a human rights problem?

2. Mary Robinson refers to governments who "refuse to address the issues" (paragraph 4). What do you think some governments will not address these issues?

3. How would improving the status of women and children be an appropriate response to HIV/AIDS?

SCIENCE AND PROFIT

The Economist

The Economist *is a weekly newsmagazine covering world politics, current affairs, business, finance, and science. It is published in England. According to its Web site (www.economist.com): "Founded in 1843 to support the cause of free trade,* The Economist *has remained a radical publication of opinion with a reverence for facts. It has become firmly established as one of the world's most authoritative and influential publications.* The Economist *is famous for its objective, factual writing, rather than for emotive journalism." This article is the cover story for the February 2001 issue.*

Once upon a time, pure and applied science were the same. Sir Humphry Davy discovered seven chemical elements, and invented the miner's safety lamp. Louis Pasteur investigated the properties of molecules, and worked out how to stop milk spoiling. Everybody thought that was admirable. Somehow, things have changed. Today the feeling is widespread that science and commerce should not—must not—mix. There is a queasy suspicion that the process of discovery is in some way corrupted if it is driven by profit.

This week saw two things that reflect this suspicion, which for many people is hardening into unshakeable conviction. One was the unease that greeted publication of the sequence of the human genome. The other was a report by Oxfam, a British charity, on the plight of people in the third world, too poor to buy the western medicines they need to stay healthy. The cases may seem unconnected, but they are not. The underlying issue is the same, and goes to the heart of the debate over science and profit: what are the terms on which scientific knowledge can be owned?

Performance Bonus

In the case of the genome, two groups have been in contention: one funded mainly by taxpayers, dedicated to the public good; the other funded privately, dedicated to the pursuit of profit. The race was acrimonious—with one side charging that the genome is the heritage of mankind, and the other seeking to establish commercial rights over it. The Oxfam report thumps away in more traditional style, denouncing western capitalism and complaining that drug companies concentrate on treatments for rich-world diseases, leaving the poor to fend for themselves, and that they keep their prices too high. In both cases, it is alleged, the ignoble search for profit distorts and corrupts.

4   These accusations are ill-conceived. Needless to say, not all science should be, or can be, driven by profit. Some fields of research are done to satisfy man's spiritual, rather than material, appetites. They seek answers to the sorts of "how did we get here?" questions which earlier generations confronted with religion. Another kind of knowledge may be useful and practical, yet too diffuse to be owned. This constitutes what economists call a pure public good. Pure public goods, when costly to produce, are nowadays funded by taxpayers and provided by governments—because, for the most part, they have to be. That leaves the rest: a fabulous vista of scientific, and commercial, opportunity.

The problem with the genome is that when it moved from the second category to the third, it took the scientists in the public project by surprise. The founders of Celera Genomics found a way to profit from the genome—or, to be more accurate, from carefully annotated and ingeniously packaged descriptions of bits of it, which drug companies are happy to buy. As a result, they got a move on. They did their work faster and in some ways better than their public-sector rivals—who would probably still be plodding towards their goal had they not had the spur of competition. The public researchers complain that Celera drew on public knowledge in order to advance their private goals. So it did—that is what public knowledge is for.

However, the genome remains a common heritage. Celera's activities do not stop other people using that public knowledge—and even packaging it for sale in other ways than those done by the firm. Genomes are not inventions and cannot be patented. Celera has no proprietary rights over the human genome per se, just over its version of that genome. In short, Celera's pursuit of profit has been good for science, and for man.

Difficult technical questions about the design of patents for particular genes (which are allowed) still need to be resolved. Any company seeking to assert ownership of scientific knowledge needs to be held to the traditional tests: advances should be original, non-obvious and useful. This standard has not always been rigorously applied. But none of this alters the basic fact that, in genome research, science and profit have mixed very productively.

8   The question of third-world drugs is undeniably more vexed—but impugning the profit motive is a fatuously inadequate answer. If not for the lure of profit, the drugs that Oxfam wants sent to developing countries would not exist in the first place. Now that the drugs have been developed, it is often argued, the cost of manufacture is, in most cases, much lower than the price charged. This is gouging, the indictment goes on: drug companies could make money even if they sold the drugs much more cheaply. Again, because of profit, the benefits of science are being withheld.

Nonsense. Developing drugs is expensive. If companies are to keep trying, they must expect to make enough profit to meet the cost of developing not only the drugs that work, but also the ones that do not. Consider another point. Presumably, as good profit-maximisers, firms would be willing to increase their sales in the third world, even at knock-down prices, if they could maintain their profits in the West. They suspect, with reason, that demands would soon arise for prices to be cut there too; "grey" re-importing would increase, as well. These concerns deserve to be taken seriously.

The case for much more generous provision of life-saving drugs to the developing countries is irresistible both morally and as a matter of economics. But it is naive, wrong and in the long run counter-productive, to expect the cost of this aid to be met out of drug-company profits. Instead, rich-world taxpayers should pay. It would be much better to spend aid money on drugs for developing countries than it is to waste it in the usual ways.

Far from compromising science, profit in both these cases—the development of new medicines and the elucidation of the genome—has animated it, and directed it towards meeting pressing human needs. It is a happy marriage. Davy and Pasteur would surely have approved.

Personal Response

Do you think, as many do, that "science and commerce should not—must not—mix" (paragraph 1)? Explain your answer.

Questions for Class or Small-Group Discussion

1. In reference to the plight of people in developing countries who are too poor to buy lifesaving medicines produced in the West, the article states: "[This is] the

heart of the debate over science and profit: what are the terms on which scientific knowledge can be owned?" (paragraph 2). How would you answer that question?

2. Respond to this statement: "The question of third-world drugs is undeniably more vexed—but impugning the profit motive is a fatuously inadequate answer" (paragraph 8). To what extent do you agree?

3. Comment on the proposal that not drug companies but "rich-world taxpayers should pay" for sending drugs to Third World countries: "It would be much better to spend aid money on drugs for developing countries than it is to waste it in the usual ways" (paragraph 10). To what extent do you agree that taxpayers and not the drug companies who discovered and produced the medicine should pay for sending it to those who cannot pay? What do you think the author means by the reference to wasting aid money "in the usual ways"?

AIDS FIGHT BOILS DOWN TO DOLLARS VS. LIVES

Tom Fiedler

Tom Fiedler covered government and politics for the Miami Herald *for twenty-five years before becoming Editorial Page Editor in 1998. He is coauthor of* Almanac of Florida Politics 2000: The Comprehensive Guide to Power, Places & Policymakers *(2000). Fiedler was in Brazil as a Pew Fellow in International Journalism when he wrote this article, which appeared in the June 24, 2001, issue of the* Miami Herald.

What if I told you that it is possible to curtail the most murderous disease to hit the world since the Bubonic Plague swept Europe in the Middle Ages; that even developing nations can master the techniques and can be positioned to afford it; that as a result millions of children will not be born with the disease, that millions more won't be left as orphans; that nations will not collapse under population and economic loss; that civilization as it is known in some parts of the globe won't go backward?

All this is true because I have seen proof of it here in Brazil.

But what if I told you that all these positive things face a towering obstacle before they may occur and it is this: Us.

4   To be specific, it is all of us acting collectively through the U.S. government. That's a harsh assessment, I know, and perhaps not entirely fair given the efforts that this country has made in myriad ways to bring an end to this plague called AIDS. But when viewed from the eyes of people who live in much of the rest of the world, the U.S. government has deliberately sided against those who have the means to virtually stop the growth of AIDS, which in time will almost certainly lead to a diminution in its effects.

And we are doing so in the name of protecting the huge profits—some call them obscene profits—of the major pharmaceutical companies in the United States that make some of the drugs that go into the "cocktails" that have proven so effective in allowing people with HIV/AIDS to continue living and participating in society.

All these issues have come to a head here in Brazil, a vast but underdeveloped nation of 170 million that has through sheer commitment become the world's model for dealing with this modern plague. Barely a decade ago the World Bank estimated that by 2000 this country would have 1.2 million people with HIV/AIDS. That statistic terrified the political and civil leadership, which responded by putting into place a program of prevention and treatment that has no rival. On the prevention side, Brazil, although nominally the world's largest Roman Catholic nation, has few if any hang-ups about openly discussing sex. Children learn about sexually transmitted diseases beginning in schools at age 7; Catholic priests in some parts of the country not only tolerate discussions of prevention, they distribute condoms and conduct classes themselves. Every year, the government also gives away $200 million worth of condoms through health clinics and programs.

But preventing AIDS, though critical, was but half the program. The government also pledged in 1996 that everyone with HIV/AIDS would receive free treatment, including the complex therapies that include taking numerous drugs under rigid conditions. The complexity of the program has been staggering, and the results no less so. Instead of 1.2 million people suffering with the virus, only 500,000 are estimated now to have it. Of these, 100,000 are in active treatment, the others not yet diagnosed.

8   In other words, the plague's casualties are below half the best estimates. And in this sort of work, success breeds success because infected people under treatment are much less apt to infect others, slowing the spread. But here is the catch: Brazil—and any country that hopes to follow its lead, especially those in Africa being devastated by the plague—may find further success blocked because they can't afford to pay for new therapies that carry astronomical price tags.

These drugs aren't expensive because of the cost to develop and manufacture them (many were actually invented at public universities using grants from taxpayers). Rather they're expensive because some of the pharmaceutical giants that market them demand huge profits, estimated by Brazil's health minister, Jose Sera, at up to 10 times cost, or 1,000 percent. And so far they've been able to get away with this because they hold patents on the drugs—essentially government-granted monopolies that keep others from copying them and selling them for pennies on the dollar. Let's be clear: The drug companies must be allowed to hold these monopolies for a certain period of time to enable them to recover their costs of development and to earn more money to invent other drugs. But the question here is how much is a fair profit? Put starkly, how many people must die without treatment until the companies are willing to lower their prices or to surrender their patents so generic makers can enter the market? Brazil answered this question in a law it passed in 1996 saying three years of a patent was enough. After that point, Brazil's law said that a local company could copy the formula and make a generic of that drug. Brazil also argued that this was the moral thing to do. In a series of newspaper advertisements aimed at American readers this month, Brazilians argued: "The drugs industry see this as an act of war. We see it as an act of life."

Incredibly, though, it isn't the drug companies that are taking on the fight to stop Brazil from making cheap substitutes for the new AIDS drugs: It is the U.S. government. Although started under the Clinton administration, the Bush administration is now asking the World Trade Organization's court to declare Brazil's law a violation of "intellectual property rights." Government officials argue, somewhat bashfully, that this isn't about AIDS, but it's about protecting trade agreements.

12   Bunk. Rather than trying to force Brazil to back down, the Bush administration should be on the other side, pushing the drug makers to agree to minimal profits, perhaps for concessions on other drugs where the stakes are clearly less high. There will be many other opportunities for this country to fight for the principles of private property, and we must. But this is an opportunity to fight for millions of people whose lives are in the balance today.

Brazil is on their side. We should join.

Personal Response

What are your thoughts on the issue addressed here?

Questions for Class or Small-Group Discussion

1. Fiedler writes: "The drug companies must be allowed to hold these monopolies for a certain period of time. [...] But the question here is how much is a fair profit?" (paragraph 9). To what extent do you agree with him that drug companies should be allowed to hold monopolies? How would you answer the question about what a fair profit is?

2. Comment on this statement from the Brazilian government in regard to their law allowing a local company to copy the formula for AIDS medicine: " 'The drugs industry see this as an act of war. We see it as an act of life' " (paragraph 9).

3. Fiedler argues that the U.S. government should be on the side of the countries who cannot afford the necessary medicine. It should, he writes, be "pushing the drug makers to agree to minimal profits" and joining in the "fight for millions of people whose lives are in the balance today" (paragraph 12). Comment on Fiedler's argument. Does he oversimplify the problem in order to make his point? Is he too quick to dismiss the viewpoint of the drugmakers? Are you persuaded by his argument?

PERSPECTIVES ON PUBLIC HEALTH

Suggestions for Synthesis

1. Drawing on Johanna McGeary's "Death Stalks a Continent" and Faith McLellan's "Human Rights: A Critical Framework for the Response to HIV/AIDS" write a paper

arguing that "the empowerment of women [is] critical to controlling the [AIDS] epidemic" ("Human Rights," paragraph 2).

2. Drawing on "Science and Profit" and Tom Fiedler's "AIDS Fight Boils Down to Dollars vs. Lives," argue either for or against the right of pharmaceutical companies to hold patents (and continue to make large profits) on drugs that could help fight AIDS in countries such as South Africa and Brazil.

3. Compare and contrast the approaches toward HIV/AIDS in Africa and Brazil, using information from Johanna McGeary's "Death Stalks a Continent" and Tom Fiedler's "AIDS Fight Boils Down to Dollars vs. Lives."

Additional Writing Topics

1. Write an essay in response to either The *Economist* article, "Science and Profit," or Tom Fiedler's "AIDS Fight Boils Down to Dollars vs. Lives."

2. Argue for or against the statement that science and commerce must not mix ("Science and Profit").

3. Explain your views on how best to educate the public about preventing sexually transmitted diseases. Or explain the role you believe schools and other public institutions should play in disseminating information about sexually transmitted diseases.

4. Argue either for or against programs to distribute free condoms to high school students.

5. If you know someone with AIDS or another grave illness, describe that person's condition, the problems it poses for the person's family, and your concerns about the person and the illness.

Research Topics

1. Research the viewpoints of drug companies, economists, and health workers, among others, on this question: Should drug companies bear the financial burden of sending lifesaving drugs to developing countries?

2. Research the contributions of either Sir Humphry Davy or Louis Pasteur in terms of not only his contributions to science but also in relation to the question of the relation of profit to science, as discussed in "Science and Profit."

3. In combination with library and Internet research, interview public health officials or representatives from the health center at your campus about a public health issue. Narrow your focus to one aspect of public health and explain your own view on the topic.

4. Research the controversy over government funding for AIDS research.

5. Research the competition between the public Human Genome Project and the private Celera Genomics in their race to get the "rough draft" of the human genome finished. What are the issues involved in that competition? How fierce was the rivalry? What is the status of the relationship between the two groups now that their initial goal has been accomplished?

6. Research and assess the importance or success of the work of either a national health agency, such as the U.S. Centers for Disease Control (CDC), or an international health agency, such as the World Health Organization (WHO).

7. Research some aspect of the AIDS epidemic in the United States (or another country) and responses by public health officials to the disease. You will discover many controversies on this subject, so identify one major controversy, explore the issues involved, and arrive at your own position on the subject. You may want to take a historical approach, for instance, by exploring various theories on the origin of AIDS, or you may want to focus on controversial treatments for the disease.

8. Research a major plague from the past, such as the bubonic plague in thirteenth- and fourteenth-century Europe, cholera epidemics, the smallpox epidemic that swept Sweden in 1764, the typhus epidemic that killed more than three million Russians during World War I, or the influenza plague of 1918 to 1919 that killed more than 20 million people around the world. Determine the consequences for the country (or countries) affected by the plague as well as its possible origins and how it was finally conquered.

CHAPTER 22
ENVIRONMENTAL STUDIES

Environmental issues such as depletion of the ozone layer, global warming, deforestation, and air and water pollution are just a few of the many causes for concern over the health of animal and vegetable life on Earth. Closely connected to these environmental problems is the rapid rate of increase in the world population. As the number of people grows, pressure increases on natural resources. Will Earth provide enough food for everyone? How can water supplies be kept safe for drinking? How does pollution produced by so many humans affect the quality of the air they breathe? How can people stop the ever-widening hole in the ozone layer that protects us from the harmful rays of the sun? How will future generations sustain the rapidly increasing worldwide population? These are just some of the questions confronting scientists, civic leaders, and ordinary people everywhere.

Although most people recognize that humans must keep their environments safe, not everyone agrees on either the nature of the problems or the severity of their consequences. For instance, resource depletion and global warming are the subjects of many debates. Researchers and scientists differ in their beliefs on questions such as Earth's ability to sustain life indefinitely and whether Earth is experiencing global warming and, if so, whether the phenomenon is cause for alarm.

In the first piece in this chapter, Aaron Sachs profiles the nineteenth-century scientist Baron Alexander von Humboldt, who, he says, is "the man most responsible for bringing the practice of science into mainstream Western culture." In "Humboldt's Legacy and the Restoration of Science," Sachs maintains that modern science would do well to adopt Humboldt's integrated vision of nature. He laments the relatively low federal allocation for furthering the understanding of the environment, and he believes that ecologists and environmentalists should adopt a broader, interdisciplinary approach to environmental problems.

Next is an essay offering practical guides to conservation in a number of areas. Paul Hawken, in "A Declaration of Sustainability," suggests actions for both individuals and groups to help the environment. According to his "strategies for sustainability," Hawken offers "twelve steps society can take to save the whole enchilada." As you read both Sachs's and Hawken's essays, think about what you already do to conserve resources and help curb environmental problems and whether these writers persuade you to do even more.

The *American Spectator* editorial, "The Galileo of Global Warming," presents critical view of environmentalists, at least those who maintain that humans are responsible for global warming. The article reviews some of the issues concerning global warning and reports on the findings of scientist Lloyd Keigwin, whose research about Earth's climate discredit the theory that it is humans who cause global warming.

D. Grant DeMan, on the other hand, maintains that he has done all he could to be friendly to the environment but is still being bombarded with messages to do more. He asserts that he is fed up with all of those who warn about the dire consequences of careless use of resources. In "Out, Damn Naturalists," he describes his efforts to be environmentally responsible and adds his opinion of environmental activists.

HUMBOLDT'S LEGACY AND THE RESTORATION OF SCIENCE

Aaron Sachs

Aaron Sachs is a research associate at Worldwatch Institute. He is author of Eco-Justice: Linking Human Rights and the Environment *(1994). He is coauthor of* The Next Efficiency Revolution: Creating a Sustainable Materials Economy *(1990) and* State of the World 1995. *This essay is from the March/April 1995 issue of* World Watch *magazine.*

On September 15, 1869, the *New York Times* ran a one-word headline: "HUMBOLDT." Every literate American knew the name. "The One Hundredth Birthday of the Philosopher," explained the subtitle. "Celebration Generally Throughout the Country." The story took up the entire front page.

It is unthinkable today that Americans would celebrate the birthday of any dead philosopher, let alone a foreign one. Yet from San Francisco to Peoria to New York, on that Tuesday afternoon, people read speeches, unrolled banners, and unveiled statues in honor of the late Baron Alexander von Humboldt. Of course, Humboldt was much more than a philosopher: He was also an explorer, a geographer, a writer, a naturalist—and the man most responsible for bringing the practice of science into mainstream Western culture.

The word *scientist* first entered the English language in the 1830s, specifically in reference to Humboldt and his disciples—Charles Darwin among them. Originally, then, the term meant "natural scientist." The new profession Humboldt had carved out and popularized took as its goal the transformation of natural history studies, to cover not just the detailed cataloging of the phenomena of the physical world, but also the formulation of a grand, unifying theory that would link all those phenomena together. Humboldt wanted to know what tied the rivers to the trees, how climate influenced vegetation, why particular animals thrived only in particular habitats; he also wanted to reveal humanity's place within these interdependent relationships. And in an early nineteenth-century culture of amateur naturalists obsessed with the romance of the wilderness, his quest struck many chords.

4   Initially, Humboldt earned his fame by exploring the New World between 1799 and 1804, when he surveyed the headwaters of the Orinoco in the jungles of Venezuela and scaled the Andes to heights never before attained in any of the world's mountain ranges. On that trip, between the ages of thirty and thirty-five, the "Rediscoverer of America" witnessed the immense diversity of humanity and nature. He saw just how different life was among the natives of the Venezuelan rainforest and the politicians of the newly formed U.S. Congress—among the insects swarming in marshlands along the Colombian coast and the birds floating above Ecuadorean volcanoes and the wildflowers lining fertile Cuban valleys. Yet he never wavered in his belief that there existed a "chain of connection," that all elements of earthly life, including humans, were "mutually dependent"—and that a knowledge of that interdependence was the "noblest and most important result" of all scientific inquiry. For the last fifty-five years of his life—he lived to age ninety—he struggled to "recognize unity in the vast diversity of physical phenomena." While acknowledging the world's chaos, he saw within it what the ancient Greeks called a *kosmos,* a beautifully ordered and harmonious system, and he coined the modern word *cosmos* to use as the title of his final, multivolume work—a book Walt Whitman kept on his desk as he was writing *Leaves of Grass.*

Today, most environmentalists would be shocked to learn that nature's interrelationships were once in the mainstream of scientific thought. The dominant theme in science over the past century has been *fission,* the breaking down of life and matter and ideas into their smaller components: Life science and its organic theories have given way to specialization, to microbiology and nuclear physics. In our rush to gain in-depth knowledge about particular elements of a complicated, seemingly chaotic world, we have tacitly decided that it would be futile to try to tie those elements together. Science has lost its delicate balance between chaos and cosmos, between diversity and unity.

It now seems clear that this century-old imbalance is inextricably linked to our global ecological crisis. If we assume that the world on which we depend is utterly chaotic, there is no reason to do anything but try to control and conquer it—which has become science's new goal. And though specialization has proved itself invaluable in the pursuit of knowledge, its narrow, short-range focus, in the absence of a complementary organic approach, is extremely dangerous. We have directed society's accumulated scientific knowledge toward constantly improving our exploitation of each individual natural resource, without recognizing the threat we are posing to the basic ecosystems that create those resources. As Rachel Carson observed in her classic *Silent Spring,* we failed to predict the environmental impacts of extensive pesticide use because chemical companies paid researchers simply to kill pests—and not to worry about the pesticides' effects on other plants and animals, or groundwater supplies, or farmworkers' lungs. Perhaps the highest goal of the environmental movement, then, is to reclaim science, to ensure that we use it not for the domination of nature but for the appreciation of our connectedness to it—to restore, in other words, the legacy that Humboldt tried to leave us.

In the nineteenth century, Humboldt's appeal was wide-ranging. Many people saw him as the world's historian, the man who would explain where we came from and how we fit into the universe. He provided an enthralled public with glimpses of exotic natural worlds they would never see for themselves. Scholars flocked to his study in Germany to soak up his wisdom, to examine his field notes and sprawling maps and native artifacts. And laypeople gathered at the newly opened natural history museums to which Humboldt had donated his famous collections of intricate jungle plants and multicolored birds. By organizing lectures and workshops all over the world, he made huge numbers of people feel involved in the progress of science. Moreover, his theories themselves were attractive for their inclusiveness, their ambitious attempts at painting a unified picture of all the world's complexities.

8   Just as every lowly plant and minute insect had a crucial role in Humboldt's vision of the world, so too did every type of human being, no matter how powerless or marginalized. Humboldt was a hero to Simon Bolivar, who used the scientist's writings in his campaigns for Latin American independence, to help prove that colonialism was wreaking havoc on both the people and the environment of the New World. And Humboldt was especially popular among Americans, by the time of the 1869 centennial, because he had been one of the world's most outspoken opponents of slavery. "In maintaining the unity of the human race," he had written, "we also reject the disagreeable assumption of superior and inferior peoples." Four years after the end of the Civil War, Americans found in Humboldt's scientific work a parallel to the political heroism of President Lincoln. Both men had staked everything on the concept of Union.

In 1869, Humboldt was as well-known and respected, globally, as Lincoln and Bolivar; he had been as influential in nineteenth-century science as Beethoven had been in music, as Napoleon had been in politics. Darwin once wrote that "my whole career is due to having read and reread" Humboldt's *Personal Narrative to the Equinoctial Regions of America,* and he often sent his manuscripts to the older scientist for comment. When the great theoretician of evolution set off on his voyage aboard *The Beagle,* he brought with him only three books: the Bible, a copy of Milton, and Humboldt's *Narrative.* Humboldt's magnum opus, *Cosmos,* bore the daunting subtitle, "A Sketch of a Physical Description of the Universe," and it had an index that

ran to more than one thousand pages. But it was translated into all the major languages and sold hundreds of thousands of copies. "The demand is epoch-making,"
Humboldt's publisher claimed. "Book parcels destined for London and St. Petersburg
were torn out of our hands by agents who wanted their orders filled for the bookstores
in Vienna and Hamburg." Science, it seems, could easily have gone in the direction
Humboldt was taking it.

Today, Humboldt's name is woven tightly into our geographical fabric: The index
of a good atlas might list it some twenty-five times, referring not only to towns like
Humboldt, Iowa, and Humboldt, South Dakota, but also to the Humboldt Mountains
in China, Venezuela, and Nevada; the Humboldt Current off the coast of Peru; and
even a Humboldt Glacier in Greenland. But almost no one today has any idea who
Humboldt was.

Science, and Western society in general, underwent a huge transformation toward the end of the nineteenth century. In 1859, Humboldt died, Darwin published
On the Origin of Species, and the modern age was born—though the full implications
of evolution did not become clear until 1871, when Darwin delivered the ultimate
comeuppance of his own species in *The Descent of Man.* The theory of evolution was
revolutionary both because it directly undermined the centuries-old assumption that
there was a divine plan separating human beings from the lowly animals, and because it posed a significant threat to the dearly held Humboldtian notion that nature
was fundamentally a harmonious, unified entity. To most educated Westerners, the
Darwinian concept of "the struggle for existence" meant that humanity's origins were
steeped in animal violence and conflict—that the different facets of nature were not
working together to form an organic whole but were competing with each other, fighting over ecological niches, fighting just to survive.

12   The one redeeming element of Darwinism, for many shocked Victorians, was that
their civilization had at least seemed to come out of the competition victorious. In
the hands of so-called Social Darwinists, "the struggle for existence" became "the
survival of the fittest," and theorizers were quick to assert that Darwin's explanation
of biological fitness proved the superiority of white, Christian Europeans. After all,
they argued, a careful reading of *On the Origin of Species* revealed that the successful animals were those that had bodies perfectly designed to perform a particular
function or adapt to a particular environment. The key to a species' success, in other
words, was *specialization*—a word Darwin probably coined in the 1840s. And Europeans were without question becoming the world's experts in specialization.

By the second half of the nineteenth century, specialization was beginning to
seep into almost every aspect of Western culture and thought. Graduate schools were
offering highly specialized training in narrow professions. Huge new businesses were
dividing their production processes into the smallest possible components, with the
aim of improving efficiency and becoming more fit competitors in the capitalist economy. Laborers no longer saw products through from start to finish, but rather performed their one limited function, over and over again. By the turn of the century,
someone had to coin the term *Renaissance man* to refer to that rare person who

hearkened back to the era before intense specialization was the norm, back when most people cultivated a variety of linked interests and skills.

Gradually, Humboldt's bigger picture came to seem neither appealing nor important, since specialization was paying off so well by making labor and the exploitation of nature so much more efficient. Now, Darwinists reasoned, man might be on his way to breaking his connections with animal savagery and freeing himself from all the other harsh forces of nature. Evolutionary progress came to mean the conquest of the natural world by science and technology, and distancing oneself from nature became a cultural imperative. Survival depended on winning an all-out competition with other living things—including other members of our own species. And knowledge depended on the ability to observe nature purely as object, as something unrelated to us and best understood when broken down mechanistically into its smallest components.

The embrace of Darwinism and the transformation of science, then, went hand in hand with rapid industrialization, the rise of free-market capitalism, and the expansion of colonialism. Social Darwinists defended empire-building on the grounds that vigorous self-aggrandizement was only natural. And they used similar arguments to validate their racism: The affluence and technological prowess of the Western world, they argued, proved that the races and nations of the "Third World" really were "less developed." As C. S. Lewis, the British writer and critic, once pointed out, the ironies of this new world order ran deep: "At the moment, then, of man's victory over nature, we find the whole human race subjected to some individual men, and individuals subjected to that in themselves which is purely 'natural'—to their irrational impulses." The leaders of a culture that worshipped civilization and science were calmly calling for the massacre or repression of several indigenous nations in the Americas, the methodical deforestation of the United States, and the military invasion of most of Africa.

16   Of course, given Humboldt's direct influence on Darwin, there had to be elements of the theory of evolution that hearkened back to the elder scientist's approach. Indeed, the most significant implication of the *Origin* may have been its assertion that man, on the most fundamental level, was but a part of nature—as Humboldt had argued for decades. Some nineteenth-century thinkers, accordingly, managed to find in evolutionary theory a spirit of cooperation and union. To the author and naturalist W. H. Hudson, for instance, Darwin's work mean that "we are no longer isolated, standing like starry visitors on a mountain-top, surveying life from the outside; but are on a level with and part and parcel of it."

Darwin was fascinated with the idea of nature as a "web"—"we may all be netted together," he mused in the late 1830s—and strong ecological currents run through many of his early writings. The word *oecologie* was in fact coined in 1866 by Germany's foremost Darwinian scientist, Ernst Haeckel. And when Haeckel defined his new scientific discipline, he invoked his mentor by name: ecology, he explained, was "the body of knowledge concerning the economy of nature . . . , the study of all those complex interrelations referred to by Darwin."

In the end, however, Darwin chose to focus on the violent, competitive aspects of his theory. He was explicitly lending his support to the colonialist ethic when he asserted the evolutionary doctrine that an "endless number of lower races" had to be "beaten and supplanted" by "the higher civilized races." Such competitive replacement was inevitable, Darwin argued, because niches in the economy of nature were only so big—as he had learned from the work of the Reverend Thomas Malthus. To Darwin, Malthus's 1798 *Essay on Population* proved that no species could rely on the myth of nature's abundance. Since our population seems to grow at a much faster rate than our food supply, Malthus argued, human society is destined to face starvation on a massive scale. Darwin made this doomsday theme the engine of his theory of evolution: Crises caused by environmental constraints brutally forced out the species that could not compete. He considered it part of his mission to convince naive Romantics that, in the words of the evolutionary biologist Stephen Jay Gould, "we should never have sought solace or moral instruction in Nature."

Humboldt, conversely, held up the natural world as a model, as something worthy of our ultimate respect. In his writings, he sought "to depict the contemplation of natural objects as a means of exciting a pure love of nature." Yet he was no naive Romantic. Just as Darwin recognized the organicist ecological perspective, so too did Humboldt recognize the elements of violence, competition, and disunity in nature. After all, he had cut his way through the swarming, dripping jungles of South America, had witnessed such bizarre events as the mass electrocution of several horses by a colony of eels—and he had seen men enslaving other men. While Darwin focused on the disunity, though, and the specialized adaptations of species to local environments, Humboldt focused on the unity, and the global forces that link different environments and their inhabitants together. Both perspectives reveal important truths. Humboldt's ideas were marginalized simply because Darwin's were more fit in the late nineteenth century—because Darwinism in effect captured the essence of the modernizing Western world.

20   In general, Humboldt's work is still marginalized, but where it is known, experts accept it as good, hard science. One representative contribution he made to the development of ecology was his theory relating the geographical distribution of plants to the effects of climate—a radical idea that remains a cornerstone of our understanding of plant ecosystems. At the base of peaks like Mount Chimborazo in the Ecuadorean Andes, he found the vines and bright orchids and tall hardwoods of the rainforest, while on the snowclad summit he found only the hardiest mosses and lichens. On mountain after mountain, vegetation got sparser at higher altitudes, as if during his ascent he were walking from the equator to one of the poles: vertical geography mirrored horizontal geography. Humboldt was the first to classify forests as tropical, temperate, or boreal. Climate, he realized, seemed to govern the development of life everywhere; all plants and animals were "subject to the same laws" of temperature.

Humboldt had traveled to a continent less touched by human influence in order to look into the past and discover the forces that had shaped nature into its present form. "In the New World," he wrote, "man and his productions almost disappear amidst the stupendous display of wild, and gigantic nature. . . . On no other part of the globe is [the naturalist] called upon more powerfully to raise himself to general ideas on the cause of phenomena and their mutual connection." This historical technique and his "habit of viewing the Globe as a great whole" allowed Humboldt to identify climate as a unifying global force, proving, in a sense, that we all live under the same roof. Changes in one locale, he pointed out, might cause, or at least signal, changes somewhere else. And by drawing lines on the map connecting points with the same mean temperature—he coined the word *isotherm*—he established permanent scientific structures that would enable future generations to think globally. Humboldt's innovations in the field of comparative climatology underlie current attempts to understand the threat of global warming.

Long before any suspicion of change in the atmosphere, Humboldt was worrying about the effect of humanity's actions on terra firma; his knowledge of ecology translated into a nascent environmentalism. Again, the New World taught him an important lesson. European systems of commerce insulated the wealthy from the ecological consequences of their consumption, but the less developed economies of the Americas could not hide their dependence on surrounding natural systems. A year in Mexico, for instance, showed Humboldt that "the produce of the earth is in fact the sole basis of permanent opulence"—and that we could not afford to use that produce wastefully.

Studying a lake in Venezuela, Humboldt used his ecological perspective to relate the lake's decline to the deforestation of the surrounding watershed. Once deprived of the trees' root systems, he explained, the surrounding soils had a greatly diminished capacity for water retention, so they could no longer recharge the springs that fed the lake. And, meanwhile, because the area was deforested, "the waters falling in rain are no longer impeded in their course; and instead of slowly augmenting the level of the rivers by progressive filtrations, they furrow [the hillsides with] sudden inundations," causing widespread soil erosion. "Hence it results that the destruction of the forests, the want of permanent springs, and the existence of torrents are three phenomena closely connected together." Humboldt saw the social consequences as well: "by felling trees . . . , men in every climate prepare at once two calamities for future generations: the want of fuel and a scarcity of water."

24   Humboldt's fear of resource scarcity reflects his own reading of Malthus's essay, which he called "one of the most profound works of political economy ever written." Yet Humboldt's analysis of environmental limits was far more sophisticated than Malthus's: To Humboldt, increases in resource consumption reflected not inevitable demographic pressures but simple, conscious decisions. If our population increased to several billion, then perhaps our basic needs might become too much for the earth to handle, but Humboldt realized that the resource scarcities of his own day were caused by overconsumption and mismanagement. Those trees in Venezuela didn't have to be chopped down.

Even more radical was Humboldt's interest in linking such problems to the injustices of colonialism. In his analysis of the resource base of Mexico, which he published as *A Political Essay on the Kingdom of New Spain*—and which ventured into the fields of demography, medicine, anthropology, sociology, political science, economics, agriculture, biology, geology, and geography—Humboldt took great pains to show that it was not necessary for so many Mexicans to go without land and food. His multifaceted approach helped him to see that such outrages were being driven not by population pressures but by basic socioeconomic structures. Many peasants were landless, he explained, because "the property in New Spain . . . is in a great measure in the hands of a few powerful families who have gradually absorbed the smaller estates." And impoverished Mexicans were starving because wealthy landlords grew cash crops for export instead of food crops for domestic consumption. "Whenever the soil can produce both indigo and maize," Humboldt noted indignantly, "the former prevails over the latter, although the general interest requires that a preference be given to those vegetables which supply nourishment to man over those which are merely objects of exchange with strangers."

Humboldt was still a man of his time: In general, he approved of the development of the New World, and he never openly demanded that the Spanish American colonies receive full independence. But his interdisplinary research did lead him to a scathing critique of colonialism. With the conviction of one who knows his subject thoroughly, Humboldt asserted that "the restless and suspicious colonial policies of the nations of Europe . . . have thrown insurmountable obstacles in the way of the . . . prosperity of their distant possessions. . . . A colony has for ages been considered useful to the parent state only in so far as it supplied a great number of raw materials." Because Humboldt was so aware of the interpendent relationships that governed the world, his science could never have been used to validate dominance over other people or the environment; he knew the Europeans' abuse of other lands would come back to haunt them. Later in the nineteenth century, politicians would repeatedly refer to Darwinism in claiming that certain human and natural resources were expendable for the sake of the evolutionary progress of "the higher civilized races." But according to Humboldt, nothing was expendable.

Today, the destruction of the developing world's environment—the burning of the rainforest, the strip-mining of mountain ranges, the appropriation of valuable croplands for the raising of tradable commodities—is still largely driven by the demands of the world's wealthiest countries. The structure of the global economy dictates that developing nations put all their efforts into raising cash—usually by exporting whatever virgin resources the industrial world might desire. They need the cash to pay off their "debt."

28   Even Humboldt accepted Darwinian conflict and chaos as basic facts of life. The whole time he was working on *Cosmos*—during the last thirty years of his life—he knew that the grand, unifying theory he sought was unattainable, because the world was too complicated and chaotic and contingent. "Experimental sciences," he wrote, "based on the observation of the external world, cannot aspire to completeness; the nature of things, and the imperfection of our organs, are alike opposed to it. . . . The attempt perfectly to represent unity in diversity must therefore necessarily prove unsuccessful."

The existence of chaos, however, does not invalidate the search for a cosmos. "Even a partial solution," Humboldt wrote, "—the tendency toward a comprehension of the phenomena of the universe—will not the less remain the eternal and sublime aim of every investigation of nature." And modern chaos theory has in fact demonstrated that beneath almost every manifestation of disorder lurks some sort of pattern or equilibrium. As Daniel Botkin, author of *Discordant Harmonies: A New Ecology for the Twenty-First Century*, has noted, it is important for us to realize, with Darwin, that nature is not calm and balanced but rather constantly changing; but we must also understand that "certain rates of change are natural, desirable, and acceptable, while others are not." It is possible to differentiate between natural and unnatural rates of change and to seek to uphold nature's dynamic equilibrium.

Up to now, unfortunately, scientists and policy makers have put far too much emphasis on bracing for disorder—on exploiting and stockpiling natural resources in ever greater quantities, and on stockpiling weapons to defend those resources. The United States, for instance, spends $50 billion annually on the development of defense and space technologies, but less than $2 billion in furthering our understanding of the environment. There is a perfectly straightforward reason why we have more sophisticated techniques for planting land mines in the desert than for planting corn on an erodible hillside.

Restoring the balance of modern science, then, would entail devoting more time and money to the search for order in nature, to the mapping of the world's interconnections. A more prominent, better-funded environmental science could help stop over-exploitation by forcing people to realize that each part of the living world is equally valuable. And a major redistribution of research dollars could produce creative, long-term solutions to the problems inherent in resource extraction. New studies could help us, for instance, to pinpoint sustainable yields from fisheries and water supplies; to harvest crops, including trees, without losing so much soil to erosion; and to harness renewable, efficient forms of energy instead of going to war to ensure a steady supply of oil.

32   In lobbying for the research dollars they deserve, ecologists and environmentalists should begin by spreading an ethic of interdisciplinary cooperation. Their unique perspective, which emphasizes holistic, synthetic thinking, is crucial to scientists and developers alike, who need to understand the full impacts of their work over the long term. Even more important, though, ecologists and environmentalists should extend their interdisciplinary approach to include the public at large. People everywhere need to realize that they have a stake in the direction science is taking. All over the world, people concerned about their environments are already clamoring for more information, so that they can hold developers, corporations, and governments accountable for their actions. But they need more help from the scientists themselves, who too often come across as aloof experts with little interest in the public sphere. Only by bridging the gap between "laypeople" and "specialists," only by building connections among ourselves, will we be able to alter the scientific research agenda and rebuild our connections with the natural world.

So far, what limited success environmentalists have had in broadening their coalitions and garnering more research grants has been due to their eloquent public warnings about the dangers of ignoring the ecological perspective. Over the last few years, for instance, by pointing out that most rainforests are probably nurturing valuable medicines, food crops, fibers, soil-restoring vegetation, or petroleum substitutes, environmentalists have convinced major drug companies and agribusiness firms to join with indigenous peoples in conserving tropical ecosystems. As the wilderness philosopher Aldo Leopold once noted, "To keep every cog and wheel is the first precaution of intelligent tinkering."

Unfortunately, though, ecological warnings sometimes deteriorate into scare tactics, and a public that already has too much to worry about is quickly becoming disdainful of doomsday scenarios. Well-meaning environmentalists too often claim that if we don't do the right thing immediately, we'll end up fighting each other for whatever resources remain—in other words, we'll be stuck in a world of Malthusian scarcity and Darwinian conflict. Yet the goal of ecological thinking should be to offer an alternative to conflict. If environmentalists truly want to restore science's balance, they will have to go beyond warnings and give us a positive reason to take an interest in scientific research priorities. They will have to popularize science the way Humboldt did—by conveying to people the exhilaration of understanding one's place in the world, the "intellectual delight and sense of freedom" that comes of "insight into universal nature."

Humboldt considered himself above all an educator, and his ultimate goal was to teach people a basic love of nature, something today's environmental movement rarely seems to do. All his life, he encouraged people simply to leave their houses and escape their specialized lifestyles, to experience the wide-open land. Once we were surrounded by nature, Humboldt felt sure, an awareness of our dependence on it would arise in us "intuitively . . . , from the contrast we draw between the narrow limits of our own existence and the image of infinity revealed on every side—whether we look upward to the starry vault of heaven, scan the far-stretching plain before us, or seek to trace the dim horizon across the vast expanse of ocean." That intuition of our indebtedness to the natural world, that recognition of our own smallness, should be the force driving scientific research.

Personal Response

What did you know about Humboldt before you read this essay? What is your impression of him now that you have read about his work and his importance?

Questions for Class or Small-Group Discussion

1. Identify a passage or a particular point in this essay that you consider especially significant or intriguing, and explain why you find it so.

2. Sachs writes in paragraph 19 that the perspectives of both Darwin and Humboldt "reveal important truths." Summarize the different perspectives of those two, and then discuss what truths their differing perspectives reveal.

3. Discuss the fact that the United States "spends $50 billion annually on the development of defense and space technologies, but less than $2 billion on furthering our understanding of the environment" (paragraph 30). Are you comfortable with that ordering of priorities? Explain whether you would make any changes in allocations if you had the authority to do so.

4. Sachs maintains that ecologists and environmentalists should spread "an ethic of interdisciplinary cooperation" (paragraph 32). How do you think that might be done?

A DECLARATION OF SUSTAINABILITY

Paul Hawken

Paul Hawken writes frequently of the need for businesses to take social and environmental responsibility. The ideas in this essay, which first appeared in the September/October 1993 issue of Utne Reader, *are from his book* The Ecology of Commerce: A Declaration of Sustainability *(1993) and from* Our Future and the Making of Things *(1994), which he wrote with William McDonough. His latest book is* Natural Capitalism: Creating the Next Industrial Revolution *(1999).*

I recently performed a social audit for Ben & Jerry's Homemade Inc., America's premier socially responsible company. After poking and prodding around, asking tough questions, trying to provoke debate, and generally making a nuisance of myself, I can attest that their status as the leading social pioneer in commerce is safe for at least another year. They are an outstanding company. Are there flaws? Of course. Welcome to planet Earth. But the people at Ben & Jerry's are relaxed and unflinching in their willingness to look at, discuss, and deal with problems.

In the meantime, the company continues to put ice cream shops in Harlem, pay outstanding benefits, keep a compensation ratio of seven to one from the top of the organization to the bottom, seek out vendors from disadvantaged groups, and donate generous scoops of their profit to others. And they are about to overtake their historic rival Häagen-Dazs, the ersatz Scandinavian originator of super-premium ice cream, as the market leader in their category. At present rates of growth, Ben & Jerry's will be a $1 billion company by the end of the century. They are publicly held, nationally recognized, and rapidly growing, in part because Ben wanted to show that a socially responsible company could make it in the normal world of business.

Ben & Jerry's is just one of a growing vanguard of companies attempting to redefine their social and ethical responsibilities. These companies no longer accept the maxim that the business of business is business. Their premise is simple: Corporations, because they are the dominant institution on the planet, must squarely face the social and environmental problems that afflict humankind. Organizations such as

Business for Social Responsibility and the Social Venture Network, corporate "ethics" consultants, magazines such as *In Business* and *Business Ethics,* nonprofits including the Council on Economic Priorities, investment funds such as Calvert and Covenant, newsletters like *Greenmoney,* and thousands of unaffiliated companies are drawing up new codes of conduct for corporate life that integrate social, ethical, and environmental principles.

4   Ben & Jerry's and the roughly two thousand other committed companies in the social responsibility movement here and abroad have combined annual sales of approximately $2 billion, or one-hundredth of 1 percent of the $20 trillion sales garnered by the estimated eighty million to one-hundred million enterprises worldwide. The problems they are trying to address are vast and unremittingly complex: 5.5 billion people are breeding exponentially, and fulfilling their wants and needs is stripping the earth of its biotic capacity to produce life; a climactic burst of consumption by a single species is overwhelming the skies, earth, waters, and fauna.

As the Worldwatch Institute's Lester Brown patiently explains in his annual survey, *State of the World,* every living system on earth is in decline. Making matters worse, we are having a once-in-a-billion-year blowout sale of hydrocarbons, which are being combusted into the atmosphere, effectively double glazing the planet within the next fifty years with unknown climatic results. The cornucopia of resources that are being extracted, mined, and harvested is so poorly distributed that 20 percent of the earth's people are chronically hungry or starving, while the top 20 percent of the population, largely in the north, control and consume 80 percent of the world's wealth. Since business in its myriad forms is primarily responsible for this "taking," it is appropriate that a growing number of companies ask the question, How does one honorably conduct business in the latter days of industrialism and the beginning of an ecological age? The ethical dilemma that confronts business begins with the acknowledgment that a commercial system that functions well by its own definitions unavoidably defies the greater and more profound ethic of biology. Specifically, how does business face the prospect that creating a profitable, growing company requires an intolerable abuse of the natural world?

Despite their dedicated good work, if we examine all or any of the businesses that deservedly earn high marks for social and environmental responsibility, we are faced with a sobering irony: If every company on the planet were to adopt the environmental and social practices of the best companies—of, say, the Body Shop, Patagonia, and Ben & Jerry's—the world would still be moving toward environmental degradation and collapse. In other words, if we analyze environmental effects and create an input–output model of resources and energy, the results do not even approximate a tolerable or sustainable future. If a tiny fraction of the world's most intelligent companies cannot model a sustainable world, then that tells us that being socially responsible is only one part of an overall solution, and that what we have is not a management problem but a design problem.

At present, there is a contradiction inherent in the premise of a socially responsible corporation: to wit, that a company can make the world better, can grow, and can increase profits by meeting social and environmental needs. It is a have-your-cake-and-eat-it fantasy that cannot come true if the primary cause of environmental degradation is overconsumption. Although proponents of socially responsible business are making an outstanding effort at reforming the tired old ethics of commerce, they are unintentionally creating a new rationale for companies to produce, advertise, expand, grow, capitalize, and use up resources: the rationale that they are doing good. A jet flying across the country, a car rented at an airport, an air-conditioned hotel room, a truck full of goods, a worker commuting to his or her job—all cause the same amount of environmental degradation whether they're associated with the Body Shop, the Environmental Defense Fund, or R. J. Reynolds.

8   In order to approximate a sustainable society, we need to describe a system of commerce and production in which each and every act is inherently sustainable and restorative. Because of the way our system of commerce is designed, businesses will not be able to fulfill their social contract with the environment or society until the system in which they operate undergoes a fundamental change, a change that brings commerce and government into alignment with the natural world from which we receive our life. There must be an integration of economic, biologic, and human systems in order to create a sustainable and interdependent method of commerce that supports and furthers our existence. As hard as we may strive to create sustainability on a company level, we cannot fully succeed until the institutions surrounding commerce are redesigned. Just as every act of production and consumption in an industrial society leads to further environmental degradation, regardless of intention or ethos, we need to imagine—and then design—a system of commerce where the opposite is true, where doing good is like falling off a log, where the natural, everyday acts of work and life accumulate into a better world as a matter of course, not a matter of altruism. A system of sustainable commerce would involve these objectives:

1. It would reduce absolute consumption of energy and natural resources among developed nations by 80 percent within forty to sixty years.
2. It would provide secure, stable, and meaningful employment for people everywhere.
3. It would be self-actuating as opposed to regulated, controlled, mandated, or moralistic.
4. It would honor human nature and market principles.
5. It would be perceived as more desirable than our present way of life.
6. It would exceed sustainability by restoring degraded habitats and ecosystems to their fullest biological capacity.
7. It would rely on current solar income.
8. It should be fun and engaging, and strive for an aesthetic outcome.

Strategies for Sustainability

At present, the environmental and social responsibility movements consist of many different initiatives, connected primarily by values and beliefs rather than by design. What is needed is a conscious plan to create a sustainable future, including a set of design strategies for people to follow. For the record, I will suggest twelve.

I. Take Back the Charter.   Although corporate charters may seem to have little to do with sustainability, they are critical to any long-term movement toward restoration of the planet. Read *Taking Care of Business: Citizenship and the Charter of Incorporation,* a 1992 pamphlet by Richard Grossman and Frank T. Adams (Charter Ink, Box 806, Cambridge, MA 02140). In it you find a lost history of corporate power and citizen involvement that addresses a basic and crucial point: Corporations are chartered by, and exist at the behest of, citizens. Incorporation is not a right but a privilege granted by the state that includes certain considerations such as limited liability. Corporations are supposed to be under our ultimate authority, not the other way around. The charter of incorporation is a revocable dispensation that was supposed to ensure accountability of the corporation to society as a whole. When Rockwell criminally despoils a weapons facility at Rocky Flats, Colorado, with plutonium waste, or when any corporation continually harms, abuses, or violates the public trust, citizens should have the right to revoke its charter, causing the company to disband, sell off its enterprises to other companies, and effectively go out of business. The workers would have jobs with the new owners, but the executives, directors, and management would be out of jobs, with a permanent notice on their résumés that they mismanaged a corporation into a charter revocation. This is not merely a deterrent to corporate abuse but a critical element of an ecological society because it creates feedback loops that prompt accountability, citizen involvement, and learning. We should remember that the citizens of this country originally envisioned corporations to be part of a public–private partnership, which is why the relationship between the chartering authority of state legislatures and the corporation was kept alive and active. They had it right.

2. Adjust Price to Reflect Cost.   The economy is environmentally and commercially dysfunctional because the market does not provide consumers with proper information. The "free market" economies that we love so much are excellent at setting prices but lousy when it comes to recognizing costs. In order for a sustainable society to exist, every purchase must reflect or at least approximate its actual costs, not only the direct cost of production but also the costs to the air, water, and soil; the cost to future generations; the cost to worker health; the cost of waste, pollution, and toxicity. Simply stated, the marketplace gives us the wrong information. It tells us that flying across the country on a discount airline ticket is cheap when it is not. It tells us that our food is inexpensive when its method of production destroys aquifers and soil, the viability of ecosystems, and workers' lives. Whenever an organism gets wrong information, it is a form of toxicity. In fact, that is how pesticides work. A herbicide kills because it is a hormone that tells the plant to grow faster than its capacity to absorb nutrients allows. It literally grows itself to death. Sound familiar? Our daily doses of toxicity are the prices in the marketplace. They are telling us to do the wrong thing for our own survival. They are lulling us into cutting down old-growth forests on the Olympic Peninsula for apple crates, into patterns of production and consumption that are not just unsustainable but profoundly shortsighted and destructive. It is surprising that "conservative" economists do not support or understand this idea, because it is they who insist that we pay as we go, have no debts, and take care of business. Let's do it.

12 **3. Throw Out and Replace the Entire Tax System.** The present tax system sends the wrong messages to virtually everyone, encourages waste, discourages conservation, and rewards consumption. It taxes what we want to encourage—jobs, creativity, payrolls, and real income—and ignores the things we want to discourage—degradation, pollution, and depletion. The present U.S. tax system costs citizens $500 billion a year in record-keeping, filing, administrative, legal, and governmental costs—more than the actual amount we pay in personal income taxes. The only incentive in the present system is to cheat or hire a lawyer to cheat for us. The entire tax system must be incrementally replaced over a twenty-year period by "Green fees," taxes that are added onto existing products, energy, services, and materials so that prices in the marketplace more closely approximate true costs. These taxes are not a means to raise revenue or bring down deficits, but must be absolutely revenue neutral so that people in the lower and middle classes experience no real change of income, only a shift in expenditures. Eventually, the cost of nonrenewable resources, extractive energy, and industrial modes of production will be more expensive than renewable resources, such as solar energy, sustainable forestry, and biological methods of agriculture. Why should the upper middle class be able to afford to conserve while the lower income classes cannot? So far the environmental movement has only made the world better for upper middle class white people. The only kind of environmental movement that can succeed has to start from the bottom up. Under a Green fee system the incentives to save on taxes will create positive, constructive acts that are affordable for everyone. As energy prices go up to three to four times their existing levels (with commensurate tax reductions to offset the increase), the natural inclination to save money will result in carpooling, bicycling, telecommuting, public transport, and more efficient houses. As taxes on artificial fertilizers, pesticides, and fuel go up, again with offsetting reductions in income and payroll taxes, organic farmers will find that their produce and methods are the cheapest means of production (because they truly are), and customers will find that organically grown food is less expensive than its commercial cousin. Eventually, with the probable exception of taxes on the rich, we will find ourselves in a position where we pay no taxes, but spend our money with a practiced and constructive discernment. Under an enlightened and redesigned tax system, the cheapest product in the marketplace would be best for the customer, the worker, the environment, and the company. That is rarely the case today.

4. Allow Resource Companies to Be Utilities. An energy utility is an interesting hybrid of public-private interests. A utility gains a market monopoly in exchange for public control of rates, open books, and a guaranteed rate of return. Because of this relationship and the pioneering work of Amory Lovins, we now have markets for "negawatts." It is the first time in the history of industrialism that a corporation has figured out how to make money by selling the absence of something. Negawatts are the opposite of energy: They represent the collaborative ability of a utility to harness efficiency instead of hydrocarbons. This conservation-based alternative saves ratepayers, shareholders, and the company money—savings that are passed along to everyone. All resources systems, including oil, gas, forests, and water, should be run by some form of utility. There should be markets in negabarrels, negatrees, and negacoal. Oil companies, for example, have no alternative at present other than to lobby for the absurd, like drilling in the Arctic National Wildlife Refuge. That project, a $40 billion to $60 billion investment for a hoped-for supply of oil that would meet U.S. consumption needs for only six months, is the only way an oil company can make money under our current system of commerce. But what if the oil companies formed an oil utility and cut a deal with citizens and taxpayers that allowed them to "invest" in insulation, super-glazed windows, conservation rebates on new automobiles, and the scrapping of old cars? Through Green fees, we would pay them back a return on their conservation investment equal to what utilities receive, a rate of return that would be in accord with how many barrels of oil they save, rather than how many barrels they produce. Why should they care? Why should we? A $60 billion investment in conservation will yield, conservatively, four to ten times as much energy as drilling for oil. Given Lovins' principle of efficiency extraction, try to imagine a forest utility, a salmon utility, a copper utility, a Mississippi River utility, a grasslands utility. Imagine a system where the resource utility benefits from conservation, makes money from efficiency, thrives through restoration, and profits from sustainability. It is possible today.

5. Change Linear Systems to Cyclical Ones.   Our economy has many design flaws, but the most glaring one is that nature is cyclical and industrialism is linear. In nature, no linear systems exist, or they don't exist for long because they exhaust themselves into extinction. Linear industrial systems take resources, transform them into products or services, discard waste, and sell to consumers, who discard more waste when they have consumed the product. But of course we don't consume TVs, cars, or most of the other stuff we buy. Instead, Americans produce six times their body weight every week in hazardous and toxic waste water, incinerator fly ash, agricultural wastes, heavy metals, and waste chemicals, paper, wood, etc. This does not include CO_2 which if it were included would double the amount of waste. Cyclical means of production are designed to imitate natural systems in which waste equals food for other forms of life, nothing is thrown away, and symbiosis replaces competition. Bill McDonough, a New York architect who has pioneered environmental design principles, has designed a system to retrofit every window in a major American city. Although it still awaits final approval, the project is planned to go like this: The city and a major window manufacturer form a joint venture to produce energy-saving super-glazed windows in the town. This partnership company will come to your house or business, measure all windows and glass doors, and then replace them with windows with an R-8 to R-12 energy-efficiency rating within seventy-two hours. The windows will have the same casements, molding, and general appearance as the old ones. You will receive a $500 check on installation, and you will pay for the new windows over a ten- to fifteen-year period in your utility or tax bill. The total bill is less than the cost of the energy the windows will save. In other words, the windows will cost the home or business owner nothing. The city will pay for them initially with industrial development bonds. The factory will train and employ three hundred disadvantaged people. The old windows will be completely recycled and reused, the glass melted into glass, the wooden frames ground up and mixed with recycled resins that are extruded to make the casements. When the city is reglazed, the residents and businesses will pocket an extra $20 million to $30 million every year in money saved on utility bills. After the windows are paid for, the figure will go even higher. The factory, designed to be transportable, will move to another city; the first city will retain an equity interest in the venture. McDonough has designed a win-win-win-win-win system that optimizes a number of agendas. The ratepayers, the homeowners, the renters, the city, the environment, and the employed all thrive because they are "making" money from efficiency rather than exploitation. It's a little like running the industrial economy backwards.

6. Transform the Making of Things.   We have to institute the Intelligent Product System created by Michael Braungart of the EPEA (Environmental Protection Encouragement Agency) in Hamburg, Germany. The system recognizes three types of products. The first are consumables, products that are either eaten, or, when they're placed on the ground, turn into dirt without any bio-accumulative effects. In other words, they are products whose waste equals food for other living systems. At present, many of the products that should be "consumable," like clothing and shoes, are not. Cotton cloth contains hundreds of different chemicals, plasticizers, defoliants, pesticides, and dyes; shoes are tanned with chromium and their soles contain lead; neckties and silk blouses contain zinc, tin, and toxic dye. Much of what we recycle today turns into toxic by-products, consuming more energy in the recycling process than is saved by recycling. We should be designing more things so that they can be thrown away—into the compost heap. Toothpaste tubes and other nondegradable packaging can be made out of natural polymers so that they break down and become fertilizer for plants. A package that turns into dirt is infinitely more useful, biologically speaking, than a package that turns into a plastic park bench. Heretical as it sounds, designing for decomposition, not recycling, is the way of the world around us.

16   The second category is *durables,* but in this case, they would not be sold, only licensed. Cars, TVs, VCRs, and refrigerators would always belong to the original manufacturer, so they would be made, used, and returned within a closed-loop system. This is already being instituted in Germany and to a lesser extent in Japan, where companies are beginning to design for disassembly. If a company knows that its products will come back someday, and that it cannot throw anything away when they do, it creates a very different approach to design and materials.

Last, there are *unsalables*—toxins, radiation, heavy metals, and chemicals. There is no living system for which these are food and thus they can never be thrown away. In Braungart's Intelligent Product System, unsalables must always belong to the original maker, safeguarded by public utilities called *parking lots* that store the toxins in glass-lined barrels indefinitely, charging the original manufacturers rent for the service. The rent ceases when an independent scientific panel can confirm that there is a safe method to detoxify the substances in question. All toxic chemicals would have molecular markers identifying them as belonging to their originator, so that if they are found in wells, rivers, soil, or fish, it is the responsibility of the company to retrieve them and clean up. This places the problem of toxicity with the makers, where it belongs, making them responsible for full-life-cycle effects.

7. Vote, Don't Buy.   Democracy has been effectively eliminated in America by the influence of money, lawyers, and a political system that is the outgrowth of the first two. While we can dream of restoring our democratic system, the fact remains that we live in a plutocracy—government by the wealthy. One way out is to vote with your dollars, to withhold purchases from companies that act or respond inappropriately. Don't just avoid buying a Mitsubishi automobile because of the company's participation in the destruction of primary forests in Malaysia, Indonesia, Ecuador, Brazil, Bolivia, Chile, Siberia, and Papua New Guinea. Write and tell them why you won't. Engage in dialogue, send one postcard a week, talk, organize, meet, publish newsletters, boycott, patronize, and communicate with companies like General Electric. Educate nonprofits, organizations, municipalities, and pension funds to act affirmatively, to support the ecological CERES (formerly *Valdez*) Principles for business, to invest intelligently, and to *think* with their money, not merely spend it. Demand the best from the companies you work for and buy from. You deserve it and your actions will help them change.

8. Restore the "Guardian."   There can be no healthy business sector unless there is a healthy governing sector. In her book *Systems of Survival,* author Jane Jacobs describes two overarching moral syndromes that permeate our society: the commercial syndrome, which arose from trading cultures, and the governing, or guardian, syndrome that arose from territorial cultures. The guardian system is hierarchical, adheres to tradition, values loyalty, and shuns trading and inventiveness. The commercial system, on the other hand, is based on trading, so it values trust of outsiders, innovation, and future thinking. Each has qualities the other lacks. Whenever the guardian tries to be in business, as in Eastern Europe, business doesn't work. What is also true, but not so obvious to us, is that when business plays government, governance fails as well. Our guardian system has almost completely broken down because of the money, power, influence, and control exercised by business and, to a lesser degree, other institutions. Business and unions have to get out of government. We need more than campaign reform. We need a vision that allows us all to see that when Speaker of the House Tom Foley exempts the aluminum industry in his district from the proposed Btu tax, or when Philip Morris donates $200,000 to the Jesse Helms Citizenship Center, citizenship is mocked and democracy is left gagging and twitching on the Capitol steps. The irony is that business thinks that its involvement in governance is good corporate citizenship or at least is advancing its own interests. The reality is that business is preventing the economy from evolving. Business loses, workers lose, the environment loses.

20 **9. Shift from Electronic Literacy to Biologic Literacy.** That an average adult can recognize one thousand brand names and logos but fewer than ten local plants is not a good sign. We are moving not to an information age but to a biologic age, and unfortunately our technological education is equipping us for corporate markets, not the future. Sitting at home with virtual reality gloves, 3D video games, and interactive cable TV shopping is a barren and impoverished vision of the future. The computer revolution is not the totem of our future, only a tool. Don't get me wrong. Computers are great. But they are not an uplifting or compelling vision for culture or society. They do not move us toward a sustainable future any more than our obsession with cars and televisions provided us with newer definitions or richer meaning. We are moving into the age of living machines, not, as Corbusier noted, "machines for living in." The Thomas Edison of the future is not Bill Gates of Microsoft, but John and Nancy Todd, founders of the New Alchemy Institute, a Massachusetts design lab and think tank for sustainability. If the Todds' work seems less commercial, less successful, and less glamorous, it is because they are working on the real problem—how to live—and it is infinitely more complex than a microprocessor. Understanding biological processes is how we are going to create a new symbiosis with living systems (or perish). What we can learn on-line is how to model complex systems. It is computers that have allowed us to realize how the synapses in the common sea slug are more powerful than all of our parallel processors put together.

10. Take Inventory. We do not know how many species live on the planet within a factor of ten. We do not know how many are being extirpated. We do not know what is contained in the biological library inherited from the Cenozoic age. (Sociobiologist E. O. Wilson estimates that it would take 25,000 person-years to catalog most of the species, putting aside the fact that there are only 1,500 people with the taxonomic ability to undertake the task.) We do not know how complex systems interact—how the transpiration of the giant lily, *Victoria amazonica,* of Brazil's rainforests affects European rainfall and agriculture, for example. We do not know what happens to 20 percent of the CO_2 that is off-gassed every year (it disappears without a trace). We do not know how to calculate sustainable yields in fisheries and forest systems. We do not know why certain species, such as frogs, are dying out even in pristine habitats. We do not know the long-term effects of chlorinated hydrocarbons on human health, behavior, sexuality, and fertility. We do not know what a sustainable life is for existing inhabitants of the planet, and certainly not for future populations. (A Dutch study calculated that your fair share of air travel is one trip across the Atlantic in a lifetime.) We do not know how many people we can feed on a sustainable basis, or what our diet would look like. In short, we need to find out what's here, who has it, and what we can or can't do with it.

11. Take Care of Human Health.   The environmental and socially responsible movements would gain additional credibility if they recognized that the greatest amount of human suffering and mortality is caused by environmental problems that are not being addressed by environmental organizations or companies. Contaminated water is killing a hundred times more people than all other forms of pollution combined. Millions of children are dying from preventable diseases and malnutrition.

The movement toward sustainability must address the clear and present dangers that people face worldwide, dangers that ironically increase population levels because of their perceived threat. People produce more children when they're afraid they'll lose them. Not until the majority of people in the world, all of whom suffer in myriad preventable yet intolerable ways, understand that environmentalism means improving their lives directly will the ecology movement walk its talk. Americans will spend more money in the next twelve months on the movie and tchotchkes of *Jurassic Park* than on foreign aid to prevent malnutrition or provide safe water.

24   **12. Respect the Human Spirit.**   If hope is to pass the sobriety test, then it has to walk a pretty straight line to reality. Nothing written, suggested, or proposed here is possible unless business is willing to integrate itself into the natural world. It is time for business to take the initiative in a genuinely, open process of dialogue, collaboration, reflection, and redesign. "It is not enough," writes Jeremy Seabrook of the British Green party, "to declare, as many do, that we are living in an unsustainable way, using up resources, squandering the substance of the next generation however true this may be. People must feel subjectively the injustice and unsustainability before they will make a more sober assessment as to whether it is worth maintaining what is, or whether there might not be more equitable and satisfying ways that will not be won at the expense either of the necessities of the poor or of the wasting fabric of the planet."

Poet and naturalist W. S. Merwin (citing Robert Graves) reminds us that we have one story, and one story only, to tell in our lives. We are made to believe by our parents and businesses, by our culture and televisions, by our politicians and movie stars that it is the story of money, of finance, of wealth, of the stock portfolio, the partnership, the country house. These are small, impoverished tales and whispers that have made us restless and craven; they are not stories at all. As author and garlic grower Stanley Crawford puts it, "The financial statement must finally give way to the narrative, with all its exceptions, special cases, imponderables. It must finally give way to the story, which is perhaps the way we arm ourselves against the next and always unpredictable turn of the cycle in the quixotic dare that is life; across the rock and cold of lifelines, it is our seed, our clove, our filament cast toward the future." It is something deeper than anything commercial culture can plumb, and it is waiting for each of us.

Business must yield to the longings of the human spirit. The most important contribution of the socially responsible business movement has little to do with recycling nuts from the rainforest, or employing the homeless. Their gift to us is that they are leading by trying to do something, to risk, take a chance, make a change—change. They are not waiting for "the solution," but are acting without guarantees of success or proof of purchase. That is what all of us must do. Being visionary has always been given a bad rap by commerce. But without a positive vision for humankind we can have no meaning, no work, and no purpose.

Personal Response

In what way or ways has this essay changed or influenced your views about your personal consumption habits and about the steps society must take to require socially responsible actions by businesses? If you are not persuaded by the essay that changes must be made, explain why.

Questions for Class or Small-Group Discussion

1. Discuss your understanding of the phrase "socially responsible" (paragraph 2). Can you give examples, other than those Hawken names, of businesses that do not meet this "socially responsible" criterion?

2. In paragraph 8, Hawken lists the objectives involved in his proposed "system of sustainable commerce." Discuss those objectives and the likelihood that the majority of commercial enterprises worldwide would adopt them and work toward such a system.

3. Discuss the twelve steps Hawken lists. Include in your discussion an assessment of how effective you believe the steps to be as reasonable conservation measures, what their adoption would entail, and how likely you think it is that Hawken's recommendations will be adopted.

4. Respond to this statement: "Democracy has been effectively eliminated in America by the influence of money, lawyers, and a political system that is the outgrowth of the first two" (paragraph 18).

5. Respond to this statement: "Computers are great. But they are not an uplifting or compelling vision for culture or society" (paragraph 20).

6. Brainstorm ways in which you personally can make changes or take action that will contribute to improving the environment.

THE GALILEO OF GLOBAL WARMING

American Spectator Editorial

American Spectator is a national opinion magazine whose target audience is leaders in business, government, and media. It covers matters of business, politics, economics, foreign policy, and culture. This editorial appeared in the May 2001 issue of American Spectator.

Now the global warming debate reveals that what Bob Tyrrell calls the plutomores (from the Greek plutos, "riches," and moros, "fools") have reached high positions in the Bush administration. Fooled entirely by the copious press and television coverage of the Democratic victory in Florida, for example, Treasury Secretary Paul O'Neill seems to believe he was summoned to Washington to serve as a token Republican in the administration of Al Gore. The Alcoa corpocrat devoted his first presentation to the Cabinet to an earnest plutomoronic tract on global warming, urging his baffled companions to save the planet from Republican religionists (apparently awaiting the Second Coming in rubber boots on Long Island beaches and golf courses). He all but said the Earth is in the Balance.

O'Neill and his Cabinet colleague Christie Whitman had provided the high point of this comic opera until this month's assault on Exxon Mobil by a group of angry shareholders, including a medley of nuns and Capuchin friars from New Jersey, inspired by Lloyd Keigwin, a good scientist panicked by pressures of political correctness. Collaborating in the panic is a writer from the *Wall Street Journal* named Thaddeus Herrick, who reports lugubriously that Exxon Mobil is "increasingly isolated on the issue, not only from the international scientific community, but also from European competitors . . . which largely accept the premise that the Earth is warming because of heat-trapping greenhouse gases."

Hardly heroic is Exxon Mobil, backpedaling from its denial of global warming risks. Its own plutomores seem increasingly ready to capitulate to the idea that their energy products imperil the planet.

4   Keigwin, though, is the more intriguing case. A 54-year-old oceanographer at Woods Hole Observatory near the Massachusetts Cape, he found a way to concoct a 3,000-year record of the temperatures of the Sargasso Sea near Bermuda through analyzing thermally dependent oxygen isotopes in fossils on the ocean floor. He discovered that temperatures a thousand years ago, during the so-called medieval climate optimum, were two degrees Celsius warmer than today's and that the average temperature over the last three millennia was slightly warmer than today's. Roughly confirming this result are historical records—the verdancy of Greenland at the time of the Vikings, the little ice age of the mid-1700s, a long series of temperature readings collected in Britain over the last 300 years documenting a slow recovery from the ice age, reports of medieval temperatures from a variety of sources, and records of tree rings and ice cores.

These previous findings, echoed by Keigwin's, are devastating to the theory of human-caused global warming. If the Earth was significantly warmer a thousand years ago, if we have been on a rewarming trend for three centuries, if, as other even more voluminous evidence suggests, the Earth has repeatedly seen mini-cycles of warming and cooling of about 1,500 years duration, then any upward drift in temperatures we may be seeing now—included scattered anecdotes of thinning arctic ice— is likely to be the result of such cycles.

Thus the case for human-caused global warming can no longer rest on the mere fact of contemporary warming. To justify drastic action like the Kyoto treaty requiring a reduction in U.S. energy consumption of some 30 percent, unfeasible without destroying the U.S. economy, the human-caused global warming advocates would have to demonstrate a persuasive mechanism of human causation. This they show no sign of being able to do. Grasping the point, scientists at Exxon Mobil recently used the Keigwin data in a *Wall Street Journal* ad and the PC bees hit the fan.

By all reasonable standards, Keigwin is a hero. Not only did he invent an ingenious way to compile an early temperature record, but he made a giant contribution to discrediting a movement that would impose a deadly energy clamp on the world economy. But soon enough his government-financed colleagues began to exert pressure. Was he a tool of the oil companies? Lordy no, he wrote, in an indignant letter to Exxon Mobil, denying that his findings had anything much to do with the global warming issue.

8   As the *Wall Street Journal* reported, "Dr. Keigwin warns that the results are not representative of the Earth as a whole. He says that the importance of his research isn't in the data per se, but rather that marine geologists can undertake such a study at all. . . . He wants to put the issue behind him." Hey, he's got a new government grant to find out "what's causing a substantial warming in the Atlantic Ocean off Nova Scotia." He has not reached any conclusion—but according to the *Journal,* "he gives a nod to global warming concerns, saying 'I'd take a guess.' "

Scores of scientists have been pressured to embrace the cult pressures that befall any critic of the cult of human-caused global warming. In a scientific establishment 50 percent financed by government, few can resist. An eminent scientist who was once the leading critic of global warming had to stop writing on the subject in order to continue his research. The source of the pressure that ended his publications was then-Senator Al Gore. Later this scientist coauthored a key paper with Arthur Robinson—organizer of a petition against Kyoto signed by 17,000 scientists—but had to remove his name under pressure from Washington.

Keigwin's denials of his own significance are all pathetically misleading. The temperature pattern he found in the Sargasso Sea is indeed a global phenomenon. Sallie Baliunas and Willi Soon of Harvard have uncovered a new oxygen isotope study that extends this temperature record another 3,000 years based on six millennia of evidence from peat bogs in northeastern China. The peat bog records both confirm Keigwin and demonstrate an even warmer period that lasted for 2,000 years. During this era, beginning some 4,000 years ago and running until the birth of Christ, temperatures averaged between 1.5 and 3 degrees Celsius higher than they do today.

Summing up the case is an article published earlier this year by Wallace Broecker in the prestigious pages of Science entitled "Was the Medieval Warm Period Global?" His answer is a resounding yes. As Craig and Keith Idso report in a March 7 editorial on their Webpage www.co2science.org, Broecker recounts substantial evidence for a series of climatic warmings spaced at roughly 1,500-year intervals. Broecker explains the science of reconstructing the histories of surface air temperatures by examining temperature data from "boreholes." From some 6,000 boreholes on all continents, this evidence confirms that the Earth was significantly warmer a thousand years ago and two degrees Celsius warmer in Greenland. This data, Robinson warns, is less detailed and authoritative than the evidence from the Sargasso Sea and from the Chinese peat bogs. But together with the independent historical record, the collective evidence is irrefutable. Thousands of years of data demonstrate that in the face of a few hundred parts per million increase in CO_2, temperatures today, if anything, are colder than usual. Temperatures in Antarctica, for example, have been falling for the last 20 years. The global satellite record of atmospheric temperature, confirmed by weather balloons, shows little change one way or another for the last three decades. Terrestrial temperature stations, on average, show more warming over the past century, but many are located in areas that were rural when the stations were established and are densely urban today, a change which causes local warming. The dominance of natural cycles globally is not surprising since, as Baliunas and Soon report, the impact of changes in sun energy output are some 70,000 times more significant than all human activity put together.

12   In the end, the global warming panic will take its place in the history books next to other environmental chimeras, such as the threat of DDT (but not of pandemic malaria), the peril of nuclear power (but not of coal mining), the brain-curdling effect of cellphones (but not of far more potent sun rays), the menace of powerlines (but not of poverty), the poison of alar (though not of rotten apple juice), the danger of asbestos in walls (but not of fire), the carcinogenic impact of PCBs (but not of carrots, peanut butter, coffee and other items that test more toxic in the same way) and the horror of radon and other sources of low-level radiation (despite is beneficial effect on health through a process called hormesis).

Overall, the situation is simple. Politicized scientists with government grants and dubious computer temperature models persuaded the world's politicians to make pompous fools of themselves in Kyoto. Socialist politicians were happy to join an absurd movement to impose government regulations over the world energy supply and thus over the world economy. The scientific claims and computer models have now blown up in their faces. But rather than admit error they persist in their fear-mongering. When this happened with DDT, hundreds of millions of people died of malaria. They continue to die. How many people would die as a result of an energy clamp on global capitalism?

Personal Response

Explore your reactions to the position this article takes on the subject of global warming.

Questions for Class or Small-Group Discussion

1. What evidence does this article present to support its major argument? Are you persuaded by that evidence?

2. Discuss your understanding of the Kyoto Treaty referred to in this article. Did you know that 17,000 scientists had signed a petition against the treaty (paragraph 9)? Does that information in any way change your thinking about the treaty?

3. Comment on the editorial's use of the term *cult* to describe the views of those who believe that there is global warming occurring and that humans are responsible for it (paragraph 9).

4. Look carefully at paragraph 12 and discuss your understanding of the implications of all of the parenthetical asides. For instance, the editorial expands on the second one—"the threat of DDT (but not of pandemic malaria)"—in paragraph 13 when it suggests that when DDT was banned, it resulted in a resurgence of malaria, which has killed hundreds of millions of people. What is your response to that claim and to the implications in paragraph 12?

OUT, DAMN NATURALISTS

D. Grant DeMan

Donald Grant DeMan (1936–2001) had many occupations throughout his life, including policeman, private investigator, management consultant, high school teacher of art, artist, and author. His articles were published in the Toronto Globe and Mail, *the* Vancouver Sun, *and the* Victoria Times-Colonist. *He was working on a book of 1950s youth adventures in conjunction with the Sociology Department of the University of Toronto when he died unexpectedly in 2001. This article was published in the May 28, 2001, issue of* McLean's *magazine.*

I've had it up to here with politicos, editorialists, naturalists, protesting leftists, rightists and plain generic loudmouths bellowing about the damage we do to our earth, water and air. Do I look like some harebrained game freak? Don't they think by now I've got the message?

It seems every time I search for news, the latest wailing of some Chicken Little group is taking up all the space. I'd like to give them space—out there alongside Pluto. By now, I think we're aware bikes are less damaging than SUV's. It's obvious that if you cut rainforest above a river the soil will wash downhill. I no longer need to hear about those things. Smoking is bad. Drinking worse, except it does a little good for the heart. Drugs devastate so we should either make them legal; hang the dealers; rehabilitate everybody; or set up more studies.

We are told the world needs fewer people. Then on the next page, we find some nincompoop praising the latest plan to extend life. "We can all live to be two hundred" raves the headline. Seems to me if the body crush were that severe the press would be chiding us to live shorter, rather than longer, lives. I've given up fish and whale products; saved birds until I'm knee-deep in feathers; and now that I've chucked the rifle, bears are stopping by for beans and rice.

4   But that's not enough.

I now drive weekly less than 10 km. Never take trips on energy-consuming air-planes, trains, buses or boats. Cut my hair with scissors. Flush every third time. Seldom shave or shower. Keep the thermostat at zero. Renew the septic system. Batten all my cracks and generally exist close to a state of donating—rather than consuming—energy. And don't even ask how often I change my underwear. But is that sufficient? Apparently not. They just keep at it.

The pain inflicted by the tree-hugging onslaught seems even more unbearable than the original issue. For they are lambasting our ecosphere with an around-the-clock verbal First World War cannon barrage, shattering my nerves with post-traumatic stress disorder.

My newspaper is like a harping spouse. I pay for the privilege of being scolded to clean up my act. During sleepless nights, I'm haunted by their clarion call: "Let's make the whole world a natural heritage park." Pipe down, guys, I've planted so much foliage that my place—known hereabouts as "that damn jungle"—grew twice as high as it is long. Thus we live under a permanent risk of being smothered and crushed by a giant fir. So call off the heralding doomsayers, I say. We know about it and are doing it, so please stop.

8   I recycle, walk softly upon the earth, breathe as little as possible and eschew harsh detergents. I refuse all packaged and imported slave-labour food. I make only green investments. I read things online in order to preserve forests, and my only newspaper not available online, I turn into mulch for a hedgerow. I return flyers. I don't own a dishwasher. I mend and fix everything. And I even spit to enrich the soil. I'll bet the farm I pollute less than 99 per cent of those thumping the door and invading my mailbox with their "Protect Momma Earth!" flyers.

For some time, I've absolutely refused to buy anything new for fear it will harm the environment. But what must transpire so the media relents and gets on to something of which we're unaware, like what the government is really up to these days? Just once I'd love to open the op-ed page to a void of environmental rage. Or turn on the television without being harangued.

Hey guys, quit picking on me.

Once more with feeling: it's not my fault!

Personal Response

What do you do to be environmentally responsible?

Questions for Class or Small-Group Discussion

1. What, exactly, is DeMan complaining about? Do you agree with him? Is he serious?

2. Explain what you think DeMan means in paragraph 6. What is "the pain inflicted by the tree-hugging onslaught"? What is "the original issue"? Where else does De-Man criticize environmentalists?

3. To what extent do you agree with DeMan about the hypocrisy of complaining about overpopulation while at the same time "praising the latest plan to extend life" (paragraph 3)?

4. Comment on DeMan's concluding statement: "Once more with feeling: it's not my fault!" Is it a fitting conclusion?

PERSPECTIVES ON ENVIRONMENTAL STUDIES

Suggestions for Synthesis

1. Incorporating the comments of at least two of the writers in this chapter, explain your own position on global warming or any of the environmental issues mentioned in the readings.

2. Incorporating the remarks of at least two of the writers in this chapter, write an essay that offers possible solutions to one of the major environmental issues confronting people today.

Additional Writing Topics

1. Write an essay in response to the *American Spectator* editorial "The Galileo of Global Warming," D. Grant DeMan's "Out, Damn Naturalists," or Paul Hawken's "A Declaration of Sustainability."

2. Taking into account the opinion of Paul Hawken in "A Declaration of Sustainability," argue on the extent to which you think pressure from lobbyists should influence the thinking of legislators considering measures that would tighten regulations on environmental issues.

3. Write a letter to the editor of your campus or community newspaper in which you urge students on your campus and citizens in the community to take actions to reverse the current abuse of natural resources. Or propose practical conservation steps that students on your campus can take.

4. Write a letter to the president of a corporation that you know abuses the environment urging him or her to make changes in the way the company produces its product. If you refuse to buy the product because of its production methods, say so.

5. Although the writers in this chapter address a wide range of environmental issues, these selections do not provide exhaustive coverage. Select an environmental issue that is not addressed in these essays, then explain the problem in detail, and if possible, offer solutions.

Research Topics

1. Research the work of Baron Alexander von Humboldt, Charles Darwin, or Thomas Malthus and write a paper arguing the relevance of their ideas to today's environmental issues.

2. Conduct library research on the impact of socioeconomic inequities on environmental issues and argue your position on the subject. Consider including interviews of environmentalists, sociologists, and/or economists from your campus in your research.

3. Research the Kyoto Treaty referred to in the *American Spectator* editorial "The Galileo of Global Warming," explain the controversy that surrounds the treaty, and explain your own viewpoint on it.

4. Select any of the environmental issues mentioned in this chapter as a research subject. Make sure that you fairly present both sides of the issue as you explain your own position.

PART 5

BUSINESS AND ECONOMICS

CHAPTER 23
MARKETING AND THE AMERICAN CONSUMER

In their characteristic consumption and materialism, Americans are both the envy of people in other nations and the objects of their criticism. America has long been regarded as the "land of plenty," with a plethora of products to buy and a standard of living that allows most citizens to buy them. Yet such plenitude can lead to overconsumption, creating a need to buy for the sake of buying that can become a kind of obsession. Some people seek psychological counseling for this compulsion, whereas others seek financial counseling to manage the debts they have built up as a result of their need to buy things.

Indeed, shopping is so central to the lives of Americans that malls have become more than places to find virtually any product people want and need; they have become social centers, where people gather to meet friends, eat, hang out, exercise, and be entertained. Some regard this penchant for spending money and acquiring goods as a symptom of some inner emptiness, with malls, shopping strips, and discount stores replacing the spiritual centers that once held primary importance in people's lives. Others, especially manufacturers of products and the people who sell them, regard consumerism as a hearty indicator of the nation's economic health.

The selections in this chapter begin with "In Praise of Consumerism," an essay by James B. Twitchell, who writes often on American consumerism and materialism. Twitchell discusses the social aspect of the consumerism concept in America, suggesting that it is the consumer who directs the marketplace, not the manufacturers and marketers of products. "We like having stuff," he asserts. As you read his essay, think about your own spending habits. Do you buy just to have things, or do you buy just those things necessary for living?

In the next article, Louise Lee, in "Can Levi's Be Cool Again?" focuses on one company that has experienced a decline in sales because it has seen a large drop in purchases by young people. She reports on the efforts of a new chief executive at Levi Strauss & Co., who has made it his goal to turn sales around in the company. Following that is Steven Levy's "Playing Fair with Copyright," which approaches the Napster issue from the point of view of the 62 million people who used Napster, before the Digital Millennium Copyright Act made it illegal to download free music from the Internet. Levy also comments on the entertainment companies' efforts to create new technologies for digital anticopying, which he sees infringing on some basic rights.

Finally, Phyllis Rose takes an amused look at consumerism in America in "Shopping and Other Spiritual Adventures in America Today." As you read each of these essays, think of your own consumer habits. Are you "addicted" to shopping? Do you like to buy for the sake of buying, whether you need a product or not? Did you take advantage of Napster before it was made illegal? Did you (or do you) actually hang out in malls, or do you visit them frequently now?

IN PRAISE OF COMMERCIALISM

James B. Twitchell

James B. Twitchell teaches English and advertising at the University of Florida. He is author of Carnival Culture: The Trashing of Taste in America *(1992),* Adcult USA: The Triumph of Advertising in American Culture *(1995), and* Twenty Ads that Shook the World: The Century's Most Groundbreaking Advertising and How It Changed Us All *(2000). This article, which is based on his book* Lead Us Into Temptation: The Triumph of American Materialism *(1999), appeared in the August/September 2000 issue of* Reason.

Sell them their dreams, sell them what they longed for and hoped for and almost despaired of having, sell them hats by splashing sunlight across them. Sell them dreams—dreams of country clubs and proms and visions of what might happen if only. After all, people don't buy things to have things. They buy things to work for them. They buy hope—hope of what your merchandise will do for them. Sell them this hope and you won't have to worry about selling them goods.

—Helen Landon Cass

Those words were spoken some years ago by a female radio announcer to a convention of salesmen in Philadelphia. *The Philadelphia Retail Ledger* for June 6, 1923, recorded Ms. Cass' invocations with no surrounding explanation. They were simply noted as a matter of record, not as a startling insight.

There are two ways to read her spiel. You can read it like a melancholy Marxist and see the barely veiled indictment of the selling process. What does she think consumers are—dopes to be duped? What is she selling? Snake oil?

4   Or you can read it like an unrepentant capitalist and see the connection between consuming goods and gathering meaning. The reason producers splash magical promise over their goods is because consumers demand it. Consumers are not sold a bill of goods; they insist on it. Snake oil to the cynic is often holy water to the eager. What looks like exploiting desire may be fulfilling desire.

How you come down in this matter depends on your estimation of the audience. Does the audience manipulate things to make meaning, or do other people use things to manipulate the audience? Clearly, this is a variation of "I persuade, you educate, they manipulate," for both points of view are supportable. Let's split the difference and be done with it.

More interesting to me, however, is to wonder why such a statement, so challenging, so revolutionary, so provocative in many respects was, in the early 1920s, so understandable, so acceptable, even so passe that it appears with no gloss. Why is it that when you read the early descriptions of capitalism, all the current bugaboos—advertising, packaging, branding, fashion, and retailing techniques—seem so much better understood?

And why has the consumer—playing an active, albeit usually secondary, part in the consumptive dyad of earlier interpretations—become almost totally listless in our current descriptions? From Thomas Hobbes in the mid-17th century ("As in other things, so in men, not the seller but the buyer determines the price") to Edwin S. Gingham in the mid-20th century ("Consumers with dollars in their pockets are not, by any stretch of the imagination, weak. To the contrary, they are the most merciless, meanest, toughest market disciplinarians I know"), the consumer was seen as participating in the meaning-making of the material world. How and why did the consumer get dumbed down and phased out so quickly? Why has the hypodermic metaphor (false needs injected into a docile populace) become the unchallenged explanation of consumerism?

8   I think that much of our current refusal to consider the liberating role of consumption is the result of who has been doing the describing. Since the 1960s, the primary "readers" of the commercial "text" have been the well-tended and -tenured of members of the academy. For any number of reasons—the most obvious being their low levels of disposable income, average age, and gender, and the fact that these critics are selling a competing product, high-cult (which is also coated with its own dream values)—the academy has casually passed off as "hegemonic brainwashing" what seems to me, at least, a self-evident truth about human nature: We like having stuff.

In place of the obvious, they have substituted an interpretation that they themselves often call vulgar Marxisms. It is supposedly vulgar in the sense that it is not as sophisticated as the real stuff, but it has enough spin on it to be more appropriately called Marxism lite. Go into almost any cultural studies course in this country and you will hear the condemnation of consumerism expounded: What we see in the marketplace is the result of the manipulation of the many for the profit of the few. Consumers are led around by the nose. We live in a squirrel cage. Left alone we would read Wordsworth, eat lots of salad, and have meetings to discuss Really Important Subjects.

In cultural studies today, everything is oppression and we are all victims. In macrocosmic form, the oppression is economic—the "free" market. In microcosmic form, oppression is media—your "free" TV. Here, in the jargon of this downmarket Marxism, is how the system works: The manipulators, a.k.a. "the culture industry," attempt to enlarge their hegemony by establishing their ideological base in the hearts and pocketbooks of a weak and demoralized populace. Left alone, we would never desire things (ugh!). They have made us materialistic. But for them, we would be spiritual.

To these critics, the masters of industry and their henchmen, the media lords, are predators, and what they do in no way reflects or resolves genuine audience concerns. Just the opposite. The masters of the media collude, striving to infantilize us so that we are docile, anxious, and filled with "reified desire." While we may think advertising is just "talking about the product," that packaging just "wraps the object," that retailing is just "trading the product," or that fashion is just "the style of the product," this is not so. That you may think so only proves their power over you. The marginalized among us—the African American, the child, the immigrant, and especially the female are trapped into this commodifying system, this false consciousness, and this fetishism that only the enlightened can correct. Legendary ad man David Ogilvy's observation that, "The consumer is no fool, she is your wife" is just an example of the repressive tolerance of such a sexist, materialist culture.

12   Needless to say, in such a system the only safe place to be is tenured, underpaid, self-defined as marginalized, teaching two days a week for nine months a year, and writing really perceptive social criticism that your colleagues can pretend to read. Or rather, you would be writing such articles if only you could find the time.

The Triumph of Stuff

The idea that consumerism creates artificial desires rests on a wistful ignorance of history and human nature, on the hazy, romantic feeling that there existed some halcyon era of noble savages with purely natural needs. Once fed and sheltered, our needs have always been cultural, not natural. Until there is some other system to codify and satisfy those needs and yearnings, capitalism—and the culture it carries with it—will continue not just to thrive but to triumph.

In the way we live now, it is simply impossible to consume objects without consuming meaning. Meaning is pumped and drawn everywhere throughout the modern commercial world, into the farthest reaches of space and into the smallest divisions of time. Commercialism is the water we all swim in, the air we breathe, our sunlight and shade. Currents of desire flow around objects like smoke in a wind tunnel.

This isn't to say that I'm simply sanguine about such a material culture. It has many problems that I have glossed over. Consumerism is wasteful, it is devoid of otherworldly concerns, it lives for today and celebrates the body. It overindulges and spoils the young with impossible promises. It encourages recklessness, living beyond one's means, gambling. Consumer culture is always new, always without a past. Like religion, which it has displaced, it afflicts the comfortable and comforts the afflicted. It is heedless of the truly poor who cannot gain access to the loop of meaningful information that is carried through its ceaseless exchanges. It is a one-dimensional world, a wafer-thin world, a world low on significance and high on glitz, a world without yesterdays.

16   On a personal level, I struggle daily to keep it at bay. For instance, I am offended by billboards (how do they externalize costs?); I fight to keep Chris Whittle's Channel One TV and all placed-based advertising from entering the classroom; political advertising makes me sick, especially the last-minute negative ads; I contribute to PBS in hopes they will stop slipping down the slope of commercialism (although I know better); I am annoyed that Coke has bought all the "pouring rights" at my school and is now trying to do the same to the world; I think it's bad enough that the state now sponsors gambling, do they also have to support deceptive advertising about it?; I despise the way that amateur athletics has become a venue for shoe companies (why not just replace the football with the Nike swoosh and be done with it?); and I just go nuts at Christmas.

But I also realize that while you don't have to like it, it doesn't hurt to understand it and our part in it. We have not been led astray. Henry Luce was not far off when he claimed in a February 1941 editorial in *Life* magazine that the next era was to be the American Century: "The Greeks, the Romans, the English and the French had their eras, and now it was ours." Not only that, but we are likely to commandeer much of the 21st century as well.

Almost a decade ago, Francis Fukuyama, a State Department official, contended in his controversial essay (and later book) "The End of History?" that "the ineluctable spread of consumerist Western culture" presages "not just the end of the Cold War, or the passing of a particular period of postwar history, but the end of history as such: that is, the end point of mankind's ideological evolution." OK, such predictions are not new. "The End of History" (as we know it) and "the end point of mankind's ideological evolution" have been predicted before by philosophers. Hegel claimed it had already happened in 1806 when Napoleon embodied the ideas of the French Revolution, and Marx said the end was coming soon with world communism. What legitimizes this modern claim is that it is demonstrably true. For better or for worse, American commercial culture is well on its way to becoming world culture. The Soviets have fallen. Only quixotic French intellectuals and anxious Islamic fundamentalists are trying to stand up to it.

To some degree, the triumph of consumerism is the triumph of the popular will. You may not like what is manufactured, advertised, packaged, branded, and broadcast, but it is far closer to what most people want most of the time than at any other period of modern history.

Trollope and The Jerk

20   Two fictional characters personify to me the great divide: Augustus Melmotte, the protagonist of Anthony Trollope's 19th-century novel, *The Way We Live Now*, and Navin R. Johnson, the eponymous hero of Steve Martin's 1979 movie, *The Jerk*.

Melmotte, a Jew, comes from Paris to London with his daughter and his Bohemian wife. When the action of the novel is over and Augustus has committed suicide because he cannot fit in to proper Victorian society, wife and daughter head off to America—to San Francisco, to be exact. Trollope is always exact in letting you know that geography determines character. So too we know that Ruby Ruggles and her bumpkin brother belong at Sheep's Acres Farm and that Roger Carbury should preside over Carbury Hall. Sir Felix Carbury, fallen from grace, must go to Germany— there is no room for his kind, no club that will accept him. Mrs. Hurtle comes from San Francisco and in the end must return there.

Any Trollope lover worth his salt can tell you much about the protagonists simply by such comings and goings. These paths are the code by which our grandparents recognized, in Dominick Dunne's felicitous title, those who are "people like us": our kind/not our kind. The Victorian reading public needed such shorthand because things had no brand personalities—manners, places, sinecures—and bloodlines did. Salaries meant little, accomplishments even less. The central acts of *The Way We Live Now* are the attempts by Augustus Melmotte to buy a titled husband for his daughter and get a named estate for himself. He can't do it, of course—how silly to try, even if he is the "City's most powerful financier." In his world, meaning was generated through such social conventions as the abstract concept of bloodline, the value of patina, your club, owning land, acceptable in-laws, your accent, the seating chart for dinner, the proper church pew—all things Melmotte could never master. It was a stultifying system—a real old-boy network, but one that to Trollope still worked. It was a system presided over by chummy squires, comfortable gentlemen, and twinkling clerics.

Compare that to the world of *The Jerk*. Here, the story is held together by the running joke that when Navin R. Johnson is being the most idiotic, he is really being the most savant. After a series of misadventures, Navin amasses a fortune by inventing a way to keep eyeglasses from slipping down the nose (the "Opti-grab"). He wins the hand of his sweetheart, buys incredibly gauche gold chains, swag lamps, outrageous golf carts, and ersatz Grecian mansions. Surrounded by things, he is finally happy. But then—curses!—he loses his possessions as a google-eyed litigant wins a class action lawsuit because the Opti-grab has made many wearers cross-eyed. Navin's wife is distraught. She bursts into tears. "I don't care about losing the money, it's losing all this stuff."

24   Navin, as innocent as he is honest, says he doesn't really care about these things, he knows who he is without possessions. His sense of self is certainly not tied to the material world. "I don't want stuff . . . I don't need anything," he says to her as he starts to leave the room in his pajamas. He sees an old ashtray. "Except this ashtray, and that's the only thing I need is this," he says, as he leans over to pick it up. Navin walks to the door. "Well, and this paddle game and the ashtray is all I need. And this, this remote control; that's all I need, just the ashtray, paddle game, and this remote control."

Navin is growing progressively more frantic in vintage Steve Martin fashion. He is in the hall now, pajamas down around his knees and his arms full of stuff. "And these matches. Just the ashtray, paddle ball, remote control, and these matches . . . and this lamp, and that's all I need. I don't need one other thing . . . except this magazine." We hear him gathering more things as he disappears down the hall. Navin, jerk enough to think he needs nothing, is sage enough not to leave home without a few of his favorite things.

Augustus Melmotte, certified world-class financier, is forever kept at bay. He never achieves his goal and finally commits suicide. Navin R. Johnson, certified consumer jerk, achieves (if only for a while) the objects of his heart's desire. He finally becomes a bum on Skid Row, true, but a bum who at least can try it all over again. In a consumerist culture, the value-making ligatures that hold our world together come from such conventions as advertising, packaging, branding, fashion, and even shopping itself. It is a system presided over by marketers who deliver the goods and all that is carried in their wake. It is a more democratic world, a more egalitarian world, and, I think, a more interesting world.

That said, commercialism can be a stultifying system too, and wasteful. It would be nice to think that this eternally encouraging market will result in the cosmopolitanism envisioned by the Enlightenment philosophers, that a "universalism of goods" will end in a crescendo of hosannas. It would be nice to think that more and more of the poor and disenfranchised will find their ways into the cycle of increased affluence without contracting "affluenza," the "disease" of buying too much. It would be nice to think that materialism could be heroic, self-abnegating, and redemptive. It would be nice to think that greater material comforts will release us from racism, sexism, and ethnocentricism, and that the apocalypse will come as it did at the end of Shelley's *Prometheus Unbound,* leaving us "Sceptreless, free, uncircumscribed . . . Equal, unclassed, tribeless; and nationless . . . Pinnacled dim in the intense inane."

28 But it is more likely that the globalization of capitalism will result in the banalities of an ever-increasing, worldwide consumerist culture. Recall that Athens ceased to be a world power around 400 B.C., yet for the next three hundred years Greek culture was the culture of the world. The Age of European Exposition ended in the mid-20th century; the Age of American Markets—Yankee imperialism—is just starting to gather force. The French don't stand a chance. The Middle East is collapsing under the weight of dish antennas and Golden Arches. The untranscendent, repetitive, sensational, democratic, immediate, tribalizing, and unifying force of what Irving Kristol calls the American Imperium need not result in a Bronze Age of culture, however. In fact, who knows what this Pax Americana will result in? But it certainly will not produce what Shelley had in mind.

We have been in the global marketplace a short time, and it is an often scary and melancholy place. A butterfly flapping its wings in China may not cause storm clouds over Miami, but a few lines of computer code written by some kid in Palo Alto may indeed change the lives of all the in habitants of Shanghai.

More important, perhaps, we have not been led into this world of material closeness against our better judgment. For many of us, especially when young, consumerism is not against our better judgment. It is our better judgment. And this is true regardless of class or culture. We have not just asked to go this way, we have demanded. Now most of the world is lining up, pushing and shoving, eager to elbow into the mall. Woe to the government or religion that says no.

Getting and spending have been the most passionate, and often the most imaginative, endeavors of modern life. We have done more than acknowledge that the good life starts with the material life, as the ancients did. We have made stuff the dominant prerequisite of organized society. Things "R" Us. Consumption has become production. While this is dreary and depressing to some, as doubtless it should be, it is liberating and democratic to many more.

Personal Response

Do you think that consumerism creates artificial values? Do you consider yourself "an unrepentant capitalist" (paragraph 4)? Explain your answer.

Questions for Class or Small-Group Discussion

1. Look at what Twitchell says in paragraph 4 about consumers demanding that "producers splash magical promise over their goods." What do you think he means when he says that consumers "insist on" a bill of goods and that "what looks like exploiting desire may be fulfilling desire"? To what extent do you agree with him?

2. Comment on Twitchell's use of the phrase "liberating role of consumption" in paragraph 8. Do you agree with him that "we like having stuff"? Do you think it is a fair representation of Americans?

3. What do you think of Twitchell's critique of academics who view consumerism as oppression (paragraphs 8–12)?

4. Twitchell seems to see consumerism as both good and bad. State in your own words what he sees as good about it and what he sees as bad. To what extent do you share his viewpoint?

CAN LEVI'S BE COOL AGAIN?

Louise Lee

Louise Lee is a writer for Business Week. *She wrote this article for the March 13, 2000, issue of* Business Week.

Marissa Emmer certainly recognizes that Levi Strauss is an all-American brand. But the 15-year-old high school sophomore from Setauket, N.Y., and her friends won't wear anything from Levi's. "It doesn't make styles we want," says Emmer, who prefers baggy pants from JNCO and Kikwear. "Levi's styles are too tight and for the older generation, like middle-aged people."

Ouch. This is what Philip A. Marineau, Levi Strauss & Co.'s new chief executive, is up against as he struggles to make the San Francisco apparel giant cool again. In the top job since September, the marketing veteran from PepsiCo Inc. is taking on a company whose fortunes in recent years have faded faster than a new pair of jeans. Marineau vows to get the venerable, family-owned company growing again. After three years of tumbling sales, layoffs, plant closings, and a failed effort to woo kids online, Levi's is gearing up for several product launches. "Levi's is a mythical brand, but our performance has been poor," says Marineau, 53. "We need to turn our attention back to customers and have more relevant products and marketing."

Manufacturing Kinks

Marineau is no stranger to makeovers. As head of Pepsi's North American unit, he directed the splashy 1998 rollout of low-cal Pepsi One and other products. He's already attacking Levi's biggest problem: its failure to respond quickly to fashion trends. In coming months, Levi's will unveil a slew of youth-oriented fashions, ranging from oddly cut jeans to nylon pants that unzip into shorts. But Marineau is not giving up on the geezers. He wants to broaden Levi's appeal to grown-ups by extending the Dockers and Slates causal-pants brands. Marineau also needs to smooth out kinks in manufacturing and shipping that prevent Levi's from rushing new products into stores.

4   Even Marineau acknowledges that a turnaround won't happen overnight. For that reason, it's probably a good thing that Levi's is privately held, owned by descendants of founder Levi Strauss. Marineau succeeded Robert D. Haas, the founder's great-great-grandnephew, who remains chairman of the board. The company has already seen sales drop steadily since 1996, when they peaked at $7.1 billion. For the year ended Nov. 30, sales slid to $5.1 billion, a 14% decline from the year before. Since the mid-'90s, the overall jeans market expanded about 4% a year. Analysts estimate that the share held by Levi's has fallen to about 17% from 31% over the past decade, snatched away by labels ranging from Gap and Old Navy to Tommy Hilfiger and Diesel.

Most of the pain from that retrenchment has already rippled through the 147-year-old company. Before Marineau arrived, Levi's closed 30 of its 51 factories and laid off about 15,000 people, or 40% of its workers. That cut annual costs by about $500 million. But Levi's was forced to rack up $1.3 billion in charges and boost its debt. Marineau says it barely broke even last year.

Some of Levi's problems can be blamed on the sliding fortunes of some of its biggest retailers, most notably J.C. Penney Co. But more damaging was the company's own inability to connect with young customers. Since the mid-1990s, Levi's mainstay five-pocket jeans have steadily lost ground to big-pocketed denim cargo and carpenter pants, says John Schamberger, head of the jeans unit at competitor VF Corp., which makes the Lee and Wrangler brands. In VF's boys' jeans business, for instance, traditional styles today make up only 20% of sales, down from more than 50% four years ago. But while VF and others jumped on this trend, Levi's largely stood still. "When fashion shifted, Levi's never caught on to what youth wanted," says Leonard Rothschilds, owner of Lark Clothing Stores Inc., a Chicago-based chain that quit selling Levi's four years ago.

Marineau acknowledges that Levi's missed trends ranging from flared jeans legs to stretchy fabrics. "We've always been a season behind," he says. To catch up, Levi's is unveiling a line called Engineered Jeans. Billed as a "reinvention" of the five-pocket style, the new pants feature side seams that follow the line of the leg and a bottom hem that slightly shorter in back to keep from dragging on the ground. The jeans also have a larger watch pocket to hold items like a pager. Under its youth-oriented Silver Tab brand, Levi's is introducing the Mobile Zip-Off Pant, with legs that unzip to create shorts, and the loose Ripcord Pant, which rolls up.

8   The new styles are designed to appeal to the sort of niche stores that kids flock to these days. But it is not clear yet whether those specialty retailers are ready for a radical shift such as Engineered Jeans from the plain-vanilla jeans supplier, which is still best known for its classic Red Tab denim cuts. "It's certainly different for Levi's because it's a fashion jean," says Norm Adams, a denim buyer at American Rag, a Los Angeles specialty jeans store that sells expensive reproductions of vintage Levi's. Some buyers say the Engineered Jeans will be a tough sell because of the unusual cut and features. "It'll be a product where sales staff will really have to explain it," says Scott Dromms, a buyer for regional specialty chain U.S. Male in Memphis, which is testing Engineered Jeans in stores.

In the meantime, Levi's can't afford to alienate its core baby-boomer customers. "It's a mistake to target only the under-25 market, because it's the most fickle," says Harry Bernard, a San Francisco marketing consultant. Marineau plans to expand the men's Slates brand into a line of skirts and trousers for women. He's also extending Dockers khakis to a business-casual line called Dockers Recode, using stretch fabrics.

But the heart of Levi's remains the flagship brand, and Marineau needs to make it just as attractive to a new generation of kids as it is to their boomer parents. How do you sell the idea that you're hip while not turning off the oldsters? New ads will showcase the products themselves rather than relentlessly trying to convey "attitude." An upcoming television campaign for frayed cutoff shorts shows a young woman throwing her jeans in front of an oncoming train, which slices them into cut-offs. Contrast that with last year's magazine ad for the Silver Tab line that showed navel-baring teens slouching nonchalantly. "Levi's is too huge a brand to be focused on such a narrow segment of the audience," says Marineau.

Wary Outsiders

Some of Marineau's other challenges are less sexy but just as critical. He has to smooth out glitches in Levi's production and logistics system, which got tangled as Levi's shifted manufacturing from company-owned plants to contractors. Stores frequently received the wrong merchandise or got it late. One major project that's under way: building a computerized "automatic replenishment" system to keep retailers' shelves full of core products. But don't look for a big e-commerce push. In January, Levi's pulled the plug on a struggling effort to sell jeans online. Sales volume was too small to justify the high costs. Also, Levi's angered retailers by blocking their efforts to sell its jeans online. Now if you try to buy jeans from Levi.com, it directs you to Macy's and Penney's Web sites.

12   Marineau projects another sales decline "in the high single digits" for this year but thinks growth will return in 2001. "There's no reason why Levi's won't recover," he says.

But outsiders are wary. Since December, Moody's Investors Service, Standard & Poor's, and Fitch IBCA have downgraded Levi's $800 million in senior unsecured debt, citing eroding sales. The company recently renegotiated its bank loans and secured them with assets that included the brand name and trademark. Until Marineau successfully woos a new generation of consumers, Levi's will be singing the blues.

Personal Response

What is your image of Levi's traditional jeans? Do you buy Levi's? If so, explain why, and if not, explain why not.

Questions for Class or Small-Group Discussion

1. Lee describes the marketing plan and new line of jeans that Levi's planned to use by the end of 2001 in order to lure young buyers back to Levi's. How successfully do you think that plan has worked? Has Levi's "successfully woo[ed] a new generation of consumers" (paragraph 13)?

2. What does this article suggest about the influence of the under-25-year-old group of consumers? Why does Levi's want to hold onto its baby boomer population as well? Do you think that any manufacturers can afford to focus on just one demographic group?

3. What do you think of Levi's decision to make their advertisements "showcase the products themselves rather than relentlessly trying to convey 'attitude'" (paragraph 10)? How important is "attitude" to young consumers?

PLAYING FAIR WITH COPYRIGHT

Steven Levy

Steven Levy, a senior editor and chief technology writer for Newsweek, *was a long-time writer of the "Iconoclast" column for* Macworld *magazine. His books include* Hackers: Heroes of the Computer Revolution *(1984),* Artificial Life: A Report from the Frontier Where Computers Meet Biology *(1992),* Insanely Great: The Life and Times of MacIntosh, the Computer That Changed Everything *(1993), and* Crypto: How the Code Rebels Beat the Government—Saving Privacy in the Digital Age *(2001). This article appeared in the February 26, 2001, issue of* Newsweek.

The appellate judges have spoken: the indiscriminate music-sharing bacchanalia must end. But can 62 million Napster users really be wrong? Almost by definition, such a massive consumer force is a market that must be served. That's why, at the same time they're trying to shut down Napster, the giant entertainment conglomerates are frantically trying to come up with their own business models to somehow combine Napster's selection and ease with a big, fat cash register on the other end. "They're engaged in Tarzan economics," says Jim Griffin, CEO of Cherry Lane Digital. "Desperately holding on to one vine—their old business model—until they can grab firm hold of the next one."

Watch out, folks. "The next vine" might present a slew of copyright problems even more difficult to untangle than the Napster case. It turns out that the entertainment industry's ultimate line of defense is not lawsuits. Instead, it plans to protect intellectual property from the new technologies of digital copying with . . . new technologies of digital anti-copying. Some of these are already in effect; the movie DVDs you buy have a complicated coding system that prevents copying. Other such technologies are in the works—including one just announced by Napster itself to "manage digital rights" by preventing users from burning CDs, and monitoring Napoids to make sure they're behaving. The moguls insist such schemes will only maintain the status quo from those palmy days when listeners didn't have CDs capable of generating perfect copies, or Internet connections that transformed sharing from a localized exchange to a global grabfest. But in many cases, these schemes actually take away certain rights from consumers. If the moguls have their way, not only will song sharing be outlawed, but certain uses that music listeners and movie viewers take for granted—like making copies for personal use or taking a snippet of a copyrighted work for an educational purpose—will go the way of the vinyl LP.

What's more, the industry has persuaded Congress to make sure nobody tries to tamper with its schemes, even if the intent is only to engage in "non-infringing" uses of music or film, like personal copies or fair use. The Digital Millennium Copyright Act, passed in 1998, makes it illegal for anyone to provide users with tools—or even publish information about such tools—that would get around anti-copying controls. But what if you wanted to circumvent the controls only for a legal use? Or what if the work in question has entered the public domain since publication, losing its copyright protection? Tough. "It was way too broad," says University of California copyright expert Pamela Samuelson. "A lot of icky consequences regarding fair use got swept under the carpet."

4   These restrictions are currently being tested in the courts, and it doesn't look good. When 2600 Magazine published the work of a 16-year-old Norwegian hacker who cracked the scheme that encodes movie DVDs (his purpose was not piracy, but a means for Linux users to view films on computers), it got hit with a lawsuit from the Motion Picture Association of America. A district-court judge wasn't swayed by the argument that the Millennium Copyright Act obliterates fair use, and the case is now under appeal. The Electronic Frontier Foundation's Lee Tien believes that the content industries will eventually use the laws to create even more controls over creative

works, engineering a pay-per-view model for all forms of intellectual property. Instead of buying a record or a book and enjoying it as often as you like, he says, you might wind up having to fork over bucks every time you reread the book or replay the tune. Tien also says that the content holders hope to use their schemes to limit consumers from other non-infringing pursuits they want to stamp out, like fast-forwarding past commercials on digital video players.

Meanwhile, it's boom time for companies concocting schemes to lock up creative works from infringers and paying customers alike. Just last week I learned that an Israeli company called TTR has created a technology called Safe Audio that allows music companies to press CDs in such a way that digital copies can't be made. If the next Jennifer Lopez disc you buy is Safe Audio-ized and you try to burn a CD copy, or even use a software program to place it in your computer jukebox, J. Lo's dulcet tones will be overwhelmed by horrible white noise. TTR's Mark Tokayer notes that though U.S. consumers might have the right to make such copies for themselves, the Sonys and AOL Time Warners of the world have no legal obligation to provide you with the means to exercise those rights. And the Millennium Copyright Act is ready to whack you if you try to take those rights back. Tokayer says that his company is negotiating with all the major entertainment powers and expects Safe Audio to be on discs sold by the end of this year.

Does this mean that we're doomed to whatever crumbs the Bertelsmanns throw us? That eventually the wonderful so-called celestial jukebox that comes from the availability of zillions of copyrighted works on demand will require not only an endless stream of nickels, but a loss of our traditional rights? Not necessarily. Pamela Samuelson believes that if the combination of law, technology and industry greed threatens to wipe out fair use, adjustments to the law can restore what's been lost—if the people make their will known to their legislators. Sixty-two million constituents can't be wrong.

Personal Response

Write for a few minutes on your view of the whole Napster controversy, whether you used its services before it was made illegal or not.

Questions for Class or Small-Group Discussion

1. Discuss your understanding of the controversy surrounding Napster, Inc. Either individually or as a class, explain the viewpoint of all interested parties—the consumers, the artists, and the entertainment industry.

2. What do you think of the entertainment industry's plan to develop anticopying devices to prevent you from copying any kind of digital entertainment? What do you think of the proposal of a "pay-per-view model for all forms of intellectual property" (paragraph 4)? What are the potential ramifications of such a model?

3. Levy raises the point that there are certain legal reasons for circumventing the restrictions against copying, that is, "fair use" conditions. What do you understand

those conditions to be? That is, under what circumstances do you think it would be all right to copy creative works without paying for them?

4. What is your response to news of "Safe Audio" technology?

SHOPPING AND OTHER SPIRITUAL ADVENTURES IN AMERICA TODAY

Phyllis Rose

Phyllis Rose is the author of the following books: Woman of Letters: A Life of Virginia Woolf *(1978),* Parallel Lives: Five Victorian Marriages *(1983),* Jazz Cleopatra: Josephine Baker in Her Time *(1989),* The Norton Book of Women's Lives *(1993),* The Year of Reading Proust: A Memoir in Real Time *(1999), and* Never Say Good-Bye: Essays *(1991), from which this essay is taken.*

Last year a new Waldbaum's Food Mart opened in the shopping mall on Route 66. It belongs to the new generation of superduper-markets open twenty-four hours that have computerized checkout. I went to see the place as soon as it opened and I was impressed. There was trail mix in Lucite bins. There was freshly made pasta. There were coffee beans, four kinds of tahini, ten kinds of herb teas, raw shrimp in shells and cooked shelled shrimp, fresh-squeezed orange juice. Every sophistication known to the big city, even goat's cheese covered with ash, was now available in Middletown, Conn. People raced from the warehouse aisle to the bagel bin to the coffee beans to the fresh fish market, exclaiming at all the new things. Many of us felt elevated, graced, complimented by the presence of this food palace in our town.

This is the wonderful egalitarianism of American business. Was it Andy Warhol who said that the nice thing about Coke is, no can is any better or worse than any other? Some people may find it dull to cross the country and find the same chain stores with the same merchandise from coast to coast, but it means that my town is as good as yours, my shopping mall as important as yours, equally filled with wonders.

Imagine what people ate during the winter as little as seventy-five years ago. They ate food that was local, long-lasting, and dull, like acorn squash, turnips, and cabbage. Walk into an American supermarket in February and the world lies before you: grapes, melons, artichokes, fennel, lettuce, peppers, pistachios, dates, even strawberries, to say nothing of ice cream. Have you ever considered what a triumph of civilization it is to be able to buy a pound of chicken livers? If you lived on a farm and had to kill a chicken when you wanted to eat one, you wouldn't ever accumulate a pound of chicken livers.

4   Another wonder of Middletown is Caldor, the discount department store. Here is man's plenty: tennis racquets, panty hose, luggage, glassware, records, toothpaste. Timex watches, Cadbury's chocolate, corn poppers, hair dryers, warm-up suits, car

wax, light bulbs, television sets. All good quality at low prices with exchanges cheerfully made on defective goods. There are worse rules to live by. I feel good about America whenever I walk into this store, which is almost every midwinter Sunday afternoon, when life elsewhere has closed down. I go to Caldor the way English people go to pubs: out of sociability. To get away from my house. To widen my horizons. For culture's sake. Caldor provides me too with a welcome sense of seasonal change. When the first outdoor grills and lawn furniture appear there, it's as exciting a sign of spring as the first crocus or robin.

Someone told me about a Soviet emigré who practices English by declaiming, at random, sentences that catch his fancy. One of his favorites is, "Fifty percent off all items today only." Refugees from Communist countries appreciate our supermarkets and discount department stores for the wonders they are. An Eastern European scientist visiting Middletown wept when she first saw the meat counter at Waldbaum's. On the other hand, before her year in America was up, her pleasure turned sour. She wanted everything she saw. Her approach to consumer goods was insufficiently abstract, too materialistic. We Americans are beyond a simple, possessive materialism. We're used to abundance and the possibility of possessing things. The things, and the possibility of possessing them, will still be there next week, next year. So today we can walk the aisles calmly.

It is a misunderstanding of the American retail store to think we go there necessarily to buy. Some of us shop. There's a difference. Shopping has many purposes, the least interesting of which is to acquire new articles. We shop to cheer ourselves up. We shop to practice decision making. We shop to be useful and productive members of our class and society. We shop to remind ourselves how much is available to us. We shop to remind ourselves how much is to be striven for. We shop to assert our superiority to the material objects that spread themselves before us.

Shopping's function as a form of therapy is widely appreciated. You don't really need, let's say, another sweater. You need the feeling of power that comes with buying or not buying it. You need the feeling that someone wants something you have—even if it's just your money. To get the benefit of shopping, you needn't actually purchase the sweater, any more than you have to marry every man you flirt with. In fact, window-shopping, like flirting, can be more rewarding, the same high without the distressing commitment, the material encumbrance. The purest form of shopping is provided by garage sales. A connoisseur goes out with no goal in mind, open to whatever may come his or her way, secure that it will cost very little. Minimum expense, maximum experience. Perfect shopping.

8   I try to think of the opposite, a kind of shopping in which the object is all-important, the pleasure of shopping at a minimum. For example, the purchase of blue jeans. I buy new blue jeans as seldom as possible because the experience is so humiliating. For every pair that looks good on me, fifteen look grotesque. But even shopping for blue jeans at Bob's Surplus on Main Street—no frills, bare-bones shopping—is an event in the life of the spirit. Once again I have to come to terms with the fact that I will never look good in Levi's. Much as I want to be mainstream, I never will be.

In fact, I'm doubly an oddball, neither Misses nor Junior, but Misses Petite. I look in the mirror, I acknowledge the disparity between myself and the ideal, I resign myself to making the best of it: I will buy the Lee's Misses Petite. Shopping is a time of reflection, assessment, spiritual self-discipline.

It is appropriate, I think, that Bob's Surplus has a communal dressing room. I used to shop only in places where I could count on a private dressing room with a mirror inside. My impulse then was to hide my weaknesses. Now I believe in sharing them. There are other women in the dressing room at Bob's Surplus trying on blue jeans who look as bad as I do. We take comfort from one another. Sometimes a woman will ask me which of two items looks better. I always give a definite answer. It's the least I can do. I figure we are all in this together, and I emerge from the dressing room not only with a new pair of jeans but with a renewed sense of belonging to a human community.

When a Solzhenitsyn rants about American materialism, I have to look at my digital Timex and check what year this is. Materialism? Like conformism, a hot moral issue of the fifties, but not now. How to spread the goods, maybe. Whether the goods are the Good, no. Solzhenitsyn, like the visiting scientist who wept at the beauty of Waldbaum's meat counter but came to covet everything she saw, takes American materialism too materialistically. He doesn't see its spiritual side. Caldor, Waldbaum's, Bob's Surplus—these, perhaps, are our cathedrals.

Personal Response

Explain your attitude toward shopping. Do you go to discount stores or malls to shop or to buy? Does shopping give you the pleasure Rose says it gives most Americans?

Questions for Class or Small-Group Discussion

1. Discuss whether you get the pleasure from shopping in American discount stores and supermarkets that Rose describes in her essay. Consider, for instance, Rose's comment in paragraph 9 that "shopping is a time of reflection, assessment, spiritual self-discipline."

2. What criticisms of American consumerism does Rose imply in her ironic descriptions of shopping as a spiritual adventure and department stores as America's cathedrals?

3. In paragraph 10, Rose describes trying on jeans in a communal dressing room and of taking comfort from other women there. Do men experience the same kind of camaraderie when shopping that women often do? To what extent do you think there are differences between the way men and women view shopping in general?

PERSPECTIVES ON MARKETING AND THE AMERICAN CONSUMER

Suggestions for Synthesis

1. Drawing on at least two readings in the chapter, write an essay on the importance of young consumers for the American economy.

2. Drawing on at least two of the readings in this chapter, explain the pressures you think America's high-consumption society puts on young people and the effects of those pressures.

3. Drawing on the comments of at least two writers in this chapter, write an essay on the image you think American consumerism presents to the rest of the world and whether you think that image is a good or a bad one.

4. Phyllis Rose suggests in "Shopping and Other Spiritual Adventures in America Today" that malls, discount stores, and supermarkets are America's cathedrals, whereas James B. Twitchell, in "In Praise of Consumerism," asserts that consumerism has displaced religion. Write an essay explaining the extent to which you agree with these writers. Can you name other structures that would be more appropriate symbols of America's spiritual center? Is consumerism America's main religion?

5. In "Shopping and Other Spiritual Adventures in America Today," Phyllis Rose refers to the "wonderful egalitarianism of American business" (paragraph 2), and in James Twitchell's "In Praise of Consumerism," he notes that consumerism makes for a "more egalitarian world" (paragraph 25). Using those comments as a starting point, write an essay on American consumerism as a social equalizer.

Additional Writing Topics

1. Imagine that you are marketing a product that has traditionally been sold to one particular segment of the market, such as white, middle-class males. Now you want to increase your sales by targeting other groups. Select a particular group and create a sales campaign aimed at that group.

2. Write a letter to Philip A. Marineau (in Louise Lee's "Can Levi's Be Cool Again?") offering advice on how to make Levi's cool again to young people.

3. Using examples of people you know, either support or refute James B. Twitchell's contention in "In Praise of Consumerism" that Americans are committed to consumerism because "We like having stuff" (paragraph 8).

4. Explain the effects on you or someone you know of a change in income, suddenly coming into money, or acquiring some coveted material possession.

5. Analyze the positive and negative effects of America's emphasis on consumerism on one particular group of people, such as young people, the elderly, working-class people, the wealthy, or those living in poverty.

6. Explain what you think shopping malls, discount stores, and overstocked supermarkets suggest about Americans' values. For instance, what impression do you think foreign visitors get of America when they see the sizes of and selections in those marketplaces?

Research Topics

1. Research the marketing strategies of a major business, perhaps one mentioned in this chapter. Assess what you see as its successes and/or failures in promoting its products.

2. Select a particular product (such as automobiles, cosmetics, clothing, or beer) or a particular target population (such as children, African-American women, or the elderly) and research the market strategies used by major companies for that particular product or group.

3. Research the controversy over Napster and argue your position on the subject.

4. Research the subject of American consumerism and arrive at your own conclusion about its effects on Americans and American values. This is a broad subject, so look for ways to narrow your focus as quickly as you can.

CHAPTER 24

THE WORKPLACE

The workplace can have enormous influence on people's lives. Most Americans work outside the home, either full-time or part-time, spending significant portions of their time on the job. The physical atmosphere of the workplace, the friendliness of coworkers, and the attitudes of supervisors or bosses play pivotal roles not only in the way workers perform but also in the way they feel about themselves. Tension, anxiety, and stress in the workplace can lower production for the company and produce actual illnesses in workers, whereas a pleasant atmosphere, good benefits, and relatively low stress can boost production and make employees look forward to going to work. The quality of life in the workplace has a direct effect on the quality of work employees do and on their general well being.

The essays in this chapter examine some of the issues related to the subject of the workplace. In "For Love or Money," Jay Matthews explains the debate over what motivates employees to do their best. Some research suggests that extrinsic rewards such as financial or other material bonuses do not necessarily result in better work or increased productivity. Rather, intrinsic rewards such as a sense of accomplishment or a feeling of contributing to the good of the company may prove to be more powerful incentives in the long run. What motivates you to do well at something? Do you respond to a promise of something tangible or material, such as a high grade, a gift, or money, or do you pursue the inner reward of knowing you have done your best work and that you are satisfied with your performance? Think about these questions as you read Matthews's review of the complex and multifaceted subject of what motivates human behavior.

Related to Matthews's piece is Matthew Boyle's "Beware the Killjoy," which discusses workplace fun, reports on low rates of job satisfaction, and suggests that corporations should find a balance between the worker-friendly culture of dot-coms and the traditional business model. If, like most college students, you have had a job or are currently working, think about the atmosphere at your workplace. Do you feel a sense of community there? Is your work fun?

Next, Barbara Ehrenreich's "Zipped Lips" treats the subject of freedom of speech in the workplace. "Most workers," she writes, have limited free speech rights, the "right of the employer to fire 'at will' " taking precedence over individual workers' rights. Finally, Terry Golway's "Rewriting the Old Rules" suggests that, despite women's advancement in the corporate world, too often women have had to adopt male values. As you read his discussion about the demands that some professions place on their employees, think about your own employment future. Are you willing to follow what he calls the traditional business model? Is your college education preparing you for the kind of work life that Golway and other authors in this chapter say men and women must accept in order to succeed?

FOR LOVE OR MONEY

Jay Matthews

Jay Matthews is a journalist who wrote this article for the December 1993 issue of the Washington Post National Weekly Edition. *In it, Matthews reviews some theories of behaviorists on what makes employees do their best work.*

In the early 1960s, two graduate students working independently on the ancient problem of coaxing the best from human beings stumbled across results they did not understand. Louise Brightwell Miller at the University of Kentucky discovered that nine-year-old boys were less likely to solve a simple identification test when they were paid for right answers than when they worked for free. Sam Glucksberg at New York University found the same result for adults given a household engineering problem.

Among the behaviorists who have dominated much of American psychology and motivational research since World War II, the notion that people would do better without a material incentive was, as Miller and her adviser said in their report, "an unexpected result, unaccountable for by theory and/or previous empirical evidence."

Thirty years later, the Miller and Glucksberg experiments have become intriguing parts of an intense academic debate over the roots of human motivation and have raised doubts about the methods that American businesses have used for decades to improve employee performance.

4   In books such as *Punished by Rewards: The Trouble with Gold Stars, Incentive Plans, A's, Praise, and Other Bribes* by Alfie Kohn, who cites Miller and Glucksberg, and *Second to None: How Our Smartest Companies Put People First* by Charles Garfield, anti-behaviorist psychologists are arguing that money not only does not buy happiness, it can also, if misapplied, kill a worker's desire to do his or her best.

"When you do something for a reward you tend to become less interested in what you're doing," says Kohn, a writer and lecturer on human behavior who cites the work of dozens of social scientists. "It comes to seem like a chore, something you have to get through in order to pick up the dollar or the A or the extra dessert. What this means is that millions of well-meaning teachers and parents and managers are killing off creativity and curiosity in their attempt to bribe people to do a good job."

To a certain extent, Kohn and Garfield and several other thinkers who take this stand are reviving an old and much-ignored argument just as the anti-reward school was having its greatest impact on Corporate America.

"We are involved in a major change in our culture," says Jim Schmitt, corporate communications director for Westinghouse Electric Corp., speaking of the redesign of jobs and work structures going on in many industries. "We have seen a culture emerging where people are more involved in the decision making regardless of their position in the organization."

8   But to those who want to encourage this trend, the day is still far off when every-one will leap out of bed eager for a day of intrinsically motivated work at the office.

"There are companies that are attempting to understand what truly motivates human beings and then there are others, and I am afraid they are the majority, that have this peculiar affection for pop psychology," including the latest ideas on how to create desire with cash, says Garfield, an associate clinical professor at the University of California at San Francisco.

Raises, promotions, stock options, performance bonuses, merit increases, trips to Disney World, and even new cars are still the prime motivators in American business. Many psychologists see nothing wrong with that. "I have worked with many people for whom a kind word doesn't mean a thing," says E. Scott Geller, professor of psychology at Virginia Polytechnic Institute and State University, "but money can mean many things to many people."

Critics of monetary rewards begin by making sure everyone understands they are not advocating a return to slavery. They say people should be paid well enough so that they are no longer distracted by worries that they are underpaid. "Managers need to divorce the task from the compensation as best they can by paying people well and then doing everything possible to help them put money out of their minds," Kohn says.

12   A material reward might work in the short term, the anti-behaviorists argue. Who wouldn't get excited about a trip to Paris for the sales agent who unloads the most Pismo Beach condominiums? But over time, the theory says, the most successful salespeople will grow tired of trips to Paris and require a motive closer to their sense of themselves or lose their spark altogether.

Kohn even cites studies by his behaviorist critics to buttress his point. In 1987 Geller and several associates reviewed the effects of twenty-eight seat-belt use programs at nine different companies. The results, Geller and his group admitted in their research paper, were "inconsistent with basic reinforcement theory." Programs that did not offer cash or prizes for buckling up reported an average 152 percent increase in seat-belt use over periods up to a year, while the long-term gain for programs with rewards was no higher than 62 percent.

Several business surveys add to the impression of money as a comfort rather than a goal. A 1978 survey of more than fifty thousand utility company applicants found pay ranked sixth out of ten job factors. (The same applicants thought others would put money first.) A 1991 poll showed that even among allegedly money-fixated salespeople, increased compensation was the least commonly cited reason for changing jobs.

But the core of Kohn's book, and its most controversial aspect, is a long appreciation of the research of Edward Deci at the University of Rochester and Mark Lepper at Stanford. The two men insist material rewards do not motivate well, and actually poison natural motivators such as curiosity and self-esteem.

16 Lepper watched children in Head Start classrooms react to an experiment with Magic Markers. Some were told that if they used the markers they would be given a special certificate. Some were given the markers with no anticipated reward. After a week, the children who were told they would get a certificate were using the markers not only less frequently than the unrewarded children, but also less frequently than they themselves had used the markers before they were told of the reward.

Deci put college students in a room and asked each to work a puzzle. Half were promised money; half were not. He then announced a pause before "the next phase of the study began" and watched what they did in those idle moments. Those who had been promised money spent less time playing with the puzzle than those who had not anticipated reward.

Deci concluded that "money may work to 'buy off' one's intrinsic motivation for an activity." Deci and Lepper speculated that people thought they were being manipulated when offered a reward. Although they might do what was necessary to receive their prize, it left a bad taste that tainted what had once been an enjoyable activity for them.

Geller says the Deci–Lepper research is flawed. "People say, 'Well, yeah, once I started playing cards for money, I didn't enjoy playing just for fun any more,' " Geller says. "It has an intuitive feel." But the experiment overlooks what Geller calls "the contrast effect"—the sudden disappointment when the reward is no longer available. If the experimenter continued to watch a card player for several months after he swore off gambling, "you might find he would again eventually want to play cards for free."

20 Kohn says studies show that the harm to intrinsic motivation is enduring.

Some psychologists complain that human motivation and its impact on productivity is just too complex a subject to reduce to debates over extrinsic or intrinsic rewards. J. William Townsend, an industrial organizational psychologist and consultant in Memphis, says he accepts much of the anti-reward research but also knows that some employees will always be motivated by money and little else.

Another factor often overlooked in the debate is talent. "People cannot outperform their abilities," Townsend says. "I don't care how much you motivate me, I'm not going to play basketball better than Michael Jordan."

The anti-behaviorists nod at this and say, fine, what we are doing is giving each person the chance to do his best with the greatest joy in the effort, and without being distracted by money. Kohn offers three ways to stimulate workers' natural desire to do well: Find ways for them to work in teams; give them variety and a sense of worthwhile work; and give them as much choice as possible of what they do and how they do it.

24 "Choice is very important," says Marion Gindes, a psychologist and president of Marion Gindes & Associates in Larchmont, N.Y. "In one very old experiment with monkeys, some were able to control to some extent when they received an electric shock and some were not. Those that had some choice ended up in better shape." Many human studies have reached the same conclusion.

Once a worker has a comfortable salary, Garfield says, "you are looking at other motivators like autonomy, the opportunity to be creative in one's work."

Human resources executives began to play with different motivational formulas in the 1970s, says Neil Lewis, management psychologist in Atlanta, "but then we got into the eighties and everybody lost sight of these things. A monkey could have made money in the eighties. We didn't have to worry about all this employee motivation stuff."

Now that corporate downsizing and restructuring have revived the interest in such research, experts warn that there is still little verifiable data to guide executives who have to decide how to get better results from fewer people. Edward Lazear, a Stanford Business School economist and senior fellow at the Hoover Institution, says some initial studies—admittedly in factories with many complicating problems—are disappointing. Even when the new techniques seem to work, he says, they appear to be tied to other motivators that include money.

28 The motives of the critics of motivational methods are often as complex as those of the workers they study. Graef S. Crystal, editor of the Crystal Report and a passionate advocate of tying executive pay to corporate financial performance, admits that more or less money probably would not motivate million-dollar executives very much. So why argue so hard for linking their compensation to the stock price?

"Because," Crystal says, indulging his love for exaggerated metaphor, "even if none of this motivates the person, it still gives the shareholders the pleasure of sitting in the stands when the stock is plummeting and seeing the executives ripped to shreds by wild animals."

The long history of the debate between behaviorists, devotees of psychologists such as B. F. Skinner, and anti-behaviorists, who prefer the work of thinkers such as Frederick Herzberg, has made many business executives skeptical of both sides.

University of Chicago psychologist Mihaly Csikszentmihalyi says it is useful to remember that different situations produce different motivational needs. "Under the right conditions, material incentives can add to the intrinsic reward," he says, "but sometimes they don't make a difference and sometimes they detract from the intrinsic rewards."

32 Crystal says that although he accepts that money can be a poor motivator, he could not resist a chance years ago to tease Herzberg when the famous anti-behaviorist haggled with him over a fee for a lecture Herzberg was to give on why money doesn't motivate.

"Money in fact doesn't motivate me," Herzberg told Crystal without embarrassment, "but it sure as hell helps me sort out my priorities."

Personal Response

Do you find that rewards—grades, money, prizes—motivate you to try harder or do better work than does a sense of satisfaction for having done a good job?

Questions for Class or Small-Group Discussion

1. What do you think of the idea that people should be paid so well that they are not distracted by money worries (paragraph 11)? Would such a plan be possible in all workplaces? Might employers see the proposal differently from the way employees see it?

2. Alfie Kohn, author of *Punished by Rewards: The Trouble with Gold Stars, Incentive Plans, A's, Praise, and Other Bribes,* says that " 'millions of well-meaning teachers and parents and managers are killing off creativity and curiosity in their attempt to bribe people to do a good job' " (paragraph 5). Now that you have read a little about the debate over incentives, do you agree? In what ways have teachers tried to "bribe" you to do well in class? Do you think you would have done just as well or better without the extra incentives?

3. Discuss the three ways to stimulate workers' natural desire to do well that Kohn suggests in paragraph 23. Do you think they would motivate workers more than the incentives of money, trips, or prizes?

4. Discuss your work experiences. To what extent did self-satisfaction or self-motivation contribute to your performance?

BEWARE THE KILLJOY

Matthew Boyle

Matthew Boyle writes for Fortune *magazine. This article appeared in the July 23, 2001, issue of* Fortune.

All work and no play has made Jon a dull boy. A former dot-commer now at a multinational telecom, Jon (he'd rather we not use his last name) pines for the days of yore. "The bright, translucent plastics, the kooky flashing lights, the scooters—it's all gone," he sighs. An information architect, Jon says his managers "would keel over at the thought of color" and doubts that traditional firms will take any further steps toward emulating the footloose environments of the dot-com phenomenon. "Who cares about job happiness? That's not a measurable benefit," he grumbles. "The closest I get to job satisfaction is a 30-minute nap in my car after lunch."

Jon may just be a disgruntled dot-communist, but his bitterness echoes throughout the American workplace. Three out of four Americans are dissatisfied with or fundamentally disconnected from their jobs, according to a recent Gallup Management Journal survey. Granted, workers have been miserable for centuries—but now that the dot-com boom, which spawned a host of worker-friendly initiatives, has ended, is the joy gone for good?

Not by a long shot. The demise of Kozmo, Pets.com, and their ilk didn't kill workplace fun any more than their arrival created it. Rather, the dot-coms accelerated and took mainstream a trend that began well before anyone had heard of Yahoo. Traditional companies scrambled to provide a more fun atmosphere, as they figured the best way to keep their staff from joining the gold rush was to emulate the Silicon Valley culture. "The dot-coms caused a lot of fury around keeping people engaged," says Sherry Perley, senior VP of human resources at Snapple.

4   The slowdown, of course, has been quite a killjoy. "We're seeing a snap back now," says Orton Varona, team leader of corporate employment and technical recruiting at Southwest Airlines. "Organizations are reeling in some of the perks that they were so liberal with in the past." When companies snap back, workers feel the sting. A survey by the Society for Human Resource Management found that only 27% of companies offered a subsidized cafeteria, compared with 37% in 1999. Company-sponsored sports teams and concierge services are also on the decline.

What's worse, a worker-friendly culture stands accused of precipitating the failure of many dot-coms. "The stuffier side of establishment America is now backlashing and making fun of what was occurring in these dot-com environments," says Nigel Morris, president and CEO of credit card giant Capital One (which itself is still committed to fun—see following box). The dot-com culture as well as the business model is under indictment.

Rather than replace one extreme (emulation) with another (rejection), a better approach is to blend what worked in dot-com land with your existing culture. Casual dress, flextime, and telecommuting are three examples. All existed before the Internet craze (Levi's began its casual-dress crusade in 1992, and Hewlett-Packard rolled out flextime way back in 1973). "Our prognostication is that we'll see blended cultures going forward," says Joan Caruso, managing director of organizational effectiveness at the Ayers Group. Indeed, in a recent survey of B-school students by academic consulting firm Universum, most respondents said they desired an informal work environment but at an established organization.

What you should avoid is segmenting fun. "There are companies that will try this as a program—like 'Send an e-mail out that we're all having fun today,'" says Art Friedson, VP of co-worker services at CDW Computer Centers. Adds Leslie Yerkes, change-management consultant and author of Fun Works: "This is a piece of your cultural fabric; don't create a department to do this." To get superiors to green-light fun, Dana Ardi, human capital partner at J. P. Morgan Partners, has a creative solution. "Call it an opportunity to be more creative in teams," she says. "Then corporations will admire it."

8   In the current climate, fun certainly isn't tops on management's list. But if you kill the fun now and ignore the lessons of the Gen X dot-commers, good luck getting

Gen Y to work for you. Three out of four high school kids surveyed by the Families and Life Institute last year said having a fun job was a must—more important than making lots of money or doing challenging work. Think about that before you cut the company softball team.

AT THESE COMPANIES, THE FUN NEVER STOPS

- Capital One. A "fun budget" of $80 per employee per quarter to spend on activities such as white-water rafting.
- CDW Computer Centers. Krispy Kreme doughnuts once a month and free Dairy Queen every summer Wednesday. If the company meets sales goals, CDW offers an "old-timer" benefit for anyone with three years' service: a free trip for you and your family anywhere in the continental U.S. (awarded every other year).
- Southwest Airlines. Spirit parties, gate- and cake-decorating contests, barbecues, and chili cookoffs are just some of the events planned by local "culture committees."
- Snapple. Theme Fridays during the summer (tie-dye day, silly-hat day), and last year the company built a makeshift miniature golf course inside its corporate headquarters, with each department constructing a hole from materials they use during the course of the day.

Personal Response

Describe the workplace environment at any of the jobs you have held. Was it "fun"? If so, what made it fun; if not, why was it not fun? If you have never had a job, describe your image of the ideal workplace.

Questions for Class or Small-Group Discussion

1. Boyle refers to "worker-friendly initiatives" of the dot-com companies (paragraph 2). What do you gather those initiatives are or were? Can you think of others that he does not mention?

2. Comment on the suggestion Boyle makes that employers would do well to adopt a balance between "an informal work environment" and the traditional ways of working at "an established organization" (paragraph 6). How do you envision such a workplace? What informalities and more traditional practices would there be?

3. Boyle reports: "Three out of four high school kids surveyed [. . .] said having a fun job was a must—more important than making lots of money or doing challenging work" (paragraph 8). Does that statement surprise you? How would you answer such a survey? Is having fun more important to you than making money or doing challenging work?

ZIPPED LIPS

Barbara Ehrenreich

Barbara Ehrenreich's articles appear in a variety of popular maga-zines and newspapers, including Time *magazine,* Ms. *magazine, and the* New York Times, *among many others. Her books include* Witches, Midwives, and Nurses: A History of Women Healers *(with Deirdre English) (1973),* Hearts of Men: American Dreams and the Flight from Commitment *(1984),* For Her Own Good: 150 Years of the Experts' Advice to Women *(with Deirdre En-glish) (1989),* Blood Rites: Origins and History of the Passions of War *(1997),* Fear of Falling: The Inner Life of the Middle Class *(2000), and* Nickel and Dimed: On (Not) Getting by in America *(2001). This article appeared in the* Time *magazine Essay column on February 5, 1996.*

Earlier this month a fellow named Sam Young was fired from his grocery-store job for wearing a Green Bay Packers T-shirt. All right, this was Dallas, and it was a little in-sensitive to flaunt the enemy team's logo on the weekend of the N.F.C. championship game, but Young was making the common assumption that if you stay away from ob-scenity, libel, or, perhaps in this case, the subject of groceries, it is a free country, isn't it? Only problem was he had not read the First Amendment carefully enough: it says *government* cannot abridge freedom of expression. Private employers can, on a whim, and they do so every day.

On January 10, for instance, a Peoria, Illinois, man was suspended from his job at Caterpillar Inc. for wearing a T-shirt bearing the words "Defending the American Dream," which happens to have been one of the slogans of the United Auto Workers in their seventeen-month strike against Caterpillar. Since the strike ended in early December, the firm has forbidden incendiary slogans like "Families in Solidarity" and suspended dozens of union employees for infractions as tiny as failing to shake a fore-man's hand with sufficient alacrity. A fifty-two-year-old worker who failed to peel union stickers off his toolbox fast enough was threatened with loss of retirement benefits.

It is not just blue-collar employees who are expected to check their freedom of speech at the company door. In mid-December, Boston physician David Himmelstein was fired for going public about the gag clause in his employer's contract with doc-tors, forbidding them to "make any communication which undermines or could un-dermine the confidence ... of the public in U.S. Healthcare ..." or even revealing that this clause is in their contract.

4   So where are the guardians of free speech when we need them? For the most part, they are off in the sunny glades of academe, defending professors against the

slightest infringement of their presumed right to say anything, at any volume, to anyone. Last fall, for example, history professor Jay Bergman was reprimanded by his employer, Central Connecticut State University, for screaming at a student he found tearing down a flyer he had posted. Now the Anti-Defamation League and the National Association of Scholars are rallying to have the reprimand rescinded. Reprimand, mind you, not firing or suspension.

Or, in 1991, you would have found the New York Civil Liberties Union defending crackpot Afrocentrist professor Leonard Jeffries of New York's City University. Thanks to such support and the fact that CUNY is a public-sector employer, Jeffries still commands a lectern, from which he is free to go on raving about the oppression of blacks by "rich Jews" and how melanin deficiency has warped the white brain.

Most workers, especially in the private sector, have no such protections. Unless their contract says otherwise, they can be fired "for any reason or no reason"—except when the firing can be shown to be discriminatory on the basis of race, sex, or religion. In addition, a few forms of "speech," such as displaying a union logo, are protected by the National Labor Relations Act, and the courts may decide this makes Caterpillar's crackdown illegal. But the general assumption is, any expansion of workers' rights would infringe on the apparently far more precious right of the employer to fire "at will." So the lesson for America's working people is: If you want to talk, be prepared to walk.

Obviously there are reasonable restrictions on an employee's freedom of speech. A switchboard operator should not break into Tourette's-like torrents of profanity; likewise, professors probably *should* be discouraged from screaming at students or presenting their loopier notions as historical fact. But it's hard to see how a Green Bay Packers T-shirt could interfere with the stocking of Pop-Tarts or how a union sticker would slow the tightening of a tractor's axle. When employers are free to make arbitrary and humiliating restrictions, we're saying democracy ends, and dictatorship begins, at the factory gate.

8   So we seem to have a cynical paradox at the heart of our political culture: "Freedom" is our official national rallying cry, but *un*freedom is, for many people, the price of economic survival. At best this is deeply confusing. In school we're taught that liberty is more precious than life itself—then we're expected to go out and sell that liberty, in eight-hour chunks, in exchange for a livelihood. But if you'd sell your freedom of speech for a few dollars an hour, what else would you sell? Think where we'd be now, as a nation, if Patrick Henry had said, "Give me liberty or give me, uh, how about a few hundred pounds sterling?"

Surely no one really believes productivity would nose-dive if employees were free to wear team logos of their choice or, for that matter, to raise the occasional question about management priorities. In fact, the economy could only benefit from an increase in democracy—and enthusiasm and creativity—on the shop floor. Or does the "free" in "free market" apply just to people on top?

When employers have rights and employees don't, democracy itself is at risk. It isn't easy to spend the day in a state of servile subjugation and then emerge, at 5 p.m., as Mr. or Ms. Citizen-Activist. Unfreedom undermines the critical spirit, and suck-ups make lousy citizens.

Personal Response

Describe any personal experiences you have had with an employer's restricting what employees can wear or say.

Questions for Class or Small-Group Discussion

1. Summarize the central issue of Ehrenreich's essay and the position she has taken on that issue. How persuasive do you find her reasoning process?

2. Discuss your opinion of each of the examples Ehrenreich gives to illustrate both the position of unprotected private sector employees and that of protected professors.

3. What dangers does Ehrenreich see in privileging employers' rights over employees' rights in this matter of free speech? To what extent do you agree with her?

REWRITING THE OLD RULES

Terry Golway

Terry Golway, city editor of the New York Observer *and a frequent columnist for* America *magazine, is author of* Irish Rebel: John Devoy and America's Fight for Ireland's Freedom *(1998),* For the Cause of Liberty: The Story of Ireland's Heroes *(2000), and* Full of Grace: An Oral Biography of John Cardinal O'Connor *(2001). This essay was originally published in the April 23, 2001, issue of* America.

Women are about to outnumber men in the nation's law schools, a development heralding yet another milestone for women and a foreshadowing of great cultural change in the way law is practiced in this country.

There can be no doubt about the former. The latter may not be so easy.

Women have been breaking through glass ceilings in the workplace for more than 30 years, and with each new achievement (the first woman to run for national office, to pilot the space shuttle, to serve as attorney general), society has changed for the better. Young girls now have role models in fields ranging from politics to the sciences to professional sports. Can there be any doubt that historians will one day agree that the civil rights movement and the women's movement were among the transforming events of the 20th century?

4   What these historians will say about the impact of women in the workforce, however, remains to be seen. At the moment, it would be fair to argue that women have not changed the American workplace as much as the workplace has changed women.

Take law, for example. Even with women pouring into law firms across the country, the macho culture of the partner track remains undisturbed. Young men and women still are obliged to perform high-end penal servitude if they wish to become partners at a white-shoe, big-city law firm. Yes, they get paid startling amounts of money—first-year associates in New York during the recently departed boom were commanding salaries approaching six figures—but they are expected to work absurd hours. It is the law culture's equivalent of boot camp, except that the military puts its new recruits through only a few months of terror, while the fresh-faced associate can expect to spend his or her 20's living and breathing for the firm and the firm alone. At the end, of course, there are no guarantees. Those long hours and work-filled weekends may be for naught, at which time an associate had best look for work elsewhere.

Not to make any sweeping generalizations, but only a man could have come up with so ruthless a scheme.

We can be grateful that some law firms have begun to concede that their associates are entitled to a life outside the office and, under pressure from women, have adopted measures like flex-time and part-time work. For the most part, however, the remorseless, endless paper chase remains a signature part of big-time law's partner-track culture.

8   It isn't only law, however, that remains in the thrall of the otherwise discredited macho ethic. In fact, in nearly every profession, in every factory, workers are expected to think of their lives and their jobs as one, to the detriment of family, friends, outside interests and other small pleasures.

Despite the historic entry of millions of women into the workforce, the workplace rules and traditions that men enforce and celebrate have not been repealed. The hoary custom of measuring one's dedication, value and, yes, toughness by the number of hours logged per week hasn't changed. And managers still shake their heads disapprovingly when, in the phrase of one former colleague, a "clockwatcher" begins packing up at 5 P.M. The clockwatcher might have children who need help with homework, or an aged parent to care for, or an anniversary to celebrate. Under the rules of the macho workplace, however, those who let such considerations get in the way of all work, all the time, are considered slackers.

The global marketplace and the technological revolution have made matters worse for those trying to balance their work lives with real life. For millions of workers, there is no escape from professional obligations. I know men and women who feel obliged to bring along their laptop computers when they are on "vacation"—a concept, incidentally, that is beginning to be thought of as yet another outdated ritual from the industrial age. I've been out to dinner with men and women who keep their cell phones ready on the table, just in case the boss (and the boss is not always a male) wants to reach them.

Recent data indicate that the culture of overwork is pervasive in American society. A survey conducted by the National Sleep Association found that 40 percent of the 1,004 adults polled said they worked longer hours than they did five years ago. The average work-week, according to the poll, was 46 hours, but 38 percent said they worked 50 hours or more a week. And then there are those, like the well-dressed fellow who sat next to me on the commuter train the other day, who keep working even when they're home. My seatmate put aside his work-related reading material to call his wife (from his cell phone) to make sure everybody at home knew he needed to use the family computer after dinner. Something to do with developments in the Asian markets.

12   Is it sexist to suggest that women—at least most women I know—have a far saner perspective on the balance between work and life? I hope not. I certainly believe it's true.

For the time being, women probably have little choice but to adhere to the old rules written by corporate America's macho men. But as more women gain power in corporate America, they will have a chance to rewrite the old rules and abolish the macho-overwork ethic for good.

Or so this macho-challenged male hopes.

Personal Response

Does it surprise you that a man wrote this essay? Do you think your response to the essay would be any different were the author a woman?

Questions for Class or Small-Group Discussion

1. Summarize what you understand Golway to mean when he refers to "the workplace rules and traditions that men enforce and celebrate" (paragraph 9), that is, what he calls "the macho culture" (paragraph 5).

2. Golway writes that women "have a far saner perspective on the balance between work and life" (paragraph 12). What do you think he means? In what ways might women have "a saner perspective" than men?

3. Golway refers to women's "breaking through glass ceilings" (paragraph 3). What do you understand that phrase to mean? What examples, other than the ones he mentions, can you give?

PERSPECTIVES ON THE WORKPLACE

Suggestions for Synthesis

1. With references to at least two readings in this chapter, write a paper on workers' perceptions of their workplaces. If possible, interview people who work full-time about their workplace experiences and combine the results of your interview(s) with the comments of writers in this chapter.

2. Referring to at least two of the essays in this chapter, describe what you see as the ideal job or ideal working conditions.

Additional Writing Topics

1. Alfie Kohn, author of *Punished by Rewards: The Trouble with Gold Stars, Incentive Plans, A's, Praise, and Other Bribes,* says that " 'millions of well-meaning teachers and parents and managers are killing off creativity and curiosity in their attempt to bribe people to do a good job' " (paragraph 5, Jay Matthews's "For Love or Money"). Argue in support of or against this statement.

2. Matthew Boyle reports on a survey conducted by the Families and Life Institute (paragraph 8, "Beware the Killjoy") in which workers were asked what they value most in a job, such as having fun, making lots of money, or having a challenging job. Write a paper explaining which your value most and why. Or conduct your own informal interview on the subject of expectations for a job and report your results.

3. Either support or argue against Barbara Ehrenreich's position on the subject of free speech in "Zipped Lips."

4. Narrate your personal experience or that of someone you know who has been in the situation of the fired employees Barbara Ehrenreich mentions in "Zipped Lips."

5. Elaborate on this statement by Terry Golway in "Rewriting the Old Rules": "Women have been breaking through glass ceilings in the workplace [. . .] and with each new achievement [. . .] society has changed for the better" (paragraph 3).

Research Topics

1. Combine library research and personal interviews with area employers for a paper on ways to motivate employees. As Jay Matthews points out in "For Love or Money," the subject is open to debate, so you will need to take a position on which works better, extrinsic or intrinsic incentives.

2. Terry Golway in "Rewriting the Old Rules" suggests that women's ways of doing things are "saner" than men's ways. Research this topic, including interviews, if possible.

3. Research the topic of the effect of workplace environment on employee productivity and morale.

4. Research the subject of free speech rights in the workplace.

CHAPTER 25

THE AMERICAN IMAGE ABROAD

The term *global village* has been used for decades to describe the myriad links among the world's countries. Given the speed of communication and travel between countries today, however, it seems a more apt phrase than ever to describe the close interrelationship of all the world's nations. Satellites link people around the globe, for instance, allowing millions worldwide to simultaneously watch a single event on television. The media of popular culture—television, magazines, and newspapers—play crucial roles in conveying certain images of America and Americans to other nations.

The image of America that is projected to people abroad creates certain stereotypes, or fixed images, of what America represents: materialism, consumerism, opportunity, power, and freedom, to name a few of the qualities foreigners associate with America. Given the place of the United States in the world market, these images can play important roles in trade and other business relations. Therefore, as you read the essays in this chapter, keep in mind the general focus of the unit on business and economics and consider the implications of the American image abroad for the U.S. economy and for conducting international business.

The first essay, Pico Iyer's "Selling Our Innocence Abroad," examines the image of America abroad as represented by American popular culture. Iyer points out that the products of America's popular culture—its movies, songs, magazines, T-shirts, and the like—make up "the largest single source of America's export earnings." These products of American pop culture convey an image that helps perpetuate certain notions about America as a land of glamour, wealth, excitement, and even a kind of innocence. Hollywood, Broadway, and Nashville have particular influence in conveying this image, according to Iyer. Before you read, think about what Hollywood suggests to you. Do you think of glamour, of classic films and famous stars, or do you think of cheap sensationalism, escapism, and money-hungry exploiters out to become rich in any way they can? What picture of America do you think today's Hollywood stars, pop recording artists, and famous Broadway actors project?

Next, writing as a British immigrant to the United States, Michael Elliott, in "Here to Stay," celebrates America as a "land of plenty." Taking a position that differs from that of many critics of American culture, Elliott thinks native-born Americans are not appreciative enough of the material goods they have. He urges Americans to show more gratitude for that plenitude and not to take for granted the many things they have that people in other countries do not. If you are a native-born American, do you take for granted the riches and opportunities that are available to you? If you are foreign born, how do you regard America?

The last two essays take a humorous look at Anglo-American relations by examining the differences between British and American English. They offer different perspectives on the English language, as two journalists explain their experiences with the vocabularies and unfamiliar connotations of words familiar in their own language. Frances Stead Sellers explains the adjustments she has made in "Terribly Sorry, but I Don't Understand." Born and reared in Britain but living in the United States since the early 1980s, she offers a combination of amusing personal anecdotes and comments of linguists and other observers of the language, both British and American, who suggest reasons for such markedly different versions of the same language. Writing from the perspective of an American living in England, T. R. Reid, in "Yobbish Prat Whinges On," uses many British words and terms to indicate the adjustment he has had to make in his English. Though these two readings are light and amusing, they also shed some light on the ways in which two countries who share such a common bond have maintained their own distinctive identities.

SELLING OUR INNOCENCE ABROAD

Pico Iyer

Pico Iyer was born in England to Indian parents and studied at Oxford and Harvard Universities. His books include Video Night in Kathmandu: And Other Reports from the Not-So-Far-East *(1988),* The Lady and the Monk: A Season in Kyoto *(1991),* Falling Off the Map: Some Lovely Places of the World *(1994),* Tropical Classical: Essays from Several Directions *(1997),* The Global Soul: Jet Lag, Shopping Malls, and the Search for Home *(2000), and* The Contagion of Innocence *(1991), from which the following piece is excerpted. Iyer lives in the United States and writes for* Time *magazine.*

There is a genuine sense in many parts of the world that America is being left behind by the rise of a unified Europe and the new East Asian powers. The largest debtor nation in the world, where ten million blacks live in poverty and whose capital, run by a cocaine addict, had a murder rate during the Eighties higher than that of Sri Lanka or Beirut, seems an unlikely model for emulation. And yet America maintains a powerful hold on the world's imagination.

A visitor today in Vietnam, one of the last of America's official enemies, will find crowds in Hue, in waterside cafes, desperate to get a glimpse of Meryl Streep on video; at night, in Dalat, he will hear every last word of "Hotel California" floating across Sighing Lake. In Bhutan, where all the citizens must wear traditional medieval dress and all the buildings must be constructed in thirteenth-century style—in Bhutan, perhaps the most tightly closed country in the world, which has never seen more than three thousand tourists in a single year—the pirated version of Eddie Murphy's *Coming to America* went on sale well before the video had ever come to America.

All this, of course, is hardly surprising and hardly new. Pop culture makes the world go round, and America makes the best pop culture. By now, indeed, such products represent the largest single source of America's export earnings, even as America remains the single most popular destination for immigrants. The more straitened or shut off a culture, the more urgent its hunger for the qualities it associates with America: freedom, wealth, and modernity. The Japanese may be the leaders in technology, the Europeans may have a stronger and more self-conscious sense of their aesthetic heritage, yet in the world of movies and songs and images America is still, and long will continue to be, the Great Communicator. The capital of the world, as Gore Vidal has said, is not Washington but Hollywood. And however much America suffers an internal loss of faith, it will continue to enjoy, abroad, some of the immunity that attaches to all things in the realm of myth. As much as we—and everyone else—assume that the French make the best perfumes and the Swiss the finest watches, the suspicion will continue that Americans make the best dreams.

4   As borders crumble and cultures mingle, more and more of us are becoming hyphenated. I, perhaps, am an increasingly typical example: entirely Indian by blood, yet unable to speak a word of any Indian language; a British citizen, born and educated in England, yet never having really worked or lived in the country of my birth; an American permanent resident who has made his home for two-thirds of his life in America, in part because it feels so little like home; and a would-be resident of Japan. As people like me proliferate, and Filipinos in San Francisco marry Salvadorans, and Germans in Japan take home women from Kyoto, the global village becomes internalized, until more and more of us are products of everywhere and citizens of nowhere.

And though Paris, Tokyo, and Sydney are all in their way natural meeting points for this multipolar culture, America, as the traditional land of immigrants, is still the spiritual home of the very notion of integration. Everyone feels at home in only two places, Milos Forman has said: at home and in America. That is one reason why

America's domination of pop culture is unlikely to subside, even if the reality of American power increasingly seems a thing of the past. The notion of America itself attracts more and more people to come and revive or refresh the notion of America. And the more international a culture is, the more, very often, it draws from the center of internationalism—the United States. The French may rail against cultural imperialism and try to enforce a kind of aesthetic protectionism by striving to keep out *le burger* and *le video*. But as soon as Madonna shows up in Cannes—so efficient is her command of all the media and so self-perpetuating her allure—she sets off the biggest stir in thirty years.

Madonna's global appeal is not unlike that of the Kentucky Fried Chicken parlor in Tiananmen Square: Both provide a way for people to align themselves, however fleetingly, with a world that is—in imagination at least—quick and flashy and rich. The lure of the foreign is quickened by the lure of the forbidden.

I got my own best sense of this in a friend's apartment in Havana some years ago. My friend was an intellectual dissident, fluent in several languages, eager to talk about Spinoza and Saroyan, and able to make a living by reading people's futures from their photographs and translating the latest Top 40 hits—recorded from radio stations in Miami—into Spanish. One night, trying to convey his desperation to escape, he pulled out what was clearly his most precious possession: a copy of Michael Jackson's album *Bad,* on which he had scrawled some heartfelt appeals to Jackson to rescue him. He did not, I suspect, know that Jackson was reclusive, eccentric, and about as likely to respond to political appeals as Donald Duck. What he did know was that Jackson was black, rich, and sexually ambiguous—all things that it is not good to be in Castro's Cuba. What he also knew was that Jackson had succeeded on his own terms, an individual who had proved himself stronger than the system. The less my friend knew about Jackson the man, the closer he could feel to Jackson the symbol. And so it is with America: Since the America that he coveted does not quite exist, it is immutable, a talisman that will fail him only if he comes here.

8   People everywhere, whatever their circumstances, will always have a hunger for innocence, and America seems to have a limitless supply of that resource. Somehow the moguls of Hollywood and Broadway and Nashville—perhaps because they were immigrants themselves, with half a heart on the streets they left—have never lost their common touch: *E.T.* and *Back to the Future* strike universal chords as surely as *Gone with the Wind* and *Casablanca* did half a century ago. These stories continue to affect us because they speak to our most innocent dreams. To renounce them would be to renounce our own innocence.

Personal Response

What does the term *global village* (paragraph 4) mean to you?

Questions for Class or Small-Group Discussion

1. Respond to Milos Forman's comment that everyone feels "at home" in America (paragraph 5). Do you agree with the statement? If so, why do you think America

makes people feel at home? If not, what do you think prevents people from feeling at home in America?

2. In what way is America "the center of internationalism" (paragraph 5) and Hollywood "the capital of the world" (paragraph 3)?

3. What dreams and myths do you think America represents to people around the world (paragraph 3)?

4. In what way or ways do you think the films Iyer mentions in the last paragraph "speak to our most innocent dreams"? Can you name any more recent films as examples of the kind of innocence Iyer is referring to?

5. How does the innocent image of America that some movies portray fit with the "quick and flashy and rich" image of Madonna and Kentucky Fried Chicken (paragraph 6)? That is, how can America seem both "innocent" and "forbidden" to foreigners?

HERE TO STAY

Michael Elliott

Michael Elliott wrote this essay for a special feature on defining America in the July 10, 1995, issue of Newsweek. *Elliott immigrated to the United States from Great Britain in 1974 and has recently become a permanent resident.*

Last month I got my green card, which is neither green, nor a card. It's a smudgy orange stamp in my passport that reads, confusingly, "Temporary evidence of lawful admission for permanent residence." In six months, if I'm lucky, the real card will arrive, though my lawyer tells me that half of them get lost in the mail. Still, "permanent residence" has a nice ring to it. I no longer have to stew in the alphabet soup of Visas A–Z. If my daughters decide to settle in the United States—and this is their home—I can, too. But that's not the whole story. I fell in love with the United States long before I had two suburban kids whose idea of joy is a sidewalk lemonade stand, and I trust I'll be in love with it long after they've left home.

I first arrived in America from Britain in the middle of a hot August night in 1974. There was nobody to meet me—arrangements had gone awry—but a student returning from a year in Paris invited me home. We were soon in Great Neck, on New York's Long Island. I was shown to my room, slept, and then went downstairs for breakfast with my hosts (whose name was Cohen, and whose address I promptly lost: if you read this, thanks). It was a classic August day, dripping with humidity. We were on a patio, beyond which a perfect lawn swooped down to a pool, and then to a dock, and then to a blue-gray slab of water, shimmering in a heat haze: Long Island Sound. I was almost precisely on the spot which, in *The Great Gatsby,* Scott Fitzgerald described as a "fresh, green breast of the world," which is just how it felt. Then came breakfast: huge jugs of coffee; bagels (bagels?); gallons of orange juice. I felt like a horn of plenty had been emptied into my lap, and I've never lost the feeling.

"Plenty" is a dangerous quality on which to base one's love for somewhere. It can sound grasping, as if the only true measure of a place is what it can give you: the more the better. Yet the idea of plenty captures America's enduring appeal better than anything else. "Whatever it is," Bill Bennett once said to me, "America has more of it: more good, more bad, more beauty, more ugliness, more everything." Crucially, more space: the magical emptiness of the intermountain West still fills me with awe.

4   Paradoxically, that endowment of "more" has proved tricky. Perhaps the problem lies in the fact that Americans thank divine providence for their good fortune, rather than hard work or, as the Australians do, dumb luck. In *People of Plenty,* a brilliantly prophetic book written in 1954, David Potter warned that America's success bore within it the seeds of its own destruction. Americans, Potter argued, had grown up to expect that life would keep on getting better—which would leave them at a loss when, as was bound to happen, their luck ran out. And, of course, luck *did* run out. In the awful five years between 1963 and 1968, political stability and social cohesion both collapsed, and then the economy stopped growing at its post-1945 rate. My arrival in the United States coincided with the end of the long postwar boom, and in large measure American opinion has never come to terms with that truth.

This inability to cope with something less than unbounded plenty has left America a place strangely unable to see its own strengths, with a mood which runs from dyspepsia to anger and then paranoia. In twelve years, nothing has so upset me as the aftermath of the Oklahoma City bombing, as the television screens filled with first, those who had grown to hate their government, and then with their sharp-suited apologists. Yet—and perhaps immigrants understand this better than natives—there is no government on earth so hemmed in by constitutive rules which limit its power to do harm. The stability of American institutions should be the wonder of the world.

And, to a large extent, is. Immigration is the acid test of a society's character; people do not immigrate to lands where they will be less free, less able to realize their dreams. By that measure, modern America is a startling success. The success, to be sure, has come at a price; America is a more messy, Babel of a place than it was in the 1950s. My children have friends whose parents were born in India, Turkey, Guatemala, France, Ireland, and other countries too numerous to list. This delights me. In the next century, *everywhere* is going to be multiethnic—it's just that in this respect (as in so many others) America has got there first. My kids are learning, better than they would anywhere else, what it means to grow up in an ethnic mosaic with shared values.

Shared values? Aren't we supposed to be "Balkanizing," or something? Oh, tosh. America has a remarkable unity on the things that really matter: In May I asked my eighty-nine-year-old aunt, visiting America for the first time, what had most impressed her. "They love their country," she said (as I knew she would).

8   This Independence Day, I'll be on Long Island Sound once more, on the "most do-
mesticated body of saltwater in the western hemisphere" (Fitzgerald again, inevitably). There'll be barbecues and flags and fireworks and ice cream (how sensible to
have a national day in high summer). I will think no great, solemn thoughts; Independence Day is too much fun for that. But at some point I will allow myself an old
wish: that native-born Americans could have as much confidence in their nation as
those of us who willingly came here from elsewhere. We are indeed a people of plenty:
Why can't we enjoy it?

Personal Response

Describe your feelings about your country. Do you have a strong sense of commitment to and belief in it? Are you critical of any aspects of it?

Questions for Class or Small-Group Discussion

1. For Elliott, the "idea of plenty captures America's enduring appeal better than
anything else" (paragraph 3). Do you feel that way about America as well? If not,
what do you find most appealing about America?

2. Elliott suggests that Americans grew so used to expecting things to get better that
they were unable to cope when "the economy stopped growing at its post-1945 rate"
(paragraph 4) and that this inability to cope is responsible for "a mood which runs
from dyspepsia to anger and then paranoia" (paragraph 5). Do you see evidence of
this unhappiness with America?

3. Elaborate on Elliott's comment about what immigrants to America "understand
[. . .] better [perhaps] than natives" (paragraph 5).

4. Do you agree with Elliott that Americans do not enjoy their position as "a people
of plenty" (paragraph 8)?

5. Why do you think Elliott quotes from *The Great Gatsby* (paragraphs 2 and 8)?
What relevance does that book have to the central idea of his essay?

TERRIBLY SORRY, BUT I DON'T UNDERSTAND

Frances Stead Sellers

*British-born writer Frances Stead Sellers, former deputy editor of
Civilization magazine, is an assistant editor of Outlook and a con-
tributor to the Washington Post. "Terribly Sorry, but I Don't Under-
stand" appeared in the Sunday, May 10, 1998, issue of the
Washington Post as part of the feature "A Look at English versus
English." It was published as a companion piece with T. R. Reid's
"Yobbish Prat Whinges On," which follows this essay.*

For almost sixteen years now, I've misused, mispronounced, and misspelt your language. And what do I get in return? Respect. It's not just that you think my British English is quaint. Many of you firmly believe that just because I call pants *trousers* (and pronounce it "trowsas"), I'm a little better educated, perhaps even a little more intelligent. So there's not much incentive for me to adapt.

Not that I speak exactly the way I used to. I try to make myself understood, so I say *mailbox* instead of *pillarbox, faucet* not *tap, truck* rather than *lorry;* I've come to understand the difference between an apartment and a condominium (they were all flats to me); I know that sometimes you add syllables we think are redundant (*burglarize* for *burgle*) and that sometimes you drop ones we consider essential (for me, *divest* means taking off clothes, which is different from *disinvesting*).

I've learnt (some habits are harder to break than others) that there's no guarantee I'll find a bath in a bathroom or get much rest in a restroom. I generally *call* people rather than *ring them up*—and I try hard to remember to do it all in reverse when I go back to England. But there are always new surprises. Just last week I found out from a friend that here *puce* means some shade of green. (In England, it means *red*—the flush that comes from exertion or acute embarrassment.) And that *diddle* (which means nothing more than *cheat* to me) suggests something rather different here—although the people I've asked can't seem to agree upon exactly what.

4   So sometimes misusing words isn't just quaint, it can actually get you into trouble. When I came to Philadelphia as a graduate student in the early 1980s, other British speakers told me war stories about America's messy linguistic traps. Hugh described what had happened when he made a mistake in a diagram and asked the student next to him if he could borrow her *rubber.* She gave him a disconcerted glance and he added, "I only need it for a second." A look of alarm came over her face. Now thoroughly confused, Hugh said, "I'll give it back when I've finished." So Hugh found out what it was—and that it didn't belong on the end of a pencil.

I was grateful for the advance warning—until one rainy day several months later. At a restaurant where I worked part-time, a customer handed me, along with his umbrella and raincoat, a large, soggy carrier bag. "Mind looking after my wet rubbers?" he asked. "I'll pick them up later." Never have I been happier to see a pair of galoshes.

At times like this, I realize how very distinct the two languages are. Though I like to consider myself almost bilingual, I think I'll never understand all the nuances. Kind as you may be about the way we speak, if we British harbour any pretensions about lording it linguistically over this former colony, some verbal slip will bring us smartly to our knees. And perhaps that shouldn't be so surprising. After all, our languages have been evolving separately for some three hundred years.

Of course, the pioneers needed new words to describe the geography they discovered and the cultures they encountered (hence *canyon* and *wigwam*). But apart from these necessary neologisms, British and American English were still very similar until late in the eighteenth century, according to Robert McCrum, coauthor of *The Story of English.* It was with the uprising you call the War of Independence that the notion of creating an independent American language gained an ideological following. And the new language of North America was not even necessarily to be English. Some suggested adopting Hebrew, French, or even Greek. English prevailed, but it was, in the words of Benjamin Rush, to be an "improved and perfected" version.

8   Noah Webster, the champion of American English and advocate of spelling reform, considered establishing a separate language a matter of nationalist pride: "Our honor requires us to have a system of our own in language as well as government," he wrote in 1789. He predicted that the Americans, mixing with non-European peoples and developing new ideas in the arts and sciences, would "produce in a course of time, a language in North America, as different from the future language of England, as the modern Dutch, Danish, and Swedish are from German, or from one another."

Despite the interest of prominent figures from Thomas Jefferson and John Adams to writer H. L. Mencken, American English has rarely enjoyed a good press, particularly on the other side of the Atlantic. Webster's English rival, Samuel Johnson, fired one of the first shots by denouncing the American dialect as a "tract of corruption." Ever since, "the English language has always been one of the battlegrounds of Anglo-American rivalry," wrote McCrum, "a fascinating window on to the tensions of the 'special relationship.' "

My (American) husband and I sometimes have found our own special relationship strained by the subtleties of language. Early in our marriage, Tim would often praise a meal I made by saying, "It's quite good." I hid my disappointment, because *quite* in British English generally softens rather than intensifies enthusiasm. All the while he believed he was flattering me, I had understood him to be telling me that my roast beef and Yorkshire pudding was "good, but not very good." And, in turn, I used to wonder why my lukewarm verdicts on a pair of earrings or brass candlesticks ("They're quite nice," I'd say) inspired him to buy them for me.

Despite the misunderstandings, there is a certain liberation to living in a country where my choice of words—let alone my accent and intonation—no longer tells more about me than I'm ready to say. When I was growing up in southeast England, people took note whether you said *serviette* or *napkin, toilet* or *lavatory, dinner* or *lunch* for the meal in the middle of the day. To say *serviette* immediately marked you as "Non-U" (not upper class), in the term that the writer Nancy Mitford popularized more than forty years ago.

12   But even in England, English has changed. Listen to a BBC broadcast from the fifties and the announcers sound far more formal and precise than they do today. My English friend Sally, who has lived in America for almost as long as I have, recently heard a tape of herself when she was fifteen. "I couldn't believe it," she told me. "I was speaking such a crystalline English."

Though I confess a certain fondness for the Queen's English (maybe because it reminds me of my mother), it no longer holds the cachet it once did in England. To many people, the old standard now sounds snooty, not listener-friendly. There is much greater acceptance, and real appreciation, of regional accents. And some Americanisms like *truck* and *apartment,* which I so carefully edit from my speech when I go home (it's quaint to be able to use *lorry* and *flat* again) have gained a new currency there.

Do these new words and Britain's more relaxed speaking style suggest that our two languages are becoming more similar? Movies, television programs, and pop songs have certainly increased the number of American words and spellings in England, but there's not much evidence, according to David Crystal, the British linguist and author of *The Cambridge Encyclopedia of the English Language,* that American English will ever hold sway over its British cousin. As Crystal says, "There remains a solid core of British/American difference, because people like to retain their identities."

And I think it is partly because of a desire to retain my own identity that I still say *trousers* and that my accent becomes more pronounced when I ring up my English relatives or even talk about England (as Cora, my eleven-year-old daughter, delights in pointing out). Of course we adapt some aspects of the way we speak to fit in, but we don't altogether change who we are. It is that need to maintain our separate identities that will keep us—Americans and British—divided by our common language.

Personal Response

Do you hold the opinion, as Sellers says Americans do, that a British accent is a "quaint" indication of both a good education and intelligence (paragraph 1)? If yes, try to explain why. If not, what opinion do you have of speakers with a British accent?

Questions for Class or Small-Group Discussion

1. Sellers writes that when she first came to America, "other British speakers told [her] war stories about America's messy linguistic traps" (paragraph 4). Explain those "linguistic traps."

2. Sellers says that misusing words "can actually get you into trouble" (paragraph 4). What examples does she give to support that statement? Do you think that statement might also be true of Americans speaking American English or the British speaking British English? That is, how might the misuse of language or ignorance of the meanings of words get one into trouble in one's own country?

3. Sellers says that in her own country, word choice used to be an indication of class membership (paragraph 11) and that British English has become less formal than it once was (paragraph 12). How does she account for the changes?

4. Sellers notes that "British and American English were still very similar until late in the eighteenth century" (paragraph 7). Why did differences between the two develop? What accounts for the continued " 'Anglo-American rivalry' " (paragraph 9)? Do you agree with Sellers that British and American English are likely to remain distinct from one another?

YOBBISH PRAT WHINGES ON

T. R. Reid

T. R. Reid, London bureau chief for the Washington Post, *has a syndicated weekly column and does commentary for National Public Radio. Author of five books in English and two in Japanese, Reid's* Confucius Lives Next Door: What Living in the East Teaches Us about Living in the West *(1999) is based on his five and a half years in Tokyo. This article ran as a companion piece with Frances Stead Sellers's "Terribly Sorry, but I Don't Understand" in the Sunday, May 10, 1998, issue of the* Washington Post *for the feature "A Look at English versus English."*

LONDON. I'm sure the "agony aunts" in the newspapers here would call me a daft whinge for saying this, but it only took a fortnight in England to leave me completely knackered. And it's all the fault of the editors of the *Washington Post.*

Of course I was dead chuffed when they assigned me to be this newspaper's new London correspondent. But I was nobbled by one worry. Before I leave for England, I told them, I'd better get some language training. Ha ha ha, the brass replied, steering me toward the airport. We've heard that joke before.

Joke? It's no joke. It hardly takes a boffin to see that my chunter to the guv'nors was bang-on. I've had so many naff verbal prangs in the past couple of weeks that I sometimes feel I'll have to become a total anorak before I can suss the strange and wonderful language spoken here.

4   Some things about England's version of English were fairly easy to learn. Once you figure out that *goal* is pronounced *jail,* that *Towcester* sounds like *toaster,* that *St. John* is *sinjin,* and that *clwyd* rhymes with *fluid,* you're at a point where you can almost read the language out loud without sounding like a hapless berk. A *berk* means a dumb jerk, and rhymes with it—which makes it all the harder to understand why *clerk* is pronounced *clark.*

It's not all that difficult to figure out that a *plaster* is a Band-aid, a *biscuit* is a cookie, and a *jumper* is a sweater. Or that the pound key on a telephone is the *hash key,* and that an organization called the *Royal Mail* delivers something called the *daily post.* Some Englishisms seem much better to me than their American counterparts. The straightforward assertion "She's ex-directory" is both simpler and snappier than "She has an unlisted number."

I'm not even sure that we Americans have a noun to describe an Ann Landers-type columnist. To fill this linguistic gap, we ought to adopt the standard British term: *agony aunt.* It's certainly livelier than *advice columnist,* or whatever an American newspaper might use. (In this category, though, I still think the Japanese have trumped us both with their *jinsei sodan,* or "human life consultant.")

In some areas of discourse, England's English is more direct. That stuff we pour in coffee under the decorous label *half-and-half* is known here, bluntly, as *half-fat*. A worker who gets axed in a corporate downsizing is not referred to as *unemployed*, or even *laid-off*. In Britain, he's *redundant*.

8   On the other hand, many of the unfamiliar words I have encountered here are draped in layers of nuance—the British generally are more than happy to explain these things to those of us who had the misfortune to learn English in the New World.

When I first came upon the mysterious adjective *twee*, for example, I turned to my friend Mary Ann Sieghart, a brilliant woman who writes editorials (sorry, *leaders*) for the *Times* of London. Over beer and potato chips (sorry, *crisps*) one day, she gave me a virtual dissertation on twee-ness.

"Now, *twee* comes from *sweet*," she began, "but it actually means a bit too sweet. *Twee* means the white picket fence around the Tudor house, and then when you go inside it's the pink floral tablecloth for high tea, plus the dried flowers in wicker baskets, plus the scented candles. That whole scene is twee. It's charming, don't you see, but too charming."

Sometimes, though, such requests for help turn out pear-shaped (the term *pear-shaped*, strangely enough, means *unsuccessful*). Reading the newspaper one day in the London subway (sorry, *tube*), I found a leader that accused Prime Minister Tony Blair of "bunking off geography." I turned to the bloke next to me and asked what *bunking off* might mean. "Bunkin'?" the fellow said. "Bunkin' off? Well, sure, mate, bunking off, it's just about the same thing as skiving, innit?"

12   Except for the occasional social blunder—I learned the hard way that you're not supposed to use the word *shag* in polite company—my struggles with the native tongue have been harmless and entertaining. But the other day, my inability to understand the English language cost me money.

I stopped in at the local turf accountant—a charming British euphemism for *bookie*—to place a bet on the famous horse race called the Derby (rhymes with *Barbie*). I picked a horse, filled in the tout slip and laid 5 pounds on the counter. To my delight, my horse came romping home at 7–1 odds.

Instead of the 35-pound ($60) windfall I had every right to expect, though, my winnings barely exceeded 8 pounds. When I complained, the clerk explained: "Your chit was an each-way, mate. A four-way punt. Quarters your quid."

"But, but, I don't understand why . . ." I sputtered before he cut me off.

"Don't go whingeing about like some yobbish wally," he said. "Don't you sodding Yanks know English?"

English to English

Anorak: a geek
Boffin: A scientist, a genius
Bunk off: See skive
Chemist: Drugstore
Chuffed: Pleased
Dead chuffed: Totally delighted

Knackered: Exhausted, worn out
Naff: Boring, tasteless
Nappies: Diapers
Paid: Put an end to
Prang: An accident
Prat: A dork, a fool
Rumbustious: Noisy, uppity
Skive: To cut class, skip work
Suss: To master, to solve
Whinge: A whiner, a tattletale
Yobbish: Rowdy

Personal Response

Explain your response to reading this essay. Were you entertained or amused by it? If you have ever been in a situation in which your vocabulary or ignorance of a word's meaning has caused you difficulty, describe the situation.

Questions for Class or Small-Group Discussion

1. Discuss aspects of Reid's linguistic difficulties and adjustments that particularly interest or amuse you.

2. At the end, Reid lists many of the words he uses in the article, but he does not include all of them on that list. Can you tell from the context what the words he does not define mean? For instance, what do you suppose the clerk's explanation about why he won only 8 pounds instead of 35 means (paragraph 14)? Locate other words that Reid does not define, and see if you can determine what they mean.

3. How important do you think language is to maintaining positive relationships with people of other countries? Do you think that in countries like America and Great Britain, which share a common language, the barriers to understanding are not as important as they might be in countries with different languages, such as America and Japan, for instance?

4. Expanding Reid's experiences as an American adopting British terminology while in Britain, discuss how important you think linguistic heritage is to identity. How important do you think it is that speakers of other languages adopt the local tongue when they visit or become residents? Would you try to learn the language of a foreign country before your visit?

PERSPECTIVES ON THE AMERICAN IMAGE ABROAD

Suggestions for Synthesis

1. Interview foreign students on your campus to gather their impressions of American people and culture, and write an essay in which you summarize your findings and analyze reasons to account for those impressions. Incorporate into your paper the views of one or more of the writers in this chapter.

2. Interview people who have immigrated to America to learn their reasons for coming to this country. Find out what images they had of America before they came and whether their impressions have changed now that they are living here. Include Michael Elliott's viewpoints in "Here to Stay" in your paper.

3. Using two or more of the essays in this chapter in combination with your own thoughts on the subject, write a paper on some aspect of the American image abroad.

4. Write an essay on the function of language as barrier or bridge in the context of either the relationship between two countries or the relationship between an individual from one country and people in another. Refer to Frances Stead Sellers's "Terribly Sorry, but I Don't Understand" and T. R. Reid's "Yobbish Prat Whinges On."

5. Write an essay explaining your conclusions about the linguistic differences between British and American English from reading Frances Stead Sellers's "Terribly Sorry, but I Don't Understand" and T. R. Reid's "Yobbish Prat Whinges On."

Additional Writing Topics

1. Write an essay explaining why you think America's popular culture appeals to people in other countries.

2. Select a recent popular film and analyze the image of America that it projects.

3. Do a close analysis of a person or object from popular culture that you think represents an aspect of American culture.

4. Define *global village,* citing specific examples from your own experiences or observations.

5. Write an essay in which you analyze an American book or story for the image it projects of America. Try to view the book or story objectively, as if you were a foreigner looking for information about America.

6. Explore the subject of cultural stereotypes by looking at the way in which Americans stereotype people in a particular foreign country. What accounts for the stereotype? How does it prevent full understanding of the culture? What can you do to help dispel the stereotype?

7. What image of America and Americans is portrayed in the most recent American book or short story you have read? What impression do you think a foreigner reading the same book or story would get of America?

8. Write an opinion essay on the relative importance of language in establishing good international relationships. If you have ever been in a situation in which language was a barrier to communication, either in your own country or abroad, narrate that experience.

Research Topics

1. Pico Iyer, in "Selling Our Innocence Abroad," describes America as "the center of internationalism" (paragraph 5). Conduct library research on this subject with a view to either supporting or refuting Iyer's assertion.

2. Conduct library research to expand on the views expressed by writers in this chapter of the American image abroad. From your research, draw some conclusions about that image. Do you find one particular image or many images? What aspects of America are responsible for the image or images? Does the image of America differ from country to country or even from continent to continent? You should be able to narrow your focus and determine a central idea for your paper after your preliminary search for sources and early review of the materials.

3. Research the subject of U.S. relations with Japan, China, the Soviet Union, or another foreign country that may figure importantly in the future of the United States. On the basis of your research, assess the importance to the United States of strengthening such relations and the potential effects of allowing relations with that country to deteriorate.

4. Taking Frances Stead Sellers's "Terribly Sorry, but I Don't Understand" and T. R. Reid's "Yobbish Prat Whinges On" as starting points, research the linguistic differences between American and British English. This is a broad subject, so do some preliminary searching on the subject to narrow your focus.

CHAPTER 26

THE UNITED STATES IN THE GLOBAL MARKETPLACE

If we live in a "global village," we also buy and sell in a "global marketplace." Manufacturers that once exported goods to other nations now build plants and sell goods directly in those countries. American businesses that once limited themselves to the domestic market are now expanding operations beyond the United States as they compete in foreign markets. Indeed, most trade analysts predict that the twenty-first century will see enormous growth in global prosperity as businesses compete for foreign trade and increase their expansion in the global marketplace. Certainly, the ease of international travel makes the process of conducting business with other countries not much more difficult than travel from state to state was in former days, and the fax machine and Internet capabilities have had enormous impacts on business communication. Combine those factors with the rise in market economies in previously communist countries, and you have some compelling reasons to account for optimistic forecasts for the global economy in the twenty-first century.

The essays in this chapter focus on the issue of globalization and the place of the United States in the global market. First, UN Secretary-General Kofi Annan, in "Development without Borders," comments on the issue of globalization, including its benefits, how to get the most out of it, and how to expand opportunities for all nations, including underdeveloped ones. Next, Vito Tanzi, in "Globalization without a Net," reports that the process of global economic integration will require a fundamental overhaul of the role the state plays in pursuing social protection policies targeted toward specific groups. He argues that globalization undermines social protection and conjectures on the likely impact of the increasing harmonization of tax policy across countries. He ends by suggesting three main policy instruments to build the modern welfare state.

In "Mixing '60s Activism and Anti-Globalization," Robert Borosage reports on the increased activism of today's college students in their efforts to oppose what they see as the exploitative aspects of globalization. Taking on the global corporation might have seemed an impossible goal, but students influenced major American corporations to make changes in the way they conduct their manufacturing abroad. Borosage writes: "Already, even pundits who disparage the demonstrators have begun to accept that worker rights and the environment, food and workplace safety can no longer be ignored in the global market."

Finally, in defense of globalization, Murray Weidenbaum's speech, "Dispelling the Myths about the Global Economy," addresses ten myths or misunderstandings that he says people have about the global economy and its impact on the American business system. Taking each one in turn, he explains why the belief is a myth and what the reality is. As you read his responses to the attacks of student groups, environmentalists, unionists, and human rights groups, among others, against globalization, consider the extent to which you agree with him. Can you offer counterarguments to his assertions? Indeed, as you read all of the readings in this chapter, consider what implications America's place in the global market has for your own future.

DEVELOPMENT WITHOUT BORDERS

Kofi Annan

Kofi Annan of Ghana is the seventh Secretary-General of the United Nations, the first to be elected from the ranks of the United Nations staff. He joined the United Nations in the early 1970s and has held many positions, including Assistant Secretary-General for Program Planning, Budget and Finance; head of human resources; director of the budget; chief of personnel for the High Commissioner for Refugees; administrative officer for the Economic Commission for Africa; and Under-Secretary-General for Peacekeeping Operations. This paper was published in the summer 2001 issue of the Harvard International Review.

What is globalization? More than ever before, groups and individuals are interacting directly across borders without involving the state. This happens partly due to new technology and partly because states have found that prosperity is better secured by releasing the creative energies of their people than by restricting them.

The benefits of globalization are obvious: faster growth, higher standards of living, and new opportunities. However, globalization's benefits are very unequally distributed; the global market is not yet underpinned by shared social objectives, and if all of today's poor follow the same path that brought the rich to prosperity, the earth's resources will soon be exhausted. The challenge we face is to ensure that globalization becomes a positive force for all people instead of leaving billions in squalor.

If we are to get the most out of globalization, we must learn how to provide better governance at the local, national, and international levels. We must think afresh about how we manage our joint activities and our shared interests, since so many challenges that we confront today are beyond the reach of any state acting on its own.

4   This should not be seen as a future of world government or the eclipse of nation-states. On the contrary, states will draw strength from each other by acting together within the framework of common institutions based on shared rules and values. Governments must work together to make these changes possible, but governments alone cannot make them happen. Much of the heavy lifting will be done by private investment and charitable foundations.

The best ideas, however, will come from nongovernmental sources: from academic researchers, nonprofit organizations, business, the media, and the arts. These elements compose civil society, and they have a vital role to play.

At the UN Millennium Summit in September 2000, world leaders resolved to halve three figures: the number of people whose income is less than one US dollar a day, the proportion of people who suffer from hunger, and the proportion of people who are unable to reach or afford safe drinking water. They resolved to accomplish these goals by 2015. History will judge this generation by what it did to fulfill that pledge.

Success in achieving sustained growth depends on expanding access to the opportunities of globalization. That in turn depends in large measure on the quality of governance a country enjoys. Countries can only compete in the global market if their people benefit from the rule of law, effective state institutions, transparency and accountability in the management of public affairs, and respect for human rights. Their people must have a say in the decisions that affect their lives.

8   If developing countries succeed in creating the right economic and social environment, new technology can put many opportunities within their reach. That is especially true of information technology, which does not require vast amounts of hardware, financial capital, or even energy, and which is relatively environment-friendly. What information technology does require is brain power—the one commodity that is equally distributed among the peoples of the world. So for a relatively small investment—for example, an investment in basic education—we can bring all kinds of knowledge within reach of the world's poor and enable poor countries to leapfrog some of the long and painful stages of development that other nations had to go through.

In short, there is much that poor countries can do to help themselves. But rich countries have an indispensable role to play. For wealthy nations to preach the virtues of open markets to developing countries is mere hypocrisy if they do not open their own markets to those countries' products or stem the flooding of the world market with subsidized food exports that make it impossible for farmers in developing countries to compete. Nor can they expect developing countries to protect the global environment, unless they are ready to alter their own irresponsible patterns of production and consumption.

Developing countries must be helped to export their way to prosperity. Everyone now agrees that the burden of debt must be lifted from the poorest countries, but developed countries have not yet come forward with sufficient resources to alleviate this burden. Nations, whether in debt or not, need help to reach the stage where they can produce goods and services that the rest of the world wants to buy. Many also need help in resolving destructive conflicts and rebuilding a peaceful, productive society.

Long ago, all members of the Organization for Economic Cooperation and Development committed 0.7 percent of their gross domestic product to development aid. Very few made good on that commitment. Private companies, as well as governments, have an obligation to consider the interests of the poor when making investment choices and when pricing their products. Companies are the largest beneficiaries of globalization; it is in their interest to make this trend sustainable, by helping it work for all.

12   Only when the lives of ordinary men, women, and children in cities and villages around the world are made better will we know that globalization is becoming inclusive, allowing everyone to share in its opportunities. This is the key to eliminating world poverty.

Personal Response

Respond to Annan's suggestion that rich countries have an obligation to help developing countries. To what extent do you agree with him?

Questions for Class or Small-Group Discussion

1. What do you understand Annan to mean when he says that "globalization's benefits are very unequally distributed" (paragraph 2)? That is, what are the benefits of globalization, according to him, and why are they unequally distributed?

2. Do you think it possible for world leaders to achieve the goals resolved upon at the UN Millenium summit (paragraph 6)? What do you think they will have to do to accomplish these goals?

3. Discuss ways in which rich or strong nations could help poor or developing countries enhance their brain power (paragraph 8).

4. Comment on this statement: "Private companies, as well as governments, have an obligation to consider the interests of the poor when making investment choices and when pricing their products" (paragraph 11).

GLOBALIZATION WITHOUT A NET

Vito Tanzi

Vito Tanzi is Director, Fiscal Affairs Department of the International Monetary Fund. He is author or editor of over a dozen books, including Taxation in an Integrating World *(Integrating National*

Economies: Promise and Pitfalls) (1995), Public Spending in the
Twentieth Century: A Global Perspective *(2000), and* Policies,
Institutions, and the Dark Side of Economics *(2000). This essay
appeared in the July/August 2001 issue of* Foreign Policy.

Today's fractious debates over economic and financial globalization often turn on
how best to care for the people most vulnerable to sudden changes wrought by new
technologies, foreign competition, or industrial relocation. On this question, however, a new consensus is emerging around a simple, compelling proposition: Countries can harness the many benefits of global integration as long as they provide
strong social protection programs that mitigate the fallout on society's weakest members. As World Trade Organization Director-General Michael Moore expressed in October 2000: "Of course, some people do lose in the short run from trade liberalization.
. . . But the right way to alleviate the hardship of the unlucky few is through social
safety nets and job retraining rather than by abandoning reforms that benefit the
many."

This call for strengthened social protection evokes similar efforts in the aftermath of World War II when many nations, particularly in Western Europe, erected formal, state-financed social protection systems to safeguard citizens from the risks
linked to old age, illness, unemployment, and poverty. Governments deployed three
main policy instruments to build the modern welfare state: first, direct public spending on social programs such as healthcare, pension benefits, and unemployment compensation; second, tax deductions for "socially desirable" spending by individuals,
such as interest payments on home mortgages and medical and educational expenses; and third, regulations that protect workers or other special groups, including
minimum-wage laws, rent controls, subsidized student loans, and reduced rates on
public utilities.

Today, however, the growing integration of economies and the free movement of
capital across borders threaten to undermine the effectiveness of these policy tools.
Even as the forces of globalization boost the demand for strong social safety nets to
protect the poor, these forces also erode the ability of governments to finance and implement large-scale social welfare policies.

4   Consider the tax revenue needed to finance social spending. Although many industrialized economies have their fiscal houses in order, with tax revenues near historical highs, several "fiscal termites" linked to globalization are nevertheless
gnawing at their foundations. These termites include increased travel by individuals,
which allows them to purchase expensive and easily transportable items in countries
or regions with low sales taxes, thus encouraging small nations to reduce taxes on
luxury products to attract foreign buyers. Similarly, the growth of global e-commerce
represents a nightmare for tax authorities, since paperless, electronic transactions
leave few footprints. Even if governments try to implement origin-based taxation of
e-commerce, stores and other sales establishments will simply relocate to places
with few or no sales taxes. And as products formerly sold only in shops and offices—
everything from music, movies, and books to financial advice, engineering plans, and

educational services—increasingly become digital products sold over the Internet, the very concept of a tax jurisdiction will seem a quaint anachronism.

The growing use of offshore tax havens as conduits for financial investments likewise weakens national tax collection since individuals or corporations holding such assets—recently estimated at $5 trillion worldwide—are unlikely to report the income they earn to the revenue authorities in their home countries. The rise of unregulated hedge funds and new financial instruments, including derivatives, also pose enormous challenges for tax authorities seeking to identify individuals, transactions, and incomes. Finally, the growth of international trade among subsidiaries of the same multinational corporation further complicates tax collection, since companies can easily manipulate internal prices to keep profits in low-tax jurisdictions—so-called transfer pricing. For example, some analysts have questioned the high profits that multinational firms record as originating in Ireland (a country that happens to offer particularly low tax rates for corporations). Put together, these elements will keep governments from maintaining current tax revenues; thus, policymakers will have little choice but to cut spending on social protection programs.

The increasing harmonization of tax policy across countries—resulting from tax competition to attract investment—will place downward pressure on tax rates and further restrict governments' ability to use tax policy for social protection. A survey of corporate tax rates in 14 major industrialized countries already shows a precipitous decline in recent years, from an average of about 46 percent in 1985 to 33 percent in 1999. Similar reductions have occurred with tax rates on individuals.

Finally, globalization undermines social protection by introducing deregulatory pressures. In an attempt to make local companies more efficient and more competitive internationally, for instance, governments may further privatize additional public enterprises and liberalize national labor and credit markets, curtailing or eliminating laws that make it difficult to fire workers or that give credit preferences to vulnerable groups.

8   Of course, the competitive pressures of globalization, as well as the need to comply with new international agreements, may push policymakers to increase spending on education, training, research and development, the environment, and on reforming government institutions. Such initiatives likely would offer broad benefits to society as a whole. Ultimately, however, the process of global economic integration will require a fundamental overhaul of the role the state plays in pursuing social protection policies targeted toward specific groups—including those adversely affected by the downsides of globalization.

Personal Response

Explain the degree to which you are convinced by Tanzi's argument that participation in the global economy will make it increasingly impossible to protect vulnerable populations.

Questions for Class or Small-Group Discussion

1. Summarize the risks that Tanzi implies are likely to befall "the people most vulnerable to sudden changes wrought by new technologies, foreign competition, or industrial relocation" (paragraph 1).

2. Explain how, according to Tanzi, "even as the forces of globalization boost the demand for strong social safety nets to protect the poor, these forces also erode the ability of governments to finance and implement large-scale social welfare policies" (paragraph 3). Are you convinced by his argument?

3. Tanzi writes: "Ultimately, however, the process of global economic integration will require a fundamental overhaul of the role the state plays in pursuing social protection policies targeted toward specific groups" (paragraph 8). Discuss how you envision such a change taking place.

MIXING '60s ACTIVISIM AND ANTI-GLOBALIZATION

Robert Borosage

Robert Borosage, professor of law at American University, is a co-founder, with Roger Hickey, of the Campaign for America's Future. He is co-editor of The Next Agenda: Blueprint for a New Progressive Movement *(2000). This article appeared in the April 23, 2000, issue of the* Los Angeles Times.

Kids today can't get any respect. First, their generation was described as apathetic, stirred only by dreams of dot-com fortunes. Then, when students stunned the world by joining turtle lovers and Teamsters to shut down the World Trade Organization meeting in Seattle last December, they were disparaged as "flat-Earth advocates." Last week, when they rallied against the World Bank and International Monetary Fund in Washington and 1,300 were arrested in nonviolent protest, they were labeled "imitation activists," filling the time between "spring break and summer vacation, and between the last body-piercing and the first IPO." At least Washington and Seattle captured headlines. For the most vibrant student movement in years is roiling America's university campuses in relative obscurity.

Here's the reality so many can't see. Activist, idealistic students are in motion once again, seized of a morally compelling cause. Their target, amazingly, is nothing less than the global corporation. They are challenging the conservative free-trade agenda that dominates both major political parties. Already, they are forcing global companies such as Nike to scramble for cover. They've only just begun.

The most vital part of this growing movement is, perhaps, the least noticed. On more than 175 campuses, students are calling global corporations to account for their exploitation of workers abroad. They are mounting demonstrations, going on hunger strikes, seizing administration buildings, confronting university trustees and administrators, and getting arrested by the dozens in nonviolent protests. The two-person staff of the coordinating group, United Students Against Sweatshops, can't keep up with the e-mail from students seeking to get involved both here and abroad.

4   This movement is less than four years old. Its roots trace back to 1996, when human-rights advocate Charles Kernaghan focused national attention on Honduran sweatshops in which young women worked at poverty wages, surrounded by barbed wire and armed guards, to sew clothes for a Kathie Lee Gifford fashion line. That summer, hundreds of university students joined worker struggles in this country as part of the AFL-CIO's Union Summer. Since then, groups of students have visited Central America to witness how women their own age work and live.

The students had a compelling moral argument: Let's not support companies that profit from exploiting workers abroad—and they acted on it. They targeted university apparel shops that buy logo clothing from global corporations with factories in Honduras, Indonesia and China, where worker rights are trampled. The $2.5-billion collegiate retail-apparel industry represents just 1% of the U.S. apparel market but is key to the youth market. So students started calling for their universities to enforce a code of conduct on suppliers.

University administrators didn't need the hassle but had no ready response for the students. The companies realized they were in trouble. Nike's swoosh symbol started being associated less with Michael Jordan than with impoverished young women abroad. Nike and others circled the wagons, enlisting a few human-rights groups to form the Fair Labor Assn., establishing their own code of conduct with the companies in control. Company-paid consultants did inspections, with factories notified ahead of time. Reports were kept private while the company "remedied" any problem. The Clinton administration pumped money into the operation. Relieved university administrators signed up.

But the students weren't buying. As Marikah Mancini, a graduate student at Purdue, said, "The basic question was whether you were empowering the companies or the workers." The result of the FLA, Sarah Jacobson of the University of Oregon argued, "would be to hide, not expose sweatshop conditions." The students insisted that any code of conduct include protections for the rights of women and workers, require a living wage and ban production from countries where workers had no right to organize. Most important, the students demanded that companies disclose the location of all factories. This would allow local church and human-rights groups to do independent monitoring. Nike and others refused.

8   So the students organized a Worker Rights Consortium to monitor company practices, financed by 1% of the revenues produced by university garment sales. It would sponsor independent monitoring by local human-rights groups and make findings public.

When university administrators resisted, the students upped the ante. At the University of Pennsylvania, the University of Wisconsin and elsewhere, students took over administration buildings. At Purdue, students camped out on the square, with several risking an 11-day hunger strike. At the University of Wisconsin, Eric Brakken was told he didn't have the student body's support. So he ran for student-government chairman on a no-sweatshops platform and won. Even at the University of Oregon, next door to Nike's corporate headquarters, students took over the president's office until he agreed to join the WRC.

Last year, facing suspension of contracts with Duke and other universities, Nike blinked and disclosed its factory locations. The other companies soon followed suit. Forty-four universities have now joined the WRC, including six Big 10 universities, Brown, Columbia and Georgetown. Two weeks ago, the entire University of California system signed up, issuing a code of conduct that demands a living wage of all contractors.

The students have identified an issue—the spread of sweatshop labor—that cuts through the cant about free trade. They have found the leverage to move not just their campuses, but global corporations—and maybe even the entire debate about globalization. They are directly challenging the laissez-faire assumptions of the last quarter-century, demanding corporations be held to some basic moral standards of conduct. Their focus on global corporations enlists the energies of many student passions, from the environmentalists to pro-Tibetan activists. And unlike the antiwar movement in the 1960s that was confronted by "hard hats," the SAS is forging links between students and workers, and between the environment and worker rights.

12   As President Bill Clinton and anyone active in the 1960s understands, when students are aroused about a moral issue, they can change the direction of the country. Already, even pundits who disparage the demonstrators have begun to accept that worker rights and the environment, food and workplace safety can no longer be ignored in the global market.

But the students are making the larger connections. Last week, SAS activists gathered in Washington for the march against the World Bank and IMF, arguing that their "structural adjustment programs," in the words of Erica Hiegelke, Smith College freshman, "press governments to attract Western investment by denying workers fundamental, internationally recognized rights."

These are not Neanderthal protectionists, nor bored kids looking for something to do. This student movement is internationalist, passionate and on the rise. And it is raising questions that might well mark the end of the conservative era of the last quarter-century.

Personal Response

Write for a few minutes about your opinion of the kind of student activism Borosage describes. Are you personally involved in the antiglobalization movement? If not, would you like to become involved or would you rather not? Explain your reasons for being involved, wanting to become involved, or avoiding such involvement.

Questions for Class or Small-Group Discussion

1. To what extent do you agree with students who argue that we should "not support companies that profit from exploiting workers abroad" (paragraph 5)? In what ways, according to this article, do companies exploit workers abroad? Can you give other examples of such exploitation?

2. Borosage writes: "[Students] are directly challenging the laissez-faire assumptions of the last quarter-century, demanding corporations be held to some basic moral standards of conduct" (paragraph 11). What do you understand by the term *laissez-faire assumptions?* What are some examples of those assumptions? How do "basic moral standards of conduct" apply to those examples?

3. Discuss your opinion of the student movement Borosage describes. Do you admire the students who are involved in the organizations he mentions, or not?

DISPELLING THE MYTHS ABOUT THE GLOBAL ECONOMY

Murray Weidenbaum

Murray Weidenbaum is chairman of the Weidenbaum Center on the Economy, Government, and Public Policy at Washington University in St. Louis. He has written and edited a number of books on business and the economy, including Business and Government in the Global Marketplace *(1995). This speech was presented to the Economic Club of Detroit on January 22, 2001.*

Today I want to deal with a perplexing conundrum facing the United States: this is a time when the American business system is producing unparalleled levels of prosperity, yet private enterprise is under increasing attack. The critics are an unusual alliance of unions, environmentalists, and human rights groups and they are focusing on the overseas activities of business. In many circles, globalization has become a dirty word.

How can we respond in a constructive way? In my interaction with these interest groups, I find that very often their views arise from basic misunderstandings of the real world of competitive enterprise. I have identified ten myths about the global economy—dangerous myths—which need to be dispelled. Here they are:

1. Globalization costs jobs.
2. The United States is an island of free trade in a world of protectionism.
3. Americans are hurt by imports.
4. U.S. companies are running away, especially to low-cost areas overseas.
5. American companies doing business overseas take advantage of local people, especially in poor countries. They also pollute their environments.

6. The trade deficit is hurting our economy and we should eliminate it.
7. It's not fair to run such large trade deficits with China or Japan.
8. Sanctions work. So do export controls.
9. Trade agreements should be used to raise environmental and labor standards around the world.
10. America's manufacturing base is eroding in the face of unfair global competition.

That's an impressive array of frequently heard charges and they are polluting our political environment. Worse yet, these widely held myths fly in the face of the facts. I'd like to take up each of them and knock them down.

1. Globalization Costs Jobs

This is a time when the American job miracle is the envy of the rest of the world, so it is hard to take that charge seriously. Yet some people do fall for it. The facts are clear: U.S. employment is at a record high and unemployment is at a 30-year low. Moreover, the United States created more than 20 million new jobs between 1993 and 2000, far more than Western Europe and Japan combined. Contrary to a widely held view, most of those new jobs pay well, often better than the average for existing jobs.

4   Of course, in the best of times, some people lose their jobs or their businesses fail, and that happens today. However, most researchers who have studied this question conclude that, in the typical case, technological progress—not international trade—is the main reason for making old jobs obsolete. Of course, at the same time, far more new jobs are created to take their place.

2. The United States Is an Island of Free Trade in a World of Protectionism

Do other nations erect trade barriers? Of course they do—although the trend has been to cut back these obstacles to commerce. But our hands are not as clean as we like to think. There is no shortage of restrictions on importers trying to ship their products into this country. These exceptions to free trade come in all shapes, sizes, and varieties. They are imposed by federal, state, and local government. U.S. import barriers include the following and more:

- Buy-American laws give preference in government procurement to domestic producers. Many states and localities show similar favoritism. Here in Michigan, preference is given to in-state printing firms;

- The Jones Act prohibits foreign ships from engaging in waterborne commerce between U.S. ports; many statutes limit the import of specific agricultural and manufactured products, ranging from sugar to pillowcases;

- We impose selective high tariffs on specific items, notably textiles; and many state and local regulatory barriers such as building codes, are aimed at protecting domestic producers.

It's strange that consumer groups and consumer activists are mute on this subject. After all, it is the American customer who has to pay higher prices as a result of all of this special interest legislation. But these barriers to trade ultimately are disappointing. Nations open to trade grow faster than those that are closed.

3. Americans Are Hurt by Imports

The myth that imports are bad will be quickly recognized by students of economics as the mercantilist approach discredited by Adam Smith over two centuries ago. The fact is that we benefit from imports in many ways. Consumers get access to a wider array of goods and services. Domestic companies obtain lower cost components and thus are more competitive. We get access to vital metals and minerals that are just not found in the United States. Also, imports prod our own producers to improve productivity and invest in developing new technology.

I'll present a painful example. By the way, I have never bought a foreign car. But we all know how the quality of our domestic autos has improved because of foreign competition. More recently, we had a striking example of the broader benefits of imports. In 1997–98, the expanded flow of lower-cost products from Asia kept inflation low here at a time when otherwise the Fed would have been raising interest rates to fight inflation. The result would have been a weaker economy. Moreover, in a full employment economy, imports enable the American people to enjoy a higher living standard than would be possible if sales were limited to domestic production.

8   In our interconnected economy, the fact is that the jobs "lost" from imports are quickly replaced by jobs elsewhere in the economy—either in export industries or in companies selling domestically. The facts are fascinating: the sharp run-up in U.S. imports in recent years paralleled the rapid growth in total U.S. employment. Both trends, of course, reflected the underlying health of our business economy.

The special importance of imports was recently highlighted by the director of the Washington State Council on International Trade. "The people who benefit most critically are families at the lower end of the wage scale who have school-age children and those elderly who must live frugally." She goes on to conclude: "It is a cruel deception that an open system of free trade is not good for working people."

4. U.S. Companies Are Running Away, Especially to Low-Cost Areas Overseas

Right off the bat, the critics have the direction wrong. The flow of money to buy and operate factories and other businesses is overwhelmingly into the United States. We haven't had a net outflow of investment since the 1960s. That's the flip side of our trade deficit. Financing large trade deficits means that far more investment capital comes into this country than is leaving.

But let us examine the overseas investments by American companies. The largest proportion goes not to poor countries, but to the most developed nations, those with high labor costs and also high environmental standards. The primary motive is to gain access to markets. That's not too surprising when we consider that the people in the most industrially advanced nations are the best customers for sophisticated American products. By the way, only one-third of the exports by the foreign branches of U.S. companies goes to the United States. About 70 percent goes to other markets, primarily to the industrialized nations.

12 Turning to American investments in Mexico, China, and other developing countries, the result often is to enhance U.S. domestic competitiveness and job opportunities. This is so because many of these overseas factories provide low-cost components and material to U.S.-based producers who are thus able to improve their international competitiveness.

In some cases, notably the pharmaceutical industry, the overseas investments are made in countries with more enlightened regulatory regimes, such as the Netherlands. "More enlightened" is not a euphemism for lower standards. The Dutch maintain a strong but more modern regulatory system than we do.

5. American Companies Doing Business Overseas Take Advantage of Local People and Pollute Their Environments

There are always exceptions. But by and large, American-owned and managed factories in foreign countries are top-of-the-line—in terms of both better working conditions and higher environmental standards than locally-owned firms. This is why so many developing countries compete enthusiastically for the overseas location of U.S. business activities—and why so many local workers seek jobs at the American factories. After all, American companies manufacturing overseas frequently follow the same high operating standards that they do here at home. I serve on a panel of Americans who investigate the conditions in some factories in China. I wish the critics could see for themselves the differences between the factories that produce for an American company under its worldwide standards and those that are not subject to our truly enlightened sense of social responsibility.

I'll give you a very personal example of the second category of facilities. While making an inspection tour, I tore my pants on an unguarded piece of equipment in one of those poorly-lit factories. An inch closer and that protruding part would have dug into my thigh. I also had to leave the factory floor every hour or so to breathe some fresh air. When I said that, in contrast, the American-owned factories were top-of-the-line, that wasn't poetry.

16 Yes, foreign investment is essential to the economic development of poor countries. By definition, they lack the capability to finance growth. The critics do those poor countries no favor when they try to discourage American firms from investing there. The critics forget that, during much of the nineteenth century, European investors financed many of our canals, railroads, steel mills, and other essentials for becoming an industrialized nation. It is sad to think where the United States would be today if Europe in the nineteenth century had had an array of powerful interest groups that were so suspicious of economic progress.

6. The Trade Deficit Is Hurting Our Economy and We Should Eliminate It

Yes, the U.S. trade deficit is at a record high. But it is part of a "virtuous circle" in our economy. The trade deficit mainly reflects the widespread prosperity in the United

States, which is substantially greater than in most of the countries we trade with. After all, a strong economy such as ours—operating so close to full employment and full capacity—depends on a substantial amount of imports to satisfy our demands for goods and services. Our exports are lower primarily because the demand for imports by other nations is much weaker.

The acid test is that our trade deficit quickly declines in the years when our economy slows down and that deficit rises again when the economy picks up. Serious studies show that, if the United States had deliberately tried to curb the trade deficit in the 1990s, the result would have been a weak economy with high inflation and fewer jobs. The trade deficit is a byproduct of economic performance. It should not become a goal of economic policy.

There is a constructive way of reducing the trade deficit. To most economists, the persistence of our trade imbalance (and especially of the related and more comprehensive current account deficit) is due to the fact that we do not generate enough domestic saving to finance domestic investment. The gap between such saving and investment is equal to the current account deficit.

20   Nobel laureate Milton Friedman summed up this point very clearly: "The remarkable performance of the United States economy in the past few years would have been impossible without the inflow of foreign capital, which is a mirror image of large balance of payments deficits."

The positive solution is clear: increase the amount that Americans save. Easier said than done, of course. The shift from budget deficits (dissaving) to budget surpluses (government saving) helps. A further shift to tax system that does not hit saving as hard as ours does would also help. The United States taxes saving more heavily than any other advanced industrialized nation. Replacing the income tax with a consumption tax, even a progressive one, would surely be in order—but that deserves to be the subject of another talk.

7. It's Not Fair to Run Such Large Trade Deficits with China or Japan

Putting the scary rhetoric aside, there really is no good reason for any two countries to have balanced trade between them. We don't have to search for sinister causes for our trade deficits with China or Japan. Bilateral trade imbalances exist for many benign reasons, such as differences in per capita incomes and in the relative size of the two economics. One of the best kept secrets of international trade is that the average Japanese buys more U.S. goods than the average American buys Japanese goods, Yes, Japan's per capita imports from the United States are larger than our per capita imports from Japan ($539 versus $432 in 1996). We have a large trade deficit with them because we have more "capita" (population).

8. Sanctions Work, So Do Export Controls

It is ironic that so many people who worry about the trade deficit simultaneously support sanctions and export controls. There is practically no evidence that unilateral sanctions are effective in getting other nations to change their policies or actions. Those restrictions on trade do, however, have an impact: they backfire. U.S. business, labor, and agriculture are harmed. We lose an overseas market for what is merely a symbolic gesture. Sanctions often are evaded. Shipping goods through third countries can disguise the ultimate recipient in the nation on which the sanctions are imposed. On balance, these sanctions reduced American exports in 1995 by an estimated $15–20 billion.

24   As for export controls, where American producers do not have a monopoly on a particular technology—which is frequent—producers in other nations can deliver the same technology or product without the handicap imposed on U.S. companies. A recent report at the Center for the Study of American Business showed that many business executives believe that sanctions and export controls are major obstacles to the expansion of U.S. foreign trade.

9. Trade Agreements Should Be Used to Raise Environmental and Labor Standards around the World

At first blush, this sounds like such a nice and high-minded way of doing good. But, as a practical matter, it is counterproductive to try to impose such costly social regulations on developing countries as a requirement for doing business with them. The acid test is that most developing nations oppose these trade restrictions. They see them for what they really are—a disguised form of protectionism designed to keep their relatively low-priced goods out of the markets of the more advanced, developed nations. All that feeds the developing nations' sense of cynicism toward us.

In the case of labor standards, there is an existing organization, the International Labor Organization, which has been set up to deal specifically with these matters. Of all the international organizations, the ILO is unique in having equal representation from business, labor, and government. The United States and most other nations are members. The ILO is where issues of labor standards should be handled. To be taken more seriously, the United States should support the ILO more vigorously than it has.

As for environmental matters, we saw at the unsuccessful meetings on climate change at the Hague late last year how difficult it is to get broad international agreement on environmental issues even in sympathetic meetings of an international environmental agency. To attempt to tie such controversial environmental matters to trade agreements arouses my suspicions about the intent of the sponsors. It is hard to avoid jumping to the conclusion that the basic motivation is to prevent progress on the trade front.

28   I still recall the signs carried by one of the protesters in Seattle, "Food is for people, not for export." Frankly, it's hard to deal with such an irrational position. After all, if the United States did not export a major part of its abundant farm output, millions of people overseas would be starving or malnourished. Also, thousands of our farmers would go broke.

The most effective way to help developing countries improve their working conditions and environmental protection is to trade with and invest in them. As for the charge that companies invest in poor, developing nations in order to minimize their environmental costs, studies of the issue show that environmental factors are not important influences in business location decisions. As I pointed out earlier, most U.S. overseas direct investment goes to developed nations with high labor costs and also high environmental standards.

10. America's Manufacturing Base Is Eroding in the Face of Unfair Global Competition

Unfortunately, some of our fellow citizens seem to feel that the only fair form of foreign competition is the kind that does not succeed in landing any of their goods on our shores. But to get to the heart of the issue, there is no factual basis for the charge that our manufacturing base is eroding—or even stagnant. The official statistics are reporting record highs in output year after year. Total industrial production in the United States today is 45 percent higher than in 1992—that's not in dollars, but in terms of real output.

Of course, not all industries or companies go up—or down—in unison. Some specific industries, especially low-tech, have had to cut back. But, simultaneously, other industries, mainly high-tech, have been expanding rapidly. Such changes are natural and to be expected in an open, dynamic economy. By the way, the United States regularly runs a trade surplus in high-tech products.

32   It's important to understand the process at work here. Technological progress generates improved industrial productivity. In the United States, that means to some degree fewer blue-collar jobs and more white-collar jobs. That is hardly a recent development. The shift from physical labor to knowledge workers has been the trend since the beginning of the 20th century. On balance, as I noted earlier, total U.S. employment is at an all-time high.

If you have any doubt about the importance of rising productivity to our society, just consider where we would be if over the past century agriculture had not enjoyed rising productivity (that is, more output per worker/hour). Most of us would still be farmers.

It is vital that we correct the erroneous views of the anti-globalists. Contrary to their claims, our open economy has raised living standards and helped to contain inflation. International commerce is more important to our economy today than at any time in the past. By dollar value and volume, the United States is the world's largest trading nation. We are the largest importer, exporter, foreign investor, and host to foreign investment. Trying to stop the global economy is futile and contrary to America's self-interest.

Nevertheless, we must recognize that globalization, like any other major change, generates costs as well as benefits. It is essential to address these consequences. Otherwise, we will not be able to maintain a national consensus that responds to the challenges of the world marketplace by focusing on opening markets instead of closing them. The challenge to all of us is to urge courses of action that help those who are hurt without doing far more harm to the much larger number who benefit from the international marketplace.

36   We need to focus more attention on those who don't share the benefits of the rapid pace of economic change. Both private and public efforts should be increased to provide more effective adjustment assistance to those who lose their jobs. The focus of adjustment policy should not be on providing relief from economic change, but on positive approaches that help more of our people participate in economic prosperity.

As you may know, I recently chaired a bipartisan commission established by Congress to deal with the trade deficit. Our commission included leaders of business and labor, former senior government officials, and academics. We could not agree on all the issues that we dealt with. But we were unanimous in concluding that the most fundamental part of an effective long-run trade adjustment policy is to do a much better job of educating and training. More Americans should be given the opportunity to become productive and high-wage members of the nation's workforce.

No, I'm not building up to a plea to donate to the college of your choice, although that's a pretty good idea.

Even though I teach at major research universities—and strongly believe in their vital mission—let me make a plea for greater attention to our junior colleges. They are an overlooked part of the educational system. Junior colleges have a key role to play. Many of these community-oriented institutions of learning are now organized to specially meet the needs of displaced workers, including those who need to brush up on their basic language and math skills. In some cases, these community colleges help people launch new businesses, especially in areas where traditional manufacturing is declining. A better trained and more productive workforce is the key to our long-term international competitiveness. That is the most effective way of resisting the calls for economic isolationism.

40   Let me leave you with a final thought. The most powerful benefit of the global economy is not economic at all, even though it involves important economic and business activities. By enabling more people to use modern technology to communicate across traditional national boundaries, the international marketplace makes possible more than an accelerated flow of data. The worldwide marketplace encourages a far greater exchange of the most powerful of all factors of production—new ideas. That process enriches and empowers the individual in ways never before possible.

As an educator, I take this as a challenge to educate the anti-globalists to the great harm that would result from a turn to economic isolationism. For the twenty-first century, the global flow of information is the endless frontier.

Personal Response

To what extent are you convinced that the "myths" Weidenbaum discusses are truly "myths"?

Questions for Class or Small-Group Discussion

1. Weidenbaum says that there are "ten myths about the global economy—dangerous myths—which need to be dispelled" (paragraph 2). Discuss each of the "myths"

in turn, examining his rationale for why they are not myths and explaining the extent to which you are convinced by his argument.

2. Respond to this statement: "Trying to stop the global economy is futile and contrary to America's self-interest" (paragraph 34).

3. Weidenbaum suggests: "More Americans should be given the opportunity to become productive and high-wage members of the nation's workforce" (paragraph 37). Does he adequately explain how those goals can be accomplished? Do you agree that both of those goals are achieveable?

PERSPECTIVES ON THE UNITED STATES IN THE GLOBAL MARKETPLACE

Suggestions for Synthesis

1. Compare and/or contrast the positions of any two of the writers in this chapter on the subject of globalization of the economy.

2. Drawing on at least two of the essays in this chapter, discuss possible solutions to the problem of how to moderate the desire of corporations to make money in the global marketplace with the altruistic goal of providing adequate attention to the needs of poor or developing countries.

3. Interview a specialist in international marketing or economics about the global market and its importance for the American economy in the twenty-first century. Then write an essay on America's future in the global economy in which you include both the specialist's remarks and those of any of the authors in this chapter.

4. Kofi Annan writes in "Development without Borders": "In short, there is much that poor countries can do to help themselves. But rich countries have an indispensable role to play." Drawing on Annan's article and at least one other article from this chapter, write an essay explaining what poor countries can do and how rich countries can help them.

Additional Writing Topics

1. Select a particular statement from any of the readings in this chapter and write a response in support of or against it.

2. Discuss the implications for both American consumers and American businesses of the rapid expansion of the global marketplace.

3. Write an essay explaining how you see changes in the global economy affecting you personally, both as a consumer and as a (perhaps future) member of the workforce. Or, assess the impact of foreign products on a typical day in your life.

4. Write an essay from the point of view of a market researcher for a new corporation looking for rapid growth through global marketing. Make up a product and a corporation name; then prepare a report for the board of directors of your company in which you recommend expanding efforts in one of the world's newest market areas.

5. Write an essay elaborating on this statement from Vito Tanzi's "Globalization without a Net": "Countries can harness the many benefits of global integration as long as they provide strong social protection programs that mitigate the fallout on society's weakest members" (paragraph 1).

Research Topics

1. Research the economic changes in the last decade in any of these geographic areas: Asia, Latin America, Eastern Europe, or sub-Saharan Africa. Read about developments in the area and projections for the future, and then report your findings and conclusions.

2. Research the global investment strategies of any major American corporation. Draw some conclusions about the effectiveness of such strategies in your paper.

3. Analyze the connections between the information revolution and the global spread of market economies. How do they affect or influence one another?

4. Select an area such as politics, technology, or economics. Then conduct library research to determine both the positive and negative implications of the enormous global changes in that area, including a prediction of the effects of these changes on the American economy in the next decade.

5. Research and assess the effectiveness of any of the following: the UN Millennium Summit of September 2000 or the Organization for Economic Cooperation and Development (Kofi Annan's "Development without Borders"); the United Students Against Sweatshops, the Fair Labor Association, or the Worker Rights Consortium (Robort Borosage's "Mixing '60s Activism and Anti-Globalization").

APPENDIX I

DEFINITIONS OF TERMS USED IN DISCUSSION QUESTIONS AND WRITING TOPICS

Abstract. A summary of the essential points of a text. It is usually quite short, no more than a paragraph.

Analysis. Dividing a subject into its separate parts for individual study.

Argument/persuasion. An argument is an attempt to prove the validity of a position by offering supporting proof. Persuasion takes argument one step further by convincing an audience to adopt a viewpoint or take action.

Book review. A report that summarizes only the main ideas of a book and provides critical commentary on it. Usually in a book review, you will also be asked to give your personal response to the book, including both your opinion of the ideas it presents and an evaluation of its worth or credibility.

Case study. A situation or profile of a person or persons, for which you provide a context and background information.

Citation. A reference that provides supporting illustrations or examples for your own ideas; the authority or source of that information is identified.

Comparison. A likeness or strong similarity between two things.

Contrast. A difference or strong dissimilarity between two things.

Debate. A discussion involving opposing points in an argument. In formal debate, opposing teams defend and attack a specific proposition.

Description. A conveyance through words of the essential nature of a thing.

Diction. A writer's word choice and level of usage, which varies in informal and formal language; slang, regional, nonstandard, and colloquial language; and jargon.

Evaluation. A judgment about worth, quality, or credibility.

Forum. An open discussion or exchange of ideas among many people. (See the *Time* magazine forum "Tough Talk on Entertainment" in chapter 9.)

Freewriting. The act of writing down every idea that occurs to you about your topic without stopping to examine what you are saying.

Hypothesis. A tentative explanation to account for some phenomenon or set of facts. It is in essence a theory or an assumption that can be tested by further investigation and is assumed to be true for the purpose of argument or investigation.

Illustration. An explanation or clarification, usually using example or comparison.

Journal. A personal record of experiences, thoughts, or responses to something, usually kept separate from other writings, as in a diary or notebook.

Literature search. A process of locating titles of articles, books, and other material on a specific subject.

Narration. Telling a story.

Panel discussion. A small group of people (usually between three and six) gathered to discuss a topic. Often each member of a panel is prepared to represent a certain position or point of view on the subject of discussion, with time left after the presentations for questions from audience members.

Paraphrase. A restatement of a passage in your own words. A paraphrase is somewhat shorter than the original but retains its essential meaning.

Position paper. A detailed report that explains, justifies, or recommends a particular course of action.

Proposition. A statement of a position on a subject, a course of action, or a topic for discussion or debate.

Reflective writing. A process of drawing on personal experience to offer your own response to something. For this kind of writing, use the first person.

Report. A detailed account of something.

Subject. A general or broad area of interest.

Summary. A shortened version of a passage, stated in your own words. A summary resembles a paraphrase, in that you are conveying the essence of the original, but it is shorter than a paraphrase.

Synthesis. Combining the ideas of two or more authors and integrating those ideas into your own discussion.

Thesis. A statement of the specific purpose of a paper. A thesis is essentially a one-sentence summary of what you will argue, explain, illustrate, define, describe, or otherwise develop in the rest of the paper. It usually comes very early in a paper.

Tone. A writer's attitude toward the subject and the audience, conveyed through word choice and diction.

Topic. A specific, focused, and clearly defined area of interest. A topic is a narrow aspect of a subject.